SO-AJE-561

THE AMERICAN NEGRO
HIS HISTORY AND LITERATURE

RICHARD J. HINTON, A LONDONER BY BIRTH, SPENT his most active years in the United States, making his home among the activist American abolitionists of the pre-Civil War decade. He devoted himself body and soul to the struggle against Southern slavery. Once, when he decided to leave Boston to ride with John Brown in Kansas' bloody civil war, abolitionist orator Wendell Phillips asked him why. Hinton answered that freedom in Kansas would lead to liberty in South Carolina.

After his return to Boston, he became a bodyguard for Phillips and a military advisor to the young abolitionists who protected Phillips and his home from pro-slavery assaults.

During the Civil War Hinton immersed himself in efforts to promote abolition and aid the freed Negroes. In 1862 he formed the Kansas Emancipation League that raised funds for the relief, education and job placement of 4,000 slaves who fled to Kansas during the war's first year. He also joined the Second Kansas Colored Volunteers as an officer and rose to the rank of Colonel.

At the conclusion of the war, Hinton edited newspapers in New York, Washington and San Francisco, and wrote two books. *John Brown and His Men* was the third biography of the anti-slave zealot to be published by men who had been part of his Kansas raiders. The interesting appendix, which is indicative of Hinton's careful research, is only a small part of the giant manuscript collection (now located at the Kansas State Historical Society Archives) which he consulted.

Despite its thorough documentation, however, *John Brown and His Men* is a personal statement. It was not intended as purely disinterested history.

William Loren Katz

American Reformers Series

JOHN BROWN
AND HIS MEN

With Some Account of the Roads They Traveled to Reach Harper's Ferry

BY
RICHARD J. HINTON

Member American Society Irrigation Engineers

Author of "Handbook to Arizona," "English Radical Leaders," "Phillip Henry Sheridan," etc. Editor of "The Poems by Richard Realf."

REVISED EDITION

FUNK & WAGNALLS COMPANY
NEW YORK and LONDON

LIST OF ILLUSTRATIONS.

CONTENTS.

A BRIEF PRELUDE.

Iᴛ is the cant of To-Day to sneer at Sacrifice. It is not "scientific" to act without a visible reward or hope of material success. It is "scientific" to assume that "sacrifice" is but another and, it may be, foolish form of Self-love.

Nevertheless, sacrifices are made! Defenders of systems always assume that the majestic forces of Religion, the exalted functions of Order and Justice, or those within the shimmering arena of Knowledge, belong to them alone. They declare that he who resists should die "as the fool dieth." Perhaps the lives I have outlined herein may help to prove that true and natural religion, that wisdom and knowledge, are also united, not divorced ! This book may show, I hope, that generosity remains to bless our human lives; that an integral part of manhood and woman-hood is service from each to all, for the life of each and the advancement of all !

It will be said that the author of this volume holds a brief for John Brown and his Men. He does not deny it; but, on the contrary, esteems it to be an honor ! He has endeavored, however, to so link their lives with historical facts along the nobler lines of American endeavor, that their careers become asso-ciated with such loftier purposes and higher im-pulses, as illustrate that true and spiritual democracy which should in very truth animate the American Federal Republic.

If no such spirit exists, and our institutions are but a mere convenience given to money making only, competitive triumph and sociological advancement of material conditions, without regard to ethical aims or considerations, let us openly enthrone Plutocracy and make Mammon the Baal of our Righteousness. Why should we have fought for the Union, if Freedom was not also our blessed reward?

If it is the fashion to sneer, this volume is not in the fashion. If America means no more than Adolphe Thiers said of the latest European commonwealth: "The Republic is the government that divides France the least" (and I do not decry the wisdom of that astute saying); if it means only light taxes, a robust police, and the best armories, guns, and street-drill for national guards, let us deny at once the existence of historical continuity and assume the folly of human Love and Service! However:

The world's saints are few, and they're costly, too—
We'll keep sweet their deeds, be they Rose or Rue!
    So much in the making of human Woe,
    Of insight deep and tender Love doth go,—
That more precious still they grow to our view,
Bringing ripe sheaves whence all bitter weeds grew—
    As the tides of endeavor swiftly flow,
    At seedlet roots their lives heroic sow!

The Scoffers, keen with bitter jest, wax bold,
While sad souls by dull Faith are growing cold,
    As memories stern, so towering wait
    On the dread footsteps slow of austere Fate!
What matters? Each lofty life finds its goal,
And answering lives in blood their names enroll.

This book, then, has been written because the
writer was impelled and desired to do it. It was
planned more than thirty years ago. The struggle
for existence, which is all that those leave us who
pervert the holy teachings of the Nazarene and the
noble naturalism of Darwin, into apologies for economic, political, and sociologic brutalities, provided only
they *exist* as institutions, has heretofore prevented the
writing of a work laid on one as a duty. These men,
of whom I have written, were for me, in a humble
sense, as dear comrades. They fell; I escaped! In
writing of them, it is with a living sense of their
worthier example. There are holier and nobler things
in Life than Life itself. They are heroic exemplars
of this !

I desire to express here my most grateful thanks
for assistance extended to me by Mrs. Anne Brown-
Adams, Mrs. Ruth Brown-Thompson, and John
Brown, Jr., of the surviving children of John Brown.
I am also specially indebted among others to George
B. Gill, of Oklahoma (commissioned Secretary of
Treasury under the John Brown-Chatham provisional
constitution); to Dr. Thomas Featherstonhaugh and
John W. Le Barnes, of Washington; Dr. Alexander
Milton Ross, of Toronto, Canada; William Hutchin-
son, one of the older and best of Kansas pioneers;
Harvey B. Hurd, of Chicago; Horace White, of
New York; Prof. L. R. Wetherell, of Davenport,
Iowa; Col. Thomas Wentworth Higginson, of Cam-
bridge, Mass.; to Edmund C. Stedman; Wm. D.
Howells; Edna Dean Proctor; Col. John Bowles,
and Richard Greener, of New York; Miss Sarah
J. Eddy, of Providence, R. I.; Franklin J. Keagy,

of Chambersburg, Pa.; Horatio N. Rust, of Pasadena, Cal., and Mrs. Crowley (sister of John E. Cook), of New York, for most valuable aid in reminiscences, letters, documents, and portraits. I desire particularly to give thus publicly my thanks to Frank G. Adams, Secretary of the Kansas Historical Society, whose untiring responses to many demands have laden me with gratitude, all the more pleasant, that I know how willingly he has served both the work I was doing for the love of it and for myself personally also. I cannot close without expressing grateful thanks to many whose abiding places are now unknown, but who years since placed in my hands letters and other papers relating to their dear ones. These are the families and relatives of the John Brown men, outside the family of their leader. If this volume shall reach any of them, they will find shortly after its publication all of such papers as I have left in the Library of the Kansas Historical Society, where I shall place the same, subject, of course, to their demands, but hoping they may be left permanently to add to the valuable collection that enriches that Library.

"MAYWOOD,"   RICHARD J. HINTON.
BAY RIDGE, N. Y.

JOHN BROWN AND HIS MEN

Your Friend
John Brown

JOHN BROWN AND HIS MEN.

CHAPTER I.

THE MAN.

John Brown's birth, ancestry, training, education, pursuits, marriage, children, and daily life—His entrance into national life and renown—Removal to Kansas in 1855.

JOHN BROWN, born at Torrington, Connecticut, May 9, 1800, was hung on a scaffold at Charlestown, West Virginia, Dec. 2, 1859. The grandson and namesake of Captain John Brown, of West Simsbury, a Revolutionary officer who died in the field; he was also the sixth in descent from Peter Brown who came to New England in the *Mayflower*, 1620. Peter was a carpenter, who married after he landed at Plymouth. Within thirteen years he married twice, and died in 1633, leaving four children. Writing about 1650 (Bradford—MSS. "History of Plymouth Plantation," 1624–57), Gov. Wm. Bradford says: "Peter Brown by his first wife had two children, who are living, and both of them married, and one of them

hath two children; by his second wife he had two
more. He died about sixteen years since." Mary
and Priscilla were daughters of the first wife, and
are the two mentioned as married. In 1644, they
were under the care of their uncle, John Brown, a
citizen of Duxbury, where also Peter Brown settled
a few years after landing at Plymouth. John Brown
outlived his brother Peter many years. Of his
family by his second wife, Peter Brown, born in 1632,
was the younger. He was the ancestor of John
Brown of Osawatomie and Harper's Ferry, and
removed from Duxbury to Windsor, Connecticut,
between 1650 and 1658, where he married Mary, the
daughter of Jonathan Gillett.

Peter Brown the pilgrim, had his home in Duxbury, not far from the hill where Miles Standish
built his house, and where his monument is now
seen. His son, Peter, lived, and died, at Windsor,
Connecticut, March 9, 1692, leaving thirteen children.
Of these, John Brown, born Jan. 8, 1668, married
Elizabeth Loomis. They had eleven children, among
whom were John Brown, the father and survivor of
John Brown, of West Simsbury, who died in
the British prison-ship in New York harbor. He
lived, and died, at Windsor, married Mary Eggle-
ston; and the Continental captain, grandfather of the
Kansas fighter, was the oldest son, born Nov. 4, 1728.
He married Hannah Owen, of Welsh descent, in
1758. Her father was Elijah Owen, of Windsor, and
her first ancestor in this country, was John Owen, a
Welshman who married in Windsor in 1650, just
before Peter Brown came there from Duxbury.

The Browns were, in fact, a distinguished family

when the sixth in descent from Peter, the Plymouth settler, made it one of the most illustrious of the world. It had embraced soldiers of Indian wars, one hero of the Revolutionary struggle, and another of the War of 1812. Its men were workmen, farmers, fighters, townbuilders, scholars, preachers, and teachers. The direct ancestor of John Brown's mother, Ruth Mills, of Simsbury, was a Protestant Hollander, Peter Van Huysenmuysen, who left that sturdy land when the Spanish Duke of Alva was harrying it. Settling in Connecticut, he built a mill and earned bread for his family. Hence the name Mills, under which the family passed into New England annals. They have bred a long line of physicians, ministers, and teachers. John Brown himself might well be counted, on the modern New York view of family place, among social " exclusives " of the first water.

A President of Amherst College, the Rev. Herman Humphrey, D.D., and the Rev. Luther Humphrey, both famous Presbyterian ministers, were his first cousins, being the sons of his father's sister. The Rev. Nathan Brown, editor of the *American Baptist*, and a famous missionary in India and Japan, was a second cousin. He translated the Bible into Japanese. Owen Brown, the father (who died in 1857), was one of the trustees of Oberlin College, and John Brown himself was associated with the affairs thereof for years. Salmon Brown, Owen's brother and John Brown's uncle, became a distinguished lawyer and judge, settling in Louisiana, and dying there. There are a score or more of other names belonging to this family, noted in New England and Ohio annals for learning, character, and service, as minis-

ters, educators, and citizens. John Brown represents in his own person, then, the best blood and
character to be found in America. Thus, in him
mingled three great racial forces, English of the
Teutonic or Saxon type, the Welsh or ancient British
stock, and the sturdy, independent Hollander, all
vitalized by the mighty conflicts for the supremacy
of civic freedom and liberty of conscience, in the
Protestant struggle of the Old World, the founding
of New England, and the fiery endurance of the War
for Independence.

John Brown was the oldest son of Owen Brown,
himself one of eleven children born to the Revolutionary captain and Hannah Owen, his wife. The
grandmother lived to see most of her own children
well established in life. One of them became a
judge in Ohio; another, John, of New Hartford, was
a man much esteemed, and a deacon of the church
there. A daughter was the mother of the Rev. Dr.
Humphrey. Owen Brown became a tanner and
shoemaker, the same trade he taught his famous
son. Owen, born and bred in Simsbury (now Canton), Connecticut, was married there to Ruth Mills,
daughter of the old minister, Rev. Gideon Mills, on
the 11th of February, 1793; they then removed to
Norfolk, where his oldest child was born, July 5,
1798, and one year later moved to Torrington. John
Brown was born there, also his brothers, Solomon
and Oliver Owen, in 1800, 1802, and 1804. In 1805
the father migrated, with his children and others of
the family, to the Western Reserve, Ohio, settling in
the town of Hudson. In the wilderness John Brown
spent his childhood and youth, though his early

recollections extended also to his Connecticut home. Hudson was a notable community of sturdy American people of anti-slavery convictions.[1]

At sixteen John Brown joined the Congregational Church in Hudson. Desiring to study for the ministry, he probably revisited Torrington in order to obtain advice of Jeremiah Hallock, who had married a relation. By him John Brown was advised to fit for college at the school of his brother, Rev. Moses Hallock, Plainfield, Massachusetts. His uncle, Hermann Hallock, D.D., was soon after made president of Amherst College, to which the sturdy student would have gone, but for a serious inflammation of the eyes from overstudy, compelling him to go back to his father's[1] tanyard in Hudson. In December, 1859, Hermann Hallock, the youngest son Gerard, of the Rev. Moses Hallock, wrote his brother editor of the New York *Journal of Commerce*, as follows:

" Your youngest brother does remember John Brown, who studied at our house. He was a tall, dignified young man. He had been a tanner, and relinquished a prosperous business for the purpose of intellectual improvement."

Soon after John Brown's return to Hudson, Ohio, he married his first wife, Dianthe Lusk, June 21, 1820. She died in childbirth, August, 1832. There were six other children of this marriage, the eldest of whom, John Brown, Jr., was born July 25, 1821; he

---

[1] See Appendix for the autobiography written for the son of George L. Stearns, of Boston, Massachusetts.

still lives, residing at Put-in-Bay Island, Lake Erie,
Ohio; Jason Brown, living at Pasadena, California,
was born January 19, 1823; Owen Brown, born
November 4, 1824, died in 1890; Ruth (Mrs. Henry
Thompson), now living at Pasadena, February 18,
1829; and Frederick Brown, December 21, 1839, killed
at Osawatomie, Kansas, August 30, 1856. By a
second marriage with Mary Anne Day, of Meadville,
Pennsylvania, in 1833, John Brown became the father
of thirteen children, seven of whom died in childhood; two, Watson and Oliver, were slain at Harper's
Ferry, and four others have survived. These are
Salmon Brown, born October 2, 1836; Anne, born
September 23, 1843; Sarah, born September 11, 1846;
and Ellen, born September 25, 1854. Anne, Sarah,
and Ellen live in Santa Cruz and Humboldt Counties,
California; Salmon recently removed from Red
Bluffs to Washington, near Tacoma. They are all
married and have families. In all, John Brown was
the father of twenty children, seven of whom are still
living. The living grandchildren number twenty-six.

John Brown was farmer, tanner, and land surveyor
at Hudson, Ohio, until 1826, then at Richmond, near
Meadville, Pennsylvania, residing there until 1835.
He then removed to Franklin Mills, Portage County,
Ohio, where he also speculated in land. He lost
heavily in the panic of 1837, and in 1839 entered upon
a new pursuit—that of wool-growing and dealing;
driving also in that year a herd of cattle from Ohio
to Connecticut. There he purchased a few sheep, the
nucleus of what became a great flock. In 1840 he
returned to Hudson, where his father, Owen Brown,
lived until 1856. In 1842 Brown removed to Rich-

field, and here his daughter, Anne, was born. Here, too, he lost four children in less than three weeks— Sarah, aged nine; Charles, almost six; Peter, not quite three, and Austin, about a year old. Three were buried in one grave and on the same date, a September day, in 1843. The next year he moved to Akron, and in 1846 to Springfield, in Massachusetts. He went there as a member of the firm of Perkins & Brown, and also as the agent of the sheep-farmers and wool-merchants of northern Ohio, whose products were then sold wholly to New England manufacturers. John Brown, to prevent loss to them by uniform low grading, initiated the system of grading wools, since then generally adopted. The manufacturers were too powerful for the Western farmer. They bribed his clerk (as he always believed) to change the wool marks, so that the stock was all paid for as low grade. This led to several lawsuits, one of which was tried and decided against him at Boston in the winter of 1852–53, after Brown had withdrawn from the business and was living in the Adirondacks. The next year he won a similar suit in a New York court, and always believed he would have won the Boston case but for the action of the counsel in compromising the same. The Boston judge was Caleb Cushing, and Rufus Choate was of counsel against Brown.

In Springfield, John Brown lived in a very modest house on Franklin street, just north of the Boston and Albany Railroad, and his warehouses were close by. Frederick Douglass visited him there in 1847. Wishing to make a market for a large stock of Ohio wool then on hand, and believing that he could sell it in

Europe to advantage, he went there in 1848–49, traversing a considerable part of England and the continent on that business. He visited both wool markets and battlefields in impartial succession. Among dealers he was noted for the delicacy of his touch in sorting different qualities, and for skill in testing them when submitted to him. After trying the markets of Europe, he finally sold his Liverpool consignment at a lower price than it would have brought in Springfield. His ill success, added to the expense of his trip, finally ruined this business, and in 1849 he gave it up and went to live, where he was afterwards buried, at North Elba, Essex County, New York.

It was in the hope of enlisting and drilling recruits for his projected company of liberators that John Brown went to live among the colored men to whom Gerritt Smith had given land in the Adirondack woods. Mr. Smith had inherited from his father landed estate in more than three-fourths of the counties of New York. In Essex, he owned several thousand acres. Farms were offered to such colored men as would live upon the land, clear, and cultivate it. On returning from England in 1849, Brown heard of the offer, and soon presented himself to Mr. Smith in Peterboro. A small colony of colored people had already gone to North Elba to clear up the forest land given them. Brown made to Mr. Smith this proposal: "I am something of a pioneer, having grown up among the woods and wilds of Ohio, and I am used to the way of life that your colony find so trying; I will take one of the farms myself, clear and plant it, and show my colored neighbors how such work should be done, will give them work as I have occasion, look after them in all needful ways, and be a kind of father to them."

Mr. Smith readily consented, and John Brown soon removed with his family from Springfield to North Elba.[1] They lived there most of the time between 1849 and 1862, and altogether, while their father was attacking slavery in Kansas, Missouri, and Virginia. Besides other inducements which this region offered him, John Brown considered it a place of refuge for his wife and younger children, where they would not only be safe and independent, but could live frugally. When he went there his youngest son, Oliver, was ten years old, Anne and Sarah were six and three years old. Ellen, his youngest child, was born at North Elba.

In 1849, there were in Essex County but few roads, schools, and churches, and only a few good farms. The life of the settler at North Elba was pioneer work; the forest had to be cut down and the land burnt over; the family supplies must be produced, mainly, within the household itself. Sugar was made from the maple trees; from the wool they raised, the women spun and wove garments; sheep and cows especially were the farmer's wealth. Winter continues for six months of the year; the short summer crops are grass, oats, and potatoes, a few vegetables, and the wild fruit of the woods and meadows. In the whole township of North Elba, Mr. Sanborn says of his first visit there in 1857, there was scarcely a house worth a thousand dollars, or one which was finished

---

[1] See Appendix for description of a visit there in the early 'fifties, written by Richard H. Dana, and published in the *Atlantic.*

2

throughout. Mrs. Brown's dwelling had but two
plastered rooms, yet two families lived in it. This
house had been built by John Brown about 1850, in
the shadow almost of the great rock beside which he
lies buried. John Brown introduced his favorite
breed of cattle, and exhibited them at the annual
show of Essex County in September, 1850. They
were a grade of Devons mixed with a particular Connecticut stock, and the first improved breed that had
been at the county fair.

Of the four sons of his first marriage who were
then living, two were married, and one, Frederick, was
engaged. Ruth, the eldest daughter, had married
Henry Thompson, a sturdy farmer of New Hampshire
origin, who lived near the Brown farm at North Elba.
He was in sympathy with, and readily consented
to join the family in Kansas. Two of his brothers
were killed at Harper's Ferry, and Watson Brown's
wife was their sister. She is still living in Wisconsin,
married to Salmon Brown, a cousin.

In the winter of 1854–55 the four older sons of John
Brown (John, Jason, Owen, and Frederick), with their
half brother Salmon, living either in or near Akron,
Ohio. made arrangements to settle in Kansas. They
established themselves the next spring in Lykins
County, about eight miles from Osawatomie. From
there they wrote their father, asking his aid. Soon
after an anti-slavery meeting was held at Utica, New
York, on behalf of the settlement of Kansas as a free
State. In this convention John Brown participated.
He was described as a gentleman standing six feet in
his boots, of thin face and dark complexion, with
flowing beard and gray hair, lithe and straight, and

about sixty years of age, being then but fifty-five. In his address he spoke of four sons already settled in Kansas, and of three others (Salmon, Watson, and Oliver) who wished to join them, but were unable to pay their way to the Territory. John Brown, referring to the declaration of the assembly that it was Abolition in sentiment, urged that something practical be done, and reminded them that " without the shedding of blood there is no remission of sin." The will of the Puritan was finding speech. He asked for arms for the sons already in Kansas, reading letters from the two eldest that gave evidence of the violent spirit of the pro-slavery people. John Brown pledged himself to go to Kansas with his three remaining sons, and " to make a good report of their doings "; this he certainly did. The funds were provided for the expenses of this segment of the Brown family to enter upon the harvest field. On the next day, Gerritt Smith in open session presented John Brown with seven muskets and bayonets, seven voltaic repeating pistols, and seven short broadswords—such as were then worn by artillerymen or sailors; a small purse was also given him,—sixty dollars had been collected the day before. The presentation of arms was a constant feature of Kansas meetings of that period on both sides of Mason and Dixon's line. John Brown's sons were already making their mark on the free-State records. They had selected claims—four of them—and the elder brothers, John, Jr., and Jason, with Frederick, were serving in free-State conventions. John, Jr., was also elected to the free-State Legislature, which convened soon after at Topeka. He and Frederick were delegates to the Big Springs Con-

vention, September 5th; Charles Robinson, James
Blood, G. W. Brown, and others of the few older
citizens of Kansas, who have since made themselves
unpleasantly conspicuous by malicious attacks and
sometimes scurrilous abuse of "Old John Brown,"
were also present. Happily for the hero's name and
family, it was found at Big Springs that there was no
relationship between an editorial defamer and the
fighting farmer of the same name. John Brown and
his kin were, at least, spared that degradation. The
two elder brothers were at Topeka in the same month
and year, assisting in framing the famous free-State
Constitution, known in political history by the name
of its birthplace—Topeka. They both opposed the
"black law" or negro-exclusion feature of the instrument, while heartily sustaining the free-State provisions.

John Brown himself arrived at the family settlement on the Pottawatomie,[1] during the first week of
October, 1855. The movement of his elder sons to
settle in Kansas was projected by John, Jr., in the
early days of January, 1855. At that time their father,
while bidding them "God-speed," declared that his
field of labor "was elsewhere." But the later call
from Kansas was that of duty, and he cheerfully
responded. John Brown had found the opening place.
For him the ruddy lights were rising, and the mystic
shadows were gathering. Up to this date his modest,
quiet, orderly life had given little objective expression to the heroic forces which, subjectively, the ag-

---

[1] See Appendix for letters by John Brown, Jr., describing their
new home.

gressions and oppressions of chattel slavery had been punctuating.   For the first time a free hand, untrammeled by compromise or party restraint, that " feared God so much that it did not fear man," was writing large a bold interrogation mark against the record of Southern domination.   It was also to write the answer thereto.   From and after that October day in 1855, John Brown was to punctuate American history with the dynamic acts of a life unawed by power and untrammeled by policy.

CHAPTER II.

PURPOSE AND PLANS.

His earliest friends and confidants—Wife and sons are vowed to the struggle—His colored allies—Frederick Douglass's account of the plans—Steadfast devotion of the family—Life at Springfield and North Elba —On the Kansas threshold.

MARY, his wife, was John Brown's first confidant and ally. His earliest recruits were sons of his loins. His faithful assistants were the daughters who had grown to years of discretion amid the plain living and high thinking so characteristic of this unique family. The husband of Ruth was one of her father's Kansas soldiers and is now in elder years the reverential supporter of his memory. The family from which Henry Thompson came—plain, simple, rustic farmers of Northern New York—gave their sons and daughters as readily to the fight as John Brown's children accepted in love their father's unflinching faith and fortitude. The sons' wives murmured no more than the sons, and the widows of Oliver and Watson went to the grave or bore their sorrow unflinchingly. John Brown's detractors never take this marvelous tally into account. Unbending, simple, and Puritanical, living hard, as severe in demands as his morals were stern, amid the nation's years of growing power and wealth that have led to personal display and social unrest, John Brown's wife, sons, and daughters, have followed without hesitation in his "path of thorns." Among the large number of published letters, written only for each others' eyes, and as exigencies arose, there can be found but one of complaint against the father, and that appears to relate to a trivial rebellion of Owen, when a youth. John Brown's friends were found, first and most faithful, within his own household. They did, and have to the end, believed in him, wholly and utterly. They would not have done so had he not been wholly worthy.

It was in 1839, at Franklin, Pennsylvania, that John Brown first announced his conviction that by blood atonement alone could chattel slavery be destroyed. De Toqueville, like Jefferson, had already partially realized this as a result not of an ideal but of conditions. It was then that he declared his purpose to live and to be with those in bonds, as if bound with them, even unto the bitter and bloody end. His three eldest sons were John, Jr., nineteen, Jason, seventeen, and Owen, sixteen years of age respectively. There was a colored preacher, named Fayette, visiting Brown about that time. He was intrusted with the purpose and place, and with John Brown's wife and three sons, took the obligation of assistance and secrecy. It is more than probable that this strong, simple man, did not hide his convictions, as long as they were unformulated in deed. In the twenty years that followed the family announcement and prayer unto the day when dying, he proved that America, like Rome, could destroy Spartacus, John Brown was not silent, but bore his testimony alike to wrong and remedy, to fitting persons and at proper times.

John Brown, Jr., records, that the only time he ever saw his father kneel in prayer was when he first vowed himself and them to attack slavery by force. The pilgrim grimly held the ark of the covenant upright when he prayed to his Creator. It was not pride but a rigid humility which thus esteemed the handiwork of the Father. Still, the soul in travail over the slave, bowed itself to the dust in mourning for the Republic dishonored by slavery. It is worth while recalling that it was to Franklin that Owen Brown steered across the rough laurel-clad spurs of the Pennsylvania Alleghanies when, with Tidd and the younger Coppoc, he escaped in October and November of 1859, from the shadow land of the slave-driver and kidnapper to the shadowed depots of the underground railway in Western Pennsylvania and Northern Ohio. It was at Meadville, near by, that John Brown was practically refused church fellowship because he insisted on breaking sacramental bread with the fugitive, and held the brother in bronze the equal before God of him whose hue was lighter. It was here, also, that the Puritan tanner refused to do militia duty, and denounced war, paying his fine for the same. John Brown never joined a church thereafter, and obeyed henceforth no man's order as a soldier. A leader of men and a born strategist, he was also a student of warfare. Von Holst says, in his admirable monograph, that no one would have gone to John Brown for a criticism of Napoleon. On the contrary, he was thoroughly able to have given keen and incisive opinions on that commander's campaigns. Colonel Philips, of Kansas, has given evidence of the careful study he had made

of the career of Spartacus.[1] He read alike of the
guerilla warfare of Spain and the Caucasus, and
could discuss aptly the movements of the Haytian
freedmen, as well as the marching and maneuvers of
European armies. John Brown equipped his brain
as well as his conscience. He made a special study
of how to subsist men, learning to make a little go
far in the commissariat—a knowledge which stood
him in good stead in Kansas. And he was always
conscious of his own power as one called to direct
and lead. He begun to both think and write, as well
as to prepare. During the following ten years
he prepared[2] the "League of Gileadites"; a paper
on "Sambo," and addresses to non-slave-holding
whites and to soldiers, among other matter. How
many knew of his purpose outside of the home
life from 1839 to 1858, it would not be easy to
ascertain. A score or so of strong, brave colored
men—Garnett, Gloucester, Loguen, Douglass, and,
later, the Langstons, with Still, Baptiste, Reynolds,
and others, who kept guard for the fugitive on the
line of "Mason and Dixon," or that of the Canadas,
knew of the Ohio farmer and Massachusetts wool-
dealer, who in a quiet, unbending way, was preparing
to precipitate a conflict to make of Jefferson's Declaration a practical fact, and of Hamilton and Franklin s Constitution something more than a mere verbal phantasmagoria. In 1839 the air was charged
with vital interest. The rugged old squire, after
whom the Ohio town of Hudson was named, typified
one side when he rejoiced at the news of a slave-

---

[1] See Appendix.   [2] Ditto.

insurrection; and the constant conflict between slave
catcher and fugitive along the dividing lines of North
and South, expressed another. The opposite view of
anti-slavery agitation and work to that held by John
Brown was rising rapidly into intellectual power.
Still, the industrial North however aroused, was at
heart peace-loving as well as profit-seeking. So the
Quaker conception of non-resistance readily became
accepted as a worthy alternative to the passion created
by knowledge of oppression. That form of action
was presented as the only means of forwarding a
crusade which inflamed the moral sensibilities.
These are always the heralds of force, and play the
rôle of couriers in the declaration of war. The South
was saved from conflagration by the underground
railroad. Mr. Garrison watered the consuming fires
while he declared slavery to be piracy and murder;
making the Constitution to be "a covenant with
Death and an agreement with Hell." The flames
thus ignited he would have restrained by withes of
straw. Wendell Phillips presented the rôle of systematic agitation, and binding the Anglo-Saxon instinct of
order to the human passion of resistance to wrong,
pointed, through his matchless oratory, the way
for the great political forces of nationality and
freedom. Conflagrations are not quenched by attar
of roses. John Brown said: "Talk was a national
institution, but it did not help the slave." The
Puritan argued from the individual to the institution, and felt, in seeking to defend the former, he
was saving the latter from the wreck and ruin injustice brings to nations as surely as vice does to
persons.

The South knew better than Garrison thought, and steadily prepared to fight. Chattel bondage combined with the cotton-gin to coin Southern fortunes, and at the same time to breed bankruptcy. The Southern States gained political power by holding human "property." Extension of bondage controlled the public policy, and the oppressor sat in the judgment seat. Still, the impossible became the efficient, and the unexpected happened.

John Brown moved to Springfield, Massachusetts, as a wool-dealer. He fought the house of Amos A. Lawrence in business, and long afterwards Mr Lawrence, after arousing the free-State men to fight, joined Brown's defamers in seeking to assail his memory. The warehouseman carried on a propaganda as well as business. There was, thirty years since, a daguerreotype, in possession, I think, of the North Elba household, which showed John Brown and a colored man, presumably Thomas,[1] a porter he employed and trusted, in which the latter carried a small banneret, lettered "S. P. W." — letters signifying "Subterranean Pass Way." Brown's hand is on the colored man's shoulder. Mr. Sanborn's biography is the authority for the statement of Thomas's early knowledge of Captain Brown's purposes. Frederick Douglass tells his own story in that exquisite English, of which the renowned slave, fugitive, freedman, orator, statesman, diplomat, and American citizen, is so perfect a master. He has given me authority to use as I wish this account, and I gladly avail myself

_____

[1] Thomas Thomas recently died at Springfield, Ill. He was in the service of Mr. Lincoln after his first election until his death.

thereof, while gratefully acknowledging the favor.
Frederick Douglass's narrative is the earliest in time
of knowledge, as it is also a most cogent account of
John Brown's views and plans.   The first public account was prepared, however, by me, under the title
of " Some Shadows Before," as a chapter in James
Redpath's book, published early in 1860.[1]   It is one
of the few prizes of a busy life that Mr. Emerson, as
stated by Henry D. Thoreau, declared this paper of
mine to be " as positive a contribution to American
history as John Brown's autobiography (also first
presented by Mr. Redpath) was to the historical
literature of the English language."

Soon after Frederick Douglass returned from his
first visit to England and had begun and successfully
carried on at Rochester, New York, the publication
and editorship of the *North Star*, he spent a night and
a day under the roof of a man whose character and conversation, and whose objects and aims in life made a
very deep impression[2] on his mind.   Other colored
men of prominence, and Douglass names Loguen and
Garnett especially, in speaking of him, would drop
their " voices to a whisper," and what they said made
Frederick " very eager to see and know him."   Being
invited to his home at Springfield, Massachusetts, for
it was John Brown they spoke of, Mr. Douglass went
there in 1847.   He was surprised at the remarkable
plainness in which the Browns lived, as the head of
the family was to all appearance a prosperous mer-

---

[1] See Appendix.

[2] Life and Times of Frederick Douglass, pp. 337–43, Chap. 8;
383–85, Chap. 10.   De Wolf, Fiske & Co., Boston.   1893.

chant doing a considerable business. Their dwelling was a small frame house on a back street, in a neighborhood chiefly occupied by laboring men and mechanics, and the inside was plainer even than the outside. In this house, writes Mr. Douglass, "there were no disguises, no illusions, no make-believes. Everything implied stern truth, solid purpose, and rigid economy." Of the head of that house, says the negro statesman, "he was, indeed, the master of it, as he would have been of any one in it if they only stayed long enough. . . . He fulfilled St. Paul's idea of the head of the family. His wife believed in him, and his children observed him with reverence." His arguments, adds Douglass, "seemed to convince all, his appeals touched all, and his will impressed all." This, too, because he was a man of truth and hid not where he trusted. Evidently the family heard what he had to say to Frederick Douglass, and this illustrates another notable fact: none of that family ever talked outside of their own circle, and, indeed, not often within it, of the vowed aim of all their lives. In their several degrees, each simple soul was wedded to ideas, and there never came to them thought of heroism or virtue; it was their daily life to be both heroic and virtuous. They have never posed for plaudits. Mr. Douglass writes that after the meal of "beef soup, cabbage, and potatoes,", which was placed before his guest and family, John Brown "cautiously approached the subject; . . . he seemed to apprehend opposition to his views. He denounced slavery in look and language fierce and bitter, thought that slave-holders had forfeited their right to live, that the slaves had the right to gain

their liberty in any way they could, did not believe
that moral sausion would ever liberate the slaves, or
that political action would abolish the system. . . .
He had been for some time looking for colored men
to whom he could safely reveal his secret." His
plan had, writes Mr. Douglass, "much to commend
it." There was no thought of a general slave rising,
much less a "general slaughter of the masters."
"Insurrection" would defeat the object he had in
view, but John Brown, says Mr. Douglass, "did
contemplate the creating of an armed force which
should act in the very heart of the South." He
designed using the Appalachian range, and declared
that in them defensive posts could be made and
camps established into which selected slaves could
be recruited or taken, and from which then raids
would soon "destroy the money value of slave property." The logic and sagacity of this idea may be
realized, when it is recalled that the Nat Turner
Virginian outbreak, in 1831, almost frightened the
people of that commonwealth into emancipation.
Only three votes stood between the affirmative and
negative of a constitutional convention. John Brown's
attack on Harper's Ferry reduced the value of Virginian slave-property by $10,000,000, and cost the State
an expenditure of about $200,000, most of it spent on
absurd acts, designed chiefly "to fire the Southern
heart," and not at all to affect Abolition activity.

"My plan," said John Brown to Frederick Douglass
in 1847, "is to take at first about twenty-five picked
men, and begin on a small scale; supply them with
arms and ammunition, and post them by squads of
five on a line of twenty-five miles. The most per-

suasive and judicious of these shall go down to the
fields from time to time, as opportunity offers, and
induce the slaves to join them, seeking and selecting
the restless and daring." With care and skill he
deemed that one hundred good men could be gotten
together, able to live hardily, well armed, and quick to
seize all advantages. His original twenty-five would
supply competent partisan leaders. When his one
hundred were secured, entrenched in the mountains,
whose Virginian portion he knew well from having
surveyed for Oberlin College, in 1840, the lands that
had been granted that institution, the area of work
would be extended, slaves run off in large numbers
and from various directions, while retaining the hardy
and brave fighting men. Of course, he designed to
subsist on the slave-holders. "If the slaves could in
this way be driven out of one county," he said, "the
whole system would be weakened in that State."
Bloodhounds might be employed, but they could be
killed as well as the hunters. He did not believe that
over any considerable area, the means of subsistence
could be cut off. Besides such men as he would train
could carry subsistence enough for several days.
They would live on game, could make jerked beef,
find roots, use the wild fruits. Unnecessary fighting
was no part of John Brown's plan. Evasion as well
as resistance; strategy equally with combat; this was
to be the rule. When attacked, resistance was to be
made as costly as possible. His field was to begin at
the northern section of the southern Appalachian
range, not necessarily at Harper's Ferry, though from
the outset he undoubtedly had that point in view as
a place of possible attack. He anticipated also being

able to arrange for sympathetic assistance along the border of Pennsylvania, and, when the progress of the movement warranted, along the Ohio also. Mr. Douglass gave favorable judgment so far as the practicability of disturbing slavery in Maryland and Virginia was concerned. He also saw that though "John Brown should be driven out of the mountains" (or even slain), that "a new fact would be developed by which the nation would be kept awake to the existence of slavery." Hence, he says, "I assented to John Brown's scheme or plan of running-off slaves."

This was the key to the letters on the daguerreotype —S. P. W. It explains also the misapprehension of Brown's movement expressed by Major Martin R. Delany, in the pleasant biography of that notable colored savant, physician, and Union soldier, who called the Chatham (Canada) Convention together in 1858. Major Delany declared, through his biographer, Frank Rollins (Mrs. Whipper, of South Carolina), that John Brown did not state that his operations were to be in Virginia, but left only the impression that the project was but a more systematic and enlarged running-off of fugitive slaves. John Brown never designed throwing his life away in such an enterprise. He would help the bondman to flee as he did in his Missouri raid, in December, 1858, and, having done so, he would not be content except he knew they were in safety. His purpose was not to populate a Queen's colony, but to save a Republic.

To fully understand John Brown and his Harper's Ferry raid, one must comprehend something of the conditions that existed during the years in which he brooded over it. Neither railroad nor telegraphs had to any large extent penetrated the Atlantic coast range. Very few towns of any size or importance existed near them or within their borders. A mobilized State force was unknown, either of armed police, country militia, or national guard organizations. The negro was not so rigidly watched as was the case in the next decade. The mountaineer and non-slave-holder knew that in the Carolinas and Virginia he and his had been for half a century deliberately pressed back and forced out of the eastern Piedmont region; were obliged to retreat to less fertile mountain fields and valleys, while the schoolhouse faded with the lowland farms. The strategical value of the Appalachian range, from the border of Pennsylvania southward, was instinctively signaled by Congress at the earlier stages of the Civil War in the creation of the State of West Virginia, and by the Executive in stubborn holding of the same at the heaviest of cost in blood and treasure. The Union holding of the upper portion of that range, was the possession of an armed and fortified promontory jutting into the furious sea of rebellion. It would have been a comparatively easy task then, given the acceptance of purpose and policy, to have at any time, between 1830 and 1850, placed a small body of trained men in that remarkable mountain formation which flows south from the Potomac and Ohio to the northern uplands of Florida, and projects westward as the Blue Ridge, Cumberland, Missionary Ridge, and Lookout ranges, into Tennessee, southern Kentucky, and northern Georgia. The ranges that split the rebel territory in twain, and the holding or successful invasion of which marked the rise and fall of Confederate and Union fortune,

3

would have been, under John Brown's original plans, a veritable land of refuge. Harriet Tubman, "the general of us all," as John Brown expressed it to Wendell Phillips in 1858, made these mountains the road by which she aided and guided over two thousand of her enslaved race from bondage to comparative freedom. The limestone formations of Kentucky are full of mountain caves—places which, till emancipation came, often served the needs of flying fugitives. John Brown had seen or heard of all these things. He had studied the census, and knew the resources of the region in which he designed to operate. I have had in my possession a memorandum, prepared by Owen Brown, quaintly written with signs and abbreviations of his own, which lets in considerable light upon the extent of the observations made. Much of this material was based upon the information of fugitive slaves. It relates largely to roads, location of plantations, and character of neighborhood supplies. The seven maps of slave States, with statistics packed on their margins, which were found in the carpet-bag of papers, etc., and captured by the Virginians, showed to Governor Wise and his councillors, that Captain Brown had contemplated more than the scare made by the attack at Harper's Ferry.

Captain Brown did not loiter over his plans, except as want of means compelled inaction. In Springfield he set to work upon the passage of the Fugitive Slave Law: to systematize resistance thereto. He organized the League of Gileadites,[1] and went also to Syracuse to aid in the rescue of "Jerry,"—a fugitive slave

---

[1] See Appendix.

whose case made a famous row at the time. In all these matters it was his aim to find fit persons for the enterprise over which he steadily brooded. For this purpose in the main, he removed himself and family to North Elba, in the picturesque but severe Adirondack region. He hoped to find fighters among the colored farmers. Gerritt Smith was settling there, and he was necessitated by business failure also to economize more closely. When he went to Europe on his wool-selling venture of 1850, he did not, one may be sure, lose sight or thought of the purpose he held. In Great Britain, Germany, Austria, and France, he visited forts, studied plans and ordnance, carefully looked at soldiers and their equipments; above all he inquired into moral, social, and economic conditions or results. More and more he clearly drew the lines he would follow in the struggle to which he was pledged without questioning. He had ideas in connection with defensive works, that bore on them the stamp of practical capacity. I saw and examined in Kagi's hands plans of John Brown, drawn by himself, for the mountain forts. They were to be used in ravines or "draws" when so situated that passage from one to another could be made. It was intended to conceal them by trees and thickets, place them on hillsides, and otherwise arrange them as ambuscades. I do not know what became of these papers, but presume, from expressions in the newspapers of the period, that they also were found stowed away in the captured carpet-bag. Frederick Douglass [1] says of a visit made to him at Rochester in 1859, by Captain

---

[1] Life and Times of Frederick Douglass, pp. 386-87.

Brown, that the latter "soon after his coming, asked
me to get him two smoothly planed boards, upon
which he would illustrate with a pair of dividers, by
a drawing, the plan of fortification which he meant to
adopt in the mountains. . . . These forts were to be
so arranged as to connect one with the other, by secret
passages, so that if one were carried, another could be
easily fallen back upon." In his Kansas warfare Captain Brown would, as at Black Jack, seek a ravine for
concealment and from which to make his first attack.
His tactics were the reverse then, as a rule, of such as
govern regular army operations when conducted on
a considerable scale.

From 1847 to 1855 no mention has been found beyond the family circle of John Brown's purposes and
plans. Much of that time was spent on the lonely
mountain farm at North Elba, or at Troy and Utica,
New York, in pursuing the lawsuits which had followed his failure in the wool business at Springfield,
Massachusetts. It is singular, in view of the subsequent relations of Amos A. Lawrence to John
Brown's Kansas activities, and his later denunciation
of the old fighter's memory, under the inspiration of
ex-Governor Charles Robinson's morbid and morti-
fied ambition, as well as of Eli Thayer's collapse as a
public man, that John Brown's wool venture, bankruptcy, and subsequent severe poverty, should have
directly resulted from the trade combination of which
the Lawrence wool dealing and manufacturing firm
of New England, were the center. The Ohio firm of
Perkins & Brown was organized, as sheep-growers,
raising good breeds and fine wool, and subsequently
undertaking to deal in American wools as presented

for market, under the system of graded qualities which John Brown first invented. The wool tariff and its custom service was practically based upon the idea of the Ohio sheep farmer In the Springfield warehouse, the wool bales consigned to John Brown were tagged and marked to indicate their grade. In some way, these marks were removed or obliterated (John Brown believed by bribery of his clerk) so that all the wool was sold as of one grade, and that, too, of a low class. The New England dealers and manufacturers had steadily monopolized the market by this practice of rating American wool in but one low class or grade. John Brown broke it up, but his opponents broke him up also. He afterwards entered suit against the buyers, won the New York case and lost the one conducted in Boston, because of compromise made without his authority, as he claimed, by his lawyers. His New York lawyers testified after he became famous alike, to the transparently honest character of his business advice and action and to the earnestness also with which he watched the progress of the fugitive slave agitation, then at its height. In 1854 he was only prevented by threat of throwing up his case on the lawyers' part, at a critical moment therein of carrying out his desire to leave Utica for Boston to participate in the Anthony Burns rescue excitement. The Kansas and Nebraska struggle went on, and closed not until John Brown was long dead. But, "His soul went marching on." At the head of battling armies, in the uproar of hilarious camps, amid the solemn savagery of the battle shock, flaming with its mighty "Hallelujah Chorus" through all the thundering octaves of

embattled conflict. It was the sign of human devotion, the unbridled recognition of courage blent and
blending with lofty conviction. It was the song of
praise fiercely tinged with that of the fighter, as when
Jeff. Davis and the "sour apple tree" were brought
figuratively into juxtaposition. It was the anthem
of reverence, the choral shout of defiance, the jubilee
of victory. John Brown's work was still a-doing.

CHAPTER III.

THE KANSAS OVERTURE.

*Slavery under arms—Freedom arousing—Slow advance
and savage persecution—John Brown's friends and
foes—Relations of the hero to the conflict—Recruits
who came; confidants who sustained—What is said—
Service without murmur made or plaudits gained.*

JOHN BROWN was not old as the years go. He
should have been in his prime on entering Kansas.
But repression tells, endurance wears, and the conflicts of the soul leave scars that are the most indel-
ible. John Brown, who had never been young with
the pride of May, or known the joyous riot of June,
was older than his fifty-five years when called to
action in that fateful summer of 1855. He knew the
summons of God had come at last, and he was ready.
With the captain were his sons, John, Jason, Owen,
Frederick, Oliver, Salmon, Watson, his son-in-law,
Henry Thompson, and his brothers-in-law, the Rev.
Mr. Adair, who is still living at Osawatomie, Kansas,
and Mr. Orson Day, his wife's brother; Ruth, his
eldest daughter, Wealthy and Ellen, the wives of John,
Jr., and Jason, with children—one having died while
these emigrants were passing through Missouri. At
first they were refused permission to bury the little

body there, and finally had to bring it on to Kansas.
These eight fighting men were a host in themselves.
To their camp came James H. Holmes, a well-educated New Yorker, fresh from college; August Bondi,
European engineer and soldier; Charley Kaiser, one
also of the brothers of Susan B. Anthony (there were
two in Kansas); the Partridge boys, John Bowles
and his brother William ; Dr. Updegraft, John
Ritchie, H. H. Williams, and a few others. Augustus
Wattles, O. B. Brown, the founder of Osawatomie,
James Hanway, E. B. Whitman, James Montgomery,
with one or two more comprised nearly all who, after
that first year, became identified with John Brown.
Some of them were advisers, not fighters. All the
earnest men on the free-state side,—that is, those who
were not temporizing for real-estate deals, political
advancement, or color-hating propensities,—held John
Brown in the sincerest respect. So far, however, as
possessing his confidence as to ultimate designs, after
all these intervening years of research, I fail to learn
of more than four or five persons, except those who
went out with him from Kansas to Iowa, and finally
as to the most of them, to Virginia itself. William A.
Phillips, besides myself, is the only one of the Kansas
men who has presented a connected account of any
such knowledge. Most of the regular Northern correspondents who were present in the Kansas fighting
years—as Phillips, of the New York *Tribune;* Redpath, of the Missouri *Democrat;* Wm. Hutchinson,
S. F. Tappan, and Mr. Winchell, of the New York
Times; John Henri Kagi, of the New York *Post;*
Hugh Young, of the New York *Tribune* and Pennsylvania papers; Anderson, of the Boston *Advertiser,* and

myself of the Boston *Traveller* and Chicago *Tribune*, with a score of others who alternated letter-writing with farm-making or town-building, and some fighting when that was required,—were earnest supporters of John Brown. Most of us believed in striking back on Missouri and slavery, and we wrote and fought on those lines. But we knew nothing till 1857 or 1858 of the reserved Alleghany campaign or of Harper's Ferry attacks. James Redpath affirmed that he went to Kansas, hoping to foment slave insurrections.[1] That, as stated, was probably an afterthought, but there can be no doubt that he, like John Brown, fully believed that American slavery would go down amid a sea of blood. Perhaps I was the only other correspondent of that date who openly announced his adhesion to the task of fighting slavery with every weapon obtainable. There is no accessible evidence that others went to Kansas with any such opinions already formed. What they accepted as the coin of that bloody mintage is another matter. Deliberate misrepresentation from men animated by disappointed ambition has been so gross that it is essential to say these things in order to comprehend some of the forces that were affecting John Brown's career. The Northern correspondents who have assailed or criticised us were merely " birds of passage," who took what was told them as gospel, or came later, like Albert D. Richardson or Edmund Babb. Professor Spring or David N. Utter belong to the later and second-hand régime. The men in the breach never assailed John Brown.

---

[1] The Roving Editor. New York City. 1858.

No one, who knows the history and internal affairs
of Kansas from 1854 down to 1866, can have the
slightest doubt as to the motives that animate
Charles Robinson. The people of Kansas after electing him Governor, have never been moved to intrust
him with any other elective office. His rival in their
regard, the late General James H. Lane, once secured
the coveted prize of a United States Senatorship, and,
with all the faults acknowledged as making part of
his character, his memory as their dead servant is
more fragrant than the living aroma that identifies
Mr. Robinson. The same galled pride of place which
aroused hostility to Lane also animates the attacks
on Captain John Brown's name and memory. Mr.
Eli Thayer, of Massachusetts, is "tarred with the
same stick," in that he realizes that his emigrant aid
organization has not given him that high rank in
current history which his own conception of its
merits and of its author's ability, would have required.
It is hardly worth while to refer to other writers who
have attempted to whitewash and rehabilitate border-
ruffian leaders and pro-slavery chiefs by minimizing
the character or services of nearly all the active
Kansas men of the free-state and war period who
did not happen to belong to the personal *entourage*
of the ex-Governor. Historical accuracy is illustrated
by the manner in which they sneer at and have
sought to belittle men who, if not always acting as
God's children should do, were always, during those
ten stern years of savage conflict, on God's side.
Charles Robinson said in 1881, on retiring from
the presidency of the Kansas Historical Society :
" The time for writing the true history of Kansas has

not yet arrived, and will not arrive till the historian shall be so far removed from the actors and passions of the hour as to be able to calmly survey the whole field, and clearly discern, not only *events*, but causes and effects as well."

It is a pity that the ex-Governor should have forgotten his own admirable maxim, and left thereby a blot on the fame of Kansas by the book which he has recently had published.

Before John Brown reached Kansas, the slavocrats had twice invaded the Territory in force, men had been slain for opinion's sake, and a code of infamous enactments, which made it a penal offense to think of freedom, or to speak, write, or act in its behalf; which dictated ball and chain with hard labor for teaching negroes to read, or to print anything against slavery, had been forced by arms upon the people. Shortly after his arrival other free-state men were slain, cabins were burned, stock stolen, towns raided, courts packed and used for oppression, armed forces were raised in the South. Missouri, as a State, and by its citizens individually, was invading the Territory, and highways of travel, such as the Missouri river, were impeded. The mails were robbed, and people left the Territory in dread of murder. And at the beginning, not over one in six of the free-state settlers owned weapons, while all the pro-slavery people, whether settlers or invaders, came armed to the teeth. A great pro-slavery organization flourished, and secret societies were active in carrying out the designs of nullifiers and secessionists. The army of the United States was as openly used as the courts to suppress free-State resistance. If its officers were better than their

instructions, which was not always the case, it was due
to the decencies inculcated by their professional
training rather than by their honor as servants
of a democratic commonwealth. Violence on behalf of slavery was found on every side. Resistance, slowly rising, became a natural consequence.
John Brown's brain had forecast these conditions, and required him to utilize the results thereof. Other men talked revolution, but they trembled at deeds. It is beyond question that all the
hours of the Kansas struggle were as replete with
intended treason on the part of the pro-slavery
leaders, as that its latter days saw the growth of
fighters for freedom who realized fully that the existence of slavery was a perpetual menace to the Republic, and who were unwilling to accept as duty the dicta
which would make them serve slavery or imperil the
Union. Charles Robinson understood this as well as
John Brown when he told William A. Phillips, on his
leaving Kansas in the second week of May, 1856, that
he designed going to the governors of the Northern
States, and urging upon them the necessity of immediate organization for armed resistance to the South
and its aggressions. The conservative newspaper
man combated the free-state leader's idea, but to no
avail. The latter went, was made prisoner at Kansas
City, brought back to Lecompton, and released
through the fighting men. He now lives in his old
age to deride John Brown and intimate that Phillips
was too radical in 1856.[1]

---

[1] "There was only one proposal," wrote Col. Wm. A. Phillips,
"that ever came to my knowledge that even looked like revolu-

John Brown's first appearance at Lawrence made him at once a conspicuous figure. Free-state confidence was not lessened by the defeat of Henry Clay Pate, of Black Jack, or by the fear which, after the Pottawatomie slaying, dwelt in every border-ruffian camp, and at the threshold of all their strongholds. Osawatomie was a dear victory for the invaders. The forty-five free-state men against four hundred ruffians could not be expected to do the impossible, though they showed that they tried to, in the slaying and wounding of as many of their assailants as themselves numbered. John Brown showed no insubordination or ambition in sinking his identity at the Washington Creek and the Titus Camp affairs, neither did he at the last defense of Lawrence on the 15th of September, 1856, unless the caustic contempt

---

tion in the country. I believed it then, as I have believed it ever, to be a mere crotchet in one man's brain, and one, too, in which he was not sincere. That man was Charles Robinson. You perhaps remember just before the sack of Lawrence by the border ruffians (May, 1856) that Robinson started East. I for one could not understand why he should want to leave at such a time, and urged him strenuously to stay, and when pressed for a reason for his departure, he told me he saw the whole country was going to be involved in civil war, and that he was going to the free States to arouse the governors and the people of them to arm, so that when an army came on us, another could strike our enemies elsewhere, if necessary at Washington. . . . I spent some time urging on him that the difficulties never need, or ought, to occupy such proportions. . . . When he left, I for the first time began to lose confidence in the man, and thought then, as I do now, that all the story about going to the free States was a mere pretense to get away from the danger." [Extract from letter of Wm. A. Phillips to James Redpath, from Lawrence, Kansas, dated Feb. 24, 1860, and published in the *New York Herald*, April 20, 1860.]

expressed for mere words by the remark that I reported at the time of "great cry and little wool; all
talk and no cider," made as he left a council where
no one agreed to aid in organizing on the street that
resistance to the Missouri invaders which the people
of Lawrence were expecting, can be so considered.
It has not been my intention to place recollections of
my own at the fore, but rather to use them as only inspiring and connecting this narrative. But as I was
a part of the conflict under consideration, and others
are busy in derogation of those who, having passed
beyond, are unable to correct misrepresentations, I
may surely be pardoned if some things are said upon
my personal knowledge :

I was in Lawrence on the 15th of September, 1856,
and ready to do my share of its defense. During the
forenoon we heard of the border-ruffian advance towards Franklin, six miles south of the little town. Of
course, it was known also that the free-state "leaders," among whom John Brown never counted himself, were sending frantic messages to Governor
Geary, then at Lecompton, eleven miles distant.
That functionary had announced his determination
to stop the fighting and protect the people. He fulfilled the former by arresting Colonel Harvey and a
free-state force under his command on its return
from Hickory Point, a border-ruffian camp north of
the Kaw river and west of Atchison. But the latter
he almost failed to do, as it took him all day to reach
Lawrence and the Missourians under Reid (the com-
ander in the attack on Osawatomie, August 30) had
already burned the cabins of free-state men, run off
their stock, and murdered one of them, Mr. David

Buffum, an unarmed cripple, who lived within eight miles of Lecompton and who was slain during the afternoon, almost in sight of Geary's slow-moving escort. The Governor had ten hours in which to have reached Lawrence. Certainly, that gallant Union soldier would never after have achieved his deserved reputation as a fighter and commander if he had shown no more alacrity than in serving Lawrence at the rate of one mile per hour on the 15th of September, 1856. At that date, I was the only correspondent in the town. By that, I mean the only one who was following that line of work exclusively. The night before I returned from Topeka where I had been sent by Colonel Harvey, on whose staff as a free-state commander I was serving. My detail had reference to warning Colonel Whipple (Aaron D. Stevens), who had moved northward with a small command to meet an incoming body of Northern men, of the Federal Governor's avowed intentions to arrest these emigrants. On my return I heard of Captain Brown, whom I had already twice met, being in the neighborhood of Lawrence, and by request of Charles Robinson, in conference with himself and others of the civil leaders. General Lane had already left for Nebraska to avoid complications with Geary and the Federal authority, and it was understood that John Brown would also "disappear." John, Jr., and Jason, his elder sons, who had been held prisoners by the United States troops, were in Lawrence with G. W. Brown, G. W. Deitzler, Judge Smith, Gaius Jenkins, and Charles Robinson, who had been hurriedly discharged by Judge Cato, after General Lane and the free-state force had " demon-

strated " a few days before in front of Lecompton.
The recollection is very distinct to me of the proceedings of September 15th.   But I am not left to
my memory, however, for there lies before me as I
write, my Boston *Traveller* letters of that date and
the 16th, written on the spot, and also the journal I
kept in those days of youthful enthusiasm.   Besides
these authorities, I am strengthened by the recollections of Col. John Bowles, now resident in New York
City, and then a young, talented, and devoted
free-state man, whose brother William was a victim
of the poor fare, bad treatment, and imprisonment of
Harvey's command, held as prisoners by Geary for
several months.   The elder brother died at Lecompton; both were Kentuckians and slave-holders, too,
by inheritance.   They emancipated their slaves.
John Bowles became a Union soldier, and, like myself,
was a commissioned officer (lieutenant-colonel) in the
first body of colored men lawfully enlisted to fight
(1862) for the Union.[1]   Colonel Bowles was on the
street with his rifle, and was among the dozen young
men, similarly armed, " directed " by Captain Brown
to take charge of the stone breastwork on Mount
Oread, the right of our position, and where the State
University now stands.   John Brown appeared on
Massachusetts street about one o'clock.   I walked
with him (he asked me for the place of meeting) to a

---

[1] The First Kansas Colored Vol. Inf'y, afterward (1864) the
Seventy-Ninth U. S. C. I.   James M. Williams, Colonel; John
Bowles, Lieutenant-Colonel; Richard Ward, Major; Adjutant,
Richard J. Hinton.   First enlistment, August 6, 1862   First
appointment to recruit colored men, to Lieutenant Hinton,
August 4th.

large stone building on the corner of Winthrop street, and just opposite the ruins of the Eldridge or Free-State Hotel. In this building were assembled a number of "leading" citizens of the town, engaged in talking about the " situation." I stood by Captain Brown's side as he listened, briefly and impatiently, refusing to participate in the "jackdaw parliament," and went out with him on to the street where about three hundred men, boys, and women were gathered, with such arms as they possessed. Among them were a portion of the "Stubbs," under, I think, a Captain Cracklin, who now hastens to declare that John Brown had no "command" and did nothing. Among the talking counselors I recall Mr. James Blood, who, in 1884, twenty-eight years after, and when Captain Brown had been dead a quarter of a century, went into cold type to argue that the old fighter was an unnecessary slayer of men or a monomaniac. I recall him listening, also with G. W. Brown and others, who have since assailed John Brown's memory, with muskets or long rifles in their hands, as the Captain mounted a dry-goods box and addressed the excited people. I reported that speech, and I find it printed in my old newspaper letter.[1]

---

[1] GENTLEMEN—It is said there are twenty-five hundred Missourians down at Franklin, and that they will be here in two hours. You can see for yourselves the smoke they are making by setting fire to the houses in that town. This is probably the last opportunity you will have of seeing a fight, so that you had better do your best. If they should come up and attack us, don't yell and make a great noise, but remain perfectly silent and still. Wait till they get within twenty-five yards of you, get a good object, be sure you see the hind sight of your gun, then fire. A great deal

4

Most of us took position in one or the other of the
two circular earthworks that had been made under
General Lane's directions the winter before. Major
Abbott was supposed to be in general command and
doubtless consulted freely with Captain Brown. Captain Sam Walker was out, I find by my notes, with a
small mounted force, watching Reid's forces, and at
the same time looking for Geary's approach. The
" Stubbs," or that portion of a company who were in
the town were armed with Sharpe's rifles that Amos
A. Lawrence, of Massachusetts, had purchased early
in 1855, and sent by Mr. Abbott to Kansas for use in
fighting the Missourians. Dr. Samuel Cabot, of
Boston, about the same time paid for and sent through
Mr. G. W. Deitzler (afterwards Brigadier-General
United States Volunteers), one hundred Sharpe's
rifles. Frederick Law Olmstead, of New York, with
the aid of other gentlemen, sent by Major Abbott,
rifles, revolvers, and one twelve-pound howitzer. All
of these arms were solicited by Robinson, Blood,
G. W. Brown, and others now attacking the memory of
Brown and Lane for revolutionary action, and of the
leading newspaper-writers also, as advocating retaliation on Missouri and attacks upon Federal authority
and the Union. These arms were in Kansas two
months before the sons of Captain Brown settled
there, and men had been drilled in their use for the

of powder and lead and very precious time is wasted by shooting
too high. You had better aim at their legs than at their heads. In
either case, be sure of the hind sight of your gun. It is for this
reason that I myself have so many times escaped, for, if all the
bullets which have ever been aimed at me had hit me, I would
have been as full of holes as a riddle.

purpose of resisting "alleged" Federal laws, at least three or four months in advance of Captain Brown's own arrival in Kansas. When I read the foolish accusations made against the facts of history, I wonder that intelligent men like Charles Robinson can forget so easily their own acts and commitments. But, to return to whether John Brown aided or not in the defense of Lawrence. The Stubbs detachment marched, by his suggestion, to an advanced point on the extreme left of our position where their long-range carbines could be used effectively against Reid's advance from Franklin. The party of which John Bowles was a member went on a run to Mount Oread, and then I find that Captain Brown came to the earthwork where I was stationed. J. W. Brown, one of his persistent defamers, was there with a United States musket in his hand; I remember two or three women, also armed, with others who were running bullets at a little fire. The Captain asked in a loud voice if any of us had Sharpe's rifles. On response he cried "Come out, quick." We never had an order or request from any one else but John Brown, and some ten or twelve responded. Others came from the street and adjacent works, and about twenty-five or thirty so armed—all young men, as far as I now recall,— marched after Captain Brown who led us to a slight ridge on the level prairie about one-third of a mile away. There we were aligned and ordered by him to lie down behind the ridge and watch the advance of a party of about three hundred horsemen we could see coming towards us from the Wakarusa. We lay there, some five or six feet apart, while John Brown, in full sight with a revolver in his hand, walked slowly up and

down giving us directions in the event of firing being
required.   We heard some shots from Mount Oread
and from a field to the East also where the Stubbs
where. This firing confused the Missourians of whom
some were wounded.   Then, as the horsemen were
coming within our range, a commotion on the California Road, indicated the arrival of Governor Geary
with two companies of United States dragoons, under
Lieut.-Col. Phillip St. George Cooke, a gallant Virginian, who remained faithful in after years to his flag
and country.   He was a courtly old gentleman, fair
and loyal, and I owe an apology to his name for some
harsh things written at that period.   I think Captain
Sackett, afterwards Inspector-General U. S. A., was in
command of one of the squadrons.   At the sight of
the "regulars" coming down Reid's advance retreated,
the town was saved, the fight did not come off, and
John Brown " disappeared," having by his presence
and encouragement, at least, prepared the way for
stubborn defense.   He always said he did not " command "; so far as my knowledge goes, no one else
did.   I remember how the Governor and his troops
failed to prevent the sky being reddened in those sun-
down hours with fiercer hues than even a prairie sunset brings, for the Missourians in their baffled rage
set to work to burn every free-state cabin and building in sight.   Late that evening I was ordered to
ride with a message of warning to the Captain,
and taking the prairie—the road not being very safe
for travel—I recall most vividly stumbling on John
Brown's bivouac, several miles west of Lawrence. He
had left immediately on Geary's arrival, disappear-
ing as suddenly as he had appeared that day.   With

him were John, Jr., Jason, Salmon, and Oliver, if I
recall aright.   They had a small wagon and one
horse, and with them was a fugitive slave, whom some
of us kept hidden about Lawrence for several days
before, while the black-law men threatened arrest
and return, and the so-called anti-slavery leaders were
asserting he had been sent into
the town to embroil us under
the Fugitive Slave Law with the
Federal authorities direct.   I
had carried him out of the town
one night, before my first Topeka
detail, and left him at a settler's
near the California road, where
John Brown's party found and
took care of him.   He made his
escape to Iowa.   This episode is
something of a digression, I
know, but its telling will be
borne with, as it illustrates a
condition of affairs in Kansas
now being actively denied and
derided.   To resume, however,

OLIVER BROWN.

during the spring and summer of 1856, the pro-
slavery people had occupied the Missouri River route
to Kansas, driving back during April, May, and June
several parties of Northern emigrants.   There were on
the road other parties, with one of which I was connected, and it was decided to make our way through
Iowa and across Nebraska, entering Kansas on the
north, and, if necessary, fight our way through to the
Kaw river.   General Lane and other free-state leaders, who had escaped the general assault by Missouri

border ruffians and the Buford contingent from other
slave States, were raising emigrants in the Northern
States. During the last week of July and the first
days of August, 1856, about twelve hundred men were
encamped on Camp Creek, a few miles from Nebraska
City, Nebraska, near the preëmption claim, then occupied by the father and sister of John Henri Kagi,
afterwards Brown's chief confidant and assistant.

The dispersal of the Topeka Legislature occurred
on the 4th of July. Captain Brown, whose limited
means were nearly exhausted, decided to take his
severely wounded son-in-law, Henry Thompson, and
the two crippled and hurt sons, Owen and Salmon—
all of them injured at the Black Jack engagement on
the 2d of June—to western Iowa, and then return himself to the field of action. The organized free-state
men set about "blazing" a road from the Kaw River
at Topeka to the Nebraska line due north, near
where Falls City now stands. Aaron D. Stevens,
then known as "Colonel Whipple," and as commander of the second or Topeka free-state regiment, was
engaged on this work. It was an absolute necessity
to open the same. The chief free-state settlements
of Kansas were then cut off and practically surrounded. They could only be succored by the bold
flanking movement, which, with insufficent commissariat and a very inadequate ordnance, gathered its
recruits, mostly young, from Massachusetts and New
York to Wisconsin and Iowa, to rescue the free-state
people. After leaving Iowa City, the last railroad
station to the West, we marched nearly six hundred
miles to Lawrence. The armed pro-slavery forces held
the eastern line of Kansas through slave Missouri, and

had flanked and surrounded the free-state communities from the Missouri border at the south and just
below Osawatomie, to Atchison on the north and
upon the Missouri river. In the huge semicircle
thus indicated, the towns of Osawatomie, Lawrence,
Leavenworth, and Topeka, with the raw farms or
settlements about them, were all embraced. Within
this arc were also the border-ruffian settlements of
Franklin, Paola, Lecompton, Indianola, Osawkee,
Hickory Point, and Kickapoo, while Leavenworth,
though near by them, had had a strong minority of
free-state men. The line thus indicated, was almost
completed and held by fortified camps occupied by
Buford's Alabamians and Georgians ; Atchison's,
Stringfellow's, and Reid's Missourians. Lane had
practically planned the overland march, and pressed
it upon the National Kansas Committee, at Chicago.
The Massachusetts Committee, of which Stearns,
Higginson, Cabot, Russel, Howe, and Sanborn
(afterwards John Brown's friends) were the more
active members, aided the Chicago movement, and
somehow the men got through. The company of
which I, a young printer and reporter, was a member,
raised principally in Boston and Worcester County,
was armed with Sharpe's rifles. My own weapons
were given to me by Theodore Parker and Dr. Henry
Channing. The Massachusetts Committee furnished
transportation and arms, and we all signed a pledge
to become *bona-fide* settlers in Kansas. Thaddeus
Hyatt, president of the National Kansas Committee,
bought and presented each of us with an Allen revolver on our arrival in New York, and I took charge
of fifteen hundred Springfield muskets. At Iowa

City, 1,500 United States guns were taken from the
State arsenal, the key of which was conveniently left
accessible to my hands on Governor (afterwards Senator) Grimes's desk. Arms were also obtained for
Lane's men from an arsenal at Ottawa, Illinois.
Several hundred Sharpe's rifles and Colt's revolvers
were taken from Massachusetts and other emigrants
at Lexington, Missouri, which were replevined next
year by those who held the evidence of ownership.
These weapons were distributed to free-state men
enrolled in 1857, for the purpose of resisting the
Lecompton Constitution movement.   Other arms,
including 400 Hall's rifles, made at the works where
Kagi, Leeman, and Leary were killed two years later,
were subsequently brought in.   There were also two
or three 12-pound guns, which subsequently helped
to make the first battery served in the War for the
Union by Kansas Volunteers.   At the Nebraska
camps many persons, then, or subsequently, of some
historical note, were assembled during 1856. Besides
Gen. J. H. Lane, Edmund Ross, afterwards United
States Senator from Kansas and then Governor of
New Mexico, was in charge of a Wisconsin party.

A young man of the name of La Grange, who subsequently as colonel of the First Wisconsin Cavalry
assisted in the capture of Jefferson Davis, was also at
Camp Creek.   To it, while we were there, came as
inspecting visitors, Thaddeus Hyatt, of New York,
a famous inventor; Dr. Samuel G. Howe, of Boston,
and Horace White, then of Chicago, and now one of
the editors of the New York *Evening Post*.   Among
others present then or shortly after was Edward
Daniel, a distinguished geologist and afterwards the

first commander of the First Wisconsin Cavalry;
Thomas Wentworth Higginson, preacher, agitator,
fighter, soldier, poet, and author; James Redpath,
journalist and editor, and S. C. Pomeroy, subsequently
United States Senator from Kansas. These are only
a few of the names that memory recalls. During
that last week in July, James H. Lane, disguised as Mr.
" Joe " Cook, with Capt. John Brown, who was known
as " Isaac Smith," under Sam Walker's escort went
southward. Lane was furnished with means, and
aided to enter Kansas only upon the understanding
with the National Committeemen that he would
avoid any collision with Federal authority, officials, or
troops, pledging himself, as he subsequently did, to
leave Kansas whenever seriously threatened with
arrest. This is a fact that I state upon personal
knowledge. It was well understood that there was
danger in Lane's immediate command, several hundred in number, breaking up for want of means.
Lane himself was under indictment for " constructive
treason." The National Kansas Committeemen then
in our camp held the point of vantage which this fact
insured. For the sake of national peace, then seriously endangered by the necessity of breaking up the
pro-slavery forces, it was well to agree.

It is part of the verities in relation to Kansas and
John Brown to say at this point that whoever planned
the summer campaign of 1856, breaking up the
pro-slavery encampments at Franklin, Washington
Creek, the Titus Camp near Lecompton, Hickory
Point, Osawkee, and Indianola, and compelling the
subservient pro-Southern administration of Franklin
Pierce to send to Kansas a Northern Democrat as

Governor, who would and did endeavor vigorously
to somewhat impartially keep the peace, it was not
the free-state " treason " prisoners held by the United
States troops at their camp adjoining Lecompton.
Their release was a part of the campaign, sedulously
forced to that point by General Lane, who retired as
he came, with a small escort when this work was
accomplished. Sifting the testimony at this late
date, as thoroughly as I am able, it appears that
Lane was the prime organizer, as he certainly was the
chief leader in that nine or ten weeks of marvelous
activity, which saw a sufficient force of earnest men
gathered, armed, and marched into Kansas from all
parts of the North, and a carefully planned conspiracy of aggression, backed by Federal acquiescence
and official power, beaten, overthrown, stamped out,
and practically driven away. The attacks on Osawatomie and Lawrence when Lane was retiring,
though severe, were but flickerings of the fires he and
his coadjutors had scattered, without any more aid
than words from the gentlemen held as prisoners at
Lecompton, on charges of " constructive treason,"
usurpation of office, etc.[1]

---

[1] In May, 1856, Chief Justice Lecompte, sitting in the United
States Court at Lecompton, charged a Federal Grand Jury as
follows :

" *This Territory was organized by an Act of Congress.* . . .
It has a Legislature in pursuance of that organic act," and, " *being
an instrument of Congress* it . . . *has passed laws.* These
*laws, therefore, are of United States authority and making, and all
that resist these laws resist the power and authority of the United
States, and are therefore guilty of high treason.*" Further on he
declared that for all combinations to resist, and all aiding in them,
the Grand Jury must " *find bills for constructive treason.*" Upon

On his way out of Kansas, during the last two weeks of September, 1856, John Brown traveled part of the road with deputy United States marshals and troops sent to arrest him, as well as to intercept the second body of Northern emigrants, whom the Missouri ruffians' seizure of the river route had compelled to march overland in Iowa from the Mississippi. The arresting parties had no idea that this sickly old man with his sons, also sick, could be the formidable partisan leader they all dreaded. Colonel Whipple (Aaron D. Stevens) was moving northward also with an armed free-state party, on parallel lines, but avoiding observation from the Federal force. Captain Brown was in Nebraska before the beaten deputies learned of his escape. He was in the Iowa and Nebraska camps of the Northern train commanded by Col. Shaler Eldridge, S. C. Pomeroy, Samuel F. Tappan, Parsons, James Redpath, and others. The Iowa muskets, under charge of Pardee Butler, a Northern preacher who had been run out of Kansas by border ruffians at Atchison, had already got through in safety. It fell to my lot to meet and convoy Butler to Topeka. Governor Geary's policy at that date was to save the Democratic party, and bring about the election of James Buchanan. By worrying the free-state movements, and by the aid of coffee-pot colored election returns of Pennsylvania, that party

---

this charge that Grand Jury did with the Judge revive Jeffrey's doctrine, and brought in a number of indictments against individuals, including Charles Robinson, and also bills against the free-state hotel and printing-offices in the town of Lawrence, which a few days later were destroyed. [Sanborn's " Public Life of John Brown," pp. 237.]

was successful in giving incipient rebellion four years more in which to prepare for an outbreak. Governor Grimes, the stalwart Executive of Iowa, waited until after the Presidential election, and then in the late winter notified the Governor of Missouri, that Iowa proposed to make the Missouri river "run unvexed" to its junction with the Mississippi, unless he should call off the ruffian people of his own State from impeding that line of travel.

There were several things to do in western Iowa before Captain Brown could take up his next rôle. His enfeebled boys had to be cared for. Owen and Watson were left at Tabor. John and Jason returned to Ohio, in which State they once more made homes. Oliver and Salmon Brown, with Henry and William Thompson, accompanied Captain Brown to Chicago, whence the Thompsons and Oliver went at once to North Elba. Captain Brown remained some days to confer with the officers of the National Kansas Aid Committee, whose headquarters were in that city. At Tabor, Iowa, a number of old arms and equipments had been left by the Northern train under Pomeroy and Eldridge. Captain Brown asked for and was refused their custody. Later, with the third Massachusetts colony under Mr. Parsons, there was brought to and left at Tabor 200 Sharpe's rifles, etc. These. arms afterwards came under Captain Brown's control, and were the rifles captured by Virginia after the defeat at Harper's Ferry.

NOTE.—Since this chapter was written, and just as this book was finished, Charles Robinson, whose career and criticisms are animaverted upon, has died If time had permitted the tone, not the facts, might have been modified.—R. J. H,

CHAPTER IV.

SHADOWS FROM POTTAWATOMIE.

A startling deed—The slaying of five men—Its causes and its effects—Aggressions of the slave-power—Preliminary to Kansas outrages—A conspiracy against the Nation—John Brown's views of duty—The roads to Harper's Ferry—Who the slain men were—The border ruffians appalled—How the critics assail and falsify—An incident at Lawrence—Opinions of contemporaries.

DURING the night of May 24, 1856, five men—William Sherman, Allen Wilkinson, and three others, named Doyle, father and two sons, were taken after midnight from their beds by armed men, who said they were of the "Northern army." They were made to go a short distance from their cabins, and there slain by those who had captured them. Their bodies were found at daylight, the skulls having been split open, evidently by a heavy broad weapon which pierced at once to the brains of the men. Only one shot was fired. The slayers were eight in number. One was an elderly man who was directing, though not otherwise personally active. The only description of the leader of the " Northern " band is given in the testimony of John Doyle and Louisa Jane Wilkinson, as presented in a report made by the minority member, Representative Oliver, of Missouri, of a Committee of the United States House of Representatives. John Doyle in his testimony, uses the following language: "An old man commanded the party; he was dark complexioned, and his face was slim." Louisa Jane Wilkinson says: "The old man who seemed to be commander wore soiled clothes, and a straw hat pulled down over his face. He spoke quick, is a tall, narrow-faced, elderly man.' There is no other description given.[1]

Another member of the party does not appear to have been actively engaged, though of late years he has repaired that sluggishness by becoming the instrument of those who find a congenial occupation in assailing the memory and fame of the leader in this tragedy. Stated thus in the plainest of words,

---

[1] In the Thirty-fourth Congress, the House of Representatives passed into the hands of the anti-Nebraska party. N. P. Banks was elected Speaker. One of the first acts was to provide for (March 19, 1856) a committee to investigate the border-ruffian invasion of Kansas, at the Territorial election just held. Lewis D. Campbell, of Ohio, and William Howard, of Michigan, Republicans, with Mordecai Oliver, of Missouri, Democrat, were, on the 24th, appointed such committee. On the 25th, Representative Campbell declined service, and Representative John Sherman was named in his place. It was this committee that was in Leavenworth when the transaction at Pottawatomie occurred. The committee never made any investigation. No evidence was ever taken at any of its sessions. The *ex-parte* affidavits referred to, were inserted by Mr. Oliver, in a minority report. They have no legal status ; still no one disputes their general correctness.

this was the deed of May 24, 1856, which is known in the free-state annals of Kansas and of anti-slavery resistance as the "Pottawatomie Massacre." I do not intend to excuse, defend, or extenuate as to guilt or innocence therein, nor to detract by any rhetorical effort from the simple sternness and severity of the deed. It will be my purpose, however, to give with equal plainness both cause and effect.

From the bivouac of the free-state farmers and settlers enrolled under John Brown, Jr., as "The Pottawatomie Rifles," then *en route* to the assistance of Lawrence, eight determined men are known to have retraced their march from Captain Shore's dwelling on Ottawa Creek, back to the Pottawatomie, where they had settled as well as the men who were slain. These eight men, like their comrades in the free-state company, had "news" of the pro-slavery doings from the settlement. The eight men were armed with breechloading rifles and repeating revolvers, while seven of them carried short, broad, heavy swords, such as artillerymen of the United States army then used as side-arms. The men who left the camp within twenty miles of the scene of death were, as is now known, John Brown; with four of his sons—Owen, Frederick, Salmon, and Oliver; a son-in-law, Henry Thompson; Theodore Weiner, a German-American settler and merchant, and James Townsley, a Marylander, identified as a settler with the free-state cause. The swords were sharpened before leaving camp, and their departure was greeted with cheers by their comrades. Information had just been received of threatened assaults upon the families who had been left behind by the free-state volunteers.

The men were slain, and the act was deliberately done. There never was any doubt of that. It was a question for some years whether or not the act was done under the influence of, and by the direct orders of John Brown. No one now doubts that it was. In passing judgment, then, on this startling deed, the issue is to be made on motive and purpose, on cause and effect. If it were dictated by a supreme need, in order to save other lives, or if it were also the overweening necessity of a situation based upon actual warfare, alive with all its imperatives, while· the results wrought righteous advantage to the cause of Freedom, then in deadly peril, the verities must reach a conclusion in no sense detracting from the lofty moral standard of the grim and sturdy Puritan fighter. Let us examine this severe act, then, in the light of all that has since occurred, and with the relief from secrecy which time has wrought to our advantage.

After thirty-eight years of perspective have been gained, we may look all around the act and decide without heat or partisanship. During those years also, this nation has passed through strangely clarifying experiences, which have made very clear the terrible righteousness of forces of which ordinarily we stand appalled. There are many worse things in human history than the taking of human life. It may be that in days of millennial joy, if they ever come, that the race can put behind it all darkness of strife, all shadows of conflict, all the lurid scarlet in whose deep currents we now see the great forces that have often made life worth living. Even altruistic halos may gain reflected luster from the blood of atonement. The currents of life are not made of perfumes. War is a stern teacher; a sterner master. When its wrath is righteous, may it not be most just? When governed by conviction and engaged in human service, its seeming is actual and without question; its inflexible decision may justly be implacable. There are some things more sacred than life itself: as when sacrilege attempts to destroy the Ark of the Covenant!

With the passage of the Missouri Compromise in May, 1820, there begun a long series of slave-holding aggressions, which culminated politically in the enactment of the "Nebraska Bill." The compromise of 1820—repealed in 1854—declared:

"That in all that territory, ceded by France to the United States under the name of Louisiana, which lies north of 36° 39′ North Latitude, not included within the limits of the State contemplated by this Act, slavery and involuntary servitude, otherwise than as the punishment of crime, shall be, and is, for ever prohibited."

John Brown was in his twentieth year when this Missouri Compromise was hailed by the slaveholders as a triumph. Good people in the North believed it would settle peacefully a great issue. Within a few years Missouri, with the aid of a National Administration, violated it with impunity and almost unnoticed. The Platte purchase became a breeding-ground for border ruffians. Dedicated to free soil in 1820, stolen to slavery in the early 'thirties, it was, during the Civil War, the supporter of bushwhacking and a hotbed of secession sympathy. The young man, turned from the pulpit training he sought by an affection of the

5

eyes, became farmer, tanner, and merchant; above all
he watched and brooded over the course of events.
To him the Declaration of Independence was almost
as sacred as the Hebrew Scriptures and the Gospel
of Christ. Each of the long line of aggressions by
slavery left, therefore, enduring impressions on his
mental character. They came rapidly: South Carolina nullification; campaigns against Indians for the
surrender of " marooned " negroes ; the forcible removal of Indian tribés beyond the Mississippi and
the Missouri, in order that slave territory might be
organized or the central continental movement of
Northern settlers might be checked; the seizure and
annexation of Texas; the War with Mexico and the
spoliation of her territory; the passage of the Fugitive
Slave Law as offset to the admission of California as a
free State, and finally the rending of the Compromise
of 1820, by the so-called " squatter-sovereignty "
dodge as the central feature of the Nebraska Act.
None of the other dark and lurid incidents of that
third of a century seemed to have escaped the notice
of John Brown. I heard him tell one evening at the
home of Augustus Wattles, Moneka, Kansas, the
obscure and forgotten stories of "Isaac," " Denmark
Vessy," " Nat Turner," and the " Cumberland Region " insurrectionary affairs in South Carolina, Virginia, and Tennessee. He showed himself perfectly
familiar with the sometime resistance to slave-
catchers in Pennsylvania, and he knew the story of
Hayti and Jamaica, too, by heart. The murder of
Owen Lovejoy was a part of his own experience,
and he had seen the principal riots against the
Abolitionists. As an illustration of how he had fol-

lowed the political workings of the slave-power, he called Mr. Wattles's attention to the policy which covered Kansas more than any other part of the trans-Missouri region with Indians removed from Ohio, Michigan, Illinois, Indiana, and other States, and stated that for over twenty-five years but one man of Northern birth had been appointed Indian agent to any one of the dozen tribes living within the section then organized as the Territories of Kansas and Nebraska ; a large portion of Colorado and Wyoming being then included. That one man, a Mr. Gay, was agent to the Shawnees. He was one of the earlier victims of border-ruffian disorder.

It must not be forgotten that for John Brown the Kansas conflict was but an episode. It drew him aside from his main design, an attack on slavery for the purpose of making the "institution" unsafe, from the Appalachian mountains in Virginia. The peril of his sons and their families, who were settlers in the prairie territory and the daily augmenting possibility of an outbreak against slavery itself being precipitated there, took him to Kansas. There was the increasing possibility also of finding recruits. John Brown had decided for himself that the slave-power designed to destroy the Republic. Did not crowding events justify that conclusion ? He was also sure, that the people of the free States were more alarmed at their own peace being disturbed than at the danger of the Union. He decided for himself, by the severe processes of his own stern conscience, that his duty as a Christian lay with those in bondage, and that, as a citizen, whatever might be the individual cost, the Republic had to be defended,

The closer one proceeds with analytical inquiry into
this chrystalline personality, and the means for such
analysis are abundant, the more evident it is that the
Puritan farmer considered himself in all his purposes
and the acts that blossomed from them, as obeying
the highest obligations of citizenship, and fulfilling,
not the promptings of his personal zealotry, but the
direct obligations due from a man to his God, his
fellows, and to his country. Nor did he misapprehend
the possible penalties, but to him the slave-holder was
a traitor to the Republic and slavery was organized
treason to its institutions. As I have already suggested, his close study of current American history
taught him the existence of a deliberate design to
work the overthrow of the Federal Union. For years
before Kansas was opened to settlement the Knights
of the Golden Circle had been systematically organized throughout western Missouri. Their offshoot,
the Blue Lodges, were organized in 1854, in order to
invade Kansas, carry elections, and make thereof
another slave State. The Constitution was in his eyes
being steadily violated. Was he not right in that
regard? To him as a Christian, if Christ were love, He
also wore a weapon and smote the money-changers. If
God were embodied mercy, He was also the enthroned
Jehovah—" Judge of the quick and the dead." If men
were the creatures of their conditions, they were to him
also and supremely the choosers of their own path;
responsible for what they knowingly left undone, as
well as whatsoever they did in daily life and action.
John Brown saw also with a marvelous precision that
seemed like the mystic's flame, the startling course
of sequences and events. He could not, therefore,

act otherwise; nor could he fail to see the grim severity of the conflict. Perceiving, he dared not turn
aside for political gain or philosophical methods. This
man lived his convictions, he did not dream that they
were available only when convenient. Neither politician nor agitator could change him; he judged by
but one thing; did they, like his compass, point to
the North? That compass "wobbled," he said, but
as the needle settled it always pointed to the North
Pole.

In Kansas the free-state politicians were bold at
times, in words at least. Reeder, the kindly, weak,
but well-meaning Pennsylvania Democrat, who had
been sent to Kansas as Governor by President Pierce,
declared, as he felt the barbarous aggressions of the
slave-power, as early as October, 1855, that—"When
other resources fail, there still remains to us the steady
eye and the strong arm, and we must conquer or
mingle the bodies of the oppressors with those of the
oppressed upon the soil which the Declaration of Independence no longer protects." Andrew H. Reeder,
to his credit be it said, never indulged in subsequent
verbal denunciations of the man who did "mingle the
bodies of the oppressors with those of the oppressed."
That weakness was left in the main to some members
of the New England Emigrant Aid Society, whose
organizers, officers, and leaders had, as the preceding chapter shows, sent to Kansas, several months
before John Brown entered the Territory, rifles, revolvers, and cannon, with which to enable free-state
men to defend themselves or to slay the assassins of
their fellow settlers. Before Captain John Brown
entered Kansas, the eight hundred legal voters of the

Territory had been overridden by the invasion of more
than four thousand Missourians who occupied the polls
and elected a citizen of Texas as delegate to Congress
from Kansas. Before John Brown's sons had started for
the West, and before even Eli Thayer, Edward Everett
Hale, Amos A. Lawrence, Thomas H. Webb, and other
men in New England had organized the Emigrant
Aid Society, which, within certain definite lines, did
excellent work for free Kansas, the South Carolina
nullifiers had publicly organized an association to aid
" armed " emigration to Kansas.

When the first legal election was called in Kansas,
John Brown had taken no public step beyond appearing with his sons four months before in defense of
Lawrence, yet, in March, 1855, over six thousand
armed Missourians marched into Kansas and took possession of the polls.   The enrolled legal voters numbered 2,905.   The invaders overrode the citizens,
defied the Governor, and made a code of slave-sus-
taining laws,[1] equaled only in atrocity by the codes
for the control of the freed people which were adopted
in South Carolina, Mississippi, and the other Southern States, and which President Johnson sought to
" restore " direct from the blistering furnace of civil
war.

After the election outrage of March, 1855, and the
subsequent determination of the free-state people,
as a body, to refuse obedience to the draconian code
that Missouri had fashioned for Kansas, it soon became evident that the secession leaders in the slave
States were determined to push their cause to the

---

[1] See Appendix for extracts from " The Border-Ruffian Code."

perilous verge of civil war. A force of about seven
hundred armed men was raised, chiefly in the cotton
States, and placed under the command of one Buford,
an Alabama fire-eater. From Arkansas, Texas, and
Louisiana, there also came several smaller bodies,
who, as they had their rendezvous at Fort Scott, the
chief pro-Southern town in Kansas, outside of Leavenworth and Lecompton, were not as well known and
conspicuous as their confrères in the central and
northern sections. From early in April, 1856, until
the increasing free-state power caused them to begin
retiring about the following October, there were certainly in the Territory never less than an organized
force of from one thousand to fifteen hundred armed
men whose residences were elsewhere than in Kansas.
A score of free-state assassinations, which included
Dow, R. P. Brown, Barber, and others not necessary to name, had already reddened the record
of the two years' occupancy of the Territory. Hundreds of cases of robbery and personal violence were
known to have occurred. Not a single unmolested
or non-blockaded way into the Territory could be
found except on the northern or Nebraska line. The
Missouri river was closed to the travel of free-state
settlers. The mails were regularly stopped, opened
and often robbed. Free-state men were maltreated,
robbed, and threatened with death, their dwellings
plundered and burned, the women of their households threatened, abused, and even assaulted. There
are hundreds of authenticated cases with a recital of
which it is not necessary to cumber these pages.
The troops of the United States were often used to
enforce pretended legalities. It became the custom

of the officers and judges of the Federal Courts to
cause the indictment and attempt the arrest of all
free-state men whose courage, activity, and ability
fitted them to advise or lead their neighbors.   John,
Jr., and Jason, elder sons of Captain Brown, were
both indicted for "usurpation of office," before the
Pottawatomie slaying took place.   Their offense consisted in being elected legislators under a State constitution which was never made operative.   Up to
the sacking of Lawrence on the 21st of May, 1856,
three days before the tragedy under review, there had
not been any really resistant act or deed perpetrated
by the free-state men, except the rescue of Branson
and the wounding in Lawrence of Sheriff Jones, the
pro-slavery leader.   This latter was a personal act
committed by one man, and without any consultation with others.   They had prepared to resist
oppression, and to defend themselves against the
border-ruffian laws.   No one need assume that the
free-state men were saints.   If they carried wings
they were not those of angels.   When they did strike
back, it was done very effectually.   The hammer of
Thor when applied to the heads of ruffians made
something crack.   Why not?

Summed up, then, the general situation when the
pro-slavery men on Pottawatomie Creek were slain,
was this: The Federal judiciary was declaring that, as
there was no right whatever (as afterwards affirmed by
Dred Scott decision) to prohibit the taking of slaves
into any Federal Territory, agitation against as well as
resistance thereto, was nothing less than treason to
the United States, while to advise or agitate on the
same line was "constructive treason." This strained

revival of Judge Jeffries's infamous doctrine was
formulated by Chief-Justice Lecompte of the Federal
Court, relative to whom Captain Brown once said
that he "had earned the right to be hanged," and
that "if the Lord had ever delivered Judge Lecompte
into his hands, it would have required the Lord God
Himself to have taken the Judge out of his (Brown's)
hands." The Captain was not without humor of the
grimmer sort. The Territorial Executive was a dis-
sipated instrument of the slave-power. A militia
force had been organized, on paper at least, with
two major-generals and four brigadiers, all residents of Missouri. Ninety-five of the officers and
eighty per cent. of the Falstaffian rank and file were
actually resident in Missouri; and, when summoned by
Jones, Stringfellow, Calhoun, Donaldson & Co., came
direct from Platte, Jackson, Clay, Lafayette, and
other Missouri counties, bearing the arms of that
State, or rather those the United States had assigned
to it, and sometimes even wearing the State uniform.
They were headed, too, by David R. Atchison, a
United States Senator from Missouri, and, at the
period now under review, presiding member of the
United States Senate, and, therefore, in the absence
of Mr. King, acting Vice-President of the United
States. The Senator was the leader of the ultra
wing of the Missouri Democracy, and the bitter opponent of Thomas H. Benton and his following. Benton
was equally as hostile to nullification and its advocates. He was the advocate of Continental Unity, as
then comprehended. Some of his declarations during
the early 'fifties now read like prophecies. The leading newspaper on his side, the *Democrat,* of St. Louis.

was the fast and wise friend, too, of the free-State
men, from 1854 to 1860, as it was also the loyal and
gallant advocate of the Union against all comers in the
five following years of the bitterest civil and even
neighborhood warfare, which any section of the
Union was compelled to wage. Missouri was the hotbed of pro-slavery aggression, violence, and final
organized resistance to the Union. It is not essential
to give details of all these acts in order to indicate
the roads that the slave-power blazed and made wide
for John Brown and his men to travel upon in reaching
Harper's Ferry. All that is suggested in this narrative
can be established, if disputed, "by bell and book." It
is not essential to parade the acts of resistance thereto
or to hold up the resisters—all of them—as priests or
heroes. But it is essential to maintain for the truth
of history, that the free-state men were never the
aggressors, and it is certainly unnecessary to exalt
the horn of special manliness for pro-slavery leaders.
As persons, apart from opinions, they may be regarded
as no worse than their neighbors who differed. But
opinions shape conduct, nevertheless. It is too late
in the day to measure great events by peanut criticisms. Still less is it writing history in fairness
to carp and sneer at or minimize the characters,
acts, services, and even the sufferings, of the men
who on the right side made that history what it is.
It has been too much a fashion in later Kansas to find
fault only with those whose unselfish and early
services aided in making that State a free commonwealth. Let me give a striking illustration of
this. The savage incidents it relates, too, occurred
five days before the Pottawatomie slaying, temporarily,

at least, awed the border ruffians into a trembling peace, and startled alike the brave and timid in free-state ranks with a triumphant, yet serious, feeling, that on their side at least a Man had arrived. In that portion of his readable, if not always fair or discriminating little volume, which treats of the sacking of Lawrence on May 21, 1856,[1] Professor Spring writes of incidents occurring on the 19th of May, two days before the actual raid, and while the "conservative" free-state leaders in Lawrence were advising the young men of the "Stubbs Rifle" company to make no resistance to the armed Missourians gathering at Franklin, six miles from the little city on the Kaw. Mr. Spring shows himself in his presentation more concerned in censuring those whose manhood counseled resistance to murder than he does in characterizing with just indignation the purveyors, to use his own elegant comparison, of "abolition wolf meat." Here is the incident, as told thirty years after by the professor:

"A detachment of the United States marshal's posse (May 19) shot a young man—mainly for the sensation and satisfaction of killing an Abolitionist. Three adventurous fellows, *presumably intoxicated* (the italics are mine, not Mr. Spring's) on hearing the news, snatched their weapons, dashed out of Lawrence to hunt the scoundrels, and begun a fusilade *upon the first travelers they encountered without any preliminary investigation. The expedition turned ont unfortunate for the assailants.* Another Abolitionist was turned into wolf meat."

---

[1] " Kansas," Commonwealth Series, Boston.

It is somewhat difficult to refrain from wrath upon reading so contemptuous and cynical an account of an incident in regard to which the author might readily find, even at this date, a hundred living citizens of Lawrence—his neighbors—who would have told him the simple facts. Here they are, based upon personal knowledge on my part, and confirmed by two of those of the "adventurous fellows" who went out to find the murderers of an inoffensive young man, named Jones, sustained also by the narrative of the New York *Herald's* Kansas correspondent at the time, and found in the columns of that journal; by the story of Col. Wm. A. Phillips, as printed in the New York *Tribune*, and somewhat later in his interesting volume on "The Conquest of Kansas." I have also examined accounts published in the Missouri border papers of that date, and in the Kansas *Squatter Sovereign*, of Atchison, and the Leavenworth *Herald*, which exulted openly over the murder of two young abolitionists, Jones and Stewart. These sources of information, except those of a personal nature, were and are accessible, I presume, to Professor Spring as to myself. But, as to the actual facts:

Several miles directly south of Lawrence on the Wakarusa, a small branch of the Kaw River, was "Blanton's," a free-state settlement. It is quite famous in the stormy annals of that period. It was here that a blacksmith, named Dow, was murdered by one Coleman, a deputy United States marshal and deputy sheriff under the bogus laws. The famous rescue of Jacob Branson by other free-state men, from Sheriff Jones's posse, which superinduced the Wakarusa War, occurred in the Blanton settlement. One of the free-state leaders,—Major Abbott, who had been sent twelve months before by Charles Robinson, James Blood, and other conservative free-state chiefs, to obtain from Amos A. Lawrence, Eli Thayer, and other Eastern friends, the breech-loading rifles, etc., which enabled the free-state men to make a successful resistance,—resided in the Blanton settlement. A bridge across the stream, so named, was indicted as a nuisance by a border-ruffian grand jury, convened and charged by United States Judge Lecompte. Its destruction was a part of the work for the doing of which a posse of 2,500 Missourians had been summoned to the neighborhood of Lawrence. There was in the Blanton settlement a widow and son, named Jones,—the latter was a quiet, inoffensive, but courageous young man of about twenty. Mr. Jones, on the day of his death (May 19, 1856), was at Blanton's store, purchasing some groceries. A party from Franklin were there, embracing among them the murderer of Dow, Deputy Marshal Coleman, with another known assassin, named, if I recollect aright, Cosgrove. Some abusive words and threats were aimed at Jones. On his part there is not a particle of proof as to any cause of offense. Though he had a small revolver in his possession he made no demonstration, but as quickly as he could gathered his goods and walked out of the store. There was no reason whatever for singling him out for assassination, but as he quietly turned his back on his assailants and walked on to Blanton's bridge, he was shot and instantly killed. Most of the free-state men were absent doing guard duty in Lawrence. The murderers mounted and rode westward towards Lecompton. Word was sent to

the free-state headquarters, and early in the afternoon the body of young Jones was carried to Lawrence in a farm wagon. Of course, it created great
excitement and indignation. Three "adventurous fellows"—all young men of less than twenty-five years
of age—left the town to overtake and capture, if they
could, Coleman and his gang. They went without
orders from the free-state committee, but their leaving was seen and their errand known and approved
of by all who saw them leave. These young men were
John Edwin Cook, lawyer, Charles Lenhart, printer,
and Mr. Stewart, a medical student from western
New York, related, I believe, to the family of Alvin
Stewart, once lieutenant governor of the Empire
State and then a well-known anti-slavery politician.
Of these three men, two had never used any intoxicating liquor, and the third, "Charley" Lenhart, left
the "case" at which he was working in the *Herald of
Freedom* office, a perfectly sober man, when the body
of young Jones was brought to rest on Massachusetts
street. Cook and Stewart had not been long in the
Territory. The former came with ample means for
his own expenses. Mr. Stewart was employed (at his
own cost) in copying the laws which had been prepared by the Topeka Legislature in the vain hope
that even squatter sovereignty might be used in removing the Missouri rule. Cook was hung at Charlestown, Va., on the 6th of December, 1859, for participation in the Harper's Ferry raid. Cook, like Stevens, Hazlett, Coppoc, Copeland, and Green, were
tried for insurrection and murder.

John Brown was tried for treason against a State of
which he was not a resident, and, therefore, under the

State-sovereignty doctrine, one to which he owned
no allegiance. The land of Washington and Jefferson
had the "honor," then, of hanging the American
Spartacus as a traitor. He is the only American so
condemned and executed. Charles Lenhart died in
1862, as a lieutenant in the Union army. Mr. Stewart
was slain by murderer Coleman. It occurred in this
wise : The fact was known that the assassins of Jones
had ridden towards Lecompton, and as Cook and
Lenhart both told me within two months after
the Jones and Stewart murders, it was believed that
they would soon return to their Franklin camp.
Stewart, Cook, and Lenhart, well armed, went towards the old California trail or road, where about a
mile south of Lawrence it crossed the lower portion
of Mount Oread and made a highway to Franklin.
They stationed themselves at this point and had been
there about thirty minutes, when three men riding
mules were seen coming down the road. Their animals, clothing, and arms, indicated they were Missourians, and as they rode nearer, Coleman, at least, was
recognized. But a moment before the young free-
state men had decided to return to Lawrence. Hesitating briefly as to what should be done (the mounted
ruffians having evidently prepared for conflict), Stewart impulsively ended the doubt by stepping forward
but without raising his Sharp's rifle, and asked—
"Where are you going, gentlemen?" The response
was immediate. A gun was raised and fired as
Coleman shouted "We're going to Franklin and
you're going to hell." Stewart fell dead as a bullet
crashed through his forehead and entered his brain.
The assassins put spurs to their animals and dashed

on to Franklin, followed by Cook and Lenhart, firing as they run. One shot from Cook's rifle wounded the murderer Coleman, who dropped his rifle. Lenhart also wounded another. But the assassins escaped, and the two gallant young men, whose memories are so shamelessly blackened by the later " historian," returned to Lawrence with the dead body of their friend. Is any further comment necessary than this plain statement? I think not. These incidents, and such as these, are of those that led up to the slaying on the Pottawatomie. The very air of the Territory was reeking with murder. If the statement is questioned, " The Conquest of Kansas " (1856, pp. 286) by William A. Phillips, will stand for proof.

On Pottawatomie Creek, near where John Brown's four sons, his son-in-law, Thompson, and a brother-in-law, Mr. Orson Day, had made their land entries and settlement, one of the pro-slavery camps had also been established. It was but a short distance from the Missouri border. Above it was the pro-slavery town of Paola, and nearer to it the free-State town of Osawatomie. There is abundant evidence to show that this post was an important link in the pro-slavery campaign of that summer. The free-State settlers south of the Pottawatomie were comparatively few. Fort Scott was left to take care of them. Practically, " Dutch Henry's Crossing," as the pro-Southern settlement was named, became the first at the southern end of the border-ruffian arc, which was forming to inclose the important free-State settlements; the Missouri border, from Bates County north to about St. Joseph, on the river, being the base of the arc, or string of the bow. Captain Brown knew

clearly that the border-ruffian forces were but pup-
pets moved on the board of secession politics, and
this understanding far more than any personal threats
or possibilities, moulded his acts. He kept himself
thoroughly well informed of their purposes. Up to
the first sacking of Lawrence (the second occurred
under Quantrill in August, 1863), the Captain was
comparatively unknown in the Territory. His only
public appearance was the one described in the preceding chapter, when with his sons he went to the
defense of Lawrence in December, 1855. But at
Osawatomie, and among the free-state settlers on
the Pottawatomie, this grave, quiet man was regarded
with increasing confidence. He made no preparations
for a continued residence, and was constantly moving
about, often appearing in Missouri and along the
border with one horse and a small wagon, loaded with
surveying instruments. He was presumed to be a
United States deputy surveyor and, therefore, " sound
on the goose " by all the Southern men in whose
camps he was constantly appearing. He allowed
them to think as they wished, shaping his replies to
questions, so as to add to their confidence. Salmon
and Oliver, his two younger sons, generally accompanied him. In this way, during the early spring
months, he became thoroughly posted not only on the
purposes of the invaders, but as to the agents they depended upon. " Dutch Henry's Crossing" was their
initiative post south of the Kansas River. Henry and
William Sherman were South Germans. Henry, for
some time before the Territory was opened to settlers,
had been employed by Ottawa Jones, the leading
member of an Indian tribe, so named, who were civil-
6

ized and Christian. Jones was an excellent farmer
and a valuable man. Educated, and married to a
white woman, formerly a missionary teacher, he was
always an open helper of the free-state men, and
Captain Brown soon became his friend. " Dutch
Henry " had left " Ottawa " before the troubles began.
He and his brother William took up claims, and opened
a small grocery and groggery. He was soon suspected
of stealing stock and doing other disreputable acts.
Both men were violent, ruffianly, and brutal. They
were constantly insulting the free-state women and
making odious threats against them. Allen Wilkinson was a man of some education and a Marylander.
He was at first disposed to be a " black law " free-
state man, and his wife did what she could to keep
him from the bad influences at Sherman's. He was
flattered into becoming actively pro-slavery and had
been elected to the Shawnee Legislature—the body
that enacted a slave code. The Doyles were a
shiftless set, of the ruder and more brutal " poor
white " sort, and they were used as tools that had an
edge on them.[1] To this nucleus came others, until

---

[1] Henry Thompson, now residing at Pasadena, California,
writes me recently, in relation to the elder Doyle, that " in Kansas
in 1855, when the fall election came off, I, with others of our
company, went to the polling-place on the Pottawatomie, thinking
there might be trouble. . . . On the way home I walked
about two miles with old man Doyle and others. Doyle had a
great many things to say about the ' nigger,' declaring they had
no human feelings and did not know anything. I told him I had
seen colored men as much smarter then he was as he was smarter
than his little dog. Doyle said that was incendiary language and
I would pay for it. So, in the spring of 1856, when they held
their bogus court at Dutch Henry's. Doyle swore out a warrant for

the Sherman's place was the center of proposed operations against the free-state people and cause. These
operations did not materialize, because the material
was missing. The Federal Judge, Cato, held court
there, and from among its frequenters, the larger
number of whom were residents of border Missouri,
were gathered the grand juries, so-called, that presented indictments against John and Jason Brown,
H. H. Williams, of Osawatomie, and other free-state
men who had become prominent.

The summary removal of Judge Cato, who presided, was afterwards demanded by Governor Geary
because of his aiding to prevent the arrest of the
murderer Coleman, who, besides slaying Dow and
Stewart, was also a party to the killing of David
Buffum.

No one knew these pro-slavery agents so well as
Captain John Brown. Scores of pages might be
filled with evidence of this, but one statement will be
sufficient. In conversation with E. A. Coleman, now
living near Lawrence, Captain Brown in reply to
questions about some of the circumstances that
doubtless led more directly to the Pottawatomie slaying, said in 1856 in the Coleman cabin near Osawatomie and just before the battle thereof:

" Mr. Coleman, I will tell you all about it. I had
heard that these men were coming to the cabin that

---

my arrest. When we heard of it, we held a little council and
decided it best for me to go and give myself up. Salmon Brown
went with me as dispatcher, so if they served the warrant on me,
the others of our company were to come into court and hand me
two revolvers. The court was to be summarily adjourned, but
the court had weakened and left before I got there."

my son and I were staying in, . . . to set fire to
it and shoot us as we ran out. Now, that was not
proof enough for me; but I thought I would satisfy
myself. . . . I was an old surveyer, so I disguised
myself, took two men with me to carry the chain, and
a flagman. The (section) lines not being run, I knew
that as soon as they saw me they would come out to
find where their lines would come. And taking a
book out of his pocket," the Coleman story proceeds
with "Here is what every man said that was killed.
I ran my lines close to each man's house. The first
that came out said, 'Is that my line, sir?' I replied,
'I cannot tell; I am running test lines.' I then said,
'You have a fine country here; great pity you have
so many Abolitionists in it.' 'Yes, but, by God, we
will soon clean them out,' he said. I kept looking
through my instrument, making motions to the flagman to move either way, and at the same time I
wrote every word that was said. Then I said, 'I hear
that there are some bad men here by the name of
Brown.' 'Yes, there are; but next Wednesday night
we will kill them.' So I ran the lines by each one of
their houses, and I took down every word; and here
it is, word for word, by each one."

At the camp, *en route* to Lawrence, intelligence was
received of the burning of Mr. Theodore Weiner's
house and store, with abundant proofs of a general
advance against the influential free-state settlers
along the Pottawatomie Creek. It was known that
the honor as well as the lives of the women were in
peril. In after years I heard some narrations as to
this that were sufficient to set any man's blood on
fire. Among others who fled hastily for security to

Osawatomie, after the younger John Brown's company had left for Lawrence, were the wives of John, Jr., and Jason Brown, as well as members of the Partridge and Updegraft, with other families. James G. Blunt, then a practising physician in that section, and afterwards a major-general of volunteers, with a distinguished record, on whose staff I served for two years, told me of the continued unrest and dread that preceded the 24th of May, and of the quiet and peace that for a considerable period followed thereafter. I never heard a free-state citizen of that section among the scores personally known to me, deprecate the act of death with which John Brown's name is there associated. I have known some of them to evade the expression of an opinion. In fact, the only upright and honorable free-state citizen I have known as always declaring the "Pottawatomie Massacre" to have been unwarranted, was the gallant Col. Samuel Walker, of Lawrence. But, he never made his view a cause of attack upon John Brown's honesty of purpose or integrity of character. He held the act to be such a case of mental aberration or fanaticism as one, for example, in criticising Calvin, might consider the burning of Servetus. Col. Walker left personal reflections to men inside of his own lines who cared more for partisan success, or personal profit and advancement, than they did for conscience and unselfish service. Some attempt has been made to have it appear that John Brown in striking the Pottawatomie blow was obeying the dictates or suggestions of a secret free-state order or council. There is absolutely no proof of such a thing, and I do not believe it to be in any way credible. Reference is made to this rumor so as to call attention to a series of "half truths" that have been made to do duty as "whole falsehoods" ever since 1860. These were started, as far as they have a place in this history of events under consideration, by ex-Governor Charles Robinson, in his volunteered testimony before the Senate Committee's "Inquiry into the Harper's Ferry Raid." In that testimony, as printed at the time in the New York *Herald* and other papers, Dr. Robinson spoke of a secret order among free-state men known, as he said, as "The Danites." He declared, that he was not a member of it, but that James H. Lane (his rival for political preferment) was. He mentions also John Brown's sons, James Redpath, Wm. A. Phillips, J. H. Kagi, killed at Harper's Ferry, and myself. When his testimony appeared, Colonel Phillips, Mr. Redpath, and myself denied fully all of Robinson's statements. He never answered our proven denials. But there was a "League of Freedom" organized in Kansas, in the fall or early winter of 1855, and Dr. Charles Robinson, then chief agent of the New England Emigrant Aid Society, residing in Lawrence, was, as I have good reason for saying, its first chief or commander. I have in my possession a paper marked "Confidential," written by a well-known and still prominent citizen of Kansas, who states this position of Robinson to be a fact, and claims for himself to have served as the first secretary. This witness states that the original minutes are all in his posession, and that they will at some future day be deposited with the State Historical Society. In writing of "Dutch Henry's" character, he says, that a messenger started and failed to reach the camp of the Pottawa-

tomie Rifles with a request for the striking of some
blow that would compel a pause on the part of the
border-ruffian assailants. [1]

John Brown Jr., has declared in recent years that a

---

[1] Henry Sherman, or "Dutch Henry," as he was called, lived on
Pottawatomie Creek and kept a store or saloon. It had become the
rendezvous for the Doyles and others who were known as border
ruffians, spies, thieves, and murderers. It was through them the
Missourians gained all information concerning the condition of the
free-state men. At this particular time, the country was full of
such ruffians, who had come up here to murder our people and
burn our homes. These men were most active and bold. They
ordered free-state men to leave under pain of death if they failed
to comply. While our men were under arms and in camp, these
marauders went to the homes of the settlers, where there was no
one but women and children; they were abusive and indecent. On
one occasion they so frightened one woman who was quick with
child that she gave premature birth to it and came near dying.
These conditions were reported, and a council was called, the
whole matter was discussed, and after a full investigation, it was
decided that "Dutch Henry" and his whole gang should be put
to death, as an example and warning to the many murderers who
infested the Territory at that time. It was believed their crimes
merited it, and the safety of the free-state community demanded
it. I do not say that John Brown's party were chosen ; probably
the decision was anticipated. I do say we decided that it must be
done. The execution of these men was the dawn of peace in
Kansas. There was no more murdering except by ruffians attached
to forces coming over in large numbers. House-burning was done
only under similar circumstances. Pro-slavery men who where
not border ruffians, and there were a goodly number, were soon
ready to aid in the protection of free-state men. They asked and
were never denied protection by the latter. It was the great beginning of the glorious ending in Kansas. I justified it then, so
did Robinson and everybody else. I have had no reason to change
my mind upon that subject since.

night or two before the last attack on Lawrence
(September 15, 1856), Dr. Robinson in his own house
told his father that the Pottawatomie slaying was
entirely justifiable, and that more of the same sort
should be done.   Captain Brown grimly advised the
doctor that if he had any such jobs on hand he
should do them himself.   The "League of Freedom"
was designed only to enable the harassed free-state
men to know each other, to aid in protection and to
assist in rapid gathering for defense.   There was no
obligation taken of a wrong or violent character;
there was no disloyalty in its pledges, and on the
whole, as I now recollect, it was less forceful even
than the Union League of America, which became so
powerful in the war period.   That League seems to
have followed the Kansas outline.   I distinctly remember that the badge of recognition was for both bodies
the same—a little piece of black tape or ribbon worn
in a button hole or at the throat.   The Kansas League
was formed into units or councils of ten.   That's all
I recall, except that I know that it was as a factor of
no great consequence.   The actors, and no "Danite"
order, alone bear the direct responsibility of the Pottawatomie slaying; and as every sincere and active
Kansas free-state man of that period, but one, of whom
I have any knowledge, indorsed or acquiesced in the
deed and its results, they must all accept a share of
responsibility.   Charles Robinson declared that the
effect was to strike terror into the hearts of pro-slavery
men; that their "party could take no exception to
it as they had inaugurated the war"   He asked:
"But was John Brown at heart a murderer in this
butchery?   I think not.   He worshiped the God of

Joshua and David, who ordered all the enemies of his people to be slaughtered; . . . and everything that breathed."[1] In December, 1859, three and a half years after the event, Dr. Robinson, at a public meeting in Lawrence, supported resolutions declaring that said transaction was not unjustifiable, but " that it was performed from the sad necessity which existed at the time to defend the lives and liberties of the settlers of that region." Again, at the unveiling of John Brown's monument at Osawatomie, August 30, 1877, twenty-one years after the Pottawatomie slaying, Charles Robinson, in his dedicatory speech, declared of the Harper's Ferry party: " They were men of conviction, though death stared them in the face. . . . The soul of John Brown was the inspiration of the Union armies in the emancipation war. . . . To the superficial observer, John Brown was a failure. So was Jesus of Nazareth. Both suffered ignominious death as traitors to the Government, yet one is now hailed as the Saviour of the world from sin, and the other of a race from bondage."

Eli Thayer, who, like Governor Robinson, has been lavish in defamatory abuse of John Brown, knew well the story of Pottawatomie and all that it suggested, yet up to 1858 he was the open and apparently sincere admirer of the Puritan fighter. In May of 1857 he paid for and made Captain Brown a present of a large gun, carrying a two-ounce ball, which had been manufactured at Worcester for Captain Brown's use by the Massachusetts Arms Company. The receipted bill made out to Eli Thayer was indorsed and

---

[1] Topeka Commonwealth, 1879.

signed on the back in his own handwriting as follows:

"Presented to my friend, Captain John Brown, for use in the cause of Freedom.   ELI THAYER."

This document was in my possession in 1860, and was used in the campaign of that year against Eli Thayer's candidacy for Congress. He was running as an Independent, and part of his stock-in-trade was denunciation of John Brown's character and memory.

Perhaps no single piece of evidence will more clearly show the immediate effect of the Pottawatomie blow, than the following letter by one who is known as the lieutenant-colonel of the First Colorado Cavalry, and, after the War, as one of the Indian Peace Commissioners, appointed by President Grant. At the date of the slaying there was considerable commotion throughout the Territory. A party of Northern emigrants which had left Illinois for Kansas by the Missouri River, had been turned back at Leavenworth by Buford's men. The Oliver Congressional Committee was in session at Leavenworth. Threats of driving out all Northern men were freely made. Colonel Samuel F. Tappan says:

"In the summer of 1856, I was at Leavenworth as clerk of the Congressional Committee, investigating free-state affairs. A reign of terror prevailed, free-state men, women, and children, were forcibly driven from their homes, put upon steamers, and sent down the river. Free-state men were arrested by a mob of Buford men, and imprisoned in the basement of a warehouse. Miles Moore, M. J. Parrott, Charles Robinson, Judge Wakefield, and others, were also held as prisoners in the city. This continued until one afternoon the *Herald* (General Easton, editor) published an extra about six inches long—giving an account of the horrible murder by John Brown, of Wilkinson and six [four] others, on Pottawatomie Creek, Southeastern Kansas. This put a stop to further demands upon free-state men, and they were all soon after released. The Buford men remained quiet, no longer appearing in the street under arms. In a few days I took passage in mail-coach for Lawrence, with S. C. Smith. Mr. Weibling, who had been a prisoner, drove the team. Judge Wakefield, having been released, was also on the coach, and we drove to Lawrence without further trouble."

So much is certain: The men who were slain represented the worst elements arrayed in behalf of slavery, and engaged in harrying the free-state settlers; the results of the deed were immediately and permanently beneficial, and the most of those who have since defamed and assailed the name and fame of John Brown under pretense of being shocked by the Pottawatomie tragedy, were conspicuous in earlier days in eulogizing the man they now assail. It is an act not to be judged by soft "lutings of my lady's chamber," or the usual conventionalities of peaceful periods. Those who are shocked always at the shedding of blood will shudder when reading the story. Those who comprehend that evolution includes cataclysm as well as continuity, will realize the nature of the forces in issue, and decide as their own conception of events and their righteousness may determine. Those who lived through those titanic days, and stood for freedom, will have no doubt in ranging themselves. For John Brown himself, no one who understands the

conditions then existing will offer apology or excuse.
The act done proved to be a potential one in the winning of free institutions for Kansas.   And that is
what they have to deal with.   John Brown always
declared that the people of Kansas would surely
sustain and justify the deed done on the 24th of May,
1856.   The marble statue erected in his honor at
Osawatomie is in evidence of the faith that was in him.
For himself, while never acknowledging participation
in the Pottawatomie slaying, he never denied it either
He always declared, however, that, as he avowed a
belief in its righteousness, he could not, therefore,
avoid a personal responsibility for the deed.   This
has been the attitude of every honorable free-state
man in Kansas.   To avoid now would be cowardice
indeed.   Time has lifted the shadows, but it has not
dulled the memory.

CHAPTER V.

John Brown leaves the Territory—Through Nebraska and Iowa to Chicago—Governor Geary and the Northern emigrants—Free-state prisoners serving as his body guard—How they were ill-treated—The political conflicts—Serving Territorial power—The Lecompton and Leavenworth Constitutions—Ballot-box frauds—John Brown in Iowa and Kansas again—A new leaf turned.

THE Missourians suddenly retired from Lawrence on the evening of Sept. 15, 1856. They had failed in their avowed design of " wiping out " the town; first, because the courage of its residents combined with John Brown's presence, gave definite direction to the defense; and, second, because the Democratic fear of Frémont's election compelled the interference of Governor John W. Geary. But he made no effort to prevent the malign pro-slavery force from wreaking such vengance as they were able when retreating, in the burning of every free-state cabin in sight. Memory still recalls the scene. Two squadrons of United States dragoons, commanded by Lieut.-Col. Phillip St. George Cooke, surrounded the Governor while occupying the crown of Mount Oread, a small range of hills upon which now stands the State university buildings. At that time it was occupied only by a rude circular wall of earth and stone thrown up for defensive purposes. Capt. Samuel Walker was conversing with Geary. Soon after he was appointed acting sheriff of Douglas County. All free-state men esteemed Captain Walker, but many of them did not like the appointment, because it involved a recognition of the " bogus laws." The sunset's glow faded swiftly from the western sky, as a low soughing wind arose. The shadows were made lurid by the red flames of a dozen fires that could be seen, marking the retreat to the Missouri border of the pro-slavery force. All of us were impatient, for murder had been committed. Rapine was free, yet the Governor was slow. His severe manner showed he felt the full importance of his strange position, while it also made manifest his mental attitude towards the free-state people. Hostile and unfriendly then, we knew soon after that he was at heart of genuine stuff. Doubtless he realized that he had by not pressing the Missouri invaders, saved for the time being that Union, for whose defense and preservation he afterwards fought so gallantly and served so well as soldier and commander. Had Lawrence been destroyed that day, the North would have arisen in its wrath, Frémont would have been elected President, and the South would doubtless have revolted four years earlier than it did. There were men in the pro-slavery camp and councils in Kansas who steadily sought to precipitate that issue. It needed, however, the crucial test of the Harper's Ferry sacrifice to educate the awakening North to a fuller measure of the work before it.

John Brown, under the friendly shadows, left the town he had helped to save, no longer to him and his a friendly refuge. John, Jr., and Jason, were with him, also a fugitive slave, hidden in the ricketty one-horse wagon that Captain Brown had moved about in when appearing as a United States land surveyor. Two others probably joined him at Topeka. They were Charles P. Tidd and William H. Leeman, afterwards known to be with him at Tabor, Iowa. Owen Brown had been left at Tabor, when Captain Brown went to Iowa, and returned to Kansas in the preceding August. This trip was made in order to convey Henry Thompson, wounded at the Black Jack fight, with Owen and Salmon, who were also injured by accidents at the same time. Owen was on his way to meet his father, and did not get to the neighborhood of Lawrence until long after dark. He had an arduous task in the night to locate the bivouac of his father and brothers. The presence of a fugitive slave in the party made necessary more than usual caution. Captain Walker directed me, after the Governor and his escort made camp and found shelter for the night, to find John Brown's camp, or at least to overtake him by the time he should reach Topeka, giving him warning of an attempt to arrest. I found them early in the morning, and shared with the party their breakfast of roasted corn ears, lean beef toasted over a little fire, and corn-coffee. In those days such parties never traveled the highway, avoided the cabins, and at night usually camped without fire in sheltered ravines.

At Topeka, the center of interest then because of the incoming Northern emigrants, the policy of the new Governor was soon made known. He sought to, and

did divide free-state councils, inducing conservatives, like Captain Walker, to coöperate in securing
what was alleged to be peace, but which in reality only
made oppression more difficult to resist. He then
directed his efforts to the arresting or scattering of the
men, organized in the Northern emigrant trains, that
were coming to the Territory by way of the long land
route through Iowa and Nebraska. The nearest railroad stations to Kansas at that time were Iowa City,
Iowa, to the north and east, and Jefferson City, Missouri, to the south, each about four hundred miles
distant. The Missouri River, from St. Louis to St.
Joseph, was in the hands of the pro-slavery forces and
practically closed to free navigation, the Federal
authorities passively coöperating. A number of
Eastern and Northern emigrant parties had been
turned back thereon, and their arms and other goods
taken from them. The Sharp's rifles, which John
Brown afterwards transported to Virginia, were originally shipped, after purchase by George L. Stearns,
from Massachusetts for Kansas *via* St. Louis and
Kansas City. They were stopped on the road and sent
to Iowa City, whence some one of the agents of the
National Kansas Aid Committee, probably Mr.
W. M. F. Amy, had them forwarded with other supplies to Tabor, a few miles from Nebraska City.
Mr. John Jones received and warehoused them at
Tabor. It is not generally known, but it is a fact
nevertheless, that there were from 1856 to 1858 more
slaves in southern Nebraska than in Kansas itself.
Less than a hundred were brought there, and most
of them were conveyed to the north star section
soon after. The first attempt to cross the Missouri

river by the new route was made by the Massachu -
setts party, under charge of Martin Stowell, of which
I was a member. We were the advance guard in
July, 1856, of " Jim " Lane's hastily gathered command. The Nebraska City ferry was worked by a
southern settler, named Nuckolds, who had brought
slaves there and who declared that our company
should not cross. Three of us, who were mounted,
rode down, called and got the ferry over to the Iowa
or eastern side of the river, with Nuckolds himself in
charge, and we held it there until our little company
of sixty-five young men with three wagons were
ferried over. These incidents are only mentioned
to show the nature of the obstacles. Mr. Nuckolds
yielded to our persuasive force, aided by that of his
neighbors, many of whom were free-state in sympathy, and, perhaps, even more by the profit he found
in the large ferriage tolls we promptly paid. Brigadier-General Persifer Smith, U. S. A., was in command, with headquarters in Fort Leavenworth, from
early in 1856 until the spring of 1857, had spies
in our camps. Southern by birth and associations,
he leaned certainly to that side. Colonel Sumner, a
cousin of Senator Sumner (then a helpless invalid
from the bludgeon of Preston Brooks, of South
Carolina), was actively commanding in the field. He
is remembered with admiring gratitude for fair play.
It is not designed to suggest, however, that General
Smith was intentionally and deliberately partisan,
but he treated the Northern emigrants as marauders,
armed to disturb the peace, and regarded the Southern and Missouri forces as composed of gentlemen,
engaged, though in mistaken ways, in the assertion of

7

their rights. This seems to be the attitude of some of our local historians, who ought to know better.[1]

Governor Geary for a time held a somewhat similar attitude as to our newcomers, though he could not be in sympathy with the brawling border-ruffian element, by which at Lecompton he was at once surrounded. Indeed, he early exhibited genuine manliness by rejecting their advice and declining personal association with them. So marked grew the divergence that within less than three months the border-ruffian leaders at Lecompton were seeking some pretext for his assassination. Perhaps Gen. Persifer Smith's tendencies were shown in no more marked way than by his treatment of Governor Geary, whose demand for troops, needed in order to prevent that assault on himself and authority, he even rudely declined to recognize. That Geary passed this peril safely was mainly due to the fact that a number of free-state men were being nominally held as prisoners at Lecompton. But of this in another place.

After the arrival in July and August, 1856, from the

---

[1] Among our army officers in Kansas during the free-state prelude, were many of the most distinguished corps and division commanders, on both sides of the subsequent Civil War. General Smith, Col. Joseph E. Johnston, Captain Longstreet, Lieutenant McIntosh, Captain Anderson, I recall as noted Confederate officers. Cols. Sumner and St. George Cooke, Majors Thomas, Sedgewick, and David Hunter, Captains Wm. B. Wood, Sackett, and Nathaniel Lyon, are some of those who made fame as soldiers and renown as Union commanders. And singularly, too, the harshest and most unfair of them all in his personal attitude and action in dealing with free-state men was a fine soldier, now relieved with rank as Major-General of Volunteers and Brigadier General of Regulars, after a notable career as a corps commander.

Northern and Eastern States of over one thousand
additional free-state men, the conditions of the conflict favorably changed. The effort then begun to dis-
integrate the free-state party. It had so far deliberately avoided either Republican or Democratic affili-
ations. With the repulse at Lawrence, the victorious
fighters, Lane, Harvey, Brown, and others, quickly
disappeared. This was in accord with the politic
demands of the National Kansas Committeemen,
who demanded non-resistance to Federal authority
as a condition of organized North-
ern support. General Lane left for
Nebraska as soon as Geary's arrival
at Kansas City was known. He
was escorted out of Kansas by a
small force commanded by Colonel
Whipple — the name by which
Aaron Dwight Stevens[1] was known
in Kansas. He was the fighting
free-state leader at Topeka, and to
him was entrusted a defense of the
open road to Nebraska and Iowa.

AARON DWIGHT STEVENS.

On John Brown's arrival at
Tabor, in the middle of August,
Henry and William Thompson,
with Salmon and Oliver Brown, started at once for
their Adirondack homes, glad to get away from war's
disorder. For a considerable period thereafter, they
were disinclined to proceed any further in their
leader's course. On the second trip north, Captain
Brown and party camped near or passed the lines of

---

[1] Hung at Charlestown, Va., March, 16, 1860.

United States cavalry, engaged in efforts to arrest
him. Colonel Whipple with his command marched
on parallel lines, but kept out of sight, arriving in
Nebraska in time to meet the Northern emigrants
who were organized and marching under Colonel
Eldredge, of Lawrence; S. C. Pomeroy, afterwards
United States Senator; Samuel F. Tappan, and James
Redpath. Preston B. Plumb was also making his
third attempt to enter Kansas, the State which sent
him to the United States Senate in after years, he
having twice before been taken prisoner by Missourians and compelled to return to Ohio. John Brown
left Topeka later (Sept. 20th) and moved with less
rapidity than Lane, avoiding also the emigrant
trains. His son Watson, then a youth of seventeen,
had left North Elba for Iowa on the arrival home of
his brothers, but he missed his father and turned
eastward before the latter's arrival early in October at
Tabor. Captain Brown proceeded direct to Chicago,
where he arrived on the 25th or 26th of October.
After conferring with the National Committee, there
began the plan of agitation which finally led directly
to Harper's Ferry. He had framed definite plans,
the character of which will develop in this narrative.

While John Brown was making his way eastward
on a missionary tour for " Beecher's Bibles " (Sharpe's
rifles) and money to sustain further active operations,
affairs in Kansas became more complex and also
quite serious in character. The " Executive Minutes "
of Gov. John W. Geary, published by the State Historical Society of Kansas, within a few years, shed
considerable light on the passing events of the period
under review.

One startling reminder of border-ruffian domination, threatening renewal of strife for more than the year following Governor Geary's arrival in the middle of September, 1856, was an alleged law passed by the Shawnee Mission Legislature,[1] providing for the convening of a so-called constitutional convention at Lecompton, the Territorial capital, with sixty delegates. These were apportioned so as to allow of electing four-fifths of the delegates from counties controlled by Missouri votes. In an apportionment for Territorial Legislature, nineteen Southern counties were given but three representatives, three counties containing the bulk of free-state voters were given nine, while seven pro-slavery counties with one-half of their population were given twenty-four members. Attempts were made to induce the Governor to authorize and recognize the arming of small bodies as militia for the purpose of preventing any election outbreaks. The leaders were to be pro-slavery partisans like Henry Clay Pate, and men of the same type. Geary did not yield to this request, nor

---

[1] The Shawnee Mission was partly in Missouri and partly in Kansas, this segment being on the Shawnee reservation in Johnson County. The missionary was a Southern Methodist, and a violent pro-slavery man. Governor Reeder convened the first Legislature at Pawnee City, Riley County, the center of the Territory. The War Department, Jefferson Davis, Secretary, decided that Pawnee was on the military reservation of Fort Riley. Colonel Montgomery was cashiered, and unjustly, for it has since been found that it was not on the reservation at all. The general belief in Kansas was that if Colonel Montgomery had been " sound on the goose," *i. e.*, slavery, he would not have been cashiered. The Missourians immediately after organizing, adjourned to the Shawnee Mission and there went on with their work.

did he to the demand of the United States marshal, J. B. Donelson, of South Carolina, for an escort of twenty dragoons to enable him to arrest a number of active free-state men, charged with resisting the border-ruffian code. The Governor expressed his aversion to the use of troops in serving civil processes, and, on that ground, declined. Among those to be so arrested may be found the name of Charles W. Moffett, one of John Brown's Regulars, and a member of the party who drilled twelve months later at Springdale, Iowa, for the Virginia raid. These rebuffs to the unqualified ruffian elements soon gave breathing space to *bona-fide* settlers on both sides. At Lecompton the situation was complicated by the holding as prisoners of 101 free-state men, who had left Lawrence under Colonel Harvey, on the 12th of September, for the purpose of attacking a fortified camp of Buford's men, located at Hickory Point, some thirty miles northeast of Lawrence. A squadron of dragoons, under Captain Wood, left Lecompton on the 14th to intercept Harvey, but did not meet and capture his command till the job they started to do had been fully completed. The captured free-state force consisted, as the Geary minutes state, of 101 prisoners, a brass cannon, seven wagons, and a large quantity of arms and munitions of war. The prisoners were conveyed to the encampment of the United States troops.[1]

---

[1] List of Prisoners confined at Lecompton, K. T., Sept. 27, 1856, and bound over on the charge of murder in the first degree:—

C. H. Calkins, Bangor, Me.; Thos. Bickerton, Portland, Me.; F. B. Swift, Brunswick, Me.; Wm. Butler, Cook Co., N. H.; J. F. Tabor, Howland, Vt.; J. L. King, Brattleboro', Vt.; O. M. Marsh, Woodstock, Vt.; Stafford J. Pratt, Boston, Mass.; W. N. Bent, Dorchester, Mass.; D. H. Montague, Springfield, Mass.;

Kagi was the correspondent of the New York *Evening Post* and the *National Era*, Washington, D. C. He and Moffett were afterwards members at different periods of the Harper's Ferry party. William Bowles was the brother of Col. John Bowles, to whom the readers of this work are indebted for the new portrait of Captain Brown, published herein. Among this list are many names of men who afterwards distinguished themselves in the Union army. The arrest, confinement, trial, and conviction with

<hr/>

A. W. Dole, Fitchburg, Mass.; Howard York, W. Brookfield, Mass.; C. L. Preston, Worcester, Mass.; " Major " Soley, Worcester, Mass.; A. H. Parker, Clinton, Mass.; Geo. S. Leonard, Franklin, Mass.; Eli D. Lyman, South Hadley, Mass.; L. D. Coleman, Southampton, Mass.; Henry Heard, Lowell, Mass., Ed. Whipple, Providence, R. I.; Wm. Owen, Central Falls, R. I.; Alonzo Crawford, Union, Conn.; C. C. Hyde, Hornellsville, N Y.; Jared Carter, Saratoga, N. Y.; Chester Hay, Madison Co., N. Y.; Theo. J. Dickinson, Newbury, N. Y.; Jas. R. White, New York City, N. Y.; A. Cutter, Central Falls, N. Y.; Henry N. Dunlap, Buffalo, N. Y.; Geo. H. Powers, Oneida Co., N. Y., Chas. J. Archinbole, Buffalo, N. Y.; John J. Howell, Utica, N. Y.; Jas. B. Haynes, Philadelphia, Pa.; Jas. J. Bower, Chester Co., Pa.; T. P. Brown, Alleghany Co., Pa.; Thos. J. Porterfield, (aged 67), Preble Co., O.; Henry H. Easter, Highland Co., O.; E. R. Farley, Morrow Co., O.; Wm. Ware, Preble Co., O.; Ed. Collingham, Preble Co., O.; S. Vogelsang, Columbiana Co., O.; Josiah G. Fuller, Oberlin, O.; Alfred J. Payne, Cuyahoga Co., O.; Thos. Bowers, Ross Co., O.; J. T. Yunker, Coshocton Co., O.; Albert F. Baker, Lake Co., O.; Chas. Sexton, Oberlin, O.; J. N. Thompson, St. Joseph Co., Mich.; Orville Thompson, St. Joseph Co., Mich.; Roswell Hutchins, Oakland Co., Mich.; John W. Stone, Detroit, Mich.; Sam'l Stuart, Detroit, Mich.; Sam'l Dolman, Grant Co., Ind.; A. G. Patrick, Greencastle Ind.; John Ritchie, Franklin, Ind.; Henry Knowles, Huntington Co., Ind.; Henry Hoover, Huntington Co., Ind.; Nath. Griffith, Huntington

subsequent treatment, had a serious effect on public
affairs and greatly intensified the Northern sentiment
on behalf of the free-state cause. Their former
residences show how wide the range of sentiment
must have been. The permitted escape of assassins
like Coleman, who had shot down unarmed or unre-
sisting men like Dow, Jones, Buffum, and others, too
vividly contrasted with the brutal starvation of men
who had met in open day an enemy under arms, and,
after a six hours' combat, captured them in three
heavily built log cabins, each side losing one man in

Co., Ind., Jas. Sinex, Wayne Co., Ind., Eph. Bainter, Henry Co.;
John Laurie, White Co., Ind.; Wm. Eptograft, Fulton Co., Ind.;
Thomas Kemp, Tippecanoe Co., Ind.; W. G. Portet, White Co.,
Ind.; Jesse Pyle, Schuyler Co., Ill.; A. D. Roy, Lyndon, Ill.;
Geo. Smith, Ogle Co., Ill.; Geo. Nebb, Bloomington, Ill.; Justice
Ketchum, Bloomington, Ill.; Geo. Pinney, Joliet, Ill.; Thos.
Leeson, Rock Island, Ill.; Gilbert Tower, Lake Co., Ill.; Jeremiah
Jordan, Ogle Co., Ill.; Thos. Aliff, Carlisle, Ill.; Adam Bower,
Schuyler Co., Ill.; J. M. Cole, St. Clair Co., Ill.; Aaron M.
Humphrey, Kendall Co., Ill.; Wm. Cline, Peoria, Ill.; Isaac
Gray, Chicago, Ill.; A. S. Gates, Hamilton, Ill.; Phineas Stevens,
Bloomingdale, Ill.; Jas. Connelly, Lake Co., Ill.; W. O. Fisher,
Madison Co., Ill.; John White, Lasalle Co., Ill.; Thos. Hankins,
Dover, Ill.; W. H. Gill, Elizabeth, Ill.; Louis Remiatte, Tazewell
Co., Ill.; R. D. Nicholls, Jefferson Co., Wis.; Robt. M. Nown,
Racine Co., Wis.; C. S. Gleason, Albany, Wis.; W. Florentine,
Jefferson Co., Wis.; Ed. Jenkins, Spring Prairie, Wis.; G. O.
Eberhart, Muscatine, Ia.; Oliver C. Lewis, Davenport, Ia.; Ed.
Jacobs, Mahaskie Co., Ia.; M. Kincle, Davenport, Ia.; Oliver
Langworthy, Poweshick, Ia.; Jacob Fisher, Jefferson City, Ia.; E.
R. Moffett, Bristolville, Ia.; Wm. Kerr, Washington, Ia.; Wm.
Reyman, Cooper Co., Ia.; J. H. Kagi, Nebraska; Wm. Bowles,
St. Charles Co., Mo.; David Patrick, Lafayette Co., Mo.; Jos.
Hicks, Platte Co., Mo.; Thos. Varner, Buchanan Co., Mo.; J. H.
York, Buchanan Co., Mo.

the fight.   It was not until the middle of March that
our men were released under "pardons" issued by
Governor Geary.   It was the writer's good fortune to
carry the printed blanks from Lawrence to Geary's
office and assist in the necessary clerical work in filling them up.   Some twenty of the prisoners had previously been transferred from Lecompton to Tecumseh, within a few miles of Topeka.   A brief visit
there under cover of night by some citizens of
Topeka, which may possibly have included a gentleman who afterwards served first as United States
Senator and subsequently as Governor of one of the
Territories, speedily achieved a big hole in the basement wall of the Tecumseh court-house through
which our men walked to freedom.   The nature of
the treatment given these prisoners may be seen from
the following transcript of a diary now in my possession.   It is worth reading.[1]

---

[1] *Monday, Sept. 20.*—Received no rations from United States
camp,—moved to Lecompton.   Received at 5 o'clock one sack of
shorts baked into bread,—one ditto not made into bread; 75 lbs.
of bacon, 6 candles; –103 men—no coffer or sugar.

Tuesday evening.—One sack of shorts, 103 lbs. of bacon, 4 lbs. of
coffee, 6 do. of sugar, 8 or 10 do. of salt; 1 do. of saleratus, 1 gall.
of molasses;—103 men.

Wednesday evening.—One sack of shorts, 5 lbs. of coffee, 5 do. of
sugar, one gall. of molasses, 1 lb. of saleratus;—105 men.

Thursday evening.—One sack of flour, 50 lbs. of bacon, 6 lbs. of
coffee, no sugar, 1 lb. of saleratus, 1 qrt. of vinegar, 3 candles, 1
gall. of molasses; no provisions brought after dark.

Friday, 2 o'clock.—Called on the sergeant of the guard for provisions, was informed that he had spoken to the Marshal, and that
we were curtailed to two meals per day.   Half-past 4 the Marshal
came; brought 50 lbs. of bacon, fore-quarter of beef—about 110

After a short detention in the military camp, the
hundred prisoners were huddled into a large log-
cabin, not fit for an abiding-place for even a score.
Colonel Titus, a notorious pro-slavery driver, was
placed in charge as jailer. Some of the number
escaped. William Bowles, for one, had this opportunity, but he refused to leave his companions, even
though his brother was near to aid him. The gallant
young man died from the confinement and semi-
starvation to which he was subjected. These privations superinduced ship's fever and pneumonia. One
of his companions was a physician, but without
medicines of any kind. All help was refused. A fee
of $10 in gold was sent to a pro-slavery physician,

---

lbs.; 125 lbs. of flour, 1 bushel green beans in the pod, 1 qrt. of vinegar, 6 lbs. of coffee, no salt, no sugar; we got about 1 quart of
salt from a neighbor. 7 o'clock.—Fresh arrival of 9 prisoners.
Marshal brought 3 candles for the whole amount of us, 111 men.
Furnished 15 mattrasses to sleep upon.

    Saturday.—Received 28 lbs. of beef, 125 lbs. of flour, 1 small
sack of salt, 1 gall. of molasses, 1 qt. of vinegar, 6 lbs. of coffee;—
111 men. Spoke to Marshal in behalf of 9 men brought here
yesterday, who had no blankets, was told that it was impossible
to furnish any for them. He afterwards brought 3 quilts for
them.

    Sunday.—About 100 lbs. of beef—much damaged, 125 lbs. of
flour, 6 lbs. of coffee, ½ lb. of saleratus, 1 peck of beans, 3 candles,
4 lbs of sugar.

    We give the above as the amount of provisions received by the
prisoners since coming to Lecompton, and are willing to make
oath to the same.

                          E. R. FALLEY,
                          ARTEMUS H. PARKER,
Commissaries for the prisoners, to distribute the provisions furnished for the same.

one Dr. J. N. O. P. Wood, and he not only refused to attend, but sent word to the effect, "that he would see every damned Yankee prisoner dead and in hell before he would either come or send any medicine for their relief." Shortly after William Bowles died. The two brothers were of Kentucky birth. John early became anti-slavery in conviction. Both inherited a few slaves, and when they moved to Missouri, the younger brother emancipated his. William, who went with John to Kansas, soon followed his example, and became also a faithful free-state citizen. John Bowles was early in the volunteer service, and, as a lieutenant in a Kansas cavalry regiment, was in association with other company officers, the active cause in bringing about an important public policy. Capt. J. M. Williams, Lieut. John Bowles, and Capt. Henry Seamen, of the Fifth Kansas, were on detached service and during it were ordered by their colonel to return to their master one or more fugitive slaves who had found refuge in their lines. The order was disobeyed (this was early in 1862), and the three officers were placed and kept under arrest for several months. The incident created excitement, was discussed in Congress, and Henry Wilson, as chairman of the Senate Military Committee, brought in a bill, which became law, enacting a new article of war, forbidding the use of the army or navy in the capture or return of fugitive slaves. John Bowles was made a field officer in the first regiment of colored men raised during the War for the Union. Capt. James M. Williams became its colonel, and the writer had the honor to be the first adjutant, as well as to legally enlist the first man of color. This seems a digression, but it illustrates how the roads to Harper's Ferry were made. It may not be out of place to mention here that William, the brother of John A. Copeland, one of the colored men hung by Virginia, December 16, 1859, was one of four men of color, commissioned and mustered, by order of the War Department, to command a light battery manned by colored soldiers. These four were the only men of their race commissioned as line officers, and actually fighting as such in the field, as they did during the Price Missouri campaign of 1864.

To return to Lecompton, Governor Geary's growing insight into the pro-slavery conspiracy and the character of the tools it used, soon made his residence there, not only uncomfortable, but very unsafe. And it is an undoubted fact that the free-state men, retained as prisoners and convicted by a border-ruffian court of murder or other crimes, practically were the only men in Lecompton he could depend upon to prevent his assassination. A fair-minded man, Kentuckian by birth, was substituted for Titus, and arms were introduced into the log-prison. Signals were arranged by which, if any attack or alarm was aimed or made at the dwelling near by, where Governor Geary had his executive office and residence, the free-state prisoners could immediately march to his defense. While the Lecompton Constitutional Convention was in session during this period, the chief reason felt for being safe in attendance thereon by the free-state correspondents was the vicinity of the prison and its armed inmates to the Convention Hall, reeking with abuse and threats from the lips of the acknowledged assassins, aimed more or less

directly at the busy men who were educating the
North to the real condition of affairs. The commercial free-state politicians and writers who have since
those days falsified the record and abused the men
whose unflinching work made it possible for them to
be safe in trade and real-estate jobbery, were soon after
seen aiding the Governors in these early efforts[1] to
divide the free-state ranks on the vital issue of recognition of the slave code made by the Missouri invaders,
and then enforced chiefly by the armed men Buford had
brought from the further South, in the guise of the
United States marshals and court posses. Governor
Geary soon saw the futility of tampering with our
integrity or dealing with the enemies of Kansas. As a
result he was compelled to retire from the Executive
office and Territory. Settlers from the North came
pouring in by the thousands and, ere the spring of
1857 awoke, at least twelve to fifteen thousand free
citizens were added to the population. Naturally,
town booms arose, and the want of titles or means of
perfecting them, as well as other administrative agen-
cies, became seriously felt. The divergencies thus
created were doubtless inevitable. Business accepts
expediency as its rule. Barter and profit control its
action. The dispute made hot contention. Every
attempt to get around the trouble was regarded by
Geary's successor, Gov. Robert J. Walker, and the
secretary, Frederick P. Stanton, ex-Congressman, of
Tennessee (both very able gentlemen, who finally
became friends of the free-state cause), as an

---

[1] Geary did a little in that direction, but Walker and Denver,
who followed, were active.

evidence of the conspiracy, they were told, existed to put into force by piecemeal the Topeka
Constitution.   It is a long and interesting record
—that of the years 1857-58 in Kansas,—but its
details belong in the main to a full and fair, but as
yet unwritten history of Kansas, not to these pages,
designed only to sketch the course of events.   John
Brown was kept faithfully advised in his Eastern
agitation of the various phases of the Kansas strife.
Among the more active of the radical section of the
free-state party were several of the young men who
afterwards followed him to Iowa, Canada, and Virginia.   Kagi, Realf, and Cook especially were active
as correspondents for the Eastern and Northern press.
They were also always ready, with other of the
Captain's friends, for any needed service.   The
divergent elements, led by Charles Robinson, G. W.
Brown, and others, were quite prominent and more
successful.   The Lecompton Constitutional Convention finished its unwholsome labors, and the need
of preventing its being forced upon the majority by
the machinery of the pro-southern minority, sustained
more or less effectively by Federal influences, were
soon beyond dispute.   It was decided at last to obtain
the needed power by voting under the " bogus laws "
of the Territory—a proposition, which, of course, met
the stoutest resistance on the part of the younger
and more radical wing.   The voting was done, and
the Territorial Legislature was seized, and as a first
result the repeal of the bogus code immediately followed.   An Act, providing for a Constitutional Convention, was then passed.   The Topeka instrument,
which had done its work as a means of holding the

free-state cause together, was abandoned and buried
for good. The abandonment was somewhat indecently
done on the part of those who had been the chief
beneficiaries of that movement.   Charles Robinson,
the Governor chosen thereunder, did not even recognize its final session.   He was too busy with certain
real-estate and town-booming operations, to con-
cern himself with funeral services over a gallant effort
of freemen.   He was, of course, active enough in the
movement to secure real-estate titles.   Looking back
over the intervening years, it may well be recognized
that no other method than the one that succeeded
could have been adopted.   But that fact made it then
no less difficult to accept.   Of course, the adoption of
such civic methods soon demoralized the foes of
free Kansas also.   The new Constitutional Convention met at Leavenworth and drafted a Constitution, quite superior in many respects to that of
Topeka.   Provision was made to elect a State Legislature and a full set of officers under it.

The pro-slavery Lecompton Constitution was not
to be submitted to the voters, but was sent to Congress direct for acceptance. But an election for State
officers under it had been provided. This the free-
state men decided to capture. An election to vote
on the Leavenworth Constitution and to choose the
officers and legislature thereof was decided upon. It
was also determined to put up the same men under
the Lecompton election, so that if Congress consented
to the proposed iniquity of admitting the State under
the pro-slavery instrument without the people's consent and against their unrecorded, yet well-known
opposition, the men chosen for the Leavenworth in-

strument would be in control. The State being admitted to the Union, it was argued that a peaceful
revolution could be at once achieved, by the substitu-
tion of the free-state for the pro-slavery Constitution,
the installation of officers, and the selection of United
States Senators. As the free-state voters numbered
fully ten to one in the fall of 1858, the programme
was certain to succeed if fraud did not intervene. Steps
were taken to meet the issues that might arise therefrom. The Territorial Legislature passed laws providing for a military organization. This they placed
under command of James H. Lane, and it was known
as " The Ballot Box Guards." It was formidable, on
paper at least, and doubtless would have done its selected work had the occasion really arisen.

John Brown was in western Iowa, sick in body and
disappointed because of the non-receipt of means he
anticipated, harassed, too, by the efforts that were
making from Kansas to get possession of the arms,
munitions, and supplies stored at Tabor, and which
had been placed under his control in Massachusetts.
He had another use than arming Lane's men with
them, as he did not believe that the real danger to
Kansas was over or could be met in the way proposed. So, partly from sickness and partly from the
desire to avoid being complicated with " authority,"
he did not respond to the urgent requests for his
presence in Kansas, made in September and October,
1858. He did not appear till November, and then
only made his presence known to a trusted few at
Lawrence and Topeka. He gathered rapidly the
nucleus of the party that went to Chatham and Harper's Ferry, to make Time's sounding-board ring with

the echoes of their footsteps and the impact of their deeds.

The Kansas elections passed over without bloodshed, though the turmoil was fierce and the attempts at frauds by the Lecomptonites among the most stupendous in any political history,—prior at least to these later days when the suffrages of a whole race of voters are practically made nugatory and of no avail. The Kansas processes were more clumsy, however. Polling places with a dozen or twenty voters were made to return, by the aid of city directories, from one thousand to three thousand votes each—all, of course, in support of the pro-slavery side. The Territorial machinery was in free-state hands and all the election officers that did not run away were speedily arrested. Governor Walker rejected these returns, and thereby prevented an outbreak which would have utterly wiped out the aggressive remnant in Kansas of the pro-slavery power, while it probably would also have involved us with the Federal authorities, bringing on another period of civil strife. This chapter of Kansas history came to an end with the action of the next session of Congress, in submitting the Lecompton Constitution to the voters of Kansas, who, of course, overwhelmingly and contemptuously trampled it out of sight under their ballots of rejection. It opened another chapter in the story of John Brown and his men. To make this clear it will be necessary to go back over the same year and trace the Captain's movements in the East and North—a year so fruitful as it was of forces that led with the irresistibility of fate to the deed he had to do—the blow it was given him to strike!

8

CHAPTER VI.

JOHN BROWN MAKING FRIENDS.

Movements eastward—The National Kansas Committee— Paper by Harvey B. Hurd—Letters of Horace White —What the political fighters meant—How John Brown was, and was not aided—The work of the Massachusetts Aid Committee — George Luther Stearns, Theodore Parker, Frank B. Sanborn and other men of Boston — John Brown's letter of auto- biography—Lowell and Emerson vs. Hay and Nicolay —Where John Brown got his money and his arms— His active itinerary—Return to Iowa—Supplies found there—Hugh Forbes, the English Garibal- dian — His relations with, and conduct to John Brown.

WITH John Brown's arrival in Chicago, October, 1856, accompanied by his son Owen, there begun a more definite development of the purposes and plans he had so long conceived. The reputation gained in Kansas opened many doors and won confidence for him in the minds of men of position and even re- nown. The whole country was quickened, and the Northern States, especially, were vibrating with a sense of danger to institutions, freedom, and union, such as had never before been felt. The overture of Kansas sternly preluded the vaster movements of the

coming slave-holder's rebellion. John Brown realized that if he openly expressed his ideas or his purposes, in their entirety, he would repel more than he
gained. But he knew that standing-room had been
achieved. The attacks made by slavery familiarized
other minds with the need of answering with blows
for freedom. His first purpose was to confer with
the National Kansas Committee, through its executive
body, resident in Chicago. In fact, that Committee
had already sent both to Kansas and Iowa, asking the
Captain to visit their headquarters at Chicago. This
National Committee had been selected in the preceding summer at a convention held in Buffalo, New
York, which was called to consider the means most
available and necessary for the protection and aid of
the free-state people of Kansas, and of the bodies of
ardent Northern emigrants who were preparing to
join them. Thaddeus Hyatt, of New York, a well-
known inventor and manufacturer, who is still living
in his seventy-eighth year, and still working, I
believe, on the problem of aërial navigation, was
made chairman of the Committee. A son-in-law of
Thurlow Weed, Mr. Barnes, of Albany, was chosen
secretary of the Buffalo Convention. Horace White,
now editor of the New York *Evening Post,* then on the
editorial staff of the Chicago *Tribune,* was an active
official of the Committee ; Harvey B. Hurd, a well-
known lawyer, and now professor in a famous law
school of Chicago, was secretary of the Executive
Committee ; George W. Dole was treasurer, and
J D. Webster, afterwards brigadier-general and chief
of artillery on the staff of General W. T. Sherman,
throughout his campaigns in the Central and Coast

States of the South during the Civil War, was vice-
chairman. I am indebted to Mr. Hurd for an interesting paper which will in large part be given in this
chapter. The first evidence of his arrival, is found
in letters of General Webster and Horace White, bearing date respectively the 25th and 26th of October.
In one of them is the significant remark that "Captain Brown says the immediate introduction of the
supplies is not of much consequence compared to the
danger of *losing* them," a suggestion which illustrated
his practical sagacity, as will be seen from what follows.

Horace White's letter mentions to Captain Brown
that "Theodore Parker, of Boston," was at the
Briggs House and wished to meet him. This was
an introduction as significant as any one of the notable incidents, which, begun, from that time forward
crowded upon John Brown's days. Hitherto the
Puritan fighter had been, outside Kansas, known only
to a few colored men and women of character, and to
his fast friend, Hon. Gerrit Smith, of Peterboro, New
York, as one of the most vigorous and determined of
resistant Abolitionists.

In order to apprehend more fully the conditions
which affected, shaped, or marred the mission he had
undertaken it will be necessary to briefly sketch some
of the movements which the National and other
Northern Kansas Aid Committees had set in operation or had then in progress at the time of John
Brown's first appearance in Chicago. At that date
(last of October, 1856) several armed emigrant trains
were congregated in Nebraska, on the northern border of Kansas. Among other members were Richard

Realf, George B. Gill and Barclay Coppoc, the first of whom was named at Chatham, Canada, eighteen months later as secretary of state for the provisional government formed there, the second was commissioned as secretary of the treasury, and the third accompanied the Captain to Harper's Ferry just three years later. Among the leaders of the Northern commands were James Redpath, John Brown's first biographer, and P. B. Plumb, who, as a Senator from Kansas, afterwards defended and eulogized him on the floor of the United States Senate. There were also with the trains, among others, Thomas Wentworth Higginson, author, preacher, soldier, poet— always faithful to the same ideal of American liberty that John Brown died for—and who, with Theodore Parker, George Luther Stearns, Dr. Samuel G. Howe, Frank B. Sanborn, the later and authorized (by his family) biographer of John Brown, and Gerrit Smith, formed later a council of friends to aid the Captain in his final efforts. I believe Mr. Sanborn visited Kansas about that date, and I know that Thaddeus Hyatt, with W. M. F. Amy, of Illinois, afterwards a Governor of New Mexico, then the general agent of the National Kansas Committee, were then or soon after *en route* to Kansas. Horace White visited Kansas also. General Lane was in Iowa making speeches, filled with his peculiar, flashing, and exciting oratory. Watson Brown, *en route* to Kansas, writes the family at North Elba from St. Charles, Iowa, under date of October 30, 1856, that " We are in the company of a train of Kansas teams loaded with Sharpe's rifles and cannon. I heard a report that father had gone east. We travel very slow; you can write to us at Tabor.

On our way we saw Gerrit Smith, F. Douglass, and other old friends. We have each a Sharpe's rifle." [1]

Finding, on arrival at Tabor, that his father had gone eastward, Watson returned to Chicago and soon rejoined him, going home later to North Elba. It is not possible to do more than outline the crowding incidents of that winter.

Captain Brown spent about two of the five weeks that passed between his last active appearance at Lawrence, Kansas, and his reporting in Chicago, at Tabor, Springdale, and Iowa City. I am greatly indebted to Prof. L. H. Wetherell, of Davenport, Iowa, for very interesting data relating to John Brown and his men during this and their subsequent visits to Iowa. The first visit was made on this journey to the Springdale Quaker settlement in Cedar County, where, just a year later, the Captain housed for several weeks eleven of the original Harper's Ferry party, and in which place four of his associates were found and recruited. At the burial of Owen Brown, Pasadena, California, in 1892, one of the pall-bearers was Mr. James O. Townsend, a liberal Quaker, formerly the landlord of the "Traveller's Rest," West Branch, ten miles east of Iowa City. Mr. Wetherell describes Captain Brown riding up to the little roadside inn, a spare, gaunt figure on a gaunt, spare mule. After dismounting, the traveler asked the landlord:

" Have you ever heard of John Brown, of Kansas ?"

Mr. Townsend eyed him sharply without reply. Having thus satisfied himself that the question identified the person, he took out a piece of chalk from his

---

[1] Sanborn's " Life and Letters of John Brown," p. 341.

vest pocket and deliberately took Brown's hat off and
marked on it a large X; as deliberately he marked
Brown's back with a XX, and ended by chalking a
large one on the mule's back, saying as he put the
chalk back in his pocket :

"Just put the animal into the stable and walk right
into the house.   Thou art surely welcome."

And Captain Brown was always a welcome guest at
the "Traveller's Rest."   Literally of Mr. Townsend it
could be said he fulfilled the injunction of the Saviour:
"I was a stranger and ye took me in; I was a-hun-
gered and a-thirst and ye gave me meat and to
drink."

Captain Brown's first advice at Chicago was characteristic.   By "supplies" were meant the arms—
Sharpe's and Hall's rifles.   An Illinois party managed
to avoid spoliation at Lexington, Missouri, but on
arrival at Leavenworth, Kansas, their arms were seized
and themselves driven back.   Several hundred Hall's
rifles, from the gun-factory at Harper's Ferry, whose
seizure was one of the objective points in John Brown's
plans, at which Kagi, Leeman, and Leary lost their
lives, were taken from this party.   The late Senator
Preston B. Plumb was a member thereof.   He refused to go back when ordered, came ashore at
Leavenworth; being threatened with lynching on the
streets he was rescued by Nicholas V. Smith (who
married one of Horace Greeley's daughters) and his
brother-in-law, Col. Hampton P. Johnson, afterwards
the first Kansas soldier killed for the Union in a conflict with Missouri rebels.   The Plumb incident was
brought to an end by the news of the Pottawatomie
slaying, which, for the time being, proved a complete

deterrent to border ruffian enterprise. The emigrants
going to Kansas by the land route were always in
danger of having their arms taken by the United States
troops under orders from the deputy marshal sent
with them by Governor Geary. In fact, some four
hundred Hall's carbines were so seized. All these
weapons were afterwards recovered. A bill of sale
was made to some competent party, whose name is
not recalled, and the rifles, etc., held at Lexington
were obtained by legal process, and brought to Kansas
in the summer of 1857. With the Northern trains,
under Redpath, Parsons, Eldridge, and Pomeroy, were
several guns, twelve-pound howitzers—three in all, I
think. These were buried near the northern border
of Kansas, to prevent seizure by the troops, and were
afterwards brought into Kansas when the struggle
against the Lecompton constitution assumed the prospect of renewed belligerency. In December, 1857, the
fraudulent election on the slavery clause of that instrument was held. The people at Leavenworth, Lawrence, knowing what was designed, took steps at once
to recover their property. The guns at Leavenworth
were replevined under a bill of sale made to a prominent free-state citizen there. Those at Lecompton
were taken from a cellar wherein they were stored,
while the acting Governor, J. W. Denver, whose office
was in the same building, was engaged in conversation upon a pretended matter of business. This transaction had its amusing as well as dangerous aspect,
and I remember laughing with great gusto at General
Denver's anger when he found out he was tricked.
This did not occur until the loaded wagon was about
to drive off. Direst threats of legal action were

hurled at us, but none was taken, for the Governor found on inquiry that he was virtually a party to holding stolen property. It is no wonder that John Brown advised as he did in the face of the Federal interference.

The conditions grew complex. Naturally gentlemen charged with a grave responsibility like that taken on the shoulders of the Kansas National Committee, grew cautious in the presence of a personality so simple and positive as John Brown's. The party political conditions were also of the gravest character. At this late date perhaps no fairer presentation of the disputed attitude of the National Committee can be given than is found in the communication sent me, under date of October 1, 1892, by Mr. Harvey B. Hurd. He says:

" The organization of the National Kansas Committee was authorized by a convention held in Buffalo in the summer of 1856. An earlier one had been held in Cleveland for the same purpose, but adjourned to meet later in Buffalo. This was presided over by Governor Reeder, and was very fully attended, something like five hundred delegates being present. The purpose was to take charge of the contest then raging in Kansas, and conduct it on behalf of the North. State Committees were formed, and it was the intention to have the States divided into districts, each under a district committee, and this was carried out to a considerable extent. There was a pretty general organization of the North, its head being the National Committee. More specifically, that Committee took charge of the contest in Kansas, as well as of the aid which the North furnished, and therefore, had much to do with the organizing of such military companies in Kansas as were necessary, and the furnishing arms, provisions, clothing, and the like, for military operations, as well as for the purpose of settling the Territory, the ultimate object being to control it with free-state settlers, and carry forward a

free-state government to success. The National Kansas Committee had a depôt at Mt. Pleasant, Iowa, where it furnished
horses, wagons, provisions, and arms for emigrants, and organized them into companies, with such commanders as were
necessary to put them in shape to defend themselves against
attacks from the pro-slavery forces. Our emigrants were forwarded by way of Tabor, Iowa, and through Nebraska, down
into Kansas, Lawrence being their objective point. Some of
the arms which were purchased for these emigrants were furnished by the Massachusetts State Committee, notably 200
Sharpe's rifles. The latter were forwarded as far as Tabor, and
were there at the time they were voted to John Brown, I do
not remember of the Massachusetts Committee or any committee other than the National Committee furnishing any other
arms directly.[1] What other arms were furnished were bought
by the National Committee, and furnished directly to emigrants.
The Committee bought many Colt's revolvers.

" An accurate account of the moneys received and expended
by the National Kansas Committee was kept at the time, but
the books of account, with the other records and papers of the
Committee, were destroyed by the Chicago fire of 1871. My
recollection of the amount of *money* contributed and expended
by the Committee is in round numbers $100,000. There was
contributed besides money a large amount of clothing. This
was gathered or made-up by local town committees and forwarded through the State Committees to the National Committee, and by the National Committee to its agents in Kansas,

[1] Arms were furnished by local committees and individuals in
New York, New Hampshire, Pennsylvania, Illinois, Ohio, and
Wisconsin, to the writer's personal knowledge. Thaddeus Hyatt,
for example, presented each member of the Massachusetts company to which I belonged, with a revolver upon their arrival at
New York. Several cases of Springfield muskets, received in
New York, were placed by T. W. Higginson, then a Unitarian
minister, resident in Worcester, Mass., and by Mr. Hyatt, of New
York, in my charge to convey to Kansas, which was safely done.

where it was distributed. No fair estimate can at present be made of the value of this clothing. I think it equaled the cash contribution.

"John Brown never had any close official relation with the National Committee. He was often at the Committee's head-quarters, and the Committee supplied him with some money,[1] and provisions and clothing at times. At the meeting of the National Committee, held at the Astor House, in January, 1857, a proposition was made by one of the representatives of the Massachusetts Committee to furnish John Brown with the arms and money to organize and drill military companies in Kansas, and to have them in readiness in any emergency, such as invasions from Missouri. I was fearful that Mr. Brown's design was to invade Missouri or some other slave State, for the purpose of bringing on a contest between the North and the South.[2] Gerrit Smith had said in the Buffalo Convention, 'that

---

[1] Only $150 in all.

[2] This suggestion is probably the result of after knowledge—born of the fact that John Brown did at later dates invade both Missouri and Virginia. The real fear of the National Kansas Committee was that Captain Brown or some other Kansas man, who was genuinely anti-slavery in feeling, would carry resistance to the bogus laws or the Fugitive Slave Act far enough to get into direct collision with the Federal authorities in the beleaguered Territory. All idea of a possible invasion was an afterthought, outside a very small number of Kansas men. In August, 1856, General Lane was compelled to promise Thaddeus Hyatt and others of the National Committee, when the Northern emigrants were concentrated in Nebraska, that he would so conduct the campaign then pending, against the border-ruffian forces harrying the Kansas free-state settlements, as to avoid in every possible way a direct collision with the Governor or United States Judges, before the means would be furnished to move forward the 1,200 men waiting impatiently to enter Kansas. Lane did as he promised. He demonstrated against, but did not attack, Lecompton, still bringing about the release thereby of the so-called "treason" prisoners in the United States camp. When the troops were sent

slavery would never be peacefully abolished, but must be
washed out with blood,' and he advocated such a course on the
part of the Committee as would bring on open hostilities between the North and the South. It was my opinion at the time
that John Brown and Gerrit Smith were in full accord, and
that Mr. Brown believed that that was the only way to abolish
slavery. One of his purposes was to bring on that contest. I
therefore opposed the Committee granting the request unless
Mr. Brown would pledge himself not to invade a slave State.
Mr. Brown was called in before the Committee, and asked if it
was his intention to invade a slave State; to which he replied,
that he would not disclose to the Committee his intentions;
that most of those present knew him well, and they would have
to trust to him in that matter. If they were not willing to do
that, he advised them not to grant him anything. The Massachusetts Committee thereupon requested to be permitted to
withdraw the 200 Sharpe's rifles, then at Tabor, from the
National Committee, for the purpose of turning them over to
Mr. Brown, and the National Committee voted to return them,
and did so. They went into the hands of John Brown, and
were the same that were afterwards found at Harper's Ferry.
The Committee did also at that meeting vote to John Brown
$5,000 in money and some clothing. The latter was furnished
to him in Kansas by the agent of the Committee, Mr. Whitman, but no money was given to him then. When he drew
upon the Committee, the Committee was out of funds and
never had the money to meet his drafts. That happened in
this way: At the same meeting at the Astor House, the Com-

---

against him he disappeared. Under his orders, when the United
States marshal, guarded by dragoons under Captain Sackett,
came into Lawrence to arrest Lane and others, no one said "yea"
or "nay," but only stood laughing at the marshal and cheering
the troops. The National Kansas Committee carried Frémont's
election on their shoulders, just as Governor Geary believed on
his arrival in Kansas that the election of Buchanan depended
upon him.

mittee had already voted to make an arrangement with the steamboat owners on the Missouri river and railroads throughout the country to sell through tickets from all principal cities in the North to emigrants in the spring of 1857, by way of St. Louis and the Missouri river. They also voted to purchase seeds for Kansas, to be forwarded as soon as it could be done, and all the money in the National Committee's hands was expended in the making of such arrangements for the transportation of settlers, and in purchasing and forwarding the needed seeds. A hundred tons of seeds were purchased and sent to Lawrence by a steamboat, purchased for that purpose.[1] The large emigration which took place early in 1857 as the result of the through-ticket arrangement, really settled the Kansas contest.

"In consequence of the Committee's failure to pay Mr. Brown's drafts on account of the $5,000 appropriation, Gerrit Smith came to Chicago to see me. He was very much offended because the Committee did not pay the drafts, but he was told that they had not the means with which to meet them, and there was no other way but to let them be protested. Drafts to the amount of $500 were given to some person in Connecticut,[2] who, as I afterward understood, had made some pikes, or same other implements of warfare, for Mr. Brown. He drew for about five hundred dollars, but his drafts not being paid, he did not draw any others.

"The National Committee's operations substantially closed with the distribution of the seeds, clothing, arms, etc., in the spring and summer of 1857. The seeds were given out to the settlers on their receipts, promising to return the amount in kind, when their crops should come in ; but these obligations were never enforced.

"Mr. Brown did not, as I understand it, remove the 200

---

[1] Thaddeus Hyatt advanced the money for this.

[2] Charles W. Blair, of Collinsville, by whom the pikes captured at Harper's Ferry, in 1859, were manufactured.

rifles from Tabor until the winter of 1857–58,[1] about the time
that he came East from Kansas by way of Iowa and went to
Canada, where he organized his raid upon Virginia. I saw him
while he was then in Chicago, at that time, and talked with him
to some extent about his operations in Kansas and his future
purposes. He had a paper about which he wished to consult
me, some parts of which he read to me. I afterwards found
that it was a draft of the constitution which he intended to
have adopted if it became necessary to form a government, as
the result of his prospective operations in Virginia. He was
exceedingly thin and worn at that time, and I remarked to him
that he was looking very feeble and much older than his years
(fifty-eight), to which he replied : ' Yes, but I feel that I have a
work to perform, and I must be expeditious if I am to do it.' I
have no doubt now, he had reference to his then contemplated
movements. I talked to him some about his operations in
Kansas, and what the newspapers had said in his justification;
that he had suffered a good deal at the hands of the border
ruffians. This plea of justification seemed to grieve him and
he said to me, ' I wish you would, whenever you have an opportunity, contradict that idea. I have done nothing out of revenge
or because I considered that I have suffered in any way. All
that I have done has been through my desire to do justice by
this oppressed race—the negro slaves. I consider it beneath
any man to avenge himself.' These are not the exact words,
but are substantially what he said to me in 1858. Mr. Brown
was at the time very poorly clad, and a number of his friends
got together and raised a purse for the purpose of buying him
a new outfit. As I was the nearest to Brown's size and form,
I went and bought the clothes, had them fitted to myself, and
sent them to him, he not daring to go on to the street at the
time, there being an offer out by the President of $3,000 reward
for his arrest.[2]

[1] He moved them from Tabor to Springdale in December, 1857,
and to northern Ohio in April, 1858.

[2] Mr. Hurd is mistaken as to the date of last seeing John Brown.
It was during the early part of February, 1859, when he was *en*

"There was, during the entire operations of the National Committee, an element having some influence before the Committee, pressing for more aggressive operations on their part—to carry the war into the enemy's camp—but those having the conduct of the affairs were unanimous in their determination to stand on the defensive alone, and to confine their operations to the protection of the free-state settlers in Kansas, so as to prevent them from being driven out or overpowered. That was the whole sum and substance of the policy upon which the Committee acted. The Executive Committee, having the matter in charge at Chicago, were J. D. Webster (afterwards General), vice-president of the Committee; George W. Dole, treasurer, and myself as secretary. I gave my entire time to the business of the Committee, and perhaps more than any other managed its affairs."

Horace White, in letters of recent date, recalls some details of value as to the relations of Captain John Brown and the National Kansas Committee of which he was so efficient an officer. It is apparent from all evidence obtainable that the anti-slavery soldier was invited to confer with that Committee, as he was also when in New York early in January, 1857, asked to visit Boston and counsel with the Massachusetts Kansas Committee. In this connection it may be well to state that outside of Mr. White's letters no evidence whatever appears that John Brown personally solicited the custody, control or gift of any of the supplies, whether consisting of arms, clothing, tools, camp equipage or teams, that had been raised exclusively for the service of Kansas and the free-state cause. Such

---

route to Canada, removing the eleven fugitive slaves rescued by him from Missouri, Christmas Eve, 1858. The document partially read was already adopted at the Chatham Convention, May, 1858. The suit Mr. Hurd purchased is the one the Captain wore when taken at Harper's Ferry.

materials or supplies as passed into his hands came
there as a volunteer act. The explanation of this
seeming contradiction is found in the probability that
Gerrit Smith was active in securing for the Captain
such control. The close relations between the two
friends will easily account for the statement made by
Mr. White. The motion to appropriate $5,000 to Cap-
tain Brown was made by the Vermont committeeman,
B. B. Newton, of St. Albans. This $5,000 was never
paid. Authority was given Captain Brown to draw
for $500 thereof, and his drafts for that amount were
dishonored in the following April. All the money he
received from this body was $150. Of course the
want of funds on the Committee's part was a sufficiently peremptory reason, but there can be little
doubt either that it was a convenient and gratifying one
also, to the committeemen who were openly opposed
to the purposes and policy of action which they felt
rather than knew that John Brown was in favor of
carrying out. When the National Committee ceased
to exist, soon after the January meeting at the Astor
House, New York City, a quantity of supplies, chiefly
clothing, bedding, and camp utensils, became John
Brown's property under the terms of their resolutions, or by reason of their being actually under
the control of the Massachusetts Committee. Of the
twenty-five Colt's revolvers sent to Kansas in September, 1856, for John Brown's use, fifteen of which had
been loaned out to various free-state men in need of
arms,[1] the Captain recovered ten or twelve. Other

---

[1] One of these revolvers thus passed into my possession and subsequently I accounted for the same to Captain Brown himself. It
was lost in my army service three years later.

articles of no great money value were also obtained
by him at Tabor and Ottumwa, Iowa, where they had
been stored, and subsequently used or sold to enable
him in part to care for his company in 1857–58, and the
fugitive slaves he carried to Canada early in 1859. It
is doubtful if all he ever received from or through the
National Committee exceeded in value a total of one
thousand dollars.[1]

Under date of September 17, 1892, Horace White
writes that the National Committee " had some arms
on hand after the struggle was over " (that is, that portion of the free-state conflict which ended with 1856);
" Brown applied for them, and Hurd, on behalf of the
Committee, required him to promise that he would
not use them to make war on slavery in the States.[2]
This he would not do. So the Committee handed

---

[1] A proposition was made at the New York meeting for the
equipment of a company of fifty picked men for special service under John Brown. The Captain's modest estimate for
camp service and teams, two of the latter, amounted to $1,774.
Later in the year the Massachusetts Committee, through Mr.
Stearns, in a letter dated May 18, 1857, writing to Thaddeus Hyatt
as chairman of the National Committee, stated that a grant of $100,-
000 was to be asked from the State Legislature, for Kansas relief,
and that a secret force should be organized under John Brown,
strictly defensive in character. A fund should also be raised in aid of
settlers who might have been impoverished through the pro-slavery
war. Mr. Stearns mentions $13,000 as the money value of arms,
materials, etc., entrusted to John Brown. Thaddeus Hyatt recently told me of his surprise at getting that letter. He contributed
personally, but the Committee did not.

[2] This suggestion probably results from that blurring of memory
which time makes with us all. No one had any thought whatever
at that date (1857), that John Brown dreamed of attacking elsewhere than in Missouri and only as a retaliatory measure for Kansas.

9

the arms back to the Massachusetts Committee from whom they were received." After referring to the action of the latter party in donating arms and money to Captain Brown, Mr. White continues: " But my recollection is that his (Brown's) principal supply of money came from Gerrit Smith."

But any responsibility for that must rest chiefly upon George L. Stearns, who manfully accepted it when giving ; though Gerrit Smith was the next largest contributor. As near as can be estimated the money received by Brown could not have exceeded $12,-000, while the supplies, arms, etc., furnished may have cost $10,000 more. Of course there were smaller contributions and support coming on, but if the total estimate be placed at $25,000, for the period between the 15th of September, 1856, when he left Lawrence, Kansas, and the 16th of October, 1859, when he moved on Harper's Ferry, Virginia, with twenty-one men, it will certainly cover all of the outlay except that of time, labor, and lives. And of this total John Brown expended not one cent for personal expenses, outside of the very moderate amounts required to enable him to keep at his work. He was in those days always economical to the verge of penuriousness, regarding the moneys in his hand as a trust. During those three years of " storm and stress," the North Elba family mainly provided for their own wants, with the exception of a sum of $1,000 raised from private contributions in the East made by Gerrit Smith, G. L. Stearns, Amos A. Lawrence, Dr. Howe, Dr. Cabot, Theodore Parker, and a few others, which amount was expended in the payments of debts incurred by reason of the Adirondack family's sacrifices for Kansas. Debts were paid

and the humble dwelling at North Elba was in some
degree repaired and made more habitable.   That was
all.[1]   The largest contributors, then, to John Brown's
enterprises were certainly George L. Stearns and
Gerrit Smith.   Francis Jackson Merriam, his latest
recruit at the Kennedy farm, who gave $600 as well
as his services, was doubtless the next largest contributor.   Mr. and Mrs. Stearns were devotedly generous
for they placed, during the early summer of 1857, at
some personal inconvenience, the sum of $7,000 to
John Brown's credit.   It was never drawn against, as
the Captain did not feel that when conditions
changed from those under which he considered the
generous proffer to have been made, that he had the
right to use any of it, no matter what the need may
have been.   The Medford family, however, certainly
gave in arms and cash not less than $7,500, and possi-
bly more, to John Brown and his cause.

In a later letter, bearing date October 6, 1892, Mr.
White makes quite clear the matter of the purchase
of arms from the funds of the National Committee.
He says:

"A meeting was held in New York, January 25,
1857, at which a statement of money received and ex-

---

[1] A large number of personal and family letters are preserved in
the archives of the Kansas Historical Society, many of which are
printed in Mr. Sanborn's volume; there are also memoranda of
receipts and expenditures.   Of all these I find only five reterences
to money sent to Mrs. Brown or to North Elba, the total being
but $403.10.   I am not quite sure that the whole of the $1,000
promised to relieve the homestead was really obtained.   Mr. Amos
A. Lawrence raised $550, and probably Mr. Stearns and Gerrit
Smith gave the balance.

pended was read by me and published in the *New York Tribune*. The expenditures of the Committee were made in the way of outfitting emigrant trains in Iowa, paying freight on clothing and other articles forwarded, and incidentals. According to my recollection, *no money was expended by the National Committee for arms, but arms passed through our hands from the Massachusetts Committee.*[1]

"My report contains an apparent discrepancy. It speaks of 763 packages of clothing as received, but of only 400 boxes forwarded. I happen to remember that the balance was stored for the winter in a barn or house owned by W. M. F. Amy, at Bloomington, Illinios.[2] The Committee voted $5,000 to Brown at the New York meeting for any defensive measures that may become necessary, but when the time came for paying it they were out of funds."

The total received by the National Committee, as given in the report published in the *New York Tribune* of January 27, 1857, show cash receipts of $85,196.46. Of this, Massachusetts contributed $26,-107.17, and New York $33,707.39. Of the latter sum the largest part was raised by the *Tribune*. The fifteen free States all contributed, though New England and New York bore two-thirds. In all, 762 packages of

---

[1] Mr. Sanborn makes it clear also in his " Life of John Brown," and it agrees with my own recollection of instructions from Mr. Higginson and Mr. Hyatt with regard to arms sent to Kansas.

[2] A considerable amount of that clothing reached Kansas early in the spring on the little steamboat. Mr. Hurd writes: Messrs. Hyatt and Arny came up from St. Louis on it. Realf and myself met it at Kansas City, and were on board during the trip up the Kansas River to Lawrence.

clothing, etc., were contributed. The estimated value
of all contributions through the National Committee
was not less than $200,000 ; as much more was con-
tributed and expended through the several States or
direct by individuals.

John Brown left Chicago early in December, visiting Albany, Rochester, and Peterboro ; also, North
Elba, for a few days. He was at the Astor House,
New York City, on the 25th of January, 1857 ; and
from thence went to Boston, being the guest, for
the time, of Judge Russell and Dr. Thayer, in that
city, and of George L. Stearns, at Medford. He also
visited Concord, having met Mr. Sanborn at Theodore
Parker's house. He doubtless met Wendell Phillips,
T. W. Higginson, and other anti-slavery people,
though he rather avoided such personal publicity and
acquaintance. James Redpath was married and living
in Boston. At Worcester, where Eli Thayer resided,
he was a frequent visitor. The well-laden archives
of the Kansas Historical Society, at Topeka, give in
the personal and family letters, as well as in other
manuscripts belonging to its large and valuable collection of John Brown papers, the close and frequent
intimacy, among others, of Captain Brown and Eli
Thayer; one, too, of decided admiration on the latter's part. Mr. Thayer evidently aided the equipment of the Captain to the extent of his ability, by
way of facilitating, at least with his purse and credit,
the procurement and repair of arms. The demand
for Sharpe's rifles had stimulated the manufacture
of that very serviceable type of weapon. The Allen
rifle, manufactured at Worcester, was one of the improvements thereon. Mr. Thayer, up to the close of

1857, maintained very friendly relations with John
Brown. He knew as much then as he did subsequently of the story of the Pottawatomie slaying.
Yet he could write upon a bill receipted by Allen &
Wheelock, that the gun it called for was presented to
his friend John Brown for use in the " Cause of Freedom," and he could advise also that the company or
command which John Brown proposed to organize,
and for the procurement of arms on behalf of which
he was striving, should be called " The Neighbors,"
as representing the scriptural story of the man who
fell among thieves and was succored by the con-
temned Samaritan, while the Levite and Pharisee
passed by on the other side.   In 1880, Eli Thayer
stated to G. W. Brown, of Rockford, Ill., a constant
assailant of Captain Brown's name and memory, that
" not long before his attack on the United States
arsenal, he (Brown) came to my house to ask for
arms . . . to protect some free-state settlements
in Kansas," etc.   As Captain Brown did not see or
call upon Eli Thayer at any date after May or June,
1857,—two and a half years—the value of Mr. Thayer's
" Memoirs " as an authority falls far below par.   John
Brown certainly conceived of Eli Thayer as his friend
as late as the spring of 1859, for he so wrote of him
at that period to his son John.   Nor is Mr. Thayer
seen of record to have been anywhere unfriendly to
John Brown's acts or character until after he failed
of election to Congress in 1860, when he ran as an
Independent and in opposition to the Republican
nominee in the Worcester, Mass., district.

All over the North, especially in the more active
centers of Republican political activity, John Brown

found friendly sympathizers, a good deal of verbal encouragement, and—a small degree of pecuniary assistance. Yet, no one who came into close contact with him could doubt but that he held firmly to a grim purpose, and that at some date, not far distant, he would probably be heard from by way of a direct attack on slavery. There never was any disguise on the Captain's part that, in his opinion, the only effectual policy would be to "carry the war into Africa." But talk was cheap. In nothing more distinctly, too, is the intellectual quality of the Captain shown than by the fact that he measured all this at no more value than it deserved. Nor was he ever thereby led into giving his confidence. This was due, not because he did not esteem in their places, men of the weight and influence of Sumner, Wilson, Greeley, Chase, *et al.*, as that he intellectually perceived that the methods he would pursue must be entirely unapproved of by them. To him they were all instruments. The analogy holds good, however, that he held no kindred sympathy or association with the methods of the non-resistant Abolitionists or their unflinching antagonism to any form of direct action other than that of agitation. John Brown was always a devoted Unionist. He would never have consented to its dissolution without fighting. He was organizing a forcible attack on slavery, because without question he held the conviction that slavery was an organized menace to the existence of the American Republic. Without freedom, it could not justly exist; with slavery it was always in peril; slavery must, therefore, be destroyed: first, because it was a crime against human life and the law of God, and, therefore, as a corollary, always a menace to free government, the Constitution, and the Union. This comprised John Brown's simple, stern political creed; the one upon which he acted with unwavering fidelity "even unto death." May he not, therefore, be classed as a Unionist of Unionists, a Loyalist of Loyalists, without evasion or guile? Naturally, such directness made him out of place in party politics. Expediencies he could not recognize; he never accepted them nor was with them, and the shortsighted capacity of the pro-slavery politicians, in endeavoring, after Harper's Ferry, to establish a connection between that action and the parliamentary leaders of Northern politics, was ridiculous enough to breed Homeric laughter. It certainly intensified, not reacted, on the opinions assailed. A letter, published in the *New York Tribune*, from the pen of Richard Realf, bearing date January 30, 1860, shortly after his escape from the South, expresses quite forcibly and, I believe, correctly, the opinions of John Brown as to political action and the Republican party. It will not be out of place, then, to append some extracts from this paper.[1]

---

[1] "To the Editor of the 'New York Tribune': Sir— Permit me, who have barely escaped from being lynched as an Abolitionist in the South, only to find myself denounced as a recreant apostate in the North, and who, therefore, can hardly be suspected of bidding for sympathy from either section, to say a word or two in answer to the allegation, asserted with so much heat and clamor, 'that the Harper's Ferry insurrection of John Brown was the natural, legitimate, and inevitable consequence of the teachings of the Republican party.' In contradicting and disproving this charge, I am moved, not by any particular regard for Republicanism, nor any particular hatred of Democracy, but only by a desire to do justice to the memory of John Brown. . . .

The meeting of John Brown and George Luther Stearns, the Boston merchant, marked for the anti-slavery fighter and idealist the beginning of a momentous end.   I hold that it was an event of deep national importance also.   Without Mr. Stearns's friendship and coöperation, the blow struck at Harper's Ferry would probably have never been delivered, as the means would doubtless have been lacking.   The Boston merchant was a leading spirit among the prominent men who gathered around Theodore Parker and the Twenty-eighth Congregational Church, of which that independent Unitarian preacher, scholar, and

---

The charge thus alleged is wholly and altogether untrue, and this for the simple reason, that the movement of John Brown was conceived and originated at least a score of years antecedent to the formation of the Republican party.   .   .   .   The Republican party had no existence until 1854 (and no national organization till 1856). The statement, therefore, that the incursion into Virginia resulted as a consequence of the inculcated doctrines of Republicanism, is now disproven.   Nor was Brown himself, nor were any of his coadjutors committed to the Republican creed.   Henry Wilson, in 1857, advised that the free-state party in Kansas secure the Legislature to themselves by voting under the provision of the Lecompton Constitution.   The advice was taken, and the result predicted was achieved.   *Not one of Brown's original party voted.* Some of us were at the time correspondents of the Eastern press; and in the interim between the Grasshopper Falls Convention, 1851 (when it was decided upon to vote), and the day on which the election occurred (in 1851), we opposed the action of the party in every possible way, by speeches, and in every available manner.   .   .   .

"Once more: the only representative of Republicanism who received any inkling of John Brown's plans, learned them from a hostile quarter, and took immediate steps to put it out of Brown's power to commit any illegal act whatever.   I allude to Senator Wilson, and his letter to Dr. Howe, of Boston."

agitator, was the pastor.   The Music Hall congregation and fraternity embraced, with the Parker household, more or less actively, very many of the cultured
men and women of Boston, often too within the pale
of the orthodox churches who were strongly, even
passionately, anti-slavery, but who could not satisfy
themselves with the policy of non-unionism and non-
resistance advocated by the American Anti-Slavery
Society.   They were the backbone of resistance to the
rendition of fugitive slaves; they were found active as
Conscience Whigs, early Free Soilers, and foremost in
younger Republican ranks.   But the men who were
inspired by Theodore Parker or aided to sustain him,
were always something more than political workers.
They were positively and practically anti-slavery,
helping every phase of agitation and effort.   Their
circle also included some of the ablest business men
of New England.   Great railroad systems in the West
received their incentive and initiative in the discussions constantly going on at Mr. Parker's residence.
The lyceum system was then in its largest vogue ; a
magnificent educator of Northern intellect and sentiment.   Theodore Parker shared with Wendell Phillips
and Henry Ward Beecher its leading honors, and he
was also its chief sacrifice, as the labor and exposure
of travel and lecturing undoubtedly hastened his un-
timely death.   It was the wide knowledge which was
thus acquired of the new West, then opening, that
aided in broadening New England's business enterprise.   To the intense interest aroused by the Kansas
struggle was in great part due the great investment
and sagacious direction that created the enlargement
of the railroads running to Missouri from Chicago, the

early construction of the Hannibal and St. Joseph railroad, the beginning of the great Santa Fé system and also of the now vast network of roads in Iowa and Nebraska, as well as of northern Missouri and Kansas. The free-state struggle, like the Civil War, vastly quickened enterprise. And out of the Music Hall Sundays, "Parker's Thursdays" at home, the Stearns's country home, and the headquarters of the Emigrant Aid Society, with the personal efforts, intellectually quickening as they were, of lawyers like Russell and Andrews, active scholars like Howe, Cabot, Thayer, Bowditch, and scores of others, an influence went that did very much to prepare New England and the great North for the mighty struggle that was impending. Parker, a pulpit Socrates, was always questioning the oracles, and as he was sincerity itself, grandly human to the core of his being, the Delphian soul always responded. John Brown came, passed through, and went away, leaving behind him an impression of a personality so simply true, a character so sternly yet impersonally fixed, a brain so honest and clear, and a courage so unfailing, that none who met him, however slightly, failed to be affected as if by the "moving of waters"; the passing of an unquestioned human force. Some were small enough to fear him; a few have since been false enough to defame a life they could not comprehend; but all of them felt his presence as that of an Ithuriel spear, touching to the very core of things. Among the noblest and sanest of all, George Luther Stearns and his wife Mary must be counted as the foremost.

Mr. Stearns met John Brown for the first time in December, 1856, and at once invited him to Boston.

They met again on the street near to the rooms of the Massachusetts Kansas Committee. It was Mr. Stearns who introduced Frank B. Sanborn to John Brown. On the first Sunday in January, 1857, John Brown went to the Music Hall to hear Theodore Parker preach. He was there introduced to Mrs. Mary E. Stearns,[1] who survives her noble husband and now resides near Boston, at Tuft's College. Their home was then at Medford. Mrs. Stearns is the niece of Lydia Maria Child, a well-known and most graceful authoress, whose pen was also and always at the service of anti-slavery work and ideas. John Brown's first visit to Medford was made on the second Sunday in January, 1857. The eldest son, Henry, was naturally attracted to the old hero, to whom, apart from a reasonable curiosity, all children and young people were irresistibly drawn. As he was telling of the privations endured by Kansas families, Henry, a boy of thirteen, brought to him a little hoard of pocket money, and, as he put it into the Captain's hands, asked if he would buy something needed " for the Kansas children," and added, as the grave old man thanked him: " Captain Brown, will you not write me, sometime, what sort of a little boy you were?"[2] This was the origin of a remarkable composition, which if, as the writer sometime over-modestly declared: " I know no more of grammar than one of that farmer's calves "—plainly shows that he was of those in whom plain living and high thinking make the noblest of spiritual and intellectual utterances.

----

[1] See Mrs. Stearns's interesting paper on " George L. Stearns and John Brown " in the closing pages of the appendix to this volume.
[2] Sanborn's " Life and Letters of John Brown," p. 18.

James Russell Lowell has, it is stated, pronounced the Brown letter to Henry L. Stearns "one of the finest pieces of autobiography extant." [1] Ralph Waldo Emerson is reported to have declared that this paper of John Brown was "a positive contribution to literature." He also regarded "in the deliberative reflection of after years," the Virginian court-room address, coupling it with Lincoln's Gettysburg speech as of "the most eloquent words of the present century." Yet, the latest biographers of Abraham Lincoln have traveled far out of their road on narrow bypaths to sneer at John Brown; discrediting his services in Kansas, decrying him as a man "of little wisdom," with a "crude visionary ideality," "ambitious to irritation;" as "clean, but coarse; honest, but rude"; with a courage that "partook of the recklessness of insanity," and of a "military ability, too insignificant even for ridicule." Messrs Hay and Nicolay, themselves among the more stupendous failures as biographers and historians in the face of the greatest of personality and subjects that human history has offered to competent capacity, have succeeded in their unnecessarily extended diatribe on John Brown, and indeed, too, of all the preluding struggle which gave to Abraham Lincoln his exalted opportunity, in making plain the smug limits of their own mental obtuseness. John Brown's reputation can stand that critical judgment far better than their literary capacity can the making of it.

It is difficult to give a correct account of the money raised in the service of Kansas. But the figures given

[1] "John Brown," by Herman Von Holst, Boston, 1889. Appendix, p. 221, by Editor Frank L. Stearns.

by Mr. Sanborn in his "Life and Letters of John Brown," must be taken as fairly approximating the facts. The National Committee is credited, as already stated, with raising and disbursing $85,196.46 in money, and in clothing, supplies, etc., to the estimated value of $110,000. The Massachusetts Committee raised chiefly through Mr. Stearns's exertions $48,000 in money; Mrs. Stearns, in supplies, at least $30,000 more. Thaddeus Hyatt probably gave $3,000 for the purchase of arms, etc., outside of his contributions to the National Committee. Previous to the formation of the National Committee, six hundred Sharpe's rifles were purchased by Amos A. Lawrence, Dr. Samuel G. Cabot, Frederick Law Olmstead and others; also two 12-pound howitzers, and several hundred revolvers; all these were sent to Kansas, at a cost in all of about $20,000. After the sacking of Lawrence, in May, 1856, when there really was the appearance of civil war, the purchase of arms and the equipment of intending settlers from the free States, was an avowed and open policy. In Massachusetts, a second and more private committee was formed to purchase arms and otherwise provide for defense and resistance; the public body chosen at a Fanueil Hall meeting having virtually agreed not to spend money for that purpose. In this, as in the general committee, Mr. Stearns was the pervading spirit. T. W. Higginson, Sanborn, Howe, Russell, Thayer, and the Cabots were all active. Many others, doubtless, came to the inner circle from time to time. It would seem to be not an extravagant statement, to estimate that the total expenditure for arms and other needed supplies for free Kansas cost in the vicinity of half a million dollars, before the books were sealed in such uneasy peace as preceded the actual outbreak of civil war. In the foregoing figures the contributions to John Brown are not included. The arms purchased for that summer's campaign, so far as they can be traced, consisted of 368 Sharpe's rifles, used to equip three companies of New England emigrants, 250 more (of which 200 were purchased by Mr. Stearns, never taken into Kansas and afterwards carried to Virginia by John Brown). In all, there were certainly bought for Kansas, between the summer of 1855 and the fall of 1856, at least 1,200 Sharpe's rifles, 400 Hall's carbines, 1,500 United States Springfield muskets, four 12-pound guns, and not less than 2,500 revolvers. Besides these about 2,000 United States muskets were obtained in Iowa and Illinois for free-state use. Of the Sharpe's carbines, 200, as already stated, came under John Brown's control and were not taken into Kansas at all.

From the departure of Captain Brown in September, 1856, to his brief and almost secret return to Kansas early in November, 1857, his days were filled with ceaseless efforts. John Brown's itinerary alone is startling. There were weeks of severe fatigue as well as wearying danger, following his departure east after the last attack on Lawrence. His visit to Chicago in the last week of October was rapidly followed by trips to New York, Boston, and western Massachusetts. Before the Astor House meeting with the National Committee during the last of January, 1857, he had previously conferred at length with the Massachusetts Kansas Committee in Boston, arranged for the custody of the Stearns rifles, that were captured by Vir-

ginia in 1859, made the acquaintance of most of those
who thereafter faithfully aided him in his work, went
to Vermont, where, at Vergennes, he probably met
one of his sons,[1] stopped at Peterboro, Rochester, and
Albany, and hastened to Boston, so that on the 18th
of February he was able to address the Massachusetts
House of Representatives on behalf of Kansas.   February, March, April, and May saw him in Connecticut,
visiting and speaking at Hartford, New Haven and
elsewhere.   At Collinsville he made with Charles Blair
a contract for the manufacture of 1,000 pikes, 900 of
which were captured by Virginia, and also arranged
for the removal to North Elba, of the tombstone over
his Revolutionary grandfather's grave, that has since
become renowned in this man's remarkable life-story.
He was at Worcester and Springfield, Akron (Ohio),
and back in New York in the last of May.   He made
his appeal to the " Friends of Freedom " through the
Tribune in April, and issued the quaint " Farewell to
Bunker Hill and Plymouth Rock," which indicated in
its tone how sharply he felt his comparative failure to
get the amount of pecuniary assistance he needed.
From Kansas reports were steadily coming of the Lecompton Constitution movement and the dangerous
conditions it was creating.   The necessity was upon
him of being near to, if not within, the Territory, and
early in June, with his son Owen, he left Hudson,
Ohio, and soon after appeared in Iowa, fitting out for
his tedious overland journey at or near Iowa City.
Two wagons and teams were purchased, the Captain

---

[1] The constant threat of arrest under Federal territorial warrants compelled him to refrain from visiting his home during the
entire period occupied by the movements under review.

driving one, and Owen the other. They were three weeks on the road to Tabor, camping in their wagons and living, as the Captain wrote to Mr. Sanborn, on herring, soda crackers, sweetened water, a little milk and a few eggs. Yet he paid for the outfit $780, and could, but for that conscientiousness which permitted all for the cause and only the barest of necessities for himself, have afforded at least decent food. This was not nearness of habit though, but a strained honesty of purpose. The Browns reached Tabor the first week in August, a letter dated the 8th being the first knowledge of his arrival. Several importunate letters and messages from General Lane and other Kansas friends, urging the need of his presence, awaited him at Tabor. Richard Realf had been sent up in July with some funds, which he left there. Hugh Forbes, the English Garibaldian with whom Captain Brown made a contract that caused much subsequent trouble, appears personally for the first time by joining the Browns at Tabor. Mention is made of his "instructions" in letters dated during September and October. He must have returned east in November, 1857, as the results of his disagreements with John Brown, for the latter was by the middle of that month on his way to central Kansas. The Captain had already sent to Concord (Mr. Sanborn being the correspondent selected between himself and the other friends who had subscribed to his efforts and expenses), an account of his expenditures with an inventory of the goods which he found in storage in Iowa City and with John Jones at Tabor.[1]

[1] Of property forwarded by the National Committee and which Captain Brown never removed, he itemizes: One brass piece,

10

The earlier details, relating to John Brown's relations with Hugh Forbes are now unknown. The
latter was then a man of about forty-five years of
age, an Englishman by birth, who had lived at Siena,
Italy, doing business as a silk merchant. He was a
man of good education and considerable accomplish-
ments, being a good linguist, an excellent master-at-
arms, and a fair military engineer. This statement is
made on the authority of General Garibaldi's chief
of staff, in the Sicilian and Neapolitan campaign,
Wm. De Rohan, an American who knew Hugh
Forbes, and for years a close friend of this writer.
Forbes early in his Italian life identified himself with
the " Young Italy " party, and was a trusted agent of
both 'Mazzini and Garibaldi. He participated in the
campaigns of 1848–49, and showed himself a man of
courage and some ability. With defeat he had of
course, to leave Italy, and for a time lived in Paris, then
in London, and some time in 1855 or 1856, he came to

---

complete; one damaged gun-carriage, some ammunition, seventy-
five old United States rifles and muskets, and twelve sabres. There
were also twelve boxes and barrels of clothing and bedding, three
hand grist-mills, some powder and lead. At Iowa City he had
obtained eleven blankets, nine tents complete, three sets of tent-
poles, and three axes, with the addition of an order for fifty dollars, given him in Chicago by Mr. Hurd, to be expended in wagon
covers, ropes, etc. These embrace all the material from the
National Committee he then received. The Stearns goods consisted of 194 Sharpe's carbines complete, with 3,300 ball cartridges,
and necessary primers. He had, besides, two repeating rifles, two
Colt's revolvers, a two-ounce gun, a few of the arms he carried into
Kansas in 1855, two wagons and four horses, with about five
hundred dollars in money. This was all of the outfit he possessed
for his great enterprise.

New York. The Italian and Garibaldian men were all on the side of the North and the Union. But Forbes, evidently, did not understand our politics. He mistook the ferment and sympathetic excitement in favor of Kansas for a deep-seated revolutionary sentiment in favor of freeing the slave by force of arms, if necessary. The arming of Northern emigrants *en route* to Kansas, he accepted as a counterpart to the probable arming of the negroes, and evidently, as his letters of complaint against John Brown show, he regarded the bold antagonism, expressed in speeches and newspapers, of Republicans to the pro-slavery Democracy and its actions, as an undoubted proof of the drift of the North towards open and armed resistance to the aggressions of the slave-power. No doubt such a feeling was manifested in very intelligent and influential circles. Men did talk boldly in those days of the need of forcible resistance; but it was not for the slave they talked, but for the free States and the institutions of the land. In the notable coteries, where European refugees of '48 were received, such a man as Hugh Forbes would be made welcome. And he undoubtedly was. Probably, also, he used his pen, as well as his skill as a swordsman, to maintain himself, wife, and daughter. What is more likely than that John Brown, who could not but have perceived from his twelve months' experience of partisan warfare in Kansas, as he well knew theoretically from his years of silent study, observation, and planning, the need of competent men to train and direct, may have cautiously suggested this need to some of the many persons he came in contact with. There were men connected with the *New York Tribune.*

for example, who knew Colonel Forbes. His name
may thus have been mentioned, and an introduction
followed. John Brown had a system of his own as
to field defenses, drill, and discipline. Such matters
would be at once discussed. Then all that followed
is simple enough. Forbes was familiar with the plans
of the European revolutionary organizations and
leaders. Among their instrumentalities were plans of
street-fighting, guerilla and irregular warfare, which
had been systematized by a French or Italian general
officer of considerable ability, who had identified himself with the European republican organization. This
system he embodied in a bulky " Manual," and Hugh
Forbes proposed to condense and translate the same
into English. Probably this proposition was first
made to John Brown, who agreed to bear the expenses
of the printing, etc. It was for this purpose that most
of the $600 drawn by Forbes from John Brown through
a banker of Hartford, Connecticut, in the spring and
early summer of 1857, was expended. It is not necessary to accuse Hugh Forbes of treachery, any more
than it is to assume that John Brown acted in this
matter with less than the careful prudence he always
showed in monetary dealings. It is more necessary to
get at the actual situation, and then for the critics, who
desire to understand and not merely accuse or make
a telling point, to put themselves in the other man's
place. Since the gun at Fort Sumter was fired at
the Union, people in our modern world, Americans
included, have made huge strides in the use and sys-
tematization of destructive forces and arms. But
before that date we knew but very little, less, too, on
this side of the Atlantic than was known on the other.

If this view is correct it will not be difficult to understand why John Brown trusted Hugh Forbes whose "Manual of the Patriotic Volunteer" was a useful book for those who were thinking, studying, and longing to act against slavery, or to defend Kansas against its assailants, as many of us were in those days.[1] As to paying Colonel Forbes a certain monthly sum, Captain Brown used his own judgment, which, granting his premises and purposes, was not so far out of the way. Forbes had no means and certainly no pecuniary credit. He had current expenses that pressed upon him, and only by regular earning could he maintain his wife and daughter. John Brown, while reducing his personal burdens to the cost of covering the narrowest margin, had more than a fair knowledge of conditions other than those to which he voluntarily limited himself. While always apart from it, he was still a man of the world, having traveled widely, transacted large business affairs, and of later years mingled with those who represented culture and embodied refinement in the best of senses. It is part of his title to leadership in his chosen path that he should apprehend the limits of men who infringed upon it. All this is not designed to defend Hugh Forbes, but only to show how John Brown and himself came together and how they also rudely separated.

At Tabor, in all probability, as to their disagreement, John Brown must have given Colonel Forbes his entire confidence, so far as naming to him, as he had done to Frederick Douglass, in 1847, and to a few others of his

---

[1] My copy of the "Manual" was burned with other books and property in Lawrence at the time of the Quantrell raid in 1863.

race before and after that date, the place or region in
and from which he designed to attack slavery.   It is
very evident that this was not at all the idea which
Hugh Forbes had associated with the expected movement.   John Brown was of course very set—dogmatic
indeed—on his own lines.   *He knew what he wanted to
do.*   The more his purposes are studied in connection
with the environment and times in which he lived, the
more must the unprejudiced student, separating himself from his own conceptions and trying to understand the growth of so strange a personality, so
unique and noble a character, be convinced that if his
intended Virginian foray had been undertaken at
such time and circumstances as can be reasonably
conceived of as possible, that there was from the point
of view of endangering slavery and making it wholly
insecure, far more than a mere probability of success.
Hugh Forbes could not see that.   He, too, was dogmatic, and possessed with a great self-pride, as his associate Garibaldian has stated.   He might, therefore,
readily come to the conclusion that he had been
" used "—not fairly dealt with—when he found John
Brown's plans so different from those which he, Hugh
Forbes, had worked out for him in his own mind.

Certain it is they parted.   There is no evidence to
show that it was in anger.   Whether John Brown
expected to find Forbes still at Tabor, on his early
return from Kansas with the eleven associates he
brought with him to study in the school and " Manual
of the Patriotic Volunteer," cannot now be ascertained.   From later letters of advice to John Brown,
Jr., then living in Ohio, it would seem as if the Captain thought Forbes might still be won over.   One

letter indicates that his son had seen the Garibaldian
and was certainly corresponding with him. There is
not an angry or reproachful word of reference to
Forbes's attitude; there is shrewd advice as to trying
to mollify his anger and threatened exposures. It
must also be said that there is not a particle of evidence to prove that Colonel Forbes went over to "the
enemy," as he must have understood that term. His
letters of angry complaint to Senators Henry Wilson
and Charles Sumner, Horace Greeley, Dr. Howe, and
others, are all explainable, though not justifiable, upon
the hypothesis suggested herein—that in Forbes's
opinion the leaders of Northern political agitation
were all more or less approving of Captain Brown's
course and were covertly, at least, sustaining him
therein. If Forbes believed also that there was a
distinct apprehension (and some purpose to definitely
prepare therefor) of a Northern outbreak "all along
the line," there is another explanation of the earnestness and even passionate nature of his warning and
demanding letters. John Brown did not stoop to
mourn over the spilled milk, or waste time and energy
by useless regrets. He endeavored to temporize, and
then, when that was impossible, made another move
which threw Forbes and others off the scent. There
is no excuse, however, for Forbes's demands but desperate necessities. His own conceptions, largely self-
imposed though they were, of the work he had expected to be engaged upon, must be considered in
making up judgment. He began to write wildly
about John Brown's course in the winter of 1857–58,
compelling thereby the movement from Chatham to
Kansas in the following summer, and then he dis-

appeared wholly from our vision, until October, 1859, and later when he was reported in command of a fortress under Garibaldi, at or near Messina, Sicily. An attack was made on him by some American newspapers,[1] and, owing to that publicity he fell into considerable discredit, dying soon from exposure and wounds, hastened doubtless by the mental mortification he underwent. Hugh Forbes was not of the higher type. He was very human in his weakness, but it remains true that he did good service elsewhere in the cause of human freedom, and that must in all generosity be weighed in his favor. John Brown cast no stone at him. Others can afford to let his memory rest. He did not send the warning letter of August, 1859, to Mr. Floyd, Buchanan's Secretary of War, for that act was left to an American to perform.

[1] The strongest criticism came from Horace Greeley's pen, and was published in the *N. Y. Tribune*, upon which I find also Col. Forbes to have been occasionally employed as a translator.—R. J. H.

CHAPTER VII.

REACHING TO A CULMINATION.

The Chatham, Canada, Convention—The refuge of the fugitives—Movements in the East—Telling Gerrit Smith and Frank B. Sanborn of his intention to raid slavery—The six friends and councilors—Martin R. Delaney's misapprehension—" The League of Liberty"—Dr. Ross, of Canada—What was meant by the Provisional Constitution—Hugh Forbes and his evil acts—Delay almost fatal—Throwing Forbes off the scent—The Lecompton Constitution—Massacre of free state men—Reuniting the little band.

JOHN BROWN arrived at the farm of Mr. Whitman, near Lawrence, on the 5th November. On the next day he sent for John E. Cook and myself. At that date I was temporarily absent and had also concluded a contract for twelve months' newspaper work. Richard Realf and Luke F. Parsons were named to John Brown by John E. Cook. On the 14th Cook, Realf, and Parsons reached Topeka, joining John Brown there, leaving almost immediately for Tabor, Iowa, with " Colonel Whipple," as Aaron D. Stevens was then known, Charles W. Moffett, from Montour, Iowa, and Richard Richardson, an intelligent man of color, who had the year before been assisted from slavery in Missouri. After reaching Canada, however.

in May, 1858, he does not again appear in the record.
Captain Brown's presence in Kansas at this period was
known to a very few persons.   The status of the Territory was by no means a settled one, owing to the
pendency of the Lecompton Constitution, and it was
a favorable element on the free-state side to have it
believed that John Brown was supposed to be mysteriously hovering along the northern line. The active
resistance at this period of James Montgomery, afterwards colonel of the Second South Carolina Colored
Volunteers, to the policy of voting under the "bogus
laws," was keeping southern Kansas in a state of ferment, which had, however, a sufficient basis in the existence of plots and ruffianly efforts to drive free-state settlers in that section from their public land entries and
settlements.¹ From Tabor John Brown soon moved to

---

¹ There were other questions embraced in the opposition to
voting for State officers under the Lecompton Constitution, besides
that of the recognition of the "bogus laws" it directly involved.
In Southern Kansas, especially, the so-called "black law" free-
state Democracy had a stronghold.   To some extent the leaders of
this faction were more unfair than were the pro-slavery party
proper.   A movement was on foot at this time to break down the
real free-state party, by substituting for it a so-called Democratic
one, which would have virtually served all the interests of the slave-
power, without having "chattelism" actually established.   Some
of the more sagacious pro-slavery men had ere this realized the
impossibility of making Kansas a slave State.   The special obstacles to this Democratic movement were the John Brown feeling,
though the Captain had no partisan relations whatever; Captain
Montgomery's defense of the free-state settlers, and the untiring
hostility of the Northern newspaper correspondents of 1855-'6-'7.
They were not many in numbers; their pens actually shaped the
policy of the free-soil and anti-Lecompton press.   Governor
Robert J. Walker found this out when he first bent his astute

Springdale, the Quaker community he had selected
for temporary residence. When assembled the party
consisted of John Brown himself, his son Owen, Aaron
Dwight Stevens, John Henri Kagi, John Edwin Cook,
Richard Realf, Charles Plummer Tidd, William Henry
Leeman, Luke F. Parsons, Charles W. Moffett, with
Richard Richardson, colored, eleven in all. John
Brown departed almost immediately for the East,
leaving Stevens in charge as military instructor. Before spring came the company was strengthened by
the accession of George B. Gill, Steward Taylor,
Edwin and Barclay Coppoc. George B. Gill and
Barclay Coppoc had entered Kansas the previous year
with the Eldridge-Perry emigrant trains and had met
therein Richard Realf and others; also met John
Brown coming out, and finding Stevens on the road
guarding the trains into Kansas.

Owen Brown's diary locates the arrival of Hugh
Forbes at Tabor on August 9th. He writes of reading
for the first time " The Manual of the Patriotic Volunteers," and mentions also George Plummer Tidd
under the name of Carpenter. On the 4th of
November Owen writes that he was thirty-three years
old. A few days later he mentions the arrival of

intellect to the task of making a free-state Democracy. Some
among us may have considered the courage of the Republican
party as not up to the measure of its occasion or duty, but there
was no hesitation in sustaining it as against an administration
Democracy and "squatter sovereignty." In this way the correspondents earned the bitter hatred of G. W. Brown, Eli Thayer,
and others it is utterly useless to name. They certainly have been
entitled by service to something different from the " cold shoulder," historically speaking, which is all their work has in the main
received from Kansas writers of later years.

"eleven desperadoes," as he jestingly termed his father
and their new comrades.

John Henri Kagi, who had visited a short time
at Camp Creek, Nebraska, with his father and sister,
soon joined the command, and remained with it until
the Chatham, Canada, movement was made in April.
The Sharpe's rifles, revolvers, ammunition and other
material which Captain Brown had found at Tabor
and taken possession of were shipped as freight to
northern Ohio in John Brown, Jr.'s, care. The original intention was to take part of the men to Ashtabula County, Ohio, Hugh Forbes being expected to be
in charge there, and Colonel Whipple (Stevens)
remain behind among the Iowa Quakers. With the
withdrawal of Forbes, concentration in Iowa was the
most reasonable plan. The men were boarded by the
Maxsons at the very small rate of one dollar each per
week,[1] the entire cost of their winter's residence not
exceeding $250. Most of the men did some work
in addition to the drilling and gun practice they regularly followed. Stevens, a very competent drillmaster
and swordsman, found apt pupils. Cook, who was
almost a phenomenal marksman and had a passion
for firearms, readily led the record at the target.
Stevens had served several years as a United States
dragoon at frontier posts, and had learned much of
rough campaigning. His lessons were all of a practical order. There was no attempt to make a secret
of their drilling, and as Gill shows and Cook stated in
his "confession," the neighborhood folks all understood that this band of earnest young men were pre-

---

[1] See the account given by George B. Gill in the Appendix.

paring for something far out of the ordinary. Of
course Kansas was presumed to be the objective point.
But generally the impression prevailed that when the
party moved again it would be somewhere in the direction of the slave States. The atmosphere of those
days was charged with disturbance. It is difficult to
determine how many of the party actually knew that
John Brown designed to invade Virginia. All the
testimony goes to show that it is most probable that
not until after the assembling at the Maryland farm
in 1859 was there a full, definite announcement of
Harper's Ferry as the objective point. That he fully
explained his purpose to make reprisals on slavery
wherever the opportunity offered is without question, but except to Owen, who was vowed to the
work in his early youth, and Kagi, who informed me
at Osawatomie in July, 1858, that Brown gave him
his fullest confidence upon their second interview at
Topeka in 1857, there is every reason to believe that
among the men the details of the intended movement
were matters of after confidence. My own experience
illustrates this : I was absent from Lawrence when
John Brown recruited his little company. He had
left already for Iowa before I returned. I met Realf
just as he was leaving, and we talked without reserve,
he assuring me that the purpose was just to prepare a
fighting nucleus for resisting the enforcement of the
Lecompton Constitution, which it was then expected
Congress might try to impose upon us. Through this
advantage was to be taken of the agitation to prepare
for a movement against slavery in Missouri, Arkansas,
the Indian Territory and possibly Louisiana. At
Kagi's request (with whom I maintained for nearly two

years an important, if irregular, correspondence), I began a systematic investigation of the conditions, roads and topography of the Southwest, visiting a good deal of the Indian Territory, with portions of southwest Missouri, western Arkansas, and northern Texas, also, under the guise of examining railroad routes, etc. The letters I wrote Kagi from time to time were

ALBERT HAZLETT.

signed William Harrison by an understanding with him. It was this name Albert Hazlett gave when taken prisoner at Carlisle, Pennsylvania, and, with John E. Cook at Chambersburg, was illegally extradited to Virginia. Under it he was tried at Charlestown, and executed in the following March, 1860. It will be recalled by those familiar with the drama of events that John Brown always declined publicly to recognize Hazlett, after the latter was imprisoned at Charlestown, as one of his men. He did not wish to throw any obstacles in the way of his possible escape before the Virginia courts.[1] It was un-

---

[1] The only witness before the Virginian Court who swore to Albert Hazlett's presence in the Harper's Ferry fight was a man named Barry, an Irish-American schoolmaster, whose life Hazlett is reported to have saved. This statement is made on the authority of George Alfred Townsend, who gives it as coming from Barry himself. The latter is the author of the pamphlet on Harper's Ferry, published under the name of "Josephus" as author, referred to and quoted in other chapters.

doubtedly the signature to my letters that made him use the name of Harrison when arrested. These letters were captured in the carpet-bag at the Virginia schoolhouse, and Governor Wise himself told me at Richmond in 1857, that two were secretly lithographed and sent to many leading men of the South and Southwest as evidence of the plots that were being formed. It is to be presumed that these were two that gave an account of discontent among the slaves in southwest Arkansas, northwest Louisiana, and those held by the Choctaw, Chickasaw, and Cherokee Indians; planning at the same time to ferment an outbreak among them, aided by Kansas men, led, perhaps, by Captain Montgomery. These things are recalled in connection with the open drilling within a Northern State of a body of men, however small in numbers, having the avowed purpose of carrying the free-state war into the Africa of slavery itself. They serve to prove how charged and vital was the public mentality in those days. A conflict seems to have been expected, denounced or tolerated by all sides. It was this condition that enabled John Brown to hold his small force together without the fullest confidence to them on his part, and, at the same time, keep from active suspicion the public feeling around himself and party. The roads they traveled would never have been so accessible but for the currents that were set in vibration by the aggressions of the slave-holders, their leaders, and politicians.

Hugh Forbes must have left Tabor immediately after Captain Brown left for Kansas, for he was at Rochester, New York, in the latter part of November. The latter with his party arrived at Springdale, and

himself moved eastward about the 20th instant, called
chiefly by the fact that Forbes had already begun a
campaign against his chief.[1]   His earlier letters were
addressed to Dr. Howe, Senator Sumner, and some
other of the more radical anti-slavery men.   He demanded that Brown be withdrawn from command,
and that he himself or some other person be placed
in charge.   Evidently he thought there was a political
revolutionary conspiracy on foot.   Of course such
letters produced commotion and caused annoyance.
Dr. Howe seems to have been most seriously affected
by them.   Forbes had received sufficient confidences
from John Brown to be able to apprehend some of
the weaker points, or rather he knew where the
joints in the armor were.   The fact that the Captain's " tools " were apparently the " property " of the
Massachusetts Kansas Committee, and that Brown had
been made their " agent," would seem to have caused
a fear that that body might be charged with a
breach of trust if Forbes's allegations should become
public property.   There is no evidence that Messrs.
Stearns, Howe, Parker, Gerrit Smith, Sanborn, Higginson, or even Senator Sumner—who knew nothing
of the Committee's work except by hearsay—were
troubled as to reprisals on slavery itself.   Mr. Stearns
certainly was not, nor Higginson, Sanborn, Parker.
Dr. Howe, sometimes overwrought by the multiplicity
of his laborious duties, was evidently excited by the
possibility of reflections on the integrity of the Kansas
Aid Committee, of which he had been an active member.   As a matter of fact, the material in John Brown's

---

[1] I am here indebted chiefly to Mr. Sanborn's " Life and Letters
of John Brown," Chap. XII., pp. 418, *et al.*, for dates, etc.

possession as "agent" was not the property of any committee, but of George L. Stearns, who had paid for and owned it. The relations of the Massachusetts Committee were protected by later letters (May, 1858) from Mr. Stearns, as chairman, notifying John Brown that said arms were to be used only " for the defense of Kansas," and shortly after their final disposition was made by his absolute and personal gift of them to John Brown direct. This action was not had, however, till Hugh Forbes found that his letters to the more intimate friends of Captain Brown in Massachusetts did not produce the effect he sought, and he had begun to extend his correspondence of assailment to public men like Senators Wilson, Hale, and Seward, as well as to Horace Greeley and William Cullen Bryant, having evidently been posted on the idea that they as party and political leaders could have no relations with direct attacks on the institution of slavery. It must be borne in mind that the aim of the new politics, its party, and policy, was simply to denationalize slavery : John Brown's purpose to render it unsafe and dangerous to hold slaves by attacks which would show the system's inherent weakness. He had no theory to substitute therefor, except that of the Declaration of Independence; and his convictions that constitutional provisions guarding and preserving, or aiming to, the rights of the individual and of the citizen, were more potential than evasive and temporary compromises. Naturally, however, the organizers and leaders of the new party, already realizing that success was before them, dreaded all action by the "fanatics" of the day. Every period has its sneer. That was the way it

11

sounded then. Now the term is "crank," or worse.
Ethics are brushed aside for "practical" success, and
faith is lost in sacerdotalism.   Plutocracy loves ceremony, and hierarchical forms are the natural product
of class and privilege.   The fanatics are denounced ;
the cranks are derided, but lo.! Time changes, and
the "practical" men who have feared or sneered,
become the active administrators of the ideas and
ideals they denounced and derided.   The administrators "win"; the others fail of personal reward and
often even of recognition. But the work they do
goes on.   So it was with John Brown.

The Captain left Iowa late in December.   Letters
had reached him there, at Springdale, and at West
Andover, Ohio, very early in January, with accounts
of the Boston-wise perturbations.   Forbes was at
Rochester, N. Y., in November, calling on Frederick
Douglass, presenting a letter from Captain Brown.
Mr. Douglass says he was not favorably impressed,
but he took him to a hotel and paid his bill while
there.   He also gave him a little money, and through
a German lady friend he received introductions also
to other Germans in New York.   For a short period
he did not attack John Brown, but that reticence soon
wore off.   Mr. Douglass did not hesitate to say that
Forbes betrayed the movement to the authorities at
Washington.   In that, however, I believe he was mistaken.   There are details of this imbroglio which
tend to show that Colonel Forbes must have about
this time got into relations with a small coterie of
clever colored men in New York City, revolving
around a well-known physician of that race, now deceased, who were notoriously at variance with the

efforts and associations of many others of their race leaders. They held the theory that it was the duty of all educated colored men to mould their people into separate and violent resistance. In their minds the reaction to race oppression and outrage led to a counter race contempt, antagonism, and rage. They wanted no help from white men, and some of them spent a good deal of misdirected intellectual effort in the endeavor to prove that somewhere in the historic past their race had been one of the ruling forces of the world. They did not realize that it mattered not to them if it ever had; the living issues were the potential ones of present wrong-doing and oppression, hurting the wrong-doer as well as the wronged ones. From such sources as these, limited though they were, Hugh Forbes received many hints of possible relations, which his imperfect conception of American affairs turned into remarks that very naturally assumed a malignant aspect when put into letters to prominent men.

A letter of John Brown to his son John, written at Rochester to West Andover, Ohio, early in February, shows the manner in which he was disposed to deal with Forbes.[1] At this date Captain Brown was fully

---

[1] After referring to a letter from the Garibaldian, of January 27th, the Captain outlines a reply to be written to Forbes by John, saying: "I am anxious to draw him out more fully, and would also like to keep him a little encouraged and *avoid an open rupture for a few weeks at any rate.*" He then adds: Suppose you write Forbes thus:

"Your letter to my father, . . . after mature reflection, I have decided to return to you, as I am unwilling he should, with all his other cares, . . . be vexed with what I am apprehensive he will accept as highly offensive and insulting, while I know

bent on delivering his intended blow, and came to the
East determined to strain every nerve to obtain the
moderate means needed to begin with. He realized
that his handful of keen-witted, brave, and devoted
young men, then at Springdale, while heated through
to the annealing point by the furnace of Kansas warfare, were liable to all the cooling influences of their
years and temperaments, and such modifying conditions as the shifting phases of Time might readily
bring to bear on them. He wanted to strike. Besides
he desired to use the colored people if possible. It must

he is disposed to do all he consistently can for you . . . unless
you are yourself the cause of his disgust." The letter then suggests the statement that he, John, understands from his father,
that $600 or " six months' pay " had already been advanced in the
face of his own disappointments, " to enable " Forbes to " provide
for his family." The contract was to be $100 per month as long
as Forbes continued to serve. " Now," continues the draft of
the letter to John Brown, Jr., " you (Forbes) undertake to
instruct him (Brown) to say that he had positively engaged you
for one year. I fear he will not accept it well to be asked or told
to state what he considers an *untruth*." The draft adds that he,
Captain Brown, will hardly take kindly to be instructed as to how
he should transact " his own business and correspondence." Reference is made to " the seemingly spiteful letters " Forbes owns to
have written as having not only done himself " great injury," but
" also weakened him (Captain Brown) with his friends to whom
they were sent." This draft is a very shrewd yet kindly forbearing
with all, and closes with suggesting that a draft of $40 may be sent
to him (Forbes) if the rebuke intended had its effect. It closes by
saying, " I do not mean to dictate to you as he does to me, but I
am anxious to understand him fully before we go any further, and
shall be glad of the earliest information of the result." No reply is
alluded to, and presumably therefore, as the facts show, the " rebuke " had no effect.—"Life and Letters of John Brown," pp.
432–34.

have been within the brooding, observant purview of his perceptive brain to understand that they, too, growing in apprehension of larger political growth, were likely to feel their personal animosity lessened. Knowing their helplessness as a despised minority they might grow timid, more or less disposed to wait upon the changes that the rising tide of northern opinion would bring in favorable drifts towards them. John Brown comprehended with undaunted clearness that respect was only won by compelling it. A blow for freedom was always a victory. That was his view. So he pushed forward on the hard and stern road he had blazed for himself.

At Rochester in January and February, staying at the Douglass House for three weeks, where he wrote industriously, combating the mischief Forbes's attacks were doing. He was urged to visit Boston, but thought it not safe for him to pass through Albany and Springfield, where he was so well known. An extract of a letter to Thomas W. Higginson shows generally how he was pressing his friends to the conclusion of such assistance as he needs. Evidently Higginson had suggested underground railroad work on a scale larger than was then practised. It was in him to do that, as he was always open to the direct conception of resistance to oppression and the duty of each of us to aid therein. Here is John Brown's suggestive note:

"Railroad business on a somewhat extended scale is the identical object for which I am trying to get means. I have been connected with that business, as commonly conducted, from boyhood, and never let an opportunity slip. I have been operating to some

purpose the past season, but I now have a measure on
foot that I feel sure would awaken in you something
more than a common interest if you could understand
it.   I have just written my friends G. L. Stearns and
F. B. Sanborn, asking them to meet me for consultation at Peterbòro, New York."

It was in Peterboro, New York, at the home of
Gerrit Smith, that the definite direction of John
Brown was made known to the friends who had so
far aided.   They were indeed few in numbers.   All
of the Emigrant Aid Society organizers had fallen.
John Brown himself still clung to the belief that Eli
Thayer might "hook on his team," as he later suggested to John, Jr., when planning out some trips of
observation and inquiry.   His experience with Amos
A. Lawrence, especially over the matter of the North
Elba homestead and the $1,000 to be raised for its
protection, did not induce any desire to ask his aid.
He had never sought assistance from the Abolitionists proper—that is, the Garrisonians.   And of course
the National Kansas Committee people were of no
avail.   The two sources of monetary support open to
him, were Gerrit Smith, his personal friend as well
as faithful anti-slavery ally, and the very small coterie
of Boston gentlemen, whose names are linked forever with his own.   Frank B. Sanborn arrived at
Mr. Smith's residence on the evening of February 22,
1858, representing also Messrs. Stearns, Parker, Howe,
and Higginson.   It was on this occasion that John
Brown unfolded in detail the fulness of his purpose,
with the possible reservation of not in words naming
Harper's Ferry, though his general purport must
have led directly thereto.   Of the three persons

to whom this high-wrought conception was thus presented, Gerrit Smith and Frank B Sanborn do not appear to have accepted it unquestioningly.[1] According to Mr. Sanborn's very interesting account, the conference lasted till after midnight, and began again briefly on the morrow, being concluded by Gerrit Smith saying:

"You see how it is; our dear old friend has made up his mind to this course and cannot be turned from it. We cannot give him up to die alone; we must support him."

Captain Brown had named $800, even $500, as the extent of his need. Then $1,000 was decided upon, and Mr. Sanborn left on the 24th for Boston, to present the matter and raise the balance of the amount. Mr. Smith's share became $500 before

---

[1] Mr. Sanborn mentioned Edwin Morton as one who was confided in. At the time that gentleman was an inmate of Mr. Smith's house as a tutor to his sons, and he acted also as secretary or confidential amanuensis. Captain Brown, Mr. Smith, and Mr. Sanborn adjourned to Mr. Morton's room. He was a classmate of Mr. Sanborn, and, in the familiar relations he bore, had necessarily to be trusted. But there is no other evidence than this of Mr. Morton's association with the movement. Mr. Smith, after the blow was struck at Harper's Ferry, had a severe recurrence of a nervous trouble he had been afflicted with at the time of the long legislative struggle in the United States House of Representatives over the repeal of the Missouri Compromise in 1854, and was sent again to the institution in which he was first treated. The family deemed it wise to send Mr. Morton to Europe for two years. No one in Massachusetts or Kansas, or in John Brown's home circle, seems, besides Mr. Sanborn, to have considered Mr. Morton as directly identified. John Brown, Jr., in letters during 1859, speaks of once meeting and talking with him.

the conclusion was reached.   In Boston, Parker
agreed, thought the matter worth trying, though except for effect on opinion, he did not believe it would
accomplish much.   Dr. Howe accepted the idea with
earnestness.   He never doubted that within the lines
to be worked upon, were real military possibilities, and
that it was not necessarily a foredoomed failure.   Mr.
Stearns accepted, with an utterly loyal belief in the
old covenanter.   Higginson also held the same view,
and Mr. Sanborn almost decided to take a personal
share in the movement.   To those who knew him
then, the wonder is that he was not found at the Kennedy Farm.   John Brown, however, knew that some
men were more valuable alive just then, than they
would be as sacrifices.

From the 23d of February the Captain was a busy
man.   The "freight" stored at Conneaut, Ohio, about
which embarrassing questions were arising, had to be
placed where John, Jr., and Jason, could control it.
Letters were written from North Elba, asking Ruth
that Henry, her husband, might "go to school"—join
in the pending raid.   The incident had a pathetic
ending in inducing Oliver and Watson to volunteer
on that which was their death-errand.   On the 4th
of March, the Captain was in Boston, stopping at the
American House, where he was visited by all his little
circle of friends.   While they resolved themselves
into a committee of aid and advice, Sanborn is convinced [1] that Harper's Ferry was never named as the
first or chief point of attack.   On leaving Boston,

---

[1] See Chapter XII. " Life and Letters of John Brown."

March 8th, he carried with him $500 in gold and assurances of other support. He passed through New York on the 2d, preferring to go round rather than take the risk of being recognized in western Massachusetts. On the 10th of March, Frederick Douglass, Henry Highland Garnet, of New York, Stephen Smith and William Still, of Philadelphia, with John Brown, Jr., met the Captain in conference at the dwelling of either Smith or Still. Others may have been present, but their names are nowhere given.

Earlier letters to his eldest son show in part what must have been discussed, among other matters, at the Philadelphia meetings. On the 4th of February, the Captain wrote John, that: "I have been thinking that I would like to have you make a trip to Bedford, Chambersburg, Gettysburg, and Uniontown, in Pennsylvania, traveling slowly along, and inquiring of every man on the way, or every family of the right stripe, and getting acquainted with them as much as you could. When you look at the location of those places, you will readily perceive the advantage of getting up some acquaintance in those parts."

He further advised with his son to visit Washington and see certain Congressmen, with the hope of "getting some money for secret service"; and then he continued,—"You can say to our friends that I am out from Kansas for that express purpose." In subsequent letters he withdrew the Washington suggestion, remarking that he had but little "faith in princes." He mentions, however, that Anson Burlingame gave him $50; and then he directs John to go to Hagerstown, Martinsburg, and *even to Harper's Ferry itself* in pursuing the inquiries he desired to have

made. Of course, the object of these was to find out
the underground railroad routes and stations, to ascertain the persons who were actually to be relied
upon, places to stop at, means of conveyance, and
especially to learn of the colored men who could be
trusted.   The Philadelphia conference must have
gone over this ground with the two Browns, and the
experience of those who were the most active of U.
G. R. R. directors in that section, could not but
have been very useful.   In the early part of April,
John Brown visited St. Catherine, Ingersoll, Hamilton, and Chatham, in Canada West, to prepare for the
convention he wished to convene just before he entered on his active work.   He was also reported at
Sandusky, Ohio, and Detroit, Michigan.   A visit had
been made to North Elba, and it was arranged, that
Henry Thompson should manage both farms, while
Oliver and Watson would "go to school" with their
father.   The Captain was hastening his steps in
order to return to Iowa and bring his men on to
Chatham, and from there, as he then expected, to the
border of Virginia, to begin working out the serious
aim of his life.

John Brown's purpose in calling and holding
the convention at Chatham, Canada West, was in
harmony with the conception and plans he had
evolved.   There was a large number of colored residents under the British flag. They were mainly fugitive slaves; among whom necessarily were many bold,
even daring men.   In the section, of which Chatham
was one of the centers, considerable direction had
been given to the settlement of these people.   There
were among them (and still are) a good many far-

mers, mechanics, storekeepers, as well as laborers. It
would not be correct to say that no prejudice existed
against them, but it was not strong enough, as in the
land from which they fled, to prevent industry and
sobriety from having a fair chance, while intelligence,
well directed, made its way to civic and business recognition.   There were probably not less than 75,000
fugitive residents in Canada West at the time of the
Chatham gathering.   Their presence, well-ordered
lives, and fair degree of prosperity, had brought also
to live with them as doctors, clergymen, teachers,
lawyers, printers, surveyors, etc., educated freemen
of their own race.   Martin R. Delany, a physician,
editor, ethnologist, and naturalist, was one of them.
Mr. Holden, a well-trained surveyor and civil engineer, at whose residence in Chatham, John Brown
stayed, the Rev. William Charles Munroe, Osborne
Perry Anderson, and others, were among these helpers.
Dr. Alexander M. Ross, of Toronto, Canada, physician and ornithologist, who is still living, honored
by all who know him, then a young (white) man
who devoted himself for years to aiding the American slave, was a frequent visitor to this section.   He
was a faithful friend of John Brown, efficient as an
ally also, seeking to serve under all conditions of need
and peril.   But it was not simply the presence of
these forces which took John Brown to Chatham.   As
one may naturally understand, looking at conditions
then existing, there existed something of an organization to assist fugitives and of resistance to their
masters.   It was found all along the Lake borders
from Syracuse, New York, to Detroit, Michigan.   As
none but colored men were admitted into direct and

active membership with this "League of Freedom,"
it is quite difficult to trace its workings, or know how
far its ramifications extended.   One of the most interesting phases of slave life, so far as the whites were
enabled to see or impinge upon it, was the extent and
rapidity of communication among them.   Four geo-
graphical lines seem to have been chiefly followed.
One was that of the coast south of the Potomac,
whose almost continuous line of swamps from the
vicinity of Norfolk, Va., to the northern border of
Florida afforded a refuge for many who could not
escape and became "marooned" in their depths,
while giving facility to the more enduring to work
their way out to the North Star land.   The great
Appalachian range and its abutting mountains were
long a rugged, lonely, but comparatively safe route
to freedom. It was used, too, for many years. Doubtless, a knowledge of that fact, for John Brown was
always an active underground railroad man, had very
much to do, apart from its immediate use strategi-
cally considered, with the Captain's decision to begin
operations therein.   Harriet Tubman, whom John
Brown met for the first time at St. Catherine's in
March or April, 1858, was a constant user of the Appalachian route, in her efforts to aid escaping slaves.
"Moses," as Mrs. Tubman was called by her own
people, was a most remarkable black woman, un-
lettered and very negrine, but with a great degree of
intelligence and perceptive insight, amazing courage,
and a simple steadfastness of devotion which lifts her
career into the ranks of heroism.   Herself a fugitive
slave, she devoted her life after her own freedom was
won, to the work of aiding others to escape   First

and last Harriet brought out several thousand slaves.[1]
John Brown always called her "General," and once
introduced her to Wendell Phillips by saying "I
bring you one of the best and bravest persons on this
continent—*General* Tubman, as we call her." William Lambert, who died in Detroit a few years since,
being very nearly one hundred years old, was another
of those of the race who devoted themselves to the
work for which John Brown hoped to strike a culminating blow. Between 1829 and 1862—thirty-three
years—William is reported to have aided in the escape of 30,000 slaves. He lived in Detroit, and was
one of the foremost representatives of his people in
both Michigan and Ontario. Underground-railroad
operations culminating chiefly at Cleveland, Sandusky, and Detroit, led by broad and defined routes
through Ohio, to the border of Kentucky. Through
that State, into the heart of the Cumberland Mountains, northern Georgia, east Tennessee, and northern Alabama, the limestone caves of the region served
a useful purpose. And it is a fact that the colored
people living in Ohio were often bolder and more determined than was the rule elsewhere. The Ohio-
Kentucky routes probably served more fugitives than
others in the North. The valley of the Mississippi
was the most westerly channel, until Kansas opened
a bolder way of escape from the Southwest slave
section. John Brown knew whatever was to be known
of all this unrest, and he also must have known of

---

[1] "Harriet—The Moses of her People." By Sarah H. Bradford.
George R. Lockwood, New York, 1886. Mrs. Tubman is still
living at Auburn, N. Y

the existence of the secret organization which George
B. Gill mentions [1] (see Appendix) in his interesting
paper. This organization served a purpose of some
value to the Government in the earlier parts of the
Civil War, a fact, that lies within my own knowledge,
and then fell into disuse, as the hours moved swifter
to the one in which the gateway of the Union swung
aside, and the pathway of the Law opened, to allow

---

[1] A letter from Dr. Alexander Milton Ross, bearing date Toronto, January 21st, 1893, contains two points of interest. The
first is that relative to the time of moving on Harper's Ferry. Dr.
Ross writes: "On the occasion of my last interview with John
Brown I asked him directly—'When do you intend to begin your
work?' After a moment's reflection he replied in these words, as
near as my recollection serves me: 'God willing, I shall move
between the 15th and 27th of October.' I replied: 'Then you will
wish me to be in Richmond between the 15th and 27th!' He said:
'Yes, not later than the 27th.'"

"Now, in reference to the 'Liberty League'—I was one of *their*
members at large—Gerrit Smith and Lewis Tappan were the
others. As to the actual members I had very little acquaintance.
I knew of George J. Reynolds, of Hamilton (Sandusky also),
George W. Brown and Glover Harrison, of this city (Toronto).
The branch of the League in Upper Canada had no connection
with the armed and drilled men along the United States border,
whose duty it was to help the slaves to escape to Canada. Of
course, I knew many of them—Liberators, as they were called—
from Erie to Sandusky and Cleveland. I never had much in them
and but little to do with the organization, *always fearing treachery.*
I never had any military taste or predilection, and but little to do
with armed men. Except to my friends, I was not known as Doctor
Ross, and my friends took pains to shield me." . . . I frequently heard the slaves speak of insurrectionary movements in
progress, but never anything definite. The slaves were very
simple, childlike, and superstitious—ready to believe anything told
them by those in their confidence."

the colored American to reach emancipation and citizenship.

These were some of the forces John Brown hoped without doubt to use. He never expected any more aid from them than that which would give a first impetus. Had he got away from Harper's Ferry and kept in the mountains for a brief period, no doubt exists whatever in my mind, that there would have been more or less sporadic outbreaks along the central lines I have suggested. The underground railroaders from Ohio and in Kentucky could not have kept out of the struggle.

The home of Isaac Holden, Chatham, Canada West, is an old-fashioned red brick, two-storied, comfortable-looking dwelling-house, nearly square, with brick gables higher than the roof, having a broad, outside chimney at each end, with the side to the street. Five low, broad windows light the parlor floor, one portion of which John Brown occupied. Mr. Holden, who had resided twenty-five years in Canada at the time of this visit, is a native of Louisiana, a man of means and liberal education. It was in John Brown's room that a committee met to examine the constitution. Dr. Delany was chairman, and J. H. Kagi and Osborne P. Anderson acted as secretaries. The meetings of the convention itself were held in a Baptist Church, of which Mr. Munroe was the pastor. Osborne P. Anderson describes some of the incidents as follows:

" The first visit of John Brown to Chatham was in April, 1858. Wherever he went around, although an entire stranger, he made a profound impression upon those who saw or became acquainted with him. Some supposed him a staid but modern-ized Quaker, others a solid business man from 'somewhere,' and without question a philanthropist. His long white beard, thoughtful and reverend brow and physiognomy, his sturdy, measured tread, as he circulated about with hands under the pendant coat skirts of plain brown tweed, with other garments to match, revived to those honored with his acquaintance and knowing of his history, the memory of a Puritan of the most exalted type." ("A Voice from Harper's Ferry," 1861, p. 9.)

Dr. Delany in the Rollins biography gives a more detailed account. The doctor's statement seems to be at variance with those made by Anderson, Gill, Realf, and Moffett, who were present. It must be borne in mind that Captain Brown had not only alternative methods of action in his own mind, but ample reason for not drawing the close attention even of friends to the one which he most desired to put into operation, viz , an attack on Harper's Ferry itself. In the first place, he knew that Forbes had sources of information, and was disposed to use them adversely to success, and, next, he never felt sure of the way in which his daring conception would be received. [1]

The "Subterranean Pass Way" represented ideas and methods in accord with and enlarging the work on the underground railroad. The essential difference was that, the rescued fugitives or runaways should be planted in or near to a Northern or Western community and not brought under the British flag. One purpose was to educate Northern people to defend fugitives, and the other would have been to teach the runaways to defend themselves. No report exists from any other source of any such plan having been

---

See Appendix for extract from the Delany biography.

discussed within the Chatham Convention itself. I have talked it over with Gill and Realf who were actively participating; incidentally I have asked Tidd and Osborne P. Anderson, but from none did I ever gather the idea of any discussion, as Dr. Delany intimates. Yet it doubtless occurred, and in all probability within the preliminary committee meeting. The convention talk was general. It is also certain that more criticism and resistant views came from colored men in the body than ever appears to have been urged at any time by the white men (except Hugh Forbes), who were knowing to Captain Brown's purposes or associated with him. It is also a fact that he received very little of the aid it was presumable he had a right to expect from colored men. Osborne P. Anderson was the only man of his race who reported from Canada, none of those who had Brown's confidence to a greater or lesser degree were on hand at the Kennedy farm, the two Ohio (Oberlin) recruits being the fruits of a near and preceding fugitive slave excitement. It is not necessary to comment on this; it is essential though to state the fact.

John Brown was at Springdale, Iowa, on the 27th of April, 1858, having arrived from Canada, *via* Chicago, on the 25th, for the purpose of removing eastward his " band of shepherds," as he termed them, or " surveyors," as they termed themselves. At this date the Boston and Peterboro friends, according to Mr. Sanborn, expected to hear of "his flock " being turned "loose about the 15th of May." J. H. Kagi, C. P. Tidd, and L. F. Parsons had preceded by a few days the main body, which left West Liberty on the

27th. At Chatham, where they arrived on the 30th
inst., they were joined by these three associates.
There were in all of the Brown party, including the
Captain himself, thirteen persons, one being colored. The convention did not assemble till the 8th
of May, and there were only forty-six present, twelve
of whom were white men. The others were all
colored men; Doctor Delany being the only one of
any wide reputation. There is no evidence to show
that Douglass, Loguen, Garnet, Stephen Smith,
Gloucester, Langston, or others of the prominent men
of color in the States who *knew* John Brown, were
invited to the Chatham meeting. It is doubtful if their
appearance would have been wise, as it would assuredly have been commented on and aroused suspicion.
But the singular fact remains, looked at in either
way, whether asked or not, that their influence had
no visible representation or presence. John and
Owen Brown, father and son, John Henri Kagi,
Aaron Dwight Stevens, still known as Charles Whipple, John Edwin Cook, Richard Realf, George B.
Gill, Charles Plummer Tidd, William Henry Leeman,
Charles W. Moffett, Luke F. Parsons, all of Kansas,
and Steward Taylor, of Canada, who had joined in
Iowa; twelve in all. Richard Richardson, a member
of this party, was a colored man. The remaining
members, thirty-three, were all colored. The president
of the convention, William Charles Munroe, was pastor
of the church in which the sessions were held on
Saturday the 8th and Monday the 10th of May.
Other delegates were Dr. Martin A. Delany, and
Alfred Whipper, Pennsylvania; William Lambert and
I. D. Shadd, of Detroit, Michigan; James H. Harris,

of Cleveland, Ohio (after the war a Representative
in Congress for two terms from North Carolina); G.
J. Reynolds, J. C. Grant, A. J. Smith, James M. Jones,
M. F. Bailey, S. Hunton, John J. Jackson, Jeremiah
Anderson, James M. Bell, Alfred M. Ellsworth, James
W. Purnell, George Aiken, Stephen Dettin, Thomas
Hickerson, John Cannel, Robinson · Alexander,
Thomas F. Cary, Thomas M. Kinnard, Robert Van
Vauken, Thomas M. Stringer, John A. Thomas (believed to be John Brown's earlier confidant and em-
ployé at Springfield, Massachusetts, afterwards employed by Abraham Lincoln in his Illinois home and
at the White House also; he died recently at Springfield, Illinois); Robert Newman, Charles Smith, Simon
Fislin, Isaac Holden, and James Smith; making
thirty-four colored and twelve white members. John
Henri Kagi was made secretary. The entire proceedings did not occupy over fifteen hours in both days,
and practically consisted of ratifying what had already
been agreed upon in the various conferences held
during the preceding three weeks.[1] The points of
difference were of no great consequence, except one.
That was a discussion of the forty-sixth article of
the proposed Constitution, which reads as follows :

THE ARTICLES NOT FOR THE OVERTHROW OF GOVERN-
MENT.

"The foregoing Articles shall not be construed
so as in any way to encourage the overthrow of any
State Government, or of the General Government of
the United States, and look to no dissolution of the

---

[1] See Appendix for minutes of proceedings.

Union, but simply to Amendment and Repeal. And
our flag shall be the same that our Fathers fought
under in the Revolution."

The motion to strike this out came from George J.
Reynolds. He is mentioned both by Dr. Ross and
Mr. Gill, as a leading member of the "League of
Liberty." When John Brown, Jr., was engaged during
August and September of the next year in the effort
to get the Chatham Convention men together for the
Harper's Ferry movement, he wrote from Sandusky,
Ohio, to Kagi at Chambersburg, Pennsylvania, that the
"Coppersmith" was "one of those men who must be
obtained if possible." This reference is understood
to be to Mr. Reynolds. In the discussion which followed, Reynolds was the only advocate of the motion.
Dr. Delany, Elder Munroe, and Mr. Kennard, all colored, were strenuous in opposing; and Captain Brown
Kagi, and Realf made earnest argument against the
motion. Article XLVI. was in fact the keynote of
John Brown's position. He was defending the Union
and the Government under it, threatened as he reasoned, by the existence of chattel slavery, having, under misapprehended provisions, political powers
which necessitated and encouraged the formation
of a dangerous and continuous pro-slavery conspiracy.
The presence of this Article makes consistent the
declaration subsequently embodied in his last speech
in the Virginia Court, in response to the usual question "Why sentence should not be passed upon
him?" In that reply he declared, as will be seen,
that he had not "raised" insurrection, committed
"treason," incited to "civil war," or "instructed"
slaves to kill their masters. Right or wrong, as he

may be judged, it is necessary to apprehend clearly, in order to estimate justly, the mental processes of this remarkable personality.   Certainly, there is nothing anarchistic in them.   The "roads" John Brown mapped out and which he sought to travel, carried, in his mind at least, the highest respect for law, and recognized to the full the responsibility to social order and equity.   The difference between him (as he saw it) and the established "disorder," was that the latter had its strength in wrong-doing, and threatened free institutions to the degree that the reserved rights of the citizen could justly be called upon for resistance.   Kennedy's motion had the support only of his own vote.   Messrs. Kagi and Realf were particularly vigorous and eloquent in their arguments, as Gill and others report.

John Brown made the opening and principal speech of the convention.   No orator, certainly no rhetorician, yet he was sententious, logical, direct, very apt in illustration, and, like all men of intellectual reserve, brooding usually on solitude and silence over large issues, quite aphoristic and terse in expression.   John Brown had read well and thought clearly within the deep lines his brain and character wrought out for action.[1]   In his evidence before the United States

---

[1] In childhood, youth, and manhood the Bible was his constant study.   Mr. Gill says that a volume of the "Sayings of Confucius," was one of his later favorites.   He read " Pilgrim's Progress," the "Life of Franklin," " Æsop's Fables," " Plutarch's Lives," " Biography of Washington," all Revolutionary material, and made a study of Marion and Sumpter's careers, "Napoleon and His Marshals," Baxter's "Saints' Rest," " Herodotus," " Josephus," and several theological works.   He read the newspapers and was well informed in current history and invention.

Senate Committee on the "Harper's Ferry Invasion,"
that was the way in which the Virginian and the
Southern Statesmen put it in order to maintain the
idea of John Brown's movement being concerted with
the aid of Republican and Northern leaders. Richard
Realf thus outlined John Brown's opening speech in
the Chatham Convention. His report is no doubt
substantially correct, though more rhetorical in tone
than were the Captain's actual words. Estimating
th: quality and temper of the latter, especially at a
" supreme moment " like this one, it may readily be accepted that John Brown's actual speech was far more
vigorous and striking even than is shown in the picturesque report of his poet follower.

" John Brown, on rising," said Realf to the Committee (p. 96–
97 of Report), " stated that for twenty or thirty years the idea
had possessed him like a passion of giving liberty to the slaves.
He stated immediately thereafter, that he made a journey to
England in 1851, in which year he took to the International
Exhibition at London samples of wool from Ohio, during which
period he made a tour upon the European continent, inspecting
all fortifications, and especially all earthwork forts which he
could find, with a view, as he stated, of applying the knowledge
thus gained, with modifications and inventions of his own, to
such a mountain warfare as he thereafter spoke upon in the
United States. John Brown stated, moreover, that he had not
been indebted to anybody for the suggestion of this plan ; that
it arose spontaneously in his own mind ; that through a series
of from twenty to thirty years it had gradually formed and
developed itself into shape and plan. He stated that he had
read all the books upon insurrectionary warfare which he could
lay his hands upon—the Roman warfare ; the successful opposition of the Spanish chieftains during the period when Spain
was a Roman province ; how with ten thousand men divided

and subdivided into small companies, acting simultaneously, yet separately, they withstood the whole consolidated power of the Roman Empire through a number of years. In addition to this, he said he had become very familiar with the successful warfare waged by Schamyl, the Circassian chief, against the Russians; he had posted himself in relation to the wars of Toussaint L'Overture, and the other phases of the wars in Hayti and the islands round about; and from all these things he had drawn the conclusion, believing, as he stated there he did believe, and as we all (if I may judge from myself) believed, that upon the first intimation of a plan formed for the liberation of the slaves, they would immediately rise all over the Southern States. He supposed that they would come into the mountains to join him, where he proposed to work, and that by flocking to his standard they would enable him (by making the line of mountains which cuts diagonally through Maryland and Virginia down through the Southern States into Tennessee and Alabama, the base of his operations) to act upon the plantations on the plains lying on each side of that range of mountains, and we should be able to establish ourselves in the fastnesses, and if any hostile action (as would be) were taken against us, either by the militia of the separate States, or by the armies of the United States, we proposed to defeat first the militia, and next, if it were possible, the troops of the United States, and then organize the freed blacks under this provisional constitution, which would carve out for the locality of its jurisdiction all that mountainous region in which the blacks were to be established, and in which they were to be taught the useful and mechanical arts, and to be instructed in all the business of life. Schools were also to be established, and so on. That was it.

"The negroes were to constitute the soldiers. John Brown expected that all the free negroes in the Northern States would immediately flock to his standard. He expected that all the slaves in the Southern States would do the same. He believed, too, that as many of the free negroes in Canada as could accompany him, would do so.

" The slaveholders were to be taken as hostages, if they refused to let their slaves go. It is a mistake to suppose that they were to be killed; they were not to be. They were to be held as hostages for the safe treatment of any prisoners of John Brown's who might fall into the hands of hostile parties.

" All the non-slaveholders were to be protected. Those who would not join the organization of John Brown, but who would not oppose it, were to be protected; but those who did oppose it were to be treated as the slaveholders themselves.

" John Brown said," continued Realf, summing up the proceedings, "that he believed a successful incursion could be made; that it could be successfully maintained; that the several slave States could be forced (from the position in which they found themselves) to recognize the freedom of those who had been slaves within their respective limits; that immediately such recognitions were made, then the places of all officers elected under this provisional constitution became vacant, and new elections were to be made. Moreover, no salaries were to be paid to the officeholders under this constitution. It was purely out of that which we supposed to be philanthropy—love for the slave. Moreover, it is a mistake to suppose, as Cook in his confession has stated—and I now get away from John Brown's speech—that at the period of that convention the people present took an oath to support that constitution. They did no such thing. Dr. Delany, of whom I have spoken, proposed, immediately the convention was organized, that an oath should be taken by all who were present, not to divulge any of the proceedings that might transpire, whereupon John Brown rose and stated his objections to such an oath. He had himself conscientious scruples against taking an oath, and all he requested was a promise that any person who should thereafter divulge any of the proceedings that might transpire, agreed to forfeit the protection which that organization could extend over him."

George B. Gill gives briefly his recollections, written to me, as follows:

" William Munroe, as president of the convention, signed the commissions issued. The sessions were not fully harmonious. There were some small points of difference, which were satisfactorily adjusted in the end. I only remember a few of the colored men; amongst them was Dr. M. R. Delany, J. J. Jackson, Wm. C. Munroe, of Chatham, G. J. Reynolds, of Sandusky City. The only whites present were members of our party. The most of us at that time did not appreciate the necessity of keeping journals. I am, however, indebted to abbreviated notes for the precision in my memory on many points.

" The main business of the convention was the adoption of a constitution, which Brown had already prepared, and the organization of a provisional government under that instrument. The election of officers occurred on the 10th. John Brown was, of course, elected commander-in-chief, Kagi, secretary of war, Realf, secretary of state, the treasurer was Owen Brown, and the secretary of the treasury was George B. Gill. Members of congress chosen were Alfred M. Ellsworth and Osborne P. Anderson, colored. I am sure that Brown did not communicate the details of his plans to the members of the convention, more than in a very general way. Indeed, I do not now remember that he gave them any more than the impressions which they could gather from the methods of organization. From those who were directly connected with his movements he solicited plans and methods—including localities—of operations in writing. Of course, we had an almost precise knowledge of his methods, but all of us perhaps did not know just the locality selected by him, or, if knowing, did not comprehend the resources and surroundings."

Had John Brown been able to have moved at once from Canada to Harper's Ferry, the result would have been more startling than even when the blow did come. The delay was caused by Hugh Forbes's letter of exposure to Senator Henry Wilson and some other leading politicians. Mr. Wilson bestirred himself actively. He had been in Kansas, some months before, and knew the intense hostility that existed, and heard both approval and adverse criticism of Captain Brown's views of aggression. He also apprehended clearly the spirit of influential persons in Massachusetts. There was no escape from his demands on the members of the Kansas Aid Committee, even though it was practically defunct. Mr. Stearns felt compelled, under pressure, to inform Captain Brown that he must not use the "tools" in his possession except "in the defense of Kansas." He was also notified that an agent would come to Chatham to see him. This policy was changed, and John Brown arranged a visit to Boston. "The news," says Osborne P. Anderson, in "A Voice from Harper's Ferry" (p. 16), "caused an entire change in the programme for a time. The old gentleman went one way, the young men another, but ultimately to meet in Kansas, where the summer was spent." Speculation may be idle, but it is reasonably certain that the movement would, had it then taken place, have been bolder and with more men in it, as there was then unquestioned earnestness in Canada and along the lake borders. Superficial students, failing to put themselves in the other man's place, condemn as insanely inadequate John Brown's force, while his organization has been derided as absurd. The fairest criticism yet published is found in the admirable monograph on "John Brown," by Dr. Von Holst.[1]

---

[1] "John Brown," by Dr. Hermann Von Holst, professor at the University of Frieberg, in Baden (not of State University, Madison, Wis.), author of "The Constitutional History of the United States," edited by Frank Preston Stearns. Boston: Cupples & Reed, 1889. Pp. 109-112.

That able historical writer speaks of the "Provisional Constitution" as "a confused medley of absurd because absolutely inapplicable forms, and of meas- ures well calculated for the end in view,—of sound common-sense and of absurd systematizing; of cool computation and of inconceivable overestimates of the resources at hand; of true, keen-sighted human- ity and of reckless severity." It was insane "to create such a Government and to want to carry on such a war," while declaring there "was no intention of overthrowing existing Governments. But the Chatham men certainly "saw farther than their noses," in seeking to provide for the negro slaves, they designed to consider as "men and citizens." It was entirely rational to form and "create a strong organization" and "sensible to appoint a supreme commander," though absurd to suppose "that a little band, . . . without influence, should secretly put their heads together, . . . to give a constitution to the United States;" this latter being, with all due deference to Von Holst, exactly what they did not intend or mean to attempt doing. The absurdity of copying the offices of the Federal Constitution is very palpable to the critics, but the logic of it is not quite so plain. To one who understands that John Brown was above all other things a plain, believing, Ameri- can citizen, there was the common-sense thought that with the impressible people to be dealt with and controlled, large forms and sounding names or titles were of value, especially if they led to such direct connection with patriotic terms and ideas as might be likely to affect the minds of other sympathetic persons. Dr. Von Holst, strangely enough in the light of the Franco-Prussian war, regards as severe provisions for taking from all who held slaves willingly, and from those who assisted them, all they possessed, whether in free or in slave-holding States."

The recognition of "any kind of neutrality," the enforcement of "fair trial," provisions against "all useless destruction of property," and forbidding the use of ill words or abuse of "defeated enemy," are esteemed by him as proofs of humanity. What Von Holst fails to see is, that these seemingly petty and even contradictory details were all used upon shrewd conceptions of the limitations of the people to be freed, and a clear understanding of the conditions that would exist in such fugitive camps as should be created. Even the learned doctor sees the significance of providing for "bringing together again of separated families, for schools, and for the furtherance of 'personal cleanliness.'"

In all criticism, the one palpable omission is the failure to perceive how far removed John Brown's mental processes were from revolutionary bias or lawless intent. The trouble is, and strangely, too, that the fact seems the hardest one to understand, that John Brown actually believed in the idea of freedom, just as he believed in the existence of God. There was no "if," "but," or "and"; no qualification for him in one or the other matters of faith. Without question, he accepted as a conviction the idea that the real and actual purpose of the Federal Constitution, and of the Union formed under it, was to "establish justice," "maintain peace," and "promote public tranquility." He could not and did not conceive of it as merely a mechanism for courts, a machine for

money-making, a means only for opening new lands
and building more towns; something by which debts
could be collected and order maintained, plus the
constable and the cannon. This was not John Brown's
conception. It is no wonder, therefore, that he was
deemed "insane."

It will be observed in the papers adopted and plans
proposed at Chatham, that certain objects were definitely kept in view:

First. That slavery was in derogation of the
Republic and contrary to just law, its righteous interpretation, and to the purposes of the American Union.

Second. That, therefore, it was slaveholders, not
liberators, who were traitors and rebels. Hence John
Brown's justification of his constitution and his
denial, when on trial, of having raised an insurrection.

Third. His purpose to organize authority among
his adherents. With this idea in view, the simple
organization John Brown projected is seen to be
admirably adapted for the conditions he anticipated
creating—a widely scattered state of resistance among
an untrained but willing set of people, to a system of
oppression,—then resistance being presumed to be set
in conditions half leaning to their own views and
necessities.

Fourth. The military plans can be seen by the
flexible form of organization, seen in " General
Order No. 1," [1] to be adapted to an insurgent warfare. The bands, sections, platoons, and companies
were designed to act separately or together. In
this will also be seen some explanation of why an

---

[1] See Appendix.

attack was made with so small a force. Each one of
that band was fitted for some separate command,
however small. If the best slaves had joined the liberators, and they, as originally designed, had gone
into the Alleghany Mountains, and not been cooped
up in the Harper's Ferry *cul de sac*, how soon would
they have been subdued? It is reasonably assured
that a number of neighborhood negroes did know of
Brown's intention. At least they knew something was
in the air. Osborne P. Anderson declares,[1] that visits
were made to plantations, " and the slaves rejoiced.
At the slaves' quarters there was apparently a general jubilee, and they stepped forward manfully,
without impressing or coaxing. In one case only was
there any hesitation. A dark-complexioned, free-born
man refused to take up arms. . . . Of the slaves
who followed us to the Ferry, some were sent to help
remove stores, and the others, . . . furnished by
me with pikes, acted as a guard to the prisoners, to
prevent their escape." Captain Brown's purpose was
to make of his white men, and of others as soon as
possible, independent commanders of some small
detachments.

The Chatham Convention adjourned on the 10th
of May, 1858. An active and acrid correspondence
had been progressing while the " Liberators " were
in council. A letter of Hugh Forbes, dated May 5th,
showed that he followed somewhat closely each of
the next moves. John Brown on the 14th wrote his
eldest son to watch him close and forward all details.

---

[1] " A Voice from Harper's Ferry," Boston, 1861, p. 60.

Following Mr. Sanborn's narrative [1] it is stated that G. L. Stearns and Theodore Parker were for postponing for a year. Mr. Sanborn was in doubt; T. W. Higginson in favor of immediate action; Dr. Howe, on the 9th of May, held the same view; on the 18th he demanded immediate postponement; Gerrit Smith on the 7th wished to go no further; Higginson, and probably Howe, suggested that " when the thing is well started, who cares what he (Forbes) will say."

Steps were taken on May 20th to change the location of the arms and material, for " reasons that cannot be written." A meeting of the Captain's friends, Messrs. Smith, Stearns, Howe, Parker, Higginson, and Sanborn was held at the Revere House, Boston, on the 24th of May, when, as Mr. Sanborn writes, it was " resolved that Brown ought to go to Kansas at once." On the 31st inst., the Captain reached Boston. He was full of regret and much discouraged by the assumed necessity of postponement. The Revere House meeting decided that no effort should be made till the next winter, when a considerable sum, from two thousand to three thousand dollars, would be raised. Brown, in the meantime, according to the notes made by Col. Higginson [2] at the time, was " to blind Forbes by going to Kansas, and to transfer the property so as to relieve the Massachusetts Kansas Committee of responsibility, and they in future were not to know his plans." To all this, the Captain objected that his force would be demoralized; " it would not cost twenty-five dollars apiece to move his thirteen men

---

[1] " Life and Letters of John Brown," p. 460, *et al.*

[2] " Life and Letters of John Brown," p. 464.

from Ohio;" he would start if he had but three hun
dred dollars.   The knowledge Forbes could give to
his opponents "would be injurious, for he wished"
them "to underrate him, but still . . . the increased terror produced would perhaps counterbal-
ance this, and it would not make much difference.
If he had the means, he would not lose a day."
Higginson's report is undoubtedly a faithful one,
and those who knew him then can realize that his
own views were coincident with Brown's.   Still, the
latter said he did not wish his friends to think him
"reckless," as they "held the purse, he was powerless
without them," that some of them were "not men of
action," and had allowed themselves "to be intimi-
dated" by "Senator Wilson's letter."   The Chatham
episode had cost him nearly all his funds; so he was
obliged to submit.   Looking back, one can perceive
that for what he was aiming at, and others were sym-
pathizing with, John Brown was right and they were
wrong.   The blow may have been severer and longer
fought.   Its direct effect as a blow would have been
more immediate and widely extended; its moral
effect would doubtless have been much less, and no
one can now judge with any reasonableness as to
what might have been the political consequences following a continued and far-spread slave uprising.
The Boston incident closed, however, with Captain
Brown leaving for the West on the 3d of June "in
good spirits," with $500 in gold, and liberty from Mr.
Stearns, their legal owner, to retain all the arms as
his own property.   Doubtless his willingness to return to Kansas, apart from the need of confusing
Forbes, which that movement most effectually did,

was due to a real emergency that had arisen in the much-harried Territory.

The Lecompton Constitution still cast its portentous shadow along the path of the free-state people. Though rejected in different ways,—the people, in order to accomplish this peacefully, having even "stooped to conquer," by voting under the fraudulent Missouri code ;—yet the national pro-slavery administration and party had endeavored in Congress to force the admission of Kansas under it as a slave State. They failed finally in this. A compromise measure, known as the "English bill" was adopted on the 18th of May, by which the Governor of Kansas (James W. Denver) was to appoint a day for voting for or against the wretched instrument. The Governor soon after named August 2d for the polling of this foregone conclusion.[1]

----

[1] The votes cast upon the final effort to force slavery upon Kansas are instructive. They were: Election of delegates to Lecompton Constitutional Convention (apportionment fraudulent), June 15, 1857, 2,200 votes. Election of State officers under the Lecompton Constitution, Dec. 21, 1857; vote for or against slavery 6,143, with 569 against; fraudulent vote proven, 3,006. The free-state men did not vote on the Constitution, but elected a majority of the Legislature; their vote on State ticket and Member of Congress averaged, 6,908; the pro-slavery vote nominally averaged 6,509, a numerical free-state majority of 399. The Constitution itself was not submitted, and Congress was asked to provide for that, or, better still, to reject the whole instrument; and, judging by the unchallenged votes on the question "with" or "without" slavery, the actual pro-slavery vote in 1857 was 3,733. But there were many small frauds perpetrated, and 2,500 would be a liberal number. The Territorial Legislature (free-state) ordered an election on the Lecompton Constitution, and it was held January 4,

But this was not all, nor the chief incident which decided John Brown's friends and John Brown himself, that it was a duty as well as the best policy for him to return forthwith to Kansas. On the 18th of May, along the eastern border of Linn County, southern Kansas, eleven peaceable, unarmed citizens, at work in field, forge, and dwelling, or on the unthreatened highway, were suddenly captured at different points within a small radius by an armed band of twenty-five men, who appeared to rise as it were from the ground, so sudden and unexpected was their presence and action. I speak from personal knowledge of the terrible deed, known as the "Marais des Cygnes" massacre. The twenty-five armed men were a remnant of the Buford gang of two years before. They were led by one Charles Hamilton, who was with most of his associates openly sheltered at Fort Smith, Arkansas, and whose terrible and unqualified act of assassination was boastingly defended all along the southwest slave borders.[1]

1858; vote was as follows: against 10,226; for, with slavery 138, without 25; total 10,389. Congress submitted the instrument over again by act signed May 18, 1858, and under it a vote was had August 2d. It stood for it 1,788; against it 11,300; free-state majority, 9,512.

[1] The names of all the assassins are not at my hands. The Hon. D. W. Wilder (" Annals of Kansas," p. 183) gives from " Kansas in 1858," William P. Tomlinson, the following names : Charles A. Hamilton, Dr. John Hamilton, Algernon Hamilton (three brothers), Luke and William Yealock, Thomas Jackson, James Tate, Lewis Henderson, W. B. Brockett, Harlin, Beech, and Mattock. The names of the other thirteen scoundrels appear to be lost—a fate that is meritted. The Hamiltons were men of education, residing, I believe, at or near West Point, Mo.; all of them

These inoffensive men, eleven in number, were marched to a point near the Snyder forge, an open log building,—sometimes called by the frightened correspondents and politicians of those days, "Snyder's Fort,"—there made to stand in line, while a volley was fired into them, killing five outright, and wounding five others very severely. It was a lovely afternoon, and the scene of murder is the centre of a landscape remarkable for its placid features and rural beauty. The deed startled the country; the North, slow of anger, was roused to passionate heat; the free-state people, who were divided into savage factions, melted and fused together again under a common horror and a single purpose. Robert B. Mitchell, a leading free-state conservative, rode with James Montgomery, the fighting radical of southern Kansas, in the endeavor to overtake the Hamilton gang. At Fort Scott, just before this deed, Sheriff Samuel J. Walker, of Douglass county, acting as deputy United States marshal, had placed Montgomery under ar-

---

were, I believe, killed as Confederate guerillas in the Civil War, and one was slain in combat in the Price campaign of 1864, at or near the point of the murder in 1858—the Chateau Trading Post. The eleven free-state men, all quiet citizens, were: William Robertson, William Colpetzer. Patrick Ross, Thomas Stillwell, John F. Campbell—killed at the first fire;—Asa and William Hairgrove, Charles Snyder, Amos Hall, and Charles F. Reed, a Methodist circuit rider and preacher. These were all severely wounded by the same fire. Amos Hall fell unhurt when the other volley was fired, and, feigning death, escaped unhurt, to be shot to death, as stated in the "Annals of Kansas," after in some later border trouble. The two Hairgroves were natives of Georgia. Mr. Snyder was a border-state man; none of the assailed party were identified with the radical wing of the free-state men.

rest, for acts previously done in defense of his neighbors' and his own rights. At the same time leaders of
the ruffian element were also arrested by this same cool
and fearless officer. Montgomery was released on his
parole; the United States Court discharged the pro-
slavery criminals. No reward was offered by any
authority for the capture of the Hamilton murderers.
The Governor of Missouri did not feel his jurisdiction
outraged, and the President offered no reward. The
Governor of Kansas contented himself with placating
the angered citizens, not in pursuing the assassins.
When, however, seven months later, John Brown rescued eleven slaves from their Missouri masters, and
Aaron D. Stevens slew one of these while he was in
the act of leveling a revolver on him, the Governor
of Missouri hastened to put a price on John Brown;
President Buchanan offered a reward for his capture;
United States marshals and posses were sent after
him, while the army of the United States was required
to join in the pursuit by Governor Medary, of Kansas.
In the one case, the lives of non-slave-holding "poor
whites" alone were sacrificed to the malignant passions of the "chivalry," while in the other the sacred
rights of property in human flesh and blood was
sternly assailed by armed "Abolitionists." The
Hamilton gang coolly and without haste made their
way further south. I learned of their movements day
after day, and soon after saw the leading assassin
strutting as a hero in the streets of Fort Smith,
Arkansas. One of the most stirring of John G. Whittier's lyrics is that of "Le Marais du Cygne," ("The
Swamp of the Swan") a picturesque name given to
the portion of the Osage River valley by the early

French voyageurs, who served at Chotteau's Trading Post, close by which the terrible deed occurred. The closing stanzas of Whittier's poem have that prophetic tone, which in the supreme moments of human conflict, always make the true poet a seer—proclaiming what will be. How prescient are the words:

> " Not in vain on the dial
>   The shade moves along
> To point the great contrasts
>   Of right and of wrong;
> Free homes and free altars,
>   And fields of ripe food;
> The reeds of the swan's march
>   Whose bloom is of blood.

> " On the lintels of Kansas
>   That blood shall not dry;
> Henceforth the bad angel
>   Shall harmless go by;
> Henceforth to the sunset
>   Unchecked on her way,
> Shall liberty follow
>   The march of the day."

The John Brown men were scattered after the adjournment of the Chatham Convention, a little discouraged, too, as Steward Taylor wrote on the 13th of May to Dr. H. C. Gill at Tabor, Iowa, by the aspect of what was "the most critical point" in their endeavors. Owen Brown went to visit his brother Jason at Akron, Ohio. Cook left Cleveland for the neighborhood of Harper's Ferry. Realf left for New York, and from there went to England, not to be heard of or from again until arrested in Texas, dur-

ing the winter of 1859–60. Gill, who tells the story
elsewhere in a simple narrative full also of unconscious art, went to work in a Shaker settlement, probably Lebanon, Ohio, where Tidd was already employed. Steward Taylor went to Illinois where he
had acquaintances. Kagi and Stevens waited Brown's
return at Cleveland. Parsons and Moffett stayed a
short time in northern Ohio, and then departed for
Iowa. Leeman got some work to do in Ashtabula
County. John Brown left Boston, as already stated,
on the 3d of June, proceeding to Vermont, where he
was joined by his son John, and both went to the
North Elba homestead for a very short visit. Kagi,
Stevens, Leeman, Gill, Parsons, Moffett, and Owen
were gathered up and the party pushed through to
Kansas, arriving at Lawrence on the 25th of June.
On that day and the following one, Captain Brown
was the guest of James Redpath and myself, at the
Whitney Hotel. How he blazed his road from
southern Kansas and Missouri through Canada back
to Harper's Ferry, must, with the four months of the
life at Kennedy Farm, be told in bold outline in the
next succeeding pages.

CHAPTER VIII.

RESCUE OF MISSOURI SLAVES.

Out of the " jaws of death "— John Brown as he looked in Kansas in 1856 and 1858—Affairs along the southwest border of Missouri — Intrigues and dissensions in both parties — Captain James Montgomery— John Brown and " Some Shadows Before " — Snyder's Fort — Harrying each other — Pro-Slavery kidnappers and free-state raiders — Fort Scott affairs — Firing on troops — John Brown's first band of freed people — From Missouri to Kansas.

JOHN BROWN in 1858 presented a somewhat different aspect to that which first impressed me in 1856. Yet the figure was the same. The picturesque portrait of him found in this volume, gives a full conception of the fighting farmer that he was. The one with the beard recalls the deeper *ensemble* left on memory, of his appearance in the summer and fall of 1858.

On the Northern emigrants' march of 1856 to the aid of their fellows at Lawrence, Topeka, and other Kansas free-state settlements, it fell to my lot to be one of a small company doing rear guard duty near the Nebraska line. But three days before we had

led the general advance across the northern line of
Kansas from Nebraska, appeals had been made that

JOHN BROWN AT THE AGE OF 58.

no arms were to
be openly carried.
Our little com-
pany, under Martin
Stowell and my-
self, rebelled, claim-
ing the right as
we phrased it, to
carry our weapons
without conceal-
ment, and we did
it. In that advance
party were two of
the men afterwards
slain in the Har-
per's Ferry fight.
One was William
Henry[1] Leeman, a
boy of eighteen
years, from Maine,
who had been
working as a shoe-
operator in Massa-
chusetts, and joined
in June, 1856, at
Worcester, Dr. Cut-
ter's party of Mas-

sachusetts men.   He turned back with them at Lex-

[1] His middle name, as designated by his parents, was "Pillsbury,"
his mother's maiden name.   He afterward adopted "Henry" and
they acquiesced.

ington, Mo., and then came up the Mississippi River from St. Louis to Davenport, Iowa, where he entered our party, which had determined to march across Iowa and southern Nebraska into Kansas, where he found his way to John Brown and Osawatomie. The other one was William Thompson, of North Elba, New York. Henry, his elder brother, the husband of Ruth Brown, was with John Brown in Kansas and had been severely wounded at the Black Jack fight, June the second. William left the Adirondacks immediately on receiving the news and joined our party at Buffalo, as we were taking the *Plymouth Rock* steamer for Detroit on our westward way. The camp where my first meeting with John Brown occurred was also named Plymouth.

"Have you a man in your camp, named William Thompson? You are from Massachusetts, young man, I believe, and Mr. Thompson joined you at Buffalo."

These words were addressed to me by an elderly man, riding on a worn-looking, gaunt gray horse. It was on a late July day and in its hottest hours. I had been idly watching a wagon and one horse, toiling slowly northward across the prairie, along the emigrant trail that had been marked out by free-state men under command of "Sam" Walker and Aaron D. Stevens, who was then known as "Colonel Whipple." Three days before, when we crossed the Kansas line, Sharpe's rifles on shoulders and Colt's revolvers at hips, a small party of mounted men was drawn up on the line to welcome us. "Colonel Whipple," who was in command as we proudly marched by—for, well I remember, we all thought the fate of the Nation was on our shoulders—gave the order in a ringing voice :

" Present arms! "

It was done, and we cheered. We then heard, " What are you doing here, men ? " in the same, clear voice.

" Holding town-meeting," was the swift reply from his own following.

" Where's your ballot-box ? " was the next question, and " Here " was the loud response, as each man brought his hand down on his Sharpe's rifle, which rang with the blow. This was a formula gotten-up for identification and encouragement.

John Brown, whose name the young and ardent had begun to conjure with and swear by, had been described to me. So, as I heard the question, I looked up and met the full, strong gaze of a pair of luminous, questioning eyes. Somehow, I instinctively knew this was John Brown, and with that name I replied, saying that Thompson was in our company. It was a long, rugged-featured face I saw. A tall, sinewy figure, too,—he had dismounted—five feet eleven, I estimated; with square shoulders, narrow flank, sinewy and deep-chested. A frame, full of nervous power, but not impressing one especially with muscular vigor. The impression left by the pose and the figure was that of reserve, endurance, and quiet strength. The questioning voice-tones were mellow, magnetic, and grave. On the weather-worn face was a stubby, short, gray beard, evidently of recent growth. John Brown never wore a beard, as a usual habit, till the attacks of Hugh Forbes seemed to make necessary a change in his usual appearance.

The lower portion of the jaws was sharp rather than broad, ending in a square, firm, but not heavy chin. The mouth was close set and wide, deep lined, firmly held. It looked like that of a man who was swift to act. The eyes first struck me, because they had in them an expression I had already begun to associate with all the free-state men I met; that was one of steadfast alertness, keen, sharp observation,—the look of the uncowed man in constant danger and always on the watch, in some respects the " hunted " look. It was the look seen in later days of war, in the eyes of men employed as scouts or secret service. I am not saying these things from memory alone, for an old manuscript journal of the period has been drawn upon and I am transcribing in the main the impressions then more effusively written. I had an excellent opportunity for making a rapid mental sketch. The face was long, as I have said; the cheek bones prominent—privation and fatigue doubtless made this more apparent. John Brown's roman nose was a very distinctive feature. Its shape was fine, the bridge well marked, while the lines were long, wide at the bridge, broad, and rather thin at the nostrils. It has been stated by a competent physiologist that this organ is a distinctive trait of the Brown family and was perceptible in the revolutionary ancestor, as it is slightly less accented in John Brown, Jr.'s, features. Our Captain's "roman" was masterful, not domineering or inquisitive in expression. The root-space was broad, and the gray, bushy eyebrows were well defined and moderately arched. The eyes, not large, were deep set, blue-gray in color, darkening almost to blackness at times. The impression was

not that of a flashing glance; it was not one that
lighted-up suddenly and quickly; it was a steady
luminous look, which inquired, but did not attack
or disturb.   They left on me always an impression of deep kindliness, as well as penetration.
Yet I recall it as one impersonal and withdrawn
in character.   They took in at once, not only the
person addressed, but all the surroundings.   The
head also was both long and broad, and carried well
forward on a long sinewy neck.   The forehead seemed
to be a low one at first glance, but it could soon be
noted that this impression was due to the short, gray
hair that grew down somewhat the front of a broad,
well-developed cerebrum.   The perceptions were finely
marked, and the space from the ears forward and
upward was quite deep, even remarkably so.   This
figure—unarmed, poorly clad, with coarse linen
trousers tucked into high, heavy cowhide boots, with
heavy spurs on their heels, a cotton shirt open at the
throat, a long torn linen duster, and a bewrayed chip
straw hat he held in his hand as he waited for
Thompson to reach us, made up the outward garb
and appearance of John Brown when I first met him.
In ten minutes his mounted figure disappeared over
the north horizon.   With him went William Thompson;—blond, sturdy, yellow-bearded, bold, generous;
a loud-voiced, fun-making young fellow of but twenty-
two—and I never saw him again.   He was done to
death in the Shenandoah River, while clinging, a
wounded man, to a pier of the Harper's Ferry railroad bridge, from which he had been thrown, after
being taken prisoner and then dragged out of
Foulke's Hotel for wanton butchery.   John Brown

was met a second and third time that year near
Osawatomie and at Lawrence. At the latter place
I heard and saw him in action, and his voice, though
a little sterner, seemed to me no louder or harsher in
tone than when I first heard his question in northern
Kansas. At Lawrence, too, I first remarked his distinctive walk. His feet were set firmly to the ground;
the whole form moved steadily onward, never sway-
ing, but walking as if on a visible line, prearranged
for the occasion. Every one gave way; a crowd
parted like the waters when a strongly-driven boat
presses through. Yet the movement never seemed
an assertive one, never left an impression of mere
push or aggressiveness. The next time we met
was on the 25th of June, 1858, at a hotel in Lawrence. In those two years he had aged more than
Time required. He was past fifty-six at the first
meeting, and had just passed his fifty-eighth birthday,[1]
when he was seated between James Redpath and
myself at that dinner-table. I can hardly define the
difference in impression that remains in memory,
unless by terms which may seem overstrained. But
I venture to say that, in 1858, John Brown looked to
me as a "Prophet" might have done; in 1856, he
certainly embodied the "Fighter." Under no circumstances could he ever have appeared common-
place. The heavy, gray beard, almost snow-white,
lent a degree of dignity as well as a grave pictur-
esqueness to his face and figure. This was enhanced
by a slower movement, manners of simple distinction,
and a grave, reticent dignity of speech, which tran-

[1] John Brown was born May 9, 1801.

scended the terseness of the fighting summer days. This impression was greatly deepened at the meeting had with him at Osawatomie, in the August following, when by his direction Kagi gave me a full insight into the whole enterprise, place, and purpose.[1]

Affairs in southern Kansas, apart from the Hamilton massacre atrocity, were in a state of seething turbulence, and had been so, more or less pronounced, ever since the summer of 1856. In large degree southeast Kansas, below the Pottawatomie basin, had not been very favorably affected by the free-state triumphs of 1856. Fort Scott, formerly an army post, had been disposed of to pro-slavery speculators for a small sum. The buildings alone substantial stone and frame post and headquarters, were worth the sum given, even as old material, while the reservation land was simply given away. A Federal land-office was established, and Clark, the murderer of Barber, a bold and violent Missourian, was the most active pro-slavery leader. Blake Little was made receiver. Later, a superannuated Democratic politician of Michigan, was made land register in defer-

---

[1] See Appendix for paper entitled "Some Shadows Before." "Five years before, when they first went to Kansas, the father and sons had a plan of going to Louisiana, trying this same project, and then retreating into Texas with the liberated slaves. Nurtured on it so long, for years sacrificing to it all the other objects of life, the thought of its failure never crossed their mind; and it is an extraordinary fact that when the disastrous news first came to North Elba, the family utterly refused to believe it, and were saved from suffering by that incredulity till the arrival of the next weekly mail." Account of a visit to the John Brown household, November, 1859, by Thomas Wentworth Higginson.

ence probably to the slightly growing strength of a
presumed sentiment among members of that party
who were originally from free States. Since Bourbon,
Anderson, Allen, McGee, and Coffee counties were
less affected than others by the violent outbreaks of
1856, as the border ruffians had things their own
way, a considerable number of so-called conservative free-state settlers—men chiefly from border
slave or western States—had taken " claims " in the
Osage, Marmaton, Neosho, and other small valleys
of the counties named. So also did the pro-slavery
men from Missouri and Arkansas. Many of Buford's
men filed upon preëmption claims in that district, and
generally, too, upon those from which other men had
been driven. There were also Indian trust lands
ordered to be sold by the ruling Buchanan administration, which, being located on the western border
of Missouri, afforded occasion for the combining and
gathering of some of the worst elements left over
from the savager days of the free-state struggle.
Later, too, a few free colored people from the Indian
Territory, southwest Missouri, and Arkansas, began
to quietly settle in this section. Among them were
farmers of some means; all were quiet and inoffensive. The chief cause of their appearance was that
growing ill-will shown in neighborhood feeling and
State law, by which they were unfavorably affected.
The history of the few years immediately preceding
the slaveholder's rebellion is deeply marked with the
harsh treatment of this unfortunate class. The disbandment of border-ruffian gangs, forced by the
political necessities of the party in power, gave zest
to land-jobs, claim-jumping, and later to negro-kid-

napping as a business, wherever the more radical
free-state feeling was not strong enough to be a persistent menace to such action.   From this same class
came at a later day (and quite as naturally as they
had become manstealers from 1857 to 1860), most of
the leaders of the guerilla bands who infested western and central Missouri, and harried the Kansas
border during the Civil War, writing in fire and blood
a record of atrocity so fearful that for the sake of a
common nationality it is better that no full record
exists nor can be made.

Resistance came.   Fort Scott, as shown, became
the seat of pro-slavery hostility, just in proportion as
the power for evil diminished in other localities.   The
free-state settlers, who had been driven or kept out
of southern Kansas from the spring of 1856 to that
of 1857, begun to return and to settle in that section.
At once violence became rampant.   The free-state
land claimants found themselves insulted and outraged by the public officials, arrested on false charges,
and in personal danger whenever they went to Fort
Scott.   Appeals were made in August and September,
1857, to free-state friends at Lawrence and elsewhere,
and volunteers soon appeared.   A squatter's tribunal
was organized.   It is not essential to this narrative to
give details.   The fact that the more violent of the
Missouri and Buford politicians and leaders made
their headquarters at Fort Scott and Paris, while
free-state black law and "conservative" Democratic
politicians were numerous at the county seats of
other counties.   Intensified quarrels and fighting
soon ensued.   It is not necessary to either defend or
narrate the history of free-state resistance.   It is

necessary to bear in mind, however, that the worst residuum of the pro-slavery force were in power. Federal interference was called for, and the disturbances arose from their usurpation of land claims. The more daring free-state men rallied around Captain James Montgomery, who, in the fall of 1857, occupied the place which had fallen the year before on John Brown. His arrest was ordered, attacks were made on his cabin, and resisted. Warrants were issued, and finally troops were sent to execute the same. An attempt was made by Blake Little, in December, 1857, to arrest and break up the squatter's court. A fight ensued, but no one was killed and the marshal retired without any prisoners. Montgomery opposed voting for State officers under the Lecompton Constitution, which was voted upon " for " and " against " under Territorial enactment, passed by the free-state majority, who, under the advice of Senator Henry Wilson and other friends, had " stooped to conquer," and thereby captured the Territorial legislative power. The Radicals did not vote as a rule. Montgomery is charged with having forcibly broken up the voting at his precinct.

Southern Kansas affairs grew warmer as 1858 lengthened. In April following, Captain Anderson, with his squadron, followed Montgomery and his men up the Marmaton and Little Sugar valleys for the purpose of arresting them. Montgomery, occupying a strong defensible position, turned and fired upon the pursuers, killing one soldier, wounding another, and the captain, too. This is the first and only time that the free-state men actually resisted United States troops. This, in all probability, would

14

not have been done, but for the notorious fact that
Anderson and his troopers [1] were practically a gang of
pro-slavery partisans, not acting as a lawful posse.
Indeed, the proceedings of that period at Fort Scott
and vicinity afford reasonable grounds for the belief
that the leading men in the pro-southern councils,
who were at heart disunionists *per se*, were endeavoring by violent persecutions, under the pretense of
law, to embroil free-state people in a conflict with
United States authority.[2] A short time before Captain Montgomery's cabin was surrounded and
attacked with firearms, after the inmates were supposed to have retired (I was a guest therein at the
time), a supposition which cost the life of one of the
assailants, at least. About the same time, a pro-
slavery occupant of a Marmaton claim, first settled
on by a free-state man (the validity of whose entry
was finally favorably decided by the General Land
Office on appeal) who had called in a force from Fort
Scott to drive away the free-state claimant, on being
visited by a posse from the squatter court, fired at
once on those who knocked and was himself killed
by a rifle shot from Montgomery. These facts are
only recalled to illustrate the existing conditions and
to show how the " Swamp of the Swan " assassinations were led up to by acts of rapine, violence, and
resistance.   In such scenes as these, Barclay Coppoc,
Jeremiah G. Anderson, and Albert Hazlett, begun to

---

[1] A number of Buford's men enlisted as dragoons.

[2] Jeremiah G. Anderson and Albert Hazlett, both emigrants of
the winter of 1856–57, were active members of Captain Montgomery's company. I was myself a witness of many of these
scenes.

traverse the roads which led them to Harper's Ferry and, for two of them, to death in Virginia.

The promotion of James W. Denver from Secretary to the position of Governor, was first followed by renewed efforts to arrest Captain Montgomery, and whether or not that was any direct emboldenment of the infuriated ruffians, the failure to arrest was followed in three days by the killing and wounding at the trading-post, Linn County, of the eleven victims of the Hamilton fury and bloodthirstiness. Immediately following, some arrests were made in connection with the trading-post crime, and for the two preceding assassinations of Denton and Hedrick, near Fort Scott. The arrested men were immediately released at Fort Scott, and Montgomery made, June 6th, a raid on the place. The assassins got away, and nothing more fatal occurred than an exchange of shots. The partisan support by the proslavery court seems to have alarmed the Territorial executive. Governor Denver moved on Bourbon County.[1]

Returning to John Brown's movements, my journal

---

[1] Governor Denver left Lawrence June 9th with Charles Robinson, Judge John Wright, A. D. Richardson (*Boston Journal*), Lewis M. Tappan, Edmund Babb (*Cincinnati Gazette*), and others, for Fort Scott. Montgomery joined the party at Moneka. The Governor's terms of peace are thus reported :

1. The withdrawal of United States troops from Fort Scott. 2. The election of new county officers in Bourbon County. 3. The stationing of troops along the Missouri frontier to protect the settlers of the Territory from invasion. 4. The suspension of the execution of all old writs until their legitimacy is authenticated before the proper tribunal. 5. The abandonment of the field by

states that he remained in Lawrence from his arrival
on the 25th of June to the morning of the 27th, when,
with Kagi, the only one of his party who then accompanied him, he left for Osawatomie.   By invitation I
afterwards visited him at the house of his brother-in-
law, the Rev. Mr. Adair.[1] A letter to " F. B. Sanborn,
and Friends at Boston and Worcester," bearing dates
July 20th, the 23d, and the 6th of August, gives an
account of his movements.   I reproduce in part
from Mr. Sanborn's volume the essential details. The
address is " Missouri Line (on Kansas Side)," and it
states that " I am here with about ten of my men,
located on the same quarter section where the terrible
murders of the 19th May were committed."   The ten
men were his son Owen, John Henry Kagi, Aaron
Dwight Stevens, Charles Plummer Tidd, William
Henry Leeman, George B. Gill, of the original Kan-
sas-Springdale, Iowa, party, with four others, were
men who escaped with their lives from Hamilton's
murderous arms.   These were the two Hairgroves,
the blacksmith, Snyder, and John Mickel or Michael.
The Captain assumed the name of " Shubel Morgan,"

Montgomery and his men, and all other parties of armed men,
whether free-state or pro-slavery.

Montgomery immediately accepted these terms.   At Fort
Scott, Governor Denver and Judge Wright made speeches. The
pro-slavery men were dissatisfied with the first, and threatened
violence over the latter. The Governor left on June 16th; Montgomery then disbanded; the United States troops left Fort Scott,
and Captain Weaver, United States Army, was stationed on the
Missouri border in Linn County.—" Annals of Kansas," D. H.
Wilder. (The truce was not of long duration, however.)

[1] See Appendix for my paper, "Some Shadows Before."

and fourteen persons signed the roll of his new company.[1] Captain Brown vividly described the prevailing feeling of terror, when he said: " Deserted farms and dwellings lie in all directions for some miles along the line, and the remaining inhabitants watch every one moving about with anxious jealousy and vigilance." "Any little affair," continued the Captain, "may open the quarrel afresh. . . . I have concealed the fact of my presence pretty much, lest it should tend to increase excitement; but it is getting leaked out, and will soon be known to all. As I am not here to *seek* or *secure revenge*, I do not mean to be the first to reopen the quarrel. How soon it may be raised against me, I cannot say, nor am I over-anxious." He then refers to misrepresentations in the New York *Tribune*, under date from Westport, Missouri, as to the existence of an alleged fort, called " Snyder's." It was said, in the Westport letter, that it was " a house built in the gorge of two mounds, and flanked by rock walls, a fit place for robbers and murderers." This was the place the Captain was occupying, and he thus described it: "At a spring in a rocky ravine stands a *very small* open blacksmith's shop, made of thin slabs from a saw-mill. This is the only building that has ever been known to stand there, yet it is called a ' fortification.' It is to-day just as it was the 19th of May,—a little pent-up shop, containing Snyder's tools (what have not been carried off), all covered with rust,—and had never been

---

[1] See Appendix for Enrollment and Rules of the "Shubel Morgan" Company. These rules should be carefully read, as expressing the spirit of all John Brown's movements.

thought of as a 'fortification' before the poor man attempted to use it in his own and his brother's and his son's defense. I give this as an illustration of the truthfulness of that whole account. It should be left to stand while it may last, and should be known hereafter as *Fort Snyder*."

The Captain's letter, under date of July 23d, describes a renewal of excitement, threatening an attack on a free-state Missourian, named Bishop. The letter says: "At present, along this part of the line, the free-state men may be said in some sense to 'possess the field,' but we deem it wise to 'be on the alert.' Whether Missouri people are more excited through fear than otherwise I am not yet prepared to judge. The blacksmith (Snyder) has got his family back; also some others have returned, and a few new settlers are coming in."

In the closing paragraph, under date of August 6th, John Brown describes his exposures and privations, being down with the ague, having " lain every night without shelter, suffering from cold rains and heavy dews, together with the oppressive heat of the days." The armed posse stationed on the line by Gov. Denver, moved to and encamped on the quarter section adjoining Snyder's, which the Captain was occupying. He wrote : "Several of them immediately sought opportunity to tender their service to me *secretly*. I, however, advised them to remain where they were. Soon after I came on the line, my right name was reported, but the majority did not credit the report."

Shortly after this last date he returned to Mr. Adair's, where I found him early in September, still quite feeble from the effects of congestive chills.

During this time the Lecompton Constitution election, as already reported, came off, creating fresh disorder and bringing warrants with posses from Fort
Scott to arrest Montgomery and his men. It must be
borne in mind that if there were dissensions as to the
policy of the free-state people, there were also very
ragged-edged ones within the pro-slavery camp.
From the first, as already pointed out, there was a
distinct and keen-witted faction determined to force
their issue to the verge of destructive fight. They
were playing "to fire the Southern heart" with Kansas free-state outrages, just as twelve months or so
later, Governor Wise, of Virginia, was doing with the
Harper's Ferry prisoners and material in his hands.
The object was disunion, pure and simple. And at
this time, the movement centered in Fort Scott. The
leaders still held Federal offices, and were able to so
harry the free-state farmers as to force them to
greater lengths. Then there were the loose and irre-
sponsible on both sides. Those of the Missouri border turned kidnappers, like William C. Quantrill
(afterwards known as guerilla and wholesale assassin),
and murderers like the Hamiltons; while on the free-
state side were men ready to risk their own lives and
the peace of the community, to free a negro and convey a pro-slavery horse or mule to their own use or
profit. John Brown and James Montgomery are not
to be so recorded, though at times men served with
them both who were adepts at such actions. The
essential difference, however, was that the one would
help a slave to escape, even if they would not steal a
horse, while the other type would rather murder a
free-state man than kidnap a negro, even into bond-

age, and the latter was their usual avocation.   Politically, then, a considerable element in the pro-slavery
party within Kansas were willing to surrender the
idea of a slave State for the maintenance of Democratic power.   Mr. Buchanan was advised by these
shrewder men, the Stringfellows, Eastin, Henderson
& Co., to let the extreme Southern wing go, and build
up a Northern or black-law Democratic party.   He
would not do it, and after him came the deluge!   It
is not possible, then, to understand the situation in the
fall of 1858, without keeping these issues in view.
John Brown understood and sought to use them.   To
a certain extent he did, acting only so far as it could
aid the spread of growing hostility to the slave-power.
Members of his party were more active than himself.
Stevens was several times threatened with attack at
Snyder's. He refused to do anything but fight, and, by
his bold attitude with a few men, caused the retreat of
a larger body.   Kagi was with Montgomery a good
deal of the time.   In the beginning of November, the
latter's cabin was fired into.   Kagi was a guest at the
time and assisted in its successful defense.   Tidd
was also on hand.   Gill was mainly with the Captain.
Stevens held "Snyder's Fort."   Jeremiah G. Anderson and Albert Hazlett were usually under Montgomery's command.   The former was several times
in arrest.   Leeman remained with Stevens.   The
Captain was chiefly at Osawatomie or Moneka, visiting with the Wattles at the latter place.   The Fort
Scott pro-slavery policy culminated on the 25th of
November in the arrest and chaining of a farmer
named B. M. Rice, under charge of murder, but
whose real offense was giving, as alleged, information

to Capt. James Montgomery. A meeting was called
on the 30th by the free-state people of Bourbon
County, Montgomery attending.   The sheriff started
to arrest " Old Brown " on the same day.   He was
living on the Snyder place with four of his men.   The
Captain had left for Osawatomie unaware of this proposed call.   One hundred men were in the sheriff's
posse, and on their arrival at " Snyder's," a demand
for surrender was made.   Stevens declared he would
fight all of them, and prepared with three others to
resist Sheriff McDaniel, who retired in good order.
The next eighteen days were filled with excitement,
ending on the 16th of December, with Montgomery's
capture of Fort Scott, rescue of Ben Rice, and the
killing of Blake Little, the pro-southern leader.
Kagi, Hazlett, Tidd, J. G. Anderson, of the Harper's
Ferry party, were certainly active in this affair.

For some days there was a lull, and then came a
startling event, which I shall leave one of the principal actors therein, George B. Gill, to describe.   In
letters to me, recently revised, he says:

"We occupied a log building on a claim owned by Montgomery's mother-in-law on the Little Sugar creek, and but a
short distance from his own dwelling.   Our family consisted of
Brown, Kagi, Tidd, and Stevens—Montgomery was with us
occasionally at night.   We threw up some earth as a barricade on the outside, and made a few concealed loopholes
between the logs in the house and called it a fort.   On the
13th of November Montgomery, with his friends, our little
company included, visited Paris, the county seat of Linn, in
search of a supposed indictment said to have been found by
the Grand Jury.   Brown accompanied us to the outskirts of
the town, saying that he would hold himself in readiness if
needed.   Later, Captain Brown, accompanied by myself, visited

Osawatomie. We returned December 1st. During our absence a demonstration was made against our fort by Mound City parties. This demonstration emanated from a public meeting held for the avowed purpose of creating sentiment against Montgomery. On the 16th of December Montgomery invaded Fort Scott and released Ben Rice, in which mêlée a deputy United States marshal, J. Blake Little, was killed. Brown's party participated, but Brown himself remained at the Little Sugar creek rendezvous.

"Returning from Fort Scott, we stopped at a settlement on the Little Osage. With the exception of Jerry Anderson, I only remember the names of two of the residents of that locality. One was Captain Bain, the other was a brother of Jerry Anderson. On the Sunday following the expedition to Fort Scott, as I was scouting down the line, I ran across a colored man, whose ostensible purpose was the selling of brooms. He soon solved the problem as to the propriety of making a confidant of me, and I found that his name was Jim Daniels; that his wife, self, and babies belonged to an estate, and were to be sold at an administrator's sale in the immediate future. His present business was not the selling of brooms particularly, but to find help to get himself, family, and a few friends in the vicinity away from these threatened conditions. Daniels was a fine-looking mulatto. I immediately hunted up Brown, and it was soon arranged to go the following night and give what assistance we could. I am sure that Brown, in his mind, was just then waiting for something to turn up; or, in his way of thinking, was expecting or hoping that God would provide him a basis of action. When this came, he hailed it as heaven-sent. Arrangements were made for Brown and his party to visit Hicklan's (the name of Daniels's owner) and others on the north side of the Little Osage, Missouri, while Stevens was to take a small party and bring in one or more applicants from the south side. Brown's party numbered about a dozen. Doctor, afterwards Colonel, Jenisson, "Pickles," a reckless young fellow of the section, and a couple of Dr. Ayres's sons, being among the number. J. G. Anderson (killed at Harper's Ferry) was also with Brown. Stevens was accompanied by Tidd, Hazlett, and others, to the number of eight. On the night of the 20th of December we wended our way slowly down into Missouri, first stopping at Hicklan's, with whom Daniels and family were staying. Hicklan, I think, had an interest in the estate, his wife being one of the heirs, but they were living on the farm at this time simply as tenants. It required a nice discrimination to tell his individual property from that belonging to the estate. All of the personal property belonging to the estate that he could find, Brown intended to take as being owned by the slaves, having surely been bought with their labor. In his view, they were entitled to all the proceeds of their labor. He would have taken the real estate as well if he had the facilities for moving it across the country to Canada. He reasoned that they, the slaves, were the creators of the whole, and were entitled to it, not only as their own, but from necessity, for they must have a conveyance and also something to dispose of in order to raise funds to defray the expenses of the long overland trip. Captain Brown had no means of his own to do this for them.

" Daniels was intrusted with the arrangements on the outside, as he was apparently the soul of honor, and a good friend of Hicklan, who, I believe, was a very fair man and, perhaps, a very good one. Daniels was very careful that nothing belonging to Hicklan should be taken or interfered with. It was also Brown's intention that nothing, if possible, should be touched that did not in his estimation belong to the slaves.

" I was intrusted with this matter in the house, and I then declared that Hicklan's effects should not be touched. I soon discovered that watches and other articles were being taken by unscrupulous members of our party. Brown caused an immediate disgorgement. Hicklan himself was consulted as to what property belonged to him and what belonged to the estate; his word being invariably relied upon. If he had any property taken it was by some sneak thief in defiance of the most explicit orders and our utmost care. The party was hastily gathered and the selections were not perfect.

"From the Lawrence estate were taken Daniels's wife, with their two children and two other chattels; also a yoke of cattle, two horses, a large old Conestago wagon, beds and bedding, with clothes and personal effects.

"From Hicklan's we went direct to LaRue's, whose house was surrounded. We found them in bed and asleep. The old man being awakened with the usual ' Hallo ' ; which, when replied to by ' What's wanted,' was answered by the old Captain stating the business thus tersely : ' We have come after your negroes and their property ; will you surrender or fight ? '

"I think that they had been rather looking for such a company and were prepared to receive us, as wc found in a few minutes that there were several men inside with plenty of arms. The immediate reply was ' We'll fight.' ' All right,' said Captain Brown, ' we'll smoke you out, then.'

"This would have been attempted forthwith, as there was plenty of fire in the negro quarters, had they not very quickly reconsidered their decision and surrendered. From this place was taken five more negroes, some clothing, bedding, and other personal effects, another yoke of cattle, wagon and several horses. The horses taken from LaRue's were probably never seen by Brown. He heard of them afterwards, no doubt, but that would be about all. Jenisson undoubtedly rode one of them away. Two or three of the white men were carried with us several miles into Kansas and then released, with the suggestion from Brown that ' You can follow us just as soon as you like.' One of them remarked in reply, ' I'll follow home ; that is just about what I'll do.' It was a very cold night, but to our contrabands the conditions produced a genial warmth not indorsed by the thermometer. One of the women pitied ' poor marsa ! he's in a bad fix ; hogs not killed, corn not shucked, and niggers all gone.' One, who was driving the oxen, inquired the distance to Canada. He was told that it was only about fifteen hundred miles. ' Oh, golly ; we 'uns never get dar before spring ! ' he exclaimed as he brought the whip down on the oxen, shouting ' Git up dar, buck ; bung along ! ' Daniels himself was very thoughtful, realizing to the fullest extent the dangers of the situation. The others seemed to have implicit confidence in their protectors.

" On meeting the other party in the morning we learned that they had succeeded in getting the contraband ' Jane ' that they had gone after, and that Stevens, much to Brown's sorrow, had killed Mr. Cruise, the so called owner of Jane. The incident was told to me by several of the party immediately after. They gained access to Cruise's house by representing themselves to be pro-slavery friends. After gaining entrance Stevens informed them of their business, and demanded his surrender, when he attempted to draw a revolver, which was conveniently near. One of his children had been playing with a ribbon or string and had created an obstruction, or an entanglement, which gave Stevens an advantage and he saved himself by killing Cruise at the first shot. I had no personal knowledge of Cruise, but he was represented as one of the most active enemies of the free-state cause, and as having accumulated much property through raids into Kansas. As reported, he was absolutely notorious. His wife was seemingly not much surprised, for she said that she had often told him that if he didn't behave himself he would get killed sooner or later. The negroes were taken first to Augustus Wattles's, from there to Mendenhall's and Adair's, close to Osawatomie, but were finally landed in some cabins, close to Garnett, under the care of Doctor (afterwards Major-General) James G. Blount. We then returned to Captain Bain's, and, in anticipation of being hunted by the Missourians, Captain Brown commenced a system of earthworks in a naturally inaccessible position on the Little Osage, close to Bain's house. The position, properly defended, would have been well-nigh impregnable, and could have been held by a handful against a small army, without artillery. Rumors of all kinds were thick and warlike, and, while waiting for the Missourians, a friendly messenger from higher up the Osage reached our camp in the night with the information that the conservative free-state men, under a prominent local leader, were organizing to either kill Captain Brown or hand him over to the Missourians. The State

authorities there had by this time offered a reward for him and
his men.

"Brown, in the estimation of these free-state men, had
exceeded his privileges by invading Missouri and interfering
with the divine institution of slavery. Their code confined all
their motions to the defensive. Missouri might invade Kansas,
but Kansas must not invade Missouri; pro-slavery men might
cross the line and steal from, harass, or murder free-state
settlers, yet free-state men must not retaliate by crossing the
line, and must be very careful not to insult the slave interest.[1]
Neither Missourians nor 'conservative' free-state men, however, came to trouble us. The company up the Osage discovered that another company had formed in the rear, which
would have given them especial attention had they moved
towards us. Besides, Montgomery was still a power behind
the throne; apparently out of the arena, yet ready in case of
need to give Brown his active support. Brown at this time

---

[1] As one result of all these conflicting conditions and disturbances, an agreement was entered into after a conference at
Moneka, Mr. Wattles acting as peacemaker. It was at this time,
when Mr. Wattles and other friends urged upon the Captain that
Kansas was too greatly harassed, that the latter replied : " He
would soon remove the seat of the trouble elsewhere." The
following is a copy of the agreement made :

"We, the undersigned citizens of Kansas and Missouri, Jan.
1, 1859 :

"1. All criminal proceedings for any action connected with
politics to be quashed.

"2. All active political men, who have been 'forcibly driven
from the Territory for their crimes . . . to remain away.'
This did not apply to those ' voluntarily' leaving ' through fear.'

"3. No troops or posse to be sent out.

"4. All parties shall in good faith discontinue acts of robbery,
theft, or violence of any kind—on account of ' political differ-
ences.'

AUGUSTUS WATTLES, JOHN BROWN, WILLIAM AULDERSON,
JAMES MONTGOMERY, O. P. BAIN, and others.

wrote his famous parallels,[1] and was exceedingly anxious to move north at the safest time for traveling with the colored people. It was found impossible to move them, in consideration of Daniels's wife, she having given birth to a boy, who was christened 'John Brown' Daniels. Dr. Blount, who had attended her, began to grow weary under the care, and sent a messenger to have them moved as soon as possible.

" It must have been on or about the 20th of January, 1859, that· we left Garnett. Captain Brown and myself were alone with the colored folks."

Mr. Gill then mentions Ottawa Jones's, Brown's Indian friend, Major Abbott's, and a Mr. Grover's, near Lawrence, as some of their stopping-places. From Grover's point John Brown visited Lawrence, sold the oxen, which were probably butchered there, and hired a team or two to help the party through as far as Tabor, one of the teams eventually going as far as Springdale, Iowa. At Lawrence the old man arranged his finances, mostly from the sale of the cattle however.[2]

" The colored folks cooked," continues Mr. Gill, "a supply of provisions, mostly obtained through the generosity of the Grovers and Abbotts. I remained with the colored folks while Brown attended to his business in town. We left Grover's on the evening of the 28th of January, I still being guide and guard, riding a fine stallion, which Brown had given Hazlett a forty acre land warrant for. The land warrant Gerrit Smith had sent Brown, and the stallion Hazlett had picked up down in Missouri. Brown afterwards sold it at auction, in Cleveland, Ohio. About midnight, and somewhere opposite Lecompton, on our way to Topeka, I noticed men behind a fence. Of course I could not tell how many. Going to the wagon in which the old man rode, I acquainted him with the fact. He was dozing when I spoke, but my news woke him up. He told me to keep

---

[1] See Appendix.

[2] It was at this time that Captain Brown had his last interview, and most remarkable interview, with William A. Phillips. (See Appendix.)

a good lookout. No one troubled us. however, but I found out
afterwards from some prisoners we took at Holton, that they
had actually ambushed us, but could not conceive of ours being
the outfit that they were looking for, until it was too late, no
oxen, no guards, or if there were guards they were behind and
of an unknown quantity, and it might be unsafe to stop us, or
it might be a stragetic movement of some kind to take them in.
·They waited to see and missed us. At Topeka, Stevens joined
us, and I stopped to rest with John Ritchie. On the 29th the
fugitives passed through and were stopped a little north of
Holton, on what was then known as Spring Creek. A messenger was hurried back by Mr. Wasson, living there, to
Topeka, and Col. Ritchie quickly raised a force, reaching Holton
in the afternoon of the 31st. We found Brown and Stevens
with the colored folks and teamsters in log houses with one
prisoner. We immediately organized and advanced towards
the ford or crossing which was in possession of the supposed
posse who were drilling on its banks. The stream was very
high and almost unfordable. We succeeded in crossing, however, and taking several prisoners without any one getting hurt.
This was known as the Battle of the Spurs. The prisoners we
kept a day or two and then allowed them to go home on foot.
It was these prisoners that it was reported were made by
Brown to kneel and pray. There was no truth in this whatever, as I guarded the prisoners myself. One of the prisoners,
to show his bravado, commenced to swear as only a first-class
expert could do. The old man hearing him sáid, ' Tut, tut, you
are not doing right, for if there is a God, it is wrong to speak
His name in that way ; if there is none it is certainly very foolish.'

" One of our boys also undertook to show his bravery by
abusing the prisoners. The Captain read him a lecture on
the cowardice of insulting a man unable to defend himself.
Some of the Topeka party accompanied us to Tabor, Iowa.
We understood at this time that troops were in our rear in
Kansas, and that there probably would be squads of armed and
organized parties to either kill, arrest, or otherwise retard our
advance. We stopped over night at a Nebraska Indian settle-

ment (the Otoes), and slept in their houses. In the morning the river had risen, and the ice floated free from each shore. We felled trees and bridged from the shore to the ice, drawing our wagons over by hand and leading the horses. Previous to passing through Nebraska City, I had, in consequence of the cold, walked behind the train. Being in quite a crippled condition, I got some distance behind ; or it is possible that the drivers were hurrying up, as it was growing dark. At any rate, I found myself intercepted by three scouts. In my efforts to throw them off, I claimed to be traveling south, which I succeeded in doing, but it delayed my getting into the city until about ten o'clock. Our folks had then crossed on the ice and passed on, I stopped over night with Kagi's brother-in-law, Mr. Mayhew, but had some difficulty in finding him, having had to inquire some. A letter from there shortly afterwards stated that I had not been gone the next morning more than fifteen minutes, before the house was surrounded by about fifty men, being a marshal's posse in search of us. Arriving at Dr. Blanchard's, midway, perhaps, between Nebraska City, at which place Brown and party had stopped, I found that the posse had preceded me, and searched thoroughly, even moving bookcases and cupboards out from the wall, to see that there were no secret recesses to hold underground travelers. How I missed coming into contact with them, or how Brown's party missed them, can only be accounted for on the supposition that different roads were traveled. On the night of the fifth of February, 1859, we arrived at Tabor, where we stayed until the 11th. At this place, meetings were held, and resolutions passed, denouncing Brown, his party, and actions. Yet Tabor had been the starting-point for the free-state movements in western Iowa, and the people continued to aid us.

"Leaving that place on the 11th, we took up our line of march for Springdale, stopping at Toole's the night of the 12th, Lewis's Mills the 13th, Porter's tavern, Grove City, the 14th, Dalmanutha, the 15th, at Murray's, Aurora, on the 16th, Jordan's on the 17th, and, about noon on the 18th, passed through Des Moines City, stopping quite a while in the streets, Kagi hunting up

Editor Teesdale, of the *Register*, an acquaintance of his; he
also proved to be an old acquaintance of Brown.   Mr. Teesdale paid our ferriage across the Des Moines River.   On the
night of the 18th we stopped at Hawley's, on the 19th at Dick-
erson's, and on the 20th reached Grinnell, at which place our
welcome was enthusiastic, Mr. J. B. Grinnell, afterwards in
Congress, personally superintending the reception.[1]   On the
25th we reached Springdale, going through Iowa City some
time during the forenoon.   No efforts having been made to

---

[1] RECEPTION OF BROWN AND PARTY AT GRINNELL, IOWA. [In
the handwriting of Captain Brown is the following memoranda
now among the records of the Kansas State Historical Society :]

" 1. Whole party and teams kept for two days free of cost.

" 2. Sundry articles of clothing given to the captives.

" 3. Bread, meat, cake, pies, etc., prepared for our journey.

" 4. Full houses for two nights in succession, at which meetings
Brown and Kagi spoke and were loudly cheered, and fully indorsed.   Three Congregational clergymen attended the meeting
on Sabbath evening (notice of which was given out from the pulpit); all of them took part in justifying our course, and in urging
for contributions in our behalf.   There was no dissenting speaker
present at either meeting.   Mr. Grinnell spoke at length, and has
since labored to secure us a free and safe conveyance to Chicago,
and effected it.

" 5. Contributions in cash amounting to $26.50.

" 6. Last, but not least, public thanksgiving to Almighty God,
offered by Mr. Grinnell, in behalf of the whole company, for His
great mercy and protecting care, with prayers for a continuance
of these Blessings.

" As the action of Tabor friends has been published in the newspapers by some of her people (as I suppose), would not friend
Gaston, or some other friend, give publicity to the above?

" Respectfully your friend,

" JOHN BROWN.

" P. S.—Our reception here among the Quaker friends has
been most cordial.   Yours truly,   J. B.

" SPRINGFIELD, IOWA, 26th Feb., 1859."

conceal our movements after entering Iowa, rumors came of an intended attempt to capture Captain Brown and the negroes. A building was selected to keep the latter in. There was scarcely any necessity for guards, as the whole community was alert, and any attempt to invade Springdale would have most likely proven very disastrous to the intruders. West Liberty, a railroad town seven miles south of Springdale, was a very hotbed of Abolitionists, and in full sympathy with Brown's idea."

Mr. Gill left the party at West Liberty on the 10th inst., as health gave out and inflammatory rheumatism prevented further travel on his part. One of the Kansas escort accompanied the party to Crookes's in Iowa, and others left at Tabor.

After leaving Iowa there was very little of special interest until arrival at Detroit and transfer to Canada. Of course, vigilant care had to be exercised. On the 12th day of March, 1859, he saw his band of freed people, augmented to twelve by the birth of a boy while camping near Dr. James G. Blunt's place on the Pottawatomie in the January preceding, carried in safety from Detroit to Windsor. John Brown, the baby born in freedom, and bearing the name of his emancipator, still lives in Windsor, having, it has been stated, never set foot in the United States. The Missouri freed people are nearly all living, doing well, and having large families about them. Of course, Captain Brown's successful raid met severe criticism on all sides, and to some extent, too, among a few of his Massachusetts friends. Neither Gerrit Smith nor George L. Stearns were counted among the critics. In Detroit, Captain Brown met Frederick Douglass, who happened to be engaged for a lyceum lecture there. A little meeting was held at the dwelling of a Mr. William Webb, and a report has been made of sharp disagreements between John Brown and the colored orator and editor. Mr. Douglass assures me nothing of the sort occurred. John Brown girded up his loins again, and with his purse a little replenished by Eastern friends, started once more on the culminating work of his life. With him at Detroit and *en route* to Cleveland, Ohio, were his son Owen, Kagi, Stevens, Leeman, Tidd, Hazlett, Edwin Coppoc, J. G. Anderson, and Barclay Coppoc of those that finally went down into the valley of shadows. Steward Taylor was waiting and working in Illinois, and Cook was in Virginia, ready for work. The hour was coming fast.

CHAPTER IX.

LIFE AND PREPARATION AT THE KENNEDY FARM.

Friends in southern Kansas and Iowa—Safe arrival of his freed people in Canada—Meeting and speeches in Cleveland—Where the men went and what they did—John Brown at home in North Elba—Peterboro and Boston—On the borders of slavery—The Kennedy farm and the hiring—Gathering there—Life within—Mrs. Anne Brown-Adams the last survivor—Martha Brown—Oliver's girl wife—John Brown, Jr., in Canada—Shipping the freight—Kagi at Chambersburg—Frederick Douglass and Shields Green—Arrival of Osborne P. Anderson and Francis J. Merriam—Return of Anne and Martha to North Elba—John E. Cook—A curious despatch—" The shot heard round the world."

JOHN BROWN's second and last campaign in Kansas left behind warm and enduring friendships. He carried to his grave, less than a year beyond the day when its prairies, made sacred with human passions and human woes, faded from his vision, a sense of enduring regard and honor, which has since made itself felt in many a brave tribute. The real free-state men of southern Kansas have never given a single recruit to the detractors of Captain Brown. "I shall remove the seat of disturbance from Kansas," were his last words to the "Squire," as he always termed his old and trusted friend, Augustus Wattles, of Moneka. Truly, he did remove it across the Continent to the Alleghanies and down to the Gulf of Mexico, and in removing it he aided beyond words in making a Nation without a slave and a Union without a foe. The meaning of the remark was well understood, though nothing would be known definitely of place and plan. That John Brown would be heard from again was certain to all, as was learned when, in the spring of 1859, I last visited that section. Among John Brown's friends and supporters many became noted in the stormier years that followed. Among the rank and file, I recall the Hairgroves and Snyder, shot in the Marais du Cygne atrocity, as gallant Union soldiers. Dr. James G. Blunt was a prominent major-general of volunteers; James Montgomery a colonel of colored troops in South Carolina; Dr. Jenison commanded a regiment of cavalry; James Hanway was a district judge; H. H. Williams a major of volunteers; Drs. Ayres and Gilpatrick army-surgeons; John Ritchie, at Topeka, a colonel, while William A. Phillips, editor, author, lawyer, commanded a loyal Indian brigade of Cherokees and Creeks, and John Bowles was lieutenant-colonel of colored infantry. There were no doubters, cowards, or trimmers among John Brown's Kansas friends when the war issues finally came. But the personal regard and friendship of the two Wattles families, at Moneka, Levin County, with the unbending Puritan leader, was an incident almost idyllic in char-

acter. Their homes were always open to him and his
men, while the Captain was loved by the charming
group of girls who made them so attractive.

Augustus and John Wattles were of Quaker origin.
They were refined, scholarly, cultivated. Augustus,
being more a man of affairs than his brother, John,
who took no public part in Kansas matters, though a
devoted anti-slavery man. He was a musician of fine
ability—the inventor of a system of musical notation,
once in considerable use. His brother was lawyer,
farmer, and editor. They came from the famous
free-soil district in Indiana, which so long sent
George W. Julian to Congress. Both had been identified as advocates and writers with the dreams of
social equity and organization, so early advanced by
the late Albert Brisbane, the disciple of Fourier and
Josiah Warren, author of an almost-forgotten form of
Bellamyism. Among such groups as these John
Brown seems always to have been understood, yet he
was apart from them all. On his way out he met
William A. Phillips at Lawrence, holding with him
the last of a series of remarkable conversations, which
are reprinted in the Appendix to this volume. John
Bowles, then about to start for California, held a long
and confidential talk with him and Kagi, being
intrusted with the general outline and location of
the movement that was made ten months later in
Virginia. In Iowa, the foremost Republicans and
anti slavery citizens, while ostensibly shaking their
heads—*a la* politician style, as at Tabor, where they
first cared for his party, and then resolved that it was
very wrong to help a human being to freedom, if he
or she happened to be dark-skinned and African in de-

scent—to the Governor and his staff ; leading men like
Hiram Price, J. B. Grinnel, Wm. Penn Clarke, Senator
Grimes's sons;—editors, lawyers, officials, prospective
Congressmen and soldiers of future prominence, vied
with each other in helping forward the liberator and
his party.   In Chicago, his presence was widely
known, and, though an "outlaw" with two rewards
for his arrest, aggregating $3,250, no one seemed to
be deterred from making him welcome.   No attempt
at arrest, no threat even, came to his ears, in either
Chicago, Detroit, or Cleveland.   The United States
marshal of northern Ohio did not attempt an arrest,
though a Federal reward was offered, but when
Captain Brown was captured and lay, with five
wounds, on the bare floor of the United States
armory guardroom, he was among the earliest of
political visitors from the North, seeking, if possible,
to glean from expected weakness an admission
against Joshua R. Giddings, Ralph M. Plumb, or
some others of the anti-slavery men of the Western
Reserve.

To Cleveland John Brown shipped the mules for
which he had traded the oxen taken in Missouri from
the estate of the slave-owners, and which had been
used in transporting his band of freed people to
"Canaan's happy land," as they had joyfully styled
the far-off north land to which they were bound,
when leaving Missouri. The stallion, which had been
purchased from Hazlett and been ridden by the Captain on his long journey with two or three other
travel-worn horses, and perhaps the two wagons used,
were on hand. His small funds were divided as far as
possible with the rescued when they were left in

Canada, and it was decided to sell the property. This was done on the public street by Captain Brown himself, who also gave due notice of the facts connected with them.   An amusing incident was narrated in a newspaper interview years after about Judge Carter, of Ohio, Chief-Justice of the District of Columbia. The Judge was narrowly critical of John Brown, who had called upon him the day after the Cleveland sale, of which he gave the lawyer full particulars, drily remarking "and they (the animals) brought good prices, too." The lawyer bought a pair of mules—at second hand, he was careful to say.   The amount was given to me afterwards at several hundred dollars, and I find a note thereof among memorabilia of the Cleveland visit, which was on the 23d of March. That evening, a well-attended meeting was held at Chapin's Hall, a small admission fee being charged.

The speakers were John Henri Kagi and John Brown, the former making the first address, while the latter in his speech made a significant declaration, which I afterwards copied from the Cleveland *Leader's* report of the same.   Interest turning on events in southern Kansas, Kagi gave a rapid review of their history, showing the border-ruffian outrages of 1856; the land-settler persecutions and the official injustice the free-state entrymen were subjected to; the constant "nagging" of the Blake-Little-Clark-Ransom pro-southern gang, with the view of producing retaliation by free-state men, the unfair interference by the Executive usually on the pro-southern side; the sending of picked squadrons of dragoons with Southern sympathy against Montgomery and his men; the constant forays, kidnapping, etc., from Missouri, with the

constant violations of all agreements made for peace,
the culminating atrocities of the Hamilton gang. Kagi
was a strong, logical, convincing, even eloquent,
speaker, with a fine presence and a good command of
language. He knew the subject, and did not seek to
either evade or defend the actions of free-state men.
He simply showed what they were and how they came
to be, leaving his audience to decide the ethics thereof.
Kagi's description of the one-sided fights, ending in
the Southerners' flight were amusing and pleased the
audience

Captain Brown's speech was like himself,—direct,
to the point, unequivocal, and animated, with his
stern conviction of righteousness. He was capable
of grouping his points well, and, from a mere brief,
presenting a close, connected statement. He told the
audience that his purpose in charging an admission
fee was to aid in reimbursing the expenses of his
recent effort. Although he had been threatened
abundantly during his last visit to Kansas, he had not
been engaged in any fight. Some of his young
men, however, had bettered the instructions of
the Southern men. He was now an outlaw, with a
price on his head. The fact did not inconvenience
him or cause any loss of sleep. He should never submit to an arrest, as he had nothing to gain by submission. This recalls the fact that Mrs. Brown said just
previous to the execution of her husband, that it had
always been her feeling, as well as the Captain's, that
if he was ever defeated, he should be killed rather
than made a prisoner. In referring to his position,
John Brown grimly remarked, that he "should settle
all questions on the spot, if any attempt was made to

take him." His purpose in liberating the Missouri bondsmen was to make familiar a direct blow at slavery. He laid it down as a platform for himself, that he considered it his duty to liberate the slave wherever he had an opportunity. He was a thorough-going Abolitionist. In referring to his life and actions in Kansas, he said that he, John Brown, " never lifted a finger toward any one whom he did not know was a violent persecutor of the free-state men. *He had never killed any body, although on some occasion he had shown the young men how some things might be done as well as others, and they had done the business.*[1] He had never destroyed the value of an ear of corn, and had never set fire to a pro-slavery man's house or property, and had never by his own action driven out pro-slavery men from the Territory, but, if occasion demanded it, he would drive them into the ground like a stake-fence, where they would remain permanent settlers." These grim declarations were probably in reply to charges and attacks made in the current Democratic newspapers. The Captain continued, as reported: " Further, he had yet to learn of any pro-slavery man being arrested or punished for any crime, while free-state men were slain even for the crime of having opinions, as was his son Frederick, the particulars of whose slaying at Osawatomie he narrated." The speeches and meeting were a remarkable success, and even the Democratic papers treated it fairly in their reports.

---

[1] This report was obtained by me in 1860 from a Cleveland paper, I believe the *Leader*, and the copy in my handwriting is before me as I write,

From Cleveland, Ohio, after short visits with his sons, John, Jr., at West Andover, and Jason, at Akron, in the same State, Captain Brown, with J. G. Anderson, left for his home at North Elba. The remainder of the party which had accompanied him as far as Detroit now provided for themselves at various points. Owen Brown remained until July at Akron, with

his brother Jason. Aaron D. Stevens, as Charles Whipple, went to West Andover, where he was employed by Mr. Lindsey on his farm until the following August. W. H. Leeman got work at Lindenville, nearby, making whips in a factory there. The two Coppocs, Edwin and Barclay, went to Medina and Salem, where they had relatives, and remained working until August, when they were summoned to the Kennedy Farm.

WILLIAM HENRY LEEMAN.

Albert Hazlett returned to his home at Indiana, Pennsylvania, where he got employment till August. C. P. Tidd remained in the vicinity of Cleveland, while J. H. Kagi divided his time until late in June, when he went to Pennsylvania, between Cleveland, West Andover, and Oberlin, being occupied, while waiting for the Captain's last return from the East, in looking after the freight shipments (*i. e.* the arms, etc.) which had been sent from Iowa to Conneaut, Ohio, and in watching the progress of the Price fugitive slave rescue case, in which a number of noted persons, professors at Oberlin, and others, were

Involved.   Several of them were imprisoned in Cleveland, and Kagi and Tidd planned with others taking them out.   The State of Ohio, however, intervened by arresting the Kentucky slave-catchers, when they came to testify against the rescuers, upon the very plain ground that the original capture of the alleged fugitive Price, was in reality a kidnapping, done without regard to the Federal law and in clear contravention of State laws.   Their arrests brought about a settlement of the whole affair, by which fugitive and rescuers were discharged, and the Kentuckians very gladly availed themselves of a chance to get out of Ohio.   Kagi acted as the correspondent of the New York *Tribune* and also wrote for the Cleveland *Leader*.   Steward Taylor was still in Illinois, not having gone to Kansas with the others.

Early in April, John Brown, accompanied by his faithful aide, J. G. Anderson, was in Rochester, and from the 11th to the 14th at Peterboro, a guest of Gerrit Smith.   The latter gave him $200.   On the 14th he started for North Elba, having been at his home but once in two years.   At this visit arrangements were made for Oliver to join him at an early day, and Watson later in the summer, after his wife Isabella's confinement.   Martha, Oliver's wife, and Anne Brown, the second daughter, it was afterwards arranged, were to go to the Maryland farm as housekeepers.   The Captain remained at home for about two weeks, and then left for Massachusetts.   He was at Concord, the guest of Mr. Sanborn, on the 7th of May, remaining till his fifty-ninth birthday, when he left for Boston.   He met John M. Forbes and a few other well-known men at this visit for the first

time, and received, with what Gerrit Smith sent,
about $500 in all. At Concord he attended and spoke
at a meeting held to hear him. Mr. Sanborn in his
volume (pp. 564–65) quotes Emerson, and Thoreau,
and Alcott; the latter as writing in his journal in
part as follows:

"Concord, May 8, 1859.—This evening I heard Captain
Brown speak, at the Town Hall, on Kansas affairs. . . .
He tells his story with surpassing simplicity and sense. Our
best people listen to his words—Emerson, Thoreau, Judge
Hoar (afterwards Attorney-General under Grant, and Congressman). . . . Some of them contributed in aid of his
plans, without asking particulars, such confidence does he
inspire in his integrity and abilities. . . . He is Sanborn's guest, and stays for a day only. A young man named
Anderson accompanies him. They go armed, I am told, and
will defend themselves if necessary. . . . The Captain
leaves much in the dark concerning his destination and designs
for the coming months, yet he does not conceal . . . his
readiness to strike a blow for freedom at the proper moment.
I infer it is his intention to run off as many slaves as he can,
and so render that property insecure to the master."

From Boston to New York[1] and Eastern Pennsyl-

---

[1] Among the manuscript letters in my possession, chiefly written
by the men, I find two from J. G. Anderson to his brother, Dr.
John B. Anderson, of Springdale, Iowa. The Doctor had served
in southern Kansas, and was trusted, so that " Jerry " Anderson
wrote quite freely. A letter of June 17th, from West Andover,
Ohio, describes their travels. The first three weeks were spent at
Peterboro, North Elba, N. Y., and in Boston and vicinity. In
New York City four days, and the young Western farmer gives a
naïve description of the impressions he received. He visited
Brooklyn, met John Hopper, son of Isaac T. Hopper, the Quaker
philanthropist, Dr. George B. Cheever, and also saw Henry Ward
Beecher on a street car, whom he described as " a very common-
looking man with very coarse features, but showing undoubted

vania and Ohio by the middle of June.   Arrangements were to complete the pikes ordered in 1857 of
Charles W. Blair, of Collinsville, Conn.   They were
partly paid for then, and Captain Brown paid the
balance, $300, ordering them finished as rapidly as
possible, and shipped to Isaac Smith & Sons, Chambersburg, Pa., where Kagi was mainly found until
the last of September.   These " tools " did not reach
the Maryland farm until late in September, where
they were stored, 950 of them, in the attic of the Kennedy dwelling.   The Sharpe's rifles and other articles
filled fifteen heavy boxes.   Curiosity had been aroused
as to their contents at Conneaut.   John Brown, Jr.,
removed them to West Andover and then to Harts-
town, Crawford Co., Pennsylvania, July 27th, shipping
by canal to Chambersburg, from whence they were
removed early in September to the Kennedy Farm.   A
log cabin, belonging to the place, just across the road
from the house was used for storage.   William

---

good sense,"—a knockdown sort of characterization that.   A visit
to Joshua R. Giddings at Jefferson, Ohio, is mentioned, and then
" Jerry " writes :

" This is an age of miracles.   I wouldn't be surprised if you
should hear of me being in some place before long.   We are going
to start from here next Monday (June 19th) for Cleveland, from there
across Pennsylvania to the border of Virginia, on a *surveying* expedition.   I think I shall write to you from that region in a few weeks.
You need not be uneasy about us *stealing niggers*, for that is not our
business, but be patient, and in due time you will be apprised of
our business, and how we succeed.   Our theory is new, but undoubtedly good, practicable, and perfectly safe and simple, but I
judge when we put it into practice, it will astonish the world and
mankind in general.   We called on Fred. Douglass again as
we passed through Rochester; he is to be one of us."

Thompson, Watson Brown, and Jeremiah G. Anderson slept therein after the tools arrived, partly as a
guard, and as a place of defense in the event of any
attack or danger.　Captain Brown arrived at Chambersburg early in June, and with his sons Oliver
and Owen, or " Jerry " Anderson, made observation
trips along the border, or went to Pittsburgh, Cleveland, and Philadelphia on business.　On the 30th of
June, with Owen, Oliver, and Anderson he went to
Hagerstown and Sandy Hook, Maryland, and on the
2d of July they were in Harper's Ferry itself.　Cook
was living there, and knew of the Captain's visits.
Interviews were had, care being taken not to appear
too public and familiar.　The party were supposed
to be prospecting for minerals.　Out in the country,
however, they were cattlemen from northern New
York, looking for grazing land, on which to fatten
their lean stock.　In an article on " The Virginia
Campaign," published in *The Atlantic*, December,
1875, Mr. F. B. Sanborn gave an interesting account
of the finding of the Kennedy Farm, in Washington
County, Maryland, but four miles from Harper's Ferry,
which was rented for a year for $35.　Starting out
from Sandy Hook, where they had stayed the night
before, on the 4th of July they went up the river
road toward the house of Mr. John C. Unseld, a Maryland slaveholder, who lived but a mile from the
Ferry, on one of the mountain roads.

"Between eight and nine o'clock that morning, as Mr.
Unseld was riding down to the Ferry, he met the party strol-
ling along the edge of the mountain.　Falling into conversation with them, in the country fashion, he learned that the
old man was named Smith, that these were his sons, Watson

and Oliver Smith, and that the other youth was named Anderson. 'Well, gentlemen,' said the Marylander, 'I suppose you are out hunting minerals, gold and silver, perhaps.' 'No,' said Brown, 'we are out looking for land. We want to buy land; we have a little money, and want to make it go as far as we can: How much is land worth an acre, hereabouts?' Being told that it 'ranged from fifteen dollars to thirty dollars in that neighborhood,' he said, 'That is high. I thought I could buy for a dollar or two an acre.' 'No,' said the Marylander, 'not here; if you expect to get land for that price, you'll have to go farther West, to Kansas, or some of those Territories where there is Congress land. Where are you from?' 'The northern part of New York State.' 'What have you followed there?' 'Farming,' said Brown; but the frost had been so heavy of late years it had cut off their crops; they could not make anything there, so they had sold out, and thought they would come farther South and try it a while. Having thus satisfied a natural curiosity, Mr. Unseld rode on. Returning some hours afterward, he again met Mr. Smith and his young men not far from the same place. 'I have been looking round your country up here,' said he, 'and it is a very fine country—a pleasant place, a fine view. The land is much better than I expected to find it; your crops are pretty good.' As he said this he pointed to where the men had been cutting grain—some white men and some negroes at work in the fields, as the custom is there. For in Washington county there were few slaves even then, and most of the field work was done by whites or free colored men. Brown then asked if any farm in the neighborhood was for sale. 'Yes, there is a farm four miles up the road here, towards Boonsborough, owned by the heirs of Dr. Booth Kennedy; you can buy that.' 'Can I rent it?' said Brown; then turning to his companions he said, 'I think we had better rent a while, until we get better acquainted, so that they cannot take advantage of us in the purchase of land.' To this they appeared to assent, and Mr. Unseld then said, 'Perhaps you can rent the Kennedy farm; I do not know about that, but it is for sale, I know.' Brown then turned

16

again to his sons and said, ' Boys, as you are not very well, you had better go back and tell the landlord at Sandy Hook that Oliver and I shall not be there to dinner, but will go on up and look at the Kennedy place ; however, you can do as you please.' Watson Brown looked at Anderson and then said, ' We will go with you.'   ' Well,' said the friendly Marylander, ' if you will go on with me up to my house, I can then point you the road exactly.'   Arrived there, he invited them to take dinner, for by this time it was nearly noon. They thanked him but declined, nor would they accept an invitation to 'drink something.'   ' Well,' said Unseld, ' if you must go on, just follow up this road along the foot of the mountain ; it is shady and pleasant, and you will come out at a church up here about three miles.   Then you can see the Kennedy house by look-ing from that church right up the road that leads to Boons-borough, or you can go right across and get into the country road and follow that up.'   Brown sat and talked with Unseld for a while, who asked him 'what he expected to follow, up yonder at Kennedy's,' adding that Brown 'could not make a living there.'   ' Well,' said Brown, ' my business has been buy-ing up fat cattle and driving them on to the State of New York, and we expect to engage in that again.'   Three days later (July 7th), the genial Unseld, jogging to or from the Ferry, again met the gray-haired rustic, who said, ' Well, I think that place will suit me ; now just give me a description where I can find the widow Kennedy and the administrator,' which Unseld did. A few days after, he once more met the new comer, and found Mr. Smith had rented the two houses on the Kennedy farm—the farm-house, about three hundred yards from the public road on the west side, where, as Unseld thought, ' it makes a very pretty show for a small house,' and ' the cabin,' which stood about as far from the road on the east side, ' hidden by shrubbery in the summer season, pretty much.' For the two houses, pasture for a cow and horse, and fire-wood, from July till March, Brown paid thirty-five dollars, as he took pains to tell Unseld, showing him the receipt of the widow Kennedy."

The Booth-Kennedy family lived at Sharpsburg, where Lee had his headquarters when the battle of Antietam was fought. The Confederates named it after the Maryland village. The Maryland farmer testified before the United States Senate's Committee on "the Harper's Ferry Invasion." The name of the Virginian Senator's Committee should be borne in mind, as a peculiar piece of direct evidence of the manner in which Mason, Davis, Wise & Co. were working towards revolution by firing the Southern heart with systematic misrepresentation of the relations of the North to the John Brown raid. Mr. Unseld said that he did "not once mistrust him, though he rode up to the Kennedy Farm nearly every week from the middle of July till the 1st of October."

"'I just went up to talk to the old man, said he to Senator Mason, when telling the story before the Senate Committee, 'but sometimes, at the request of others, on business about selling him some horses or cows. He was in my yard frequently, perhaps four or five times. I would always ask him in, but he would never go in, and of course I would not go in his house. He often invited me in; indeed, nearly every time I went there he asked me to go in, and remarked to me frequently, "We have no chairs for you to sit on, but we have trunks and boxes." I declined going in, but sat on my horse and chatted with him. Before the 20th of July he saw there "two females," who were Martha, the wife of Oliver Brown, and Anne, the eldest unmarried sister of Oliver. Both of them were but girls in their seventeenth years, as they were born in 1843. "Twice I went there," says Unseld, and found none of the men, but the two ladies, and I sat there on my horse—there was a high porch on the house, and I could sit there and chat with them—and then I rode off and left them. They told me there were none of the men at home, but did not tell me where they were. One time I went there and inquired for them, and one of the females answered me, " They are across there at the cabin ; you had better ride over and see them." I replied it did not make any difference, and I would not bother them, and I rode back home.'"

The region is semi-mountainous, and is still sparsely settled. Within three years after John Brown's advent, it passed into national history as the scene of McClellan's defeat of Lee. Across it passed in part the great armies that met in a decisive battle shock at Gettysburg. But it will always be recalled more readily as the location of John Brown's final preparations for the Harper's Ferry attack, which sent the old fighter's soul "marching on" until chattel slavery, by the will of the Nation and the fearful cost of civil war was abolished in the land. It is ruggedly picturesque, quiet, rural, well wooded, and with no great stretches of open, arable lands. The section is quiet, the residents are easy-going and the landscape is the most attractive thing connected therewith. Of late years it has become somewhat noted for the summer residences of well-to-do families, chiefly from Washington and Baltimore. Osborne Perry Anderson, in "A Voice from Harper's Ferry," wrote that "To a passer-by the house and its surroundings presented but indifferent attractions. Any log (frame) tenement of equal dimensions would be as likely to attract attention. Rough, unsightly, and aged, it was only those privileged to enter and tarry for a long time and to penetrate the mysteries of the two rooms it contained — kitchen, parlor, dining-room below, and the spacious chamber, attic, storeroom, prison, drilling-room, comprised in the loft above—who could tell how we lived at Kennedy Farm?"

The question may in a fair fashion be answered, as besides other sources, I am fortunately endowed with permission to use the vivid recollections of Anne Brown (now Mrs. Adams, of Petralia, Humboldt County, California, and the mother of six children, who was called by her father his " watch dog ") who has written me valuable notes and memoranda, full, as I name them, of thumb-nail sketches, which illustrate the scenes of that summer, and the men, too, who were actors in them. Coming from the only survivor of the little band who lived at the Kennedy Farm,[1] these recollections have a special biographical and historical significance.

Anne Brown and Martha Evelyn, the loving young wife of Oliver, who was as much slain as if she had fallen by a Virginian bullet, arrived at the Maryland camp in the third week in July. "Josephus," the Harper's Ferry annalist often quoted in these pages, says, that the Captain and his sons, with Jerry Anderson, first boarded with Mr. Osmond Bulter, at Sandy Hook, Maryland. The Virginian pamphleteer adds, "their conduct was unexceptionable. They

---

[1] It is necessary to emphasize the fact that Anne Brown Adams is the only one alive of the Kennedy Farm party. Besides George B. Gill and Charles W. Moffett, of Iowa and Kansas, there are none alive of those who went " to school " at Springdale, Iowa, and participated in the Chatham, Canada, Convention, in 1857–58, unless it be Richard Richardson, a colored man, of whom I learn nothing. Others are living who were actively aiding and trusted by John Brown, but these named were actually at the farm, in the fight, or trained therefor.

paid in gold for whatever they purchased, and as their manners were courteous to all, they were, on the whole, very popular." Kagi came down from Chambersburg, and remained two or three days with them at Sandy Hook, but his likeness to the Virginian "Keagys," as his uncle's family were called in the neighborhood, compelled him to make a quick retreat to Chambersburg. He was born in southern Ohio, his father having removed from the Shenandoah Valley, but himself went to school, and taught also in the section, when about sixteen years old. He distinguished himself even then by assisting a fugitive slave, and was obliged to return to his father's home in Ohio. There was danger that he would be recognized. A memorandum in John Brown's handwriting found in the captured carpet-bag and printed in a State document some time after, gives a good idea of Captain Brown's care for details. It was evidently written for Kagi's guidance, and on the back of it a rough, topographical road sketch, with the names of the towns in Kagi's own handwriting.   John Brown wrote:

" Look for letters directed to John Henrie; at Chambersburg inquire for letters (there) directed to J. Smith & Sons; for Isaac Smith inquire for freight at the depot, at Chambersburg, for J. Smith & Sons; and write them at Harper's Ferry *as soon* as any does come. See Mr. Henry Watson, at Chambersburg, and find out if the Tribune comes on.[1]   Have Mr. Watson and his *reliable* friends get ready to receive company (about this time Leary and Copeland were to arrive from Oberlin, Ohio, Anderson and others from Canada were expected).   Get Mr. Watson to make you acquainted with his reliable friends, *but*

[1] A memorandum exists of a subscription of $3 sent early in June.

do not appear to be any wise thick with them ; and do *not often be seen with any such* man.   Get Mr. Watson to find out *if he can*, a trusty man or men to stop with at Hagerstown (if any such there be), as Mr. (Thomas) Henrie (A. D. Stevens) has gone there.   Write Tidd to come to Chambersburg, by Pittsburg and Harrisburg, at once.   He can stop off the Pittsburg road at Hudson and go to Jason's (Akron) for his trunk.   Write Carpenter (Edwin Coppoc probably) and Hazlett that we are all right and ready as soon as we can get our boarding-house fixed ; when we will write them to come on and by what route. I will pay Hazlett the money he advanced to Anderson for expenses traveling.   Find yourself a comfortable, cheap boarding-house at once.   Write J. Smith & Sons, at Harper's Ferry.   Inquire after your four Cleveland friends, and have them come on to Chambersburg if they are on the way; if *not on the road* let them wait till we get a little better prepared. *Be careful what you write to all persons. Do not send or bring* any more persons here until we advise you of our readiness to board them."

The " four Cleveland friends " referred in all probability to colored men: Lewis Sherrard Leary, and John A. Copeland, of Oberlin, who did report for duty; Charles Langston and James H. Harris, of Cleveland, who were for some reason unable to come. The date of the foregoing must have been about the 10th or 12th of July, as about that time Kagi first appeared in Chambersburg, and letters began to reach different parties pledged to the enterprise. I received inquiries relating to Richard Realf and Charles W. Leonhardt, of whom further mention will be made.

Oliver Brown was sent at the same time that Kagi left for Pennsylvania to North Elba, to bring his wife and Anne to Maryland.   On their return to the Adirondack homestead, seventeen days before the outbreak, Oliver escorted them as far as Troy, New

York, where, on the 2d of October (Sunday), they parted to meet no more on earth. Mrs. Adams describes the love of the young couple as an exquisite thing, so happy were they "in the enjoyment of each other, that they did not feel the need of much of this world's goods." They were married on the 7th of April, 1858, he being but nineteen and she but sixteen. Their married life lasted only a few months, nearly three of which were spent at the Maryland Farm, in the shadow almost of Death. Martha was cook and housekeeper, and Anne aided as best she could, her chief duty being, as she writes, to serve as "outside guard," and to meet all who called, parley long enough on porch and steps for those inside to remove all suspicious things. If surprised while eating, the men would each seize his dishes and food, and then the table-cloth, quietly going upstairs, till the visitor had left. Her father demanded "constant watchfulness" on her part; others could help with the housework, and the men aided in turn. She sat on porch or at inside door, sewing or reading, with a constant lookout on the road, listening to the katydids and whippoorwills. " I used to enjoy watching the fireflies," she writes, " in the evening and looking at the lights and shadows on those fine old trees and the mountain ridge upon moonlight nights."

By the first week in August, then, there were assembled the brothers Owen, Oliver, and Watson Brown, William and Dauphin Thompson, Edwin and Barclay Coppoc, C. P. Tidd, J. G. Anderson, and Aaron D. Stevens; while close after came Albert Hazlett, William H. Leeman, and Steward Taylor. Captain Brown and one of his sons, usually Watson, were away a good deal of the time. Owen, at first, was on the road between Chambersburg, Hagerstown, and Harper's Ferry, the farm being in general charge of shipment, both men and freight. Kagi remained at Chambersburg, under the name of "John Henri." He boarded at the house of Mrs. Ritner, the widow of a famous ex-governor of Pennsylvania, known in State history as being a sturdy man of anti-slavery sentiment and the first organizer of free or public schools, also as an early friend and political associate of the "great commoner." Thaddeus Stevens, "Isaac Smith," and his sons also stopped at Mrs. Ritner's. Occasionally Tidd, Merriam, and one or two others stopped there ; Mrs. Virginia Cook, also most of the men, as they arrived, went to Bedford or Hagerstown. The colored men were chiefly booked at Chambersburg by Henry Watson, a trusted colored agent of the " underground railroad."

" The pictures of the men do not do them justice," writes Mrs. Adams; " Oliver Brown, Edwin Coppoc, J. G. Anderson, and John H. Kagi, whose faces are given as shaven, all had full beards at the Kennedy Farm, and were really handsome men. Cook had a mustache, and Leeman a mustache and imperial. They were all," writes Mrs. Brown Adams, "much better looking than the pictures convey an idea of." The Oliver Brown picture was taken before he went to Kansas in 1855, when he was but seventeen.

"All questions on religion or any other subject were very freely discussed by the men, and father always took an interested part in the discussions, and encouraged every one to express his opinion on any subject, no matter whether he agreed with him

or not.   Stevens had a copy of Paine's ' Age of
Reason ' there; that was read by some of the men and
discussed.   Father subscribed for the Baltimore *Sun*,
and Kagi used to send down a bundle of papers and
magazines from Chambersburg when the wagon went
up.   They had a manual of military tactics that was
studied a good deal.[1]   Cook obtained directions for
browning or coloring rifle-barrels in the arsenal at
Harper's Ferry, and the men spent a part of the time
in this work on their Sharpe's rifle-barrels, making
belts, pistol holsters, etc.   They also played checkers,
cards, and other games, and sang a deal of the time.
Stevens and Tidd were very fine singers, the former
having an excellent baritone.   They often sang ' All
the Old Folks Are Gone,' substituting ' All the Dear
Ones' for the first words; 'Faded Flowers,' and
' Nearer My God to Thee.' "

The live stock consisted of a mule and " Cuff," a
mongrel pup, but very vigilant and noisy when any
stranger or a neighbor appeared.   There was no cow
or chicken, and very little furniture.   Boxes were
used for seats, and the men slept on the floor, camp
fashion, in the large room upstairs.   A small log-
building across the road was later on used by several
of the men.   Some housekeeping articles had been
brought from North Elba, and a few purchased at
Chambersburg.   A stout, though small, wagon and
a mule was their only conveyance, and by its means
the 198 Sharpe's rifles and belongings, with 950 pikes,
shipped from Connecticut and Ohio to "Isaac Smith

---

[1] Forbes's " Patriotic Volunteer." W. H. Tinson, printer, 43–45
Centre street, New York.   1857.

& Sons " at Chambersburg, were brought from there *via* Hagerstown to the Farm. The section of Pennsylvania over which they passed was then a more dangerous one to them than the neighborhood of Harper's Ferry itself. " Hunting niggers " was a regular occupation at that date, and small, " covered " wagons were often objects of suspicion, as fugitive slaves were occasionally so transported, so as to enable the friendly Quaker, Dunker, or colored farmer along the route to declare they had not seen any fugitive. Provisions could be taken by drivers to these wagons, and no one appeared at all but the driver. Usually the movements of colored men were made on foot. Mrs. Adams describes an incident which occurred about the 19th or 20th of August.

" When Owen was bringing Shields Green down to the farm some men got after them and they were chased into the woods. While the pursuers went back for reinforcements, Owen took Green on his back and swam across the river. As they were traveling south, the slave-hunters did not look in that direction, naturally supposing Green to be a fugitive making his way to the North Star. After that Owen staid at the farm, for fear he might be recognized. The Captain with his son Watson or J. G. Anderson made the journeys to and from Chambers‑ burg to the Kennedy farm, rendered necessary by the removal of their freight, some of which remained at the Pennsylvania town, and was discovered there after the blow was struck. The Kansas recruit, whose arrival at Hagerstown, on the 14th of October, is elsewhere mentioned, was sent back therefrom to Chambersburg by Captain Brown and Kagi who had met him with instructions to ship this freight. He had the means to obtain a team for that purpose. He reached too late on the 15th to attend to any business, and the 16th, being Sunday, he kept close out of the town in the dwelling of a trusted colored man. The next the news of the attack came, and the Kansan made his way to Harrisburg and Cincinnati, thence returning East. He has since accounted, in his own mind, and from greater familiarity with the details of events, for the condition in which he was placed, by the possibility of Kagi's desire to save his life, for that heroic soul had no doubt of personal defeat. On a letter summoning him (the Kansas man), the 23d and the 25th of October was named as the beginning of operations. The dispatch of the 15th, however, may have had the effect of determining a sudden movement. A horse and mule with a small covered wagon formed their only quartermaster train. One would drive and the other ride, before or behind, so as to keep a lookout for suspicious movements. People along the road were beginning to be very inquisitive, often stopping them and asking questions as to their business. Kagi being well known in this section, having resided as a boy in the upper Shenandoah Valley with an uncle, and got himself into trouble too, by aiding a slave to escape, was compelled to remain most of the time at Chambersburg. The Browns, with " Jerry " Anderson and himself, first boarded at Sandy Springs."

While the strange, quiet life at the farm went on, John Brown was busy through the correspondence of Kagi from Chambersburg in bringing together his entire band. Several letters of inquiry about Realf had already reached me in Boston and Kansas, and I referred them to William Hutchinson, of Lawrence, Kansas, Thaddeus Hyatt, and Charles Yeaton, of New York. During my stay in Boston in the fall and winter of 1858, I outlined to James Redpath and Francis Jackson Merriam the plan of attack on slavery without, however, at the time naming Harper's Ferry to either of them. In a letter from Kansas to Merriam, during the spring of 1859, I told him of the point of assault, and advised him, if I now remember aright, that he ask Mr. Sanborn to put him in communication with Captain Brown.   Mr. Redpath never knew till the telegraph brought the startling news from Virginia on the 17th of October, 1859. C. W. Moffett, at Montaur, Iowa, and George B. Gill, then with his brother, Dr. Gill, at Springdale, and still suffering from the rheumatic fever he got during the slave rescue trip from Missouri to Iowa, were written to. Luke F. Parsons was also addressed, but it was learned, that he had withdrawn entirely under the advice of Col. Wm. A. Phillips, settling at Salina, Kansas. Another person addressed was Charles W. Leonhardt, a Polish gentlemen from Posen, Prussia.   The Slav "ski" had been dropped from his name when he first came to the United States about 1851 or '52.   He was a member of a well-to-do family of old Polish stock, who had been educated for a Prussian soldier and had served as lieutenant in some guard corps at Berlin.   He was very handsome, dark, with black silken hair, fine eyes, prominent features, and a soldierly aspect.   In 1848 he joined the German and Polish revolutionists, and soon after found his way with Dembrowski and the Polish army to Hungary, where he served against Russia.   He was made a staff officer with the rank of colonel, serving with Klapka, distinguishing himself for great gallantry. Leonhardt escaped to Turkey with his general, and came to America when Kossuth did.   He became fluent and eloquent too in his command of English. During the fall of 1856 Leonhardt arrived in Kansas. He wrote for German, American, and other papers, and commenced the study of law.   He was an enthusiastic anti-slavery man, active in helping fugitives,

became well known as a free state speaker, and identified himself with Montgomery in 1858 and '59. At
this time he became known to Kagi, and through him
to Captain Brown. It is certain that he agreed to
serve and was entrusted with the plan and intended
movement. Early in 1859 Leonhardt removed to Cincinnati and entered as a student and clerk the office of
Chase (Salmon P.) and Ball. During subsequent
months Colonel Leonhardt received several notes
from Kagi, as he himself informed me shortly
after the Harper's Ferry attack. Edmund Babb,
an editorial writer on the Cincinnati *Gazette*, now
dead I believe, had been in Kansas two or three
times during the troubles that followed the arrival of
Governor Geary. I recall his first arrival at Lawrence,
Kansas, in December or January, 1856–57; he was a
close friend of Leonhardt. From the first, as a Kansas correspondent, Babb was critical, censorious, and
carping, decrying the journalists and other men who
had been " in the breach" for the preceding two
years. He personally identified himself with the
views of Charles Robinson and George W. Brown,
editor of the *Herald of Freedom*, who was especially
hostile to all other Northern newspaper men, or "letter-
writers," as they were then termed. Mr. Babb was with
Governor Denver in 1858, when that Executive visited
southern Kansas to stop the Fort Scott Blake Little-
Montgomery troubles. His correspondence, though
written to a strong Republican paper, was always
hostile in tone to the resistant free-state men and
their actions. Leonhardt, a generous soul, was apt
to trust those about him. He gave me distinctly to
understand that he made a confidant of his editorial

friend, after receiving early in August letters from both "Isaac Smith" (John Brown), and John Henri (Kagi) from Chambersburg, Pa., informing him that the "mines" were ready, and the "workmen" needed. These were the terms agreed upon between Kagi and myself, as well as to Leonhardt and the others. Almost immediately after confidence was given to Mr. Babb the following letter was sent to John B. Floyd, secretary of war, who, it will be recalled, took no notice of the same. He was probably too much engaged himself in preparing for a coming civil war by a systematic distribution of United States arms and munitions from Northern to Southern Government arsenals, to take any notice of the Cincinnati warning. Here is the letter:

CINCINNATI, August 20, 1859.

SIR—I have lately received information of a movement of so great importance that I feel it my duty to impart it to you without delay. I have discovered the existence of a secret association, having for its object the liberation of the slaves at the South by a general insurrection. The leader of the movement is "old John Brown," late of Kansas. He has been in Canada during the winter, drilling the negroes there, and they are only waiting his word to start for the South to assist the slaves. They have one of their leading men (a white man) in an armory in Maryland,—where it is situated I have not been able to learn. As soon as everything is ready, those of their number who are in the Northern States and Canada are to come in small companies to their rendezvous, which is in the mountains of Virginia. They will pass down through Pennsylvania and Maryland, and enter Virginia at Harper's Ferry. Brown left the North about three or four weeks ago, and will arm the negroes and strike the blow in a few weeks ; so that whatever is done must be done at once. They have a large quantity of arms at their rendezvous, and are probably distributing them

already.   As I am not fully in their confidence, this is all the
information I can give you.   I dare not sign my name to this,
but trust that you will not disregard the warning on that
account.

What this letter contains is, in effect, what I understood from Colonel Leonhardt, that he told Edmund
Babb.   The latter then, and successfully too, labored
with the law student not to go further in the John
Brown movement.   At the time, inquiring in Cincinnati also among earnest anti-slavery friends as to Mr
Babb's standing on matters of direct help to fugitives,
etc., and with the reluctant belief, too, of his friend
Leonhardt behind me, I soon after made public the
allegation that Edmund Babb wrote the letter to Secretary Floyd.   I still hold that view, and repeat it
now as part of the narrative, without the slightest
feeling one way or the other relative to the person
whom I believe wrote the same.   Mr. Babb never
denied the authorship, though that is not, of course,
conclusive or affirmative.   Captain Brown knew
nothing whatever of this letter and of the peril it
indicated, until his attack and defeat caused its publication.

It is almost startling now, in view of the many
statements to relatives and friends, that were made
in letters written during this period by members of
the party, as well as the great public interest that
attended John Brown's movements, that there was
not an undue exposure and arrest of the whole party.
I have in my possession a score of letters from
Anderson, Leeman, and Taylor, very plainly setting
forth the general purpose.   Anderson, it is evident,
was better informed than most of them as to the

place and date. In visits after the war to London County and other parts of the valley of Virginia, I gathered many details of Cook's movements, as a writing-teacher, map and book agent, etc., and of his rather loose talk. He never concealed his identity with the Kansas free-state cause, and was quite open, at least among the Quaker and Dunker farmers of that section, in declaring that there might be "disturbance" or "active uneasiness" among the "darkies."

In one letter Leeman tells his mother he is in Virginia, engaged in a movement to attack slavery at Harper's Ferry. Steward Taylor was engaged in writing farewells to intimate friends and his brother, and letters found in the carpet-bag, captured in Virginia, shows that even Tidd had been very frank in his hints to his brother and sister as early as 1858. Some of these matters reached John Brown and aroused his anxiety, if not anger. The sharpest letter from his pen I have seen was

STEWARD TAYLOR.

written to Kagi, though not designed for him, and is as follows:

"WASHINGTON, MD., 11th August, 1859.

"J. HENRIE, ESQ.:

"DEAR SIR—I got along Tuesday evening all right; with letters, etc. I do hope all corresponding except on business *of the Co. will be droped for the present*. If every one must write some *girl;* or some other *extra* friend, telling or shoing

17

our location; and telling (*as some have done*) all about our matters; we might as well get the whole published *at once*, in the *New York Herald*. Any person is a *stupid fool* who expects his *friends* to keep *for him;* that which he cannot keep himself. All our friends have each got *their special friends;* and they *again have theirs;* and it would not be right to lay the burden of keeping a secret on any one; at the end of a long string. I could tell you of some reasons I have for feeling rather keenly on this point. I do not say this on account of any tale-bearing that I accuse any—you of. Three more hands came on from North Elba on Saturday last. Be sure to let me know of anything of interest.

"Yours in TRUTH."

There is another fact to account for the feeling this letter manifests. At this time there was evidently considerable and earnest discussion in progress at the Kennedy Farm. The men there were made acquainted with the fact that John Brown intended to first capture Harper's Ferry. Even his own sons did not regard it as a wise or practicable step. Mrs. Adams's memoranda gives warrant to this. It would seem as if the men had a desire to only repeat but on a larger scale the Missouri episode and run off a large body of fugitive slaves. The discussions were "warm." Even his sons Owen, Oliver, and Watson, unwillingly consented to the attack on Harper's Ferry. Kagi came down from Chambersburg to take part in that decision. Cook was also present from Harper's Ferry. Charles P. Tidd got so warm, writes Mrs. Adams, that he left the farm and went down to Cook's dwelling near Harper's Ferry "to let his wrath cool off." He remained away for over a week. Kagi, when telling me of the plan, had emphasized the intention of getting out of the place before the frightened people could get organized for an attack in force. This, as we know, was not done. Cook favored the capture quite forcibly, and made many visits to examine and report on the Government buildings, their contents, weak or strong points, habits of their watchmen, and other matters of value. Kagi, the adjutant-general, did not oppose Captain Brown. Stevens, Anderson, Leeman seem also to have been with their leader. Owen, Oliver, and Watson, all men of ability, Oliver especially, had visited the Ferry quite often, and saw readily what a deathtrap it might become. This brave, clean-souled lover and husband, young and ardent, with a beautiful girl-wife near him, closed the discussion, for the sons at least, with the remark: "We must not let our father die alone." The Captain had declared that he would go to the Ferry with the half dozen, who had signified that they, at least, would follow him anywhere and under all conditions. He also proposed to resign the command and follow Kagi, Stevens, or whoever the men might choose. On that question their vote was a united negative. The following letter was written two days before Frederick Douglass and Captain Brown had their last meeting in the old stone quarry, near Chambersburg.

Here it is:

HARPER'S FERRY, August 18, 1859.

DEAR SIR—We have all agreed to sustain your decisions, until you have *proved* incompetent, and many of us will adhere to your decisions so long as you will.   Your friend   OWEN SMITH.[1]

---

[1] For "Smith" we should, of course, read "Brown."

" The men generally," writes Mrs. Adams, " did not
know that the raid on the Government works was
part of the 'plan' until after they arrived at the
farm in the beginning of August. We knew," she
writes, " that he had planned the taking of Harper's
Ferry long before he or any member of his family
ever went to Kansas. It was father's original plan,
as we used to call it, to take Harper's Ferry at the
outset, to secure firea. ms to arm the slaves, and to
strike terror into the hearts of the slaveholders; then
to immediately start for the plantations, gather up
the negroes, and retreat to the mountains; send out
armed squads from there to gather more, and eventually to spread out his forces until the slaves would
come to them, or the slaveholders would surrender
them to gain peace. He expected . . . that if
they had intelligent white leaders that they would be
prevailed on to rise and secure their freedom without
revenging their wrongs, and with very little bloodshed. . . . He changed his plan as to the places
for commencing while in Kansas, and at one time
thought of going down to the vicinity of New Orleans
and working north from there." [1]

John Brown, Jr., begun active work "hiving the
bees," as his father told Frederick Douglass, at
Chambersburg, he wished him to do; after shipping
the precious freight of tools, etc., the Captain had

---

[1] This may account for a series of memoranda relative to Louisiana slave plantations, routes, etc., which, in Owen's peculiar
hand, are now in possession of Mrs. Ruth Thompson, the eldest
sister. It may also account for Kagi suggesting to me the trips I
made into the Indian Territory and even further south, reporting
observations to him by letter.

procured with such labored efforts, July and part of
August was taken up with this work.   The first trip
was made to Boston, August 10th, where he succeeded
in raising about two hundred dollars. He wrote Kagi
from Syracuse, under date of August 17th, that he
dined at Medford, with George L. Stearns, who said
as he left: "Tell friend Isaac that we have the *fullest
confidence* in his endeavor, whatever may be the
result."   John Brown, Jr., adds: "I have met with no
man on whom, I think, more implicit reliance can be
placed." Of other Boston friends whom he met or
had communication with, he says; "Our cause is
their cause in the fullest sense of the word."   On the
same day he sends a brief note from Rochester, announcing that Frederick Douglass had left *via* New
York and Philadelphia, to meet "friend Isaac."   He
also states "That other young friend went on from
here, to visit you yesterday," referring to the negro
Shields Green, whom Douglass had enlisted in his
place. John Brown, Jr., then went northward to
Canada West, taking with him a colored man, the
Rev. Mr. Loguen, of Syracuse, of whom he afterwards
wrote as "too fat" for real use. St. Catherine,
Hamilton, Chatham, London, Buxton, and Windsor
were all visited. Branches of the League, of which
mention has been made in chapter seven, were
organized. John's letters are full of information, but
all of them indicate delay on the part of the small
number relied upon. He was in Detroit, conferring
with De Baptiste, and at Sandusky and Cleveland,
urging others to work and assist. In a letter from
Sandusky to "John Henri" (Kagi), bearing date
August 27th, John, Jr., writes of "a coppersmith," sup-

posed to be Reynolds, who was at the Chatham Convention and one of the sharpest of would be fighters, saying, " I think he is one of those men who must be obtained if possible," but he had been out of work, and now " has a job, which he cannot leave until finished." At another man's " an association " was formed, " the business of which is to hunt up good workmen and raise the means among themselves to send them forward." None of these things materialized. John, Jr. believed that "they will take hold and do something." At Chatham " I met a hearty response," he writes and that's all, except that the brave, modest, reticent O. P. Anderson, paid his own way and reported for duty shortly after. Robinson Alexander, also a member of the Chatham Convention, "thinks," writes John, " he can now close out by 1st November, and in the meantime to prove his devotion will furnish means to help on two or three himself." But if he did that, they fell by the wayside somewhere. Mr. Holden, also a member of the convention, had "gone to the Frazier River," British Columbia. Even Richard Richardson, the fugitive, who had been helped out of Missouri, and was afterward one of the men " at school" in Iowa and a member of the Chatham Convention, was "away harvesting." All, indeed, appeared to be otherwise busy or to misapprehend. Canada, and the freed refugees therein, proved a broken reed, indeed. Harriet Tubman, "the General of us all," fell sick and could not travel. Frederick Douglass's refusal to finally join the enterprise has never, to me, appeared to warrant adverse criticism. His position before the land justified, in 1859, a choice between both conditions, nor failed of endeavor. Certainly he was doing a large work, compelling, by his intellectual power and eloquence, a fast-growing recognition for the oppressed race, of which he was an able leader. He might well weigh, as he did, the question of casting this upon the "hazard of a die." The "logic of events" at least has justified Frederick Douglass, and his faithful services must silence critics ; those at least who also had the opportunity and did not follow John Brown. On the 2d of September John, Jr., writes again to "John Henri," dating from his home at West Andover.

In this he mentions sending letters to Canada points, and says that "friend L—y (Leary), of Ob—(erlin) will be on hand soon." He brought a recruit, too, in the person of John A. Copeland "C. H. L—n (Langston) will do all he can, but his health is bad." Another one has "married a wife and cannot come." So had Oliver Brown, but he had never been a slave. John, Jr., inquires as to the "frame of mind" in which the Rochester friend (Frederick Douglass) returned. On the 8th of September, another letter reaches Kagi, in which John, Jr., says: "I had supposed you would not think it best to commence operations opening the coal banks before spring, unless circumstances should make important." This misapprehension, if such it was, seems to have been the cause of delays on the Canada side. I do not myself believe that beyond a dozen in all, there was any real expectation of competent recruits arriving. Mrs. Adams's statements confirm this view.

Reasons grew for pressing to a conclusion. Disbandment was not hinted at even ; a forward movement was therefore necessary. Life in the little farm-house went on, becoming almost unbearable at times ; the men, who, in spite of their devotion, good humor, and discipline, necessarily feeling the vigorous caution and confinement demanded by it　Their singing was a great relief when it could be indulged; Stevens and Tidd especially having fine voices, the former being an excellent baritone of superior timbre　Among their favorite songs were "All the Dear Folk have Gone," "Faded Flowers" and "Nearer My God to Thee." No spiritual "seances" were held at Kennedy's, at least while Anne and Martha were there. John Brown was always good to his neighbors, and his acts of personal kindness and charity, as well as his skill as veterinarian with sick cattle and horses, are remembered to this day, and have become parts of the neighborhood traditions. At the "Ferry," he and his sons became favorites, and were noted for their courtesy and willingness to oblige. Owen especially used to spend hours in talking with the railroad men and others, learning thereby, without arousing suspicions, of the people, topography, the best and worst slaveholders, and of the "tools," etc., in the United States Arsenal. Cook at this time was constantly on the move, selling maps through the country as an excuse. The people around the Kennedy Farm were mainly of the Dunker sect or church, and of a division therein which were non-resistant and did not believe in slavery. Captain Brown used to go nearly every evening to a little church close by, and join with these quaint people in their religious exercises, often exhorting or preaching to the small congregation. Mrs. Adams says of the result of one of these occasions:

"There was a family of poor people who lived near by who had rented the garden on the Kennedy place, directly back of the house. The little barefooted woman and four small children (she carried the youngest in her arms) would all come trooping over to the garden at all hours of the day, and, at times, several times during the day. Nearly always they would come up the steps and into the house and stay a short time. This made it very troublesome for us, compelling the men, when she came in sight at meal times, to gather up the victuals and table-cloth and quietly disappear up stairs. One Saturday father and I went to a religious (Dunker) meeting that was held in a grove near the schoolhouse, and the folks left at home forgot to keep a sharp lookout for Mrs. Heiffmaster, and she stole into the house before they saw her, and saw Shields Green (that must have been in September), Barclay Coppoc, and Will Leeman. And another time after that she saw C. P. Tidd standing on the porch. She thought these strangers were running off negroes to the North. I used to give her everything she wanted or asked for to keep her on good terms, but we were in constant fear that she was either a spy or would betray us. It was like standing on a powder magazine, after a slow match had been lighted."

The Pennsylvania border was more suspicious. It floated slowly over to Maryland, and rumors began to be heard of possible domiciliary visits, of calls by the sheriff, and other symptoms of distrust. They did not crystallize into action, but it is most probable that an exposure of some sort must have soon occurred, if Captain Brown had not himself made the same. The men themselves were overstrained. The exaltation they were feeling would have broken and fallen down. "One day, while we were alone in the yard," writes Mrs. Adams, "Owen remarked as he looked up at the house—'If we succeed, some day there will be a United States flag over this house—if we do not, it will be considered a den of land pirates and thieves.' "

On the 29th of September, the two young and brave women left the Kennedy Farm for North Elba. Martha's babe was born, and died five months after, and in a few days she parted with life also. Oliver escorted them to Troy, and then returned direct. Virginia Cook, the wife of John Edwin, spent one night, the 13th of October, on her way from her home to Chambersburg, where she was left with her babe almost destitute for some days. When Anne and Martha, with Oliver, were on their way to Chambersburg to take the train and ere they had left Maryland, a constable, or deputy sheriff, rode up and compelled Oliver to stop, while he searched the little wagon. When the train reached Harrisburg, the three young folks met their father and Kagi, returning from Philadelphia, and there in the depot bade them farewell,— the last one as it proved. It was difficult to make any of the Brown family believe their father's plan was to prove a failure. When the startling news reached them at North Elba, and it came in even worse than the actual shape, they could not be induced to give it full credence.

The last of the party closed in. Osborne P. Anderson arrived at Chambersburg on the 16th, and reached the farm on the 25th of September. Dangerfield Newby, who had been living in a border town of Pennsylvania, was on hand, Captain Brown, Kagi, Leary, and Copeland alone were absent. The two last arrived on the 2d of October. Merriam reported at Philadelphia on the 10th or 11th of the last month, met Captain Brown there, and, after conference, left immediately for Baltimore, where he purchased a large amount of primers and caps. The dealer testified afterwards that he supposed the purchase to be for some filibustering expedition. On the 15th, Merriam arrived at the Kennedy Farm. From Harper's Ferry he sent the following inexplicable dispatch:

HARPER'S FERRY, Oct. 15, 1859.

LEWIS HAYDEN,[1] Secretary of State's Office, State House, Boston.

Orders disobeyed. Conditions broken. Pay S. immediately balance of my money. Allow no further expenses. Recall money advanced, if not sent.

FRANCIS J. MERRIAM.

The meaning of this dispatch is unknown. It can only be conjecturally understood. There is not the slightest ground for supposing it to relate to any dissatisfaction with Captain Brown. Merriam brought with him to the point at which he first met John Brown several hundred dollars in gold, and transferred to him in large part what he did not expend at Baltimore on the 13th or 14th of October in the purchase of 40,000 Sharpe's rifle primers and percussion caps, etc. It is evident, therefore, that the message could not have referred to affairs at the Maryland rendezvous, and must have related to some undue gossip or complaints made in Boston. The five men of color that Lewis Hayden states agreed to, but did not go to join John Brown, were to have traveled on funds advanced by Frank J. Merriam, who had drawn $600 from his uncle before he left Boston, leaving part of it with Mr. Hayden. My information,

---

[1] A well-known colored man, of Boston, now deceased, himself a fugitive slave.

though not quite verified, goes to show that he gave and spent for Captain Brown and the enterprise about $400 in all; fortunately retaining some for himself, thus enabling him to make his escape from Chambersburg north to Canada, after the defeat.

Frank B. Sanborn (on the authority of Hayden himself), in an *Atlantic* article, December, 1875 (" The Virginia Campaign of John Brown "), states that Lewis Hayden was informed of the movement by John Brown, Jr., after conferring with Mr. Stearns and Dr. House in June, 1859, of his father's purposes and plans. The *Atlantic* article says:

" Mr. Hayden entered warmly into the work, and undertook to enlist a few colored men in Massachusetts. . . . According- ing to his recollections he did enlist six such recruits . . . only one . . . reached Harper's Ferry, before the attack, and even he took no part in the fight." In a footnote to the same article, it is said, on Mr. Hayden's authority, that " John Anderson was a different person from Osborne (Perry) Ander- son; that he was the only one of the colored recruits from Massachusetts who reached Harper's Ferry, but that he took no part in the fight and returned to Boston, where he has since died." [I have been unable to find the slightest trace of such a person.—R. J. H.]

This much is certain, that with the arrival of the Boston recruit, Francis J. Merriam, the tally was closed, the list put away, the die was cast! Within thirty hours, at sunrise of the 17th of October, 1859, a " shot was fired " that, like that of the embattled farmers of Concord and Lexington, eighty-two years before, led, too, by the grandfather of the Reverend Theodore Parker, one of John Brown's warmest friends, " echoed round the world."

CHAPTER X.

"THE ORDER OF MARCH."

Gathering the last recruits—Date of assault—Was it changed?—Arrivals from Canada—Ohio – The young Bostonian—A colored man who cannot be traced—Lewis Hayden and John Brown, Jr., as recruiting agents—The Kansas notification—Night rides from Chambersburg to Hagerstown—The last Sunday services at the farm—A council of war—Assignments to duty—Down the moonlit road.

THE movement upon Harper's Ferry begun at eight in the evening of the 16th of October, that being the hour at which the little band assumed their weapons and left the Kennedy farm. John Brown returned from Philadelphia *via* Hagerstown, during the night of the 14th, reaching the farm early in the forenoon of the 15th. All who participated in the attack answered the roll call. It remains uncertain whether the actual blow was suddenly decided on or not. Dr. A. M. Ross, of Toronto, Canada, states that he was notified that the blow was to be delivered between the 15th and 27th, and, according to a previous understanding, the doctor went to Richmond and was in that city when the startling news arrived. John Brown, Jr., evidently did not anticipate as early a movement. His letters from Canada, found in the captured car-

pet-bag, showed that there were colored men from
Canada and Ohio who expected and were preparing
to join during the last week of October.   One hand
from Kansas reported to Captain Brown himself,
between the 10th and 14th, while the latter was
absent from the farm.   This Western man was sent
to Hagerstown and Chambersburg, receiving a distinct impression that a week would elapse before
positive action.   He managed to remain from the
15th to the 18th in the neighborhood; and then, finding it impossible to assist in any direct way the
party headed by Owen Brown who had escaped into
the laurel hills of southern Pennsylvania, successfully
made his way to Cincinnati, returning immediately
to the border counties of Pennsylvania.   As a newspaper correspondent, being recognized or suspected
of being, moreover, a "Kansas" man—not a safe
designation in those days,—he soon left for Harrisburg and Cleveland, and finally went to Boston.

Details multiply to show that "Isaac Smith's"
appearance, with the presence of Owen Brown and
his brothers and of Jerry Anderson, in such a quiet
neighborhood and upon so small a farm, excited
active suspicions among those who were always alert
to guard the interests of slavery.   The presence of a
colored man at the farm-house, known as it was,
according to Dauphin Thompson's letter, could but
excite alarm.   The Pennsylvania border was a more
dangerous neighborhood than that of Maryland.
The "peculiar institution," as Ralph Waldo Emerson
once wittily termed chattelism, was never without
assets, however, when assault was threatened or dangers feared.   A large draft of alarm was always ready

for discount. The type of Pennsylvanians by whom
Cook and Hazlett were afterwards done to death,
were as "mediumistic" as the border slaves and free
people of color. In Maryland, county peace officers
were somewhat anxiously inquiring about "Isaac
Smith & Sons," a mining firm that did not mine—
cattle buyers who were not trading in stock. Annie
Brown (Mrs. Adams), whom her father called his
"little watch-dog," because so vigilant when at the
farm, recalls in her California home that, when she and
Isabel, her brother Watson's wife, left the Kennedy
farm for North Elba, nearly a month before the outbreak, that persons were already prying about the
place. James Redpath [1] puts the expected date as
the 24th of October. He was in communication with
Lewis Hayden and Francis J. Merriam, and had, as
he wrote, all the current data at command. During
August, I received at Leavenworth, from J. H. Kagi,
a letter referring to a proposed "expedition" to
"Central America," being about to start later in
October. From "Isaac Smith" there came to me
in the middle of September, bearing date at Chambersburg, a brief note by which I was notified that
"mining operations" would begin in October, and
that if I still wished to enter upon the speculation,
I should report by the middle of that month at
a point named. Under the tense excitement of
that period, I destroyed this note, and have ever
since been apologizing to myself for the only bit of
fear or evasion as to my own feelings or purposes,
of which I was in any way guilty during all the fierce

---

[1] "Public Life of Capt. John Brown," Boston, 1860.

days that followed the 17th of October, 1859. In
subsequent conversation with Charles Plummer Tidd,
while in northern Ohio, and later with Barclay Coppoc in Boston and at North Elba, the following July,
I had my view strengthened into conviction, that the
final order to move was based upon a sudden emergency. Osborne Perry Anderson's graphic and in-

valuable little monograph "A
Voice From Harper's Ferry,"
must after all be the best authority. Summarizing his testimony, he states that, after his
own arrival at Chambersburg,
Pa., from Chatham, Canada, on
the 16th of September, 1859,
there was a council or conference held, presumably at Mrs.
Ritter's, the boarding-house
where "Isaac Smith" and "John
Henri" always put up, and
where boarded also the Car-
penters (the two Coppocs),

OSBORNE PERRY ANDERSON.   George Plummer (Tidd),Watson
and Oliver "Smith" (Brown),
and to which Mrs.Virginia Cook, the young wife of that
abolition partisan, went on the night of the 12th or 13th
of October, from Martinsburg, *via* Hagerstown, Md.
The colored hands were usually accommodated, it is
presumed, by men of that race, like Henry Watson,
the barber. There were others who tilled small
areas of land and worked "round," that could also
be depended upon. Mr. Anderson, in conversation at
Washington during 1870, estimated that there were at

least one hundred and fifty actively informed slaves. He spent eight days at Chambersburg. On the 20th and 24th, conferences as before referred to, were held, and upon the latter date Anderson started afoot for Middletown, a village on the borders of Maryland and Pennsylvania. He arrived there at dark and found Captain Brown awaiting him in a one-horse covered wagon he used. The underground railway work of that border was usually done in such vehicles, when "Walker's express" was not employed. It was this little experience that helped Anderson to escape. If the party which Owen Brown afterwards led, had taken the same general direction northwards that Anderson did, probably all of them would have got away. Cook's anxiety to get news of his young wife, then at Chambersburg, and Owen Brown's knowledge of western Pennsylvania, led to the route, west and south of the range—the road watched by the professional kidnappers and fugitive slave-hunters of those days—which they finally followed. Hazlitt's divergence at Chambersburg from the north star line, also led to his arrest at Carlisle. But to return to Anderson's experiences.

After meeting Captain Brown on the outskirts of Middletown, they drove at once to the Kennedy Farm, arriving there about daybreak. As a necessary precaution against surprise all the four colored men who went from the North to the farm and ferry made the journey from Chambersburg to the Kennedy Farm in the night. Anderson says: "A more earnest, fearless, determined company of men it would be difficult to get together." On the 12th of October John A. Copeland and Lewis Sherrard

18

Leary, colored men from Oberlin, Ohio, arrived at Chambersburg. Captain Brown on the 10th or 11th of October was in Philadelphia, meeting F. J. Merriam there, and sending him over to Baltimore to buy gun caps, rifle primers, tools, etc. Why these were not purchased in Philadelphia has never been explained. The large quantity of 40,000 caps Merriam purchased aroused suspicion of a filibustering movement and almost caused his arrest. Some days before, Merriam, who had learned from me a few months previously of the proposed attack on slavery, was met on a Boston street and asked by Lewis Hayden for $600, which was furnished, Merriam well knowing it was intended for " secret service " purposes. Lewis Hayden always said one " John Anderson," a colored man, went from Boston and never returned. Mr. Sanborn in his " Life and Letters of John Brown " gives this name. But I have never been able to trace any such person, and if John Anderson did go to join John Brown, he must have been slain on the road after the fight commenced.

FRANCIS JACKSON MERRIAM.

The party who assembled then in council at the Kennedy Farm after the Captain returned from the little Winebrenarian (Dunker) chapel and the evening prayer-meeting therein, consisted of John Brown and his three sons—Owen, Oliver, and Watson; William and Adolphus Dauphin Thompson, brothers of Henry, husband of the Captain's eldest daughter Ruth; John Henri Kagi, Aaron Dwight Stevens, John Edwin Cook, who had come the same day from Martinsburg, Maryland, where he had lived for about fifteen months with his wife's people ; William H. Leeman, George Plummer Tidd, Jeremiah G. Anderson, Albert Hazlett, Steward Taylor, Edwin and Barclay Coppoc, and Francis J. Merriam, white men, and Osborne P. Anderson, William Copeland, Lewis Sherrard Leary, and Shields Green (known usually as "the Emperor"), colored. No mention is made as being at the farm of Dangerfield Newby, the Virginian free man, who fought and died at Harper's Ferry, in the evident hope of making his wife free. She was a slave woman who lived about thirty miles south of Harper's Ferry and was then, as letters show, about to be sold to a Louisiana trader. She was subsequently so sold and still lives, I learn, in the Pelican State, made free by the civil war.

JOHN EDWIN COOK.

Of the twenty-one followers assembled in the Kennedy dwelling, thirteen of them, including the Browns and William Thompson, had all seen service in Kansas. Of the younger whites—Dauphin Thompson was a North Elba recruit, the brothers Coppoc were from Iowa, and Francis Jackson Merriam, a grandson of the president of the American Anti-Slavery Society, came naturally with his hostility to chattel bondage,

though his feeling did not take the non-resistance form of Francis Jackson. Adolphus Dauphin
Thompson and Barclay Coppoc were both in their
twentieth year; Merriam was not over twenty-one.
The unmarried men were besides these three young-
sters,—Owen Brown, Kagi, Stevens, Tidd, Leeman,
Edwin Coppoc, Taylor, " Jerry " Anderson, his colored
namesake, Osborne, and Shields Green—twelve out
of the twenty-two. During the summer months the
wives of Oliver and Watson Brown had both been at
the Kennedy Farm on short visits. Virginia, the
wife of Captain Cook, was then at Chambersburg,
Pa., waiting with her young child for the news of an
event whose nature she but half suspected. The
wives of the Browns were all in North Elba. The
roads by which the little band of heroic emancipators
had traveled to reach Harper's Ferry that fateful
Sunday evening, were indeed sufficiently defined.
Five through slavery and fugitive days; thirteen in
the miry smoke and red flame of Kansas aggressions;
the remaining five of the party had been trained by
the seeing of events and through their associations.
Only one recruit came direct from Canada. There
was also one unknown colored Virginian left at the
Maryland farm to assist Owen's party in moving
goods.

That suspicions were aroused became even more
evident on the Pennsylvania border, where the
profit of fugitive slave-hunting had trained its
human bloodhounds, than it was in the sleepy
fields of Maryland. A letter of Dauphin Thompson to his North Elba home gives a reason for
this:

"PARTS UNKNOWN, September 4, 1859.

" DEAR BROTHER AND SISTER—   . . .   I am sitting in the door of an old log-house, in which we have stored some of our freight. It is about fifty rods from the house in which we live. We are all well and in capital spirits. The girls have gone to meeting this morning, and some of the boys. They call the meeting a bush-meeting. They have meetings in a grove during the daytime, and at evening in the house. The meeting is conducted by a sect, called Winebrenarians. They are opposed to slavery, so much so that they will not have anything to do with the institution in the least. If a strange minister comes along, they will not let him preach until they find out whether he is in favor of slavery or not.

" We have to be very careful here how we act in everything. We have one colored man in our company who has been seen by a neighbor woman, but she thinks he is a fugitive, and that we are trying to help him to his freedom. She has promised to keep dark about it, and we are going to trust her honesty. It is rather a bad job, but it can't be helped, as we are not ready to begin operations yet. Probably you will hear from us about the 1st of October, if not before. The girls will be sent home before we begin operations. I have been over into Virginia a number of times since I have been here. There are some of the best farms in Jefferson County I ever saw. There are two nephews of George Washington over there. They own large farms and lots of slaves." He then inquires after home and neighborhood affairs, and writes: " I suppose the folk think we are a set of fools, but they will find out we know what we are about."

It is also known that Captain Brown had learned
of orders to remove a large number of arms at an
early day from the Harper's Ferry Arsenal to other
points, chiefly in the South. Indeed, the removal had
already begun, for when on the 17th the citizens
began to arm themselves, it was United States muskets they obtained from boxes stored in the town
previous to transfer elsewhere. There can be little
question to a student of the period, that the removal
of which Captain Brown heard, was commenced in
pursuance of the Secretary of War's policy of loading
the Southern arsenals with the military property of
the general Government.[1]

Mr. O. P. Anderson's narrative continues by saying
that a tried friend (Dangerfield Newby) had given
information of the state of public feeling without, and
of the projected search. Captain Brown, therefore,

---

[1] Valuable documents of an historical character were obtained
during the Civil War, by army seizures, etc. Among such finds
were a number of letters taken from Jefferson Davis's plantation
house in Mississippi, bearing dates from 1851 to 1856. They were
from various Southern Senators; all of them urged secession if the
new Northern party should prove successful, and several demanded
of Mr. Davis, as Secretary of War, the replacing of old arms in
Southern arsenals with the best at command of the War Department. Senators Butler (South Carolina) and Mason (Virginia)
were especially earnest. The latter, under date of September 30,
1856, writes Davis, after urging the supply of arms as indicated,
that " in the event of Frémont's election the South should proceed
at once to immediate, absolute, and eternal separation," adding,
that " I am a candidate for the first halter." It were a pity that
he did not get it also. This, and other letters, first appeared in
print in *The Republic* (May, 1876), a political monthly then issued
at Washington, of which I was one of the editors.

concluded to strike the blow immediately, and not, as at first intended, to await certain reinforcements from the North and East, which would have been in Maryland within from one to three weeks. Captain Brown was not seconded in another quarter as he expected at the time of the action, but could the fears of the neighbors have been allayed for a few days, the disappointment in that respect would not have had much weight. It is not of much moment to speculate as to the disappointment Anderson refers to, but it seems most probable that the reference is made both to the failure to make connection with the Canada colored recruits, who had been expected, and to the declination of Frederick Douglass to participate in the Harper's Ferry movement, as there is some evidence that other colored men made their possible activity contingent on that of their leading orator and statesman.

"On Sunday," writes Anderson, "October the 16th, Captain Brown arose earlier than usual and called his men to worship. He read a chapter from the Bible applicable to the condition of the slaves and our duty as their brethren, and then offered up a fervent prayer to God to assist us in the liberation of the bondmen." After breakfast the Captain called the roll, a sentinel was posted outside the door to warn if any one should approach, and at 10 o'clock the council assembled ; Osborne P. Anderson was appointed to the chair. John Brown preserved the moral logic of his attitude by putting this competent colored man into the presiding place. After the council adjourned the constitution was read for the benefit of the four who had not before heard it and the necessary obligations

taken. Mr. Anderson used the word "oaths," but
the records show that it was a parole of honor which
was taken at Chatham when the "Constitution" was
adopted. Men who were to hold military positions
in the organization, and who had not received commissions before then, had them filled out by J. H. Kagi,
and gave the required promises of obedience. In the
afternoon eleven orders were made out by the Captain and were afterwards carried out in all particulars by the officers and men. They were as follows:

1. Captain Owen Brown, F. J. Merriam, and Barclay Coppoc to remain at the old house as sentinels, to
guard the arms and effects till morning, when they
would be joined by some of the men from the Ferry with
teams to move all arms and other things to the old
school-house in Virginia, located about three-quarters
of a mile from Harper's Ferry. It is a place selected
beforehand by the Captain.

2. All hands to make as little noise as possible
going to the Ferry, so as not to attract attention till
we could get to the bridge; and to keep all arms
secreted, so as not to be detected if met by any one.

3. The men to walk in couples, at some distance
apart; and should any one overtake us, stop and detain him until the rest of our comrades were out of
the road. The same course to be pursued if we are
met by any one.

4. That Captains Charles P. Tidd, and John E.
Cook walk ahead of the wagon in which Captain
Brown rides to the Ferry. They are to tear down the
telegraph wires on the Maryland side along the railroad; and to do the same on the Virginia side, after
the town should be captured.

5. Captains John H. Kagi and A. D. Stevens to take the watchman at the Ferry bridge a prisoner when the party get there, and to detain him until the engine-house upon the Government grounds shall be taken.

6. Captain Watson Brown and Steward Taylor to take positions at the Potomac (covered) bridge, and hold it till morning. They to stand on opposite sides, a rod apart, and if any one entered the bridge, they are to let him get in between them. In that case, pikes to be used, not Sharpe's rifles, unless they are offered much resistance, and they meet with refusal to surrender.

7. Captains Oliver Brown and William Thompson are to execute a similar order at the Shenandoah bridge; remaining until morning.

8. Lieutenant Jeremiah Anderson and Adolphus (Dauphin) Thompson to occupy the engine-house at first, with the watchman from the bridge and the watchman belonging to the engine-house yard as prisoners, until the one on the opposite side of the street and the rifle factory be taken, after which they would be reinforced, to hold that place with the prisoners.

9. Lieutenant Albert Hazlett and Private Edwin Coppoc to hold the armory opposite the engine-house after it has been taken; remaining through the night and until morning, when arrangements would be different.

10. That John H. Kagi, Adjutant-General, and John A Copeland (colored), take positions at the rifle factory through the night, and hold it until further orders.

12. That Capt. A. D. Stevens proceed to the country with his men, and after taking certain parties prisoners, bring them to the Ferry. In the case of Col. Lewis Washington, who had certain arms in his possession, he must, after being secured as a prisoner, deliver them into the hands of Osborne P. Anderson. Anderson being a colored man, and colored men being only *things* in the South, it is proper that the South be taught a lesson upon this point.

Preparation had been made for the means of firing the bridges, buildings, etc., by tow balls steeped in oil. The making of these was probably due to Annie and Isabel Brown before they left. These articles were taken to the Ferry, but no use was made of them. It was the intention, evidently, to set fire before leaving that place for the mountains.

Captain Brown did not omit, it is said by a former neighbor of the Kennedy farm party, to proceed to the nearby Dunker or "Winebrenarian" Church, and conduct there the services in which he had participated or led during the preceding months of his life in Maryland. But that is doubtful, as the order to move was made so early. When all was ready, Captain Brown then gave his final charge to the men, in which he said among other things, as Anderson reports:

"And now, gentlemen, let me impress this one thing upon your minds. You all know how dear life is to you, and how dear your life is to your friends. And in remembering that consider that the lives of others are as dear to them as yours are to you. Do not therefore, take the life of any one if you can possibly avoid it; but if it is necessary to take life in order to save your own, then make sure work of it."

The several parties had been chosen. John H. Kagi being second in command, the capture and holding of Hall's Rifle Works was naturally assigned to him. To Aaron D. Stevens was assigned the capture of several prominent slaveholders. He selected for his assistants Charles P. Tidd, John E. Cook, Osborne P. Anderson, Lewis Sherrard Leary, and John A. Copeland. Stevens was to send over from Virginia to Owen Brown at the farm a wagon with negro help for the removal of the pikes and guns, etc., stored at the farm. Captain Cook had several times traveled thus along the Valley turnpike and collected information needed. He thus learned of Lewis Washington's possession of the historic arms of Frederick the Great and General Lafayette that were afterwards captured. [1]

DAUPHIN ADOLPHUS THOMPSON.

It would hardly be necessary to repeat the startling story, except to bring out the actions of the party as a whole and as individuals. One thing must be realized from the first moment: not one faltered, quailed, or failed. From the two country lads, who had not yet crossed the path of manhood, Dauphin Thompson and Barclay Coppoc, neither of whom had

---

[1] The Lafayette pistol or pistols were afterwards restored by Owen Brown; the sword was retaken from Captain Brown.

reached his twentieth year, to Kagi and Stevens and Cook—the three whose experience of the world had most assuredly given some mental maturity, fitted them to understand as they did, the desperate chances of their startling venture—all the associates at Harper's Ferry failed not in obedience, courage, and combat, to their veteran and idealistic leader. From the outset, intelligently and intellectually—sentimentally and by feeling—new recruits as well as long-time comrades, all knew or felt that the attack on slavery they were about making, whether lost or won at the moment, would assuredly "pay," and it did. John Brown was right when he said so in the jail and on the road to the sacred gallows.

CHAPTER XI.

RENDING THE FORTRESS WALL.

*The first blow—An Irish watchman—Twenty-two cap-
ture the United States arsenal, armory, and works
—Stopping the train a fatal blunder—The town
people's fright—Sunrise brings aid—Capture of
Lewis Washington—Attack on the little band—
Beginning of the fateful end—The fight was on—
Two thousand held at bay by seventeen men—Bar-
barities and brutalities — Courage and calmness
—The United States marines—The Virginians' own
verdict on their own acts—Where the roads ended.*

DOWN the still road, dim white in the moonlight,
and amid the chill October night, went the little
band, silent and sober. Tidd and Anderson stated
afterward that they saw no sign and felt none themselves of any special excitement. Cook and Tidd
were so busily engaged in cutting the telegraph wires
along the road that they had no time to think. Near
the Maryland entrance of the Ferry bridge the wagon
stopped and the men assumed their carbines and
cartridge-boxes. No one had seen them on the road.

John H. Kagi and Aaron D. Stevens led the march
and were first to cross the bridge. Williams, the
watchman there, was captured without disturbance.
Captain Brown with the wagon and the balance of

the force went on and into the **Arsenal grounds.**
Watson Brown and Stewart Taylor were placed as
guards, and the engine-house was then occupied. The
watchman in the armory began to shout and would
not open the door, which was forced. The two prisoners were left under charge of Jeremiah G. Anderson
and the younger Thompson. Stevens then moved
to take possession of the armory. Kagi and Copeland

were left at Hall's rifle works,
and Albert Hazlett and Edwin
Coppoc held the United States
armory. William Thompson and
Oliver Brown held possession of
the Shenandoah railroad bridge.
Up to this point not a shot had
been fired. Returning to the
engine-house, where Captain
Brown had already stationed
himself, Stevens with Cook, Tidd,
Leary, Shields Green, and O. P.
Anderson, left to secure Lewis
Washington, Terence Burns, and
Alstedt as hostages, with their
slave men as recruits, according

JOHN HENRI KAGI.

to the arranged programme. The capture of the place
was effected before eleven on the 16th. At midnight
the relief watchman for the railroad bridge came
down. He may be left to tell his own story of
events. The first shot fired was at that watchman.[1]

---

[1] Patrick Higgins is a watchman of the Baltimore and Ohio
Railroad, who is still at Harper's Ferry, where, in the employ of
that corporation, he has resided for nearly forty years, recently
gave to Dr. Thomas Featherstonhaugh, of Washington (to whom

On the night of the 16th of October, 1859, Patrick
Higgins went to his post at midnight, waiting as
usual at the end of the bridge till the half hour
came in order to pull the indicator, as required by
the railroad regulations.   He noticed that the lamps
at each end of the bridge were out, and thought
it strange but did not light them.   A little alarmed,
with a lantern in his hand he passed the watch-house
looking for the other man, Bill Williams.   When
nearly over the bridge he was suddenly halted by two
men; keeping on, however, he was seized by one
(Oliver Brown, he afterwards learned) who, grasping
his arm, told him to "come along."   Higgins walked
on, remonstrating quietly, till he saw by the light of
his lantern a half dozen pikes leaning against the
bridge rail.   Terrified at this, he struck Oliver a
savage blow on the right ear and knocked him back
to the rail.   Then he ran towards the Foulke's Hotel,
while William Thompson, the other guard, immediately fired upon him, sending the bullet from his Sharpe's
rifle through Higgins's hat, and grazed his scalp, leaving a mark which is still visible.   This shot and Higgins's story gave the alarm to the Hotel people, but
as to the party in possession, nothing was known.   The
barkeeper ventured out from curiosity soon after and
was captured.   Captain Brown exchanged this man
in the morning for breakfast for forty men, which

I am greatly indebted for detailed local and other important information), his recollection of the capture of that place by John
Brown and his men.   Mr. Higgins is a man of recognized probity
and character.   His courage and manliness was conspicuously
manifested during the remarkable scenes of which he speaks
clearly and with so much interest.

number included his prisoners. The careful Virginians afterwards deducted from such remnants of
the Captain's property, as could be recovered from the
ravenous hands of enemies or relic-hunters and sold
for his benefit, the price of these meals. After his
escape, Higgins went to Williams's house, and found
that he had not returned and was a prisoner. The
train was in when the watchman got back. Accompanying the conductor (Mr. Phelps), they went to
the armory grounds, saying loudly "What's the matter,
boys?" The answer was:

"We want liberty; the grounds, bridge, and town
are in our hands."

By this time the passengers were swarming in the
depot and much excited; no one knew, and the watchman could not tell them, what was the matter. It was
generally thought to be a strike of dissatisfied men,
working on a government dam. As the dawn broke,
John Brown told Mr. Phelps to "proceed, that he had
no intention of interfering with the comfort of passengers or hindering the United States mails." Captain Brown was apparently unarmed, and with cool
deliberation and as much unconcern as if carrying on
an ordinary business proceeding, walked with the
conductor across the bridge. He waited with Mr.
Phelps till the signal to proceed was given, and then
walked back over it alone.

The four-horse wagon load of Colonel Washington's
slaves, etc., had already been brought in. Just as the
train was leaving, Cook recrossed the bridge, with a
companion (a colored man) driving the wagon, to
the school-house and Kennedy farm. Heyward
Shepherd, the Hotel porter, was shot soon after.

Higgins aided in his removal to the depot, where the watchman remained with the dying man. Early in the forenoon, Heyward asked for water, and Higgins started to the pump to get some. On starting to return William Thompson halted him and asked for a drink. The bucket was handed him. After drinking he asked Higgins to go to the bridge and give some to two men. They were Oliver Brown and a negro. As he did so, Oliver said:

" You're the buck that hit me last night, eh ? "

Replying affirmatively to Oliver, the latter continued:

" Well, you did an unwise thing; it was only this leg that saved you "; showing a cut near his left knee, which he received on striking the bridge from Higgins's blow. The latter then asked:

" What's all this fuss about, anyhow ? "

" Oh, its a darkey affair," laughingly replied Thompson, pointing to the smiling negro, and adding: " I am one, and here's another."

" I'm on a darkey affair, too," responded Higgins, " and that's to get water for a negro whom you have shot."

" All right," replied Oliver, " go along. He brought it on himself by refusing to obey orders."

Soon after, the Mayor, Mr. Beckham, was shot and his body lay exposed by the water tank for some hours. It was not molested by the invaders. Citizens in the town had got arms and others were arriving from the valley and from Maryland. A party from that side, says Higgins, opened the fight in earnest, coming upon the bridge and firing a volley. A negro ran towards the arsenal and was shot down while

19

getting over a fence. People came along, says this
eye witness, and cut pieces from his ears and face,
and the pigs ate from a neck wound. The latter incident is told of Dangerfield Newby's body, but as
he was shot at the armory gate, it is probably untrue.

DANGERFIELD NEWBY.

Mr. Higgins describes Aaron D.
Stevens as the boldest man of the
party. He stood in the open entrance of the bridge, firing upon
the Marylanders, and that, too,
after he was desperately wounded.
The watchman reached him when
he fell face downward, taking a
pistol from his person, and assisting in removing the wounded
man to the Galt House. William
Thompson had in the meanwhile
been taken prisoner, carried to
Foulke's, and then brought out
upon the bridge, shot, and thrown
over into the river mortally
wounded. He managed to swim or wade and reach
one of the piers, where he was discovered and
riddled with bullets.

Mr. Higgins's description of the scenes of the day
and night of the 17th is certainly terse and graphic.
" The people, who came pouring into town," he says,
" broke into liquor saloons, filled up, and then got into
the arsenal, arming themselves with United States
guns and ammunition. They kept shouting, shooting at random, and howling." Day passed in this way,
and evening came. During the night the United
States marines came. He saw the attack upon and

capture of the engine-house. Oliver's body was, the watchman says, thrown into a cart and carried to a shallow grave across the Shenandoah. Shots came from the side of the mountains during the afternoon of the 17th from Cook, as he believed then, and as we now know. It was supposed that Cook had quite a command in the range, and even as late as 1887, Andrew Hunter, John Brown's prosecutor at the Charlestown trial, asserted that the mountains and woods were full of John Brown's men. It is proper to say at this point, that the few shots Cook was able to fire in the futile though gallant effort that courageous but unfortunate young man made to assist his leader and comrades then in the engine-house and arsenal building, with a few more fired by Albert Hazlett and Osborne Perry Anderson later in the day from the Maryland Heights, after they had succeeded in crossing the river unharmed from the arsenal building, was all the firing actually known to have been done outside of the United States grounds by any of the John Brown party. There is reason to believe that a small band of neighborhood negroes fired a few desultory shots from the upper shore, but that cannot be positively stated. Mr. Higgins remained at Harper's Ferry all through the war, saw both armies in possession, and all the fighting, but the nights of the John Brown raid stand alone in his memory for their terror and the fury and excesses that prevailed. Higgins knew Cook well, had often talked with "Isaac Smith," remembers Owen's arrival and asking for the "Smith place." He assisted in placing John Brown's body into the freight car, and saw Mrs. Brown, who was, he quietly remarks, "a nice-looking little woman." He closes his narrative with the suggestion that "It was not healthy to be out in sight of the armory during the fray."

With the moving of the train, early in the morning, the alarm was given to the country. And what a startling one it was! From Penobscot to Mobile, and from New York to San Francisco the story flashed! Extras were issued! The headlines were ablaze! Here are some culled from the dailies of the period:

HARPER'S FERRY. FEARFUL AND EXCITING INTELLIGENCE!

NEGRO INSURRECTION AT HARPER'S FERRY!!

EXTENSIVE SLAVE CONSPIRACY IN MARYLAND AND VIRGINIA!

HUNDREDS OF INSURRECTIONISTS IN ARMS!

SEIZURE OF THE UNITED STATES ARSENAL AND WORKS!

TELEGRAPH WIRES CUT—BRIDGE SEIZED AND FORTIFIED!

DEFENDED BY CANNON—TRAIN SEIZED AND HELD—FIRING ON BOTH SIDES—SEVERAL KILLED—CONTRIBUTIONS LEVIED—TROOPS ON THE WAY!

LATER IN THE DAY—ADDING NEW FUEL TO THE FLAME OF EXCITEMENT—THE NAME OF THE LEADER APPEARED AS OSAWATOMIE BROWN, OF KANSAS.

On the road the Stevens party met several colored men who promised to at once arouse their fellows. The designated hostages were then captured ; Colonel Washington being the first. The Virginian gave the sword of Frederick the Great and the pistols of Lafayette to O. P. Anderson. Shields Green and Leary were placed on guard, one at the side and the other in front of the house. Of course Colonel Washington was excited and alarmed. Stevens, who was dramatic in manner as well as commanding in appearance, briefly told him that they would take his slaves, not his life, and that he must go to the Ferry with them as a prisoner. The slaves in the meanwhile had been aroused and harnessed up a family carriage and a four-horse wagon. Whiskey was offered and refused, and when he found the handsome, tall, full-bearded invader was not to be moved, Colonel Washington broke down utterly. Amid the cries of his family he was placed in his carriage, and with the addition of his slaves, who filled the big wagon, the party started back. O. P. Anderson writes that all the colored people they met were eager to aid. Seventeen men were armed and added to the force. The only shot fired that first night was at the railroad bridge and that was the only act also of direct personal violence. Sunrise on the 17th was, however, greeted with stirring action on both sides. O. P. Anderson says that, in consequence of the movements of the night before, we were prepared for commotion and tumult, but certainly not for more than we beheld around us. Men, women, and children could be seen leaving their homes in all directions, climbing up the hillsides,

evidently impelled by a sudden fear. Captain Brown
was all activity, though at times he appeared somewhat puzzled. He ordered Lewis Sherrard Leary,
and four slaves, to join Kagi and Copeland at the
rifle factory. Copeland was the only man of the
seven (Leeman afterwards joining them) who
escaped from the dangerous post. Kagi early realized
the perilous position, and ineffectually sent for orders
to join Captain Brown. Tidd, Leeman, and Cook,
with some fourteen slaves were ordered to take
Washington's four-horse wagon and proceed to the
Kennedy farm where Owen Brown, Merriam, and
Barclay Coppoc had been left to guard the place and
the arms. Cook, Leeman, and Tidd returned to the
schoolhouse, Leeman subsequently reporting to
Kagi. Owen Brown then began to move the arms
and goods down to the schoolhouse in the mountain,
three-fourths of a mile from the Ferry. Cook and
Tidd, with the help of armed slaves, busied themselves in the capture of Terence Burns, Mr. Alstedt,
and some other neighboring slaveholders, whom they
sent into the Ferry. Their orders required them also
to hold the schoolhouse, to which it was understood
Captain Brown, Kagi, Stevens, and comrades, with
such negroes as might follow from the Ferry, would
retreat, bringing any arms, etc., that it should be
deemed advisable to remove. Up to and about noon
this could have been accomplished. Early in the
morning it could have been done without loss; in the
waning hours of the forenoon, there would have
been some sporadic fighting. The noon sun, however,
saw the liberators encircled. Even then a bold
sortie would have opened the ring, though pursuit

had surely followed.   The United States reservation
was to them a trap of death.   O. P. Anderson remained
at the Ferry, and, by Captain Brown's orders, proceeded to arm slaves in the grounds with the pikes
brought by the wagon from the farm.   Among those
who eagerly accepted the weapons were several farm-
hands who had come in on hearing the reports from
"underground wires."   Colonel
Washington's "Jim" was one of
the boldest of the new fighters.

Outside the gates the excited
citizens gathered.   Arms were
found and began to be used.
Desultory firing commenced in
the middle of the forenoon.
Kagi's position was chiefly assailed, as the Virginia and Maryland farmers could fire on the
rifle works without getting within
the deadly range of the engine-
house squad.   O. P. Anderson's
arming of the negroes led to the
early report that the commander
was a colored man named Ander-

EDWIN COPPOC.

son.   Edwin Coppoc, on guard at the arsenal gates,
was fired upon from the outside.   He was not struck.
Immediately after, writes Anderson, an old colored
man armed with a double-barreled shotgun, taken at
the Washington's and loaded by Leeman with buck-
shot, was ordered by Captain Stevens to arrest a citizen.   The latter refused to obey the order to halt,
and the old man fired both barrels into him, causing
his death immediately.   A rifle-shot from the engine-

house had also wounded the man who fired at Coppoc. From the rifle works where Kagi, Leeman, Leary, and Copeland, with four freed men held the fort, came fresh messages urging immediate withdrawal. It was at this point that John Brown lost control of his judgment, and acted with hesitation unusual to him, halting between two views of the situation. He tried to be both teacher and fighter at once and necessarily failed, not that the characters are incompatible, but that if fighting to achieve a moral result is accepted, then fighting rather than teaching is the order of the day. In his anxiety to prove that the movement was one not of outlawry and destruction, but of beneficence, of justice, and lofty purpose, the logic of the method chosen was temporarily overlooked. Just then the business of the liberators was to have got out of Harper's Ferry and into the mountainous region nearby, leaving Virginians, prisoners, and citizens alike to settle for themselves as best as they might, whether their assailants were freebooters or freedommakers. It may well be supposed also, that the long strain of mental effort and agony he had endured, combined with undoubted debility consequent upon intermittent attacks of chills and fever with malarial tendencies, had some temporary effect on his intellectual powers. Though possessing a sturdy frame, an iron constitution, enriched and endowed with a temperate life, he was over fifty-nine years of age and showed it. But, whatever was the cause, Captain Brown delayed, and when the October sun reached its meridian on that memorable Monday, he and his little band were practically hemmed in by fire from five hundred guns, held and used by infuriated men, with more coming and the certainty also that a Federal force was on its way to the scene of action.

This tardiness was fatal, and the general encounter commenced in all its fury. With Frederick the Great's sword on his hip, the Captain went on the street, sending for the men at the arsenal, Stevens, Anderson, Dauphin Thompson, Dangerfield Newby, and several colored Virginians. A fight impending, no indecision existed. Anderson reports the scene in a vigorous style:

" The troops are on the bridge coming into town; we will give them a warm reception," said Captain Brown as he walked around among us, giving words of encouragement:

"Men! be cool! Don't waste your powder and shot! Take aim, and make every shot count! The troops will look for us to retreat on their first appearance; be careful to shoot first."

His men were all supplied with rifles, but Captain Brown had only the sword mentioned. The troops soon came out of the bridge and up the street facing us, we occupying an irregular position. When they got within sixty or seventy yards, Captain Brown said:

" Let go upon them ! "

Which we did, when several of them fell. Again and again was the fire repeated, creating consternation among the troops. From marching in solid marching columns they became scattered. Some hastened to seize upon and bear up the wounded. They seemed not to realize at first that the raiders would fire upon them, but evidently expected they would be driven out by them without firing. Captain Brown seemed to understand this, Anderson wrote,

and in defense undertook to forestall their movements. The consequence of their unexpected reception was after leaving several of their dead on the
field, the Marylanders beat a confused retreat into the
bridge and stayed there under cover until other reinforcements came to the Ferry. On the retreat of the
troops, Brown ordered his men back to their former
posts. While going, Dangerfield Newby was shot
through the head from the window of a brick store on
the opposite side of the street. Anderson writes:
" He fell at my side, and his death was promptly
avenged by Shields Green, the Zouave of the band,
who afterwards calmly met his fate on the gallows
with John Copeland." Newby was shot twice. At
the first fire he fell on his face and returned it; as he
lay, a second shot was fired and the ball entered his
neck. Green raised his rifle and brought down the
assailant before the latter could even get his gun and
face from the window.

The hillsides grew more lively with the frightened
people, and for a time even that refuge became unsafe, as armed slaves were seen in some numbers.
Cook's later statement and the escape account given
years later to Ralph Keeler for magazine publication
by Owen Brown, shows that the laborers on the canal
above the Ferry, and, indeed, generally the non-
slave-holding white workmen of the neighborhood,
took very little part in the fighting, and, while alarmed
at the tumult, were evidently somewhat disposed to
feel kindly to the liberators. Cook, at least, testified
to this. He was given coffee and food, as well as
warned of the location of armed men and the danger
of capture he ran.

For some time after the Maryland militia fell back, nothing of moment occurred until William Thompson was slain on the railroad bridge. Shortly after the Mayor, Fountain Beckham, was shot dead from the engine-house and all the furies were released. Thompson was dragged out of the Foulke House. Oliver Brown was mortally wounded at the arsenal gate and Stevens soon after receiving several wounds, was captured and taken to the Galt House. The men at the rifle works were in the deadliest peril, and the difficulty of communication became greater. Jeremiah G. Anderson was sent with a message to Kagi, requesting him, " to hold out a few moments longer." But that was the last. An hour's severe fighting ensued. More troops were on the ground, from Frederick, Baltimore, Hagerstown, in Maryland, and Winchester, in Virginia. From current accounts at the time, a list of twelve companies is obtained, numbering in all from 700 to 800 men. Officers were numerous. Colonel Baylor, who evidently had some military knowledge, assumed command, and from that moment all chances of escape from the self-made trap had passed. The flag of truce, pressed for and accompanied by some of Brown's Virginian prisoners, was fired upon after the hostages had escaped, which they swiftly did. In this way, Oliver and Watson Brown, with A. D. Stevens, were slain or wounded and the latter was captured also. " Jerry ' Anderson, carrying a last message and making his way to the rifle works, was fired upon and returned to the engine-house. Continuous firing was kept up till dark on both sides. The little garrison at the rifle works had all been slain. The men at the armory were isolated, all slain but two, and they crossed the river and escaped. Captain Brown, with four men and ten prisoners, his dead son Oliver, and with Watson dying, settled himself grimly for the night to "hold the Fort." The United States marines, less than a hundred in number, commanded by General Scott's chief-of-staff, Robert E. Lee, were on the ground at night to regain control of the Federal reservation. The incidents of that night, with the early morning attack, may fully be told by eye witnesses who were prisoners. It will not then be said, the story is the concoction of an advocate or admirer. John Brown selected eight prisoners to hold as hostages after he was compelled to retreat to the engine-house. Among these were Jesse W. Graham, armory workman, and acting United States paymaster or pay clerk, John E. R. Daingerfield, who had been taken on the 17th. Mr. Daingerfield tells of his capture,[1] and of being taken to "Captain Smith," and adds:

"Upon reaching the gate I saw what, indeed, looked like war—negroes armed with pikes, and sentinels with muskets all around. When I reached the gate I was turned over to 'Captain Smith.' He called me by name, and asked if I knew Colonel Washington and others, mentioning familiar names. I said I did, and he then said, 'Sir, you will find them there,' motioning me towards the engine-room.

"We were not kept closely confined, but were allowed to converse with him. I asked him what his object was; he replied, 'To free the negroes of Virginia.' He added that he was prepared to do it, and

---

[1] *Century* for June, 1885. John Brown at Harper's Ferry.

by twelve o'clock would have fifteen hundred men with him, ready armed."

This is evidently a mistake or misconception of the paymaster's memory. After describing briefly from his own point of view the excitement, massing, and arming of the citizens, by which Captain Brown and three unwounded men, one dead, and one dying, with eight prisoners, were driven to keep within the engine-house, Mr. Daingerfield says:

"After getting into the engine-house with his men, he made this speech: 'Gentlemen, perhaps you wonder why I have selected you from the others. It is because I believe you to be the most influential, and I have only to say now that you will have to share precisely the same fate that your friends extend to my men.' He began at once to bar the doors and windows, and to cut port holes through the brick wall."

Firing ceased at nightfall, but the men were vigilant, responding to their Captain's voice and commands. After the arrival of the United States marines, the paymaster says:

"When Stuart was admitted, and a light brought, he exclaimed, 'Why, aren't you old Osawatomie Brown, of Kansas, whom I once had there as my prisoner?' 'Yes,' was the answer, 'but you did not keep me.' This was the first intimation we had as to Brown's true name. He had been engaged in the Kansas border war, and had come from there to Harper's Ferry. When Colonel Lee advised Brown to trust to the clemency of the Government, he responded that he knew what that meant,— a rope for his men and himself,—adding, 'I prefer to die just here.' Stuart told him he would return at early morning for his final reply, and left him.

"When he had gone, Brown at once proceeded to barricade the doors, windows, etc., endeavoring to make the place as strong as possible.

"During all this time no one of Brown's men showed the slightest fear, but calmly awaited the attack, selecting the best situations to fire from upon the attacking party, and arranging their guns and pistols so that a fresh one could be taken up as soon as one was discharged. . . .

"When Lieutenant Stuart came in the morning for the final reply to the demand to surrender, I got up and went to Brown's side to hear his answer. Stuart asked, 'Are you ready to surrender, and trust to the mercy of the Government?' Brown answered promptly, 'No! I prefer to die here.' His manner did not betray the least fear."

He then pays the stern partisan this tribute:

"During the day and night I talked much with John Brown, and found him as brave as a man could be, and sensible upon all subjects, except slavery. Upon that question he was a religious fanatic, and believed it was his duty to free the slaves, even if in doing so he lost his own life.

"During a sharp fight one of Brown's sons was killed. He fell; then trying to raise himself, he said, 'It is all over with me,' and died instantly.

"Brown did not leave his post at the port-hole, but when the fighting ceased he walked to his son's body, straightened out his limbs, took off his trappings, then, turning to me, said, 'This is the third son I have lost in this cause.' Another son had been shot in the morning and was then dying, having been brought in from the street. While Brown was a murderer, yet I was constrained to think that he was not a vicious man, but was crazed upon the subject of slavery. Often, during the affair in the engine-house, when his men would want to fire upon some one who might be seen passing, Brown would stop them, saying, 'Don't shoot; that man is unarmed.' The firing was kept up by our men all day and until late at night, and during this time several of his men were killed; but, as I said before, none of the prisoners was hurt, though in great danger."

WATSON BROWN.

Mr. Daingerfield's description of the entrance of the marines is very vivid and worth reproducing here:

"I had assisted in the barricading, fixing the fastenings so that I could remove them upon the first effort to get in. But I was not at the door when the battering began, and could not get to the fastenings until the ladder was used I then quickly removed the fastenings, and after two or three strokes of the ladder the engine rolled partially back, making a small aperture, through which Lieutenant Green of the marines forced himself, jumped on top of the engine, and stood a second in the midst of a shower of balls, looking for John Brown. When he saw Brown he sprang about twelve feet at him, and gave

an underthrust of his sword, striking him about midway the body and, raising him completely from the
ground. Brown fell forward with his head between
his knees, and Green struck him several times over
the head, and, as I then supposed, split his skull at
every stroke.

"I was not two feet fro... Brown at that time. Of
course I got out of the building as soon as possible,
and did not know till some time later that Brown was
not killed. It seems that in making the thrust Green's
sword struck Brown's belt and did not penetrate the
body.   The sword was bent double."

Two years after this was prepared and published,
Mr. Hunter in a paper printed in a New Orleans
journal, declared that Captain Brown was "shamming" sickness and feebleness from his wounds. He
is the only Virginian of repute who saw Captain
Brown at that time, that has, since his death, gone
aside to defame him, supplying material for the same
purpose to others.[1]

Mr. Graham gave Dr. Featherstonhaugh (in 1892)
interesting details of his experience, from which I
extract some significant details. When Mr. Graham
was brought to Captain Brown, he reports the latter
as saying in response to a question as to reason for
capture, that he "had no time to make breastworks,
and I mean to use you as such." Graham went
soon after (the prisoners were then all in front of

---

[1] "Trial of John Brown," pamphlet. By Gen. Marcus J.
Wright (ex-Confederate Major-General, and then, 1889, in charge
of Confederate records, War of the Rebellion, War Department). A
review of Professor Von Holst's paper on John Brown, Richmond,
Va., 1889.

the engine-house) to Stevens, who was walking up and down as a guard, and begged for leave to go home for twenty minutes and tell his family. After a while Stevens yielded and told the Captain he'd be responsible for his, Graham's, return, then led him to the gate where he was placed in charge of "a small man" (probably Steward Taylor) who was directed to escort and bring Graham back, which was done. Coming back, Daingerfield was captured by Graham's guard. Firing had then begun, and soon after Newby having fallen near the gate, Graham saw Mr. Burleigh shot by Shields Green. The party, prisoners and all, were obliged to take shelter in the engine-house. Shields Green, or "Emperor," was the only negro taken out of the engine-house when the capture was made. Mr. Graham and others, who were there, mention "negroes" as being in the early hours of the fight in and around "John Brown's Fort." One of these, says Mr. Graham, commenced making a hole in the wall for firing. Some one in a building near by—only a road and fence intervening —saw what was in progress and fired at the hole. Pieces of brick, etc., flew about the negro and he never ventured near the spot again. Shields Green is spoken of as "very impudent." Probably that was true from a chattel owner's point of view. When Mr. Beckham was shot Graham remonstrated, and Green pointed a pistol at his head telling him to "shut up." Before the engine-house was finally occupied, a number of prisoners escaped to the back of the building. Mr. Graham is interesting when describing the scenes inside the engine-house just before and at the attack on the doors. He says:

20

"Early on Tuesday morning I peeped out of a hole and saw Colonel Lee, whom I had seen before at the Ferry, standing close by with the troops behind him. A negro stood near him, holding a large military cloak. Just then Edwin Coppoc thrust me aside, and thrust the muzzle of his gun into the hole, drawing a bead on Lee. I interposed, putting my hand on the rifle and begging the man not to shoot, as that was Colonel Lee, of the United States army, and if he were hurt the building would be torn down and they'd all be killed. Green again put up his pistol and Coppoc readjusted his rifle. During this momentary altercation, Robert E. Lee had stepped aside, and thus his life was saved to the slaveholder's Confederacy. After the demand for surrender had been made and rejected, the attack begun. A hole was made by a sledge-hammer in one of the doors, and Quinn, who crawled through, was shot at by J. G. Anderson, who a few moments after, when with a ladder the doors were battered in, raised his gun to fire on another marine. The gun snapped and the marine made a savage bayonet thrust. The weapon passed clean through Anderson's body and pinned it to the wall where in the dying struggle it turned clear over, so that Anderson hung with his face downward, a horrible sight. Lieutenant Green struck at Captain Brown, who stood by the side of

JEREMIAH G. ANDERSON.

the engine, wounding him over the left eye, so that he fell to the ground, where, as the Lieutenant himself testified on the trial and before the United States Senate Investigating Committee, as since in letters published in current newspapers, he struck at him several times in the shoulder and in the stomach and abdomen.

Mr. Graham tells of visiting Stevens after his own release, and states that while talking with him, a citizen armed with a bayonet rushed in and pressed the point on Stevens's neck saying "I'm minded to kill you." The wounded man cooly looked up and said :

"If I were up and had a pistol in my hand, you would jump out of that window," pointing to an open one. Mr. Graham adds that Stevens was brave, cool, and kindly, too.

The fight was over; the work was done. John Brown was a prisoner, surrounded by politicians, soldiers, reporters, and vengeful spectators. His son Owen, with his followers, Cook, Tidd, Barclay Coppoc, and F. J. Merriam, as also Albert Hazlett and O. P. Anderson, on their own account, were fugitives. Of these, Cook and Hazlett were captured, tried, and executed. Stevens, Edwin Coppoc, Copeland, and Shields Green were hung, while Oliver and Watson Brown, William and Dauphin Thompson, John H. Kagi, Wm. Leeman, Steward Taylor, Lewis S. Leary, Jeremiah G. Anderson, and Dangerfield Newby were killed in combat or as prisoners. If "John Anderson" was present and slain, the deaths were ten of the attacking party, and during the fighting; afterwards seven were executed, and five escaped. It is known

and allowed that seventeen colored men were slain,
though the policy of Virginia minimized the action of
the slave-population.   On the side of the citizens and
soldiery, eight were killed, seven whites and one
colored.   Nine persons were wounded.   John Brown
held eight prisoners in the engine-house during the
night, all of whom testified during the subsequent
trial to the uniform kindness of the leader, and as to
the civility of the men.   The attitude of other Virginians seems to have been different.

From a pamphlet,[1] still sold at Harper's Ferry, interesting details are given of the raid, and especially
of the treatment of men, shot, wounded, and slain,
by one who was an eye witness to the defense against
and attacks on John Brown's party.

The village annalist says: that "he encountered
four armed men at the arsenal gate—two white and
two black,"—on the morning of the 17th. They saluted
him civilly and "one of the white men asked if he
owned any slaves.   On his answering in the negative, the strangers told him there was a movement on
foot that would benefit him and all people who did
not own such property."   His curiosity then led him
to look in and speak to some of the prisoners within
the arsenal gates that he knew, and the result was
that he had to run to escape being himself taken.
Four Sharpe's rifles were raised and his chances of
escape seemed small, when a colored woman, who
was crouched in a doorway in the alley, rushed out

---

[1] " Annals of Harper's Ferry," by Josephus, Jr., Hagerstown,
Md., 1869, pp. 64.   The author's name is Joseph Barry, formerly
a school-teacher.

between him and the guns, and extending her arms begged of the men not to shoot. They did not, but the pamphleteer finds no space or words to thank the brave woman for her timely and courageous kindness.

The treatment of prisoners and wounded captives, as well as the indignities inflicted on the dead, are described with apparent gusto by this village pamphleteer. He says: " William Thompson was dragged to the bridge and riddled with bullets. He even, however, tried to escape by letting himself drop through the bridge into the river. He had been left for dead, but it appears he had vitality enough left to accomplish this feat. He was, however, discovered and a shower of bullets was discharged at him. He was either killed or drowned, as he could be seen for a day or two after lying at the bottom, and with his ghastly face still exhibiting his fearful death agony."

Jeremiah G. Anderson, slain by the bayonet in the engine-house, had, says the Harper's Ferry annalist, " three or four bayonet stabs in the breast and stomach. When dragged out of the engine-house to the flagged walk in front, he was yet alive and vomiting gore from internal hemorrhage. While he was in this condition a farmer from some part of the surrounding country, came up to him and viewed him in silence, but with a look of concentrated bitterness. . . . He passed on to another part of the yard, and did not return for a considerable time. When he came back, Anderson was still breathing, and the farmer addressed him thus: ' Well, it takes you a hell of a long time to die.' . . . After death, also, this man Anderson appeared to be marked out for special

honors and the most marked attention. Some physicians from the valley of Virginia[1] picked him out as
a good subject for dissection, and, *nem. con.*, they got
possession of his body.   In order to take him away
handily, they procured a barrel and tried to pack
him into it.   Head foremost they rammed him in,
but they could not bend his legs so as to get them
into the barrel with the rest of his body.   In their
endeavors to accomplish this feat, the man's
bones, or sinews, fairly cracked.   The praiseworthy
exertions of these sons of Galen, in the cause of
science and humanity, elicited the warmest expressions of approval from the spectators.   The writer
does not know what disposition was finally made of
him."

The would-be humorous brutality of this incident
is only equaled by the evident delight the annalist
takes in the following description of Dangerfield
Newby's death.   He was a colored man, and native
of that section of Virginia, whose wife Harriet was a
slave living some thirty miles below.   By letters
found in the famous carpet-bag, afterwards published
in State Legislative Document No. 1, accompanying
Governor Wise's message relating to the outbreak, it
appears she was the mother of their children, and
about to bear another, while in hourly dread of being
sold to a New Orleans trader.   She was afterwards
found in Louisiana.   Dangerfield Newby was killed

---

[1] Winchester doubtless, as there was a medical college there,
and, some years after the war, the bones of Oliver and Watson
Brown were recovered there and taken away by John Brown, Jr.,
for burial with their brothers.

about 11 A. M. on the 17th, and lay where he fell, his body exposed to nameless brutalities until the afternoon of Tuesday the 18th of October. A writer for a Maryland paper stated that infuriated people beat the body with sticks, put them in the wounds, showered curses on the dead and otherwise degraded themselves. The annalist shows that Newby was fired at from above, a house window probably, as "the bullet struck him in the lower part of the neck and went down into his body. From the relative position of the parties, the size of the bullet, the hole in his neck was very large," and it was remarked that "a smoothing iron had been shot into him. Shortly after his death a hog came rooting about him. . . . Suddenly the brute was seized with a panic, and, with bristles and tail erect, it scampered away as if for life. This display of sensibility was very creditable to that hog, but soon a drove of the same genus crowded round the dead man, none of which appeared to be actuated by the same generous impulse as the first. . . . The King of Terrors himself could not exceed those hogs in zealous attention to the defunct Newby. They tugged away at him with might and main, and the writer saw one run its snout into the wound and drag out a stringy substance of some kind, which he is not anatomist enough to call by its right name. It appeared to be very long or elastic, . . . one end being in the hog's mouth and the other in the man's body. This circumstance," says the gloating annalist, "could not fail to improve the flavor, . . . and value of pork at Harper's Ferry next winter."

Of the fate of others the annalist, already quoted,

says, that Lewis S. Leary " was mortally wounded "
early on the 17th, " at the rifle factory, and died in a
cooper's shop on 'the Island.'" He suffered great
agony, but was left alone by the infuriated defenders.
Of the circumstances attending the death of Dauphin
Thompson, little is known, except that he was shot
outside and died in the engine-house. Steward Taylor

LEWIS SHERRARD LEARY.

was killed near the rifle works.
The bodies of Kagi, Leary, and
Wm. Thompson were taken out of
the river on the 18th, and buried
in shallow holes upon the river
bank, where the dogs soon rooted
them out. They were partly destroyed before the Winchester
doctors took the remains away
for dissection. Hazlett and O.
P. Anderson, who served with
Kagi, managed to cross the border in safety and get away from
Maryland into Pennsylvania,
where Hazlett was arrested and
extradited at the demand of
Virginia. After W. H. Leeman

had cut off his accoutrements and wounded as he was
plunged into the river at the rifle works, a Virginia
militiaman waded after him. Leeman threw up
his hands and said appealingly, "Don't shoot."
The maddened pursuer thrust his pistol in the boy's
face, fired, and blew it into an undistinguishable and
bloody mass. He then cut off the skirts of his coat.
gathered the weapons of his victim, and returned to
the bank, where he was loudly applauded by his

fellows. With him in the river or lying on the rocks were the riddled bodies of Kagi, Steward Taylor, William Thompson, and Lewis S. Leary.

It is related by a Maryland newspaper man that some time after Leeman had been killed as described, another militiaman waded out to where it lay and set it up in a grotesque attitude as a target. Finally he was pushed off and floated down stream, lodging near William Thompson's body. The correspondent remarks that " being outlaws," they " were regarded as food for carrion birds and not as human beings." The same writer stated the " dead lay . . . subjected to every indignity that a wild and madly excited people could heap upon them. Dangerfield Newby's wounds had sticks 'ran into' them, they were used 'to beat him,' while the assailants 'wished he had a thousand lives' wherewith to appease their fury." In striking contrast with this, was the fact that when Mr. Beckham, the Mayor, was killed, his body lay for some time exposed on the road, till the hotel porter volunteered to bring it in. A lady also went out, and as soon as the reason for their presence was seen, the anti-slavery men ceased their fire and the body was recovered.

It is almost in order to apologize for quoting such brutalities. They would not be given here but for the illustration afforded thereby of the temper and tone of the occasion, flickering down into verbal indecencies several years after the occasion. They are of a piece with the sad and savage spirit the wretched Mahala Doyle, of the Pottawatomie affair, was induced to exhibit when she signed the letter written for her in which she desired to furnish the rope wherewith to hang John Brown.

Very different in tone, though no less inexorable in spirit and purpose, were the unqualified tributes which the power of character wrung from Messrs. Wise, Hunter, Mason, Vallandigham, and Voorhees, pro-slavery sympathizers as they were. These direct if unwilling estimates to the convictions, high courage, stoical endurance, and the moral purpose of John Brown, were given by them under conditions which would have certainly excused opinions to the contrary. Hunter, the prosecuting attorney; Avis, the jailer; Campbell, the sheriff; and Parker, the judge, have also given unmistakable evidence of the moral magnetism and personal grandeur of the man. As a rule, it is not among the Virginian survivors of the Harper's Ferry raid, it is not in Southern books and newspapers that one will find abuse and denunciation, assault on motives, denial of honesty, and general effort to belittle and degrade the memory of a great soul or besmirch the luminous apotheosis of a special and sacrificial deed. It is left to Kansas defamers, and Northern cynics and sciolists to do these things, and credit themselves with honor in the doing.[1]

---

[1] It is not my purpose to shoot parthian arrows in the dark. I have especial reference in this allusion, among a few other assailants, to ex-Governor Charles Robinson, of Kansas; to Eli Thayer, of Massachusetts, and to Mr. David N. Utter for his indefensible article of November, 1883, in the *North American Review.*

CHAPTER XII.

JOHN BROWN, wounded and prone, gibed and
wondered at by those he had scared to the verge
of hysterical fury, was captured by a party of eighty
United States marines, commanded by Major Russell
and Lieutenant Green, who were directed by the
chief-of-staff of Lieutenant-General Winfield Scott—
Colonel Robert E. Lee—he being also accompanied
by a dragoon officer, afterwards to be the most

famous of Confederate cavalry raiders—Lieut. J. E.
B. Stuart. Nine hundred armed Virginians and
Marylanders! Nearly one hundred Federal soldiers
with the power of army headquarters behind them!
All these were necessary to capture one old man, a
dying son, and four young men, one seriously
wounded. Harper's Ferry had practically been held
for fifty-eight hours by seventeen men.[1] For more
than half that time not over a dozen men of the
party were actually in the fighting.

It was a wonderful object-lesson in the weakness of
a slave-holding community. But there were more
forcible ones yet to be taught. The old man lay
for eighteen hours on the floor of the armory superintendent's office, which thus became an improvised
guardroom. His wounds remained undressed for all
that period: wounds, too, administered by bayonets
of marines and sabre of officer, Lieutenant Green,
after firing had ceased, and both Coppoc and Anderson had announced their surrender, while the latter,
too, had been fastened by Marine Quinn's bayonet to
the wall of the engine-house. Brown's gun[2] was in his
hand when Russell and Green entered the engine-
house, and either of them could have been slain by
him. He lowered the muzzle and was immediately
struck down. Aaron D. Stevens, also shot while

---

[1] Owen Brown, Barclay Coppoc, and Francis J. Merriam were
not at the Ferry at all. John E. Cook and Charles Plummer
Tidd took no active part in the fighting, being ordered to the
Virginia schoolhouse in the forenoon of the 17th, and then being
unable to afterwards return.

[2] One of his prisoners, Mr. Graham, states that he had taken up
a pike.

carrying a flag of truce, lay by his Captain's side, with six bullet wounds, five of the bullets being imbedded in head and neck. He, too, was unarmed when shot. In fact, Virginia's victims were so taken, and the most of her shots were directed against unarmed prisoners, or men dying or already dead. It was Henry Hunter, son of the State's special attorney, Andrew Hunter, who testified on John Brown's trial, upon call to the witness stand by his father, that he shot William Thompson, an unarmed prisoner, and only regretted that he was not quite sure of having killed him, as some one else fired into his head at the same time. Another Virginian, George Schoeper, of Harper's Ferry, is reported to have shot Leeman, after he fell dying into the Shenandoah, wading out into the stream and setting up his poor body against a rock, to enable a Maryland company to make a target thereof. Schoeper cut off the tail

WILLIAM THOMPSON.

of the boy's coat in which he found his commission as a lieutenant. George Chambers, of Williamsport, Virginia, is reported as the man who shared with Henry Hunter in the massacre of William Thompson, and boasted of it. James Holt, of Harper's Ferry, was seen to club the body of Leary, after the capture of the raiders, and long after life was extinct. A farmer spat his tobacco expectoration into the throat of the dying Jerry Anderson. But the Virginians who had been John Brown's prisoners, resisted the cruelty of their fellows, and it was they who testified as to the capture, as witnesses at the trial and ever since to their deaths, to the uniform kindness and courtesy of manner of John Brown and to his anxiety to prevent their being unnecessarily exposed to the reckless firing of their own people. The bodies of Oliver, dead, and Watson, dying, were brought to the armory. The latter died about three in the afternoon with his head pillowed on the knees of Edwin Coppoc. Two wounded men, three unwounded, ten of the raiders dead, and seven fugitives was the tally which Governor Wise was greeted with upon his arrival from Richmond, about 9 A. M. on the 18th of October. In the New Orleans *Times-Democrat* of September 5, 1887, the late Andrew Hunter published a long and somewhat remarkable account of the John Brown raid and trial. In this paper Mr. Hunter sought to prove that the Liberator's wounds were slight, only one, he said, and that was on the temple, from whence the blood spread down his face and breast. The garments, afterwards mended by Mrs. Rebecca Spring, of New Jersey, and in which his body was clothed, were in proof of the reverse of this. One severe bayonet wound in the left kidney caused Captain Brown to suffer until his execution had ended the account.

Federal soldiers were necessary for the protection of the prisoners. The wonderful vitality and mental force of Captain Brown kept him alert throughout the long strain of examination and interviewing, to which he was subjected. Immediately upon the Governor's arrival, the Baltimore Grays went to the Kennedy Farm-house and the mountain

school-building, and soon brought in the famous
carpet-bag, containing the historic John Brown's
papers, and also a large number of letters, etc.,
belonging to the men.   The arms, etc., found at the
schoolhouse, were legally John Brown's property.
A small wagon and mule, compass, and other personal property, were brought from the Maryland
farm into Virginia and there confiscated; the wagon
and mule being seized by Foulke, the Harper's Ferry
hotel-keeper, to pay for meals which Brown had
obtained to feed his prisoners and his men.   It was
well that the money found on Brown's body, when
captured (about two hundred and ninety dollars in
gold and silver), had been taken by Federal officials,
or otherwise he would not have any means whatever
to aid in defraying the small expenses of a trial
and prison life.   Even that, he did not obtain the use
of till the 30th instant, after Northern counsel had
arrived.   Virginia had a somewhat obsolete law,
sequestrating the property of a convicted person found
within the State.   While Judge Parker said nothing
and Sheriff Campbell was ignorant, wrote Counselor
Hoyt of its existence, Andrew Hunter, claiming
kindly treatment to his prisoners, and even writing
his will, exacted however the State's full pound of
flesh.   The military stores of the raiders proved a
somewhat rich " loot " for the captors.   To this day
the " pikes " are being offered for sale from distant
points in Alabama, and elsewhere, to which it is
claimed they were carried early in the Civil War.
Of arms there were not less than 180 Sharpe's rifles
and 75 Allen revolvers, a little less in size than the
Colt navy-pistol, with 950 pikes, and primers, caps,

powder, tools, etc. The following were reported on
the trial as received by the State authorities: 108
Sharpe's rifles, 12 revolvers, 455 pikes, several kegs of
powder, 40,000 rifle and 20,000 revolver percussion
caps, with a quantity of rifle primers, several reams
of cartridge paper, lead for bullets, ladles, a small,
portable furnace, and a swivel gun, with some other
articles. The swivel gun, carrying a two-ounce
ball, was found in the Kennedy house, and it was the
weapon presented to John Brown by Eli Thayer, "for
service in the cause of freedom," in April or May,
1857. The Sharpe rifles and Allen revolvers were
those turned over to the Captain in 1857, and finally
presented to him as a personal gift, in 1858, by
George Luther Stearns, of Massachusetts.

By noon on the 19th of October, the armory-room
was crowded by local magnates, press men, and
military officers, while the train soon brought leading
men from Richmond, Washington, Baltimore, and
Ohio,—Senator Mason and Clement L. Vallandigham, among others—representatives of some leading
newspapers, and the agent of the Associated Press,
from Baltimore, connected with the *American* of that
city. They certainly manifested a fair and manly
spirit in all dispatches, and, even at this date, they
can be admired for their candid, almost judicial
temper. These dispatches, still present a remarkable
tribute to the character and personality of the anti-
slavery raider. " Porte Crayon " (General Strother),
artist for *Harper's Weekly*, a Virginian born, was
among the earlier arrivals. His graphic pencil,
made furious by the thoughts of an avoided slave
insurrection, spared no line in savage realism.

Captain Brown's identity had been settled the day before.[1] Governor Wise and Senator Mason arrived during the early afternoon of Tuesday. Lieutenant Stuart, who had been stationed in Kansas during the fighting summer of 1856, also recognized the leader as Black Jack and Osawatomie. A remarkable intellectual duel at once ensued.

From the outset, Governor Wise, who dominated the situation by virtue both of public position and erratic zealotry as a representative Southerner, sought to shape questions and entrap replies into the mould he had already formed, viz., the idea that John Brown was but the agent of an extended and powerful combination of Northern politicians and persons opposed to slavery. Vallandigham seconded, and rudely even, this effort of the Governor. Senator Mason, as the report shows, aimed more at ascertaining the Captain's motives and pleas in justifica-

---

[1] Col. Robert W. Baylor, "Colonel-Commandant" of the State forces, then about six hundred in number, in his report to Governor Wise, published the following cartels. It was 3 P.M. of the 17th, Stevens had already been shot while carrying a flag of truce and bearing John Brown's first proposition to retire, releasing his prisoners, forty in all, as he got beyond Harper's Ferry. Baylor than assumed command, pouring in a heavy fire, rescuing thirty of the hostages and compelling Brown to retire with five men and ten prisoners to the shelter of the engine-house. Having driven them under cover, Baylor also withdrew his own troops out of range. A second flag of truce appeared; Isaac Russell, a prisoner, being used to bear a verbal message. Baylor replied:

HEADQUARTERS, HARPER'S FERRY.
CAPT. JOHN BROWN: SIR—Upon consultation with Mr. Isaac Russell, one of your prisoners, who has come to me on terms of capitulation, I say to you, if you will set at liberty our citizens we

21

tion. The evidence then and afterwards indicates
that the author of the Fugitive-Slave Law gave but
little weight to the apparently excitable conceptions
which dominated Henry A. Wise. All, however,
were eager for any means of " firing the Southern
heart," for the disunion struggle up to which their
efforts were leading. John Brown, still bleeding,
stiff, sore, and dazed; in blood-stiffened and dirt-
begrimed garments; suffering from hunger, thirst,
and want of even the rudest care; with his project
defeated, his men slain, captured, or scattered; himself a prisoner, one son dead, another expiring while
the Southern politicians questioned, and a third a
fugitive with his fate wholly unknown, held himself
with such firmness, intellectual clearness, stoic
grandeur and manly directness, that the harsh floor

---

will leave the Government (Federal) to deal with you concerning
their property, as it may think most advisable.

ROBERT W. BAYLOR, *Colonel-Commandant.*

The following written reply was then received:

In consideration of all my men, whether living or dead, or
wounded, being soon safely in and delivered to me at this point,
with all their arms and ammunition, we will then take our prisoners and cross the Potomac bridge, a little beyond which we will
set them at liberty; after which we can negotiate about the Government property as may be best. Also we require the delivery
of our horse and wagon at the hotel.

JOHN BROWN.

Baylor returned the following:

CAPT. JOHN BROWN: SIR—The terms you propose I cannot
accept. Under no considerations will I consent to a removal of
our citizens across the river. The only negotations upon which I
will consent to treat are those which have been previously proposed to you.   ROBERT W. BAYLOR, *Colonel-Commandant.*

on which he lay became, as it were, the enthroned seat of true courage, while his bearing compelled the unwilling attention of all present and the unstinted and admiring respect of some of them. There was a persistent demand to know " who paid " and " who sent" John Brown to Virginia. Vallandigham endeavored to lay all sorts of verbal traps in which to catch the Ohio or other Republicans. Governor Wise showed to greater advantage than others, and his questions were straightforward and direct, being such as his position gave him the right to ask. To the Ohio politician John Brown said: " No man sent me here; it was my own prompting and that of my Maker; or that of the devil, which ever you please to ascribe it to. I acknowledge no master in human form." To Senator Mason's question of " How do you justify your acts?" he turned the tables by saying: " I think, my friend, you are guilty of a great wrong to God and against humanity—I say it without wishing to be offensive—and I believe it would be perfectly right to interfere with you, so far as to free those you wickedly and willfully hold in bondage."

In reply to other questions he declared that he did what "he thought right", that he "applied the golden rule " to his own conduct, and that it was "a duty to help others to gain their liberty." In reply to a question of the Senator, as to whether he considered the Provisional Constitution (copies of which in pamphlet form were in the hands of his examiners, as the carpet-bag with his papers had been brought from the Kennedy Farm-house to Harper's Ferry), Captain Brown said: " Yes, in some respects. I wish you would give that paper your close attention."

To Lieutenant Stuart, who remarked in comment
on some expression of the wounded man—"The
wages of sin are death "—John Brown replied with
quiet dignity, " I would not have said that if you had
been a prisoner and wounded in my hands." When
asked under " whose auspices " he went to Kansas,
he told Vallandigham—" Under the auspices of John
Brown and no one else." To Governor Wise he said
he was an " instrument in the hands of Providence,"
and that he considered the work he attempted " the
greatest service man can render to his God." During
the long examination to which he was subjected,
Captain Brown avoided all names; all recriminatory
speech, and contented himself with courteous but very
direct replies as to his motives and purposes; declaring that he had none but the freeing of slaves; that
he had treated his thirty prisoners well and with
humanity. Those who were present promptly confirmed this. He asserted that the only reason for his
defeat and capture was that he considered too long
the feelings of families of those he was holding as
hostages. But for that he would have got away. To
the reporters present he said:

" I claim to be here in carrying out a measure I
believe to be perfectly justifiable, and not to act the
part of an incendiary or ruffian; but, on the contrary, to aid those suffering a great wrong. I wish
to say, furthermore, that you had better—all you,
people of the South—prepare yourselves for a settlement of this question. You may dispose of me very
easily. I am nearly disposed of now; but this question is still to be settled—this negro question, I mean.
The end of that is not yet."

Governor Wise, before leaving for Richmond, directed that the bodily necessities of the prisoners be properly cared for, and also declared that Captain Brown and his men should have a fair trial. How little he meant this became soon apparent. There were five alive and in their hand,—John Brown and A. D. Stevens, wounded; Edwin Coppoc, Shields Green, and John A. Copeland (the two last colored), unwounded, retained in the army guardroom till noon of the 19th, when all were removed to Charlestown. They were then placed in the jail, a moderate-sized brick building, which still stands. It was surrounded by State troops under Colonel Baylor's orders, and two guns were also placed in position to command the jail. The scare begun. Rage had taken the place of the first alarmed surprise. It had vented itself in a saturnalia of abuse and outrage on the bodies of those whose lives had been given in return for their daring. But when the first excitement flickered down a little, a terrible dread then arose as to how far the movement extended among the slaves and free people of color. This dread reached Richmond, Baltimore, and Washington. It caused vigilance and guards at Charleston and New Orleans, and put the entire South into a ferment, illustrating John Brown's biblical comment—"The wicked fleeth, when no man pursueth." That it was a terror need not be denied or evaded. In Virginia and Maryland one effect was to cause a rapid sale at reduced prices "down South" of all slaves who were "suspects," unruly, or turbulent. The loss from this source has been estimated at $10,000,000 in Virginia alone. For a considerable period thereafter some of John

Brown's friends kept a record, so far as newspaper
information permitted, of the enforced movement
southward of slaves from the border States. It was
very rapid and extended from Virginia to Missouri.

There and then began another marvelous struggle,
not for life, but for recognition; for a clear apprehension of motives, conditions, and results. History
holds no record more memorable. It was waged
against the entrenched Slave power, embattled insti-
tutionalism, aroused legal ties sure to avenge themselves if the taking of life would accomplish that;
but, more than all, it was set to conquer and convict
the Northern States, with all their compromising
tendencies, their commercial needs, and social demands excited and in hostile array. More, too, than
that, there was a growing power in public affairs to
be influenced, whose dominance aiming only and
wholly for the advancement of the Nation, was
threatened in its very heart, apparently, by this
seemingly frantic blow at Harper's Ferry. To meet
all these there was but a simple, upright, crystalline
manhood, physically sure of only but one thing—
DEATH! To him, however, there was also, and without questioning, GOD! Convinced of his cause, sure
of his motive, purged of all desire but service, and
confident that such sacrifice was victory, John Brown,
knowing what he was doing and whither it led, was
supremely the Idealist,—transendental and transparent, too, in the eyes of the world. To this end
the men most opposed, most actively aided. The
manhood of men like Wise and Vallandigham run,
for the time being, with their schemes, aims, and

policies, so far as John Brown's character and motives were concerned.

The Harper's Ferry raid was at once used as a means of attack on Northern and anti-slavery opinion. More than that, however, the attack was moulded so as to arouse every hostile feeling in the South. The effort to prove that Republican leaders, voters, and newspapers were parties to the movements of John Brown soon failed of their own inanition. But the larger purpose of preparing for revolution, by inflaming Southern sentiment, gathered force with every day, and the words of the hour served John Brown, his men, and their cause most admirably. So far as affecting fierce and fusing public opinion, as well as the colder verdict of history, Henry A. Wise stamped on the latter his representation of John Brown, when he said in a public speech, upon his return to Richmond, from Harper's Ferry, that—

"They are themselves mistaken who take him to be a madman. He is a bundle of the best nerves I ever saw, cut, and thrust, and bleeding, and in bonds. He is a man of clear head, of courage, fortitude, and simple ingenuousness. He is cool, collected, indomitable, and it is but just to him to say that he was humane to his prisoners, as attested to me by Colonel Washington and Mr. Mills [an armorer at the United States works], and he inspired me with great trust in his integrity, as a man of truth. He is fanatic, vain, and garrulous, but firm and truthful, and intelligent.[1] His men, too, who survive, except

---

[1] Governor Wise is the only man of weight who ever criticised John Brown as "garrulous." Those who knew him best always considered him a reticent man. He was able to talk, however, on proper occasions, and this, with the listening ears of men wide open, waiting on his utterances, was certainly one that he improved upon, and wisely too.

the free negroes with him, are like him.　He professes to be a
Christian in communion with the Congregational Church of the
North,[1] and only preaches his purpose of universal emancipation; and the negroes themselves were to be the agents, by
means of arms, led on by white commanders.　When Colonel
Washington was taken, his watch, plate, and jewels, and
money were demanded, to create what they call a 'safety
fund'[2] to compensate the Liberators for the trouble and expense
of taking away his slaves.[3]　This, by a law, was to be done
with all slaveholders."

---

[1] This seems to be an error.　If John Brown was a regular
church member, it would have been with a small Presbyterian or
Cameronian sect, the chief seat of which was in Pittsburg and
western Pennsylvania, and which was positively anti-slavery in its
tenets and action, not fellowshipping with those who were actively
or tacitly in favor of slavery.　He seems not to have been in
regular standing with any church body after being ostracised early
in the 'forties on account of his recognition on equal terms of
colored Christians.

[2] The "safety fund" mentioned by the Governor was never
designed for "compensation to liberators" or any one else.　Its
purpose was simply that which its name implied, or for what, by
the light of war experiences, we should now term "secret service" work.

[3] "ARTICLE XXIX.

"SAFETY OR INTELLIGENCE FUND."

"All money, plate, watches, or jewelry captured by honorable
warfare, found, taken, or confiscated, belonging to the enemy *shall
be held sacred, to constitute a liberal intelligence or safety fund;* and
any person who shall improperly retain, dispose of, hide, use, or
destroy such money or other article above named, contrary to the
provisions and spirit of this article, shall be deemed guilty of
theft, and on conviction thereof, shall be punished accordingly.
The treasurer (Owen Brown) shall furnish the commander-in-chief
(John Brown) at all times with a full statement of the condition
of such fund and its nature."

After referring to the taking of Frederick the Great's sword by Stevens, Governor Wise went on to say of John Brown:

"He promised. . . . to return it when he was done with it. And Colonel Washington says that he, Brown, was the coolest and firmest man he ever saw in defying danger and death. With one son dead by his side, and another shot through, he felt the pulse of his dying son with one hand, and held his rifle with the other, and commanded his men with the utmost composure, encouraging them to be firm, and to sell their lives as dearly as they could."

In the light of historic evidence, events, and conditions, such as can now be seen, it is quite apparent that the Virginian managers sought to prove that John Brown represented a wide-spread, organized, and active hostility in the North, deliberately aiming to injure the South and destroy its slave institutions. Such careful examination of the "John Brown papers," as Governor Wise and Senator Mason, with their counselors and aids must have given, could but have convinced them that the range of Brown's active support was very limited indeed. The Virginian Executive secured the services of the ablest detectives, lawyers, newspaper men, etc., to examine these papers and to follow up the clues afforded. These men and their rumors, or reports, fooled him to the top of his bent. They led nowhere and ended in nothing, until early in November the paper prepared by John Edwin Cook, under the pressure brought upon him by his brother-in-law and other relatives, gave the names of Dr. Howe, F. B. Sanborn, Thaddeus Hyatt, and Gerrit Smith as being active in support of the Captain's movements. In all

the papers and letters printed in " Appendix No. I."
to the messages of Governor Wise, or in the Harper's
Ferry raid report of the United States Senate Investigating Committee, there are but few clues to any
names.[1]

After removal by United States marines to Charlestown, six miles beyond the direct jurisdiction of the
general government, four of the prisoners—Brown,
Coppoc, Copeland, and Green—were kept until the

---

[1] The " Appendix to Message I. Documents relative to the
Harper's Ferry Invasion," is a thin octavo of 154 pages. With
some exceptions as to personal letters, it probably contains nearly
all the manuscripts or printed matter found in the Captain's
carpet-bag or at the Kennedy Farm-house, in addition to a letter,
addressed to President Buchanan, dated November 25th, and the
reply thereto; also letter of Wise to the Governors of Maryland,
Ohio, and Pennsylvania, with replies, all relating to the " invasion" for "rescue" purposes, of which Governor Wise claimed
he had positive information; with reports of State militia commanders, Cols. J. T. Gibson and Robert W. Baylor. There
is a letter from one Henry Hudnall to the Governor, setting forth
at some length the contents of the captured carpet-bag. Hudnall
was probably a lawyer-clerk, employed to look over this material,
and his comments are not especially marked by acumen or ability
of any value. The formal documents are the " Provisional Constitution and Ordinances for the People of the United States;"
" No. I. The Duty of the Soldier;" " Blank Form of Commission
under the Provisional Government." The three were printed;
the first and last having been " set up " at St. Catherine's, Canada.
Then follows the manuscript journal of that convention, with the
autographs attached of the delegates thereto. Outside of John
Brown's own name, there is not one known at the time beyond a
neighborhood circle, unless Dr. Delany is an exception, as having
been editor of a weekly paper. A remarkable document was
" A Declaration of Liberty. By the Representatives of the Slave
Population of the United States of America." This was in the

25th without further disturbance. On the 22d, the Captain wrote letters to the North appealing for counsel. At John Brown's home in North Elba— shut away amid the mountains from rapid communication with the world—the news of disaster and death had been slow in its merciless movement. It was not until the afternoon of Friday, the 21st inst., that a young man, their neighbor, brought to the lonely dwelling under the shadow of Whiteface and

---

original, bearing, wrote Mr. Hudnall, "strong internal proof of having been the work of Brown, parodied on the colonial declaration, with some very original variations and interpolations by Brown himself, the whole being copied by his son, Owen, and fixed upon a roller." There are 102 letters in this "Appendix," mainly written to and from the men of the party, and a few by friends at Springfield, Ia., or Cleveland, O. There is a business note of Horace Greeley & Co. inclosing to Kagi a check in payment of work done for the *Tribune;* one from Gerrit Smith, forwarding $200, and nothing else directly relating any one to Captain Brown's movements. Reference is made under initials, or assumed names, to Messrs. Stearns, Howe, Sanborn, and Parker, as persons having relations with his efforts. The correspondence must have been a disappointment to the Virginians. What became of these papers and the historic carpet-bag is unknown, though there is reason to believe they were kept in the Virginian State Library at Richmond until 1865. When the Federal army was about entering the ex-Confederate capital, it is stated that the librarian threw the carpet-bag and contents into some receptacle between the walls of the dome of the Capitol, from which, if so, they have never been recovered. This statement is not vouched for, however, but yet it seems to have some foundation in fact. What is of interest in the carpet-bag papers is the unquestioned fact that they offered little or no foundation for the inflated structure of hysteria and suspicion, Governor Wise sought to build upon them.

amid the somber Adirondack woods, a copy of the
New York *Times* of the 18th. The day before an
exaggerated report of the defeat had reached them,
but this they would not believe. But the newspaper
with all its startling details could not be denied. To
them the shock was lessened by the sacrificial, expec-
tant atmosphere in which they had all and so long
moved. Within the small frame-house, dim and un-
painted, were Mary, the wife and mother; Annie,
Sarah, and Ellen, the younger daughters—the latter
still a child—and Martha, the pregnant widow of
Oliver Brown, who was so soon after to join her
boy-husband in death; also Salmon, the remaining
brother and son, while Henry and Ruth Thompson
were close neighbors. The dwelling of the elder
Thompson was one of mourning also. Two of
its boys had fallen, their sister was the widowed
wife of Watson Brown, while in another home
William Thompson's wife wailed in loneliness her
sudden widowhood. Five households and four
families were stricken by the blow at Harper's Ferry,
and yet no recognized murmur ever escaped any of
them, unless it were from the parents of Oliver's
widow, who were very hostile to the anti-slavery sentiments of the Browns and Thompsons. The neighborhood, too, was somewhat unfriendly on account
of political feeling, but the overwhelming nature of
the defeat and the reluctant admiration extorted by
the way the sorrow was borne, soon changed hostile
indifference into active kindliness. How vividly does
memory recall the facts relating to their devotion,
the Spartanlike simplicity of their lives, the courage
which came because it must and never thought to

vaunt itself. No one murmured, and each sought to
lift the burden of the two fated mother-lives—the
wife who had borne sons for freedom, and the young
bride who was so near death in her coming mother-
hood. The sorrow and endurance at North Elba
was felt elsewhere. In Jefferson County, Ohio, the
homes of John, Jr., and Jason Brown, at Dorset and
Akron, were abodes of care and suffering. It was
known that one brother—Owen—had escaped, but
his fate remained in tedious uncertainty. It was
also certain that John, Jr., would early be an object
of suspicion, as many of his letters were among the
captured papers. The inaccessibility of North Elba
doubtless prevented annoyance and insult to the
elder household; in the Western reserve the organized courage and open determination to resist attempts at arrests, kept the Federal and State agents,
officers and detectives, at a respectful distance. John
Brown, Jr's, home at Dorset soon became for John
Brown men the safest place in the land. There was
mourning in southern Nebraska, where father and
sisters lived, for the able and gallant John Henri
Kagi; at Chambersburg, Pennsylvania, the wife of
John E. Cook, cowered in bewildering dread, saved
only at first from insult and possible arrest by the
courage of Mrs. Ritner, in whose boarding-house she
had temporary shelter. In the homes of his own
relatives, in Connecticut, New York, and Indiana
sorrow and anxiety felt for Cook was made bitterer
by open hostility of feeling felt towards his cause.
The father and sisters of Aaron Dwight Stevens,
whom he had not seen since, as a youth of nineteen,
he had enlisted in the United States army, were in

accord with his nobler aims, and cheered him unre-
mittingly through the four and a half months of
brave prison life that followed. In Springfield, Iowa,
the Coppoc boys left home and mother behind them,
and there were other hearts drawn by tender feelings
towards some of the party. Edwin's Quaker mother
bore her burden well, rejoicing at least that one of
her sons came safely through the fiery furnace. In
Maine, two households were affected, that of Leeman
unto death, and that of Tidd, until his safety was
assured. In Oberlin, the widow of Leary was
mourning for her beloved, while Harriet Newby, her
Virginian sister in affliction, weighted too with bondage, was hurriedly sold to a Louisiana dealer. The
range of interested and sympathetic excitement ran
over a wide area. Danger, too, shadowed some well-
known door-steps. One family neither affirmed or
denied. The household of George Luther Stearns, im-
plicated as was its generous head, made no change
and took no precautions. Dr. Howe found it advisable to visit Canada. Gerrit Smith was stricken
under the excitement with severe recurrence of a
former nervous disorder which necessitated his being
placed in perfect quiet and care. Frederick Douglass soon and wisely, too, left for England   Mrs.
Gloucester, of Brooklyn, who was known to have
freely assisted John Brown, took no outward heed of
the talk aimed at her, as well as others, while in
other directions men marked for suspicion and
known at least to have been trusted, went unfearing
about their work of moulding opinion for John Brown
and his acts, or for at least his character and purposes. From startled surprise and deprecation, even

savage criticism, Northern opinion begun to mellow
and glow in the light and heat of the calm unflinching courage and sincerity that aura-like enveloped
John Brown. Orator, writer, and poet, expressed
their true thoughts. Among those who, without in-
dorsing John Brown's acts, still felt the force of John
Brown's character, was the poet from whose stirring
"Old Brown of Osawatomie," the following verse is
given in autographic fac-simile:

THE STEDMAN FAC-SIMILE.

The hot passion of Virginia, which was perfectly
natural at first, degenerated as details came out of
the manner in which twenty-two men had throttled
the State and five had held 800 of its armed citizens

at bay for at least eighteen hours, into a very drivel
of hysterical fears, which fed a nervous and almost
ruffianly panic at every stupid rumor or darkling
fear that crossed those trembling days. Northern
newspapers, of any character, were compelled to
resort to all sorts of subterfuges to gain information.
Edward House and Mr. Olcott, since known as
a teacher of modern theosophy, went to Virginia in
disguise, the latter joining a Richmond volunteer
company sent on guard duty to Charlestown. Other
correspondents were stationed at Baltimore, Washington, Harrisburg, and various points in Maryland
and Pennsylvania, to whom letters were sent from
" within the lines," it being unsafe to direct them
openly to the several journals. Harper's Ferry was
the chief outpost of this strange encampment, in
which, first and last, Virginia massed about four thousand militia at a cost of $200,000,[1] maintaining an
armed force about Charlestown throughout of not
less than from one thousand to three thousand men,
with artillery, and yet it may safely be affirmed that
there never was *over one hundred men* in all of the
United States directly involved or knowing in any
positive degree, the character of John Brown's intended movement. That the " wicked flee when no
man pursueth," was never more vigorously illustrated. In the North for weeks the leading brains
on the anti-slavery side, that spoke out boldly, could
be counted on one pair of hands. Garrison doubted
the use of it, Beecher denied wisdom and depre-

---

[1] Andrew Hunter's paper of 1887 put the cost at $250,000 ; a
carefully prepared statement of a New York paper, published in
December, 1859, made the bill up to that time $193,000.

cated responsibility, and, as a matter of course, the Northern political leaders denied, avoided, or denounced. The bitter taste left of Mr. Seward's assailing speech, has not yet departed. The newspapers grew slowly to understand, brought thereto more rapidly by the stupid folly of the South itself. Even its readiest servants in the North, like the New York *Herald*, were denied access to information or opportunity for proper publication. That great journal was able only to get its interesting matter by the fact that it had as a correspondent a cousin of editor Gallagher, of the Jefferson County *Times-Democrat*. He was a native of Charlestown, who secured employment as a jail guard, and so got to the prisoners occasionally. He did his work well, for at the execution he drove the undertaker's wagon in which John Brown was seated.

The provisions of law under which the State's attorney, Andrew Hunter, and his associates were proceeding, are in substance as follows: Treason was defined as an offense against the " sovereignty of the State," and the provision of the Code of Virginia (1859–60), Chapter CXC., read as follows:

I. Treason shall consist only in levying war against the State, or adhering to its enemies, giving them aid and comfort, or establishing, without authority of the Legislature, any government within its limits, separate from the existing government, or holding or executing, in such usurped government, any office, or professing allegiance or fidelity to it, or resisting the execution of the laws, under color of its authority; and such treason, if proved by the testimony of two witnesses to the same overt act, or by confession in court, shall be punished with death.

22

Sections 2 and 3 relate to " accessories," etc.   The
fourth defines conspiracy with slaves as follows:

4. If a free person advise or conspire with a slave to rebel
or make insurrection, or with any person induce a slave to
rebel or make insurrection, he shall be punished with death,
whether such rebellion or insurrection be made or not.

The general laws of the State provided for the
holding of special term of courts, and for immediate
process on indictments for felony, and for trial
on such indictments at the same term of court.
They also authorized *immediate execution of the death-
sentence in cases of insurrection or rebellion.*   This class
of cases was excepted under the existing code out of
the general provision of law, allowing thirty (30)
days to intervene between sentence and execution.

Under these statutes, then, John Brown and his
fellow prisoners could have been tried, convicted,
sentenced, and executed on the same day they were
arraigned, had the court so minded, and the execution could also have been conducted in private, if so
ordered. These provisions were undoubtedly intended
for the defense of a slave-holding community. They
probably had their active origin in the Nat Turner
insurrection of 1839, though the " patrol law," and
other provisions, run further back, even to colonial
days, when attempts at insurrections seemed more
frequent.   It was perfectly, then, within the legal
power of Virginia to have tried, sentenced, and executed the Harper's Ferry raiders in its custody within
the ten-days " emergency " law, of which Andrew
Hunter wrote in 1887, and upon which, but not avow-
edly, he attempted to proceed in 1859. The reason for

holding back Aaron Dwight Stevens is apparent under the light of these provisions. With the rest swept
away, his case could have been used to foment sectional feeling and to hunt down the Northern men
and women, whose love of liberty may have drawn
them to John Brown. Mr. Hunter's disingenuousness,
in his paper of 1887, is only equaled by Governor
Wise's double dealing, in so emphatically promising
John Brown a fair trial.   It is a matter of uncertainty
as to how far the Captain's knowledge of the State
Code then extended, but it is certain that his determination to make clear his own objects as well as
the methods that were being pursued by the State
authorities, completely baffled the latter, and led to
that full understanding of a simple, moral, and intellectual courage, which, combining lofty aims and
intentions, has made the name and history of John
Brown that of one of humanity's nobler servants and
leaders.

The Examining Court met under orders. John
Brown, manacled to Edwin Coppoc, supported on the
other side by an armed man, and surrounded by
eighty men with fixed bayonets, was taken to the
courtroom and arraigned. The presiding justice was
a slaveholder named Davenport. He was ordered to
plead to the charges made, and in response replied as
follows, as reported by the Associated Press:

"VIRGINIANS : I did not ask for quarter at the time I was
taken. I did not ask to have my life spared. Your Governor
assured me of a fair trial. In my present condition this is impossible. If you seek my blood, you can have it at any time
without this mockery of a trial. I have no counsel. I have
not been able to advise with any one. I know nothing of the

feelings of my fellow prisoners, and am utterly unable to attend to my own defense. If a fair trial is allowed, there are mitigating circumstances to be urged. But if we are forced with a mere form—a trial for execution—you might spare yourselves that trouble. I am ready for my fate. I beg for no mockery of a trial—no insult—nothing but that which conscience gives or cowardice would drive you to practice." In conclusion he added: "I have now little further to ask, other than that I may not be foolishly insulted, as only cowardly barbarians insult those who fall into their power."

No attention was paid to this trenchant statement. Attorneys Lawson Botts and Charles J. Faulkner[1] were assigned by the examining court as the prisoner's counsel. On being asked if he accepted their services (Attorney Green, ex-Mayor of Charlestown, and now a State judge, was afterwards substituted for Mr. Faulkner, who could not attend), Captain Brown stated he had sent for counsel, and there was no time given for their arrival. He had no wish to trouble any gentleman, and with such mockery of trial. In reply to Harding's statement that he would have "a fair trial," the Captain said: "I want counsel of my own. I have been unable to have any conference with any one. Let these gentlemen exercise their own pleasure." The other four agreed to the assignment, but in no affirmative way did John Brown acknowledge them as his counsel. The proceedings went on, and eight witnesses testified to the attack on, the fighting, and results at, Harper's Ferry. The prisoners were at once committed. The Grand Jury

[1] The latter served the Confederacy as a diplomatic agent, and has since been elected from West Virginia as Congressman and United States Senator.

met on the 25th, and remained in session. A true bill was found with three counts against John Brown, and at a later session, October 25th, bills were also presented against the others for slave conspiracy, murder, and robbery. John Brown was charged with

—Conspiracy with slaves for the purpose of insurrection; with

—Treason against the Commonwealth of Virginia; and with

—Murder in the first degree.

The trial was set for the next day, Wednesday, the 26th of October. Still the prisoners were practically penniless and defenseless. No matter what might have been the courage and uprightness of Messrs. Botts and Green, it was simply an impossibility for them to have martyrized themselves by vigorous showing. In the Andrew Hunter narrative of the trial, there is abundant testimony, even if unconsciously given, to this state of feeling. It is asserted that "Brown's men" were "swarming" in the one street of Charlestown, that the jail was approached by them, and that they were constantly managing to converse with either him or some of his men through the cell windows of the jail, which, as the diagram shows, were in the back part, looking into the yard. All these statements are without foundation in fact. That it was impossible to communicate with John Brown or his men, may be understood when it is known that the jailer's house occupied the front, and that the yard inclosing the brick jail was surrounded on three sides by a wall fourteen feet in height.

Here is a rude plan of the building and its yard :

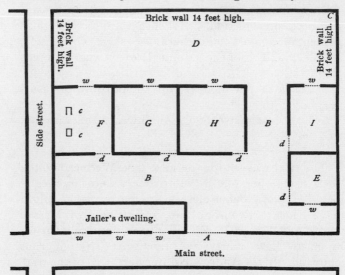

A Main entrance; *B* Space between walls, Avis's house, and the
jail building; *C* Point of wall which Cook and Coppoc reached
on the night of Dec. 15th in their attempt to escape; *D* Jail yard
d d d d d, cell doors; *E* Reception-room; *F* Cell occupied by
Brown and Stevens, afterwards by the latter and Hazlett; *G* Cell
of Green and Copeland; *H* Cell of Coppoc and Cook; *I* Cell
first occupied by Albert Hazlett, *w w w*, *w w*, windows, those of
cells look into the jail yard; *c c* cots of Brown and Stevens.

At this date, too, the building was guarded by a
heavy force, two cannons were planted so as to cover
the same, the inside guards were heavily armed and
increased in number, several hundred State troops
were encamped about the town. Harper's Ferry, the
nearest railroad point, was occupied as an outpost,
and no one was allowed to pass from the earliest

days of the raiders' imprisonment at the county seat without passes from Governor Wise or Mr. Hunter himself. All this procedure seemed to be decided upon as a means of forcing any issue justifying the execution of John Brown and of breeding sectional ill will. Espionage and vigilance were increased, not diminished, as the trial, etc., went forward.

Mr. Hunter's explanation (New Orleans *Times-Democrat*, September 5, 1887) of the haste shown in the preliminary examination is, that " according to a very anomalous system peculiar to Virginia, it was necessary that from the time of issuing the warrant, calling for the examining court, not less than five nor more than ten days should expire." So Mr. Hunter proceeded to enforce the law to almost the rigidest letter thereof, by putting the examination on the sixth day. The State warrant for John Brown's commitment was not issued till October 19th. The examining court, which had to consist of not less than five justices of the peace (a Mr. Davenport presided, and eight were summoned), could acquit, but not convict a prisoner. The October term of the county court began the next day, the 20th. The preliminary inquiry was ordered for the 25th; the trial for the next day. The Hunter programme, defeated by the arrival of Counselor Hoyt and the sagacious courage of Captain Brown, would, if unchecked, have had the chief prisoner examined, committed, indicted, tried, convicted, and sentenced by the 28th of October, and probably also, executed the next day—all being done within the ten days permitted by Virginian law.

Captain Brown was unable to stand more than a

few minutes at a time. The wound in his head had
affected both his sight and hearing, and he was without friendly counsel or money, as the Federal agent
at Harper's Ferry yet retained what was taken from
his person. On the 26th the trial proceeded, and it was
only by a fortunate series of incidents (for Captain
Brown and his cause) that conviction did not transpire on the 28th or 29th of the same month. It has
been left to men like Hunter, however, who had
motives to present, ambitions to serve, and records
to maintain, to accuse John Brown of trifling and
trickery. He accuses him of shamming weakness, of
declaring he wanted no trial, while at the same time
he did all he could to delay the proceedings. It must
be borne in mind that John Brown had not the
slightest expectation of escape from the severest legal
penalty. His only interest was in securing time
sufficient to make evident to the country and the
world the motives that animated him, the objects he
had pursued, and the manner in which he had acted.
He was confident of his historical vindication, or,
rather of that of his cause. It was the interest of
Virginia and of the larger issues of Southern policy
which at once developed themselves, that John
Brown's motives should be questioned and his action
left obscure. Hence, in spite of the tribute to
character already wrung from Henry A. Wise and
others, it becomes at once plain that the intention
was to press the examination, trial, conviction, sentence, and execution to as rapid a consummation as
possible. The current press records show this; they
were not in John Brown's interest, and offer therefore
the best of evidence. Virginia was afraid of a better

understanding of John Brown on the part of the
country and of the world.   John A. Andrew voiced
the growing public opinion when he said at this time:
" *Whatever may be thought of John Brown's acts, John
Brown himself is right!* "

The court begun its business early.   Judge Parker,
who presided, lived to the age of eighty-three, dying
in 1893, was then a man of about forty-nine years,
handsome and dignified, with a severe look, rather
small in stature; personally, a very social and agreeable gentleman.   He was a native of the section, and
connected by family and marriage with all the noted
Virginians therein.   Charles B. Harding, the County
Attorney, is reported in the current dispatches as a
man of intemperate habits, unprepossessing, morose,
and even ferocious in manners.   He was soon blotted
out of the case, however.   Captain Avis, who is still
a resident of Harper's Ferry, was then a man
approaching middle age, short and stout, with a
humorous-looking, pleasant face, but of serious manners.   He was always kind, and the testimony to that
effect is without a negative.   The sheriff, Mr. Campbell, was a tall, stout man, of middle age, who, like
Avis, won the respect of his prisoners.   Indeed, he
did for them, and willingly, even more than common
humanity required.   The most comical, pompous
apparition of the period was a militia officer, to whom
the " protection " of the court and " security " of the
prisoners was committed.   This was Col. J. Lewis
Davis, a very queer-looking dignitary indeed, especially profuse in his hirsute appendages.   He wore
his hair braided in two queues tied by a bow-knot
over his forehead, and with arrogant manner and

strident voice, armed with a Sharpe's rifle, "looted"
by him from Captain Brown's stock, which he always
carried, he was the ever present, conspicious, and
unendurable figure about the courthouse. His special
purpose seemed to be the hunting out of newspaper
men and annoying them all he could. He was brutally offensive to Counselor Hoyt, and it was by his
order that Mr. Jewell, a newspaper artist or illustrator,
and Mr. Hoyt were driven from Charlestown. Col.
Lewis A. Washington was naturally also a conspicuous figure. A handsome man, of medium height,
with slow, grave speech and walk, he looked like
Trumbull's portrait of his great-uncle. Lieutenant
Green, of the Marine Corps, was another personage
of the period. He is an undersized, dull-look-
ing man, compact of build, and with the air of a
stupid sort of a swashbuckler. Andrew Hunter, the
State's special attorney, fully represented Virginia, in
both her strength and weakness. His, was the dominant figure in the prosecution. Governor Wise made
no mistake in selecting Hunter. About fifty years of
age, six feet in stature, well proportioned, active,
elegant in manner, generally suave, quiet, and grave
in speech, from the first carrying everything with a
high hand, confident, as a matter of course, of conviction, he could still be very overbearing in act and
coolly insolent in manner. This was his attitude at
first to the brave, quick-witted, keen-brained, but
inexperienced young lawyer, George Henry Hoyt, of
Massachusetts, who appeared so opportunely in that
Virginia courthouse, disarranging thereby the short,
swift plans of the haughty Virginian prosecutor.
Afterwards he gauged Hoyt's ability more fully and

got him out of Virginia as early and rudely as he could. He did not care even to assume the virtue he had not, and made it quite clear that he proposed to drive matters red-handed. This became very apparent at the afternoon session of the 29th, when, as Hunter states in his last paper (1887), " the court reassembled after dinner," and the " word came from the jail that Brown was too sick to appear that evening. I at once suggested to the court to have the jail physician summoned to examine, whether he was too sick, and to report. This was done, and the physician, who was Dr. Mason, promptly reported that he was not too sick, and that he was feigning. On my motion, the court directed him to be brought into court. . . . He was conducted through the line of soldiers into the courthouse and placed (still on the cot) in the bar, with one of his lawyers (Mr. Hoyt) fanning him. The trial went on to a certain extent, but every effort was made to protract it. I resisted it, but at last, late in the evening, the judge called me up and said he thought we'd better agree, to avoid all further cavil at our proceedings, to let the case be adjourned over till Monday, which was done. Brown did not require to be carried back to jail that evening; he walked back." In this statement, it is possible that Mr. Hunter was as wrong as in his writing that the trial ended on Monday night, October 30th, when, in fact, the verdict was not rendered until Wednesday, November 2d. Mr. Hunter's own statement shows how incapable he and all his associates were of understanding the representative character of John Brown. He was at that moment the embodied moral sense of the free States; he had sought to be

the mailed hand thereof. It was essential that intellectual courage should serve the conscience of freedom better even than armed action has sought to do
it, and he was not found wanting. Privilege never
can understand the resistance planted on the basis of
right dealing. Scratch its veneer ever so slightly,
and the brutal grain always appears. Attorney Hunter
demonstrated this in many ways. As a pleader, his
manner was subdued, his diction strong and earnest,
his voice deep and full, and he could make it ring at
will. He did this, and with a touch of ferocity, too,
when making his final argument for the conviction of
Shields Green, till the crowd in and around the courthouse blazed with fury at his denunciation of the
black man who had attempted to free his race, and
both as fighter and prisoner showed in rude, but
vigorous manner, his utter disdain of men who sold
mothers, dealt in men, bred children for sale, making
concubines for profit of every ninth woman in the
land.

The Virginian lawyers selected by the Examining
Court to defend these prisoners had an ungracious
and thankless task assigned them. Mr. Green was
described by Correspondent House, of the New
York *Tribune*, as a " most extraordinary man to look
upon, . . . long, angular, uncouth, and wild in
gesture, . . . deficient in all rhetorical graces.
His words rush from his mouth scarce half made
up. He speaks sentences abreast. . . . His
. . . ' whar and ' thar ' are the least of his offenses.
His demeanor, altogether, is of unrivaled oddity;
and yet his power is so decided that, while he is
upon his legs, he carries everything before him.

He is the most remarkable man I have seen here, although not so impressive in his bearing as Mr. Andrew Hunter, who is a man of real nobility of presence." Mr. Lawson Botts is also mentioned in the Cook trial as having all the while "sat coiled together in his chair, . . . watching for opportunities of springing upon his antagonist at the least sign of weakness, he has darted upon Hunter and striven, . . to destroy the fabric of his argument."

George Henry Hoyt served an excellent purpose for the defense by his presence, and won a deserved place for both courage and ability. Mr. Chilton, of Washington, was selected by Montgomery Blair, who at one moment, under the solicitation of John A. Andrew, was almost ready to go himself. Chilton was a Virginian by birth, connected with leading Valley families, thoroughly familiar with the State laws, and quite able to measure the needlessness of the extreme alarm, which was driving the community into such violent excitement. He understood the political drift of the positions taken by Mr. Hunter and Governor Wise, and afterwards aided Blair and other conservative Republican leaders to make the most of it. Judge Griswold, of Ohio, was a strong, conscientious, able lawyer, who did not at all like the work he had undertaken at the request of Judge Tilden, John Brown's former lawyer and personal friend. He did his work well, as a lawyer, and got away as soon as it was done. George Sennott, the young Boston Democratic lawyer who volunteered, working for only his bare expenses, did a man's part as well as a lawyer's in the defense of Copeland and Green, the colored men, as also for Stevens, Coppoc, and Hazlett.　His avowed Democracy gave him a better chance than Mr. Hoyt would have had. Indeed, it was probably fortunate for himself that the latter did not have occasion beyond the first day he was in court, to make a plea for his friend and client, as his warm and impassioned speech and earnest anti-slavery feeling—Hoyt was a man of genuine eloquence even then—might have led him to expressions that would have been unwise and readily have proven dangerous, too.　The most picturesque and powerful figure connected with any defense was that of Daniel W. Voorhees, now the veteran Democratic leader and United States Senator, of Indiana; then in the full zenith of his ability as a pleader, and gifted with the soaring power of speech which so well befitted Western and Southern juries of the period.　John E. Cook had wealthy relations— opposed to him in opinions, but strongly attached to him personally,—and they made for his life a forensic and legal fight of the most vigorous character.　It was unsuccessful, for he had lived and married among the neighborhood people.　With that strange belief in the iniquity of disbelieving what they believe, still a characteristic of our Southern brethren, the Virginians would have almost let Brown go in preference to Cook, if a peremptory choice had been thrust upon them.　These were some of the salient features of that courthouse drama, though when the curtain rolled up for the first act, it was on a scene all one-sided.　The gray-bearded, worn old man, so imperturbably lying or half raised on his dirty cot; the intense, almost savage faces of spectators, the alert dignified judge, the already decided jury wait-

ing with barest patience for the hour in which their inevitable verdict would be recorded, the armed attend-
ants, subdued but still eager for force; yet dominated all over by the strident will of Andrew Hunter,
pursuing his end with contemptuous disregard of
practice, caring nothing for the bungling form of
papers and pleas, brushing aside all dilatory motions,
declaring that the cost of waiting was too great, and
demanding a swift ending;—these made a somber
prologue to the powerful tragedy.

Cannon were trained on the courthouse. The
building and vicinity swarmed with armed guards.
Brown's face was less swollen, but he managed to
walk only with great difficulty. Stevens, supported
by two bailiffs, was held up, breathing with great
difficulty ; afterwards he lay on a mattress placed
upon the floor. Coppoc, Copeland, and Green stood
behind. All four were removed to the jail after the
indictments were read, Captain Brown being left
alone. Before the indictment was read, the prisoner
said:

" I do not intend to detain the Court, but barely wish to say,
as I have been promised a fair trial, that I am not now in circumstances that enable me to attend a trial, owing to the state
of my health. I have a severe wound in the back, or rather in
one kidney, which enfeebles me very much. But I am doing
well, and I only ask for a very short delay of my trial, and I
think I may get able to listen to it; and I merely ask that, as
the saying is, ' the devil may have his due '—no more. I wish
further to say that my hearing is impaired, and rendered indis-
tinct, in consequence of the wounds about my head. I cannot
hear distinctly at all. I could not hear what the Court has
said this morning. I would be glad to hear what is said on
my trial, and am now doing better than I could expect to under

the circumstances. . . . I do not presume to ask more than a very short stay. . . . If that could be allowed me, I would be very much obliged."[1]

This is certainly a remarkable speech for a man "shamming weakness," defiant of proceedings, and desirous of "embarrassing" justice. It was objected that the request was premature, and the reading of the indictments were proceeded with. A plea of "not guilty" was made and separate trials asked for in each case; the State electing to try John Brown first. Lawson Botts, of counsel, then made the formal plea for a short delay on the ground of the prisoner's physical disability. The Court after brief discussion, ordered the jail physician, Dr. Mason, to examine the Captain. He did so and swore that Brown was able to stand trial, upon which the Court ordered it to proceed. During the afternoon the jury was made up. Not a single member of the panel was challenged by Mr. Botts, though prejudice and preconceived opinion was necessarily evident in a majority. At five o'clock the Court adjourned. On the 27th, Captain Brown was brought into court on a cot. The illustrated papers of the date give pictures of the carrying of him to and fro, accompanied by armed guards. A press dispatch describes the prevalent opinion, as follows :

" There is an evident intention to hurry the trial through, and execute the prisoners as soon as possible—fearing attempts to rescue them. It is rumored that Brown is desirous of making a full statement of his motives and intentions through the press; but the Court has refused all access to reporters—

---

[1] See Associated Press dispatches of date.

fearing that he may put forth something calculated to influence the public mind, and to have a bad effect on the slaves. The reason given for hurrying the trial is that the people of the whole country are kept in a state of excitement, and a large armed force is required to prevent attempts at rescue."

On entering court, Captain Brown was confronted with a dispatch sent from Cleveland, Ohio, alleging his insanity and urging delay, in order to prove the same. This emanated from persons unable to grasp the ethical nature of the situation. Jeremiah L. Brown, half-brother of the Captain, was one of the most persistent of those who asserted that John Brown's brain was affected. Others, and a majority, desired only to save, if possible, the life of the old covenanter, and were ready for any method that offered. As a matter of fact, no saner man lived or died than John Brown. In the court, when Attorney Botts presented the dispatch, the Captain, slowly getting on his feet, said:

" I will add, if the Court will allow me, that I look upon it as a miserable artifice and trick of those who ought to take a different course in regard to me, if they took any at all, and I view it with contempt more than otherwise. . . . I am perfectly unconscious of insanity, and I reject, so far as I am capable, any attempts to interfere in my behalf on that score."

This little speech and other details again proved that the accused did not seek to obstruct, or cause any unnecessary delay.

The jury being sworn, and the indictment read, a plea of " Not guilty " was entered. Mr. Hunter then stated the evidence he propossd to present and urged absence of prejudice, but demanding celerity in the proceedings. Mr. Green argued in reply, that

23

the indictment for "treason" was faulty, as it must be shown that an attempt was made to "set up" a separate State government, and to show the treasonable purpose of all acts done, not by the prisoners' confessions, but by two separate witnesses; that the alleged conspiracy with slaves must be shown by competent testimony to have existed within the State of Virginia itself. The Court could not punish for acts done in Maryland or within the Federal jurisdiction at Harper's Ferry, and this applies also to the charge of murder committed on the United States reservation there. Mr. Hunter replied, that the treason was shown by the effort made, backed by the evidences of a new form of government being ready, if the effort was successful. On his own confession, Brown was guilty of conspiracy. The murder was notorious, and the prisoner was in command. The United States had always recognized the local jurisdiction over criminal offenses committed at Harper's Ferry. Testimony was given, among others, by the train men to the effect that Captain Brown expressed regret that the train had been stopped and that no one should be hurt, adding that it was not his intention that "blood should be spilled." The stoppage was bad management on the part of the men stationed on the bridge. He walked over the bridge with the conductor, as a guarantee that the passengers and people would not be injured. Messrs. Washington, Allstadt, Ball, and others, who had been held as hostages by Captain Brown, testified as to his directing them to keep out of range of the firing as far as practicable, and of the unvarying courtesy of manner and speech he showed towards them; also, as to his

steadfast coolness and courage, and of a declaration
to them, that "his object was to free the slaves and
not to make war on the people, . . . that it was
no child's play he had undertaken; that he was only
obeying the Bible and following the law of God."
He assured all in his hands that he was not making
war on property, but defending liberty.

During this afternoon and early the next morning,
he offered no obstacles whatever to the progress of
the trial, identifying as handed him all the documents, papers, and letters, found in the Kennedy
Farm-house, or at the Virginia schoolhouse, declaring
as documents were handed him by the prosecuting
attorney through Sheriff Campbell (who had made
himself familiar with Captain Brown's handwriting)
that he was " ready to face the music," and save all
trouble in such matters.   Adjournment on Thursday
afternoon was had at a reasonable hour.   The
arrival about midnight of George Henry Hoyt, a
young Massachusetts lawyer, who proposed to serve
as junior counselor for John Brown, marked the
beginning of historical incidents of importance.   Mr.
Hoyt was not allowed to enter the jail; Messrs. Botts
and Green called at the hotel and notified him that
they declined his or any other man's assistance, while
the public hostility was eagerly and loudly made
apparent.   By Judge Parker's direction, with the
aid of Sheriff Campbell, Mr. Hoyt was permitted to
enter the courtroom and seat himself by the cot of
the prisoner.   During the early part of the Friday
(October 28th) morning session, the evidence of the
leading " hostages," and the identification of the
John Brown papers proceeded.

It soon became evident that the prosecution was about to rest. Witnesses subpœnaed were called, but did not respond, though, as Mr. Hoyt stated in after years, John Brown himself pointed out to him several he desired to testify as being then in the courtroom. The position was a very plain one. Mr. Hunter had called enough of John Brown's more prominent " hostages " to give some color to the prosecutor's desire for " fairness," and did not want any further testimony of that character. He had brought out the seizure of buildings and train, the capture of prisoners and property; the presence of negroes, free and slave; the firing, wounding, and killing of persons; and, to emphasize this latter, put his own son on the stand to show the death of Mr. Beckham—" his grand-uncle "—and his subsequent seizure and slaying, with others, of Wm. Thompson. A good case had been made and none of the testimony disproven. Why, then, should John Brown be permitted in a Virginia court, under plea of defense or " mitigating circumstances," to make anti-slavery arguments or prove that his aim was to attack slavery as " the sum of all villainies "? Why, indeed! The instinct of self-preservation leads clearly to the tacit understanding, as existing between prosecution and defense. Counselor Hoyt always charged this. And here comes in the narration of events, described to this writer and others, by Mr. Hoyt, and established, too, by the exhibition of a brief, or memorandum, in John Brown's handwriting, which, during the earlier years of the Civil War, was in Colonel Hoyt's possession. As this gentleman sat by the Captain's cot, his attention was called by a silent motion of the Captain's eyes and head to a paper with writing on it, lying near the chairs occupied by Messrs. Botts and Green. My recollection of Hoyt's statement was that it lay close to Mr. Green's chair. He managed to secure the same, attention being directed to Captain Brown's rising from his cot and addressing the Court as follows:

May it please the Court,—I discover that, notwithstanding all the assertions I have received of a fair trial, nothing like a fair trial is to be given me, as it would seem. I gave the names as soon as I could get at them, of the persons I wished to have called as witnesses, and was assured that they would be subpœnaed. I wrote down a memorandum to that effect, saying where those parties were, but it appears that they have not been subpœnaed, so far as I can learn. And now I ask if I am to have anything at all deserving the name and shadow of a fair trial, that this proceeding be deferred until to-morrow morning; for I have no counsel, as I have before stated, in whom I feel that I can rely, but I am in hopes counsel may arrive who will see that I get the witnesses necessary for my defense. I am myself unable to attend to it. I have given all the attention I possibly could to it, but am unable to see or know about them, and can't even find out their names; and I have nobody to do my errands, for my money was all taken from me when I was hacked and stabbed, and I have not a dime. I had two hundred and fifty or sixty dollars in gold and silver taken from my pocket, and now I have no possible means of getting anybody to go my errands for me, and I have not had all the witnesses subpœnaed. They are not within reach, and are not here. I ask at least until to-morrow morning to have something done, if anything is designed. If not, I am ready for anything that may come up.[1]

---

[1] Associated Press report of period.

This bold address created a sensation. Messrs.
Botts and Green withdrew peremptorily. An examination of the paper Mr. Hoyt had secured, showed it
to be a memorandum made by John Brown for the
use of counsel, containing the names of witnesses,
with notes of what was to be shown by the testimony. It was written on legal foolscap (blue) and occupied nearly the whole four pages thereof. The handwriting was unmistakable. When I saw it in 1862
this document still bore the marks of tobacco juice
and bootheels with which its place on the courtroom
floor had caused it to be decorated. Evidently it
had been rejected by "counsel" and flung away.[1]
Nothing else was left, of course, to Messrs. Botts and
Green, than to retire at once from John Brown's case.
Mr. Hoyt was perforce compelled to assume charge,
and first made a request for an adjournment until
morning in order to enable him to examine the indictment papers in the case and the Virginia statutes,
etc. In resisting and refusing this motion both the
Judge and State's Attorney were contemptuously ungracious in speech. John Brown at this time suggested to Hoyt that a motion for time be made on
account of the non-appearance of witnesses for the
defense and the lack of subpœnas for them. On
this ground Mr. Hoyt was at home, fresh as he was
from his common-law studies, and aroused to the full
significance of the delay asked, by the arrival of telegrams to Captain Brown, announcing that Mr. Gris-

---

[1] Of what has become of this document I have no knowledge. **A**
statement or replica of its contents was once published, if I recollect aright, in the daily *Conservative*, Leavenworth, Kansas, D. W.
Wilder, editor.

wold had already left Cleveland, that Mr. Samuel
Chilton, of Washington, would leave by the evening
train, so that both would be in the courtroom next
morning.   The interest and excitement of the afternoon was added to by the arrival later in the day
under heavy guard, of John E. Cook, captured two
days before at Chambersburg, Pennsylvania, and returned under the stimulus of Governor Wise's reward,
without waiting the full legal execution of the process of extradition.   Mr. Hoyt's earnestness and per-
sistence coupled with the news that the other counsel
were to arrive, brought about an adjournment till
morning. Cook, in the meanwhile, was being arraigned
before the examining court.   Mr. Hunter was baffled,
he did not dare to meet the issue made and used the
full power of the law to end the trial !   The young
lawyer was admitted to a conference with Captain
Brown, Jailer Avis being present.   He managed to
place in Brown's hand a private note from a Boston
friend, the purport of which is hereafter shown, and
proceeded with the larger duty that had fallen upon
him, spending the night in an examination of the
State laws.

The trial proceeded; Messrs. Chilton and Griswold
taking full control of the defense on Saturday morning.   Both gentlemen asked for a few hours delay, in
order that they might have time to read the indictment at least.   Mr. Chilton had expected to assist
the Virginia lawyers, and finding they retired from
the case, had hesitated to take charge, but at the
solicitation of Captain Brown and Mr. Hoyt, and
friends elsewhere, he had consented to serve.   A few
hours' delay only was essential for Judge Griswold

and himself to become informed.   Judge Packer was
almost surly in his rejection of this motion, referring
with marked asperity to the speech made by Captain
Brown the day before.   "The trial must proceed," he
ordered.   The witnesses Brown desired were secured,
and the evidence of Master-Armorer Mills, Paymaster
Daingerfield, and Samuel Snider, of the United States
Arsenal, Captain Sims, a Maryland militiaman, with
others testified strongly to the general aim and speech
of Captain Brown and the men under him, in the care
for prisoners and other matters, and equally as general
inhumanity on the part of all the Virginians who
directed the attack.   The evidence of Captain Simons,
Fredericksburg, Maryland, Guards, is worthy repro-
duction as to the essential points :

"Brown complained (at the time of the first proposition on
17th, for withdrawal) that his men were shot down like dogs,
while bearing a flag of truce.   I told him they must expect to
be shot like dogs, if they took up arms in that way.   Brown
said he knew what he had to undergo when he came there.
He had weighed the responsibility and should not shrink from
it.   He had had full possession of the town, and could have
massacred all the inhabitants, had he thought proper to do so ;
but as he had not, he considered himself entitled to some
terms.   He said he had knowingly shot no one who had not
carried arms.   I told him that Mayor Beckham had been killed,
and that I knew he was altogether unarmed.   He seemed
sorry to hear of his death, and said, 'I fight only those who
fight me.'   I saw Stevens at the hotel after he was wounded,
and shamed some young men who were endeavoring to shoot
him as he lay in his bed, apparently dying.   .   .   .   I have no
sympathy for the acts of the prisoner, but I regard him as a
brave man." [1]

---

[1] Condensed from the current press reports.

An attempt was again made to force the prisoner's counsel to proceed to a finish. As the ten days of the "Emergency" law had expired, the effort was altogether needless. Hunter made his opening speech and the Court then adjourned until Monday at nine. Late in the afternoon, of Monday, October 31st, after about six hours were consumed by the arguments of Messrs. Chilton, Griswold, and Hunter, the case was delivered to the jury. An absence of less than an hour occurred and then the jury returned. The clerk asked:

"Gentlemen of the jury, what say you? Is the prisoner at the bar, John Brown, guilty or not guilty?" The offense charged had previously been recapitulated.

" Guilty," was the foreman's reply.

"Guilty of treason, and conspiring and advising with slaves and others to rebel, and of murder in the first degree," officially queried the clerk.

"Yes," slowly and seriously responded the foreman.

Strange as it seems under the high-pressure excitement that existed, not a word or sound, beside the natural stir of the audience, was heard. All seemed to feel that a deep tragedy, to be met with befitting stillness, was in progress around them. Counsel Chilton entered a motion for arrest of judgment, on errors to which he had taken exceptions in both indictment and verdict ; Hunter even then wanted, or said he did, to proceed with the arguments. But the Court adjourned till next day, when the closing arguments were heard. Edwin Coppoc was called to the bar, and his trial proceeded, lasting less than two days. So on the second day of November, while the jury was out on the verdict thereof, Captain Brown was brought into court. He still walked with difficulty, every step being attended with evident pain. His features were firm and com posed, but within the dimly lighted courtroom, showed wan and pallid. He seated himself near his counsel, and resting his head upon his right hand, remained motionless, apparently the most unheeding man in the room. He sat upright with lips compressed, looking direct into the chilled stern face of the judge as he overruled the exceptions of counsel. When directed by the clerk to say " why sentence should not be passed upon him," John Brown rose slowly to his feet, placing his hands on a table in front of him, and leaning slightly forward, in a voice singularly quiet and self-controlled, with tones of marked gentleness and a manner slow and slightly hesitating, made this memorable speech:

I have, may it please the Court, a few words to say: In the first place, I deny everything but what I have all along admitted,—the design on my part to free the slaves. I intended certainly to have made a clean thing of that matter, as I did last winter, when I went into Missouri and took slaves without the snapping of a gun on either side, moved them through the country, and finally left them in Canada. I designed to have done the same thing again, on a larger scale. That was all I intended. I never did intend murder, or treason, or the destruction of property, or to excite or incite slaves to rebellion, or to make insurrection.

I have another objection: and that is, it is unjust that I should suffer such a penalty, Had I interfered in the manner which I admit, and which I admit has been fairly proved (for I admire the truthfulness and candor of the greater portion of

the witnesses who have testified in this case), had I so interfered in behalf of the rich, the powerful, the intelligent, the so-
called great, or in behalf of any of their friends—either father,
mother, brother, sister, wife, or children, or any of that class
—and suffered and sacrificed what I have in this interference,
it would have been all right; and every man in this court
would have deemed it an act worthy of reward rather than
punishment.

This court acknowledges, as I suppose, the validity of the
law of God. I see a book kissed here which I suppose is the
Bible, or at least the New Testament. That teaches me that
all things whatsoever I would that men should do to me, I
should do even so to them. It teaches me further, to "remember
them that are in bonds, as bound with them." I endeavored to
act up to that instruction. I say, I am yet too young to understand that God is any respecter of persons. I believe that to
have interfered as I have done—as I have always freely admitted I have done—in behalf of His despised poor, was not
wrong, but right. Now, if it is deemed necessary that I should
forfeit my life for the furtherance of the ends of justice, and
mingle my blood further with the blood of my children and
with the blood of millions in this slave country whose rights
are disregarded by wicked, cruel, and unjust enactments,—I
submit: so let it be done.

Let me say one word further.

I feel entirely satisfied with the treatment I have received on
my trial. Considering all the circumstances, it has been more
generous than I expected. But I feel no consciousness of
guilt. I have stated from the first what was my intention, and
what was not. I never had any design against the life of any
person, nor any disposition to commit treason, or excite slaves
to rebel, or make any general insurrection. I never encouraged any man to do so, but always discouraged any idea
of the kind.

Let me say, also, a word in regard to the statements made
by some of those connected with me. I hear it has been
stated by some of them that I have induced them to join me.

But the contrary is true. I do not say this to injure them, but as regarding their weakness. There is not one of them but joined me of his own accord, and the greater part of them at their own expense. A number of them I never saw, and never had a word of conversation with, till the day they came to me; and that was for the purpose I have stated. Now, 1 have done!¹

On that act the curtain fell, without a sound. Over

---

¹ At a later date (November 22d), under pressure from Andrew Hunter, John Brown wrote a letter to explain the apparent discrepancy between his statement to Governor Wise, on the day of capture, and the above speech. The Captain declared he was taken by surprise in court, not having anticipated so early a sentence. Hunter wrote, in 1887 (New Orleans *Times-Democrat* paper), that he informed Governor Wise, at his visit to Brown in jail, on the 20th of November, that the latter's speech in court "was deliberate, cool, and evidently prepared beforehand." Not a word of such preparation has ever been heard of, and the speech itself bears internal proof of unexpectedness on his part. Governor Wise declared that Brown represented to him and the examining court that he designed to free slaves on the soil, and did not primarily design to turn them off. Under date of November 22d, John Brown addressed Andrew Hunter a letter, in which the apparent "confliction" was dealt with. Of what he said in court, John Brown wrote: "I was taken wholly by surprise. . . . In the hurry of the moment I forgot much of what I had intended to say, and did not consider the full bearing of what I did say. I intended to convey this idea: that it was my intention to place the slaves in a condition to defend their liberties, if they would, without any bloodshed, but not that I intended to run them out of the slave States. I was not aware of any such apparent confliction until my attention was called to it. . . . A man in my then circumstances" could not be "superhuman in respect to the exact purpose of every word he might utter." What he said to the Governor "was intended for truth," and what was said in court "was equally intended for truth, but required a more full explanation than I gave."

all sounds were the echo of those firm but gentle
tones !

The letters of George Henry Hoyt, furnished me
by J. W. Le Barnes, Esq.[1] (now a practising lawyer

---

[1] In a recent letter, this gentleman writes : " Hoyt went to
Charlestown, at my instance, and I furnished him the money for
his expenses. He was living at Athol, Mass., with his parents,
having then recently graduated at law. The morning that the
news was received of the raid and capture, he came at once to
Boston, and I met him at the Republican Headquarters and told
him I wanted him to go to Charlestown and act as counsel for
John Brown. My suggestion was that so youthful and physically
fragile a person in appearance (he was not more than twenty-one,
and looked not more than nineteen, and was slight in figure)
would not create the suspicion that a more mature man might do,
and I believed that for this reason he would be more likely to
succeed in being allowed access to Brown than another, and did
not believe he would be in as much personal danger as another
might be. The purposes for which I wanted him to go were:
first, to watch and be able to report proceedings, to see and talk
with Brown, and be able to communicate with his friends anything Brown might want to say; and, second, to send me an
accurate and detailed account of the military situation at Charlestown, the number and distribution of troops, the location and
defenses of the jail, the nature of the approaches to the town and
jail, the opportunities for a sudden attack, and the means of
retreat, with the location and situation of the room in which
Brown was confined, and all other particulars that might enable
friends to consult as to some plan of attempt at rescue. Hoyt
was willing to accept the commission, if his expenses could be
paid, as he had no money himself." Le Barnes and Hoyt visited
Dr. Howe, at South Boston, who threw cold water on the project,
declaring that John Brown's execution would have a good effect
on public opinion. Such a view naturally seemed cold-blooded to
these earnest young men. It was probably a surprise when they
found John Brown holding the same and living up thereto, para-
doxical as that seems in statement. Le Barnes furnished Hoyt

of Washington, D. C.), by whom Mr. Hoyt was induced to volunteer for the Virginia work, and who supplied the modest means required to defray his expenses, give details of the trial and prison life, which will be of interest here.

Under date of Sunday, October 30th, Hoyt writes Mr. Le Barnes, that—

"Pursued with unrelenting zeal by the prosecution, who intended to have had Brown *convicted* and *sentenced* last night, even if the session continued until twelve o'clock. By ingenious devices, counsel have got the case continued until to-morrow (Monday, October 31) for concluding arguments. We are fortunate in having here Mr. Chilton, of Washington, a Virginian, and a very eminent lawyer, . . . also a relative of the Judge and the family friend of most of the wealthy and respectable people hereabouts. . . . Associated with him, also, is Mr. Griswold, one of the eminent Ohio lawyers, who was for many years the Reporter of the State. He was sent on by Judge Tilden, who is a personal and family friend of B's relations in Ohio. . . . After referring to the legal points

---

seventy-five dollars "in silver," and afterwards sent him other small remittances. The funds for paying Messrs. Chilton & Griswold, as counsel, $1,000 each, with the expenses for copying records, etc., were probably raised through John A. Andrews and Judge Thomas Russell. Mr. Le Barnes's original purpose was probably never known to either of these gentlemen. Hoyt's first letter to Le Barnes set this forth most plainly, and it was, of course, scrupulously obeyed. Mr. Le Barnes writes: "There was a letter from Hoyt, written after he had seen (the night of the 28th of October) and talked with Brown, in which he gave the information desired in respect to the situation at Charlestown, the defenses, etc., and which inclosed a diagram of the jail, showing Brown's cell, the approaches, etc., etc., and in which he stated *that Brown positively refused his consent* to any movement looking to a rescue."

raised and reserved as exceptions, by Mr. Chilton, on which subsequently sound (as to treason, but useless as to prejudices) appeal to the State Supreme Court was made, Mr. Hoyt goes on—' Providentially, things have been conserved to obtain delay. It certainly was most fortunate for Brown that I was with him when he dismissed Botts and Green. In justice to them I must say that their management of the case was as good for him as the *circumstances of their position* permitted. You must be told that the morning of my arrival I was visited by them and informed, that they had decided not to be associated with anybody in the defense, so if I then went into the case they would wholly withdraw. Of course, my only alternative was to remain *passive* and wait for developments. I was not permitted to see Brown until that night (October 28th), when the case was thrown upon me. I never offered a sincerer thanksgiving, than when the morning light brought to us the eminent gentlemen now conducting the case. Here let me say, as it is unnecessary for me to explain the exact condition of the case—the very fine report of the Associated Press agent being minute and particular—that Brown is well pleased with what has transpired; is perfectly satisfied, and more than all the rest, seems to be inspired with a truly noble resignation.

" This morning, Mr. Chilton, Mr. Griswold, and myself were closeted with him three or four hours. I confess, I did not know which most to admire, the thorough honor and admirable qualities of the brave, old border soldier, or the uncontaminated simplicity of the man. My friend John Brown is an astonishing character. The people about here, while determined to have him die for his alleged offenses, generally concede and applaud the conscientiousness, the honor, and the supreme bravery of this man. His fate is sealed, undoubtedly. Whether he will in the course of further judicial proceedings be condemned and executed upon a Virginia scaffold, or whether he will die by the rough hand of violence, I do not decide in my own mind. . . . There is *no chance* of his ultimate escape. There is nothing but the most unmitigated failure and the saddest consequence which it is possible to conjure up to ensue upon an attempt at *rescue*. The country, all aroused, is guarded by armed patrols and a large body of troops are constantly under arms. If you hear anything about such an attempt, for Heaven's sake do not *fail to restrain the enterprise."*

Under date of the 31st, Mr. Hoyt again writes, acknowledging receipt of a small draft, and stating that he had been sending for witnesses, and in the incidental payments due thereon, says he is regarded by all the lawyers, and indeed by everybody else, as representing an infinitely rich somebody in Boston." He explained the facts, of course, to Messrs. Chilton and Griswold, assuring them, however, that their fees, etc. will be duly met, until the writ of error to be filed before the Supreme Court is decided upon. He then adds:

"In regard to the other prisoners, Coppoc is now on trial, Griswold and I are counsel, and Green and Stevens are yet to be tried. Cook (who was brought from Pennsylvania on the 28th) is making a confession. Griswold and I accidentally found that out. . . . Stevens is in the same cell with Brown. I have frequent talks with him. He is in a most pitiable condition physically, his wounds being of the most painful and dangerous character. He has four bullets in his body, two or three being about the head and neck. He bears his sufferings with grim and silent fortitude, never complaining and absolutely without hope. He is a splendid-looking young fellow. Brown says it was a great mistake, and Stevens agrees that it was a great mistake, chaffering, to save the lives and shedding of the blood of men. They might have got away into the mountains, where no body of men could have captured them, had it not been for this mistake. Brown says—he doubts not it is all right in the providence of God and is resigned to his fate. . . . I am assured by everybody that there is no danger of violence to these men. I am not so much of a fool, however, that I cannot read a devilish countenance when I see it face to face, and I tell you there have been too many *silent* people about this courthouse to-day, and I am quite sure there are a few . . . who want no better pretext than a delay, such as we are endeavoring and hope to obtain to set the assassin's hand upon our brave, old friend. John Brown is too good to live among men. .I never imagined it possible for a man to be so desperately cool and calm under such terrible circumstances. It may be he has fulfilled his appointed mission on earth (if there be such a thing). . . . I don't believe that John Brown will ever leave this town a live man." (Hoyt had described the lawyers' hopes of having their writs of error sustained and a new trial ordered, all of which proved fallacious.) "There is a disposition," he continues, "in a measure, to prevent it being said, that he had no formal trial, but the people are bound he shall die. Beckham, one of the killed at the Ferry, . . . was a relative of Hunter, and mayor of that town. H. Turner, another of them, was a respectable and highly connected citizen, and they (the citizens) are bound to have the blood of this entire lot of prisoners."

In another letter (November 2d), Mr. Hoyt refers to the defense of Coppoc by Mr. Griswold and himself, and then states that Mr. George Sennott, of Boston, who had been sent down, a volunteer, to defend Stevens and the colored prisoners, " had fought with extraordinary pluck and most astonishing zeal the cases of Copeland and Green." Mr. Hoyt urged on Boston friends the necessity of engaging Mr. Chilton to prepare and carry appeals to Richmond in all the other cases, declaring that it would never do to have one case better cared for legally than the others. " Brown will protest against it, and so will the entire North. Brown wants (he says) to share everything with the others."

Commenting further on the state of feeling, Mr.

24

Hoyt wrote about the 10th of November, after his return from Philadelphia, that he expects "to get a notice to quit" owing to excitement aroused by the Northern press, especially the letters of Mr. House in the New York *Tribune*. The feeling had grown so abnormal that Hoyt had difficulty in seeing Captain Brown, but in the presence of the "kind-hearted jailer, Captain Avis," contrived to have a long interview with Brown. "They allege," he writes, "fears that poison or some other means of death will be conveyed to the old hero. They need not fear suicide from him!"

Mr. Hoyt was kept busy at Baltimore, Philadelphia, and Washington, in such duties as junior counsel usually perform in cases of the magnitude of that of John Brown. He was also serving and making that first, as the personal friend of the Captain in gathering the property and belongings of the Captain for the benefit of Mrs. Brown. The Boston friends were desirous of having all that could be rescued brought there for sale as "relics." Sheriff Campbell, aided all he could in getting the material together. The money taken from Captain Brown's person after capture by the Marines, had been held for some time in the custody of the United States Army Superintendent at Harper's Ferry, but was finally paid over to aid in defraying expenses of the defense. Foulke, the hotel proprietor, levied upon the wagon and mule found at the Kennedy Farm, to pay for the food which Captain Brown impressed from him, chiefly for the feeding of his forty prisoners. A Virginia law, Mr. Hoyt found out, carried judgment for costs against the property of a convic-

ted prisoner.   He thought the sheriff was not aware
of it, and that Judge Parker would not speak of it.
In all this, however, he reckoned without Andrew
Hunter, who was bound to have not only the pound
of flesh, but all the surroundings and belongings,
thereto.   Boston got none of the relics, and Mrs.
Brown received little or nothing from property found
in Virginia.   The order to quit that Counselor Hoyt
expected, came on the 12th of November, and he
writes on the 13th from Baltimore that he, with Mr.
Jewett, Frank Leslie's artist, whom he writes of "as
a gentleman and a deuced good fellow," was "compelled to leave the town of Charlestown. . . .
We got a polite, but decidedly peremptory notice to
quit, which, considering that the town was in a state
of wild excitement with barns and wheat stacks
burning,[1] and the lynching of these prisoners as well
as tar and feathers imminent (for us), we concluded
to deny ourselves the pleasure of facing a mob and
make discretion the better part of valor. . . .   It
was the merest suspicion that set them on to us."

Under date of Washington, November 14th and
16th, whither he had gone on the appeal business,
Hoyt sends very interesting letters, showing the
opinions of important persons and why certain action
was taken.   He writes:

  . . . Found Chilton had crossed over to Alexandria where
he had cases to be postponed in order to go to Richmond. (In
another note, Mr. Chilton's explanation is given.)   Sought and
found Montgomery Blair ; . . .   his judgment in this matter

---

[1] These fires must have been made by the slaves ; there was no
one else to do it.   The Virginians, of course, declared that it was
the work of Northern emissaries.

is the best possible.   Hoyt was very earnest as to securing for
the men as good and complete legal service as given to Captain
Brown. " The expense," he writes, " must be shouldered. How
will the world and especially John Brown regard an omission
to secure to the same last extremity, the rights of the associates
of the captive chief ?   .   .   .   Certainly it is expected to make
a clean fight in this matter.   .   .   .   I have had a long talk
with Mr. Blair and have got his ideas pretty thoroughly in my
mind.   In regard to this, Hoyt's going to Richmond, he waited
on learning whether ' John A. Andrews is going ' as had been
discussed.   No statement can, therefore, be made by him, as
the ' expulsion from Charlestown ' by the Mayor's order and
under threats of mob violence " until it is settled that he, Hoyt,
is to go to Richmond or not." .   .   .   " Mr. Blair thinks," continues Mr. Hoyt, " a demonstration of Brown's insanity might
please Wise.   He says he has seen something in the Richmond
Inquirer (*Examiner*)—probably the statement he exhibited to
Andrews—which looks like an invitation. .   .   .   Mr. Blair
is very anxious that all those persons who have any reason to
suppose that Wise has any reason to summon them down to
this Federal Court (and he will soon have some, as number one
detectives are hunting them up) should quit the country."
(About this time Dr. Howe and Frederick Douglass left for
Canada and England ; no one else retired except to the Western
Reserve and Kansas.)   " He says they are sure to be outraged
and insulted by the usual programme of ' tar and feathers,' if
they are not killed, and he thinks they are likely to meet the
other treatment.   I want you, Le Barnes, to see that Sanborn
and the rest are put on guard, and if possible are either ' hived
up ' or sent away, for they are surely to be summoned.   .   .   .
Mr. Blair thinks that Mason and Company are bound to stir up
disruption out of this affair, and that they will go to every extremity to do it.   He is confident of a Republican victory in '60,
and says disunion must be avoided.   I agree mainly with this
doctrine, provided victory is sure in 1860.   But I feel like a
frantic disunionist.   I cannot help saying—I hate with all my
heart the detestable despotism into which I cannot venture to

set foot for an honest purpose without suffering violence.

I suppose Mr. Blair has inferred that I am very bitter in my heart toward the South, for he has kindly entered into an exposition of the plan of the Republican party for the future. It is a most persuasive and inspiring thing. . . . I think that Mr. Blair, senior, is a man who understands the people of the South better than we at the North, and his emancipation theory is great! Under date of the 16th, Mr. Hoyt says that Mr. Blair deems it unsafe for him (H.) to go to Richmond, denounced as he had been 'as the agent of the Boston abolitionists.' Mr. Chilton has been arranged with 'to look after other appeals.' The article in Wise's Richmond organ, the *Examiner*, is considered by Mr. Blair 'as an invitation to make a demonstration.' Hoyt was, therefore, to proceed and gather affidavits needed."

On the matter of insanity affidavits, Governor Wise evidently felt himself obliged, after Brown's execution, to make some sort of a case. In a message to the Legislature, under date of December 13th, he said that "no insanity was feigned, even the prisoner, Brown, spurned it. Since his sentence, Samuel Chilton, Esq. (of counsel), has filed with me a number of affidavits for delay, in order to show such alleged insanity." Mr. Hoyt's letter, already quoted, explains this, and Mr. Chilton, in a letter published December 18th, in the *National Intelligencer*, states that he had no hand in the preparation or presentation of such affidavits; that Mr. Hoyt had *pro forma* only attached his name (Chilton's) to a petition for a hearing, making himself the affidavit required of counsel, and that he, Hoyt, was undoubtedly led into such procedure by a statement, made in the Richmond *Examiner* (credited with being Governor Wise's organ), that it "was not too late to have the question of insanity upon an issue, and relief afforded, if it was found to exist." The statement was misleading, as only the Legislature could have acted.

An undated letter from Philadelphia gives an account of Mrs. Brown there, and must have been written about the 8th of November. Mr. Hoyt says, " I found Mrs. Brown at the house of Wm. Still, on Locust street. . . . She was stopped at Baltimore (on her way to Harper's Ferry and Charlestown) by my dispatch (due to a conviction that it was not safe for her then to go to Charlestown) to Mr. Fulton (of the *American*). . . . We have this P.M., heard news, which seems to demand instant action. It has been explained by Mr. McKim to Mr. Webb. *There are three refugees now in the mountains.* They must be Tidd, Owen Brown, and Coppoc (brother of the prisoner). . . . We telegraphed for Redpath. It is important that funds should be placed in Mr. McKim's hands to assist them—poor fellows! (Owen, who was the leader, took care that no one approached them till they reached western Pennsylvania. I tried it from Harrisburg, Redpath and colored men from Chambersburg, but it was of no avail.) . . . I think it prudent, if the cases of Cook and Stevens (which was discussed) be turned over to the Federal Courts, that those parties who feel they are likely to be summoned as witnesses, keep out of the way *of all United States processes.* I hope there is *pluck* enough and *ammunition* enough in Massachusetts to prevent the forcible attachment of any Massachusetts man— in this regard. . . . I wish I could describe my interview with Mrs. Brown. 'Tell my husband, I can spare him for the sake of the cause!' . . . 'I can resign him to God, sure that it is His hand that strikes the blow ! ' Every word she utters breathes the spirit of trust and resignation. When I bade her good-bye, the lips quivered, the voice trembled, and the tears flowed freely, but the words were firmly spoken and were worthy the wife of John Brown."

Captain Brown had discouraged the visit of Mary, his wife, at this time, as, owing to the local anger and excitement, due in large degree to the successful defeat of the plan to try and execute on an " emergency " plea, there was really personal danger to all visitors, especially, he feared, of any of his family. It was the energy also of J. E. Cook's defense, as well as the personal feeling against him, that re-aroused at this time the bitter hostility and mob-feeling in the town and vicinage. " The shadow of an unconquerable terror " still hung over the people. Evidence of the feeling was found in the exclusion of Lawyer Sennott from the jail at this time, and the wild, almost unappeasable fury which arose, over the arrival of a kindly Quaker lady from Eagleswood, New York, who, expecting to find Lydia Maria Child also at Charlestown, had come to aid in caring for the prisoners.

Edwin Coppoc, defended by Messrs. Griswold, Green, and Hoyt, was soon disposed of, having been put on trial at the afternoon session of November 1st, and convicted late on the 2nd inst. Brown was brought in and sentenced on that day. Hunter's "latter-day pamphlet," stated that he was not sentenced till the appeal on the writ of error was decided adversely, November 16th. Shields Green and John A. Copeland were placed on trial November 3d, and convicted the next day, and sentenced to be hung on the same day as Coppoc, December 16th. Mr. Sennott fought vigorously for these men, and went the length of justifying them in their resistance to the enslavement of their race. The State Attorney, Hunter, was almost ferocious in his philippics against Shields Green, whose boldly careless bearing had aroused all the brutal malignity that slave ownership and race prejudice necessarily produced. Cook's trial began immediately after, and was hotly contested until its close on the 9th, when at nine in the evening the jury brought in a verdict of guilty on the same charges that Brown was convicted upon. The trial was remarkable on the part of the defense for its ingenuity and ability. Cook's brother-in-law, Lieutenant-Governor Willard, led the array of counsel. Besides himself, from Indiana were other two lawyers, Daniel W. Voorhees being most prominent. Botts and Green were also retained. The debates were "very keen," and sometimes "very severe." Hunter "vigorously repelled these attacks, and sometimes turned them to his own advantage."

Just before this came, the visit of Judge Thomas Russell and his wife, of Boston, had excited a great fury. Mr. Hoyt in one of his letters to Le Barnes refers graphically to them, wondering how she managed to get away unhurt. He himself fell under greater suspicion because of leaving Charlestown with the Judge. Hunter, it is stated, would have arrested the lady, except for her sex, on a charge of "treason." Mrs. Spring was at first refused admission to the jail, but Judge Parker interfered, took her himself to the jail, accompanied by a guard, and for her protection waited till the interview was closed. Captain Brown himself was greatly disturbed by these ill-timed, though well-meaning visits. Mr. Hoyt, on the 13th of November, writes to Mr. Le Barnes, from Baltimore:

" Do not allow Mrs. Child to visit B. He does not wish it because the infuriated populace will have new suspicions aroused, and great excitement and injurious results are certain. He is comfortable and has all his wants supplied kindly, and is not sick enough to be nursed. He don't want women there to weaken his heroic determination to maintain a firm and consistent composure. Keep Mrs. Child away at all hazards. Brown and his associates will certainly be lynched if she goes there. This ought to be shown Mr. Andrews and others, but let no public exhibition be made."

One of the curious incidents in the legal proceedings, which at the time and since has escaped notice, was reserved from trial by the State authorities until early in February, 1860. Up to that date Stevens was retained, it was understood, as a Federal prisoner under indictment by a Federal Grand Jury, sitting for the Western District of Virginia, in the County jail at Charlestown. No record is at hand as how this was brought about, nor, by what process he was transferred to the State for a judicial slaying. The object, however, is self-evident. Andrew Hunter gave it away in writing in 1887, that Governor Wise and himself came to the conclusion " that this Brown raid was the beginning of a great conflict between the North and the South, and had better be regarded accordingly," and he adds significantly, that " it was not alone for the protection of the jail and the repelling" of rescuing parties who were " not," in spite of

his declarations otherwise, organizing for the "rescuing of Brown and the prisoners, *but it was for the purpose of preparing for coming events.*" Part of that preparation was to involve the Federal government favorably to the South, hence the Federal indictment
against Stevens, the sending of troops to Harper's
Ferry as a *posse comitatus*, the proposed making by
Federal court and United States Senate Committee
of drag-nets, into which to bring all sorts of prominent personages in the North, and the deliberate
threat made by Wise of invading Northern States in
" alleged " emergencies, existing mainly in his " mind's
eye," coupled with a demand that the general government act with Virginia against other neighboring
States upon these frantic declarations of an envenomed
Governor. In tracing the "roads" leading *from*
Harper's Ferry as well as *to* it, it is seen most clearly
that in the evolutionary providence of events the
wrath of the slaveholders was made to serve the cause
of Union and Freedom. The common sense of the
North soon perceived the truth; that while there was
a great sentiment and a growing force of reason acting
steadily against the aggressive spirit and acts of
slavery, that also there never was any inclination
amounting to serious danger, of a desire to put the
institution down by force. The right or wrong of
such a situation need not be debated. It is essential
here and only to understand the situation. There
never was at any time from 1840 till John Brown's
pendent shadow clouded the December sunshine,
more than one hundred men who had any positive or
direct knowledge and affiliation at any one time with
John Brown's plans and purposes. At the time of the

raid there certainly were less than that number
in all, counting in every delegate who sat in the
Convention at Chatham, Canada West, May 10, 1859.
it was the South which made of the raid a conspiracy
against the Union! John Brown's action was indeed
startling. Nobody denies that. Dealt with according to the accepted legalities, it would have failed of
the aims its commander had in view. But Virginia
fanned it into a greater success, because moral and
righteous in character, than could have resulted from
even its partial trial as a test of conflict. John
Brown saw the possibility of this when he laid a
wounded captive under Wise's examination. How
aptly then could the young and now eminent Ohio
poet, himself nurtured with anti-slavery ideas and
convictions, say as he did:—

> O, patience, flower of the hour!
> Over thy ghastly gallows-tree
> Shall climb the vine of Liberty;
> With ripened fruit and fragrant
>   flower.
>
>   W. D. Howells.
>
> (Columbus, Ohio.
>   1859.)

Perhaps in no better way can a more suggestive
conception be given of the state of alarm in which
the people of the Virginia Valley had lashed them-

selves than by summarizing a few of the statements
made by Mr. Andrew Hunter in the notable paper to
which several references have already been made. It
cannot be said to be unfair. The prisoners, when captured, says Mr. Hunter, were to be, by railroad, sent
to Charlestown from Harper's Ferry, via Winchester.
Hunter told Governor Wise this would not do, as
the militia company (Captain Rowan's), to be sent as
a guard, " will massacre them before they reach the
jail." He then advised Wise to go himself, accompanied by a party of United States marines, taking
the highway from Harper's Ferry for the trip. This
was done, and Mr. Hunter, telling the story twenty-
eight years after, cannot see the awful irony involved
therein. The attorney says that he told John Brown
that " anything he wanted, consistent with his condition as a prisoner, he should have "; yet he states
that he himself retained (in the name of the State, of
course) some, at least, of the money which friendly
persons were sending the prisoner in letters from the
North. All letters to the prisoners, by " his " direction, were placed by the postmaster, a United States
officer, in the box of the State Prosecutor, not
delivered at the jail, as was the postmaster's duty.
It was, of course, within the power of the State, after
the letters were delivered to the jail, actually or con-
structively to examine and read the same. Hunter
retained those that he pleased, " between seventy
and eighty in all," he stated. Many letters contained
small sums, generally one-dollar gold pieces. He
seems to believe it was generous to allow these small
amounts to reach the condemned men, while retaining others of larger value. There was a letter from

a Mrs. Russell, of Boston, mentioned as sent to Governor Wise by Mr. Hoyt, which evidently never reached John Brown. In the matter of the arms and other property, some of it wholly personal, which had been captured by Virginia, it would seem, in the face of all the evidence obtainable, that every State officer but Hunter was willing that the barbarous State law which sequestrated the property of convicted persons, and which had long 'been practically unenforced, should remain in that status, so far as John Brown was concerned. Hunter led the Captain to believe, even to drafting for him a second will, on the day of his execution, that he might dispose of his property as he wished; none of it, however, seems to have got out of Virginia, that the State's Attorney could trace. Mr. Sennott, a Boston Democrat, in defending the colored prisoners, spoke of slavery as "illogical and absurd," and was, as a result, for a time, denied admission to his clients within the jail. Among the strangest of half confessions which let in unconsciously the light upon the character it illuminated is one resulting from Hunter's quoting approvingly, twenty-eight years after date, from a New Haven Doughface paper, which hopefully suggested that if "any other party 'ever' invades the territory of Virginia . . . they may be caught and, without judge or jury, burned alive in a fire made of green faggots." Funny, to quote this, for both the " respectable " Connecticut paper and the old Virginia lawyer, in the light of the vast invasions that came so soon upon the kibes of John Brown's execution. Funnier still, however, is the attorney's recollections of the projected invasions and rescue plots which did not

materialize, and which yet, even as late as 1887, this
venerable "survival" actually believed had an existence.   Hunter "chuckled" almost audibly in his
New Orleans article over the "adroitness" with
which he imagines he met these men in buckram.
He sustains his claims by telling of an alleged fire at
a neighbor's house, which local papers afterwards
said, so the despatches state, was the result of a
smoky chimney, and by describing how he and his
son Henry (the unblushing butcher of the unarmed
prisoner, William Thompson) heard a great clamor
on the road adjoining their house, and, seizing the
Sharpe's rifles "conveyed" to them from Brown's
stores, went out, to find some drunken men from
Harper's Ferry riding wildly by.   It would be cruel
to repeat these senile reminiscences, but for the fact
that the incidents were first used in aid of breeding
civil war, and were later repeated to justify it and to
show the "chivalry and courage" of a slave-rearing
oligarchy.   By means, as he alleges, of Brown's "intercepted" correspondence, and other sources, such
as the paid detective, it is presumed, who falsely
reported, for example, being with John Brown, Jr.,
at Oberlin, while plotting a rescue of his father.   Mr.
Brown did not leave the county of Jefferson, and
seldom his home at Dorset there, for many months.
All the plots he was connected with were simply as a
defense against attempts, by kidnapping, to carry
him to Virginia, or, later, to make him appear as a
witness before the Harper's Ferry United States
Senate Committee.   When Owen Brown and Barclay
Coppoc found refuge on the Western Reserve, the
best people joined in a movement to warn them and

to prevent efforts to get hold of them without due process of law, as was done in Pennsylvania in both Cook's and Hazlett's cases. The same was true in Iowa, to which Barclay Coppoc went later, and in Boston, with relation to the effort to secure F. B Sanborn as a witness at Washington. All the rest, so far as Hunter's story of John Brown's "rescue plots" are concerned, is mere sensation. It is true, probably, that many letters were sent to John Brown, expressing a wish for his release, by force or otherwise; and it is certain, also, that huge jokes were perpetrated at the expense of Virginia's frightened officials. James Redpath and myself were responsible for filling one credulous detective, who called on us in Boston, having a forged letter of introduction, with a most exciting yarn of our scheme to get John Brown out of jail. It was so Munchausen in style that we hardly dared to hope for its being retailed. But it was, and Hunter sent for 500 more troops at once, while Wise appealed solemnly to the President, Mr. Buchanan, for aid. Hunter tells (1887), as sober truth, a lot of stuff about men "drilling" in Huntington County, Penn.; about an organization at Oberlin and Bellaire, Ohio, which involved the seizure of trains in Ohio; also of an alleged movement from Kentucky, of all places in the world, and under charge of a man named "Day from Missouri." This, probably, had some blundering reference to Dr. Doy, of Kansas, who had been stolen by force from Kansas and imprisoned in jail at St. Joseph, Mo., from which he was afterwards rescued. Dr. Doy was lecturing on his adventures, in Michigan or Massachusetts, and, being apt to talk with a loose mouth, doubtless

filled another of Wise's detectives with a mare's nest.
The only direct tale Hunter reported in 1887 related
to information received by him from Pennsylvania.
It had, however, nothing to do with John Brown, for
he had been executed two months before. Hunter
was warned of " rescue " movements *designed on behalf
of Stevens and Hazlett*, the last two victims. This
incident will be told in its proper place, and correctly, too, as the writer was an active organizer
thereof. Now, as a matter of fact, and this is said
with the fullest possible knowledge, the most serious
attention was paid, and immediately, too, to the
desire, nay, demand, of Captain John Brown that no
such attempt should be thought of or prepared for.
Stevens and Hazlett also made the same declaration,
and, like John Brown, said that even if any prospects
of success could be shown, the result could not be
achieved without the slaying of Captain Avis, the
jailer, and to that none of them would agree. All
three assumed that they would be most useful to the
cause they loved as sacrifices.

Governor Wise, under date of November 25, stated
to the President, that " a conspiracy, of formidable
extent in means and numbers (was) formed in Ohio,
Pennsylvania, New York, and other States, to rescue
John Brown and his associates," was a simple absurdity. The barn and hayrick fires, few probably in
number, were made by the negroes, naturally aroused
and cognizant of events about them. Governor Wise
says that he has 1,000 men under arms, " and, if
necessary, shall call out the whole available force of
the State." He declared that " places in Maryland,
Ohio, and Pennsylvania have been occupied as depots

and rendezvous by (these) desperadoes, unobstructed
by guards, or otherwise intend to invade " Virginia
and he then proceeds to declare, that while his " purpose is peaceful," that " if another invasion " occurs,
he " will pursue the invaders wherever they may go,
into any territory, and punish them wherever arms
can reach them." The President was called upon to
"take steps to preserve peace *between the States.*" The
words " between the States " and " Confederate," as
political terms, seem to be extensively introduced by
Wise at this time. A copy of this rodomontade was
sent to the executives of Maryland, Ohio, and Pennsylvania. Mr. Buchanan replied on the 28th of November to Wise, reminding him that he " did not communicate the facts " on which his charges " are
founded." He could not conceive of such "atrocious
wickedness," and expressed the conviction that Virginia was "abundantly able and willing to carry her
own laws into execution." To protect United States
property and to act as a *posse comitatus* to the United
States marshal for western Virginia, who still held
Stevens in custody, "charged with the crime of
high treason against the United States,"[1] Mr. Buchanan announces that two companies of artillery have
been ordered "to proceed immediately from Fortress
Monroe to Harper's Ferry." Mr. Buchanan, in further
reply to the Virginian's demand to "take steps to
preserve peace between the States," proceeds to lay

---

[1] No other of the raiders was proceeded against by the Federal
authorities. Stevens, then, was the only man indicted for treason
against the United States. He was held until early in 1860, and
then tried by the State of Virginia as a conspirator and homicide.

25

down that doctrine of imbecility upon which he acted when " the States " went into "rebellion " and prepared for the real " invasion " of other States, on a large scale. It was the duty, he said, of the several States themselves to prevent such invasions as Wise feared, and that if "the Federal executive, however, were to enter these States and perform this duty for them, it would be a manifest usurpation of their rights. Were I thus to act, it would be a palpable invasion of State sovereignty, and, as a precedent, might prove highly dangerous."

Mr. Lincoln would certainly have found it a bar to earlier Union preparations. Governor Wise may have brought himself into the frenzy of fright which his preparations indicate his being in, but a more reasonable hypothesis, based at least upon his acknowledged possession of considerable ability, and the certainty that he had quite correctly gauged the inside facts as to the extent and character of the support John Brown had received, is found in the conception that a plot against the Union was in process of realization. The same purpose that gave the most vigorous direction to the pro-slavery attacks on Kansas, was enlarging the opportunity in Virginia. Memory is often at fault, but sometimes even its senility may serve to clinch a condition. Reference has already been made to Andrew Hunter's late-in-the-day defense of Virginian justice in connection with John Brown and his men. The Hunter paper of September 5, 1887, gives as reason for not sparing the lives of the raiders, "that in the coming war they would be found to the South ugly customers, and," he writes, " I have no doubt that if Brown, particularly, had survived the result of this raid the most dangerous military leaders would have been found in him and some of his associates."

The replies of Governors Hicks, Maryland ; Packer, Pennsylvania ; and Chase, Ohio, to the terrified "squeal" of Governor Wise, are characteristic. The Marylander will "coöperate"; the Pennsylvanian says that Wise's statement as to that State will "be found, in the sequel, utterly and entirely without foundation," and that in "all circumstances " Pennsylvania will see "that her honor is fully vindicated." Governor Salmon P. Chase, like Governor Packer, resented the tone of the Wise letter, and notified him that, while "unlawful combinations" against Virginia or any other State would be broken up, the State of Ohio would "not consent, however, to the invasion of her territory by armed bodies from other States, even for the pursuing and arresting of fugitives from justice." John Brown's action placed large issues in the scales. Governor Wise and his fellow conspirators on behalf of the "war between the States" worked the "Invasion" issue for all it was worth for their aims—in the South, while their impotent demands on States to so act upon the personal showing of Wise, "that their confederate duty" be performed, had just a contrary effect on the States that were addressed. Even Maryland was held to her fealty when the time came and Governor Hicks aided.

Events moved forward to the taking of life on the second and sixteenth days of December. Albert Hazlett, under the name of "William Harrison," was, early in November, brought from Carlisle, Pennsylvania, having been sent to execution in Vir-

ginia by a United States Commissioner, upon evidence
that certainly did not fully identify him with the
Harper's Ferry raid. Application for his extradition
as Albert Hazlett was made; his identity as such
was not shown even before the Court that condemned him to death; only one witness actually testi-
fying to his presence at the Ferry, and he was shaken
by Mr. Sennott's cross-examination. Of course, no
moral doubt of his connection ever existed; but it
remains true that the legal evidence was imperfect.
For this reason, Captain Brown always refused to
recognize Hazlett as one of his men, and wrote of
him to "Aunt Fanny" (Mrs. Mary A. Gage) the 2d of
November, as being among those reported as killed.
The tally of the raiders was now complete. Five had
been tried and convicted, and were now awaiting execution; two were in prison as yet untried; five had
escaped, and were known to be in safety, and ten
had been slain. Seventeen other men, colored, also
fighting on the side of liberty, have been reported
killed in the Harper's Ferry struggle. The North
was arousing, the South was on fire; while the prisoners, all of them, inspired by the calmness and courage
of their leader, awaited death in simple and manly
fashion. That fact, no record blackens, and no advocate can deny. John Brown's correspondence went
forth; each letter as it was published, became as a
winged fire in the testimony it bore. This is not the
time nor place to reproduce them. The days moved
onward with austere tread. The calm man in the
prison cell steadily replies to his correspondents. On
the 1st of December, Mary, his wife, came, surrounded
by an armed guard, and compelled to leave the

friends, Messrs. Miller McKim and Hector Tyndale, who had escorted her from Philadelphia, behind at Harper's Ferry. One of them was afterwards Brigadier-General Tyndale, of the Union Army, and commanded for a time the Union forces in the upper valley, with headquarters at Harper's Ferry.

The narrative of Andrew Hunter of the execution of John Brown (see New Orleans *Times-Democrat*, Sept. 5, 1887) may be accepted as generally accurate. Its cool and cynical recognition of the prisoner's fortitude and courage is in itself a tribute worthy of more enduring preservation than a newspaper file. He says:

" On the morning of the 2d of December, a messenger from Brown came to me to my office in Charlestown, saying that Captain Brown wanted to see me at the jail. Though extremely busy making arrangements for the execution that day, I dropped everything and went at once to the jail. There, to my surprise, I learned from Brown that he wanted me to draw his will. He had been previously advised by me, that as to any real estate he had, the disposition of it would be governed by the laws of the State where it was situated, as to which, of course, I could not advise him, but as to any personal property he possessed, he could dispose of it here in Virginia. He accordingly asked me to draw his will. I said to him, ' Captain, you wield a ready pen, take it, and I will dictate to you such a testament as to this personal property in Virginia as will hold good. It will be what is called a ' holographic will "; being written and signed by yourself, it will need no witnesses.' He replied, ' Yes, but I am so busy now answering my correspondence of yesterday, and this being the day of my execution, I haven't time and will be obliged if you will write it.' Thereupon, I sat down with pen and ink to draw the will, and did draw it according to his dictation. After the body of the will had been drawn, he made suggestions which led to drawing the codicil. It was drawn as he suggested it, and both the will and the codicil are attested by John Avis and myself, and was probated in Jefferson County.[1] This all occurred a short

---

[1] The first will was a holographic one, made by John Brown and prepared the day before. It reads like him:

CHARLESTOWN, JEFFERSON COUNTY. VA., Dec. 1, 1859.

I give to my son John Brown, Jr., my surveyor's compass and other surveyor's articles, if found; also, my old granite monument, now at North Elba, N. Y., to receive upon its two sides a further inscription, as I will hereafter direct; said stone monument, however, to remain at North Elba so long as any of my children and my wife may remain there as residents.

I give to my son John Brown, Jr., my silver watch, with my name engraved on the inner case.

I give to my son Owen Brown my double spring opera-glass, and my rifle-gun (if found), presented to me at Worcester, Mass. It is globe-sighted and new. I give, also, to the same son $50 in cash, to be paid him from the proceeds of my wife's estate, in consideration of his terrible suffering in Kansas and his crippled condition from his childhood.

I give to my son Salmon Brown $50 in cash, to be paid to him from my father's estate, as an offset to the first two cases above named.

I give to my daughter Ruth Thompson my large old Bible, containing the family record.

I give to each of my sons, and to each of my daughters, my son-in-law, Henry Thompson, and to each of my daughters-in-law, as good a copy of the Bible as can be purchased at some book-store in New York or Boston, at a cost of $5 each in cash, to be paid out of the proceeds of my father's estate.

I give to each of my grandchildren that may be living when my father's estate is settled, as good a copy of the Bible as can be purchased (as above) at a cost of $3 each.

I desire to have $50 each paid out of the final proceeds of my father's estate to the following named persons, to wit : To Allen Hammond, Esq., of Rockville, Tolland County, Conn., or to George Kellogg, Esq., former agent to the New England Company

time before the officers came to take Brown out to execution. As evidence of his coolness and firmness, while I was drawing the will he was answering letters with a cool and steady hand. I saw no signs of tremor or giving away in him at all. He wrote his letters, each one of which was handed to me before it went out, while I was drawing the will, so as to get done by

at that place, for the use and benefit of that company. Also $50 to Silas Havens, formerly of Lewisburg, Summit County, Ohio, if he can be found. Also, $50 to a man of Stark County, Ohio, at Canton, who sued my father in his lifetime, through Judge Humphrey and Mr. Upson, of Akron, to be paid by J. R. Brown to the man in person, if he can be found ; his name I cannot remember. My father made a compromise with the man by taking our house and lot at Munroeville. I desire that any remaining balance that may become due from my father's estate may be paid in equal amounts to my wife and to each of my children, and to the widows of Watson and Oliver Brown, by my brother.

JOHN AVIS, Witness.   JOHN BROWN.

To this document he added the following " codicil " next morning early, and as will be seen, mailed to his wife.

CHARLESTOWN, JEFFERSON COUNTY, VA., Dec. 2, 1859.

It is my desire that my wife have all my personal property not previously disposed of by me ; and the entire use of all my landed property during her natural life ; and that, after her death, the proceeds of such land be equally divided between all my then living children ; and that what would be a child's share be given to the children of each of my two sons who fell at Harper's Ferry ; and that a child's share be divided among the children of my now living children who may die before their mother (my present beloved wife). No formal will can be of use when my expressed wishes are made known to my dutiful and beloved family.

JOHN BROWN.

MY DEAR WIFE—I have time to enclose the within and the above, which I forgot yesterday, and to bid you another farewell. " Be of good cheer," and God Almighty bless, save, comfort, guide, and keep you to the end.

Your affectionate husband,   JOHN BROWN.

the time the officers came to take him out.   When they finally
came to take him he grasped me by the hand and thanked me
in the warmest terms for the kindness I had shown to him from
the beginning down to that time.

"I left the jail about ten o'clock and stood at the corner
above the jail until the procession went out.   The military was
drawn up, he was received out of the jail into a spring wagon,
and the procession moved around the corner of the jail and out
George street to the field.   I saw everything from beginning to
end of that morning's operations, and preceded the procession
by a few minutes in getting out to the field.   That whole
story about his kissing a negro child as he went out of the jail
is utterly and absolutely false from beginning to end.   There
is not a word of truth in it.   Nothing of the kind occurred—
nothing of the sort could have occurred.   He was surrounded
by soldiers, and no negro could get access to him.

"I had a party, called my suite, of some fifteen or twenty on
that day, and David H. Strother ("Porte Crayon," of *Harper's
Weekly*) was among the number.   We were standing near the
scaffold, or immediately under it, when the drop fell.   When
Brown was led forward and placed on the drop, and Campbell,
the sheriff, and Avis, the jailer, had stepped back, I distinctly
heard him say in a plaintive tone, 'I hope they will not keep
me standing here any longer than necessary.'   Immediately
upon hearing which, the signal was given to cut the rope that
supported the drop, which was done, and that ended John
Brown's career.   I did not hear him say 'be quick,' as mentioned by Captain Avis, though I have no doubt it occurred as
he has narrated it.   At the time the order was given to cut
the rope, the military had not completed their dispositions
around the scaffold, but I promptly determined that Brown,
according to his wish, should not be kept longer in this state
of painful suspense.   Though very close to Brown (we had
gotten there to see how he bore himself) we could see nothing
of tremor ; his hands were clinched, and he was as cool and as
firm as any human being I ever saw under such circumstances.

"While the body was hanging, Strother slipped up, raised

the cap from his face and took a sketch of him hanging. He said that the celebrated Maria Lydia Child had published that she wanted to have a portrait or likeness of Brown in every condition of life to hang in her room, and that he had taken this sketch to send her, that 'she might have him, too, when he was finished.' If he sent it she has the best portrait of Brown ever taken.

"After Brown had hung some eight or ten minutes the doctors began to go upon the scaffold, Dr. Mason, the jail physician, first. He examined the body and pronounced him dead. Some ten or fifteen other physicians then went up, examined the body and concurred that he was dead. The body was then cut down, placed in the coffin box prepared for it, and returned to the jail. It remained there until toward the close of the afternoon, when it was sent to the depot and transmitted to his wife and friends at Harper's Ferry to be carried North."

The will drawn by Mr. Hunter is as follows;

I, John Brown, a prisoner in the prison of Charlestown, Jefferson County, Va., do hereby make and ordain this as my own true last will and testament. I will and direct that all my property, being personal property, which is scattered about in the States of Virginia and Maryland, should be carefully gathered up by my executor, hereinafter appointed, and disposed of to the best advantage, and the proceeds thereof paid over to my beloved wife, Mary A. Brown.

Many of these articles are not of a warlike character, and I trust as to such, and all other property that I may be entitled to, that my rights and the rights of my family may be respected.

And lastly, I hereby appoint Sheriff James W. Campbell, executor of this, my true last will, hereby revoking all others.

Witness my hand and seal this 2d day of December, 1859.

JOHN BROWN.   [SEAL.]

Signed, sealed, and declared to be the true last will of John

Brown, in our presence, who attested the same at his request, in his presence, and in the presence of each other.

JOHN AVIS.

ANDREW HUNTER.

Codicil—I wish my friends, James W. Campbell, sheriff, and John Avis, jailer, as a return for their kindness, each to have a Sharpe's rifle of those belonging to me, or, if no rifle can be had, then each a pistol.

Witness my hand and seal this second day of December, 1859.

JOHN BROWN.   [SEAL.]

Signed, sealed, and declared to be a codicil to the last will and testament of John Brown, in our presence, who attested the same at his request, in his presence, and in the presence of each other.   ANDREW HUNTER.

JOHN AVIS.

This will was written on a plain white quarter sheet of paper, with the usual faint blue lines, but with no side-rulings or other customary incidentals of a legal document. The seals were merely pen-scrawls inclosing a small circular space in which was placed the word "seal." The black ink in which the body of the paper was indited has turned brown with age, and the edges of the folds are much worn and tawny in color. Across the back of the main fold are these indorsements:

51.

John Brown's will and codicil. 1859, Dec. 19th. Will and codicil proved by the oaths of John Avis and Andrew Hunter, and ordered to be recorded. Teste:

F. A. MOORE, C. C.

Recorded Will Book No. 16, page 143.

This document is now in the City of Washington. It was "of record" for years at Charlestown, West Virginia, but when the county seat was removed to Shephardstown, temporary accommodations were rented. Having but a limited space at his disposal, the then clerk of the court exercised his own discre-

tion in the premises, and threw out what he considered to be "unnecessary and unclaimed" papers.
Among the rest was this original will.   It was
promptly rescued by a prominent citizen, who recognized its historical value, and afterward by bequest
it came into possession of relatives at the Federal
City.   It has been carefully examined, signatures
authenticated, and the document was then photo-
graphed.   Copies of this fac-simile are in my possession.   Mr. Andrew Hunter testified before the Senate
Committee on "The Harper's Ferry Invasion" in
reply to a question of Jefferson Davis, that John
Brown " sent for me to write his will."

"Did you write it?" was the next question.

"Yes, sir," answered Mr. Hunter, " *about an hour
and a half before his execution.*"

One of the correspondents of the New York *Herald*,
a Mr. Gallagher,[1] cousin of the editor of *The Democrat*,
a weekly published at Charlestown, was allowed about
the jail during the last week of John Brown's imprisonment.   In order to see the last of the tragedy,
Mr. Gallaher drove the undertaker's wagon in
which a coffin was placed.   On this John Brown and
the undertaker were seated.   The latter said : " Captain Brown, you are in better spirits to-day than I."

"I have good cause to be," was the quiet response.

---

[1] New York *Herald*, Dec. 3, 1859.   Mr. Gallagher, who died at
Washington in 1893, confirmed this account to me personally.   He
left behind him a number of interesting relics, among them being
a copy of a paper containing a sermon of Henry Ward Beecher,
sharply critical of John Brown.   The latter covered the margins
with tart replies.   This document is doubtless in possession of the
old reporter's son, who is employed, I believe, in the library of
the United States Geological Survey.

At the scaffold, while standing waiting Talliaferro's fussy maneuvers, using, according to Hunter, a "criminal" execution as a field for training men to thereafter seek the "execution" of the American Union. Sheriff Campbell said in a kind, low tone to his prisoner, "Are you not tired?"

"Not tired," was the reply, "but don't let them make me wait longer than is absolutely necessary."

Three thousand Virginian uniformed militia inclosed the scaffold, a hollow square. According to Mr. Hunter they were only trying to get into formation when he gave the signal for the drop to fall. One Northern man, at least, saw the execution. Correspondent Olcott, of the New York *Tribune*, who, in order to be present, took another's place in the ranks of a cadet company from Richmond. Another young man was there with pallid, handsome face, and lithe well-moulded form, whose name has since become almost as widely infamous as that of the man whose death he then gloated over has become renowned. John Wilkes Booth, the assassin of Abraham Lincoln, served as a volunteer in the ranks of the Jefferson Guards. In all probability, too, a Kansas man—one of John Brown's men—was in the same file with him. Charles Lenhart, a printer, before mentioned in this volume, is known to have left his home in Kansas some time before, and there is good reason to believe that he went to Virginia, passing himself off as a pro-slavery Missourian. As he possessed the sign, etc., of the secret Blue Lodge Society, and was thoroughly informed, Lenhart could have done this. Of course he told a good story of John Brown outrages, and then was enabled to obtain work

at Charlestown, where he remained till after the execution of Cook on the 16th inst. They were close
friends and comrades, and Lenhart desired to aid
him, if possible. The printer died in the Union Army
in 1862. For miles around the rugged-looking country town, every road was crowded with scouts and
pickets, so it would have been impossible for Northern men, as Mr. Hunter asserted was the case, to have
left the railroad before reaching Harper's Ferry,
which was under strong guard of both Federal and
State troops, while Maryland had troops on guard at
approaching stations and towns, and crossed Loudon
County for the purpose of being present at the execution. Several cannon were drawn up and pointed
at the scaffold, and not until the quivering form of
the brave old man ceased its muscular action, did the
shivering commonwealth recover even its braggadocio. It had forgotten before in its wild terrors, to
do that. William Jackson Armstrong (of California),
writer and lecturer, standing years after on the small
rounded knoll upon which the rude scaffold had
stood, thus described the landscape :

" The beauty of the earth, as on that fair, soft December noon
it shone in on his sight over the Blue Ridge mists, might have
unmanned, at the last moment, any man who had had lower
than a martyr's purpose for his deed. But John Brown's was
not an unfledged fancy, and his imagination had only lent itself to human sentiments. He said to his jailer as he mounted
this hill: ' This is a beautiful country. I have never noticed it
before.' From the spot of the scaffold, on the ridge of a
plowed field, the country dips away into a valley of superb
picture—a sweep of wild fields, broken into vistas by ribs of
mountain here and there pitched up through the soil and bearing fringes of forest. On the edge of this landscape, five miles

away, glides the Shenandoah River, and around that lifts and
sweeps the magnificent crescent of the Blue Ridge, closing the
vision under thirty miles of eastern sky. That vision, beyond
the gaudy military parade at his feet, caught at last John
Brown's eye before he dropped from the scaffold."

His last written words, penned in the jail-room as
he was about to leave it for ever, were a prophecy. His
last spoken words were those of calm and pleasant resignation. The last writing was in chirography clear,
firm, strong; in sentiment solemn, prescient, majestic:

CHARLESTOWN, VA., 2d December, 1859.

I, John Brown, am now quite certain that the crimes of this
guilty land: will never be purged *away;* but with *Blood.* I
had *as I now think vainly* flattered myself that without very
much *bloodshed;* it might be done.

Truly could it be said and sung—

They may hang him on the gibbet; they
  may raise the victor's cry
When they see him darkly swinging
  like a speck against the sky;—
Ah! the dying of a hero that the right
  may win its way;
Is but sowing seed for harvest in a
  warm and mellow May!
Now his story shall be whispered by
  the firelight's evening glow,
And in fields of rice and cotton when
  the hot noon passes slow,
Till his name shall be a watchword
  from Missouri to the sea,
And his planting find its reaping in
  the birthday of the Free!
        Edna Dean Proctor.

Between the second and fifteenth of December there was little of interest in Virginia, at least. The people of Charlestown and vicinity managed, however, to keep up the abnormal excitement on which they had been feeding. At the North, the effects of John Brown's execution was not all pleasant to the gentlemen of Virginia who had made use of it as a means of training their cohorts for an attack on the United States itself in the near future. Some demonstrations may have been satisfactory to them, such, for example, as the breaking up by a Boston " mob in broadcloth " of a sympathy meeting in Tremont Temple. But, as a rule, the rising tide of opinion expressed nothing but sympathetic opinion, not at the " raid " made by John Brown, but at the cruelty and cowardice the slaveholders had shown. The body of the Liberator had been carried in solemn sorrow from Harper's Ferry to North Elba and there laid beside the grand granite boulder, which now, in monumental letters, boldly chisseled, bears the words:

JOHN BROWN.

" Marvelous old man !" said Wendell Phillips at the side of his grave.[1] " We have hardly said it when the loved form of his sons, in the bloom of young devotion, encircled him. We remember he is not alone, only the majestic center of a group. . . . How resolute each looked into the face of Virginia, how loyally each stood at his forlorn post, meeting death cheerfully, till that master-voice said, 'It is enough.' And these weeping children and widows so lifted up and consecrated by long, single-hearted devotion to his great purpose,

---

[1] From speech delivered at the grave of John Brown, North Elba, December 8, 1859.

that we dare, even at this moment, to remind them how blessed they are in the privilege of thinking that in the last throbs of those brave, young hearts, . . . thoughts of them mingled with love to God and hope for the slave. He has abolished slavery in Virginia. You may think this is too much. Our neighbors are the last men we know. The hours that pass us are the ones we appreciate the least. . . . History will date Virginian Emancipation from Harper's Ferry. True, the slave is still there. So, when the tempest uproots a pine . . . it looks green for months,—a year or two. John Brown has loosened the roots of the slave system ; it only breathes,—it does not live,—hereafter. . . . I feel honored to stand under such a roof. . . . Thank God for such a master. . . . What lessons shall these lips teach us ? . . . His words, they are stronger even than his rifles. These crushed a State. Those have changed the thoughts of millions, and will yet crush slavery. . . . God make us all worthier of him whose dust we lay among these hills he loved. Here he girded himself and went forth to battle. Fuller success than his heart ever dreamed God granted him. He sleeps in the blessings of the crushed and the poor, and men believe more firmly in virtue, now that such a man has lived."

A movement was made to secure a commutation of Edwin Coppoc's sentence. Governor Wise seems to have entered frankly into this, and it went so far that a committee of the State Legislature were in favor of making his sentence one of "imprisonment for life." Edwin's family were Quakers, and the great influence of that sect was brought to bear in his favor. It was, however, rejected by the Legislature. Wise could not, under the law, commute the sentences of any of the men convicted of treason, he was able, therefore, to shield himself behind the Legislature. At Charlestown, the relatives of Cook and Coppoc were permitted to see them. The latter's grandfather and uncle, from Salem, Ohio, and Cook's sister and husband, Mr. and Mrs. Willard, with Miss Hughes, a cousin, were prolonging their farewells. In the town was a Kansas man, Charles Lenhart, who, under disguise, had secured a position where he was striving to be of service.   On the night of the 14th of December, Lenhart was on guard and at the angle of the jail wall where, the next night, the spectacle of their heads above its edge created the alarm of a faithful pro-slavery sentinel.   The attempt was not made on the 14th, because Mr. and Mrs. Willard were still in the town.   They had bade their brother farewell and were expected to leave so as to reach an evening train to the West, but at the last moment Mrs. Willard broke down and was obliged to remain till the next day.   Knowledge of this compelled the two prisoners to postpone their attempt until the next night, when they failed.   The Associated Press report states:

"The sentinel stationed near the jail reported that at 8.15 o'clock he observed a man on the jail wall.   He challenged him, and, receiving no answer, fired at him.   Another head was also seen above the wall, but it disappeared as soon as the first one had been fired at.   The man on the top of the wall seemed at first determined to jump down, but the sentinel declared his intention of impaling him on his bayonet, and he then retreated into the jail-yard with Coppoc, and both gave themselves up without further resistance.   Cook afterwards remarked that if he could have got over and throttled the guard, he would have made his escape.   The Shenandoah Mountains are within ten minutes' run of the jail wall, and had he reached them, with his thorough knowledge of the mountains, his arrest would have been difficult—especially as but few of the military could have followed him during the night.

26

They acknowledged that they had been at work a whole week
in making the aperture in the wall.   Their cell being on the
first floor, the aperture was not more than five feet above the
pavement of the yard, and when freed of their shackles their
access to the yard was quite easy.   Here, however, there was
a smooth brick wall, about fifteen feet high, to scale. This difficulty was, however, soon overcome with the aid of the timbers
of the scaffold on which Captain Brown was hung, and which
was intended also for their own execution.   They placed these
against the wall and soon succeeded in reaching the top, from
which they could have easily dropped to the other side, had
not the vigilance of the sentinel on duty so quickly checked
their movements."

    The account written on the morning of the execu-
tion by John E. Cook differs slightly from that of the
Associated Press.   It is as follows :

    " Having been called upon to make a fair statement in regard
to the ways and means of our breaking jail, I have agreed to do
so from a sense of duty to the sheriff of the county, our jailer,
and the jail guard.   We do not wish that any one should be
unjustly censured on our account.   The principal implements
with which we opened a passage through the wall of the jail
were a barlow knife and a screw which we took out of the
bedstead.
    " The knife was borrowed from one of the jail guards to cut
a lemon with.   We did not return it to him.   He had no idea
of any intention on our part to break out, neither did the
sheriff, jailer, or any of the guard, have any knowledge of our
plans.
    " We received no aid from any person or persons whatever.
We had, as we supposed, removed all the brick except the last
tier, several days ago, but on the evening previous to our breaking out, we found our mistake in regard to that matter.
    " We had intended to go out on the evening that my sister
and brother-in-law were here, but I knew that it would reflect

on them, and we postponed it—but I urged Coppoc to go and I would remain, but he refused. We then concluded to wait.

"I got a knife blade from Shields Green, and with that made some teeth in the barlow knife, with which we sawed off our shackles. We had them all off the night previous to our getting out. Coppoc went out first and I followed. We then got up on the wall, when I was discovered and shot at. The guard outside the wall immediately came up to the wall.

"We saw there was no chance to escape, and as it was discovered that we had broken jail, we walked in deliberately and gave ourselves up to the sheriff, Captain Avis, and the jail guard. There was no person or persons who aided us in our escape. This is true, so help us God.

JOHN E. COOK.
EDWIN COPPOC.

The regular Press reports are drawn upon for an account of the excitement following the attempted escape and of the proceeding at the double executions of the following day.

"At daybreak this morning the *reveille* was sounded from the various barracks, announcing the dawn of the day of execution, and soon the whole community was astir. The weather was bright and beautiful, and much milder than for several preceding days. At nine o'clock the entire military force in attendance was formed on Main street, and the officers reported ready for duty at headquarters. Those companies detailed for field duty around the gallows immediately took up the line of march, and at 9.30 o'clock were in the positions assigned them in the field. Those companies detailed for escort duty took up their positions in front of the jail, awaiting orders.

"At 10.30 o'clock General Taliaferro, with his staff, numbering about twenty-five officers, having given orders to prepare the two negro prisoners, Shields Green and John Copeland, for execution, took their departure to join the main body of the troops on the field. The military then formed in a hollow

around the jail, and an open wagon, containing the coffins of
the prisoners, drew up in front, with a carriage to convey
Sheriff Campbell and his deputies. The crowd of citizens and
strangers was very great—at least five times as numerous as
on the occasion of Brown's execution—most of whom were
already on the field, while others wanted to see the prisoners
come out."

Religious services were performed in the prisoners'
cell, and at a quarter to eleven their departure was
made. According to the report,

" Copeland and Green seemed downcast and wore none of
that calm and cheerful spirit evinced by Brown under similar
circumstances. They were helped into the wagon and took
their seats on their coffins without scarcely looking to the right
or left. . . . They mounted the scaffold with a firm step,
and were immediately joined by Sheriff Campbell. . . .

" Green died very easy, his neck being broken by the fall.
The motion of his body was very slight. Copeland seemed
to suffer very much, and his body writhed in violent contor-
tions for several minutes. The bodies were placed in poplar
coffins and carried back to jail. They will be interred to-morrow on the spot where the gallows stands, but there is a party
of medical students here from Winchester who will doubtless
not allow them to remain there long."

John Edwin Cook and Edwin Coppoc were called
from their cells at half past twelve, the religious
services having closed. The report says that—

" They were reserved and rather quiet. Cook gave directions in regard to one or two articles: one, a breast-pin, he
did not want taken off, then, nor at the scaffold. He wished
it given to his wife, or to his boy if he lived. Within
his shirt-bosom, on the left side, was a daguerreotype and
lock of his son's hair, which he wished given to his wife.
During these proceedings, Coppoc was struggling to keep

down his emotion and Cook was striving to be calm.   The
Quaker gentleman remarked that 'it was hard to die,' to which
Coppoc responded, 'It is the parting from friends, not the
dread of death, that moves us.'   On the way down stairs they
were allowed to advance to the cell of Stevens and Hazlett, and
bid them farewell.   They shook hands cordially, and Cook
said to Stevens, 'My friend, good-by.'   Stevens said, 'Good
by, cheer up ; give my love to my friends in the other world.'
Coppoc also made a remark to Stevens, which was unheard by
the crowd, but Stevens replied, 'Never mind.'   Both then
shook hands with Hazlett, and bade him 'good-by,' but did
not call him by name.   On emerging from jail, Cook recognized several gentlemen and bowed politely.

   "After the cap had been placed on their heads, Coppoc
turned toward Cook, and stretched forth his hand as far as
possible.   At the same time Cook said, 'Stop a minute—where
is Edwin's hand ?'   They then shook hands cordially, and Cook
said, 'God bless you.'   The calm and collected manner of
both was very marked.   On approaching the scaffold, Cook
shook hands with a large number of persons, and bowed
politely to Mayor Green. . . .   They both exhibited the most
unflinching firmness, saying nothing, with the exception of
bidding farewell to the ministers and sheriff.   After the rope
was adjusted, Cook exclaimed, 'Be quick—as quick as possible,' which was also repeated by Coppoc.   After hanging for
about half an hour, both bodies were taken down and placed
in black walnut coffins, prepared for them.   That of Cook was
placed in a poplar box, labeled and directed as follows: 'Ash-
bell P. Willard and Robert Crowley, No. 104 William street,
New York, care of Adams's Express.'   Coppoc's body was
placed in a similar box, to be forwarded to his relatives in
Salem, Ohio."

From the 16th of December, 1859, until the 2d of
February, 1860, when Aaron Dwight Stevens and
Albert Hazlett were arraigned, little transpired at
Charlestown of any moment.   From a constant

parade of from 1,000 to 3,000 armed militia (the first
named force were, it seems, necessary to secure the
peaceful execution of Green, Copeland, Cook and
Coppoc, the latter number that of John Brown) the
guard had diminished, first to two companies, and
finally to one of about sixty men. Judge Parker
being too reluctant to continue the task, another
district judge, Mr. Kenny, took his place on the
bench. Andrew Hunter represented the State; George
Sennott, of Boston, with undiminished energy, defended the prisoners. Before the proceedings fairly
begun, Mr. Sennott read a letter he had addressed to
President Buchanan, with the reply thereto.[1]

---

[1] To His Excellency JAMES BUCHANAN, President of the United
    States:

The undersigned respectfully invites the attention of the President to the case of Aaron D. Stevens, whose counsel he is.

Mr. Stevens was arrested in the armory grounds at Harper's
Ferry, during the late disturbances there. He was committed for
examination under the authority of the United States. Afterwards, and before any such examination was made, he was indicted
for treason and other capital offenses, in and against the Commonwealth of Virginia. He was forced to plead; but he was so dreadfully wounded as to be in a dying condition, and the humanity of
the court would not urge his trial, which was indefinitely postponed.

Contrary to expectations, however, he did not die of his five
desperate and all but mortal wounds, and it was thought fit to try
him. The people, who had shown little sympathy for the other
prisoners, were deeply moved when this young man was brought
in on a bed and laid on the courthouse floor. A jury was partly
empaneled, and the undersigned, who had asked for delay without
success, was present and ready to proceed with the trial. All at
once, without any consultation with the defendant, proceedings
were suspended, and a dispatch, said to be from the Governor of

In his reply to a demand of Governor Wise, dated
Nov. 25, 1859, for use of United States troops to pre-

Virginia, recommending the defendant to be given up to the
authorities of the United States, was read in open court. In this
arrangement the defendant, being asked to do so by the counsel
conducting the case for the Commonwealth, acquiesced, and consented to the suspending of the trial with the understanding that
he was to be delivered into the custody of the United States, and
to be tried in their courts.

But now, from private advices and fron the public acts of the
Legislature of Virginia, we learn that the Commonwealth is about
to retract its own proposition, made to and accepted by Mr.
Stevens in good faith on his part, and without any, the slightest
shadow, of constraint upon the part of the Commonwealth, Mr.
Stevens is to be again taken from the marshal's custody, and a
special session of the Circuit Court of Jefferson County is proposed to try him, though the regular session comes on as early as
May.

Such, according to the best of his information and belief, being
the facts, the undersigned, as it was his duty to do, respectfully
inquires of the President what action, if any, the authorities of the
United States have taken, or propose to take, in the case of Aaron
D. Stevens. The forlorn and desperate condition of the man, and
his uncomplaining fortitude, appeal for an answer to the well-
known humanity of the President much more strongly than any
claim which the undersigned imagines he has to be answered.
The answer is plainly of the last importance to the defendant, and
is awaited with great anxiety and respect by his counsel, the
President's humble, obedient servant.   GEO. SENNOTT.

WASHINGTON, Dec. 16, 1859.

DEAR SIR—I have received your favor of the 13th instant, and
immediately telegraphed to Andrew Hunter, Esq., to ascertain
whether Mr. Stevens had been actually delivered to the United
States authorities according to the current report. His answer,
dated to-day, is as follows: "Stevens has not been delivered to
the authorities of the United States. Undecided as yet whether
he will be tried here. He is still in the Charlestown jail." Yours
very respectfully,   JAMES BUCHANAN.

vent alleged "invasions" of the State of Virginia,
from Pennsylvania and Ohio, Mr. Buchanan said that

. . . "There is one measure which, on the presumption
that your information is well founded, it is both my right and
my duty to adopt: that is, to reinforce the guard already at
Harper's Ferry." This is necessary, he wrote, to protect public property as well as to prevent "insurgents" from "seizing
arms," and he adds, "Besides it is possible the additional
troops *may be required to act as posse comitatus on the requisition of the marshal* of the United States for the western
district of Virginia, to prevent the rescue of Stevens, *now in
his custody, charged with the crime of high treason.*"

When, however, the question is that of Stevens's
trial and execution by Virginia, the President who
could send troops to keep him as a Federal prisoner,
transmits his counsel the baldfaced acknowledgment of legal fraud in the form of a dispatch from
the United States marshal to the effect, that "*Stevens
has not been delivered to the authorities of the United
States.*" A curious dilemma this to be impaled upon.

Mr. Sennott moved for Stevens's discharge on the
ground that the Commonwealth had offered a trial
in the United States Court, and that the offer had
been accepted. Hunter denied that such a proposition had ever been made in court. Governor Wise
had recommended it to be done, "in order to reach
Brown's confederates." He withdrew that, however,
on the appointment of the Mason Committee by the
United States Senate. Harding, the inebriated and
snubbed county attorney, took the occasion to say
that Hunter had proposed the same thing as Governor
Wise, and that he, Harding, did then and would have
resisted in court the carrying out of any such con-

tract.   Sennott's motion was overruled and the trial proceeded rapidly to conviction and sentence.[1]

---

[1] A copy of the first count of the indictment against Stevens is given below with a statement of the other two counts. It will be seen that the charges of treason and murder were abandoned in his case, as also in that of Albert Hazlett. They were presented "for advising" certain "slaves" to "rebel and make insurrection," as per the first count here given, of "conspiring" to do the same thing in the other two. The quaint phraseology is of interest, and the historical significance of the document warrants the quoting of this count:

Virginia, to wit: In the Circuit Court of Jefferson county, Thirteenth Judicial Circuit of Virginia, Jefferson county, to wit:

First count—The Jurors of the Commonwealth of Virginia, in and for the body of the county of Jefferson, duly empanneled and attending upon said Court, upon their oaths present, that Aaron D. Stevens, being a free person, on the sixteenth and seventeenth days of the month of October, in the year eighteen hundred and fifty-nine, and on divers other days before and after that time, in the county of Jefferson and the Commonwealth of Virginia aforesaid, and within the jurisdiction of that Court, not having the fear of God before his eyes, but moved and seduced by the instigations of the devil, did maliciously, willfully, and feloniously, advise certain slaves of the county and Commonwealth aforesaid, to wit: slaves called Jim, Sam. Mason, and Catesby, the slaves of Lewis W. Washington, and slaves called Henry, Levi, Ben, Jerry, Phil, George, and Bill, the slaves of John H. Allstadt, and each of said slaves severally, to rebel and make insurrection against their said masters respectively, and against the authority of the constitution and laws of the said Commonwealth of Virginia, to the evil example of all others in like case offending against the form of the statute in that case provided, and against the peace and dignity of the Commonwealth.

*   *   *   *   *   *   *   *

Lewis W. Washington, Alexander Kelly, William D. Copeland, John McClelland, Jesse Grimes, Benjamin F. Beall, Lewis P. Stary, and George H. Furtney—witnesses sworn in open court

It will be observed that the fact of " slaves " assisting the raiders is herein judicially and historically
acknowledged. Virginian authorities at that time
endeavored to minimize the sympathetic position
of the enslaved people. Ten slaves are named as
being "advised" with, but, in the third count, the
indictment for conspiracy runs against those already
named and divers other slaves to the jurors unknown,
The trial of Albert Hazlett, as "William Harrison,
alias Albert Hazlett" was opened on the 8th of February. There was really, as before stated, but little direct
proof of his connection with the Harper's Ferry raid.
Except in the case of one witness, who identified Hazlett as the raider by whom he was captured and treated
well, even to risking himself to prevent injury to the
prisoner, the chief testimony was of the flimziest circumstantial character. Another point which told
for identification was the fact that when captured,
Albert Hazlett carried a Sharpe's rifle, pistol, and
cartridge-belt and box. It is safe to say that had
Hazlett's arrest occurred in Ohio, he would not have
been surrendered to Virginia by that State, and upon
the evidence offered. At a later date a test was given
in the case of Francis J. Merriam, whose surrender
was demanded. Governor Chase replied that no evidence was offered that Merriam had even been in Virginia. He never had, except as a passenger on a rail-

this first day of February, 1860, to give evidence to the Grand Jury
upon the bill of indictment.

ROBT. T. BROWN,
Clerk of the Circuit Court of Jefferson County.
ROBT. T. BROWN, County Clerk.

road train. Nor was there any proof of Hazlett's presence in Virginia submitted to the examining officer at Carlisle, Pennsylvania, showing that the arrested man had ever been in the State demanding his surrender. All this, however, passed for nothing. Virginia demanded her victim and got him. All the idle talk of Governor Wise's "merciful" desires, which were rife in the sad and tragic panorama, between the 19th of October, 1859, and the 16th day of February, 1860, are blown away like thistledown in the breeze, when the execution of Stevens and Hazlett is recalled. It was a piece of pure savagery, demanded only by the merciless voracity of slaveholding fury. Stevens or Hazlett never became parties to any appeals for mercy. They neither expected or asked it. Their able and energetic counsel, Mr. Sennot, did all that he could; all that any lawyer might, but against the inexorable maw of public opinion, excited by dread of attack on "property" in human beings, and excited to fury by the exaggerations of political conspirators seeking to rend apart the Federal Union, nothing but death could be the outcome. And these young men, handsome, gallant, unflinching, and true in their manly fortitude, with "malice towards none and charity for all," went to the gallows on the 16th of March, 1860, with a debonair courage befitting their years and a dignity of mien and manner that exalted the cause for which they, with the others, had so ungrudgingly lived and died.

So John Brown and his men battered the citadel wall—a forlorn hope, which perished in the doing. Lo! the wall was rent in twain, revealing all the

creeping, slimy horrors that oppression creates in the
hearts and brains of the oppressors themselves! We
learned, as never before, the truth of Lamartine's
saying that man never fastens a chain around the
heel of his fellow man, but what God fastens the
other end around the neck of the oppressor!

CHAPTER XIII.

AS SEEN BY HIMSELF, FAMILY, NEIGHBORS, AND FRIENDS.

John Brown, the farmer—His characteristics—The father and teacher—Business illustrates integrity—Leader of the slave—How he reasoned—In prison and his cheerfulness—Religious philosophy—A modern Franklin—The North Elba home—How the family bore it—Oliver's and Watson's wives.

THEY held themselves "as the Lord's free people, to walk in all His ways made known, or to be made known to them, according to their best endeavors, WHATEVER IT MAY COST THEM."

This was a part of the covenant which Peter Brown, the carpenter, nearly two hundred and fifty years before his sixth descendant, John Brown, swung from a Virginian gallows for the " crime " of seeking to overthrow chattel slavery, signed in the cabin of the *Mayflower*, one December morning in the seventeenth century. Oliver Wendell Holmes, in "Elsie Venner," writes of a man's brain and body as being an omnibus, filled with his ancestors. Surely, John Brown's Pilgrim progenitor drove the vehicle that rumbled to the scaffold at Charlestown, while the revolutionary grandfather must have served as its conductor. If a man ever obeyed the law of heredity, it was John Brown! If a citizen ever made an apotheosis of such loftier civic duties, as came to him, it was John Brown! And all that led thereto was as but part of his daily life and hourly walk. To him it was not necessary to exalt the horn of righteousness; yet every note or blast thereof fell on ears attuned to understand. There is not in American historical literature more quaint, sincere materials from which to weave, as a living fabric, the life of an American and New England family—such a life as was constantly lived within the first six decades of this century, than can be found in the published letters, or mass of unpublished reminiscences and manuscripts still existing, written by John Brown, or by members of his family to him and to others. The homely details of a severe and Spartan life are, however, gilded therein by a frank simplicity of spirit. The animating forces of noble, redemptive subjectivity of soul, always active and informing, touches each seemingly severe detail into that clearness of outline which heat brings back to an incrusted and battered die or medallion. Every line glows, and the beauty of true endeavor burns from the inner life to the outer environment. It is not designed to give John Brown's letters and papers here—the important ones may be found in the Appendix—but enough may be quoted from himself, his "most familiar acquaintances—his family," as he once quaintly expressed it, and his immediate neighbors and friends, to show in truth what manner of man it was that American slavery thought fit to hang with such awesome pomp and fearsome ceremony. Hung as a lawbreaker, of course, and according to "law," but no defense of the great

lawbreakers, from Moses to Washington, can be
made that will not count John Brown as a saint
among them all. Let us see, then, what manner of
man he was, apart from the deeds that sent his soul
" marching on."

His boyhood and its conditions have been described
in the Stearns autobiographical paper, and by his
father, Owen Brown, in an autobiography which first
saw the light in Mr. Sanborn's volume.[1] So, at twenty-
four, of simple ways,[2] one of the neatest of men, and
very particular as to personal cleanliness, he would
never wear expensive clothing, however, for the reason
that their cost was a useless waste of money which
might be given to the poor. Often jocose and mirthful in speech he was hotly resentful to all vulgar
words and profane talk. Helpful to his neighbors,
and anxious to assist new settlers, but suspicious of
those whose standards differed from his own. Active
in favor of free schools, abstemious in food, never
using tobacco or intoxicating liquor, which custom
then made common and deemed no offense. He was
masterful in disposition, but open to reason; dislik-
ing to be accused of unfairness or harsh judgment,
but argumentative, somewhat set and disputatious.
He never, however, respected those who always agreed
with him. He knew the Bible thoroughly and could
use it with more aptness of illustration than any of
those about him—lay or clerical. Rigid and unbending in his religious views, he was kind and friendly

---

[1] See " Life and Letters of John Brown."

[2] This characterization of earlier life and habits in Western
Pennsylvania are condensed from a lengthy letter from W. C. Neff,
of Bradford, Pa., written in the winter of 1859–60.

in all his personal conduct and intercourse. In local affairs he was always an active organizer of good roads and free schools, a stern opponent of Sabbath-breaking, and a liberal supporter of the church he belonged to; always foremost in good citizenship. He was then a Presbyterian—a better and more ready theologian, too, than most of the preachers known in those years. Anti-slavery to the core—as then understood; in politics he was a supporter of John Quincy Adams, and, therefore, a Northern Whig. He would not vote for Henry Clay, because he defended slavery and had fought a duel. He early refused to do military duty and paid a fine in preference. Becoming a Mason in his younger manhood, he soon abandoned the fraternity, and after the Morgan excitement became strongly anti-secret society in his views. In business affairs he was shrewd and energetic, but rigidly upright and honest, " no trader " said a later friend He made good leather, and would not allow a single pound to leave the tanyard until there could by no means be any more water squeezed from it. His customers were often compelled to submit to return without their goods, as he would take no pay until the hides were completely dry. An excellent judge of timber—he owned five hundred acres of hemlock—and a good surveyor, he was in constant demand in timber lot purchases. Even then he was noted for terse, epigrammatic speech, and a quaint humor which was no respecter of persons. Having a public theological dispute with a Baptist clergyman, on the doctrine of predestination, in which John Brown was an earnest believer, he afterwards criticised his clerical opponent with considerable plainness of speech. The clergyman, who was one that magnified his office and exacted all the deference that in those days was generally tendered thereto, was quite indignant at the tanner's presumption, and called to ask if Brown had said that he, the minister, had not behaved in a gentlemanly manner? "I did say you were no gentleman. ·I said more than that, sir," was the slow response.

"What did you say?" queried the indignant cleric.

"I said, sir, it would take as many men like you to make a gentleman as it would take hens to make a cock turkey."

The Baptist preacher felt compelled to give the Presbyterian farmer another chance to debate. The complaint made of the preceding discussion was that the clergyman talked too fast, overrode his slower antagonist, and agreed to no rules. In the second debate, twenty-four questions were propounded, a moderator chosen, and both sides kept down to strict time and methods. John Brown was considered successful on this occasion..

In the early 'thirties it was a common saying in Crawford County (Pa.), when speaking of a man who won the respect of the people, that he was as honest as John Brown and as good to his country; no higher praise could be given.

It is told of him, by Mr. Neff, and the incident is one he vouched for, that a journeyman working in Brown's tanyard was suspected, and, after quiet investigation, proven to be guilty of stealing a calfskin hide. Orders were issued to say nothing. After some time, however, the brother of the delinquent was known to have offered the stolen goods for sale.

27

John Brown called the two men into his barn and
there told them of his knowledge, convicting the thief
so clearly, that he confessed. John Brown's punishment was to tell him to go to work again, be honest
in all his actions, and nothing should ever be said of
it. He charged his household with silence. The
young man became foreman in the tanyard and the
early fact was unknown until years after he told it
himself to the honor of his benefactor. Incidents of
charity are many, extended alike to those whom he
held under suspicion. To a debtor whom he had
relieved in distress, and who was unable, at the time
set, to discharge the debt of thirty dollars, he said:
"Return home and take care of your family and let
me hear no more of this debt. It is part of my religion to assist those in distress and comfort those who
mourn."

A man stole a cow and John Brown was among the
more active in bringing him to trial and punishment,
yet all through the following winter the tanner traveled regularly through the heavy snow to furnish the
imprisoned man's family with sufficient supplies for
their needs.

He was never interested in hunting or fishing,
though active in other athletic sports, being an excellent wrestler and a fair horseman. He loved good
stock ; sheep, cattle, and horses. After he moved to
Ohio he bred fine horses, two of them becoming
noted racers. This pursuit, however, he abandoned,
because of the doubtful associations of racing and
horse-trading. He was not a graceful rider, but
knew how to manage a horse and could not be easily
thrown. He loved the land and all work upon the

soil, once congratulating his sons, John, Jason, and Frederick, on following the "pursuit of the patri- archs." He loved the mountains, and was "enam- oured of all out-o'-doors." Music delighted him, and he felt the strains of Schubert as well as the spur of martial playing. Just before his death, his old friend, Mr. Lowry, of Pennsylvania (afterwards a Representative in Congress), was permitted to see him. While conversing in his cell, the strains of a military band were heard, Governor Wise being en- gaged in reviewing the garrison. The Captain was asked if it did not disturb him. "Not at all," was the reply, "it is inspiring." His favorite hymn was "Blow ye the Trumpet, Blow." "He sung us to sleep by it," wrote one of his daughters, "when we were little ones." The Psalms of David and the Prophecies of Isaiah and Jeremiah, with the poetic grandeur of Job, fed with their splendid fervor his own winged imagination. The night with its planetary display, was a constant study and delight. His fail- ure, in 1842, was due to buying land in that way, and though legally relieved by bankruptcy proceedings from his liabilities, he was seeking always to the day of his death to meet the obligations then incurred. In his will he directed $50 to be paid on that account. While unable to fall in successfully as a merchant with the conditions of competitive traffic, every one with whom he came in contact during his thirty-five years of such activities testifies to his integrity and uprightness. It has taken the latter-day politicians, who benefited by his struggles for free Kansas, to suggest a want of veracity in speech and honesty in purpose. Even the New England editor who ad-

duced as proof of insanity the statement that if John
Brown as a wool merchant believed a thing was
right, he would wreck all his affairs in the effort to
do the same, declared that, at the banks John
Brown's word was as good as another man's note.
An old associate, Mr. Baldwin, of Ohio, who had business and personal relations with him for years, wrote
of him as a "man of rigid integrity." George Leach,
another of his earlier friends, declared he was
"strictly conscientious and honest, but of ardent im-
pulses and strong religious feelings." Mr. Otis, of
Akron, Ohio, wrote in 1859 that "I always regarded
him (John Brown) as a man of more than ordinary
mental capacity, a kind neighbor, a good Christian,
deeply imbued with religious feelings and sympathies. . . . I never knew his integrity to be
questioned by any one." A former chief-justice of
Massachusetts, Judge Rufus Chapman, was Brown's
counsel at Springfield, and his characterization of his
famous client is a good one: He was "a quiet and
peaceable citizen and a religious man," whose "integrity was never doubted; honorable in all his dealings," he was "peculiar" and possessed of "great
obstinacy." Mr. E. C. Leonard, who knew him well
in the Springfield wool-dealing years (1847 *et al*),
says that "Uncle John was no trader; he waited until
his wools were graded and then fixed a price; if this
suited the manufacturers, they took the fleeces; if
not, they bought elsewhere, and Uncle John had to
submit finally to a much lower price than he could
have got. Yet he was a scrupulously honest and upright man—hard and inflexible, but everybody had
just what belonged to them." There is no need of

inquiring further why John Brown was not a successful "trader." He emphasized in business, it
seems, what he advised his daughter Ruth when a
young girl, that is, "to be all that to-day, which she
intends to be to-morrow." In his connection with
the litigation, which arose over this wool business, a
gentleman connected with the New York law firm
(Vernon near Utica) that served as his counsel said that
his "memory and acuteness often astonished" them.
He was then 54 years of age, "a clean-shaven, scrupulously neat, well-dressed old gentleman." Is it any
wonder, then, that John Brown could write to his son
John, that "It is a source of the utmost comfort to
feel that I retain a warm place in the sympathies,
affections, and confidence of my own most familiar
acquaintances, *my family ;* a man can hardly get into
difficulties too big to be surmounted if he has a firm
foothold at home. Remember that."

Indeed, John Brown had strange conceptions of
business and was not in harmony with its more
ordinary precepts. All his troubles, he said, arose
from trying to do business on credit. In 1847, he
wrote that "to get a little property together to leave,
. . . is really a low mark to be firing at through
life. . . . Running into debt includes so much
evil," he declares, "that I hope my children will shun
it as they would a pestilence. . . . Regular out-
of-doors labor I believe to be one of the best medicines of all that God has yet provided. . . . A
world of pleasure and success," he writes John, "is
the sure and constant attendant upon early rising.
It makes all the business of the day go off with peculiar cheerfulness, while the effects of the contrary

course are a great and constant draft upon one's
vitality."

"On our first visit to the Adirondacks," writes
Ruth, "Father wanted us to notice how fragrant the
air was, filled with the perfume of the spruce, hem-
locks, and balsams. Soon after we had settled there,
he one day called us together and asked if he should
spend a little money he had to spare in furnishing
the parlor, or spend it in paying for clothing for the
colored people, who may need help in North Elba
another year. We all said (the older ones present),
' Save the money.' " Once, when asked by Ruth to
write a long letter of " good advice," he wrote a short
one, saying, " Would you believe that the long story
would be that ye *sin* not, that you form no foolish
attachments, and that you be not a companion of
fools." Another time he writes, that "God is carrying out His eternal purpose in them all." And he
hopes to his sons, " that entire leanness of soul may
not attend any little success in business." His letters
are full of aphorisms like these: "Who can tell or
comprehend the vast results for good or evil that are
to follow the saying of one little word." " Everything worthy of being done at all is worthy of being
done in good earnest, and in the best possible manner." . . . Of the little house at Elba, on taking
possession, he remarked, "It is very small, but
the main thing is, that we all keep good natured."
Writing his wife from Springfield, he declares that
"It is my growing resolution to promote my own
happiness by doing what I can to render those about
me happier." Mingling husbandry with faith, he says,
"Sheep and cattle are doing well; and I would be

most happy to add that in wisdom and good morals we are all improving." Of his first visit (1840) to the Virginia Alleghanies, in the interest of Oberlin College, Ohio, has already been mentioned. He wrote his wife from Ripley, that "Were the inhabitants as resolute and industrious as the Northern people, and did they understand how to manage as well, they would become rich, but they are not generally so. . . . By comparing them with the people of other parts of the country, I can see new and abundant proofs that knowledge is power. I think we might be very useful to them on many accounts, were we so disposed."

How vividly and forceful comes his words as the period of probation shortens and the days of action begin. From Kansas he writes, in 1856, that "We have, like David of old, had our dwellings with the serpents of the rocks and wild beasts of the wilderness, being obliged to hide away from our enemies. We were not disheartened, though nearly destitute of food, clothing, and money. God, who has not given over to the will of our enemies, but has moreover delivered them into our hands, will, we humbly trust, still keep and deliver us. We feel assured that He, who sees not as men see, does not lay the guilt of innocent blood to our charge." To his wife, after the Osawatomie fight, he says : " I was struck by a partly spent grape, canister, or rifle shot, which bruised me some, but did not injure me seriously. Hitherto the Lord has helped me, notwithstanding my afflictions." He saw the issues plainly, writing home that " The slaveholders are neither disheartened as yet, nor indifferent, nor inactive. . . . They

are gathering assurance and determination. They
see the magnitude of the issue; . . . a prominent
Missourian declared that, to prevent Kansas from
becoming a free State, Missouri should pour half her
population 'temporarily, at least,' into the Territory.
. . . We are in the midst of a revolution, as you
will see by the papers. How we shall come out of
the furnace, God only knows. That we have got to
enter it, some of us, there is no doubt; but we are
ready to be offered."

After the second sacking of Lawrence, Kansas, in
May, 1856, Captain Brown's comment was, that
"Their leading men had (as I think) decided in a
very cowardly manner not to resist any process having any government official to serve it." Before the
Massachusetts Legislature, on the 18th of February,
1857, he remarked tersely, "We want men who fear
God too much to fear anything human." To Mr.
Stearns, and other gentlemen met at Medford, Mass.,
he declared, "I believe in the Golden Rule, sir, and
the Declaration of Independence. I think they both
mean the same thing; and it is better that a whole
generation should pass off the face of the earth—
men, women, and children—by a violent death than
that one jot of either should fail in this country. I
mean exactly *so*, sir."

He was emphatic when occasion arose, in saying,
"Do not allow any one to say I acted from revenge.
It is a feeling that does not enter my heart. What I
do, I do for the cause of human liberty, and because
I regard it as necessary." To William A. Phillips, in
Kansas, when the colonel pointed out danger in a
conflict with the United States troops, the stern and

uncompromising old man replied: "And why not? The people of Kansas are doing nothing here but what they have a right to do as American citizens. If the regular army interferes, they have no right to do it. It is the act of a blackguard, whoever does it; and if a blackguard, doing a blackguard's business, should happen to desecrate the United States livery, we cannot help it. It is our duty to protect our rights." Some mention being made of farcial judicial proceedings, common to early Kansas history, Captain Brown grimly said to Mr. Stearns that "If the Lord had delivered Judge Lecompte into my hands, I think it would have required the Lord to have taken him out again." When first invited to call at Medford on "his business," it being Sunday, deference was paid to his views. But, on being asked, he said, "Mr. Stearns, I have a poor little ewe that has fallen into the ditch, and I think the Sabbath is as good a day as any to help her out. I will come." There was a grim directness in his suggestion to the National Kansas Aid Committee, in February, 1857: "Gentlemen, we had rather have one rifle without contingencies than two hundred with them."

John Brown thought "a standing army the greatest curse to a country, because it drained off the best of the young men and left farming and the industrial arts to be managed by inferior men." "Give a slave a pike, and you make him a man. . . . Deprive him of the means of resistance, and you keep him down." To colored men organized to resist arrest as fugitive slaves, he advised that they "Do not delay one moment after you are ready; you will lose all your resolution, if you do. . . . No jury can be

found in the Northern States that would convict a
man for defending his rights to the last extremity.
. . . Your plans must be known only to yourself,
and with the understanding that all traitors must
die, wherever caught and proven to be guilty. . . .
Collect quietly, so as to outnumber the adversaries
who are taking an active part against you; make
clear work of all such, and be sure you meddle not
with any other. . . . Stand by one another and
by your friends while a drop of blood remains, and
be hanged, if you must, but tell no tales out of
school; *make no confessions.*" And he required them
to pledge that "We will ever be true to the flag of
our beloved country, always acting under it." He
told Mr. Sanborn, early in their friendship, that he
"had much considered the matter, and had about
concluded that the forcible separation of the connection between master and slave was necessary to fit
the blacks for self-government. . . . When the
slaves stand like men, the nation will respect them;
it is necessary to teach them this." "Negroes behaved
so much like folks, he almost thought they were so."
"A few men in the right, and knowing that they are
right, can overturn a mighty king. Fifty men,
twenty men, in the Alleghenies would break slavery
to pieces in two years. . . . The mountains and
swamps of the South were intended by God as a
refuge for the slave, and a defense against his
master. . . . Slavery, being maintained by force
must be overthrown by force." To Judge Russell, of
Boston, he said, "It would be better that a whole
generation should perish from the earth than that
one truth in the Sermon on the Mount or the

Declaration of Independence should be forgotten among men." Also, when it was reported that an attempt might be made to arrest him, he said, very quietly, to Mrs. Russell, "I should hate to spoil your carpets, but, you know, I cannot be taken alive." In his eyes, as he declared "the slaves were prisoners of war"; their masters had taken them by force, that is by "the sword, and must perish by it." "Tell General Lane"—during the Kansas days in 1856—"that when he wants me to fight, to say so; that is the only order I will obey." Writing on "The Duty of the Soldier," he declared that the test of "Legitimate Authority is right, and to maintain that authority soldiers are not required to be mere living machines." When it was suggested that he should fight the fellows who killed Frederick, as long as he lived, Captain Brown replied, "That is not a Christian spirit. If I had one bit of that spirit I would not lift my hand. I do not make war on slaveholders, but on slavery." In conversation with James Redpath, after the Black Jack fight, he said, "It's a mistake, sir, that our people make when they think that bullies are our best fighters. Give me men of good principles, God-fearing men, men who respect themselves, and with a dozen of them I will oppose any hundred such men as these Buford ruffians." To Henry Clay Pate, commanding the border ruffians, who was trying to parley with John Brown, the reply was : "Captain, I understand exactly what you are, and do not want to hear more about it. Have you any proposition to make to me?" "Well, no ; that is—" "Very well, Captain, I have one to make to you—your unconditional surrender."

His courage is shown when he writes: "Things now look more favorable than they have, but I may still be disappointed. We must all try to trust in Him who is very gracious and full of compassion as almighty power; for those that do will not be made ashamed." His practical view was shown when he wrote to a New England friend: "I was told that the newspapers in a certain city were dressed in mourning on hearing that I was killed and scalped in Kansas, but I did not know of it until I reached the place. Much good it did me. In the same place I met a more cool reception than in any other place where I have stopped. If my friends will hold up my hands, while I live, I will freely absolve them from any expense over me when I am dead."

In a letter from Brown to his men, written on the 18th of May, 1858, he advises them to keep up their courage, seek out farms, and say they were traveling, got out of money, etc., wanted work, offer to do it for board, and thus save in that way, and adds: " I and three others were in exactly such a fix in the spring of 1817, between the seaside and Ohio, in a time of extreme scarcity, not only of money, but of the greatest distress for want of provisions. . . . It was the next year after the 'cold summer,' as it was called, and would you believe it, some of the company are on their legs yet."

This bit of cheerful philosophy will bear quoting: " I have often passed under the rod of Him whom I call my Father; and certainly no son ever needed it oftener; and yet I have enjoyed much of life, as I was enabled to discover the secret of this somewhat early. It has been in making the prosperity and happiness of others my own; so that really I had a good deal of prosperity. I am very prosperous still."

John Brown, while certainly not without a due sense of his possible place in history, had no vanity to favor. Mrs. Stearns was very anxious to have a cast or drawing made from which the sculptor Brackett could work. He told the artist over and over again, "Its nonsense! All nonsense! Better give the money to the poor. It is of no consequence to posterity how I looked. Give the money to the poor." He only yielded when convinced that his doing would be a pleasure to Mrs. Stearns. He wrote Mrs. Child not to come to Charlestown, but if she wished to be of real aid, to start a fund, asking fifty cents from each for the benefit of his wife and children. In the movement made in 1857 to pay $1,000 for the North Elba homestead, in order to make his wife secure, he wrote Frank B. Sanborn that, if attempted the amount should be promptly raised; adding— "This, I think, much the cheapest and most proper way to provide for them (his family), and far less humiliating to my wife, who, though not above getting her bread over the washtub, will never tell her trials or wants to the world. This I know by the experiences of the past two years, while I was absent; but I would never utter a word in regard to it were I not conscious that I am performing that service which is equally the duty of millions, who need not forego a single hearty meal by the efforts they are called on to make." He was not unmindful of what he regarded as due to his name in all these matters, as is shown by his removal of the Torrington, Conn., gravestone to North Elba, and the inscriptions placed thereon.

In a letter dated Hudson, Ohio, May, 1857, he writes his wife:

"If I should never return, it is my particular request that no other monument be used to keep me in remembrance than the same plain old one that records the death of my grandfather and son; and that short story, like those already on it, be told of John Brown the fifth, under that of grandfather. . . . I would be glad that my posterity should not only remember their parentage, but also the cause they labored in."

When Governor Henry A. Wise, in his last visit to Charlestown, warned him to prepare for eternity, John Brown replied: "Governor, I have from all appearances not more than fifteen or twenty years the start of you in that eternity of which you kindly warn me; and whether my term here shall be fifteen months, or fifteen days, or fifteen hours, I am equally prepared to go. There is an eternity behind, and an eternity before, and the little spec in the center, however long, is but comparatively a minute. You all (referring to slaveholders) have all of you a heavy responsibility, and it behooves you to prepare more than it does me."

John Brown repudiated the ministrations of all the local clergymen, whenever they showed a desire to defend chattelism. To one who declared he would not fight for or aid in freeing the slaves, the stern Puritan said: "I will thank you to leave me alone; your prayers would be an abomination to my God." A preacher who argued that slavery was a "Christian institution" was told that he knew nothing about Christianity; "you," he said, "will have to learn its A, B, C; I find you quite ignorant of what the word Christianity means." Seeing that his visitor was disconcerted, John Brown added, "I respect you as a gentleman, of course, but it is as a heathen gentleman." "There are no ministers of Christ here," he wrote. "These ministers, who profess to be Christians, and hold slaves, or advocate slavery, I cannot abide them." In a letter found by Mrs. Brown after his death, he wrote: "I have asked to be spared from having any mock or hypocritical prayers made over me when I am publicly murdered;" and to Mrs. Spring he said during her prison visit: "I do not believe I shall deny my Lord and Master, Jesus Christ, as I should if I denied my principles against slavery. Why, I preach against it all the time; Captain Avis knows I do;" referring to the kindly humored jailer who was present. He told another Methodist that he "would not insult God by bowing down in prayer with any one who had the blood of the slave on his skirts."

In a letter to the Rev. H. L. Vail, his old schoolmaster, dated during the middle of November, he said: "You will not, therefore, feel surprised when I tell you I am joyful in all my tribulations; that I do not feel condemned of Him whose judgment is just, nor of my own conscience. . . . As to both the time and manner of my death—I have but very little trouble on that score, and am able to be of good cheer." To his excellent friend, Judge Russell, of Boston, he declared: "I have no kind of fault to find about the manner of my death. The disgrace of hanging does not trouble me in the least. In fact, I know that the very errors by which my scheme was marred were decreed before the world was made." His cousin, the Rev. Luther Humphrey, was told that—" The fact, that a man dies under the hand of an executioner (or otherwise) has but little to do with his true character, as I suppose. . . . I should be sixty years old were I to live to May 9, 1860. I have enjoyed much of life as it is, and have been remarkably prosperous; having early learned to regard the welfare and prosperity of others as my own. I have never, since I can remember, required a great amount of sleep; so that I conclude that I have already fully enjoyed an average number of working hours with those who reach their threescore years and ten. I have not yet been driven to the use of glasses, but can see to read and write quite comfortably. But more than that, I have generally enjoyed remarkably good health. I might go on to recount unnumbered and unmerited blessings, among which would be some very severe afflictions,—and those the most needed blessings of all. And now, when I think how easily I might be left to spoil all I have done or suffered in the cause of freedom, I hardly dare wish another voyage, even if I had the opportunity."

He considered himself, he declared, " worth inconceivably more to be hung in this cause," than to be used in any other way. He could wait the hour . . . with great composure of mind and cheerfulness. In no other possible manner could he be used to so much advantage to the cause of God and humanity. . . . " I expect nothing but to endure hardship, but I expect to achieve a great victory, even though it be like the last victory of Samson." In a last letter to Mr. Vail, he wrote, " The Captain of my salvation, who is also a Captain of liberty, has taken away my sword of steel, and put into my hands

a sword of Spirit ";—and that, " As I believe most
firmly that God reigns, I cannot believe that anything that I have done, suffered, or may yet suffer,
will be lost to the cause of God or humanity. And
before I begun my work at Harper's Ferry, I felt assured that in the worst event it would certainly *pay*."

Henry Ward Beecher preached in Plymouth Church
on Sunday morning, October 30th, 1859, twelve days
after the attack begun on Harper's Ferry, from Jeremiah vi: 12–19, using the text as a basis for a remarkable sermon on John Brown, his movement, and
character. This sermon was widely published and
commented on, more or less caustically all over the
land. It did not suit the grim old covenanter when
it reached through the pages of a spiritualist weekly,
The Telegraph. Captain Brown wrote a series of running comments on the margin, and this paper passed
into the possession (with certificates of its genuineness from Captain Avis, A. D. Stevens, and Sheriff
Campbell) of W. W. B. Gallaher, one of the *New York
Herald's* correspondents,[1] who was serving also as a

---

[1] " CHARLESTOWN, Dec. 10, '59.

" I hereby certify that W. W. B. Gallaher sent to Captain John
Brown a copy of some newspaper with a request that he would
give his opinion of a sermon therein published of the Rev. H.
Ward Beecher; that Captain Brown did make comments upon the
same, in his own handwriting upon the margin, and other blank
places of said paper.

" I also certify that I heard Captain Brown deny that his comments were correctly printed in the *New York Herald.*

" I also certify that the certificate of A. D. Stevens was signed
in my presence.

[Test]   J. W. GALLAHER, Jail Guard.

JOHN AVIS, Jailer.

" Jail Guard." Mr. Beecher's opening references to
the attack and characterization of John Brown himself, is quietly sat upon by the latter with the remark
that it is "mere rhetoric," and Mr. Beecher is "not
well posted." To the references to Kansas and the
Federal treatment of the free-state men there, as
compared with President Buchanan's eager display
of troops against John Brown, the latter's marginal
note with an admiration point, is "Truth!" but to
the remark that he (Brown) "received his impulse"
from Kansas, the quiet comment is, "He does not
understand his subject." When Mr. Beecher begins
to deal in causistry, and says that for the negro "reasonable liberty is required, possessed with the consent
of the master," and that freedom sometimes "is a
mischief," while vague insurrection speech is a great
and cruel wrong to them "—the slaves,—John Brown
appreciates the point involved in the latter remark,
but adds "it is not strictly true." The right way to
deal with "the African," said Mr. Beecher, is to
"begin at home"—make him fit for freedom. On
that "I am willing to be weighed in an even balance
on this score," commented Captain Brown, as indeed
he might well be, but added—"His remark is, however, true." When Mr. Beecher commented sharply
on the inconsistent treatment of the negro in the

" CHARLESTOWN JAIL, Dec. 10, 1859.

" I hereby certify that Captain Brown wrote, with his own hand,
comments upon H. W. Beecher's sermon published in the *Spiritual Telegraph.*

A. D. STEVENS, W. B. GALLAHER, Witness.
Copied in my presence, read, and found correct.
THOS. FEATHERSTONHAUGH."

North, with its comments on slavery in the South, John Brown underscored the passage and wrote marginally that, "these are truthful remarks, but were never applicable to my case. God is my witness on this point." Beecher said the "air must be made vital with love of liberty," and the Captain underscored "Truth! very well," three times, and then added, "my own practice has been correct in this matter." When the Plymouth preacher suggests that "the shot that struck his child, crazed the father's brain." John Brown wrote he "is mistaken in the individual." Captain Brown wrote "Good" on the margin, after underscoring the words that follow: "Let no man pray that John Brown be spared! Let Virginia make him a martyr! Now, he has only blundered. His soul was noble; his work miserable. But a cord and a gibbet would redeem all that, and wind up Brown's failure with a heroic success." The sentences next marked do not meet with as hearty an approval. The preacher declares "that men who tamper with slaves and incite them are not themselves to be trusted . . . conspirators, the world over, are bad men " . . . wouldn't trust "such men with money " nor " place any confidence in them "—they must crafty and "unreliable." Such a statement, wrote Captain Brown, is "an utterly false assumption as applied to this case. . . . It is a boastful and false insinuation" if directed "to me." When Mr. Beecher declared that he would help the fugitive who came to his door, Brown waxed sarcastic and wrote, a " very brave man" this; " must be a very good man, too; glad to know it." To a remark of Beecher's that "breeding discontent is not good for the slaves

themselves,"—Captain Brown savagely indites—
"Another vile assumption," and underscores the remark. When Beecher talked against "insurrection,"
Brown writes, "I never counseled it." "The right of
a people to revolt in order to achieve liberty," said
Beecher, must "conform" in "its use" "to reason
and to the benefits" to be achieved. Captain Brown
notes this as a "false assumption," but marks as
"Truth" the further remark, that " a man who leads
a people has no right to incite that people to rise,
unless there is a reasonable prospect that they will
conquer." To the optimism of Beecher, which said:
There is "a nobler spirit" rising; a "fearless assertion of truth" to the South, and a declaration to them
that we "love you; we hate your slavery"; Captain
Brown writes, "so say I!" To a remark on Paul's
direction to servants and masters, Brown writes—
"Why don't Beecher come South to preach?" When
the preacher said, that the establishment of "a few
virtues" among the slaves, "houshold love," "personal chastity," "the right of parents to their
children," would revolutionize the moral conditions
of "both masters and slaves"; John Brown wrote—
"This is true, but is there any progress making in
this direction?" There follows a number of eloquent
sentences on this subject, to which John Brown's
comments give pungency. "Let the champion come
here to preach!" "Good, if spoken here!" "How
can he stay away?" When Mr. Beecher, referring
to the slave mart, said—"It is no use to preach a
gospel without protection to the family," Brown
cynically remarks, "Come on, Beecher." To a series of
other sentences in relation to practice and principles,

Brown wrote that they "were truth and error inter-
mingled"; that they were also "sophistical," and in
the nature of "a plea in avoidance." "No relief," said
Beecher, "could come from inciting or organizing"
slaves "to run away" or "abscond," and Brown sar-
castically writes, "a great man may be mistaken—
he's very wise, indeed." To the Plymouth orator's
declaration that—"Emancipation, when it comes,
will come either by revolution or by a change of public opinion in the *whole* community," Brown underscored the whole sentence and writes, "*Truth!*" and
when the great preacher closed with the hope—"that
bondsmen may become free, that the ignorant may
become wise, that the master and slave may respect
each other, so that at length we may be an evangelized
and Christian people! May God in His own way and
time speed the Day!"—John Brown heavily underscored the words, and added: "Amen! So says old
Brown; Amen!"

John Brown was not a dreamer, nor an enthusiast;
nor was he visionary or fanatical. That he miscalcu-
lated his forces is doubtless true, from the limited or
immediate point of view. But who will deny that he
was a man of cléar mentality and spiritual insight,
when we recall with what distinct and non-personal
sagacity he built, from his own errors of command, a
strategy of peaceful victory, which laid bare the
weakness of his enemy and made marvelously clear
the lucidity of purpose and the idealistic rarefication
of atmosphere in which he breathed. He was never
a schemer, but yet he manifested intellectual craft,
while always simple in aim and action. He was an
idealist with a human intent. As Henry Q. Thoreau

said, he would have "left a Greek accent slanting the wrong way and slanted up a falling man." He probably never thought of the cynical saying, that " no man is a hero with his valet," because he dreamed not of being a hero and never would have accepted a valet. If his simplicity of action made him the victim of inadequate means, the grandeur of his purpose served him to a loftier realization. In the first family letter, he wrote after defeat, he expressed this when he wrote:

" Under all these terrible calamities, I feel quite cheerful in the assurance that God reigns, and will overrule all for His glory and the best possible good. I feel no consciousness of guilt in this matter, and I feel perfectly assured that very soon no member of my family will feel any possible disposition to blush on my account."

And this was written after describing the death of Oliver, the mortal wounding and subsequent death of Watson, the massacre of William Thompson, the slight wounding on the first day and the killing of Dauphin, his young brother, on the second, while he himself became a prisoner, saber cuts on his head and bayonet wounds in his body. He could tell his wife and children to " never forget the poor, nor think anything you may bestow on them to be lost to you," and ask them, after being sentenced to death, " not to grieve on my account "; adding, " I am still quite cheerful, God bless you ! " Nor was he seeking to blame any one but himself for apparent failure: " It is solely my own fault . . . that we met with disaster . . . I mean, that I mingled with our prisoners and so far sympathized with them and their families, that I neglected my duty in other respects." In an appeal to Mrs. Child and others to aid in raising funds for the wives and children made widowed and fatherless at North Elba, his object was to secure means to "supply themselves and children with bread and very plain clothing, and to enable all the children to receive a common English education."

He pleaded with his wife Mary not to come on to Virginia, because it would use up the little money she had, and because there was but little more of the romantic in helping poor widows than there is about trying to relieve the poor negroes. Indeed, he believed that more generous sympathy would flow out to them all by their staying at home. "There is," he wrote, "no night so dark as to have hindered the coming day, nor any storm so furious or dreadful as to prevent the return of warm sunshine and a cloudless sky." "God will surely attend," he declared, "to His own cause in the best possible way and time, and He will not forget the work of His own hand." "Jesus of Nazareth suffered a most excruciating death on the cross as a felon," he tells his wife, "under the most aggravating circumstances. Think, also, of the prophets, and apostles, and Christians of former days, who went through greater tribulations than you or I, and try to be reconciled. May God Almighty comfort all your hearts and soon wipe away all tears from your eyes! To Him be endless praise! Think, too, of the crushed millions who have no comforter. I charge you all to never, in your trials, to forget the griefs 'of the poor who cry, and of those who have none to help them.'" And that last letter to his household at North Elba, how full of faith and sincerity of devotion; with what simpleness in wants and singleness of purpose does he advise with his children. The courage is unfaltering; indeed, it is something more than courage, for it practically takes no account of death, only as such result may affect others. No wonder that his young men murmured not; that his wife and children accepted unflinchingly!

CHARLESTOWN PRISON, JEFFERSON COUNTY, VA.,
November 30, 1859.

MY DEAR BELOVED WIFE, SONS, AND DAUGHTERS, EVERY ONE—As I now begin probably what is the last letter I shall ever write to any of you, I conclude to write to all at the same time. I will mention some little matters particularly applicable to little property concerns in another place.

I recently received a letter from my wife, from near Philadelphia, dated November 22, by which it would seem that she was about giving up the idea of seeing me again. I had written to her to come on if she felt equal to the undertaking, but I do not know that she will get my letter in time. It was on her own account, chiefly, that I asked her to stay back. At first I had a most strong desire to see her again, but there appeared to be very serious objections; and should we never meet in this life, I trust that she will in the end be satisfied it was for the best at least, if not most for her comfort.

I am waiting the hour of my public murder with great composure of mind and cheerfulness; feeling the strong assurance that in no other possible way could I be used to so much advantage to the cause of God and of humanity, and that nothing that either I or all my family have sacrificed or suffered will be lost. The reflection that a wise and merciful as well as just and holy God rules not only the affairs of this world but of all worlds, is a rock to set our feet upon under all circumstances,—even those more severely trying ones in which our own feelings and wrongs have placed us. I have no doubt but that our

seeming disaster will ultimately result in the most glorious success. So, my dear shattered and broken family, be of good
cheer, and believe and trust in God with all your heart and with
all your soul; for He doeth all things well. Do not feel ashamed
on my account, nor for one moment despair of the cause or
grow weary of well-doing. I bless God I never felt stronger
confidence in the certain and near approach of a bright morning
and glorious day than I have felt, and do now feel, since my
confinement here. I am endeavoring to return, like a poor
prodigal as I am, to my Father, against whom I have always
sinned, in the hope that He may kindly and forgivingly meet me,
though a very great way off.

Oh, my dear wife and children, would to God you could know
how I have been travailing in birth for you all, that no one of
you may fail of the grace of God through Jesus Christ; that no
one of you may be blind to the truth and the glorious light of
His Word, in which life and immortality are brought to light.
I beseech you, every one, to make the Bible your daily and
nightly study, with a childlike, honest, candid, teachable spirit
of love and respect for your husband and father. And I beseech
the God of my fathers to open all your eyes to the discovery of
the truth. You cannot imagine how much you may soon need
the consolations of the Christian religion. Circumstances like
my own for more than a month past have convinced me,
beyond all doubt, of my own great need of some theories
treasured up, when our prejudices are excited, our vanity worked
up to the highest pitch. Oh, do not trust your eternal all
upon the boisterous ocean, without even a helm or compass
to aid you in steering. I do not ask of you to throw away
your reason; I only ask you to make a candid, sober use of
your reason.

My dear young children, will you listen to this last poor
admonition of one who can only love you? Oh, be determined
at once to give your whole heart to God, and let nothing shake
or alter that resolution. You need have no fears of regretting
it. Do not be vain and thoughtless, but sober-minded; and let
me entreat you all to love the whole remnant of our once great

family. Try and build up again your broken walls, and to make the utmost of every stone that is left. Nothing can so tend to make life a blessing as the consciousness that your life and example may bless and leave others stronger. Still, it is ground for the utmost comfort to my mind to know that so many of you as have had the opportunity have given some proof of your fidelity to the great family of men. Be faithful unto death; from the exercise of habitual love to man it cannot be very hard to love his Maker.

I must yet insert the reason for my firm belief in the divine inspiration of the Bible, notwithstanding I am, perhaps, naturally skeptical—certainly not credulous. I wish all to consider it most thoroughly when you read that blessed book, and see whether you cannot discover such evidence yourselves. It is the purity of heart, filling our minds as well as work and actions, which is everywhere insisted on, that distinguishes it from all the other teachings, that commends it to my conscience. Whether my heart be willing and obedient or not, the inducement that it holds out is another reason of my conviction of its truth and genuineness; but I do not here omit this; my last argument on the Bible, that eternal life is what my soul is panting after this moment. I mention this as a reason for endeavoring to leave a valuable copy of the Bible, to be carefully preserved in remembrance of me, to so many of my posterity, instead of some other book at equal cost.

I beseech you all to live in habitual contentment with moderate circumstances and gains of worldly store, and earnestly to teach this to your children and children's children after you, by example as well as precept. Be determined to know by experience, as soon as may be, whether Bible instruction is of divine origin or not. Be sure to owe no man anything, but to love one another. John Rogers wrote to his children: "Abhor that arrant whore of Rome." John Brown writes to abhor, with undying hatred also, that sum of all villanies, Slavery. Remember, " that he that is slow to anger is better than the mighty," and " he that ruleth his spirit than he that taketh a city." Remember, also, that " they being wise shall shine, and they that turn many to righteousness, as the stars for ever and ever."

And now, dearly beloved family, to God and the work of His grace I commend you all.

Your affectionate husband and father,

JOHN BROWN.

And that lonely mountain home at North Elba. The somber beauty of its surroundings were harmonious with the solemn moods and sad thoughts that dwelt therein. How slow were the hours and how infrequent the communication they necessarily had with all that animating life, laden with a quickening sympathy and regard, wherewith their father's life and acts had endowed the world. We may sneer in cold blood at the fanatics. We may deride those who give that others may live, but in the presence of one flaming deed all mankind are kin. "When souls reach," said Emerson, "a certain clearness of perception, they accept a knowledge and motive above selfishness. . . . It is the air which all intellects inhale and exhale, and it is the wind which blows the world into order and orbit." Character is a weapon for the accomplishment of great deeds, but the forging of the weapon is done in the furnace of environment, and the home-life of John Brown was a large part of his character. Moulded by him, mother and children—older ones and younger, too—also moulded and uplifted this Cromwellian soul unto the hour of his and their supreme sacrifice! "Does it seem as if freedom were to gain or lose by this?" This was the wife's expression—the mother's question: "I have had thirteen children, and only four are left; but if I am to see ruin of my house, I cannot but hope that Providence may bring out of it some benefit to the poor slave." And in this atmosphere and hope they had lived for thirty years. John Brown said to Frank B. Sanborn, early in that last, fateful year of his life: "I always told them that when the time came to fight against slavery, that conflict would be the signal of our separation. Mary made up her mind to have me go along before this; and when I did go, she got ready bandages and medicines for the wounded." The wife and mother who "got ready bandages and medicines," wrote her husband, as he lay under sentence of death (on the 15th of October, 1859): "I have often thought that I would rather hear you were dead than fallen into the hands of your enemies: but I don't think so now. The good that is growing out of it is wonderful. If you had preached in the pulpit ten such lives as you have lived, you could not have done so much good as you have done, in that one speech to the Court." It was Salmon Brown who said, "I sometimes think that's what we came into the world for—to make sacrifices," and it was his eldest daughter, Ruth, who had once given up her beloved husband to the field and saw brought home to her, bleeding, upon "his shield," who wrote her father in May of that last year:

"DEAR FATHER—You have asked me rather a hard question. I want to answer you wisely, but hardly know how. I cannot bear the thought of Henry leaving me again, but I feel that I am selfish, when I think of my poor, despised sisters, that are deprived of both husband and children, I feel deeply for them; and were it not for my little children, I would go most anywhere with Henry, if by going I could do them any good. . . . I should be very glad to be with him, if it would not be more expense then what good we could do. I say *we;* could I not do something for the cause?"

There were others, too, who suffered, and from whom no murmurs came. In the many letters from all directions, faulty in grammar, halting in expression and awkward in chirography, the writer of this volume has received from those who survived their sons, brothers, and lovers, were as true in unselfish and unregretting love and remembrance, as the plain farmer families at North Elba who suffered so much and lost so largely. For it was not one family, but four that mourned amid the Adirondacks. Anne Brown illuminates the life of the household, and describes the bearing of the members when she writes:

"You ask me to tell you how the family at North Elba received the news of the Harper's Ferry affair. That is a time that I do not like to think of or speak of. We only had a weekly mail at that time. I do not now remember whether we had heard any rumors before, but I think we had. It was the Tuesday evening that the mail usually came, when a young man, a neighbor, brought us a paper (the *New York Times*) with a full account in it, some one said ' Let Annie read it, for she can read faster than any of us can'; so I read that long account from beginning to end, aloud, without faltering. I was stunned, and my senses so benumbed that I did not comprehend the meaning of the words I pronounced. There was very little 'weeping or wailing' or loud demonstration on the part of our brave household; we were most of us struck dumb, horrorstricken with a grief too deep and hard to find expression in words or even tears. I do not think I have ever fully recovered from the mental shock I received then. Mother, Salmon's wife, and I were all down sick shortly after that, and Martha patiently did the work and cared for us, until she became ill herself. I never saw her smile but twice after that, once when she same upstairs in the morning to see me while I was sick, and I told her that an ' angel came in the night with a bright light and gave me some water,' and showed her

a bowl of water beside the bed to prove it; she smiled and
said she was 'my angel.'   The other time was the night after
her baby was born, when she told me to 'write to Tidd and
tell him he had a little sister.'   C. P. Tidd used to call Martha
and Oliver 'Mother and Father,' to tease them, while we were
at Kennedy Farm.   The only time after that I ever saw her
shed a tear was when I held her little dead baby at her bed-
side, for her to take a last look at it before they put it into the
coffin; a few great scalding drops fell on its little, waxen
face."

Anne Brown (Mrs. Adams) unconsciously illustrates
her own sincere self and shows how with what true
courage they all walked within the valley of shadows.
Martha Evelin Brewster was born in 1842, and died
in March, 1860, being, therefore, but eighteen years of
age.   Wife, widow, and mother, within two years.
She married Oliver on the 17th of April, 1858, of
medium height, well formed, with regular features,
hair of a pale gold brown, and blue-gray eyes, she was
a very woman, sedate and dignified in manners, full
of character, writes Mrs. Adams, even as a little
child.   "I remember," writes Mrs. Adams, "William
Thompson telling me, that one day soon after her
father moved on to the farm adjoining the Thompsons' home, he was going by the house and saw three
little girls on the fence by the roadside; he stopped
and talked to them inquiring their names; the little
Martha after telling her name added, 'I'm Mom's
lady.'   He said, 'I think she is Mom's lady still,' and
so she always continued to be.   As her father was an
easygoing, thriftless man, with a large family poorly
provided for, she preferred to work for the farmers'
wives around, where by her own labor she could procure better clothing and in most places a more con-

genial home." Oliver married her while waiting for
his father's next movement towards Harper's Ferry,
"so that she might," writes his sister, "have a legal
right to a home with his family during his absence,
as most of her relatives were rabidly pro-slavery and
opposed to us politically," though not personally.
It was as characteristic of the Essex county neighbors
as elsewhere, that John Brown and his family were
held in the highest respect for their good qualities.
There was a considerable modicum of the pro-southern, hardshell Democracy among its men, and John
Brown was counted as a "crazy Abolitionist," but
always esteemed as a good citizen and excellent
neighbor.

Isabella Thompson, the widowed wife of Watson
Brown, lived with her parents—the Thompson family
which furnished two fighters for Kansas and two victims of Harper's Ferry—the sons, William and
Dauphin. Henry, the eldest brother, is the husband
of Ruth, John Brown's eldest daughter. They are
both still living at Pasadena, California. A child was
born to Watson and Bella, but two weeks before the
young husband started in June, 1859, for the Kennedy
Farm. "Freddie," the little one, lived four years.
William Thompson's widow, Mary Brown, lived close
by. Though of the same name she was no relative.
A young, good-looking, brave-minded woman of about
twenty years, she bore her part well and murmured
not. Death's harvest had not spared that lonely
mountain section—four widows, and six fatherless
children, with other parents, relatives, and grandchildren in mourning. Yet, with what fortitude it was
all borne, and but for the profound regard that the

land fastened upon those stricken homes, no word or wail would have ever floated beyond the Au-Sable valley.

And so John Brown passed beyond. And so was the tidings borne, and these were the manner of persons that wore their robe of sorrow with a quiet dignity that exalted. They were not unknowing of the sacrifices. To them their dead was sacred. To the cause they gave, if not joyfully, yet with a sober, sweet earnestness, that added grace to their deep sorrow. Nor have they thrust themselves ever into the world's notice, but lived their lives; hardworking, honorable men, loving, motherly women; all an honor to the name they bear and the strong life of which they are a part. Was he not, indeed, the largest of "Connecticut schoolmasters," as Wendell Phillips said, and did he not withal prove himself a " great commander," as Richard Realf affirmed before the Senate Committee of investigation ? Northern or Kansas defamers may malign and deride, but as against the hero-life and the martyr's crown, their venomous spittle is blown back but to scorch their own names and fames. We may say with D. W. Wilder, of Kansas, and there is no more competent critic: "Common men live for years in despair, with only ordinary bad luck to contend with; but here is a man absolutely alone, exiled from family, among hostile strangers, where barbarism is made popular by law and fashion,—yet never in despair. Why this contrast ? He believed in God and Justice, and in nothing else; we believe in everything else, but not in God."

CHAPTER XIV.

JOHN BROWN'S MEN : WHO THEY WERE.

Their rightful place in history—Kagi, philosopher and scholar—Cook, ardent, poetic, and generous—Stevens, soldier and hero—Hazlett, simple and brave—Osborne P. Anderson, the faithful colored leader—Danger-field Newby, the Virginian freeman, fighting for family and race—Copeland, Leary, Shields Green, resisting like men, dying as heroes—Arrests and renditions of Cook and Hazlett—Col. A. K. McClure's account—Travesty of justice at Carlisle—Story of an attempt at rescue.

TWENTY-ONE men marched with John Brown on the night of October 16, 1859. That was the fighting array with which he invaded the "sacred soil" of Virginia, and begun a "sympathetic strike" against the "chattel slavery" which enthralled labor, while threatening the peace of the Republic and the safety of the Union. Sixteen of these men were of the master race; five of the one that was in bondage, two only of whom had, however, been born slaves. Three of the white men were sons of the leader; two were related by marriage and years of close and neighborly friendship. They were all Northern and anti-slavery by association and training; positive in such

29

opinion by the force and blending of serious conditions and experiences. All but two of them were
country born and bred. All who participated were
"native and to the manner born." Anna Brown,
one of the two brave girls from the family, who
walked, worked, and watched with her comrades in
the "valley of shadows" at the Kennedy Farm, says
of them collectively, and she knew all but one of the
white men, F. J. Merriam, and four also out of the
five men of color, that—"taking them all together, I
think they would compare well (she is speaking of
manners, etc.) with the same number of men in any
station of life I have ever met";—and her experience
compasses the homes of Ralph Waldo Emerson and
George Luther Stearns, as well as that of her father's
household and the wholesome dignity of her own
abode. All of her comrades possessed more than
the average of intelligence and character. Some of
them would have made a broad place for themselves
in the stirring drama to which their sacrifice was the
tragic overture. In telling, as I shall try very briefly
to do, from whence these men came—we know where
they went—I shall hope to work in the spirit suggested by Anna Brown (Mrs. Adams), in writing
me: "I have always had a feeling that I wished some
one would write of these men who felt like a friend
and companion; who was in sympathy with them,
and did not condescend to look down from a high
pedestal of culture at such common mortals as they
were. . . . It takes very much more of school
education to write of the lives of good people, than
it did for them to live those lives. Some of the best,
noblest, and most heroic people I have ever known

were men and women who could neither read nor write, and still they lived beautiful lives. The young men of these days do not know that there is some good bread that is not college bred." The homely pun may be forgiven for the wholesome lesson it teaches.

The youngest of the whites was not yet nineteen; the oldest had just reached twenty-eight, when, after an imprisonment of 169 days, Virginia sent his nobly-equipped life and soul into eternity. Of the colored men the youngest was barely twenty-one and only one had passed his twenty-fourth year. That was Danger-field Newby, who fought for his family as well as race. Captain Brown and he were the two men of mature years in the fateful band. This group of devoted men in any other of our modern lands (except, perhaps, Russia) would have been embalmed long ere this in historical record. Practically, they have remained unknown for a third of a century and may remain so during the passing of time. As an immediate result this was due to the pervading personality and record of their Captain. But as a permanent condition it is due most directly to the strange fact that their lives were given for the negro; that they fought for those who were then the poorest and most wretched of all Americans. That in itself is an hostility to the canons of good taste and an offense against a spirit which worships success—even in altruism.

"We will endure the shadow of dishonor but not the stain of guilt." These words of John Henri Kagi express the spirit of John Brown's men and, in an especial sense, the character of the young and brilliant man who fell riddled with bullets into the waters of the Shenandoah. Thirty miles below, the blood-tinged stream flowed through the lands of his father's family. Kagi was related to Virginia by more than one hundred years of American progenitors. One of the same family[1] writes:

"The first Kagy of whom I have authentic record in this country was one John R. Kagy, who came to this country from Switzerland in 1715, with others who suffered persecution in the fatherland on account of their religious faith, they being followers of the great reformer Menno Simon. My ancestor was among the first settlers in Lancaster Co., Pa., having settled on the Conestogue, in the township of Conestogue, then a vast wilderness inhabited by wild beasts and Indians. Here in the primitive forest, Hanse Kagy reared his family of four sons and three daughters. One of his sons, Henry, born 1728, went to Virginia in 1768, and located on Smith Creek, in the county of Shenandoah. He raised seven sons and three daughters, one of these sons was named Abraham, and he had sons, one also named Abraham, who was the father of the subject of this sketch by John Henri Kagi. The descendants of Hanse, or John R. Kagy, are numbered by hundreds and are to be found in all the States of this Union and in Canada. I never knew but two instances of the Kagys owning slaves, one in Pennsylvania, the other in Virginia. A large number of our people belong to the German Baptist and Methodist Churches."

John Brown's adjutant-general had just passed the seventh month of his twenty-fourth year when slain at Harper's Ferry. He was tall and somewhat angular, with a slight stoop in the shoulders, about

---

[1] Franklin H. Keagy, Chambersburg, Pa.

five feet eleven inches in height, and weighing one
hundred and fifty pounds. The insufficient portrait
that has been the only one obtainable was taken in
1854, at an age when thoughtful young men are apt to
look older than they really are. At the time of his
death, Kagi wore a short, full, dark-brown beard; his
face was thin and worn-looking, complexion pallid
but healthy, hair thin and dark brown. His cousin
Franklin, who got well acquainted with him in the
ten or eleven weeks of his life spent at Chambersburg, but without then knowing the relationship
between them, writes that he " had more the appearance of a divinity student than a warrior. His manner
was reserved almost to bashfulness, but when addressed or engaged in conversation he spoke freely
and fluently, commanding attention. His language
was elegant, his deportment unassailable, his habits
strictly temperate, kind in his feelings to every one,
especially to children, whose confidence he acquired
at first acquaintance." It was John Henri Kagi
whom John Brown permitted to tell me fully in the
summer of 1858, as to his startling design, and who
replied to me when I involuntarily exclaimed that all
would " be killed "; " Yes, I know it, Hinton, *but the
result will be worth the sacrifice.*" I recall my friend
as a man of personal beauty, with a fine, well-shaped
head, a voice of quiet, sweet tones, that could be penetrating and cutting, too, almost to sharpness. The
eyes were remarkable— large, full, well-set beneath
strongly arched brows. Ordinarily they wore a veiled
look, reminding me of a slow-burning fire of heated
coals, hidden behind a mica door. Hazel-gray in
color, irridescent in light and effect. The face

gave you confidence in the character that had already wrought it into a stern gravity beyond its years. One would trust or turn away at once, according to the purpose sought. Kagi was not a man of expressed enthusiasms; on the contrary, he was cold in manner, and his conclusions were stamped with the approval of his intellect. Mentally, he was the ablest of those who followed John Brown to Harper's Ferry. In the best sense, too, he was the most scholarly and cultured. George B. Gill, who was closely associated with him for twelve months, writes:

"That he was a logician of more than ordinary ability. In speaking or debating, he would stand slightly bent with his hands behind his back. To a superficial listener perhaps he would not have been very attractive, but the thinking, thoughtful listener would not tire of him. In mental fields he possessed abundant and ingenious resources. He was full of a wonderful, enduring vitality. Disappointment gave him just as results as a successful termination. All things were fit food for his brain. No road was so lonely that he did not see hope beckoning in the distance; somewhere see the sun peering through the clouds. . . . He was an agnostic of the most pronounced type, so grounded in his convictions that he gave but little thought to what he considered useless problems. His disposition was a model one. No strain or stress could shake his unruffled serenity. His fertility of resources made him a tower of strength to John Brown."

Osborne Perry Anderson, the colored annalist of the Harper's Ferry party,[1] writes that:

"Kagi was indifferent to personal appearance, he went about with slouched hat, only one leg of his pantaloons properly ad-

---

[1] "A Voice from Harper's Ferry," p. 15.

justed, and the other partly tucked into his high boot-top; un-
brushed, unshaven, and in utter disregard of the 'latest style,'
but to his companions and acquaintances a verification of
'Burns' man' in the clothes.   He had improved his time; for
he discoursed elegantly and fluently, wrote ably, and could
occupy the platform with greater ability than many a man
known to the American people as famous in these respects."

Realf once described Kagi as the "Horace Greeley" of the John Brown party.

Kagi was an only son, born March 15, 1835, at
Bristol, Trumbull County, Ohio, where his father,
Abraham Neff Kagy, had moved some years before
from Shenandoah County, Virginia.   Abraham was
born in 1807, and died in Kansas about 1890.   His son
John was fifth in descent from Hanse Kagy, who, with
other Swiss Mennonites, settled in 1715 on Paquea
Creek, Conestoga township, Lancaster County, Pennsylvania.   It was the grandson of this emigrant that
moved to Virginia.   The root of this life, like John
Brown's, ran deep it will be seen into the volcanic
soil of struggle for liberty of conscience and civic freedom.   The father was a blacksmith, all of the earlier
Kagys were farmers and mechanics; good stock to
be citizens of a great nationality, the whole of whose
stirring history, made and making, has sprung from
the shaping hands of industry; fuses only in the
heated crucible of toil and its correlative issues.
Kagi's mother was Anna Fansler, born in Virginia,
and to them four children were born.   This mother
died when he was three years old.   John went to
the district school, and became an example for his
assiduity in study.   So marked was his devotion that
his uncle Jackson Neff sent him to an academy in

Virginia. He commenced teaching in that State before he was seventeen and remained till he was nineteen, when his quietly outspoken dislike of slavery
put him under the ban. He was a good mathema-
tician and English scholar, and knew his Latin well
enough to teach it. He taught himself phonography
and French, and had commenced the study of German, when he found it conducive to physical safety
to retire from the "Old Dominion." On his return
to Bristol he taught in the neighborhood, begàn the
study of law, made a practise of attending the
country lyceum and debating clubs, and worked also
at his reporting. His father went to California late
in 1850, and returned East in 1853, settling at last in
southern Nebraska, at Otoe, on Camp Creek. John
had to keep hard at work. During this period he was
at Lexington, Kentucky, reporting the State Constitutional Convention. It was excellent drill and
made of him a proficient verbatim reporter. Kagi
was admitted to the bar somewhere in the West in
the early part of 1856 at the age of twenty-one. He
grew firmer and sterner in his anti-slavery convictions,
identifying himself in 1854 with the local free-soil
agitation of southern Ohio.

Arriving at Topeka, Kansas, on the fourth day of
July, 1856, he was a deeply interested observer of the
disposal by the United States Dragoons, under the
command of Colonel Sumner (who was afterward
killed in command of the Sixth Army Corps, in Virginia), of the body known in free-state annals as the
"Topeka Legislature." It will be worth while to
briefly re-indicate here the historical relation of that
body : After Missouri and its Southern allies had

violated the so-called "squatter sovereignty," or home-rule dogma of the Territorial organic act, by invading Kansas, electing citizens of Missouri as a Legislature and then passing the draconian slave-code, known as the "bogus laws," the free-state citizens, who were six to one of all other *bona-fide* residents, framed through a constitutional convention a free-state constitution and form of government. It had asked for admission as such into the Union. That was pending, and to prevent the "constructive treason," for which Judge Lecompte indicted, when the Legislature met *pro forma*, under orders (subsequently repudiated), the gallant Massachusetts soldier who commanded the United States troops, was obliged to disperse by a show of force. Kagi's future, his life, and death, were fixed by that event. He at once actively identified himself with the free-state party, joining Company " B," of what was known as the Second Regiment of the Free-State Volunteers, under command of Colonel "Charles Whipple"—afterwards hung at Charlestown, Virginia, as Aaron D. Stevens, March 16, 1860, for participation in the Harper's Ferry raid. In all subsequent details of the Topeka movement, Kagi was one of the most active, serving as its reporter, writing appeals to the American people on Kansas affairs, and to the Topeka Legislature, urging the members to assemble and maintain, as will be seen, that policy to the last.

Kagi became, in every sense, active in free-state warfare. He served for one year in the Whipple regiment, and was a prisoner at Lecompton for a period of four months, half starved and abused all the time. He was beaten with a club and wounded by a pistol

for writings he sent to Eastern journals. He was the
regular correspondent of the *National Era*, Dr.
Bailey's paper, at Washington, and of the New York
Evening Post, the latter over the signature of " Kent."
He was a writer for the Kansas *Tribune*, at Topeka,
and the *Republican*, Lawrence, Kan., from 1857 to the
early spring of 1859. He wrote a good deal also for
the Chicago *Tribune*, Cleveland *Leader*, and the New
York *Tribune*. As such writer, he possessed the faculty
of knowing what was news and stating the same
clearly and forcibly. A small volume might readily
be made interesting from the materials in my hands
—school compositions, drafts of lectures, essays, including one in which he outlines the theory that all
forms of matter are the result of ether in motion;
in other words the alleged law of vibration. In his
early Kansas life, like all the free-state correspondents, he was a shining target for pro-slavery persecution It was not an uncommon thing, in those
days, for the Territorial Grand Juries to be manip-
ulated into rendering indictments against them under
their pen names. Kagi was once indicted by the
name of "Kent." Hugh Young had a charge made
against him as " Potter," hat being the signature he
used in the New York *Tr bune*. I also had the honor
of being so served. Against Kagi, indictments for
highway robbery, arson, e ., were found. His arrest
was achieved by a rather disgraceful trick, under
cover of Gov. Geary's presence, at Topeka. It was
published early in October, 1856, that the Governor
would address the free-state men of Topeka in the
interests of peace. Kagi attended to report his
speech and was arrested while so engaged on account

of his alleged participation, early in August, in an attack upon a fortified position held by Titus, the border ruffian, near Lecompton. The purpose of the arrest was evidently to stop his pen. But it only increased its usefulness, for prison letters bitterly incisive in their exposure of brutal cruelty, were of great value in the creation of Northern public opinion. The man whose alleged buildings he was said to have aided in burning, was the jailer in charge of such accused prisoners. Kagi resorted to all sorts of ingenious expedients to get his letters out of prison and properly mailed. In January, his health failing him rapidly, he procured bondsmen and was admitted to $5,000 bail. Judge Lecompte was glad to get rid of him. When the pro-slavery Constitutional Convention assembled soon after, in February 1857, Kagi came down to Lecompton to report its proceedings, and was almost immediately rearrested; giving this time bonds of $8,000. All these charges were frauds, and were never brought to trial. Such persecution not only shaped his early ended career, but prevented attention to his own interests and that of his father and sisters. There are many family letters of the period showing this, and also illustrating Kagi's sincere and affectionate character. He notifies his father in Nebraska of his intended home-coming, and of the necessity of returning in April, the date set for his trial. He asks that his projected return by way of the Missouri River be kept " perfectly quiet," as his life would not be safe. " I shall be compelled," he says, " to go under an assumed name " as I am otherwise known all along the border and pro-slavery men " would not hesitate to assassinate me." While in the Lecompton prison he wrote to his sister, that—

"Our friends will take us out the moment I say so. A regiment, the same in which I was lieutenant, will come to our rescue any night I give the order. I hesitate only because we may get out some other way, and a forcible rescue would bring on a fearful winter war, which I do not wish to see. Be cheerful!"

In March, 1857, an incident occurred of great moment to Kagi. Tecumseh was a pro-slavery town, which the border-ruffian Legislature had made the county seat of Shawnee. Topeka is in the same county, and it was almost wholly free State. Constant disturbances occurred at Tecumseh. Free-state men were not safe in it alone. One of its residents was robbed by a pro-slavery townsman. An appeal for protection was made to friends at Topeka. The law of force was the only one that was respected on either side. The Topeka boys arrived and proposed arbitration. A committee was appointed, consisting of the accuser and the accused, with Rush Elmore, a lawyer from Alabama, who had served a brief period as one of the United States Judges. The free-state man proved the loss of his goods and traced them into the other man's hands. Of this latter there was no doubt, for the goods were afterwards seized and restored to the rightful owner by free-state men, who announced their responsibility for the act. The burden of deciding fell on the ex-Judge, and he avoided by declaring that he "could not tell." In his letter, describing the farce, Kagi said that—

"President Pierce need not have sought a pretext for dismissing Elmore, on account of his extra-judicial investments, as it was self-evident that a person who could not decide a case when the clearest evidence was given, whether a convicted robber should return stolen goods or retain them, was hardly qualified for a seat on the supreme bench of the Territory."

Shortly after the receipt of this publication in Kansas, Kagi had occasion with a few others to visit Tecumseh, in order to attend the United States Court in session there. Elmore approached him armed with bludgeon and revolver. Kagi did not know the ruffian personally and when spoken to as to his identity politely responded. Elmore immediately struck him a savage blow over the head, and, dodging behind a pillar, commenced firing on Kagi. One ball struck him in the breast, passing through a heavy memorandum book, and glancing made a severe wound in his left arm. The blood streaming from the wound in his head, half blinded Kagi, who nevertheless, revolver in hand, advanced steadily on the burly and fugacious Alabamian, dodging round the pillar and firing wildly at his antagonist until the latter's only shot, penetrating the groin, laid him low. The lawyer lived, but the house of Elmore was ended by this incident. Kagi, however, never quite recovered from the effects of the blow on his head. Mr. Gill, in his recollections, says he required watching at times, especially when suffering from fever. Becoming melancholic and moody for brief spells, his comrades would deem it necessary to hide his weapons and otherwise care for his safety. But this was never serious, and resulted more from the effects of privation than any cerebral difficulty.

The lasting contact with John Brown did not occur till October, 1857, when these two met at Topeka. Aaron D. Stevens also entered that service at the time. The party was formed which went to school at Springdale, Iowa, to Chatham, Canada, back to southern Kansas, thence to Pennsylvania, Maryland, Virginia—and Death. Other chapters have sketched in outline the events which moved along this route, and have indicated the part John Henri Kagi played therein. A memorandum found in the carpet-bag of papers seized by the Virginian authorities had the following written thereon by Kagi. Evidently this was intended as the basis of a fuller paper or lecture. It shows the working of his mind, the spirit in which he acted: "Slavery," the paper declares, "must be abolished by war. Peaceful abolition would result in a war of races. Slaves will grow in war and fit themselves for (civic) equality. A republic cannot abolish it. Slavery and its increase is a bribe" to the politicians. The suggestion as to the incapacity of a republic to the task he had in mind is not without incisive vigor, when the subsequent course of civic suppression and ballot-box inanity pursued "down South," is duly considered. Writing to William A. Phillips, of Kansas, in 1859, but a few weeks before his death, he showed the intensity of his sympathetic hostility to chattelism, by declaring, that

"I shall long remember that your house was one of the only two in Lawrence into which I dared, and that in the night only, to enter; and solely because I was opposed to theft, robbery, murder—for slavery is all of these. It steals babes in the cradle; I might say in the mother's womb. It robs women of their chastity and men of their wives. It kills, with sorrow, uncheered labor and the various forms of cruelty, more slowly, surely, but more in number than the sword."

In all the twenty-four months of close intimacy that followed the meeting of John Brown and John Henri Kagi, there is not one discordant note. It is a tribute to his closest associate, that from the first the old Captain trusted him to the uttermost. It was not Kagi that ever murmured or opposed. It was Kagi that planned, worked, conceived, fought, and obeyed, without question. He was the best of counselors and showed it in his last communication with the leader at Harper's Ferry, when in the noon hour of the 17th of October, he sent "Jerry" Anderson from Hall's Rifle Works, half a mile distant, to John Brown at the Armory Yard, urging a uniting of all their small force, with a view to fighting their way out of the trap they were in. It could have then been successfully done and have carried out also fifteen or twenty of the pluckier men of color. The fatal glamor of judgment which made John Brown place, at the moment, more importance on the fair impression he tried to, but never made, on such brains as those of Lewis Washington, Alstadt, Burns, *et al.*, than he did upon gaining a vigorous foothold for the partisan warfare he had started, induced him to urge another hour's delay on Kagi's suggestion.

With some manuscript letters of Kagi, filed by the late Col. William A. Phillips, of Kansas, in the State Historical Society's Library, there was attached a note in which he describes briefly Kagi's fate, and says that "he was not hopeful of the result of the attack, but accompanied Brown." There is no justification for the remark in any extant letter or writing left by John Henri Kagi. On the contrary, he always wrote hopefully, cheering every one addressed. On

September 23, 1858, he wrote his father and unmarried sister, who had met Captain Brown and others, and knew, in a general way, that their purpose was to attack slavery in its own domain, that—

"I believe there are better times dawning, to my sight at least. I am not now laboring and waiting without present reward for myself alone; it is for a future reward for mankind, and for you all. There can be no doubt of the reward in the end, or of the drawing very near of the success of a great cause which is to earn it. Few of my age have toiled harder or suffered more in the cause than I, yet I regret nothing that I have done, nor am I in any discouragement at the future. It is bright and good, and treads on to meet the hopeful with rapid strides. Things are now quiet. I am collecting arms, etc., belonging to J. B., so that he may command them at any time."

From Tabor, Iowa, on the 7th of February, 1859, he writes "expecting to get actively to work by July," and from Cleveland, Ohio, under date of June 8th, he says: "I now expect to leave here next week and go into my business in earnest;"—and he also advises his sister that she should "always keep in good spirits and hopeful, believing that all is for the best and not thinking that you were singled out by Fate from living chessmen in his game of horror and of death. Follow this and you will never regret being alive."

Under date of Cleveland, Ohio, March 18, 1859, he wrote the following:

DEAR HINTON—I have to-day written Redpath and Merriam respecting our proposed Nicaragua emigration, and wishing them to meet me in Boston at an early day. The careless action of our government and the evident backing down in view of the virtual European interference seem to offer advantages never possessed by Walker.   I wrote to them in care of Francis Jackson.   I need not say that I would like to see you also at that time, which I am now unable to name.   Will you see that Redpath and Merriam get the word ? "

But the letter which most expressed confidence was the last one written to his home in Otoe, Nebraska, bearing date, Chambersburg, Pa., September 24, 1859, twenty-two days before the little party started down the dim moonlit road from the Kennedy Farm to Harper's Ferry.   Kagi writes:

" My business is progressing finely.   I could not ask for better prospects.   My *partners* are all about sixty miles this side of Uncle Jacob's, and enough of them to put the business through in the best of style.   Our freight is all on the ground with them in safety, and we are now only waiting a *few days* more for two or three hands, not so much because we *want* them, but because they want a share themselves.   So that in a very few days we shall commence.   You may even hear of it before you get this letter.   Things could not be more cheerful and more certain of success than they are.   We have worked hard and suffered much, but the hardest is down now, and a glorious success is in sight.   I will say—can say—only one word more. I will write soon after we commence work. When you write, give me all the news—for I shall hereafter have only three correspondents in all—Mr. Dana (Charles A., then managing editor) of the *Tribune*, and Mr. Wm. A. Phillips, of Lawrence (Kansas), so that I shall look to you for all news about our friends and acquaintances.   Direct the letters like this: H. K., and put them into another envelope and direct it as follows: Mrs. Mary W. Ritner, Chambersburg, Pa.   But don't let no one else know how you send them.   Be cheerful. Don't imagine dangers.   All will be well."

He remained at his post, fighting and dying in the same lofty temper which made him declare to me the

30

year preceding that, whatever it was, life or death—
"the result would be worth the sacrifice." No word
of surrender came from his lips. Pierced with bullets, his riddled body lay in the Shenandoah till late
in the afternoon of the nineteenth, when it was pitched
with others in a shallow trench dug on the east bank,
to be afterwards carried off for dissection by the Winchester medical students. No braver man or more
unselfish soul ever blessed the earth than John Henri
Kagi.

John Edwin Cook was in his twenty-ninth year
when hung by Virginia, having been born in the
summer of 1830, at Haddam, Connecticut. The family
were well-to-do, cultivated people, of old Puritan
stock, and John was the favorite boy-child among a
family of handsome sisters. He was well educated,
and was early admitted to Yale. It remains uncertain
to the writer whether he graduated, but he studied
law in Williamsburgh, with a Mr. Stearns, and resided
in the home of his elder sister Mrs. Crowley, the wife
of a prosperous Englishman, acting as agent in this
country for a famous English make of needles. He
afterwards served as a clerk in the office of Ogden
Hoffman, a famous New York lawyer of that day.
But his love of adventure was irresistible, and when
the Kansas excitement broke out, he could not be
persuaded to pursue his profession further. Of his
life as law student, the Rev. Elder J. Porter, editor of
the *Christian Intelligencer* writes that—

"He was, a few years ago, a member of the congregation of
which the writer is the pastor. He was then a law student in
Williamsburgh, and a young man of blameless morals and industrious habits. As an attendant at church, and a teacher in

a then mission Sabbath-school, he displayed tendencies of disposition at once amicable and admirable.   When the Kansas
war broke out, when preachers and politicians strove together
to inflame the public mind with diabolical resentments, Cook,
young, sentimental, visionary, and adventurous, emigrated to
Kansas."

Cook was about five feet, seven inches in height,
slender but strong in frame, active in movement,
quick, impetuous of speech, even sometimes stammer-
ing a little through his vocal, nervous haste.   His
appearance was always attractive.   Memory recalls
him as he rode up to a campfire near Fall City, Nebraska, about the 20th of July, 1856, accompanied by
Charles Lenhart, his devoted comrade, a young,
curly, and blonde haired, fresh-faced, intensely blue-
eyed boy, for he looked not to be over twenty years
of age, though five years older, with a good horse,
handsome clothing, and a brilliant array of weapons
on his person. He captured all present at once. Even
Ira Stewart (afterwards the organizer of the New England Eight-Hour League), our cynical and somewhat
depressing critic, gave way to the spell that Cook possessed.   For myself, we became friends at once, and
this was constant until we parted in the early November days of 1857.   Cook was ingenuous, fervid,
passionate, eloquent; always cheerful and sentimental,
because affectionate and tender to a fine degree.   He
would talk and rattle on about himself.   After all, it
will be difficult to recall that he ever really talked of
any one's opinion or purposes but his own.   This,
however, was an indiscretion at times and under the
conditions in which John Brown's men were placed.
Anna Brown doubtless expresses the facts, when she

writes, that—"Cook favored the plan of taking the town (Harper's Ferry), government buildings, visited them and obtained a good deal of valuable information. The idea of taking Colonel Washington and his relics was his, and he called on that gentleman and found out where he kept them. Cook wanted to go among the plantation negroes and give them vague hints of what was coming. This father positively forbade him doing, and he lived in constant fear all that summer that Cook would make a confidant of some one who would betray us. He never doubted his bravery, honesty, or good intentions, but considered him impulsive and indiscreet."

It is unnecessary to follow the details of his life, from the early summer of 1856 to the early winter day of 1859, when he was done to death on a Virginia scaffold. His course has generally been outlined in tracing the roads followed from Kansas to Harper's Ferry. In Springdale, Iowa, as in Kansas, he was a good comrade to all men; beloved of all women,— mothers as well as maidens. He had a good deal of poetic fancy and excellent taste in rhyming. From a forgotten Kansas newspaper I rescue one little lyric, written in reply to one sent from Boston, demanding that we "Don't give up" the free-state cause. One of Richard Realf's stirring free-state lyrics was penned in reply, and John E. Cook responded with—

WE'LL NOT GO BACK!

From the bleak New England hills,
From the forest, dark and old,
From the side of murm'ring rills,
Came the hardy and the bold—

Came they here to seek a home,
On the prairies' boundless plain.
Here, to Kansas, they have come,
Found a home—and will remain.

Rest they here; though clouds may lower,
O'er Freedom's glowing sky,
Fear not they the tyrant's power,
Nor the Ruffian's battle-cry.
If the storm should o'er them roll—
Battles' lightnings round them glow,
Still, with firm, undaunted soul,
They will meet the coming blow.

Meet it, as the sons of sires,
Who, in bye-gone days of yore,
Stood where Bunker's awful fires
Strewed the field with crimson gore.
Sires, who died that Freedom's light
Here might glow with undimm'd ray,
Freedom theirs; and truth and right
Hallows tombs where now they lay.

This our home; and Kansas sod
Free from slavery's stain shall be.
Here the tyrant's chast'ning rod,
Bows no neck, nor bends no knee.
This our home; and we'll never
Leave a land we so much love,
Till life's ties shall sever,
And we seek a home above.

Here, on Kansas' wide-spread plains,
We shall dwell, through weal and woe;
Keep it pure from slavery's stains,
Till life's fountains cease to flow.

> Leave it—never! nevermore,
> While the blue sky bends above,
> Woods and plains, and valleys o'er,
> Are our home—the home we love.

LAWRENCE, Dec. 17, '56.

His letters, and many have been in my poseession, are all clean, sweet, and manly, filled with a poetic sentimentality, but never one embraces a sentence unworthy of light, or detracting from the strong, manly quality of his character. Writing, after the Chatham Convention, to Iowa friends, he says:

"I came as a stranger; I was treated as a friend and brother, and in return you have my undying gratitude and affection. . . . Higher, holier duties called me and I left you, probably for ever. But wherever I may roam, through all the changing scenes of life, and in that hour when the scenes of life are closing, I shall think of you and shall love you with a brother's love. And may I not hope that the golden links of the chain that thus unites us will remain unbroken in life and grow brighter in eternity. Then *only* can you know me as I am. And when upon your bended knees, 'Oh! if at no other time you think of me, do not forget me then. Alone, before your God, in the stillness of your chamber, I would most wish to be remembered,' till I left you that there was so much selfishness in my nature; that there would be so great a struggle between the desires of a selfish heart and my manifest duty. But, so it is. We do not know ourselves until we are tested in the great crucible of time and circumstances. . . . The prospects of our cause are growing brighter and brighter. Through the dark gloom of the future I almost fancy I can see the dawning light of freedom breaking through the midnight darkness of foul wrong and oppression. That I can almost hear the swelling anthem of Liberty rising from the millions who have but just cast aside the fetters and shackles that

bound them. But ere that day arrives I fear that we shall
hear the crash of the battle shock and see the red glare of the
cannon's lightning. . . . Inclosed you will find a few
flowers that I gathered in my rambles about town. They are
the earliest flowers that blossom in this region. Accept this
with my best wishes for your earthly and eternal bloom." [1]

In another letter of the same period he writes:

"I am in the worst situation I ever was in in my life. I am
here among strangers, and, what is strange, have no wish to
make acquaintances. I also wish to write to my parents, sisters, and brother, but dare not at present on account of future
plans. For, should they know that I was stopping here, it
would awaken suspicion as to the cause of it. And then,
beside, Mr. B. says he rather we would not until we leave here;
for which request he has good reasons. . . . Time hangs
heavily on my hands while waiting, and there is but one thing
that keeps me from being absolutely unhappy, and that is the
consciousness that I am in the path of duty. I long for the
10th of May to come (this was the date set for the Chatham
Convention to meet). I am anxious to have my mind occupied
with the great work of our missions, for amid the bustling,
busy scenes of the camp, I should be less lonely and therefore
more happy than at present."

His Springdale friendships were maintained to the
last hour of his life, and on the morning of his execution he wrote to Mr. and Mrs. Townsend there,
before he indited the farewell letter to his wife and
child. On the 3d of July, 1859. he writes:

. . . I shall start up among the mountains to gaze upon
the grand and beautiful. . . . God's blessed air sweeps
over them, and the winds, as it were, breathe a mournful song
of Liberty. . . . Time passes slowly . . . as I idle

---

[1] To Miss Ella F. Lewis, of Springdale, Iowa.

thus. Heart and soul are all absorbed in the thought of what I owe my country and my God. . . . To-morrow is the Fourth! the glorious day which saw our Freedom's birth, but left sad hearts beneath the slave lash and clanking chain. . . . I feel self-condemned whenever I think of it. . . . The contents of the cup may be *bitter*, but, if it is our duty let us *drain it to the very dregs.*

On the 10th of August he writes to the Lewis family that:

"A light is breaking in the Southern sky, and my glad eyes are gazing on its beams, for well I know that they are heralds fair of the bright glories of the coming day. My hours of watching and waiting now are over, and my glad heart is thrilled with the joy which the morning light has brought. My spirit seems to drink the inspiration of the scene, and I scarcely feel the weakness of my body. I am ready, waiting for my task. *I shall not have long to wait.* The harvest is ripe, and the husbandman is almost ready. He has gazed over the field, and found that *all was good.* I but await his mandate. How I want to see you now. I have no words to tell my yearning after friends and home. Oh, I would love to gaze upon them now; to hear the tones that taught my infant lips to utter father, mother, sister, brother. But this may not be. God be with and bless them."

In this letter he sent the following stanzas:

We see the gathering tempest in the sky,
We see the black clouds as along they roll,
We see from out the gloom the lightnings fly,
O'erthrowing all who would their course control!

We see their flashes as they light the gloom,
Which o'er the morning's deep-blue sky was cast;
We hear the deep thunder's echoing boom,
That tells the Death-descending bolt has past.

We see the sunlight pierce the gloom of night,
Which those dark clouds o'er mornings had cast,
And roll them back upon their rapid flight,
That we may hail the rainbow's beam at last.

John E. Cook left Captain Brown at Cleveland,
Ohio, in the latter part of May, 1858, proposing to
him to go to Harper's Ferry, or neighborhood, procure
employment, and make investigations. John Brown
consented, a little reluctantly at first, as Cook's indiscreet speech always disturbed him. But there is no
doubt that his hearty consent was finally given. Gill,
Tidd, Parsons, Realf, have all agreed to that. Andrew
Hunter, examining the correspondence in the captured carpet-bag, found two or three letters, one
being written by Richard Realf, criticising Cook for
indiscreet talking, and, with the craft of the petty
prosecutor, thought he had lighted on evidence of a
divided feeling. He set himself to work it up, hoping to,
in some way, find one of his prisoners weak enough to
fall into the shallow trap he set. It was given out that
Copeland had confessed and Edwin Coppoc adjured
his Captain, while Cook's statement, wrung from him
by the desire to see his wife and babe again, but more
through the pleadings of his sister and cousin, Mrs.
Willard and Miss Hughes, of Indiana, was heralded
as a "confession" of importance. How little significance it had is apparent by the comments of the
New York *Tribune's* correspondent (Nov. 10, 1859),
when it was sensationally introduced into court.
The Captain's daughter writes relative to these mat-

---

[1] The spectators had begun to withdraw, expecting no continuance of the interest, when, suddenly, all attention was arrested by
Mr. Hunter's announcement that he had a confession rendered by

ters, that both Cook and Coppoc were "warm-
hearted and impulsive, willing to work for the cause,
but would rather not die for it, unless forced to."

Arriving in Virginia early in June, 1858, Cook
stopped at Martinsburg, boarding with Mrs. Kennedy,
whose daughter Virginia he soon after married.
He taught district school, and also gave writing lessons. He peddled maps and traveled as a book
agent in the Valley of Virginia. He kept in touch
with his Captain, who wisely destroyed the letters as
they came. Hence there were none found in the carpet-bag. For some time he kept the canal lock at the
north end of the United States grounds. He was
often in the armory and gathered considerable information. Cook formed the plan for capturing Lewis
Washington and obtaining his historical relics. He
also advocated the seizure of Harper's Ferry, wanted
to burn the buildings and railroad bridges, carrying
off such United States arms as their means of transportation would allow. He was a favorite with his

---

Cook, which he was about to read. The intelligence soon spread
about, and the courtroom was speedily crowded again. All hoped
for a complete and satisfactory revelation. . . . but all were
disappointed. For the confession, which occupied some twenty
large pages of manuscript, and was not read in less than half an
hour, was very little beside a record of some of Cook's experiences in Kansas, Iowa, Ohio, Canada, and elsewhere, in which,
to be sure, Brown was concerned all through, but which, excepting the latter portions, bore very remotely upon the Harper's
Ferry question. . . . Beyond the interest that attaches to an
ostensible full avowal from one of Brown's party, his confession
has none. It is thought by the court that Cook has played a
double game in preparing it—that he has pretended to reveal to
the authorities in good faith all that he is able to, and at the
same time attempted to preserve his fidelity to his old master.

neighbors, and was well treated and warned of danger by the people along the canal, when, on the afternoon of the 17th of October, he was the only one of the band not in the Ferry, who risked his life to aid his comrades that were fighting there.   Mr. Boteler, then in Congress from that district, has told of the close call he received from a bullet sent by Cook from the side of Maryland Heights.   The mark is still seen, made as he fell fifteen feet that afternoon, when a shot from one of the militia cut a small tree branch to which he was clinging.   Cook never lacked the courage which Napoleon termed the "three o'clock in the morning" type.   In Ralph Keeler's account, from Owen Brown's notes and statement, of the final escape of Owen, Barclay Coppoc, and F. J. Merriam, the earlier pages are of interest as illustrating the influences that acted upon Cook in his fatal move at the Mount Alto or " old " furnace.

The counsel of John Edwin Cook, at Chambersburg, is a man honored in his native State and esteemed throughout the nation.   In a recent volume[1] the editor of the *Philadelphia Times*, Hon. Alexander K. McClure, has written an account of his connection with my beloved comrade and friend.   It is a pathetic story, having the great merit of personal knowledge by one whose word will not be gainsaid, and it embodies a real tribute to a brilliant, brave, erratic but earnest manhood.   I condense:

When Hazlett was captured near Shippenburg

---

[1] " Abraham Lincoln and Men of War Times." By A. K. McClure, LL.D., Philadelphia, The Times Publishing Company, 1892 " An Episode of the John Brown Raid," pp. 307-326.

and taken to Carlisle, Pennsylvania, he was believed
to be Captain Cook. A reward of $1,000 was offered
for the latter's capture, and of $2,000 for Owen Brown,
Charles Plummer Tidd, Barclay Coppoc, and Francis
J. Merriam. Attached to the proclamation was a
fair description of each of the fugitives. A requisition was obtained from Richmond for the rendition
of Cook. When the mistake was discovered, the
Cook requisition was retained in a sheriff's hands,
thirty miles from Chambersburg. This proximity
cost Cook his life. Thus, as a matter of fact, he was
practically sacrificed; the arrest of Hazlett being one
direct cause, and the rather quarrelsome disposition
of Tidd being the other, though unintentional, force
which, with hunger, induced or drove Cook down from
the mountains. Col. A. K. McClure says: "I was the
counsel of John E. Cook at Chambersburg, and the
only person entirely familiar with the inner history
of his capture and the plans of escape."

The hunters, slave or otherwise, of the "South
Mountain" region, had seen that the line of retreat
must be in that direction. "Cook was known as a man
of desperate courage," "reckless," and "expert" in the
use of weapons, and "his capture alive was not expected." He was, however, arrested on the 24th of
October, and, says Col. McClure, he "walked into the
hands of the only man in Franklin County who combined with the courage and skill the purpose to capture him. The Logans were mountaineers, Southern
in sympathy, "natural-born detectives," accustomed
to the hunting of fugitive slaves. Daniel Logan, the
capturer of Cook, lived at Lancaster, until 1892. He
is described as a man who "did not believe that either

slavery or freedom was worth dying for." His brother Hugh went South and joined the Confederate Army, dying at last in its ranks from wounds. Daniel, possessing "the highest measure of courage," was a man of complete "physical strength," having clean-cut features and a symmetrical form. "A born detective, silent, cunning, tireless, and resolute," without a conviction, he was just the man for the act. Captain Cook, in his wanderings in search of food, found himself suddenly in an "open space" and "within fifty yards of a number of workmen." He boldly declared himself to be a hunter. Cleggett Fitzhugh, manager of the Mount Alto Furnace, where Cook was first seen, was a man of Southern birth and sympathies. He is reported in the newspapers of the period as a nephew, by marriage, of Gerrit Smith, John Brown's friend and supporter. Logan was conversing with him, when Cook emerged from the thickets. He quietly said: "That's Captain Cook; we must arrest him; the reward is $1,000." Cook advanced carelessly, stated he had been hunting and wanted to "replenish his stock of bread and bacon." Logan heartily invited Cook to go to "his store" for supplies. Without noticing how he was flanked, with his gun carelessly on his shoulder, Cook was suddenly seized. After a brief and hopeless struggle he asked "why?" "Because you are Captain Cook," replied Logan. No answer was made to this. Afterwards, the captor said all he wanted was the reward or its equivalent. "Cook's naturally bright face beamed at once with hope." He told Logan that the amount and more was not to be a consideration, for his brother-in-law, Willard, of Indiana, and Crowley, of New

York, could raise the same on learning the conditions. The statements were of course distrusted by such a man, but Logan named Col. McClure as a Republican and lawyer who would act as counsel and might otherwise aid. They went to Chambersburg, put up at a small hotel and started to find the now famous editor. He could not be found easily, and Logan, fearing for his reward, took his prisoner, about dark, to Justice Reisher. Mr. McClure was passing and, seeing a gathering crowd, stepped into the office. Logan whispered, "with a betrayal of excitement," unusual in him: "My God, Col. McClure! where have you been? I have been hunting you for more than an hour. That's Captain Cook, and I had agreed to bring him to you. Can't you get him yet·?" Logan had promised Cook to take McClure's word for the reward or its equivalent. There was, of course, nothing to be done, but let Cook be committed. Everybody, says the editor, would have been content if Cook had "been able to bounce through a window and escape . . . Logan repented . . . when he saw he had surrendered a life for a price," and as they passed out he said: "Get Cook away, reward or no reward." McClure was counsel for the sheriff, who would also have been glad to have his prisoner escape. Cook, however, agreed not to try until the next night. At the next noon, the sheriff rushed to McClure's office "wild with excitement and his eyes dimmed with tears," exclaiming, "Cook's taken away." A requisition had arrived from Carlisle, in the hands of the sheriff of Cumberland County. The officer accompanied by a Mr. Kimball, Judge Jeremiah G. Black's brother-in-law, arrived in town on the morning train, accompanied, as press reports state, by a Virginian lawyer named Douglass. A presiding judge (State) happening to be in town, was called upon, instant delivery demanded, and acceded to. The papers being regular, Cook was at once turned over to the Virginian. The whole transaction was finished in twenty minutes. He was borne away before his lawyer even knew of the action taken, loaded with irons, placed in a wagon and driven to the station. Gov. Willard had been notified and was already on his way from Indiana to Chambersburg.

Here is Col. McClure's description of his famous client:

"When the lawless little captain had got comfortably seated in his cell, I had my first opportunity to note his appearance and quality. His long silken blonde hair curled carelessly about his neck; his deep blue eyes were gentle in expression as a woman's, and his slightly bronzed complexion did not conceal the soft, effeminate skin that would have well befitted the gentler sex. He was small in stature, . . . nervous, and impatient. He spoke in quick, impulsive sentences, but with little directness save in repeating that he must escape from prison."

It was pointed out that it would be dangerous to all for him to try that night—no one knew of the waiting requisition, and time seemed to be unpressing. The next night it was decided that the attempt should be made. A conference was then held by the lawyer and his partner as to the best means of delaying or fighting a requisition. At ten o'clock McClure returned to the jail and had his last interview with Cook. "As he never dreamed of a requisition reaching him before the second day," and felt confident of escape, Cook "threw off the cloud of despair that shadowed him in the early part of the evening, and startled me with the eloquence and elegance of his conversation," making "one forget that he was in a chilly prison cell, and imagine that he was in the library of some romantic lover of literature and the fine arts. . . . He was evidently a man of much more than common intellectual qualities, and thoroughly poetic in tastes and temperament, with a jarring mixture of wild, romantic love of the heroic." He talked of Kansas and his adventures, while "his soul," writes McClure, "seemed to be absorbed in avenging the Kansas slavery crusades by revolutionary emancipation in the slave States. When asked whether he would not abandon this, 'when he escaped,' his large, soft eyes flashed with the fire of defiance, as he answered, with an emphasis that unstrung every nerve in his body, 'No! the battle must be fought to the bitter end, and we must triumph, or God is not just.'"

Col. McClure states that Cook, at any time that night, could have escaped within thirty minutes, but refrained from action "for it would have compromised both the sheriff and counsel." Arriving at home at eleven o'clock, Mrs. McClure and Miss Virginia Reilley, a devoted friend, were found prepared with a bundle of female apparel, and ready to go to the jail, admission to which would not be denied them. There they proposed that Cook should assume the garb, and while one remained in his place he should walk out with the other. It took more than persuasion to prevent their doing this, and they have since then many times "reproached themselves for not acting upon their woman's intuition."

Justice Reisher, before whom Logan brought Cook, said: "In the short time I was with him, I thought him a gentleman. There was a good deal of candor about him. He is evidently a very brave man." In conversation, Cook spoke of his own companions in the mountains, except Merriam, but gave no clue to their whereabouts. He denied all knowledge of the Bostonian, who had luckily got on the train five miles from Chambersburg and was then in safety. He also refused to talk of Hazlett, of whom he said he had no knowledge, either as "Harrison," or by his own name. He did not mention him in his so-called confession and the only vexatious admission therein was the use of this writer's name. Realf was at the time believed among the John Brown party to be dead, and when I had left Boston, the spring before, I had designedly stated my intention to join Gen. Frederick Landers, on a United States wagon road expedition to Oregon. So that in no way did Cook ever designedly mention the name of any one not already known to the Virginian authorities as in some way or fashion contributing to the John Brown movement. Mr. Franklin Keagy writes, that "in the early part of October, 1892, Daniel Logan was struck by an engine on the Pennsylvania railroad at Lancaster City, and had his right leg so badly mangled that it had to be amputated, and the shock killed him. It is but justice to Mr. Logan to say, that he greatly regretted he had arrested John C. Cook." Mr. Keagy describes the arrival of Mrs. Cook at Chambersburg, she hav-

31

ing been brought in Brown's covered wagon from the
Kennedy Farm. He writes that:

"Mrs. Cook was assigned a room in the rear of the parlor
on the first floor. She was under the impression that a party
from here were going West, of which she was to be a part.
They were to start in a few days. . . . When Mrs. Cook
learned of the outbreak at Harper's Ferry, and her husband's
connection with it, she was terribly distressed and frenzied
with grief. Her situation was pitiable in the extreme. She
was a total stranger, with a young babe, and not a dollar to
pay her boarding or assist her to go away. In this extremity
she appealed to the writer hereof for advice. She desired to
go back to Harper's Ferry. I thought it best she should not
go there at that time. The intense excitement and possibility
of her being arrested, harassed, or insulted, was pointed out to
her. She feared, too, to go there. On inquiry I learned from
her that she had an uncle residing at Brooklyn, N, Y., and I
advised her to go there. It was then I was informed that she
was penniless. I told her if she wished to go the means would
be furnished her. I appealed to Capt. Thomas G. Cochran
for assistance, and in a few hours had more than enough to
defray her expenses. I shall never forget the look of speech-
less gratitude when I placed the money in her hands. I started
to leave the room. She awoke as it were from a dream, and
breaking out in a flood of tears, with clenched hands raised
above her head, she exclaimed: ' Oh, sir, how can I thank you
for your kindness to me. God bless you.' At her further
request I ordered the 'bus to call for her the next morning,
and she started for Brooklyn, N. Y. Late in the afternoon of
that same day her uncle arrived here with the purpose of looking after her. They had passed each other on the road."

Mrs. Ritner, in whose house "Dr. Smith," John
Henri, Watson, Owen, and Oliver, Merriam, and Tidd
had boarded for varying periods, was the widow of a

Mr. Ritner, son of the famous farmer-governor of
Pennsylvania, who secured, about 1830, the first laws
for a free-school system, which he inaugurated.   He
was a warm personal friend of Thaddeus Stevens,
and therefore of the old political free-soil stock.
Mrs. Ritner and her daughter live in Bridgeport,
Connecticut, where also resides, as a merchant and a
man of family, the son of John E. Cook.   Mrs. Cook
remained for some time in Williamsburg, but early in
the spring of 1860 went to Boston, working for a
time at "the case" in James Redpath's office, until
she finally decided to take her son and return to her
mother at Martinsburg, Virginia.   This she did, and,
though it was not a pleasant experience that beset
her in unneighborly ill will, she bravely remained
through the war period, marrying, in 1864, an officer
of Illinois volunteers, named Johnson, with whom
she removed to Bloomington, and now resides in
Chicago.   Virginia Kennedy Cook was an attractive
young woman, large, regular featured, blonde
in complexion, modest, quiet in manner, blameless in life, devoted to her husband's memory,
possessed a reserve of will and character that well
befitted her sad position.   Mrs. Willard still lives in
Indianapolis, and Mrs. Robert Crowley in New York,
both widows.   Another married sister, Mrs. Carpenter, and an unmarried one reside in Connecticut, the
latter at Haddam, the family home.   Cook's counsel
were Daniel W. Voorhees and J. E. McDonald, both of
whom have served as United States Senators, and his
brother-in-law, Governor Willard, of Indiana. Messrs.
Bott & Green were also engaged.   One of the most
frequently repeated stories about the relations of

Captain Brown and John E. Cook is that of a slight put upon the latter as the former was going to his execution. On the 9th of December, Cook set that at rest, in a letter, given below, which is of interest for other reasons:

" The statements that have been made in regard to my companions and myself are totally false. There has not been one single instance in which I have felt or shown any signs of fear or nervousness since I have been here. Neither has my comrade, Coppoc, since he has occupied the cell with me, shown any such weakness or dread of death. We dislike the mode of death to which we have been doomed. But, notwithstanding, we are cheerfully and calmly awaiting our fate, and trust we shall meet it like men. I will frankly admit that on one or two occasions I have been agitated by the reception of touching letters from my wife and other relatives, whose happiness are dearer to me than my life. The doom that awaits me has not in the least affected my appetite, nor has it occasioned any loss of rest. I sleep as calmly here as I would if in my boyhood home."

As to the farewell interview, Cook wrote:

" Captain Brown came in smiling, and shook both Coppoc and myself warmly by the hand. He asked kindly after our health. He then said to me that he was very sorry that I had made a statement that was not true, as I would only gain contempt by it. I asked him what I had said that was untrue. He told that it was the statement which I had made, 'that he had sent me to the Ferry.' I told him he most certainly did tell me to go there. He said he had no recollection of anything of the kind, but that he remembered distinctly of telling me not to go there. I replied that I had a good memory, and had not the slightest recollection of anything of the kind. He remarked that he thought that my memory must be treacherous then, but it would do no good to talk about that; but that if we had got to die, to meet our fate like men, that we had gone into a good cause, and not to deny it now. He then turned to Coppoc, and said that he had heard that he had made some false statements, but was glad to learn that those reports were untrue. He then asked if he could do anything for us. We answered in the negative. He then pressed our hands warmly, and bade us a last farewell. There was no one present except Captain Avis Captain Brown, Coppoc, and myself. Captain Avis will, I think, vouch for the truth of this statement, as will Mr. Coppoc."

Among the papers left by Cook are a number of musical and pathetic lyrics, written during his imprisonment. One of them, written in pencil, on a leaf of his note-book, was brought to me by George Henry Hoyt. Another was received by the Lewis family at Springdale, Iowa, and in his exquisite farewell letter to " wife and child," penned on the morning of his execution, was enclosed some stanzas expressive of both affection and religious resignation. Virginia had a spasmodic generosity and allowed his body to be taken North by his relatives. The cowardice and doughfacism, then too prevalent, culminated in insulting refusals to permit public funeral services over the dead soldier's body. The consistory of Dr. Porter's church refused to allow funeral services therein over Cook's body. Mr. Robert Crowley and his wife were members of the church. So also did the consistory of Dr. Tompkins's church (the New England). A Baptist Congregation offered the use of their small chapel, but the funeral services were finally held in Mr. Crowley's dwelling, where Virginia Cook by the coffin of her husband for the first time met any of her relatives. He was buried in the Cypress Hills Cemetery.

Loving their heroic relative though they did, some

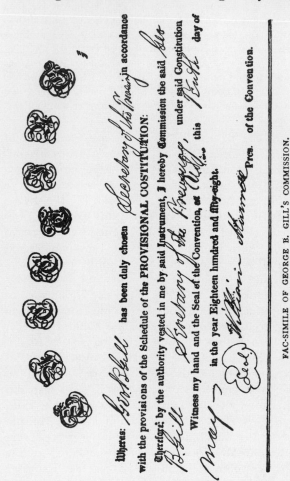

FAC-SIMILE OF GEORGE B. GILL'S COMMISSION.

of John Edwin Cook's " respectable " kin, undertook

to do a considerable amount of explaining for him. Richard Realf, in a letter dated from Washington in 1860, responded to this spirit in words of tribute, which are gladly adopted here: "You will, I am sure," he wrote, "pardon me for saying that in relation to 'John Edwin Cook' I cannot consent to adopt as my own the sentiments with which you appear to regard him. I cannot, that is, consent to call him unfortunate. . . . We have been friends. Permit me to say of him that his faults were such as belong to a warm, impulsive, chivalrous nature. He was quickhearted, swift-blooded, brave unto recklessness, generous unto prodigality. We have been together on the stump, in the solitude of the far prairies, in the social circle, in the retirement of our own homes, and I never knew him other than that which I have stated." Here let it be added, that knowing Cook closely in personal relations, and critically scanning for years everything to be found written by or about him, this writer regards his errors or rather his mistakes, as matters of temperament; his qualities were those of a noble soul, an aspiring, abiding brain, a vivid and hopeful imagination. He was a man of deep convictions; a genuine comrade; more than brave, for he had often shown himself ready in the faithfulness that abides even into death for its higher ideals.

Quakers are esteemed to be good fighters when the paradox is illustrated of their being engaged in fighting. Edwin Coppoc was Quaker bred, and showed it in his grave, quiet, reserved, even rustic, ways. But he was faithful in fight and unflinching before death. A letter written by him to friends in

Iowa illustrates his character.   It bears date November 22d, and deserves this place in the record. It is valuable, too, as a simple, succinct statement of personal knowledge.   It reads in part:

" And with them are the forms and faces of those that, to me, were more than comrades, who fell in a fearful struggle. Eleven of our little band are sleeping now in their bloody garments with the cold earth above them.   Braver men never lived ; truer men to the plighted word never banded together.   Five of them fell while fighting in self-defense for the cause for which they had enlisted ; three on the afternoon of the 17th ; the first a negro by the name of Dangerfield Newby; he fell on the street by my side, whilst we were running to the aid of some of our friends who were surrounded by the enemy.   Two men, Steward Taylor and Oliver Brown, fell by the engine-house. Taylor lived about three hours after he was shot ; he suffered very much and begged of us to kill him.   Oliver died in about fifteen minutes after he was shot ; he said nothing.   During these last moments we could not administer to their wants such as they deserved, for we were surrounded by the troops who were firing volley after volley, so that we had to keep up a brisk fire in return to keep them from charging upon us.   Two more fell in the engine-house on the morning of the 18th, when the last charge was made—Jeremiah Anderson and Dolph. Thompson.

" They both had surrendered after the first charge, which was repulsed, but, owing to the noise and confusion, they were not heard.   Captain Brown and I were the only ones that fought to the last.   The negro Green, after I had stationed him behind one of the engines, the safest place in the house, laid down his rifle and pulled off his cartridge-box, and passed himself off for one of the prisoners.   He and I were the only ones not wounded.

" Watson Brown was wounded about 10 o'clock on Monday at the same time Stevens was, while passing along the street with a flag of truce, but was not so badly wounded but he got

back in the engine-house.   During the fight in the afternoon he
fought as brave as ever any man fought, but as soon as the
fight was over he got worse.   When we were taken in the
morning he was just able to walk.   He and Green and myself
were put in the watch-house.   Watson kept getting worse from
then until about three o'clock Wednesday morning when he died.
I did everything in my power to make him comfortable.   He
begged hard for a bed, but could not get one, so I pulled off my
coat and put it under him, and placed his head in my lap, and
in that position he died.

" Cook and Tidd had left the Ferry early in the morning, by
order of Captain Brown, to cross the river for the purpose of
taking some prisoners and to convey the arms to a schoolhouse
about one and a half miles from the Ferry, there to guard them
until the Captain came, but, hearing a heavy firing. Cook went
down to learn the cause.   On gaining the side of the river
opposite the Ferry, he found we were surrounded, so he ascended the mountain in order to get a better view ; while there
he saw parties firing on us.   In order to relieve us he fired on
them and in doing so he drew the fire on himself, the result of
which was the cutting of a limb and giving him a fall of about
fifteen feet down the mountain side, tearing his clothes, and
lacerating his flesh.   There were thirty or forty men in the first
party he fired on who after the second shot were taken with a
sudden leaving, having no doubt important business elsewhere.
The Virginians who were present give him the credit of being
a splendid shot at a long range, as they admit they made a very
near acquaintance with some of his bullets.

" But enough of this.   Whatever may be our fate, rest assured we shall not shame our dead companions by a shrinking
fear.   They lived and died like brave men.   We, I trust, shall
do the same.   And our souls with no sin of intention on their
robes will gaze unmoved upon the scaffold and the tomb.   We
were deceived in some things.   Even Captain Brown acknowledges that ; but all is over now, so let it pass.   There are true
and brave men in Virginia who deeply sympathize with us in
our misfortune.   I suppose within the last two days from eight

hundred to one thousand persons have visited us, some through sympathy, but more through animosity.

"Among those who called to-day were three young ladies from Harper's Ferry, friends and acquaintances of Cook. They stood and gazed on us for a moment with deep earnestness and then burst into tears. One of them told Cook that all of his friends and acquaintances at the Ferry, had formed the highest opinion of him and regretted he should have gone into such a scheme. They parted from us with tear-dimmed eyes and the deepest expression of sympathy for us in our sad position. . . . I have not seen the Captain or Stevens since our trials, but the jailer tells me they are doing well, their wounds will soon be healed. J. E. Cook sends his love to all."

Edwin Coppoc's days before the early part of 1859 were uneventful. Born near Salem, Columbiana County, Ohio, June 30, 1835, he was, when hung by Virginia on the 16th of December, 1859, twenty-four years, four months, and sixteen days old. He was reared by his grandfather, having lost his father early in childhood, going to district school and working on the farm. As pupil, studious; as a boy, industrious; as a youth, enterprising, with good business traits. Mr. Gill, who knew him intimately, writes of Edwin as a young man of force and decision of character, accompanied by winning manners and most amiable ways. He was brave, persistent, active, and athletic, intelligent, "honorable, loyal, and true;" full, too, of "pleasant mirthfulness," a "magnetic person," and a "capital chum." Edwin Coppoc, says Anne Brown, was of fair skin, had a well-balanced, large head, dark brown hair and eyes, short beard, "quite simple and fascinating in his ways." He was "a rare young fellow; caring for and fearing nothing, he yet possessed great social traits and no better comrade have I ever met." His mother was a woman of uncommon intelligence. Barclay was killed in the Civil War. Two sisters and another brother died of consumption. The Rev. Joseph Coppoc, a Baptist preacher, resident in Iowa, is the only living brother. He was a major in a colored infantry regiment during the Civil War. Edwin's brief record begun when John Brown went through Iowa, early in 1859, with his band of rescued slaves from Missouri. He and his brother Barclay bade their mother farewell in the early summer, and at their own cost went to Chambersburg and reported for service. A quaint incident, characteristic of the Captain's care for details, is told as occurring on the morning of his execution. Barclay Coppoc spent about forty dollars in the "cause," and this amount John Brown considered as due him. He handed Edwin fifty cents—all the change that remained to him as he was leaving the jail, recalling, as he did so, the amount Barclay had expended. The latter never considered it as a debt, however. It is unnecessary to recount again the story of Edwin's attempt with Cook to escape, or of his quiet, manly farewells. "It is not the manner of death that troubles, it is the leaving of dear friends," and with these words, and hand clasped in Cook's, this young life went gallantly into the unknown.

"What happiness there is in thinking or knowing that we are doing the best we can for the good of humanity, although we meet hardships on our journey." Thus wrote Aaron Dwight Stevens in a letter from "Post of Duty" (Kennedy Farm), dated September 9, 1859, and directed to Miss Jennie Dunbar, at

West Andover, Ohio. When a condemned prisoner, he said to a Virginian who railed at him: "I am a poor man myself, but I never yet saw the day when I would have exchanged liberty for riches." Anne Brown wrote of Stevens: "He tries the hardest to be good;" and he himself declared, after conviction and sentence, that "I am cheerful and happy, ready to die at a moment's warning, although I would like to live as long as anybody." The young man who wrote thus of duty, liberty, riches, and death, was born at Lisbon, New London County, Connecticut, March 15, 1831, and was hung on March 16, 1860, at Charlestown, Virginia, for the "crime" of attacking chattel slavery. Stevens was also of the best New England stock, and of ancestral strains that go deep into the roots of the struggle for liberty of conscience and civic freedom. His great-grandfather, Moses Stevens, was a revolutionary officer, and his grandfather served in the war of 1812. The record goes back to early colonial days, when his progenitors were always found with the people's cause and against the aggressions or arrogance of the crown. The paths of heredity, as well as the roads of action, moulded tendencies and created forces, leading direct to Harper's Ferry and a Virginian gallows-tree.

The boy was father of the man. Taught till fourteen in the common school, he early went to work to maintain himself. Handsome and active as a young Greek gladiator, overflowing with abundant life, impetuous, passionate, generous, warm-hearted, and hasty, it is not surprising that this boy found his daily life monotonous, and that during the first years of war with Mexico he enlisted and served until its

close. He was honorably discharged, and remained
at home until 1851, when he enlisted as a bugler in a
United States dragoon regiment, commanded by Col.
Sumner, being drafted to the West at once. He
became the colonel's bugler-orderly. He served in
Western Kansas and Nebraska, in Wyoming, Colorado, and New Mexico. Stevens was hard to discipline, and could seldom restrain his disposition to
resist the daily tyrannies. One who knew the circumstances attending his desertion, has told that,
after a considerable period in New Mexico, watching,
and sometimes fighting Navajo and Apache, the
command, early in 1855, was ordered into Fort
Leavenworth. Soon after the march commenced, a
soldier disobeyed some petty order and was inhumanly
punished therefor by order of the major in command.
Maddened by the outrage, Stevens fell upon the major,
and, beating his bugle out of shape over his head,
chastised him, as he richly deserved, within an inch
of his life. For this performance he was marched
across the plains, with a ball and chain attached to
his ankle, to Fort Leavenworth, where he was court-
martialed, and sentenced to be shot. On application
of some of the officers at the fort to the President,
his sentence was commuted to three years' hard labor
in the guardhouse or the shop, with the ball and
chain to his ankle. He served the government in
this way till early in January, 1856, when he deserted,
and concealed himself among the Delaware Indians
on the Kaw River. He remained with them till about
the 1st of March following, when he made his appearance in Topeka. Stevens at once identified himself
with the Free State cause, assuming his mother's name

and being known as "Charles Whipple." He filed a
preëmption claim on a quarter section of land in
Shawnee County.

It was of course soon apparent that he had had a
military training, and this was accounted for by his
acknowledgment of having served in the Mexican
War. Whipple became useful at once, and during
the spring of 1856, organized several mounted companies which were formed into the Second Regiment
of Free-State Volunteers. This was not disbanded
until the next summer, when, being in possession of
the Territorial Legislature, the free-state people
authorized the creation of a militia of which James
H. Lane was made major-general in command, Stevens being offered a brigadier-general's commission.
Under Col. "Whipple," the Second Free-State Regiment did service at Indianola, Tecumseh, Osawkee,
the Titus Fort, Lecompton, and other points. These,
as already explained, were armed camps of Buford's
men, or towns controlled by and serving as rallying
points for the Missouri invaders. Whipple himself
was exceedingly serviceable also in keeping open the
Northern emigrant route to Nebraska. When Col.
Sumner with dragoons was in Topeka, on the 4th
of July, and later with Governor Geary in the following December and January, the free-state colonel
always found a convenient excuse for being absent.
They would have hardly recognized however, in the
stalwart man, "bearded like a pard," the down-
bedewed cheeks of the daring youth who had served
as orderly among the Rocky Mountains.

In describing the roads to Harper's Ferry, the
actions of Aaron D. Stevens and his general charac-

teristics have been sufficiently outlined to make of
him a distinct figure. The Baltimore *American's*
special correspondent, under date of October 18th,
1859, thus writes of Stevens, then a prisoner, with
six bullet wounds in various parts of his body:

" He is the only one of the lot that I have seen, excepting,
of course, the negroes, who has not light hair. His hair and
long beard are of a fine black (it was really a dark brown) ;
his face partakes of the handsome and noble ; his eye, though
restless, has a sharp brilliancy; and he, too, is a six-footer.
A stout, strong man, whose condition, lying upon the floor,
obedient to the last to the command of ' my Captain,' as he called
him, wounded with three or four buckshot wounds—two in the
head and one in the breast, certain of death—I could not but pity.
He, too, showed a marvelous courage. Ever and anon, groan-
ing with excessive pain, he did not, however, forget himself for
an instant, but calmly, although in such pain, listened to the
conversation as it progressed. Both men seemed prepared for
death, seemed to court it rather, perhaps under the idea that
they will be acknowledged martyrs, but more possibly under
the conviction of having performed a sacred duty. However
much the writer hereof may differ from them, there must arise
a feeling of respect for them in their bold rashness."

Stevens stood six feet two inches in his stocking-
feet, was a perfectly proportioned man, with hands
and feet that were small for stature and bulk, a long
arm, having remarkable skill in the use of a sabre,—he
was a perfect drillmaster for cavalry and irregular
warfare. His head was large, round, with full, high
forehead, well proportioned, good features, and remarkably brilliant, clear, speaking eyes. He had
decidedly soldierly qualities and would have won
place and fame if he had lived and occasion arose
before him. He wrote fairly and read much in Eng-

lish, and coming of a decidedly musical family, with a magnificent baritone voice, was, of course, fond of singing. His father and elder brothers both taught music, and all the family were choir members. To Mrs. Spring, replying to that lady's proposal to bury both himself and Hazlett at Eagleswood, he wrote:

"I have a dear father, a very kind, benevolent man. I have also a stepmother, my own mother's sister, and I have also two sisters, and two brothers, all very near and dear to me. They are somewhat different from me—more quiet and steady than me. My oldest brother is a music teacher—in fact, we all understand music, more or less. My father has led a choir ever since he was sixteen—he is now over sixty. I have written him to know if he will want to claim my body, if I am sent to the spiritland through the *kindness* of Virginia. It makes very little difference to me what becomes of the body after the spirit has left it. My father is a poor man; I do not know as he will be able to come on here and get it. I wrote him, telling him he had better give up his right to you, and that he could come to your place, if he chose, and see me buried. I hope he will comply; if not, please accept my thanks for your kind offer."

Nothing can give a better conception of Stevens— bold, brave, full of courage and passionate vigor as he was—than some brief sentences from the numerous letters at my command; enough, in fact, to fill a small volume. To his sister he said:

"I am glad that I did not die of my wounds; for I believe that my execution upon the gallows will be a better testimony for truth and liberty."

In reply to a question why he went to Harper's Ferry with John Brown, the reply was:

"It was to help my fellow men out of bondage. *You* know nothing of slavery—*I* know a great deal. It is the crime of crimes. I hate it more and more the longer I live. Even since I have been lying in this cell, I have heard the cryings of slave-children torn from their parents."

"We are in the right, and will resist the universe," was the answer thundered back at a Kansas sheriff in the fall of 1858, when arrests were to be attempted for resistance to pro-slavery murderers and robbers. "There is so much happiness," he said, "in trying to make others happy." To Mrs. Spring, with whom he maintained a long and remarkable correspondence, he wrote, at different dates:

"I wish you a long life and a happy one, and in your last days the thought of having helped the world forward instead of back. . . . The bouquet you sent me is very beautiful. I have hung it up south of the window, over the little table I have to write upon. It always has a smile of love and kindness. . . . My trial comes on to-morrow. I shall soon know my destiny. I have not much hope short of anything but the better land. . . . I hope your soul is so strong that sorrow cannot find a lodging there. I am cheerful and happy, patiently awaiting the fate of man—death. . . . I could bear all the sorrow of the world, if I had it on my shoulders. . . . It makes my soul overflow with sorrow to see men with great talents use them in defending what is both a curse to themselves and to all mankind. . . . I hope you will always, as you love yourself, as you love woman, as you love man, as you love God, work with hands, head, and heart for the happiness of all mankind. . . . I am glad I did not die of my wounds; for I believe my execution upon the gallows will be a better testimony for truth and liberty. . . . Give those little children my love and thanks for their bounteousness; tell them I hope they will live to be an ornament to the world, and lovers of freedom and justice to all the human family. . . . Mr. Sennott (his lawyer) left here this morning; I suppose you will see him before you get this. He has

32

done all a man could for me, for which I am very *thankful*.
. . . I hope you will not hesitate a moment about speaking
to me of death, for it gives me no more pain than it would to
talk about living. It would give me much more pain to have
you tell of some poor human being trodden down by some
tyrant. Death has no terrors for me; at the same time, I
should like to live as long as I can do any good."

To Anne Brown, in closing a letter, he said: "Give
my love to all good people—to all who love the
truth." Again he writes, eight days before his execution, that:

"It is hard to look back on those that are gone; but, thank
God, they died for liberty, and ere the 17th of March I expect
to meet them in the spirit land. I am very cheerful and happy,
and never felt more so in my life. . . . My comrade, Mr.
Harrison, is getting along nicely."

He tells Wealthy Brown that he cannot "laugh"
because of his facial paralysis, owing to a wound, and
that it is impossible to sing, which is the worst of all.
He read much and was amply supplied with books.
Gerald Massey's poems and "Abou Ben Adhem," by
Leigh Hunt, were among his favorites. Copies of
verses in Stevens's neat handwriting are quite plentiful.
His songs seem to have been " The Messenger Bird,"
a lyric often sung in spiritualist meetings, "Just as I
Am," " Come to Me," " The Eden Shore," and others.
Ellen Francis Watkins Harper, a colored woman of
poetical and oratorical ability, then living in Phila-
delphia, was a constant and cheering correspondent,
and sent him several very pretty lyrics of her own.

When Captain Brown was bidding a final farewell
to his young comrade, he wrote the following:

"CHARLESTOWN PRISON, 2d December, 1859.
"John Brown to Aaron D. Stevens. ' He that is *slow* to anger

is better than the mighty; and he that ruleth his *spirit*, than he that taketh a city.'—*Solomon*."

Stevens added:

"This was given me an hour or two before he was executed.   A. D. S."

Unlike Captain Brown, his gallant soldier associate did not affect the faith of a Christian. He was a devoted spiritualist, however, and died believing absolutely in the immortality of life. To Mrs. Spring he wrote:

"I suppose you have heard before this, that I am not a believer in the Christian religion, and I never judge a person by their belief. The Christian religion never looked consistent to me, and therefore I had to look elsewhere for religion, and found it in the great *Bible of Nature*. Christians think, as a general thing, that a person that believes that way never has the feeling that comes over a person when they experience religion; but that *is not so*. That feeling will come upon every one who will put away the *great self*, and try to do unto others as they would have others do unto them; then they will feel happy and ready to die at any time. There is a natural feeling to live in the bosom of all as long as they can, but I mean they will have no fears of going into the hands of the Supreme Being, or Ruling Power of the universe." Of his prison life, under date of January 14, 1860, he says: "I have many letters to write to many dear friends which employ a good part of my time, and the rest is taken up in sleeping, exercise, and reading. The chain only gives me room to take a half step, so you will see I cannot walk very fast, but I get some exercise that way, which gives me rest from sitting or lying." After regretting his inability to write freely, he goes on: "Without going into the mysteries of death, what a field of thought and action there is here to find out *how* to live and *how* to do our duty to our brothers and sisters, or to everything that lives. How little can we learn in the few years we spend here of the truth found in the infinite ocean of mind and matter." He then mentions the books sent him by friends as having been read with pleasure ' in the snug home," wherein he was confined.

The trial of Stevens and Hazlett begun on the 2d of February, 1860. The indefatigable and faithful Boston lawyer, Mr. Sennott, was on hand, able and untiring in his unpaid and volunteer labors. He harried the prosecutor Hunter a good deal over the pretense of having transferred Stevens's case to the Federal Court, and endeavored to secure from Judge Kenny an order permitting such choice on the prisoner's part. It was all useless, of course. Stevens was in prison one hundred and sixty-nine days and then executed ; Hazlett was held for one hundred and fifty; Coppoc, Copeland, and Green for fifty-nine each; Cook for forty-eight, and John Brown for forty-five days.

In his brief address, when sentence was pronounced, he denied that he ever proposed the burning of Harper's Ferry, as had been sworn to, and closed by saying: "When I think of my brothers slaughtered and my sisters outraged, my conscience does not reprove me for my actions. I shall meet my fate manfully." The coolness of these men is shown by an incident. Captain Avis tells of finding Hazlett and Stevens engaged the day after their sentences, in "chucking" pennies. As the jailer stood there Stevens tossed the coin again and called out: "Head or tail?" "Tail!" shouted Hazlett. "It's head— I've won!" exclaimed Stevens, as he went over and picked up the coin. "What have you won?" asked the jailer. "The privilege of selecting you to put the hangman's noose around my neck!" was the cool reply.

The jailer's kindness had made a deep impression on both men, and they had discussed the question as to which should be the first to be noosed by his hands. Stevens had won, and as they mounted the gallows in company he whispered to the jailer: "Captain, remember that I won the first choice!"

Of course, the inevitable military parade was had, though the pompous General Taleifiero had departed and Col. John Gibson was in command of the six companies of State militia, it was thought necessary to "call out" to see executed two men who deemed their deaths better for freedom than their lives could possibly be. During the middle of February a secret message was received by the prisoners and a reply returned. An intoxicated man was arrested in Charlestown on a Saturday evening and locked up over Sunday in jail. To all appearances he was a jolly, devil-may-care young Irish laborer, in whom whisky left nothing but boisterous fun. As he sobered up, he became a delight to the jailer's family by his funny songs and witty words. Discipline had relaxed, vigilance nodded, and the careless Irishman was enabled to communicate with Stevens and Hazlett. He made himself known and told them that their comrades, James Montgomery, Richard J. Hinton, Joseph Gardner, "Preacher" Steward, and six other Kansas men, with Thomas Wentworth Higginson, J. W. Le Barnes, and W. W. Thayer, of Boston, assisted by some New York German-Americans, were ready at Harrisburg, Pennsylvania, to make a move through the South Mountain section of that State, into Virginia,

and attempt their rescue. They were told that Montgomery was even then in the adjacent mountains,
making a reconnaissance as to practicability. Both were
deeply affected, but without hesitation declared it to
be impossible. Stevens emphatically asserted that
the attempt could not be made without causing other
deaths, especially that of the jailer, Mr. Avis, who
would resist to the last. He would not take his
liberty at such a cost. The constant armed force consisted of eighty men, and, while it was possible to get
away if Montgomery could reach and attack the place
suddenly, yet the lives to be sacrificed would not
warrant the saving of their own. Hazlett sent a personal message to the writer of this volume, who had
been deeply stirred by the fact that his comrade was
tried and condemned under a name himself assumed
in writing to Kagi. There was nothing to be done.
The daring young Kansan, who had so successfully
used his powers of mimicry, was discharged next day
by an unsuspecting justice of the peace and made his
way out of Virginia as rapidly as he dared. Montgomery
had already returned to Harrisburg and his associate
rejoined him in Boston, bearing there his message to
myself.

Mrs. Pierce, Stevens's sister, and Miss Jennie Dunbar, of Ohio, visited the prisoners the day before
the execution; the latter having just returned from a
visit to Richmond, where she pleaded with Governor
Letcher (Wise retired at the close of 1859) for the
lives of Stevens and "Harrison." In a letter, still
unpublished I believe, Miss Dunbar tells how she
arrived at Richmond on the 14th. Mr. Sennott had
already left, having unsuccessfully been on the same

mission. Miss Dunbar was received, she wrote, with what the Governor called "civility," but which she thought might have had a harsher name. After reading Mrs. Spring's letter—the servant being gone from the room—Letcher said in substance that Stevens was the worst of the Harper's Ferry insurrectionists; that at the trial he saw that he was "reckless, hardened, and dangerous to society"; that he (Letcher) felt it to be a duty to rid the world of him. In short, that Stevens "should not be pardoned." Miss Dunbar describes her reception by the friend she had sought to succor. He expressed regret that she had pleaded with the Governor, whose hardness as one with the slave-power he had fully expected. He soon became calm and cheerful; "quite himself," writes the young lady, "talking and laughing as he had done under other and happier circumstances." On the last morning they all breakfasted together. Miss Dunbar writes, that he was dressed in fresh clothing, his chains had been removed, and "I had never seen him looking better; he seemed fitter to live than ever on the morning of his execution." His sister was quite overcome, and had to leave the table to recover herself. Tears welled from Miss Dunbar's eyes. "You must not give up here," said the brave brother and friend; "wait until you reach Mrs. Spring, you can weep upon her bosom." They all grew calmer. He packed a little trunk, designating various gifts for different persons, chatted as if he were going soon to meet us again, polished his shoes and brushed his clothes, saying "I wish to look well when I go upon the scaffold." Miss Dunbar, in taking her last farewell, said: "You have done a great deal for me, inasmuch as you have shown me that the moralist's faith will do to die by."

"Oh! yes," he quickly replied, "I am perfectly confirmed in the belief that God is over all and that He is too loving a God to make His creatures unhappier than they make themselves." Miss Dunbar tells that a minister called on Stevens a few days before the execution, saying he " was not going to help him out of the trouble in *this* life, but wished to help him to security in the *next*." Stevens told him, he " required no help after leaving the body; that, if the minister could not help him then, he did not wish his services at all." At half-past eight they left, to wait at Harper's Ferry for the remains of the two brave young soldiers of liberty. They embraced and kissed on the scaffold, were unattended by any one but the officers, bore themselves both bravely, but evidently died hardly. Lawbreakers! yes; but more to be commended in spirit and purpose, or character either, than the makers and administrators of the laws they violated.

The colored men who are known to have borne their part in the raid at Harper's Ferry, were Osborne Perry Anderson, born free in Pennsylvania, a printer by trade, working at Chatham, Canada West, where he first became connected with John Brown; Shields Green, a fugitive slave from Charlestown, S. C., who came with Frederick Douglass to Chambersburg, Pa., on the 19th of August preceding the outbreak, and entered the party at Kennedy Farm as in sort a representative of Mr. Douglass; Dangerfield Newby, a freeman of the Shenandoah Valley, Virginia; John A. Copeland and Lewis Sherrard Leary, both born in

Raleigh, N. C., but reared from childhood at Oberlin, Ohio. Copeland was free born; Leary was a fugitive slave. Newby and Leary were married men, the first had a wife and seven children, the second a wife and one child. Green had left a boy in slavery; his wife dying before he made his escape. Copeland was unmarried. Newby was about thirty years of age, Green twenty-four, Anderson twenty-four, and the Oberlin men were twenty-two and twenty-four years of age. Green was a full-blooded black; Newby "was a tall, well-built mulatto, aged about thirty, with a pleasing face." [1]   Anderson and Copeland were good-looking, bright, mulatto in color, the latter having bushy head and nearly straight hair, while Leary was nearly or quite a quadroon. They were all intelligent, Green looking the least so, though possessed of considerable natural ability, vigor of character, and a courage which showed that if better trained he might have become a marked man Anderson was well educated, a man of natural dignity, modest, simple in character and manners. He wrote a very interesting pamphlet account of the raid, after his escape, served during the latter part of the Civil War in the Union Army, and died in Washington, in 1871. Anne Brown writes that his treatment was not altogether creditable to the people of his own race, upon whom he was compelled to call for aid, when escaping. He gives very few particulars in his own account, and they are in acknowledgment of favors received. In the early summer of 1860, he visited North Elba, entering the door yard and stop-

---

[1] Barry's "Annals of Harper's Ferry."

ping at the grave of the Captain, where he appeared
to the friendly eyes watching him from the house to
be weeping and praying. At last, as he turned to
leave, Watson's widow, Belle, suggested he might be
a fugitive, and Anne Brown, looking again, declared
that perhaps she knew him. On going out, his identity was established. He expressed himself as delighted to meet her, asked after all the family, and
then with a " God bless you, you dear girl," he started
to go. Anne insisted on his coming into the house,
seeing Watson's boy, Freddie, and meeting her mother.
"I might not be welcome; I have seen you and the
Captain's grave, and now I'll go." The harsh manner in which, among others, some of his own relatives
had received him, threatening even his arrest in their
selfish and cowardly alarm, had made the refined and
sensitive man timid even of this hospitality. However, he staid, and for a number of days, being present at the Fourth-of-July celebration held at John
Brown's grave, in 1860, at which F. J. Merriam and
Barclay Coppoc were also present, while Thaddeus
Hyatt, James Redpath, and R. J. Hinton were active,
papers and letters being read, by the latter, from
Wendell Phillips, Frederick Douglass, and Henry D.
Thoreau. When Anderson was leaving the modest
but very hospitable " House of the Gods," which had
received him so cordially, he told Anne, in explanation of his strange behavior, how he had been treated,
and that he had hardly had a kind word spoken to
him until he came to their house. He apologized,
she writes, "for staying so long and said he dreaded
to go back and into the world where he would be so
friendless and alone. He was a dignified and sensible

man, modest, and unassuming in his conversation, a printer by trade. At the Kennedy Farm, the night before we were leaving for home (Martha and Anne), he came downstairs to listen to the 'Emperor's' (Shields Green) farewell speech, as he called it. This was the greatest conglomeration of big words that was ever piled up. Some one asked Anderson 'if he understood it,' and he replied, ' No, God Himself could not understand that.'"

But the negro man with Congo face, big, misplaced words, and huge feet, knew instinctively what courageous manhood meant and how devotion acted. Frederick Douglass tells how, when he turned to leave the Chambersburg quarry, where his last interview with John Brown was had, that, on telling Green he could return with him to Rochester, New York, the latter had turned and looked at the strong but bowed figure of John Brown, weighted with the pain of Douglass's refusal to aid him in, as he termed it, "hiving the bees," and then asked: "Is he going to stay?" An affirmative answer being made, he looked again at the old leader, and slowly said, "Well, I guess I's goes wid de old man." When, a short time after O. P. Anderson and Albert Hazlett had decided the resistance then making to be hopeless, Green came, under fire, with some message, over to their station at the arsenal on the Potomac. Anderson told him he'd better go with them. He turned and looked toward the engine-house, before the door of which stood its few defenders, and asked: "You think der's no chance, Osborne?" "Not one," was the reply. "And de old Captain can't get away?" "No," said both the men. "Well," with a long look and slow utterance, " I guess I'll go back to de old man." In the prison, Green, with Copeland and Leary, were constantly sending messages of regard to Captain Brown and Stevens, and on the morning of John Brown's execution he sent him word that he was glad he came, and that he waited willingly for his own death.

Lewis Sherrard Leary was a bright, and quite well-educated young man Leary was the first Oberlin recruit, and introduced Copeland to Kagi. In an alleged "confession," which was merely statements that Mr. Hunter, by adroit examination, got out of Copeland, it appears that Ralph and Samuel Plumb, of Oberlin College, gave them fifteen dollars to defray their expenses to Chambersburg; that they came by way of Cleveland, stopping with Mrs. Isaac Sturtevant, a distant relative of C. W. Moffet, meeting Charles H. Langston there, and from thence coming on to Chambersburg, where they were received by James Watson, a col-

JOHN A. COPELAND.

ored man. Andrew Hunter spent a good deal of time in the effort to get some one of the prisoners to tell something they did not know, but he utterly failed. Letters of Copeland, written from the jail, to his father and mother at Oberlin, are as notable for cheerfulness and religious resignation as any of John Brown's correspondence. He wrote, shortly before the execution of December 16th, that:

" I am not terrified by the gallows, which I see staring me
in the face, and upon which I am soon to stand and suffer
death for doing what George Washington was made a hero for
doing." . . . " While, for having lent my aid to a general
no less brave, and engaged in a cause no less honorable and
glorious, I am to suffer death. Washington entered the field
to fight for the freedom of the American people—not for the
white man alone, but for both black and white. Nor were they
white men alone who fought for the freedom of this country.
The blood of black men flowed as freely as that of white men.
. . . And some of the very last blood shed was that of black
men. . . . It was a sense of the wrongs which we have suffered that prompted the noble but unfortunate Captain Brown
and his associates to attempt to give freedom to a small number,
at least, of those who are now held by cruel and unjust laws,
and by no less cruel and unjust men. . . . And now, dear
brother, could I die in a more noble cause ? Could I die in a
manner and for a cause which would induce true and honest
men more to honor me, and the angels more ready to receive
me to their happy home of everlasting joy above ? I imagine
that I hear you, and all of you, mother, father, sisters, and
brothers, say—' No, there is not a cause for which we, with
less sorrow, could see you die.' Believe me when I tell you,
that though shut up in prison and under sentence of death, I
have spent more very happy hours here, and were it not
that I know that the hearts of those to whom I am attached
. . . will be filled with sorrow, I would almost as lief die
now as at any time, for I feel that I am now prepared to meet
my Maker. . . . You may think I have been treated very
harshly since I have been here, but it is not so. I have been
treated exceedingly well. . . . My jailer, Captain John
Avis, is a gentleman who has a heart in his bosom as brave as
any other. He met us at Harper's Ferry, and fought us as a
brave man would do. But since we have been in his power,
he has protected us from insult and abuse which cowards
would have heaped upon us. He has done as a brave man and
gentleman would do. Also one of his aids, Mr. John Sheats,

has been very kind to us, and has done all he could to serve us. And now, Henry, if fortune should ever throw either of them in your way, and you can confer the least favor on them, do it for my sake."

On the morning of the execution he wrote a long letter to his family at Oberlin, from which the following may well be quoted:

" I am well both in body and in mind.   And now, dear ones, if it were not for those feelings I have for you—if it were not that I know your hearts will be filled with sorrow at my fate, I could pass from this earth without regret.   Why should you sorrow ?   Why should your hearts be racked with grief ?   Have I not everything to gain, and nothing to lose by the change ? I fully believe that not only myself, but also all three of my poor comrades who are to ascend the same scaffold (a scaffold already made sacred to the cause of freedom by the death of that great champion of human freedom, Captain John Brown), are prepared to meet our God. , . . I pray daily and hourly that I may be fitted to have my home with them, and that you, one and all, may prepare your souls to meet your God ; that so, in the end, though we meet no more on earth, we shall meet in heaven, where we shall not be parted by the demands of the cruel and unjust monster, slavery.   But think not that I am complaining, for I feel reconciled to meet my fate.   I pray God that His will be done, not mine.   Let me tell you that it is not the mere fact of having to meet death which I should regret (if I should express regret, I mean), but that such an unjust institution should exist as the one which demands my life, and not my life only, but the lives of those to whom my life bears but the relative value of zero to the infinite.   I beg of you, one and all, that you will not grieve about me, but that you will thank God that He spared me to make my peace with Him.

" And now, dear ones, attach no blame to any one for my coming here, for not any person but myself is to blame.   I have no antipathy against any one. I have freed my mind of all hard feelings against every living being, and I ask all who have anything against me to do the same."

Virginia's cruel hostility to the negro, even when imprisoned and dead, is shown by Hunter's attack in court on Shields Green, and more than all by the petty maliciousness of Governor Wise's refusal to give up the dead bodies unless "white men came after them." Andrew Hunter says, Copeland "died with unwavering fortitude and perfect composure." Professor Munroe, of Oberlin, who secured admission to the prisoners, declares that Green was "patient, manly, and enduring." Copeland was sent with Leary under Kagi's command to the Hall Rifle Works, half a mile distant from the armory and engine-house. Leary was riddled to pieces in Shenandoah River about two o'clock on the 18th of October. Copeland was compelled to surrender, and his life was saved for the scaffold through the interposition of Congressman Boteler. Newby was in the thickest of the early fighting at the armory gate, shooting, it appears, both Turner and Boerly, being himself shot by Armorer Boerly from an upper window of a dwelling on the corner of High and Stevenson streets. The gun was loaded with a spike or shot bolt, which entered into Newby's neck, inflicting a frightful wound and killing him instantly. Boerly was himself slain by a bullet from a Sharpe's rifle, fired by an old slaveman of the neighborhood, who distinguished himself by reckless courage. He was probably killed soon after. "Jim," Colonel Washington's coachman, also fought, says O. P. Anderson, "like a tiger." Anderson and Green went with Stevens to Washington, and Newby, from

there with Cook to Alstadt and Burns. Anderson
and Hazlett were sent to the arsenal and ordered to
hold it.   After they crossed the river, late on the 17th,
they had quite a sharp skirmish with some of the
militia; a proceeding which led the Virginians ever
since to write of the " reinforcements" that sought
to aid John Brown.   Osborne P. Anderson deserves a
fuller account, but, after all, the record, though
meager, is sufficient to insure his place among the
heroes of mankind.   He possessed, among other qualities, good literary ability.   It may speak well for
shrewdness and sagacity, but not for the " higher
power " which Emerson says, is " the wind that blows
the world into orbit and order," that amid the forty
or fifty more or less representative men of color,
cognizant of John Brown's plans; the unassuming
Anderson, the young Oberlin recruits, the negro
fugitive slave from South Carolina and " clothes
cleaner " from Rochester, were the only ones that
answered the call.   Even Richardson failed in Canada,
and Thomas kept still at Springfield.

Albert Hazlett, returned to death by his native
State of Pennsylvania, without justifiable and legal
identification, was hung by Virginia on the 16th of
March, 1860, after being held more than 140 days in
jail and on trial, never clearly shown to have been at
Harper's Ferry.   Even his name was never clearly
established, for he was tried as " William Harrison,
alias Albert Hazlett," the first being the name given
by him when arrested between Chambersburg and
Carlisle, on the 21st of October.   The writer of this
volume was sympathetically drawn more closely to
this young man than to any other of the John Brown

party, a number of whom were his personal friends
as well as anti-slavery associates, by reason of the
fact in using the name " William Harrison," he took
that which this writer had signed for prudential
reasons to letters sent during 1858 and 1859, to John
H. Kagi. It may have been but an accidental coin-
cidence, but it influenced the writer to the organization of the only definite attempt made towards rescuing any of the Harper's Ferry raiders.[1]

Albert Hazlett was born at Indiana, Pennsylvania,
September 21st, 1837. At the date of his death,
therefore, he was in his twenty-fourth year, that is
twenty-three years, six months, and eleven days old
He went to Southern Kansas very early in 1857, and

---

[1] In referring to the " Harrison " letters to Kagi, it may not be
improper for me to say that Henry A. Wise told me, in 1867, at
the Spottswoode Hotel, Richmond, that three of these letters
were found, giving an account of a trip through the Indian Territory, with especial reference to the slaves found among the Cherokees, Choctaws, Chickasaws, and Creeks, as well as to the descendants of the " marooned " negroes among the Seminoles,
both in the territory and in Nuevo Leon, Mexico. There
were also extended details of slave conditions in northeastern
Texas, northern Louisiana, western and central Arkansas. The
topography of all this region was referred to with reference to a
plan of attack on slavery therein. This was vigorously outlined in
one of the " William Harrison " letters. Part of them were in
stenographic (not phonographic) signs, arranged between Kagi
and myself, and were never deciphered by Wise, Hunter & Co.
It would have caused some loss of life had they been able to read
the names and places such signs referred to. Gov. Wise informed
me these letters had been taken from the famous John Brown
carpet-bag with the consent of Senator Mason, privately lithographed, and carefully circulated in the South, as an illustration of
the extent of the " abolition " conspiracy. The authorship of

33

soon became actively identified, on the free-state
side, with the troubles there.   In the latter part of
1858 he joined John Brown's company, was with him
on the Christmas-Eve raid into Missouri, and aided
in escorting the rescued slaves to Canada.   After
this was done, Hazlett staid a short time in
northern Ohio and then returned to his home in
western Pennsylvania, where he remained at his
brother William's doing such work as he could obtain
until the early part of September, 1859, when he
joined the party at Kennedy Farm, reporting first to
Kagi at Mrs. Ritner's, Chambersburg.   In the latter
part of May (21st) he wrote: "I wish it would come
off soon, for I am tired of doing nothing;" and

---

these letters was a matter of uncertainty to the Virginian authorities, and when Hazlett first gave the name " Harrison " they
hoped to have secured the writer.   From other reference, and a
comparison with letters, signed by my own name, they reached
the conclusion that I was the author of those they deemed important enough to keep secret and use as a breeder of future civil war.
Recently, on a visit to South Carolina, I found a curious pamphlet
allusion to these letters, and to a subsequent plan of insurrection
which was prepared and sent out from Boston during the fall of
1860, more as a scare or means of agitation than anything else.
In the library of a Northern gentleman, who has resided and done
business in the Palmetto State ever since the surrender of Lee, and
who has collected a large amount of Civil-War matter, especially
Southern, I found a pamphlet printed in Charleston, which
quotes from the Boston plan and refers mysteriously to the carpet-
bag letters under consideration.   General Albert L. Lee and other
officers of the 7th Kansas Cavalry, who served in northern Louisiana, told me also of finding several partially mutilated copies of
the lithograph letters in places that were raided.   Their attention
was first called to them because of Kansas places and dates.—
R. J. H.

again, July 14th, he wrote: "I will be ready when
you want me, if nothing happens." Mrs. Adams
(Anne Brown) writes of him, that he was "a bright,
kindly, obliging young man," not, perhaps, as
"refined" in manners as the others, but always frank
and willing. Mr. Gill writes of him in the same
vein, suggesting mildly, as also of Leeman, that he
was one who did not impress you as especially
striving to "climb the golden stairs." And yet he did
his "dering do," with the same modest and chivalrous acceptance that characterized all the party, and
not less unflinchingly than did their wonderful old
leader. He was tall, quite five feet eleven in height;
slender, small, well-shaped head, with marked oval
face, very fair complexion, blonde, curly hair, open
expression, genial in ways, truthful, and brave to the
last degree. Hazlett was busy under Captain Brown's
direct orders all of the 17th, until after a large number of the Virginian militia were driven to the
Potomac bridge, falling back to the other side. Hazlett, with O. P. Anderson and Shields Green, were
directed to hold the arsenal, it being the Captain's
obvious purpose, at the time, to effect a retreat that
way. The arrival of other militia prevented this by
compelling Captain Brown to retire into the engine-
house. Green returned to him, and the other two
made their way, by a culvert, into the stream and
then across the same to the Maryland side. Osborne
P. Anderson, in "A Voice From Harper's Ferry,"
stated that:

"Hazlett and I crossed over to the Maryland side after the
skirmish with the troops about nightfall. When we descended
from the rocks, we passed through the back part of the Ferry

on the hill, down to the railroad, proceeding as far as the saw-mill on the Virginia side, where we came upon an old boat, tied up to the shore, which we cast off and crossed the Poto-mac. The Maryland shore once gained, we passed along the tow-path of the canal for some distance, when we came to an arch which led through under the canal, and thence we went to the Kennedy Farm, hoping to find something to eat and to meet the men who had been stationed on that side. But the old house had been ransacked and deserted, and the provisions taken away. . . . Thinking that we should fare better at the schoolhouse, we bent our ways in that direction. The night was dark and rainy, and after tramping for an hour and a half we reached it about two in the morning. The school-house was packed with things moved there by the party the previous day, but we searched in vain, after lighting a match, for food, our great necessity. . . . Thinking it unsafe to remain . . . from fear of oversleeping ourselves, we climbed up the mountain in the rear of it, to lie down till daylight. It was after sunrise when we awoke. Hearing . . . shooting at the Ferry, Hazlett thought it must be Owen Brown and his men, trying to force their way into the town, as they had been informed that a number of us were taken prisoners. When we got in sight of the Ferry, troops were firing across the river to the Maryland side, . . . and to our surprise we saw that they were firing upon a few colored men who had been armed the day before by our men at the Kennedy Farm, and stationed at the schoolhouse by C. P. Tidd. One of the colored men came toward us; we hailed him and inquired the particulars. He said that one of his comrades had been shot and was lying on the side of the mountain ; that they thought the men who had armed them the day before must be in the Ferry. We told him ' no,' and asked him to join us in hunting up the rest of the party, but he refused.

" While in this part of the mountains we could see the troops take possession of the schoolhouse. Our shelter was gone and we had no hope of meeting our companions. We then con-cluded to make our escape North, and started at once. Having eaten nothing for forty-eight hours, our appetites were exceedingly keen. So, under cover of the night, we sought a cornfield, gathered some of the ears and, having matches, struck fire and roasted and feasted. As a result of our hard journey and poor diet we became nearly famished and very much reduced in strength. Poor Hazlett could not endure as much as I could. With his feet blistered and sore, he gave out at last ten miles below Chambersburg. He declared he could go no further, and begged me to go on as we should be more in danger if seen together in the vicinity of the towns, that after resting that night he would throw away his rifle and go to Chambersburg, where we agreed to meet again. The poor, young man's face was wet with tears when we parted."

Anderson found it impossible to retrace his steps, and was barely able to get away in safety from the colored man's dwelling where he had obtained food. He felt compelled to make his way out of the town northward, and was therefore able to move with less suspicion. It was the fourth day before this occurred, after Anderson had left him, Hazlett endeavored also to reach Chambersburg. This was on the 21st of October. The reward of $1,000 offered by the State of Virginia for the capture of Cook, had aroused the cupidity of all the fugitive kidnappers and thief-catchers of the border counties of Pennsylvania. An experience had, three months later, enabled the writer to assert that even the armed bands of western Missouri, arrayed at that period for the business of capturing fugitives, or kidnapping free men of color sheltering or living in Kansas, were no more brutal in their cupidity and zeal, if more courageous in the exercise of those amiable qualities, than were some of the kidnappers on the Virginian border. Hazlett took the railroad, believing,

doubtless, that, as he was in a "free" State, the
chances were in his favor. It was the vigilance
aroused at the appearance of Hazlett that aided
materially in the capture of Cook on the 24th. Hazlett, arrested near Newville, having followed the
Cumberland Valley railroad, was turned over to the
sheriff of Cumberland County, and by him taken to
Carlisle. He was first carried to a justice court,
and then arraigned before a United States commissioner. The stories are all incorrect to the effect that
Mrs. Cook or Mrs. Ritner saw and warned Hazlett,
or that any other of the fugitives were endeavoring
to rescue Cook. The pursuit against them was too
hot for any such action on their part. Hazlett gave
the name of William Harrison. It was quickly found
that he was not "Captain Cook." Douglass and
other attorneys of Virginia and Pennsylvania, found
themselves at fault. Their witnesses could not
identify the prisoner as one of the raiders. They
never did. A requisition for him as Albert Hazlett
would not hold. On the 29th inst. a writ of *habeas
corpus* was returned, and "the court," says a dispatch
of that date, "took the ground that the requisition is legally and formally right, but there is no
evidence that we have any man in our custody
named Hazlett whom we can deliver on this requisition. We are satisfied that a monstrous crime has
been committed, and that the prisoner was there and
participated, and therefore recommit him to await a
requisition from the Governor of Virginia."

He had been in prison then for eight days, and the
jail officials are believed to have pointed him out to
a man named Copeland from Virginia, who swore to

seeing him at Harper's Ferry in the act of firing a rifle. On the trial at Charlestown this fellow's evidence was discredited and abandoned by the prosecution itself. Yet Hazlett was held long enough to secure a requisition for " William Harrison," and, after two weeks of effort, he was sent back by a judge in his native State, without a single direct or even circumstantial proof of his ever having been in Virginia. He escaped on the 18th of October, was arrested on the 22d, extradited on the 5th of November, and reached Charlestown on the 8th, the day that the trial of Cook and Coppoc begun before Judge Parker.

His own trial, or the farce so called, begun on the 2d of February following. Mr. Sennott contested strongly for the defense, and it was the 14th of the month before sentence was passed. In receiving it, Hazlett said:

' I have a few words to say. I am innocent of the charge on which I have been convicted. I deny ever having committed murder, or ever having contemplated murder, or ever having associated with any one having such intentions. Some of the witnesses here have sworn to things which I deny, and which were positively false. But I forgive them all. I have been treated kindly." . . . He thanked officers and his Virginia counsel, and closed by saying : " I repeat, I am innocent of murder, but I am prepared to meet my fate."

The spiteful brutality of Virginia is forcibly illustrated by the execution of this young man. In law there was more than a reasonable doubt of his identity, and in any event his part in the raid was comparatively unimportant. Governor Letcher was as savage but less politic, than his predecessor Henry A. Wise.

Mrs. Rebecca B. Spring, the good woman who
visited "those in bonds" at Charlestown, writes that
the delay in executing Stevens and Hazlett was because of the former's wounds, and also from the fact
that they " were not sure that Hazlett . . . was
really one of John Brown's men." There never was
any doubt by the officials of his participation in the
raid; there was difficulty in procuring or manufacturing evidence thereof. The delay held out the hope
of rescuing these two gallant men.

The special reason for my desire in that regard has
already been given. In Boston were a few persons
who would have risked everything to have saved
John Brown or any of his men. If I give as most
active and earnest in this desire John W. Le Barnes,
Thomas Wentworth Higginson, W. W. Thayer (of
the publishing firm of Thayer & Eldridge), F. B.
Sanborn, James Redpath, Dr. David Thayer, George
Henry Hoyt, Brackett, the sculptor, and Richard J.
Hinton, I shall cover not only those I am permitted
to name, but all that were most actively interested in any such conception. As to John Brown,
that was ended by his message through Hoyt, from
his prison cell. But knowing myself that in Kansas
there were men brave enough to try the odds, when
the relaxation of vigilance begun after the 16th of
December, the desire to save Hazlett and Stevens
grew into a hope, and from that into a plan, which
was ably seconded by John W. Le Barnes and T. W.
Higginson, as well as supported by Redpath and W.
W. Thayer, was pushed thoroughly up to the point
where an actual reconniassance proved it could not be
accomplished. Money was raised, and about the

middle of January I started for Kansas. For prudential reasons I adopted in traveling my mother's
name of Read, except, of course, in Kansas, where I
was well known.   Proceeding direct to the southern
portion of the Territory, I consulted with Captain
James Montgomery, laying before him topographical
maps of the section, plans of the jail, with the railroad
and country highways.   Careful inquiry had been
made as to possible " underground railway " routes
and stations, and as to the trust that could be reposed
in the latter.   It was very slight, indeed.   Messrs.
Higginson, Le Barnes, and publisher Thayer were to
look after the pecuniary part of the plan.   By the sale
of Redpath's " Life of John Brown " a small fund for
the benefit of the families had been obtained.   With
Mrs. John Brown's consent, this fund might be used
temporarily, and that was readily obtained.   Sculptor
Brackett promised $200; Mr. Le Barnes gave liberally
and advanced more, and Mr. Higginson, who was
treasurer, obtained other amounts and met the costs
fully, with what, besides the men, was obtained in
Kansas.   From that section seven volunteers returned
with me, including James Montgomery, Silas Soule,
James Stewart, Joseph Gardner, Mr. Willis, and two
others (from Lawrence) whose names have escaped
me.[1]   We reached Leavenworth early in February,
and I found that money expected had not arrived.

---

[1] The omission of some of the names is due to the fact that one
of my notebooks was loaned in 1880 and never returned, to a writer
who prepared an article for the Philadelphia *Times*.   It was published, but having no copy, I am writing mainly from memory,
except some letters of Col. Higginson placed in my hands by Mr.
Le Barnes, to whom they were addressed.

Taking Col. Daniel R. Anthony [1] into my confidence
he at once contributed the money needed, placing
in Captain Montgomery's hand $150, and an equal
amount in mine.   It was deemed best I should go by
way of Weston, Missouri, direct to St. Joe, and that
Montgomery and his associates should go by private
teams to Elwood, Kansas, directly opposite that place,
then the railroad terminus for the section.   Hon.
Edward Russell, now of Lawrence, Kansas, gives me
a brief but interesting account of the party's arrival
there and of the aid extended to them. [2]

---

[1] Under date of January 31, 1893, he writes me as follows:
" You ask me about using my name in connection with the attempted rescue. Yes, of course, I always felt proud of my action
in that case, but have forgotten much. I had forgotten to whom
I paid the $150. My memory is that I paid it direct to Captain
Montgomery when he stopped with me over night. You probably
was the active agent managing the rescue, and I may have paid
this sum to you, but I think I paid it to Captain Montgomery, and
he left for the East *via* St. Joseph, Mo."

[2] Lawrence, Kansas, February 14, 1893: . . . I have made
some statements at a meeting of the Historical Society in connection with the paper read by Major Abbott on the Doy rescue; but
I never wrote out my recollections of this matter, so far as I now
recall; at least, I did not for the State Historical Society. To save
you a little bother and time, I will give you the facts as I recall
them. One afternoon, just before dark, Captain Montgomery appeared in Elwood, Doniphan County, with letters to several of us
living there from friends in Leavenworth, and probably in Lawrence,
requesting any assistance upon our part which we could supply to
enable the captain and his company to secure transportation over
the Hannibal and St. Joseph railroad on their way to West Virginia, for the purpose of rescuing John Brown or some of his
party. Just how many men were with Montgomery I do not recall; but I do know that when I had them loaded into a skiff, it

On the way to Harrisburg, though traveling by the same train, the party were apparently unacquainted with each other. By the Higginson-Le Barnes letters

---

sank into the water so that there was less than an inch of her gunwale above the river. After a consultation it was found that there were three of us who held passes over the Hannibal and St. Joseph railroad, through our connection with the press in Elwood,—D. W. Wilder, Albert L. Lee (afterwards brigadier-general), and myself. We very cheerfully offered our passes to Montgomery, and wrote a note also to the station-agent in St. Joseph (Joseph Howard), requesting him to help the party, if possible, over his line. He was in thorough sympathy with the free-state men of Kansas. We knew, also, that the men who owned and controlled the Hannibal and St. Joseph railroad and the general management thereof, were in sympathy with us and opposed to slavery. We trusted not a little to that; and, as I recall it, they secured transportation upon our passes and also got additional passes, so that nearly or quite all of them were carried over the Hannibal and St. Joseph railroad, and without charge. They had reached Elwood so late in the short winter evening, that due preparation could not be made for their crossing the river. The only skiffs convenient to be reached belonged to the gentleman, Mr. Ebenezer Blackiston, the Ferry owner. It was not safe for him to know anything about the proceedings. Through his daughter (Mrs. Russell) I obtained possession of the boathouse keys and also the oars, which were in his house, and between nine and ten o'clock that night (one of the darkest I ever knew), we proceeded to the river and loaded the company with their weapons. We furnished them two or three of the Sharpe's rifles which we had among us in Elwood, and also some ammunition. After getting them loaded, and enjoining them to keep quiet lest the skiff should dip water and we should all be dumped out, I headed it for the opposite shore. There was a long pull and we reached there, but it was still so dark that we could not see the shore until we bumped against it, and came very near being swamped thereby. The company landed, bade me adieu, went upon their journey, and I returned to report progress,"

I find we arrived on February 17th. The men were housed as cattle-ouyers and drovers at a little tavern in the outskirts. Higginson had been lecturing in Ohio and was awaiting our arrival, stopping, I believe, with Dr. Rutherford, a well-known Quaker abolitionist and physician. At his residence I know, however, that all our conferences were held. The prospects were very dubious. At Pittsburg we had encountered a heavy snow-storm. Another storm occurred on the 18th. Arms (revolvers) had been obtained by Mr. Higginson as a loan, unless used. Arrangements were made for five or six men from New York, ex-German revolutionary soldiers, these. Le Barnes, with Higginson himself and " Read," they would have made sixteen " machines," as in our correspondence we were termed. Under date of the 18th, " C. P. Carter " (Higginson) writes:

" The machinist (Montgomery) is strong in hope, and he is a man to inspire infinite hope in others. Nothing stops him but the snow that now lies—that is a hopeless obstacle to the working of the machines,—but a few days will probably take it away, and he does not consider the season such an obstacle as T. (Thayer) did, and I believe it can be done."

Captain Montgomery started from Harrisburg on a reconnaissance of the mountain section to the west of Harper's Ferry and Charlestown. Gardner, as having been a Pennsylvania Quaker, was sent to exploit the " underground " routes to see what aid could be secured in that way. He trusted his Quaker brethren too much, and, as a result, was threatened with exposure to Governor Parker, who had already made undue haste in returning Hazlett. It was from this source that Attorney Andrew Hunter received his only reliable "rescue" information. In his later years he misplaced the dates, and thought it related to John Brown himself. Silas Soule was sent into Virginia to find out what he could; the others were put at various details, and I went direct to New York and Massachusetts to see our German friends and also to hurry Publisher Thayer's arrival at Harrisburg. In New York, by Le Barnes's introduction and through an acquaintance with the late Dr. Adolph Douai, I met Frederick Kapp, the German historian, then editor of the *New Yorker Demokrat*, also Col. Richard Metternich, nephew of the famous diplomat (who afterwards fell in the Union army). The matter was discussed with both, and the latter was to arrange the military contingent. Rockets were purchased, arms and ammunition provided for, and also various other tools. All these things were prepared, but the reports from the field were of the worst. Heavy and frequent snows made all mountain movements impossible. At last, Thayer having arrived, and Higginson returned to Harrisburg from lecturing in Chicago, a conference was held at Dr. Rutherford's. It was purposely convened before my return, in order to relieve me of responsibility for the decision, which was entirely adverse to the attempt. In writing, about this date (February 25th), to Le Barnes, Higginson says: "Perhaps Read saw you; I sent him to New York to clench the Teutons, and for other objects. He has proved himself very efficient." Again, he writes that Montgomery "was the very man of all the world. Read could not have done better, both as to the whole or the parts." The cost of the expedition, of which Higginson writes Le

Barnes that he was glad that an attempt had been made, is placed at about $1,800; of this, $300 was obtained in Kansas. Le Barnes advanced $200 in all; of which, $74 was returned to him. Higginson took $250 and W. W. Thayer $471 to Harrisburg, making in all, with $300 paid to me on starting for Kansas, $1,721. I have been a little precise in these details, because of a desire to settle for good the matter of "rescue" talks or attempts. This is the only effort made, and it was necessarily abandoned.

In a few days after, Albert Hazlett also died on a Virginia scaffold. His brother visited him on the 15th of March, under the name of Harrison. A letter of that date to Mrs. Spring, who had promised to receive his body with that of Stevens, will illustrate the simple courage of the simple-hearted boy—for such he really was.

"CHARLESTOWN, VA., March 15, 1860.

"DEAR FRIEND—Your letter gave me great comfort to know that my body would be taken from this land of chains. You spoke of my friends; I never wrote to them, but my brother has come to see me. He left the matter to me, and I thought it best to let you have my body. You wanted to know who was dear to me ; I say everybody that is good is dear to me. I am willing to die in the cause of liberty; if I had ten thousand lives, I would willingly lay them all down for the same cause. My death will do more good than if I had lived. Farewell, my dear friend."

On the 1st of March he had written to Anne Brown at North Elba, in reply to a letter of hers. His letter deserves a place in this prison literature :

"CHARLESTOWN JAIL, VA., March 1, 1860.

"MY DEAR FRIEND ANNE—Your kind letter gave me

much pleasure to know there was some who had sympathy for me in my prison home. I am very thankful to you for your kind and cheering letter to me. Do not grieve about the past, but take all things for the best. I think, as you do, that my fate is hard and very unjust. But I shall try to meet it like a man. I do not see that my death will do them any good, but 'the Lord s will, not mine be done.' I do not think the citizens here thirst for my blood; they have treated me very kind and humane; the ladies come in to see us most every day, and gentlemen also. Good-bye, Anne, I am your friend,

"W. H. HARRISON."

On the 3d of the month he also sent to Wealthy, wife of John Brown, Jr., a copy of some simple but pathetic stanzas, headed "Harrison's Farewell." In them he bids his mother, sweetheart, and friends farewell, saying:

"Oh, do not mourn for me,
Remember that I die
In the cause of Liberty.'

So feeling and so saying he went to his death, without regret, passion, or denunciation, and my tally of the gallows is complete!

CHAPTER XV.

MEN WHO FOUGHT AND FELL, OR ESCAPED.

*The North Elba families—Owen's mountain journey—
Roswell Thompson and sons—Tidd, Barclay Coppoc, Merriam—Owen's devotion—The Boston boy's
escape—Deaths of J. G. Anderson, William H.
Leeman, Steward Taylor, the two Thompsons—Oliver
and Watson Brown—Who begun the war that ended
slavery—The words of Frederick Douglass.*

NORTH ELBA gave ungrudgingly to the attack on
slavery, made by John Brown and his men. One
household lost father, two sons, the wife and child of
one of these. Another household suffered almost as
heavily; two sons slain and one daughter widowed. No
one has heard from this one a word of complaint; a
single demand for recognition. William and Dauphin
Thompson were both slain—the first named having
been brutally butchered. That act was done under
the fierce passion of alarm and combat. But the
boasting thereof was cold-blooded and ruffianly in
the extreme. The younger brother was at least slain
in combat. Their sister, Isabel, was the wife and
widow of Watson Brown. Henry, the elder brother,
is the husband of Ruth, John Brown's eldest daughter,
and he, too, served his apprenticeship to freedom's
fighting.

There were twenty children born to Roswell
Thompson and his wife Mary. There were four pair
of twins, of whom William and Willard were one set.
Only ten children lived to maturity, the others dying
in infancy. William was born in August, 1833.
Adolphus Dauphin Thompson, the youngest son, was
in his twenty-second year when shot in the Harper's
Ferry engine-house. He was born April 17, 1838. Barclay Coppoc was therefore the youngest member of
the party. William married in the fall of 1858, Mary
Brown, the daughter of a neighboring farmer, not related to the historic family. She was eighteen years of
age when married, was left by her husband with his
brother Henry and family. She was a quiet, brave,
young woman, fortunately without any child, and
left North Elba for the West in the next summer,
where she remarried within a few years. Watson's
widow lives in Wisconsin, having married Salmon
Brown, a cousin of her first husband. William was a
strong, bold, rustic-looking man, with large features,
ruddy complexion, very fair hair, bold but kindly
blue eyes. Anne Brown writes that—

" William Thompson and his twin brother, Willard, were
noted as boys for their mischievous pranks. No one could tell
which one did the mischief, not even their own mother. William was a complete and successful mimic, imitating speech
and gestures perfectly. He was lively and full of fun, but
could be as sober and earnest as any man when occasion
required. His brother Willard served in the Union army, was
taken prisoner and sent to Andersonville, finding, on his
return, his wife insane, his children scattered, and his mother
mourning him as dead."

William was " kind, generous-hearted, and helpful
34

to others. Dauphin was," she writes, "very quiet, with a fair, thoughtful face, curly blonde hair, and baby-blue eyes. He always seemed like a very good girl," to her. The family came from Keene, New Hampshire, and Mr. Roswell Thompson was a nephew of Dr. "Lobelia" Thompson, as he was called, founder of the botanic school of medicine.

William Thompson was assigned, with Oliver Brown, to the capture of the Potomac railroad bridge. By some accident a collision occurred with the watch-man, just about to go off duty, and that led to the un-successful attempt to capture Patrick Higgins, who is still watchman there. This brought the detention of the midnight train, and then, when it was allowed to go on, to the acceleration through the neighboring section of the alarm created by the attack. It was intended to evacuate the town and burn the bridges in doing so. At least, fire-balls were prepared of tow, placed on sticks, and saturated with oil. The two Thompsons were kept with Captain Brown in the armory grounds. Soon after noon William was cap-tured and taken to Foulke's hotel. Heywood, Tur-ner, and Boerly, of the Ferry, had been killed. About forty citizens were prisoners. Newby, "Jim" Washington, and another man of the raiding party were also slain, when the mayor, Fountaine Beck-ham was killed, having incautiously shown himself. This roused great anger. Henry Hunter, a grand-nephew of the dead mayor, headed a party and dragged the prisoner from the hotel. The land-lord's daughter, C. C. Foulke, who was reported as endeavoring to prevent the prisoner from being lynched, wrote, for a St. Louis daily, an apologetic

account of her action.[1] He was dragged out, shot at
and wounded almost before he was past the door-
step, beaten as he was hauled to the bridge, where
several guns were fired at his head and breast. He
was then thrown over the bridge into the river, and
again wounded as he struck the water. After a little
while, he was discovered, still alive, clinging to the
pier, when he was literally riddled with bullets. He
lay in the river, face upward, until the next day,
when his body was taken out and carried to Winchester for dissection. His young brother was
wounded slightly during the firing on the 17th, and
retreated to the engine-house with the Captain. He
was shot dead when the marines attacked the little
building.

In all movements, involving personal danger, there
will some one be found with fateful forebodings.
The Kennedy Farm party did not prove an excep-

---

[1] " While I was talking to Thompson several of the friends of
Mr. Beckham, who were justly enraged at his cold-blooded
murder, came in with the avowed determination to kill Thompson
on the spot. As they appeared with leveled rifles I stood before
T. and protected him, for three powerful reasons: first, my sister-
in-law was lying in the adjoining room very ill under the influence
of a nervous chill, from sheer fright, and if they had carried out
their design it would have proved fatal to her, no doubt. In the
second place, I considered it a great outrage to kill the man in the
house, however much he deserved to die. Thirdly, I am emphatically a law-and-order woman, and wanted the self-condemned man
to live that he might be disposed of by the law. I simply shielded
the terribly frightened man, *without touching him*, until Col.
Moor (I think it was) came in and assured me, on his honor, that
he should not be shot in the house. That was all I desired. The
result everybody knows."

tion, for Steward Taylor, one of the younger members, was quite confident he would be the first man
slain.   Anne Brown tells how he was affected and
with what cool equanimity he went forward with the
" duty " he had assumed.   She writes that—

" Taylor somehow got the notion that he would be shot as
soon as the party took possession of Harper's Ferry.   We
could not persuade him out of this.   It did not seem to make
him cowardly in the least, or act like flinching from what he
considered his duty.   He wrote farewell letters to his relatives
and friends, and sent them off.   Then he seemed as calm and
content as ever, even laughing when one of the men found him
writing one day, and called out : ' Boys, Steward is writing his
will.'   He was one who could never have betrayed a friend or
deserted a post."

Edwin Coppoc tells in a letter to Iowa friends just
how and when Taylor fell.   He was wounded in the
afternoon fighting on the 17th inst., and died in the
engine-house soon after.

Steward Taylor's birthplace was a Canadian town,
named Uxbridge, north of Toronto, and the date was
October 29, 1836.   At the time of death, then, he was
within twelve days of his twenty-third birthday.   His
mother, Jane Taylor, married a Mr. Foote, while
Steward was still a child.   He received a fair English
education and went to work in his youth, remaining
in Canada with his grandfather, David Taylor, till
his seventeenth year, when he started for the United
States, intending to settle in Kansas.   He did not
enter that Territory, having been quite ill in Missouri, and upon his recovery, after visiting Arkansas,
he returned north to Iowa, where, at West Liberty,
Cedar County, he obtained employment in a wagon

factory. He early became acquainted with George B. Gill, who, in the early spring of 1858, introduced him to the John Brown party, and to John Brown himself at the house of a Mr. Painter. He joined as Mr. Gill did and went to Chatham, Canada, to participate in the convention held there. After that body adjourned, Steward Taylor found employment in Illinois, and remained until Kagi addressed him from Chambersburg, early in July, 1859, when he responded at once, bearing his own expenses and reporting for duty as soon as required. That he had deliberately engaged himself in the enterprise is shown by the fact, that for a year he had no communication with any of the party, yet he writes to an Iowa friend, in 1859, that—

" My condition seemed rather unfavorable. I expected momentarily I would be relieved of my doubts, which arose from my losing communication with my friends. I keep waiting day after day for word and at last gave it up. Then my hopes were partly crushed, I felt as though I was deprived of my chief object in life. I could imagine no other cause than want of ability or confidence. I believe that fate has decreed me for this undertaking. . . . Although at one time . . . I had given up being wanted, but all came right when necessary. It could not seem to be wrong, in spite of my trying to believe to the contrary. But truth will, if it has a chance, appear to the sincere."

In his reply from Illinois to Kagi under date of July 3d, he writes:

" It is my chief desire to add fuel to the flame. The amount may be small but every little helps. My ardent passion for the gold fields is my thought by day and my dream by night. I often think that I am with you bringing it forth in masses that will surprise the world. Please let me know as soon as possible, for if it is very sudden, I might be sore troubled to get my money."

Taylor was of medium height, stout and stocky in form, quite strong and capable of physical endurance. His head was large, round, well balanced. In that respect he was of striking appearance. Very quiet in his ways, helpful, a good comrade, always even tempered. Complexion dark, reddish-brown hair, closely cropped, his eyes were dark brown, large and full. He was smooth-faced and immature looking for even his age. He was given to day-dreaming and writing a great deal; phonographic shorthand especially. Like Stevens, " Jerry " Anderson, Edwin Coppoc, Taylor was strongly disposed to spiritualism, but with Kagi, he leaned more to what may be termed "rationalism." He was somewhat excitable on such questions, was always an "odd genius," and would nowadays be branded " crank " by the flippant formalists. Very persistent in any purpose, he learned to play the violin quite fairly, though he had but little musical ability. He was a constant student and always had some book or study on hand. In disposition, benevolent and affectionate—his brother says very tender,—he proved himself faithful to his convictions unto death.

William Henry Leeman, slain at Hall's Rifle Works, was a native of Maine, where members of the family still reside. The youngest member of the party, born March 20, 1839, and therefore, when slain, but twenty years, seven months and three days old, his life had been for over three years as full of stirring adventure as his death was tragic. He was sent out of the Ferry in the early morning, under Tidd's command, to capture Terence Burns, and on returning took four of the rescued slaves with him to reinforce Kagi, who with Leary and Copeland had taken possession of Hall's Rifle Works. The eight men were trapped when the Virginia militia got ready to take a hand in the proceedings. A Harper's Ferry doctor, after the shooting of the railway porter, Heywood, had gotten out of town, and, riding hard, roused the country. By noon the Virginians begun to cross the Shenandoah, and the men in the Rifle Works were soon discovered. The four colored Virginians made their escape without fighting,.and the other four held the untenable place for over an hour, until at last the quartet of anti-slavery fighters made a break from the back of the factory. They fell before the fire of a hundred rifles. Leeman lay on the gray rock dying with ten or twelve bullets in his body. A militiaman waded out, put a pistol against his face and firing blew half his head off. Cutting off the boy's coattails and cartridge-box and belt, he sat the mangled form against the rocks, and then with a grim humor of the pro-slavery type, spent, with others, the afternoon in target practice on the dead body. Captain Leeman thus completed a service begun for free Kansas in June, 1856. He became a fighter for freedom in the early part of his seventeenth year, and died in the seventh month of his twentieth year. Leeman was six feet in height, slender but well built, fair complexion, small featured, with good steady eyes, bluish gray in color, light brown hair, ingenious in the use of tools, quiet in manners, and always reliable. He received a moderate degree of education in the common schools of Saco and Hallowell, and at the age of fourteen went to Haverhill, Mass., to work in a shoe factory. From earlier boyhood, as his letters show, he identified himself with anti-slavery politics and, in the spring of 1856, decided to go to Kansas. He left Massachusetts, in June of that year, with Dr. Cutler's party, and was with it when armed Missourians, at Lexington, turned the company back and down the Missouri River. Leeman found his way to Keokuk, Iowa, and there joined the second Massachusetts colony, under charge of Martin Stowell and Richard J. Hinton, entered Kansas with them, after marching afoot across the State from Iowa City and through southern Nebraska to Fall City. He then pushed southward and was soon in the midst of the fighting, joining "John Brown's Regulars,"[1] as the record shows, September 9, 1856. He was at the third attack on Lawrence where we met again and for the last time.

Leeman's life thereafter was a part of the record of John Brown. He was at the Springdale, Iowa, school, a member of the Chatham Convention, and his signature was the fifteenth in order to the roll of the convention, and of the provisional constitution there adopted. He was also a member of the committee appointed to fill the offices under it. Letters to his parents and sisters have been in my possession, and many evidences are given by them of his adventurous disposition, as well as the underlying steadfastness of his character. His people were poor, struggling constantly, and naturally sought his assistance. Some touching letters were found from them, showing

---

[1] See Appendix.

their trouble at his absence as well as affection for the wandering son and brother. His replies were all as affectionate in tone, and there are proofs that he sent small amounts of money at different periods. He wrote of going to Utah, when he was about some dangerous movement for the Captain. Of his early Kansas experience he writes, early in November, 1856, that after "we had cleaned out the border ruffians, the government troops got after us and I had to get away to Nebraska, where I shall work at my trade. (He was a bootmaker.) If Fremont is elected, there will be more trouble in the spring. You have heard how we whipped them at Osawatomie. We had thirty men and wounded thirty-two; they had 400, all mounted." There is no trouble in following the roads by which Leeman traveled to his death at Harper's Ferry. In 1858 and '59 there are several letters giving hints, more or less plain, of the purposes he was following. In one Ohio letter the youthful partisan says he "can't tell till he hears from Kansas." This was in 1858, and then he adds:

"I think a great deal of my mother and sisters, and I know they do of me, and it makes me unhappy to think that mother worries so much about me, but I feel myself amply repaid for denying myself the pleasure of seeing them by realizing that I have been engaged in a good cause—a noble cause. For the last year I have been engaged in the cause of freedom, and ere long it will be shown to the world. If we succeed in our undertaking, it will pay me for years of toil."

The last letter sent from Harper's Ferry is dated October 2, 1859, and makes no disguise of his position. It reads:

"DEAR MOTHER—I have not written you for a long time,

and have not heard from you for a longer one. I am well, and
anxious to hear from you. I am now in a Southern *slave State*,
and before I leave it, it will be a free State, and so will *every
other one in the South.* Yes, mother, I am warring with
slavery, the greatest curse that ever infested America. In
explanation of my absence from you for so long, I would tell
you that for three years I have been engaged in a secret association of as gallent fellows as ever pulled a trigger, with the
sole purpose of the extermination of slavery. We are now all
privately gathered in a slave State, where we are determined
to strike for freedom, incite the slaves to rebellion, and establish a free government. With the help of God we will carry it
through. Now you will see, mother, the reason why I have
stayed away from you so long—why I have never helped you
when I knew you was in want, and why I have not explained
to you before. I dared not divulge it. Now we are about to
commence, and it does not make any difference; but, mother
dear, I charge you not to divulge a word in this letter outside
of the family, until you hear from me in actual service. I don't
want you to worry yourself about me at all. I shall be in
danger, of course, but that is natural to me. I shall not get
killed. I am in a good cause and I am not afraid. I know my
mother will not object. You have a generous heart. I know
you will sacrifice something for your fellow beings in bondage.
I knew one lady in New York that bid her husband and four
sons to take up arms in our cause, and they are here with us
now."

With what courage, then, these young men entered
upon their tragic work is illustrated by such letters,
scores of which testify to the purposes and devotion
of their writers. They show also, however mistaken
in their hopes, that no unworthy thoughts ever dwelt
in their manly brains. Their paths were clean; their
aim noble; their lives full of high bravery, and in
their deaths were justified the sacrifice of their lives.

Barclay Coppoc, brother of Edwin, one of the younger members of the party, was born at Salem, Ohio, January 4, 1839, and was, therefore, twenty-one years of age when left under Owen Brown's command, with Merriam, to attend to the removal of the arms and tools from the Kennedy Farm to the little Virginia schoolhouse, where they were afterwards seized. In the fall of 1856, Barclay was in Kansas for a short time and there became possessed of the spirit of the
free-state movement. He was a
little taller and more slender than
his brother Edwin, with the rest-
lessness of one touched with consumption, full of an adventurous
spirit, and more inclined to audac-
ity. He had scant brown hair, bold
large eyes, irregular features, a determined expression. During the
perilous period of escaping, though
frail in strength, Owen's narrative
shows that the brave youth bore his
share without complaint, of the

BARCLAY COPPOC.

thirty-six days of hunger, cold, fatigue, and danger they passed in the rough laurel hills and semi-mountain areas from the neighborhood of Harper's Ferry to Center County, western Pennsylvania, where the three comrades—Owen Brown, Tidd, and the young Coppoc parted, November 24, 1859. Barclay made haste to reach Iowa. His presence there was concealed slightly, and the young men of Springdale, and Liberty township, in Cedar County, organized for his protection. George B. Gill and Charles W.

Moffett, two of the Chatham Convention delegates,
were resident there also. Both were in some danger. Virginia sent agents to secure Barclay Coppoc's arrest,[1] but Governor Kirkwood (afterwards
United States Senator and Secretary of the In-
terior) had no desire to extradite the young
adventurer. Arrangements were made, if not with

---

[1] The following letter illustrates the feelings and actions of the
period:

"SPRINGDALE, CEDAR COUNTY, IOWA, Feb. 12, 1860.

" The object of thy anxious inquiry (Barclay Coppoc) has not
been taken from Springdale, nor is it intended that he shall be
taken. Springdale is in arms and is prepared at a half-hour's
notice to give them a reception of 200 shots; and it will be necessary for the marshal to find him before he can be taken. There is
a well-organized body here. They meet two or three evenings in
each week to lay their plans and take the necessary steps to have
them carried out in case of necessity, There are three of their
number who always know of his whereabouts, and nobody else
knows anything of him. He is never seen at night where he was
during the day, and there are men on the watch at Davenport,
Muscatine, Iowa City, Liberty, Tipton, and all around, and the
first sign of an arrest in any quarter a messenger will be dispatched
to Springdale, and larger companies than the Virginians can raise
will follow immediately after them. Muscatine has offered to send
400 men at the very shortest notice. But it is intended to baffle
them in every possible way without bloodshed if possible. The
marshal was at Des Moines City some two weeks for a requisition,
and the Governor refused to grant it on account of informality,
then swore they would take him by mob. The citizens dispatched
a messenger immediately to this place. He rode four horses down
on the way, and came through in two nights and a day, it being
165 miles. We understand that the marshal has gone the second
time to Des Moines for his requisition, and his return is looked
for daily. But I have no doubt but he will be baffled in some way,
for be assured Springdale is right on the goose.

" F. C. GALBRAITH."

the Governor's direct consent, not without his
knowledge, to give Barclay's friends due notice
of any legal action upon a requisition from Virginia
that the Iowa Governor might feel himself formally
bound to obey. As a matter of fact, he was never
forced to such action. The Virginian sent to accomplish the arrest proved to be worthless, drunken, and
cowardly. He succeeded in getting arrested for debt
on account of a board bill. After a visit East to Ohio,
New York, and Massachusetts, in the early summer of
1860, Barclay went to Kansas. In the fall of that
year Coppoc aided to run off some Missouri slaves.
Quantrile, afterward so infamous as a Missouri rebel
guerilla (he was himself of Ohio birth), then known
as "Charley Hart," and pretending to be in sympathy
with the helpers of the fugitives, trapped the boy,
two of his cousins, and four or five others, into
a movement to help some Jackson County, Missouri,
slaves. They were ambushed; Barclay and others of
the party escaped, but two or three were killed. For
several months after this he remained quiet, but, when
the Civil War began, he at once entered the Union
army, and was commissioned in June a second lieutenant in the Fourth Kansas Volunteer Infantry,
commanded by Col. James Montgomery. Coppoc
was sent to Iowa to collect as recruits some young
men of Cedar County, who desired to serve in a
Kansas regiment. On his return with them he met
his death, on the 30th of August, on the Hannibal
and St. Joseph Railroad, by the precipitation of a
train eighty feet into the Platte River, owing to
guerillas having burned away the timbers of the
bridge across it. The rebel force had attacked and

taken St. Joe, which they held for a few hours. It was supposed that a heavy train of Union troops was on the road; it had, however, fortunately been detained at Palmyra, but the trap set for them was filled by the ordinary passenger train. Barclay Coppoc, with several others, were killed, and seventeen more were severely injured. His body was taken to Leavenworth, Kansas, and buried there in the Pilot Knob Cemetery. That of his brother Edwin was grudgingly surrendered to Quaker friends and buried at his birthplace, Salem, Ohio. The lives of these young brothers, with their comrades, were indeed

> " Built of furtherance and pursuing,
> Not of great deeds, *but of doing*."

Revolutionary blood was in the ascendancy in the John Brown party; as the Browns and Thompsons, Kagi, Cook, Stevens, " Jerry " Anderson, the Coppoc brothers, and Merriam, could all tell of progenitors serving in that and earlier fields of civic and religious freedom. Anderson, slain by a United States soldier after he had thrown down his rifle, was the great-grandson of two soldiers of the American War for Independence. They were both Virginians. On his mother's side, Col. Jacob Westfall, of Tygert Valley, in the " Old Dominion," was a partisan commander of considerable local reputation. Soon after the war ceased he moved to Kentucky. He was a slaveholder, as was the other grandfather, Captain Anderson. John, his son, abjured slavery, and after his marriage moved first to the Territory of Black Hawk (Wisconsin), and then to that of Indiana, settling at the town of Indiana, Putnam County, where his son Jeremiah was born, April 17, 1833. " Jerry " was therefore in his twenty-seventh year when killed in the raid. The family, his father having died, then moved to Des Moines, Iowa. Jeremiah was fairly well educated, attending the district schools, and at Galesburg, Illinois, and Kossuth, Iowa, entering the academy or high school. Hon. James W. McDill, ex-Congressman from Iowa, and now a member of the Interstate Commerce Commission, writes that when, in 1854, he was teaching in the Kossuth Academy, "one of the students was Jeremiah G. Anderson. My recollection of him is quite distinct. He was a morose, eccentric young man, quiet and very studious." The moroseness alluded to doubtless arose from the fact that Anderson found himself out of his element in a Presbyterian seminary, where he had been placed with the idea of becoming a minister. He soon kicked over the theological traces, having, by an essay he wrote, declared himself a Universalist. At the time of his death he was accounted a Spiritualist. A score of essays and compositions, placed before me, show he was a thoughtful and industrious student. Leaving the academy, then, before graduation, owing to poor health, he took up an active out-of-door life, investing in a steam sawmill and working industriously therein. One brother studied medicine and graduated. He went to Kansas, was concerned in the Southern troubles of 1857–58. He now lives in Iowa. Harrison, another brother, went to California, after a short stay in Kansas. Jeremiah also moved there in the fall of 1857, purchasing a "claim" on the Little Osage. His youthful essays show a strong, free-soil bias, due, doubtless, to the teachings of his father.

So, when the Fort Scott outbreaks were renewed, it
was natural for the young man to range himself at
once at the free-state side. He became active, was
one of Montgomery and Bain's most trusted men, and
got himself under arrest several times. He was in
the fight of resistance with Montgomery against
Captain Anderson, a dragoon officer, already referred
to. In a letter to his brother in Iowa, Jeremiah
writes, Camp near Luella, Kansas Territory, February
17, 1858, as follows:

. . . "There is considerable excitement here at the
present time. A free-state man was robbed at Fort Scott some
time ago. His name was Johnson, and he came here to see if
he could get help to recover his property. Our company,
under Capt. Bain, and the Sugar Creek company, under Capt.
Montgomery, responded. We marched into the fort on the
14th inst., met with no resistance, for the bloody villains
had heard of our coming and fled into the State (Mo.) that
night. . . . We have just now heard that a company left
the fort to-day, and expect them to attack us to-night, but I
don't think they will attempt it again, they got whipped so bad
the other time. . . . We have so many alarms that I cannot get half a chance to work. . . . It has been this way
for three months or more, but not always so bad."

Naturally, the young settler drifted into John
Brown's camp, when, as "Shubel Morgan," he took
position on the border near the "Trading Post," the
scene of the "Marias du Cygne" massacre. He was
with Captain Brown at Christmas, 1859, when the
raid of freedom was made on Missouri slaveholders.
From Lawrence, on the 14th of January, 1859, he
writes his brother that, after getting away from an
arrest, attempted by the pro-slavery officials, he had:

. . . "A call to go into the service, and went to Fort

Scott to help relieve Benjamin Rice. We were fired upon by one John Little Blake, ex-deputy United States marshal. Our men fired back,[1] and a ball hit him in the forehead, which done him up just right. I was also engaged in liberating the Missouri slaves Captain Brown brought in."

After giving a short account of the rescue, Anderson continues:

"I am now three miles from Lawrence with 'Old Brown,' as they call him. We are looking out a railroad route, establishing depots, and finding watering-places. Our road is a long one, terminating in Canada. . . . Montgomery came out of Lawrence to stay with us to night, and has just told us of a plan laid to assassinate Brown and himself."

Anderson did not leave the Territory in January, 1859, but joined John Brown early in the spring, as he was with him in Rochester, Peterboro, and North Elba, New York, in the following March and April. He seldom left him afterwards, Captain Brown having evidently grown much attached to him. He said to Mr. Putman, of Peterboro, that Anderson "was more than a friend; he was as a brother and a son to him." To J. Q. Anderson, writing on the 29th of November, three days before his execution, Captain Brown states that his brother Jeremiah "was fighting bravely *by my side*, at Harper's Ferry, up to the moment when I fell wounded and took no further notice of what passed for a little time." Anderson was pierced with a death wound by the bayonet of a marine whose weapon first struck the buckle of a pistol belt and sliding off pierced his body through till he was pinned to the opposite wall. One of the prisoners described Anderson as turning completely

---

[1] J. H. Kagi fired that shot.

35

over against the wall in his dying agony.   He lived
a short time, stretched on the brick walk without,
where he was subjected to savage brutalities, being
kicked in body and face, while one brute of an armed
farmer spat a huge quid of tobacco from his vile jaws
into the mouth of the dying man, which he first
forced open.

All the evidence shows Anderson to have been regarded as singularly reliable; quiet, grave, and
modest in manners and temper.   He was about five
feet nine inches in height, quite spare, of black complexion, quiet but penetrative dark eyes.   His features were of the Abraham Lincoln type; one common
to the Blue Range Scotch-Irish stock from which he
came.   George B. Gill writes of him:

"I remember that he was considered quite a valuable aquisi-
tion to the party, based mainly on his appearance and motions,
and from his undoubted reliability, carrying, I think, his whole
being into the cause.   He was probably as earnest a member
of the party as Brown had with him."

He wrote good letters and just before the attack
informed his brother in Iowa fully of the purposed
assault.   On the 5th of July he writes:

"I am stopping (Sandy Hook) one mile from Harper's Ferry,
in Maryland, on the Potomac.   The railroad is one side, the
house and the canal is on the other.   This is a mountainous
country and the scenery is very beautiful.   Crops look well,
especially wheat, of which there is a vast amount."   He describes the fruits, berries, etc., tells of cool weather, and says,
"there was nothing going on for the Fourth but 'drinking,
dancing, and fighting,' so he spent the day in 'berrying' and
long walks," and adds, "I am going to be on a farm about five
miles from the Ferry engaged," he adds, "in agricultural pur-

suits,' and then warns his brother not to write of the institution."

A letter, bearing date September 28th, evidently written from the Kennedy Farm, says:

"Our cooks (Anne Brown and Martha, wife of Oliver) are going to start back to Essex County, New York, in the morning (Sept. 29). They are the old man's daughter and daughter-in law. The old man (Osawatomie) has gone to Philadelphia for a few more hands and will be back in a few days, and then we will commence digging the precious metal sometime next week without doubt."

He writes hopefully of a future visit to Iowa, and then adds, that:

"At present I am bound by all that is honorable to continue in the same cause for which I left Kansas and all my relations. Millions of fellow beings require it of us; their cries for help go out to the universe daily and hourly. Whose duty is it to help them? Is it yours, is it mine? It is every man's; but how few there are to help. But there are a few who dare to answer this call, and dare to answer it in a manner that will make this land of Liberty and Equality shake to the center. If my life is sacrificed, it can't be lost in a better cause. Our motto is, 'We go in to win at all hazards.' So if you should hear of a failure it will be after a desperate struggle and loss of capital on both sides. But that is the last of our thoughts; everything seems to work to our hands. . . . The old man has had this operation in view for twenty years and last winter was just a hint and a trial of what could be done."

Anderson then refers to a picture which would seem to be a view of Harper's Ferry, as he writes:

"It is not a large place, but a precious one to Uncle Sam, as he has great many tools there. I expect (when I start again traveling) to start at that place and go through the State of Virginia and on South, just as circumstances requiring mining, and prospecting, and carrying the *ore* along with us; you can just imagine while you are reading this what we are doing and see how near you guess the truth. 'Great excitement!' 'New gold discoveries in Virginia!' I judge the excitement will be so high that the slaveholders will have all the *darkies* out digging gold for THEMSELVES. I believe a hint to the wise is sufficient. I suppose this is the last letter I shall write before there is something in the wind. . . . Farewell till you hear from or see me and hope for the best."

The hopeful courage of all these young men, as manifested in these simple, unaffected home letters, is not the least remarkable fact the records show. It stands as proof alike of their intelligent fidelity to principle, and of the confidence their leader inspired them with. Anderson was one of the minority who in the debate at the Kennedy Farm sustained the proposed attack on Harper's Ferry.

After the arrest of Cook and Hazlett, Governor Wise issued another proclamation. In these days he seems to have maintained a factory for their production :

TWO THOUSAND DOLLARS REWARD—A PROCLAMATION BY THE GOVERNOR OF VIRGINIA.—Information having been received by the Executive that Owen Brown, Barclay Coppoc, Francis J. Merriam, and Charles P. Tidd (who are severally charged with the crimes of treason, murder, and conspiring and advising with slaves to rebel in the county of Jefferson, in this commonwealth), have escaped from justice, and are now going at large, therefore I do hereby offer a reward of five hundred dollars to any person who shall arrest either of said fugitives and deliver him into the jail of said county of Jefferson, and I do, moreover, require all officers of this commonwealth, civil and military, and request the people generally, to use their best exertions to procure their arrest, that they may be brought to justice.

Given under my hand as Governor, and under the Less seal

of the commonwealth, at Richmond, this third day of November, 1859.   HENRY A. WISE.

The Richmond papers appended the following descriptions to the above:

" Owen Brown is thirty-three or thirty-four years of age, about six feet in height, with fair complexion, though somewhat freckled—has red hair, and very heavy whiskers of the same color.   He is a spare man, with regular features, and has deep blue eyes.

" Barclay Coppoc is about twenty years of age; is about five feet seven and a half inches in height, with hazel eyes, and brown hair, wears a light mustache, and has a consumptive look.

" Francis J. Merriam is about twenty-five years of age; is about five feet eight and a half inches in height, has black hair and eyes, and brown mustache.   He has lost one eye—sometimes wears a glass eye.   His face is somewhat blotched. Complexion dark.

" Charles P. Tidd stands five feet eleven inches ; has broad shoulders, and looks like a very muscular and active man; has light hair, blue eyes, Grecian nose, and heavy brown whiskers; looks like a fighting man, and his looks in this respect are in no way deceptive."

With John Edwin Cook, the other four men started on the morning of the 18th of October, across the South Mountain spur, to escape from the clutches of Virginia, and reach, if possible, the western part of Pennsylvania, where John Brown had married his wife, Mary Anne Day. It was natural, then, for Owen to make that section his objective point. Not only could they then reach the Ohio northwestern reserve, where John, Jr., and Jason Brown lived and in which nearly all of the party had recently been staying, but in the western counties of the Keystone State there were prominent persons, like the Delameters, who had in earlier days avowed their sympathy with John Brown's acknowledged purpose. Three of the four proclaimed in Wise's proclamation never got a chance at the fighting; Tidd was actually in the Ferry between midnight and daylight of the 17th, and then went with a party to capture Terence Burns, a slaveholder of the neighborhood. He returned to the Ferry and was immediately sent out again with a four-horse wagon and a party of negroes to assist at the schoolhouse and protect the arms, etc., that Owen Brown's party was removing from the Kennedy Farm. He was the first to hear the news of failure. Owen declared, "We must not desert our friends," and started to arm with rifles the colored men, with them who had been brought from the Washington, Alstadt, Burns, and other plantations; take position as near the Ferry as possible, and open firing at long range, at least so as to enable the others to fight their way out. Tidd was hopeless, and the colored men soon showed they were unwilling. It was late in the afternoon; John Brown had been driven into the engine-house, and the report Tidd returned with, having volunteered to go as near the Ferry as possible and obtain news, was: "Your father was killed at four. Oliver and Watson are reported dead. Only two or three men are left alive." It appeared evident, then, that the only hope was in making their escape. They made up some provisions, Cook having joined them after his unsuccessful firing at the Virginians from a perch on the side of Maryland Heights. A negro man who had been left at the Kennedy Farm also appeared. The six men then went to the Maryland house, got supper, and immediately after took to the range.   The negro was directed to let loose a horse he had.   This he refused and that night he disappeared.   "None of us," said Owen, in after days, "made much pretension to being scared."   They were alarmed, however, at the negro's flight, and made on the 18th as good time as they could.   Owen naturally assumed command, and declared that they must follow the mountains, making to the Northwest as steadily as possible.   It was determined to keep out of sight and travel only by night.   If the party had gone directly north from the Kennedy Farm, as Anderson and Hazlitt, they would probably have met the latter, been on ground the topopraphy of which they understood, and would in all probability have had a better chance of getting away.   Anderson was in Chambersburg on the night of the 20th.   Cook did not go down to the old forge in the Cumberland Valley, where he was captured, until the 24th inst.   By Owen's directions, all traveled roads were shunned, except to cross them at night ; no fires were built, though the cold was bitter; at first they got along without getting food except a few ears of corn, eaten raw.   After they were able to travel more directly west they succeeded in either raiding on farmyards or, preferably, in buying provisions.   After finding, early in the morning, that the negro had fled, they crossed the nearest range.   Cook, bold, fiery, quick-thinking, wanted all to go together on to the roads and then move, at night, as rapidly as possible. Tidd was severe in his criticisms of what he termed Cook's "braggadocio."   It took all of Owen's genuine kindliness and tact to prevent open quarrels.   Another difficulty supervened in the inability of Merriam to withstand the severe fatigue. " He never complained," Owen said in after years, though he avoided also telling how he carried the young Bostonian over streams and difficult places. Barclay Coppoc was not strong, being consumptive in tendency, but he had a brave, enduring spirit, had lived in the open air, worked at manual labor, as Merriam had not, and got through without serious drawbacks. After Cook's descent to the valley, and his capture within fifteen miles of Chambersburg, the others pushed on to that burg, hoping to get food and aid their unfortunate comrade. Another reason for venturing, as it were, into a trap, was to enable Merriam to get away by railroad, and in this they succeeded. Fortunately, he had retained some of the $600 drawn from his trustee and uncle, Mr. James Jackson, of Boston. He divided with his comrades, retaining only sufficient to reach a place of safety. Tidd and Coppoc left Owen and Merriam hidden nearby and made their way to Mrs. Ritner's dwelling. Mr. Franklin Keagy thus describes this adventure:

"On the morning after Cook's capture and the day on which he was surrendered so hastily to Virginia, Tidd and Coppoc came to Mrs. Ritner's house, and awakened her by knocking at her bedroom window with a bean pole. Mrs. Ritner put her arm out and motioned them to leave. Tidd said, 'Don't you know me? I am Tidd.' Mrs. Ritner whispered in a frightened manner, 'Leave, leave!' Tidd said, 'We are hungry,' to which Mrs. Ritner replied, 'I can't help you, if you were starving, leave! the house is guarded by armed men!' The men then hurriedly left and secreted themselves in a thicket on the outskirt of the town; there they remained all day, and that night they left their hiding-place and started northward. It is well they did, the next morning was Thanksgiving Day, and the country about town was alive with boys and men rabbit hunting. The arms left by them were soon found, and it was surmised that there was some of the party in the town yet. Merriam left the party at Chambersburg, and, going on the railroad track as far as Scotland, distant five miles, took the early morning train east. The rest of the party, Owen Brown, Coppoc, and Tidd, crossed the North Mountains and escaped capture."

An account, published at the time in the New York *Tribune*, dated Chambersburg, says that the four men remained several days near that place. This and other statements are incorrect, as James Redpath met Merriam in Philadelphia on the 26th, and sent him northward, while also dispatching previously arranged for telegrams to his mother and uncle. A quiet, but well-organized and vigorous effort was made to reach Owen's party at the time, and several times friends were within rifle shot. It was impossible, however, to communicate with them even when the messengers were of the colored race. The same thing was true in the neighborhood of Harrisburg, where both Colonel Hoyt and myself conducted well-planned efforts. After leaving Chambersburg, which they did after learning in some way of Cook's return to Virginia at noon of the 25th, they were compelled to wander in more or less danger, and it was not until the 4th of November, twenty days after they had left the Kennedy Farm that they were able to obtain an old newspaper and learn that John Brown and Stevens, severely wounded, with Edwin Coppoc, Green, and Copeland had been captured and were on trial for their lives. It was Owen's birthday and he read the proclamation of Governor Wise offering rewards for

their capture. Owen stated that Tidd got the paper,
and he (Owen), " with a tremor in the voice, read the
news aloud." At this time they adopted other names;
Owen taking that of Edward Clark, Tidd becoming
Charles Plummer, and Coppoc assuming to be George
Barclay. They began to get among Quakers and
farmers who asked no questions, gave them food and
directed them on their way. On one occasion they
were hotly pursued, and Benjamin Wakefield, near
Fawnville, Crumford County, a Quaker, managed to
put the pursuers off on a wrong road. He fed and cared
for the fugitives, letting them understand he knew
who they were, would take no money, and directed
them to find a cousin, forty miles distant, at Half
Moon. At Half Moon they were at first reluctantly
received, but well treated after the household got
over its fright. Here they bought large carpet bags
and were thus enabled to hide their weapons. They
reached Center County, Pennsylvania, where Owen
had relatives, in the latter part of November, and then
separated. Under date of November 28th, Hoyt
wrote Mr. Le Barnes from Cleveland: "Coppoc passed
this place this morning. Before this gets to Boston
he will be safe enough in Canada. Owen Brown is
in Ashtabula County and will soon be here *en route*.
Where Tidd is I don't know, but he is safe." He was
very careful about his address, and, as late as July,
1860, his actual whereabouts—he being then in Massachusetts—was withheld directly from all but members of the Brown family, Barclay Coppoc, and L. F.
Parsons. Owen, who had gone to his brother at
Dorset, did not leave Ohio for many years. On the
8th of March, 1860, Governor Letcher made a demand

for Virginia on Governor Dennison, Ohio, for the surrender of Owen Brown and Francis J. Merriam. The
latter had been sojourning a brief period at Cleveland, while passing to and from Chatham, Canada,
where I find by O. P. Anderson's letters to me, he
made his residence until the summer of 1860. The
attorney-general of Ohio, to whom Letcher's demand
was referred, stated that no "le-
gal" demand had been made or
proper papers submitted. He
said: "In all these documents,
from beginning to end, there is
no word, no letter, from which
human ingenuity can draw the
vaguest hint that Owen Brown
or Merriam had fled from Virginia, nor was there any proper
proof of either of the men being
within the bounds of Ohio."

OWEN BROWN.

Owen Brown showed in his
conduct of the escape, as in his
life in Kansas and elsewhere, the
best qualities and the true stuff
of which the Browns were all
made.   George B. Gill, who knew him well, writes a
bit of analytical description. He says:

"Owen Brown came as near being a philosopher, in many
ways, as I ever saw. A thorough optimist, too, often express
ing approbation of life by wishing that he could live a thousand
years. Apparently organized like his father, yet having but
few of the latter's severe peculiarities, every idea had to pass
through the cynical test of logic. In contradistinction to his
father's views, Owen was an avowed agnostic. He was moral

and upright, very kind, and very willing to sacrifice his personal comforts, if by doing so he might benefit others. To induce me to quit the use of tobacco he offered to live upon two meals a day. Very firm, yet entirely free from vindictiveness: the very soul of honor and honesty. The equanimity of his temper I have never seen equaled.

"He must have been six feet in height and well proportioned, with red or sandy hair and full, long beard. He had been physically unfortunate, when younger, in the injury of an arm or shoulder, I think, through which he had suffered so severely as to prematurely age him, and produced a trouble of some kind by which he was subject to drowsiness. This, as well as being crippled in his arm, rendered him incapable of any very hard labor. His father, in planning for him, was ,always taking this into consideration, and most likely had this in mind when leaving him in charge of the house and arms at the Kennedy Farm. He inherited from him a dislike for buttermilk and cheese. Owen became much attached to a young lady at Springdale, Iowa, but owing to the peculiar conditions, he considered that it would be dishonorable in him to make any advance. I have, however, understood that he retained for her an undiminished affection to the day of his death."

Owen lived for several years at Gibraltar (Jay Cooke's residence) in Sandusky Bay, Lake Erie, John, Jr., and Jason residing at the same time on Put-in-Bay Island, nearby. John, with his wife, Wealthy, and their son and daughter, still live at the vineyard, whose planting was begun in 1860. They are among the rarest of gentlefolks, well mannered, and cultivated in the best sense, honored by all who know them, and beloved by those who are endowed with their friendship. Early in the 'eighties the Brown family removed to California, with the exception of John, Jr., and his family, who remain in their Island home, Lake Erie. A portion of Jason's family still live at Akron, Ohio. The North Elba homestead, purchased, raised through the energy of Kate Field, is now in the hands of trustees and in charge of a family related by marriage to the Browns. The unmarried daughter, Sarah, lived in San Francisco, where the widowed mother died two years before Owen's death. Ruth, Jason, and Owen settled in, or near, South Pasadena; the two sons holding small ranches on Las Cacitas, a neighboring table-land. Ellen, with her husband, settled in the Santa Cruz Valley, where also Sarah now resides. Salmon, with his family, recently removed to Yakima Valley, Washington, from the neighborhood of Red Bluff, while Mrs. Anne Brown-Adams resides at Petralia, Humboldt County. Owen Brown died on the 9th of January, 1891, greatly beloved by all who knew him. His powers of description were marked and made his conversation very attractive. His memory of places, incidents, and scenes, though not of names or persons, remained vivid until his death. In July, 1860, at North Elba, he wrote in an autograph album the following, and it is quoted here because it clearly illustrates his mental habits and his way of putting things :

"How much better is defeat while struggling for the right than the greater success in an evil work. That nation which will rob and oppress its laboring citizens must experience all the horrors of a revolution. It is a necessary result of a war upon the natural and most sacred rights of man. I am sorry that any member of the human family should think so much of self, or have so tight a hold upon the great silver and golden god of the United States, that they cannot be just. From this source springs all oppression. The welfare of man is the *first* great law. Then let all, male and female, irrespective of nation or complexion, be governed by one and the same laws."

A native of Maine, born at Palermo, Waldo County, in 1832, Charles Plummer Tidd was in his twenty-seventh year when he escaped from Virginia, October 18th, 1859. Anne Brown-Adams writes that, after the discussion at the Kennedy Farm in September, ending by the decision to follow John Brown's plans, Tidd was so dissatisfied that he left the farmhouse and went to stay with Cook, and a week passed before he gave way to the general verdict. At this point, it may well be assumed that the real objection to the Harper's Ferry raid was against Captain Brown's desire to hold the place long enough to leave a startling impression on the country, and then by a disappearance, to be followed swiftly by raids elsewhere, add to the alarm that would exist. What John Brown · seriously believed was, that slavery, being vulnerable in all directions, could be frightened quite as much as fought out of existence. I have found no evidence whatever that there was any difference of opinion among his men as to this, but evidently the experienced Kansas members of the party questioned the wisdom of the special demonstration at Harper's Ferry, which Captain Brown projected, and which he finally failed to carry to a finish, as planned. I know, from conversation and correspondence with Kagi, and from constant examination of all the facts since accessible, that the idea of raids from the Appalachian ranges into the farm and plantation regions below them was well understood and fully accepted by Tidd as well as the others. Cook's essentially dramatic way of putting things, as well as his minute knowledge of affairs at Harper's Ferry, had, doubtless, something to do with John Brown's adherence to his conception of the value of a blow well struck at the Ferry. Kagi never opposed, because he probably believed that a speedy evacuation of the place would follow. Tidd never gave a hearty consent to the attack, but would not, because of this difference, abandon the leader he and all of them personally trusted in so implicitly.

CHARLES PLUMMER TIDD.

A man of sturdy frame, about five feet nine inches in height, with a large, well-shaped head, set well forward on broad shoulders, Charles Plummer Tidd had the look of a clever, handy mechanic. His perceptives were active and dominant. Of bilious, nervous temperament, his complexion was dark, eyes, beard, and hair also, features strongly marked, expression grave, even stern. In temper, he was somewhat saturnine and dominant. A little overbearing, and fond of practical jokes and sharp teasing. This led to quareling at times. Stevens and Tidd were excellent friends, and depended greatly on each other, but Stevens was quick to wrath while Tidd was cool, provoking, and sarcastic. Yet he was faithful, a true comrade, courageous, and wholly trustworthy, with more than ordinary mental capacity. Somewhat reticent, not given to writing, and more apt to repress than to

express, he has left little accessible matter behind
him.　A personal friend, writing in a Maine paper at
the time of the raid, when it was believed he was one
of the slain, says:

"I have been privileged with looking over many letters to
his mother and sisters, and if what a man says to his most intimate and dearest friends, if the whole tenor of numerous
letters to a mother, continued through a period of nearly four
years, is an evidence of a man's motives, Charles P. Tidd deserves a monument to his memory, rather than execration and
reproach.　He minutely relates the tragical scenes in which he
was engaged in Kansas ; describes the sufferings which he
endured from pro-slavery violence, and yet there is not in all
his letters a single revengeful, vindictive, or cruel sentiment
uttered relative to his enemies."

Reference is made in the same article to the winter
passed at Springdale, and to the regard entertained
for the Varney family at that place, the maternal head
of which was always called "mother" by Tidd and
Stevens.　He tells his family of a course of Bible-
reading and of the abstinence from liquor and tobacco
which the party had all agreed to.　He declared that
he had himself refrained from tea and coffee and
used but little meat for the two years past.　In the
last few of these letters, Tidd hinted clearly that he
was engaged in an undertaking which he could not
divulge, but in every letter he assured his friends that
it was one which they would heartily approve if they
knew all the particulars.　It was one, too, from which
he could reap no personal benefit, but was all for the
good of the oppressed and downtrodden, although
it was fraught with danger to himself, yet he was
willing to risk all for the good of others.　In his last
letter he informed his parents where what property

he had would be found if anything should befall him, who had his miniatures, and closed by saying that, "this is perhaps the last letter you will ever receive from your son. The next time you hear from me, will probably be through the public prints. If we succeed the world will call us heroes; if we fail, we shall hang between the Heavens and the earth."

He entered Kansas in August, 1856, having joined the Dr. Cutter party from Massachusetts, and he was with it when the Missourians blockaded the river at Lexington forcing his return to Chicago and thence overland through Iowa and Nebraska to Kansas. Tidd made the acquaintance of John Brown and his sons Owen and Oliver at Tabor, Iowa. He was trusted fully, and justly esteemed as one of the reliables. Having received a fair English education, he wrote well, had good business faculties, and would have been a successful man in ordinary circumstances. Owen Brown had a good deal to endure from the willfulness of both Tidd and Cook. The two younger men, Coppoc and Merriam, seem to have implicitly followed his directions and obeyed his requests. The presence of Mr. Cook at Chambersburg was the loadstone which, with hunger, drew my unfortunate friend from obeying Owen's more sagacious counsel. It was the latter's plan to avoid Chambersburg, but the other two insisted on their chance to get food there. Tidd seems to have been more than persistent—he was obstinate, even after the failure of Cook to return on the 24th inst. in his determination to call at Mrs. Ritner's house. Owen urged that the lady had doubtless denied knowledge of them all, and it would not be fair to bring her into trouble. One incident,

36

graphically related to Mr. Keeler by Owen, well illustrated the trials and temptations of the trip. It was about the 21st or 22d of October, and they were keeping in the range.

"Leaving Cook, Merriam, and Coppoc in the timber, I took Tidd and went to see if we could prudently cross that valley by daylight. We had gone on, Tidd and I, about a mile and a half, when we came in sight of a road with teams going and coming on it. Farther on we could see a farmhouse. While we were discussing the matter, and deciding that it would not be safe to cross the valley by daylight, there came wafted to our keen, hungry nostrils, from that farmhouse, at least forty rods away, the smell of something like doughnuts cooking. . . . It was too much for Tidd's endurance. . . . We were both weak and faint enough to stagger. Tidd vowed he wouldn't go a step farther without food. 'You'll be all winter,' he said, 'and never get through after all; you'll starve and freeze to death. It is just as well to expose ourselves one way as another,' and he took a long breath of the distant frying. I had the two arguments to withstand, Tidd's and the lard-laden air. The latter was the more powerful, but I withstood them both. I promised him, as I had promised to others, that as soon we got three nights north of Chambersburg, I would steal all the chickens, milk, and apples we needed. It would not do, I contended, to go to buying or even stealing provisions now. I am not in the habit of stealing, by the bye. But anti-slavery men would have been glad to give what little we needed to the cause, and pro-slavery men certainly owed it that much. That was the way I argued. Tidd, however, clung to the delightful, maddening odor, and his determination to go and buy food. As a great favor, I at last prevailed upon him to go first with me back to the place where we had left the other boys. And every one but myself agreed with Tidd. I had a large red silk handkerchief with white spots in it, given me by Mrs. Gerrit Smith. Well, this, with the empty shot-bag for salt, mentioned before, I gave to Cook, and told him, if they insisted on having food bought he could wield the glibest tongue, and tell the best story; he should go. Still, I didn't want—and I feel just as agitated now, almost, when I tell it—I didn't want him to go. I needed food, I told them, as much as any of them; and if they *would* go and get it, it would be foolish in me not to help eat it. So, as I had more funds than the rest, I made him take my money to pay for it, begging him to the last not to go. In Cook's confession, he says we sent him for food. That is the way it was.

" Cook was gone two or three hours, perhaps. He came back with a couple of loaves of bread, some salt in the bag, some good boiled beef, and a pie. He had had a pleasant visit, he said. He had stayed to dinner—which happened to be a little late that day—with the people of the farmhouse; had made himself very agreeable, and told them the story we had concocted beforehand about our being a hunting party, too far from home to get back to our dinners. If you have never been a great deal more than half starved, you can form no idea how marvelously good that feast was that day. I felt more or less gloomy about it at the time, keeping it to myself, though. But the shadow of the danger hanging over us did not seem to affect the other boys, who were exceedingly merry. And after dinner we all went to sleep for an hour or so."

A bitter quarrel soon arose between Cook and Tidd, owing to the former insisting, after the procurement of this food, on firing off the Washington horse-pistol he had in order to keep up the pretense of being hunters. Tidd undertook to take the pistol away and fell upon Cook. It took all the efforts of the three to prevent a serious personal termination of this quarrel.

The first detailed news the three received of the fighting, losses, and subsequent trials in Virginia, was obtained early in November, near Bellefonte, Pa., where a farmer sheltered them one night. He

handed them his newly arrived weekly paper to read.
In the Keeler narrative, Owen says:

"Tidd's stoicism broke down first ; he arose and caught up
the paper and began reading aloud. The first thing that
caught his eye was the account of Cook's capture. You can
imagine how eagerly Coppoc and I listened to the first we had
heard of Cook since he had left us in the mountains. Our host
interrupted the reading to assure me that one son of old Smith,
who had proved to be old Brown of Kansas, had escaped with
Cook and others, and was supposed to be still at large somewhere. Old man Brown was not dead, as we had heard. No,
he was just severely wounded; it was not certain yet whether
he would live to be hanged, for he had been tried and found
guilty. To me, who had so long thought my father dead, this
somehow had the effect of good news. In the meantime, Tidd
had gone on, silently devouring the paper. I could see that he
was much moved by what he read. He was probably reading
how his friend Stevens was shot down while going on an
errand of mercy and bearing a flag of truce."

Upon separating from Owen Brown and Barclay
Coppoc, Tidd, after a trip to Canada and Ohio,
under the name of Charles Plummer, lived for awhile
at Edinboro, Erie County, Pa., where he got interested in the oil business and made then and subsequently some money. In the summer of 1860 he
settled in Massachusetts and became intimate in the
family of Dr. Cutter. In a letter to Owen Brown,
dated Salem, Ohio, December 9, 1859, he writes that
he didn't stay in Erie County at first, on account of
the excitement, but went to Cleveland, where he remained but two days.

"I met there," he writes, "a person as unexpected to me
as that of the 'old man' himself would have been. The first
two letters of his name Al (as we used to call him) 'Chatham

Anderson.' He escaped from below with Hazlett but before they got to Chambersburg, 'Al' gave out. and so Anderson had to leave him. He got through safe as his presence showed. From Windsor we went to Chatham together, where I also found Merriam, so there were three of the originals together. From there I went to Rochester, where I found Dr. Doy, of Kansas. He wanted me to go lecturing with him, but I had made other arrangements and could not break them."

He then tells of his return to Salem, sends his regards to "George Barclay" (Coppoc), says the "box is all right." They had shipped their arms to Salem, Ohio, after reaching Center, Pa. He adds, at the close, "I see that I have been arrested and am now in Charlestown jail." From Cleveland he wrote, before the execution of Captain Brown, a vigorous letter to the New York *Tribune* in response to an attack by the *Observer*, the Presbyterian weekly, which was especially severe on John Brown. The basis of this attack was an article from the Kansas *Herald*, written by the editor, George W. Brown. Tidd's *Tribune* letter, bold, well-put and keen, declared that the Kansas editor's animosity was due to John Brown's plain characterization of him as "cowardly" as well as an "old granny." He charged the editor with maintaining a secret correspondence with Missourians and betraying Lawrence into border ruffians' hands. This charge is without foundation, I believe, except in so far that George W. Brown was always assailing, gossiping about, and backbiting every other prominent free-state man.

During the early part of the Civil War, Tidd enlisted as Charles Plummer in Company " K," Twenty-first Regiment Massachusetts Volunteer Infantry, and was soon made orderly sergeant. The regiment was detailed as a part of the Burnside expedition to North Carolina in the early months of 1862, and was shipped on the steamer *Northerner* with the expedition. Walcott's " History of the Twenty-first Regiment" (p. 42) refers to him. The landing on Roanoke Island was successfully accomplished, and the author says:

"On the 17th of February, soon after we left the *Northerner*, one of our men died on her who is worthy something more than a passing mention. His true name was Charles Plummer Tidd. He had been a trusted comrade of John Brown in Kansas and Virginia, and was one of the four men who evaded the thousands of armed foes who blockaded every outlet of escape from the scene of that grand historic precursor of the War, at Harper's Ferry. He dropped his surname Tidd, and called himself Charles Plummer, to aid in escaping detection. Following that staunch abolitionist, Dr. Cutter, our surgeon, who was a father to him, he brought his fierce enthusiasm for freedom into the Twenty-first, and was made first sergeant of Company K. He was too marked a man to escape Colonel Maggi's vigilant eye, and was selected to command a band of sixty scouts, organized by the colonel while on the *Northerner*, whose duty it would be to scour the country around us after we were on hostile ground : every man of the sixty was a good shot, fearless and strong, and Tidd was the strongest and bravest of them all. Shortly before we landed he was prostrated with inflammation of the bowels (enteritis), but could not reconcile himself to being left behind without a chance to fire a shot under the flag (perhaps at Governor Wise himself, commander of the rebel forces on the island), to avenge the death of his old leader and his own sufferings from hunger and cold during the terrible month when, hunted like a wolf, he painfully worked his way along the mountains of Maryland and Pennsylvania north from Harper's Ferry. Forced to remain in bed when the regiment entered the boats, every cannon shot excited and inflamed his mind beyond his shattered powers of physical endurance, and he died just after we landed, more from the fearful strain of his deep and bitter disappointment than from his disease. His eyes were closed by his true and loving friend, Miss Carrie E. Cutter, the Florence Nightingale of the Twenty-first, the delicate and accomplished daughter of our surgeon, who followed her father and the regiment to nurse our sick, until she, alas, so soon, shared the grave of her noble and admired friend."

The men who escaped from Harper's Ferry, or who were immediately and perilously connected with the movement, will be found in line, when able, serving the Union cause when that issue came. Two of John Brown's living sons, John Brown, Jr., and Salmon, held commissions. John was captain of Company K, Seventh Kansas Volunteer Cavalry, until inflammatory rheumatism compelled his resignation. Salmon was a second lieutenant in a New York infantry regiment. O. P. Anderson served as a non-commissioned officer in a colored regiment. William, brother of John A. Copeland, was commissioned as second lieutenant in a colored light artillery company. Barclay Coppoc was killed in the service. Parsons, Moffett, and Realf, of the men who were with the Iowa party and at the Chatham Convention, were commissioned officers, and Realf, especially, had a notable career. Dr. Delany was a major of colored troops. A brother of J. G. Anderson was also major in the same service. Charles W. Leonhardt had the rank of lieutenant-colonel. Richard Metternich, who was to have gone with me to the rescue of Stevens and Hazlett, was killed in Texas, it is stated, as a lieutenant-colonel. F. J. Merriam was in the service in some capacity throughout the War. George W. Stearns aided materially in raising troops, spending large sums of money for that purpose. James Montgomery and Thomas Wentworth Higginson were both regimental commanders. George Henry Hoyt was a brilliant cavalry officer, retiring with a brevet as brigadier-general. John W. Le Barnes served also as lieutenant and captain. The list can be lengthened, but these will serve for illustrations of service and loyalty.

Francis Jackson Merriam, born November 17, 1837, at Framingham, Mass., handsome, well-to-do, cultivated, and traveled, was in his twenty-second year when he made his escape. He was about five feet seven inches in height, slender in frame, having no pretension to possession of special powers of endurance, or even of courage. Yet Merriam was as absolutely fearless as he was personally unrestrained in his hostility to slavery and his determination to resist it, at all hazards, personal, social, or civic. He was the child of the anti-slavery agitation, his grandfather being Francis Jackson, the president of the American Anti-Slavery Society, whose house in Hollis street was attacked on one occasion by a mob of Boston "Conservatives." There was a meeting of women, and his mother, not long married, was present. So, also, was the mother of Colonel Hoyt, and two men never existed within my range of acquaintance who scorned and assailed slaveholders so bitterly as young Merriam and Hoyt. Francis was educated in the public schools, attending the "Brimmer," not entering college, but traveling in Europe and living in Paris for some time.

His father, Charles, died when the boy was young, and the mother married again. The daughter, Sarah J. Eddy, resides in Providence. Merriam was decidedly good-looking, with dark, long, brown hair and beard, good features, somewhat disfigured by blotches, though; he had a thoughtful, rather dreamy look. I am primarily responsible for Merriam's recruitment, having informed him, as I did James Redpath (with Kagi's consent), during the winter of 1858–59, of the general purpose and plan of John Brown. I spent that winter in Boston, leaving early in the spring for the West. Merriam's letter[1] to Captain Brown was sent to Lawrence, Kansas, by my direction. We were occupying the same rooms in Boston at the time, and Merriam proposed devoting his means to this work. He had already visited Kansas, where I first met him.

In one of his *Atlantic Monthly* articles, Mr. Sanborn gives this interesting account of the meeting of Hayden with Merriam. F. B. Sanborn suggests that Merriam had no direct knowledge of John Brown's

---

[1] " BOSTON, December 23, 1858.

" DEAR SIR—I have heard vaguely of your general purpose, and have been seeking definite information for some time past, and now Mr. Redpath and Mr. Hinton have told me of your contemplated action, in which I earnestly wish to join you to act in any capacity you wish to place me as far as my small capacities go. I am now about starting for Hayti with Mr. Redpath, to pass the winter there, and shall return in time for all movements. In case you should accept my services, I would return at any time you might wish me to, and in the spring at any rate. Is there anything it would be well for me to study meanwhile? Of course, I shall pay all my own expenses, and shall acquire the use of the proper tools for the work which I have bought. Any letters

movements until early in that month which witnessed
the attempt at consummation:

" One early day in October, Lewis Hayden got word at the
State House in Boston, by a letter either from Chambersburg
or from John Brown, Jr., in Ohio that Captain Brown's men
were in need of more money, and could not begin their movements until it reached them. Going down from the State
House to the post-office, which was then in State street, he
met Merriam near the old Province House, and it occurred to
him that here was a friend who would perhaps contribute
something. He therefore accosted Merriam, and, after a few
words, said. " I want five hundred dollars and *must have it*."
Merriam, startled at the manner of the request, replied, " If
you have a good cause, you shall have it." Hayden then told
Merriam briefly what he had learned from John Brown, Jr.,
that Captain Brown was at Chambersburg, or could be heard
of there, that he was preparing to lead a party of liberators
into Virginia, and that he needed money ; to which Merriam
replied, " If you tell me John Brown is there, you can have my
money and me along with it." For it was well known to Merriam that Brown had the general purpose of freeing the slaves
by force, and he had even written to him the winter before,
offering to join the party upon his return from Hayti in the
spring. Being thus prepared in mind for Mr. Hayden's communication, he received it as a call from heaven, and prepared
at once to obey.

" Within a day or two—probably that same day—Merriam,

---

addressed to the care of my grandfather, Francis Jackson, 31 Hollis
street, Boston, will be safe, and will be forwarded to me. I
already consider this the whole present business of my life. I am
entirely free from any family ties which would impede my action. I
was much disappointed in not meeting you in Kansas last winter,
with a letter of recommendation from Wendell Phillips. Immediately upon my return in the spring I should wish to be employed
in any manner to be of service to you; and, if convenient, to go
through your system of training, which I propose studying."

whom I had never seen before, made me an evening visit in Concord, where he spent the night.   He came to say that he had learned something of Captain Brown's plans."

Merriam was not without other direct information, however, as I had forwarded to the care of his grandfather two letters from Kagi, that reached me in the far West—one in May and the other during August of 1859.   I know the first was received, and have reason to suppose the second also, as Mr. Redpath wrote to that effect.   Merriam's visit to Hayti, mentioned in the letter I give, was designed as a study of the effects of a struggle for freedom on the negro character.

Merriam arrived at Chambersburg on the 9th of October; the date being fixed by notes afterwards found in Kagi's handwriting, and by own knowledge of John Brown's presence in Philadelphia from the 10th to the 13th thereof.   Col. A. K. McClure, in his book "Lincoln and Men of War Time" (page 309), writes that—

" In the early part of October two persons, unknown to me, entered my office and asked to submit some legal matters in private. . . .   The younger of the two, an intelligent and evidently positive man, gave his name as Francis Jackson Merriam, of Boston, and his companion gave his name as John Henri.   This was Kagi.   Merriam said that he was going on a journey South; that he had some property at home, and that he desired me to draw his will.   I did so, and was not surprised that a young Boston traveler, after making a few special bequests, gave his property to the Abolition Society of his native State.   There was nothing in his appearance, manner, or conversation to attract any special attention to his proceeding, and his will was duly executed, witnessed, and, in obedience to his orders, mailed to his executor in Boston.   When I asked

Merriam's companion to witness the will, he declined, saying
that he was a traveler also, and that both the witnesses had
better be in the same town."

On the 11th Merriam was in Philadelphia; on the
13th and 14th he was in Baltimore purchasing supplies, and on the 15th (Saturday) at the Wager
House, Harper's Ferry. John Brown and Kagi
arrived at the Kennedy Farm the night before, from
Chambersburg. At Harper's Ferry Merriam sent
the following telegram to Lewis Hayden in Boston:
"Orders disobeyed; conditions broken. Pay S.
(probably Sanborn) immediately balance of my
money; allow no further expense; recall money
advanced, if not spent." The only probable explanation of this is that finding John Brown designed
moving at once he regarded prior Boston arrangements
as "broken," or else he found that the "recruits,"
for whose expenses he had left in Hayden's hands a
considerable sum, had not arrived as per "conditions." The latter seems the most likely explanation.
One thing, however, is certain, that he did not break
his own promise, but went to the farm early in the
morning of the 16th to take his share of the work.

The care required to bring Merriam through from
the Virginia schoolhouse to the point five miles from
Chambersburg, Pa., where he was able to take the
Philadelphia train and so make good his escape, is
clearly brought out in Ralph Keeler's narrative,
though in it Owen seemed unconscious that he was
making for himself a tribute to that good comrade-
ship and devotion, to the exercise of which Merriam
undoubtedly owed his final safety. At one time in
their flight they were moving along a Cumberland

Valley road and found themselves approaching a tollgate, from which, of course, they sheered at once.

" The baying of the hounds had not yet wholly ceased. A few moments after we were obliged to wade quite a large creek. We were hurrying on from that towards the mountains, when I happened to look back and found that Merriam was nowhere to be seen. Hurrying back to the steep bank of the creek we had crossed, I discovered him, poor fellow, unable to climb it. I tried to hold him up, but was too tired and weak. I called Tidd and he took hold of Merriam rather impatiently, and, in pulling him up together, we bruised him against a projecting root,"

When within a few miles of Chambersburg, after Cook's arrest, Tidd and Coppoc announced their intention of leaving Owen and Merriam; the former having declared he would not abandon his almost helpless comrade. They started off, arranging to return to one of the two hiding-places Owen Brown had discovered on the road to Hagerstown when taking the colored men to the Kennedy Farm. Owen and Merriam followed steadily and kept within a short distance of the others till they reached the outskirts of the town. Tidd and Coppoc entered and the former approached Mrs. Ritner's house, as has already been stated. Thoroughly alarmed at their reception the two made their way back to where the others had concealed themselves. It was then decided that Merriam must be got away by rail and as quickly as possible.

" They succeeded after a severe effort, during which Merriam had to be dragged along or supported, in concealing themselves in a thicket about daybreak." Owen describes how he mended Merriam's overcoat, which had been torn in the mountain travel, " to a state of what I considered suspicious shabbiness. I had a pair of scissors with my needles and thread; and so when the tempest got worse, and it was safe to sit up a little, I clipped off his beard as close as I could shingle it. What was especially fortunate for Merriam just then was the fact that he wore a glass eye; and this glass eye fitted him so well that he could turn it, or at least seemed to turn it nearly as well as he did the other one. That and his beard gone, Merriam was pretty thoroughly disguised. We discussed Merriam's leaving, more or less, all day long. The poor fellow was so weak and worn that he couldn't have walked any further anyhow."

They saw the train passing that conveyed Cook to his trial and death. In the briar patch where they were hidden, they concluded to leave Merriam's arms and ammunition, and their own Sharpe's carbines, all except the pistol that could be concealed on their persons. Owen tells of the final parting, saying that—

" Merriam had furnished a good deal of money to the cause. He would take only five dollars from me when making his preparation to part with us. He said he had money enough to get through with. A driving snow set in that night, and it was as dark as I ever saw it in my life. We could see almost nothing at all. We started together for the road bordering the side of the field opposite the railway. In this road Tidd and Coppoc bade Merriam good-by and Godspeed. Leaving them in a fence corner, I took Merriam by the hand—it was so dark and he was so feeble—and led him to the railroad. Then I walked a little way on the track with him, so that he would be sure to take the direction away from Chambersburg, and reach the first station outside of that town before taking a train. Our plan was that he should thereafter go north as directly as he could. So I left him on the track and found my way back to Tidd and Coppoc, through the darkness and blinding snowstorm."

There remains little more to be said of Merriam. He went direct to Philadelphia and thence to Chatham, Canada, where, as Tidd's letter to Owen Brown shows, he was at the time of the executions of December 2d and 16th. He returned to Boston in the latter winter and was there at the time of Stevens's and Hazlett's (March 16th) execution. He was at North Elba on the 4th of July, and O. P. Anderson wrote under date of October 13, 1860, in answer to my inquiry that Francis was then at Chatham, Canada. Merriam visited Hayti again in the summer of 1860, this time in the interest of a more extended insurrectionary or revolutionary movement, which embraced not only a projected uprising of colored American slaves, but the possible organization of such a racial nationality in the Gulf States, the mid-continental islands, and portions of South America. This is not the place to detail that scheme, which ended with the precipitation of civil war by our own slaveholders. When the first stern throes of that struggle were visible to the most skeptical, Merriam wrote in a little autograph volume, under date of January 31st, 1861, dating it " Third Month of the Crisis," that—" I hail with exultation the emancipation of six millions of Southern whites—I care not for the abnormal manner they use their newly acquired liberty.

" They seized power to rivet the claims of their black fellows,—they have freed themselves and will soon accomplish the freedom of the remaining four millions.

" While others see only anarchy and the ruin of our country, I see permanent peace, founded on justice through a veil of thin, though dark, war-clouds."

Early in the Civil War, Merriam married Minerva Caldwell, of Galena, Ill., the daughter and sister of physicians, who also became herself a physician of note. In some relation or other, Merriam was in the field constantly. Dr. David Thayer, of Boston, writes that "it was reported that his (the doctor's) brother-in-law was killed in the Battle of Fredericksburg. I went down," he says, "to Washington to obtain his body. . . . In my search through all the hospitals of the District of Columbia I saw thousands of wounded soldiers. In one large field hospital, as I was going along, I heard some one call out, 'Dr. Thayer, is that you?' I halted and said, 'Who is it?' and went in the direction of the voice. The day was already far advanced and it began to be dark. Some one said 'It is Francis.' I looked and found it was Merriam. I said to him, 'Francis, this is wrong.' He replied, 'My friends in Chicago know where I am. But I could not keep out of it.' He had been in battle and was wounded in the leg, a gunshot wound." Merriam was on the South Carolina Sea Islands, during 1863, recruiting colored soldiers.[1] In 1864 he was under Grant. His death occurred November 28, 1865.

-----

[1] CAMP 3D REGT., S. C. INFANTRY, July 7, 1863.
BRIG.-GENERAL A. H. TERRY:

GENERAL—I respectfully request permission to visit Fort Pulaski with a small squad of men, for the purpose of obtaining colored men as recruits for the 3d S. C. Infantry, and return.

Very respectfully, your ob'd't servant,

F. J. MERRIAM, *Capt. Co. E, 3d S. C. I.*

APPROVED:

By order of E. R. FOWLER, *Capt. Com'g 3d S. C. Inf'y.*

But little more remains to be said of those who only fought and fell. The final words on Watson and Oliver Brown, the fifth and seventh of John Brown's sons; the ninth and twelfth of his twenty children, and the second and fifth born to Mary, his second wife and widow, remain unwritten. So much might still be said, while so many references have already been made, that the pen hesitates at further description. Watson was born October 7, 1835, and when he died from his wounds on the 18th of October, 1859, he had passed but eleven days into his twenty-fifth year. He was the only one of the living boys who did not serve in Kansas, though he started therefor, reaching Tabor, Iowa, in the latter part of 1856. Watson married Isabella M. Thompson, Henry's sister, in September, 1856, and when he fell was the father of a boy, born in May preceding, who lived to the age of four. The mother is still living and is now the wife of Salmon Brown, a cousin of her first husband. Watson was tall and rather fair, of finely knit frame, athletic, and active. He was a man of excellent natural ability, fair education, and had in fine poise the good qualities of this wonderful family. Oliver was born March 9, 1839, and was therefore, when slain, on the afternoon of October 17th, at Harper's Ferry, still within four months and twenty-two days of his twenty-first year. He was in Kansas with his father from June until October, 1856, and received his "baptism of fire" at Black Jack. The two brothers were about six feet in height, and of large muscular development. There was a marked difference, however, in the physiognomical and phrenological cast of the brothers. The features of Oliver

37

were regular and the head was evenly developed, the organs most prominent, in phrenological idiom, being those of individuality and eventuality. The head of Watson was broader and more fully developed above and behind the ears, while the cheek bones were more prominent.

Oliver married Martha Evelyn Brewster on the 7th of April, 1858, and she died in childbirth early in 1860. Watson suffered greatly, being desperately wounded by shots fired at the armory gate at the same time that Newby fell. After the capture on the morning of the 18th, he was able to inquire after his father's welfare. Edwin Coppoc, in a letter to Mrs. Brown, described the last hours of her son, writing:

"I was with your sons when they fell. Oliver lived but a very few moments after he was shot. He spoke no word, but yielded calmly to his fate. Watson was shot at ten o'clock on Monday morning, and died about three o'clock Monday afternoon. He fought bravely against the men who charged on us. When the enemy were repulsed, and the excitement of the charge was over, he began to sink rapidly. After we were taken prisoners he was placed in the guardhouse with me. He complained of the hardness of the bench on which he was lying. I begged hard for a bed for him, or even a blanket, but could obtain none for him. I took off my coat and placed it under him and held his head in my lap, in which position he died without a groan or struggle."

On the 16th of September, Watson, writing to his wife, says:

"We have only two black men with us as yet, but we expect more. One of them has a wife and seven children in slavery. I sometimes feel as if I could not make this sacrifice, but what would I not want others to do were I in their place."

In still another letter to his home, he writes:

" I received your letter of September 14th, the night the girls got home, which I was very glad to get.   Oh, Bell, I do want to see you and the little fellow [the young babe born in the father's absence] very much, but I must wait.   There was a slave near here whose wife was sold off South the other day, and he was found in Thomas Kennedy's orchard, dead, the next morning.   Cannot come home so long as such things are done here."

In the last letter sent to Isabella at North Elba, dated October 14, he also writes:

"We are all eager for the work and confident of success. There was another murder committed near our place the other day, making in all five murders and one suicide within five miles   .   .   .   since we have lived here. They were all slaves, too."

Pages might be filled with such extracts and others, as manly and sympathic. Touch these men and women—the sons and daughters of John Brown— when and where you will, and the response is always virile, wholesome, clean, upright; glowing with courage and white with the clear light of firmness and faith. Mrs. Brown spoke of her son Oliver as among the most promising of her children, gifted with a thoughtful character and great intelligence. His last letter to his lovely child-wife bears date, "Home, October 9, 1859," and she did not receive it until after his death:

" MY DEAR MARTHA—Having opportunity to write you once more, I improve it, with the greatest pleasure to myself, and with the hope of pleasing you. I arrived here two days sooner than father and Watson. They have gone back once more. We are all well at present.

"You can hardly think how I want to see you, or how lonesome it was the day I left you. . . . Nothing else could strengthen me to do the right so much as the thought of you. It is when I look at your picture that I am wholly ashamed of my every meanness, weakness, and folly. I would not part with that picture for anything on earth—but the original. I have made a morocco case for it and carry it close around my body. I am more and more determined every day to live a more unselfish life.

"Now, Martha, you can hardly conceive my great anxiety about you in your present situation, and you will certainly allow me to suggest some ideas to you for your own good. Let me ask you to try and keep up good, cheerful spirits. Take plenty of sleep and rest, plenty of outdoor exercise. Bathe often. And, finally, do read good books, such as Parker's 'Sermons' and Combe's 'Constitution of Man.' These books will do much to keep you from being lonesome. Finally, Martha, do try to enjoy yourself. Make the best of everything. Remember your affectionate husband."

The most amazing fact one finds in these dramatic events, is the systematic savagery of all the slave-holding acts and forces. When the South Carolina rebel commander replied to a request for the body of Col. Robert Shaw, who fell at Fort Wagner, that he was "buried with his niggahs," he only phrased for himself an echo of the brutality which animated the Virginians less than three years before. The bodies of the slain men were refused the consideration of decent burial; the passions of the hour seeking a fancied revenge in the defilement of their dead forms. Oliver's body was thrown on its back into a shallow grave or trench, and in his arms was placed the body of Dangerfield Newby, the bold, brave, free man of color, who fought to save his wife and children from the slavedealer's pen. These white Virginians actually believed they hurt the dead heroes by laying such comrades upon each other. Anderson, Leeman, and Taylor, were flung together into the same grave, to remain there a short time. The ghoulish young medicos of Winchester quickly rifled this pit, and that also into which, upon the Shenandoah's bank, the bodies of Kagi and others had been thrown. The skeleton of Watson, as it had been made an exhibit of at the Virginian Medical School, was identified as late as 1882, and then removed to North Elba from Indiana, whither it had been taken from Winchester, Va., by a Union surgeon in 1862. There is no reason for doubting this to have been Watson's frame, and it was sent to the lonely homestead to be interred in the grave of his father.

The tally of the Harper's Ferry dead was completed, when the soul of Martha passed beyond. " Other women give money," she said, "but I have given all; my beloved and my life!" So it was. Their sacrifice, however great it became, was not without majestic return. The roads to Harper's Ferry are all emblazened with Union and Emancipation. The words of Frederick Douglass, spoken at the place where the blow fell, illustrate the historical weight and significance of that reward. In a commencement address to the colored students of Storer College at Harper's Ferry (May 30, 1882), the eloquent negro orator said:

" *If John Brown did not end the war that ended slavery, he did at least begin the war that ended slavery. If we look over the dates, places, and men for which this*

honor is claimed, we shall find that not Carolina, but Vir-
ginia, not Fort Sumter, but Harper's Ferry, and the
United States Arsenal—not Major Anderson, but John
Brown began the war that ended American slavery and
made this a free Republic. Until this blow was struck,
the prospect for Freedom was dim, shadowy, and uncer-
tain. The irrepressible conflict was one of words, votes,
and compromises. When John Brown stretched forth his
arm the sky was cleared—the time for compromise was
gone—the armed hosts stood face to face over the chasm of
a broken Union and the clash of arms was at hand!"

APPENDIX.

Containing the principal and more important documents prepared by John Brown, or relating directly to the enterprises against American slavery in which he was actively engaged.

PART I.

"WORDS OF ADVICE.

" Branch of the United States League of Gileadites. Adopted January 15, 1851, as written and recommended by John Brown, also'

AGREEMENT AND RULES.

[This interesting paper, written at Springfield, Massachusetts, was first published in " The Independent," 1870, by William Wells Brown. The manuscript, written shortly after the passage of the Fugitive Slave Law, is still in existence, is in the Captain's quaint and peculiar chirography. It was signed by forty-four men and women, chiefly colored, resident in Springfield. Mr. F. B. Sanborn published in his "Life and Letters of John Brown" (pp. 125-26), the agreement, rules, and signatures, from which volume they are transcribed here.]

"UNION IS STRENGTH."

" Nothing so charms the American people as personal bravery. The trial for life of one bold and to some extent successful man, for defending his rights in good earnest, would arouse more sympathy throughout the nation than the accumulated wrongs and sufferings of more than three millions of our submissive colored population. We need not mention the Greeks struggling against the oppressive Turks, the Poles against Russia, nor the Hungarians against Austria and Russia combined, to prove this. *No jury can be found in the Northern*

States that would convict a man for defending his rights to the last extremity. This is well understood by Southern Congressmen, who insisted that the right of trial by jury should not be granted to the fugitive. Colored people have more fast friends amongst the whites than they suppose, and would have ten times the number they now have were they but half as much in earnest to secure their dearest rights as they are to ape the follies and extravagances of their white neighbors, and to indulge in idle show, in ease, and in luxury. Just think of the money expended by individuals in your behalf in the past twenty years. Think of the number who have been mobbed and imprisoned on your account. Have any of you seen the Branded Hand? Do you remember the names of Lovejoy and Torrey?

"Should one of your number be arrested, you must collect together as quickly as possible, so as to outnumber your adversaries who are taking an active part against you. Let no able-bodied man appear on the ground unequipped, or with his weapons exposed to view; let that be understood beforehand. Your plans must be known only to yourself, and with the understanding that all traitors must die, wherever caught and proven to be guilty. 'Whosoever is fearful or afraid, let him return and depart early from Mount Gilead.' (Judges, vii. chap., 3 verse; Deut., xx chap., 8 verse.) Give all cowards an opportunity to show it on condition of holding their peace. *Do not delay one moment after you are ready; you will lose all your resolution if you do. Let the first blow be the signal for all to engage, and when engaged do not do your work by halves; but make clean work with your enemies, and be sure you meddle not with any others.* By going about your business quietly, you will get the job disposed of before the number that an uproar would bring together can collect; and you will have the advantage of those who come out against you, for they will be wholly unprepared with either equipments or matured plans; all with them will be confusion and terror. Your enemies will be slow to attack you after you have once done up the work nicely; and, if they should, they will have to encounter your white friends as well as you, for you may safely calculate on a division of the whites, and may by that means get to an honorable parley.

"Be firm, determined, and cool; but let it be understood that you are not to be driven to desperation without making it an awful job to others as well as to you. Give them to know distinctly that those who live in wooden houses should not throw fire, and that you are just as able to suffer as your white neighbors. *After effecting a rescue, if you are assailed, go into the houses of your most prominent and influential white friends with your wives, and that will effectually fasten upon them the suspicion of being connected with you, and will compel them to make a common cause with you, whether they would otherwise live up to their profession or not. This would leave them no choice in the matter.* Some would, doubtless, prove themselves true of their own choice; others would flinch. That would be taking them at their own words. You may make a tumult in the court-room where a trial is going on by burning gunpowder freely in paper packages, if you cannot think of any better way to create a momentary alarm, and might possibly give one or more of your enemies a hoist. But in such case the prisoner will need to take the hint at once and bestir himself; and so should his friends improve the opportunity for a general rush.

"A lasso might possibly be applied to a slave-catcher for once with good effect. Hold on to your weapons, and never be persuaded to leave them, part with them, or have them far away from you. *Stand by one another, and by your friends, while a drop of blood remains; and be hanged, if you must, but tell no tales out of school. Make no confession.*"

AGREEMENT.

"As citizens of the United States of America, trusting in a just and merciful God, whose spirit and all-powerful aid we humbly implore, *we will ever be true to the flag of our beloved country, always acting under it.* We, whose names are hereunto affixed, do constitute ourselves a branch of the United States League of Gileadites. We will provide ourselves

at once with suitable implements, and will aid those who do
not possess the means, if any such are disposed to join us.
We invite every colored person whose heart is engaged for the
performance of our business, whether male or female, old or
young. The duty of the aged, infirm, and young members of
the League shall be to give instant notice to all members in
case of an attack upon any of our people. We agree to have
no officers except a Treasurer and Secretary, *pro tem.*, until
after some trial of courage and talent of able-bodied members
shall enable us to elect officers from those who shall have
rendered the most important services. Nothing but wisdom
and undaunted courage, efficiency, and general good conduct
shall in any way influence us in electing our officers."

SAMBO'S MISTAKES.

[*Part of an unfinished pamphlet, so called, which Captain
Brown begun to write for publication in a small anti-
slavery paper, called " The Ramshorn." The manuscript
is now in the library of the Maryland Historical Society
at Baltimore. It was first printed in Sanborn's " Life
and Letters of John Brown." pp. 129–131.*]

I.

MESSRS. EDITORS.—Notwithstanding I may have committed a few mistakes in the course of a long life, like others
of my colored brethren, yet you will perceive at a glance
that I have always been remarkable for a seasonable discovery of
my errors and a quick perception of the true course. I propose
to give you a few illustrations in the following chapters.

For instance, when I was a boy I learned to read; but,
instead of giving my attention to sacred and profane history,
by which I might have become acquainted with the true character of God and man, learned the true course for individuals,
societies, and nations to pursue; stored my mind with an endless variety of rational and practical ideas; profited by the

experience of millions of others of all ages; fitted myself for the most important stations in life, and fortified my mind with the best and wisest resolutions, and noblest sentiments and motives—I have spent my whole life in devouring silly novels and other miserable trash, such as most newspapers of the day are filled with; thereby unfitting myself for the realities of life, and acquiring a taste for nonsense and low wit, so that I have no relish for sober truth, useful knowledge, or practical wisdom. By this means I have passed through life without profit to myself or others, a mere blank on which nothing worth perusing is written. But I can see in a twink where I missed it.

Another error into which I fell in early life was the notion that chewing and smoking tobacco would make a man of me, but little inferior to some of the whites. The money spent in this way would, with the interest of it, have enabled me to relieve a great many sufferers, supplied me with a well-selected, interesting library, and paid for a good farm for the support and comfort of my old age; whereas I have now neither books, clothing, the satisfaction of having benefited others, nor where to lay my hoary head. But I can see in a moment where I missed it.

Another of the few errors of my life is, that I have joined the Free Masons, Odd Fellows, Sons of Temperance, and a score of other social societies, instead of seeking the company of intelligent, wise, and good men, from whom I might have learned much that would have been interesting, instructive, and useful; and have in that way squandered a good deal of most precious time, and money enough, sometimes in a single year, which, if I had then put out the same at interest and kept it so, would have kept me always above board, given me character and influence among men, or enabled me to pursue some respectable calling, so that I might employ others to their benefit and improvement; but as it is I have always been poor, in debt, and now obliged to travel about in search of employment as a hostler, shoe-black, and fiddler. But I retain all my quickness of perception; I can readily see where I missed it.

II.

Another error of my riper years has been, that when any meeting of colored people has been called to consider any important matter of general interest, I have been so eager to display my spouting talents, and so tenacious of some trifling theory or other that I have adopted, that I have generally lost sight of the business on hand, consumed the time in disputing about things of no moment, and thereby defeated many important measures calculated to promote the general welfare; but I am happy to say that I can see in a minute where I missed it.

Another small error of my life (for I never committed great blunders) has been that I never would (for the sake of union in the furtherance of the most vital interests of our race), yield any minor points of difference. In this I have always had to act with but a few, or more frequently alone, and could accomplish nothing worth living for; but I have one comfort, I can see in a moment where I missed it.

Another little fault I have committed is, that if in anything another man has failed to come up to my standard, notwithstanding that he might possess some of the most valuable traits, and be most admirably adapted to fill some one important post, I would reject him entirely, injure his influence, oppose his measures, and even glory in his defeat. But I have the great satisfaction of being able to say, without fear of contradiction, that I can see very quick—that I can see where I missed it.

III.

Another small mistake which I have made is, that I could never bring myself to practice any present self-denial, although my theories have been excellent. For instance, I have bought expensive, gay clothing, nice canes, watches, safety guards, finger-rings, breast-pins, and many other things of a like nature, thinking I might by that means distinguish myself from the vulgar, as some of the better class of the whites do. I have always been of the foremost in getting up expensive parties, and running after fashionable amusements; having indulged my appetite freely whenever I had the means (and even with borrowed means), have patronized the dealers in nuts, candy, etc., freely, and have sometimes bought good suppers, and was always a regular customer at livery stables. By these, and many other means, I have been unable to help to benefit my suffering brethren, and am now but poorly able to keep my body and soul together, but do not think me thoughtless or dull of apprehension, for I can see at once where I missed it.

Another trifling error of my life has been, that I have always expected to secure the favor of the whites by tamely submitting to every species of indignity, contempt, and wrong, instead of nobly resisting their brutal aggressions from principle, and taking my place as a man, and assuming the responsibilities of a man, a citizen, a husband, a father, a brother, a neighbor, a friend—as God requires of every one (if his neighbor will allow him to do it); but I find I get for all my submission about the same reward that the Southern slavocrats render to the dough-faced statesmen of the North, for being bribed and troubled, and fooled and cheated, as the Whigs and Democrats love to be, and think themselves highly honored if allowed to lick up the spittle of a Southerner. I say, I get the same reward. But, I am uncommon quick-sighted. I can see in a minute where I missed it.

Another little blunder that I made is, that while I have always been a most zealous Abolitionist, I have commonly been at war with my friends about certain religious tenets. I was first a Presbyterian, but I could never think of acting with my Quaker friends, for they were the rankest heretics; and the Baptists would be in the water, and the Methodists denied the doctrine of election, etc. Of later years, since becoming enlightened by Garrison, Abby Kelly, and other really benevolent persons, I have been spending all my force on my friends who love the Sabbath, and felt that all was at stake on that point; just as it proved to be of late in France, in the abolition of slavery in their colonies. Now, I cannot doubt, Messrs. Editors, notwithstanding that I have been unsuccessful, that you will allow me full credit for my peculiar quick-sightedness. I can see in one second where I missed it.

JOHN BROWN'S REGULARS.[1]

*[Its contents are from " Life and Letters of John Brown,"
F. B. Sanborn, page 287, given here, as to spelling and
punctuation, in exact accordance with the original.]*

ARTICLES OF ENLISTMENT AND BY-LAWS OF THE
KANSAS REGULARS, MADE AND ESTABLISHED BY THE
COMMANDER, A.D. 1856, IN WHOSE HANDWRITING IT IS.

We whose names are found on these and the next following pages do hereby enlist ourselves in the Free State cause under John Brown as Commander: during the full period of time affixed to our names respectively and we severally pledge our word and sacred honor to said Commander; and to each other, that during the time for which we have enlisted we will faithfully and punctually perform our duty (in such capacity or place as may be assigned to us by a majority of all the votes of those associated with us : or of the companies to which we may belong as the case may be) as a regular volunteer force for the maintenance of the rights & liberties of the Free State Citizens of Kansas : and we further agree ; that as individuals we will conform to the *by Laws of this Organization* & that *we will insist* on their regular & punctual *enforcement* as a first & last duty : & in short that we will observe & Maintain a strict & thorough Military discipline at all times until our term of service expires.

Names, date of enlistment, and term of service on next Pages.

---

[1] This represents the free-State men who fought at Osawatomie and elsewhere in 1856.

Term of service omitted for want of room (principally for the War.)

2. Names and Date of Enlistment.

Aug. 22. Wm. Patridge (imprisoned), John Salathiel, S. Z. Brown, John Goodell, L. F. Parsons, N. B. Phelps, Wm. B. Harris.

Aug. 23. Jason Brown (son of commander; imprisoned).

Aug. 24. J. Benjamin (imprisoned).

Aug. 25. Cyrus Taton, R. Reynolds (imprisoned), Noah Frazee (1st Lieut.), Amos Alderman, August Bondie, Charles Kaiser (murdered Aug. 30), Freeman Austin (aged 57 years), Samuel Hereson, John W. Troy, Jas. Holmes (Capt.).

Aug. 26. Geo. Partridge (killed Aug. 30), Wm. A. Sears.

Aug. 27. S. H. Wright.

Aug. 29. B. Darrach (Surgeon), Saml. Farrar.

Sept. 8. Timothy Kelly, Jas. Andrews.

Sept. 9. W. H. Leman, Charles Oliver, D. H. Hurd.

Sept. 15. Wm. F. Haniel.

Sept. 16. Saml. Geer (Commissary).

3. By-Laws of the Free-State Regular Volunteers of Kansas Enlisted under John Brown.

Art. I. Those who agree to be governed by the following articles & whose names are appended will be known as the Kansas Regulars.

Art. II. Every officer connected with this organization (except the Commander already named) shall be elected by a majority of the members *if above a Captain;* and if a Captain; or under a Captain, by a majority of the company to which they belong.

Art. III. All vacancies shall be filled by vote of the majority of members or companies as the case may be, & all members shall be alike eligible to the highest office.

Art. IV. All trials for misconduct of Officers; or privates; shall be by a jury of Twelve; chosen by a majority of Company, or companies as the case may be. Each Company shall try its own members.

Art. V. All valuable property taken by honorable warfare from the enemy, shall be held as property of the whole company, or companies, as the case may be: equally, without distinction; to be used for the common benefit or be placed in the hands of responsible agents for sale: the proceeds to be divided as nearly equally amongst the company: *or companies* capturing it as may be: except that no person shall be entitled to any dividend from property taken before he entered the service; and any person guilty of desertion, or convicted of any gross violation of his obligations to those with whom he should act, *whether officer or private:* shall forfeit his interest in all dividends made after such misconduct has occurred.

Art. VI. All property captured shall be delivered to the receiver of the force, or company as the case may be; whose duty it shall be to make a full inventory of the same (assisted by such person, or *persons* as may be chosen for that purpose), a copy of which shall be made into the Books of this Organization; & held subject to examination by any member, on all suitable occasions.

Art. VII. The receiver shall give his receipts in a Book for that purpose for all moneys & other property of the regulars placed in his hands; keep an inventory of the same & make copy as provided in Article VI.

Art. VIII. Captured articles when used for the benefit of the members: shall be receipted for by the Commissary, the same as moneys placed in his hands. The receiver to hold said receipts.

Art. IX. A disorderly retreat shall not be suffered at any time & every Officer & private is by this article fully empowered to prevent the same by force if need be, & any attempt at leaving the ground during a fight is hereby declared disorderly unless the consent or direction of the officer then in command have authorized the same.

Art. X. A disorderly attact or charge; shall not be suffered at any time.

Art. XI. When in camp a thorough watch both regular and Piquet shall be maintained both by day, & by Night: and visitors shall not be suffered to pass or repass without leave from the Captain of the guard and under common or ordinary circumstances it is expected that the Officers will cheerfully share this service with the private for example sake.

Art. XII. Keeping up Fires or lights after dark; or firing of Guns, Pistols or Caps shall not be allowed, except Fires and lights when unavoidable.

Art. XIII. When in Camp neither Officers shall be allowed to leave without consent of the Officer then in command.

Art. XIV. All uncivil ungentlemanly profane, vulgar talk or conversation shall be discountenanced.

Art. XV. All acts of petty theft needless waste of the property of the members or of Citizens is hereby declared disorderly: together with all uncivil, or unkind treatment of Citizens or of prisoners.

Art. XVI. In all cases of capturing property, a sufficient number of men shall be detailed to take charge of the same; all others shall keep in their position.

Art. XVII. It shall at all times be the duty of the quarter Master to select ground for encampment subject however to the approbation of the commanding officer.

Art. XVIII. The Commissary shall give his receips in a Book for that purpose for all money provisions, and stores put into his hands.

Art XIX. The Officers of the companies shall see that the arms of the same *are in constant good order* and a neglect of this duty shall be deemed disorderly.

Art. XX. No *person* after having first surrendered himself a prisoner shall be *put to death,* or *subjected to corporal punishment*, without *first* having had the benefit of an impartial trial.

Art. XXI. A Waggon Master and an Assistant shall be chosen for each company whose duty it shall be to take a general care and oversight of the teams, waggons, harness, and all the other articles or property pertaining thereto: and who shall both be exempt from serving on guard.

Art. XXII. The ordinary use or introduction into the camp of any intoxicating liquor, *as a beverage:* is hereby declared disorderly.

Art. XXIII. A Majority of Two Thirds of *all the members* may at any time alter or amend the foregoing articles.

4. LIST OF VOLUNTEERS EITHER ENGAGED OR GUARDING HORSES DURING THE FIGHT OF BLACK JACK OR PALMYRA, JUNE 2, 1856.

1. Saml. T. Shore (Captain). 2. Silas Moore. 3. David Hendricks (Horse Guard). 4. Hiram McAllister. 5. Mr. Parmely (wounded). 6. Silvester Harris. 7. O. A. Carpenter (wounded). 8. Augustus Shore. 9. Mr. Townsley (Potawatomie). 10. Wm. B. Hayden. 11. John Mewhinney. 12. Montgomery Shore. 13. Elkana Timmons. 14. T. Weiner. 15. August Bondy. 16. Hugh Mewhinney. 17. Charles Kaiser. 18. Elizur Hill. 19. William David. 20. B. L. Cochran. 21. Henry Thompson (wounded). 22. Elias Basinger. 23. Owen Brown. 24. Fredk. Brown, horse guard ; (murdered Aug. 30). 25. Salmon Brown. 26. Oliver Brown. 27. This blank may be filled by Capt. Shore as he may have the name.

JOHN BROWN.

5. LIST OF NAMES OF THE WOUNDED IN THE BATTLE OF BLACK JACK (OR PALMYRA) AND ALSO OF THE EIGHT WHO HELD OUT TO RECEIVE THE SURRENDER OF CAPT. PATE AND TWENTY-TWO MEN ON THAT OCCASION, JUNE 2, 1856.

1. Mr. Parmely wounded in Nose & Arm, obliged to leave. 2. Henry Thompson, dangerously wounded but fought for nearly one Hour afterward. 3. O. A. Carpenter Badly wounded and obliged to leave. 4. Charles Kaiser, murdered Aug. 30. 5. Elizur Hill. 6. Wm. David. 7. Hugh Mewhinney (17 yrs old). 8. B. L. Cochran. 9. Owen Brown. 10. Salmon Brown. Seriously wounded (*soon after by accident*). 11. Oliver Brown—17 years old.

In the battle of Osawatomie Capt. (or Dr.) Updegraph ; and

Two others whose names I have lost were severely (*one of them shockingly*) wounded before the fight began Aug. 30, 1856.

JOHN BROWN.

JOHN BROWN AND THE FIRST ATTACK IN THE "WAKARUSA WAR," 1855.

OSAWATOMIE, K. T., 16th Dec., 1855.
Sabbath evening.

DEAR WIFE AND CHILDREN, EVERY ONE—I improve the first mail since my return from the camp of volunteers who lately turned out for the defense of the town of Lawrence in this Territory; and, notwithstanding, I suppose you have learned the result before this (possibly), will give a brief account of the invasion in my own way. About three or four weeks ago news came that a free-State man by the name of Dow had been murdered by a pro-slavery man by the name of Coleman, who had gone and given himself up for trial to pro-slavery Governor Shannon. This was soon followed by further news that a free-State man, who was the only reliable witness against the murderer, had been seized by a Missourian, appointed sheriff by the bogus Legislature of Kansas, upon false pretexts, examined, and held to bail under such heavy bonds to answer these false charges as he could not give; and that, while on his way to jail in charge of the bogus sheriff, he was rescued by some men belonging to a company near Lawrence, and that in consequence of the rescue Governor Shannon had ordered out all the pro-slavery force he could muster in the Territory and called on Missouri for further help; that about two thousand had collected, demanding a surrender of the rescued witness and of the rescuers; the destruction of several buildings and printing-presses, and the giving up of the Sharpe's rifles by the free-State men; threatening to destroy the town with cannon with which they were provided, etc.; and that about an equal number of free-State men had turned out to resist them, and that a battle was hourly expected or sup-

posed to have been already fought. These reports appeared
to be well authenticated ; but we could get no further account
of matters, and left this for the place where the boys are settled
at evening, intending to go to Lawrence the next day to learn
the fact. John was, however, started on horseback ; but
before he had gone many rods word came that our help was
wanted immediately. On getting this last news it was at once
agreed to break up at John's Camp and take Wealthy and
Johnny to Jason's Camp (some two miles off), and that all the
men but Henry, Jason, and Oliver, should at once set off to
Lawrence under arms ; those three being wholly unfit for duty.
We set about providing a little cornbread and meat, blankets,
cooking utensils, running bullets, loading all our guns, pistols,
etc. The five set off in the afternoon and after a short rest in
the night (which was quite dark) continued our march until
after daylight next morning, when we got our breakfast, started
again, and reached Lawrence in the forenoon, all of us more or
less lamed by our tramp. On reaching the place we found that
negotiations had commenced between Governor Shannon
(having a force of some fifteen or sixteen hundred men) and
the principal leaders of the free-State men ; they having a
force of some five hundred men at the time. These were busy
night and day fortifying the town with embankments and circular earthworks up to the time of the treaty with the Governor, as an attack was constantly expected, notwithstanding the
negotiations then pending. This state of things continued
from Friday until Sunday evening. On the evening we left, a
company of the invaders of from fifteen to twenty-five attacked
some three or four free-State men, mostly unarmed, killing a
Mr. Barber, from Ohio, wholly unarmed. His body was afterwards brought in, and it lay for some days in the room afterwards occupied by a part of the company to which he belonged,
it being organized after we reached Lawrence. The building
was a large, unfinished stone hotel, in which a great part of
the volunteers were quartered, and who witnessed the scene of
bringing in the wife and the friends of the murdered man. I
will only say of this scene that it was heart-rendering and cal-

culated to exasperate the men exceedingly, and one of the sure results of civil war. After frequently calling on the leaders of the free-State men to come and have an interview with him, by Governor Shannon, and after as often getting for an answer that if he had any business to transact with any one in Lawrence to come and attend to it, he signified his wish to come into the town, and an escort was sent to the invaders' camp to conduct him in. When there the leading free-State men, finding out his weakness, frailty, and consciousness of the awkward circumstances into which he had really got himself, took advantage of his cowardice and folly, and by means of that and the free use of whiskey and some trickery succeeded in getting a written arrangement with him much to their own liking. He stipulated with them to order the pro-slavery men of Kansas home, and to proclaim to the Missouri invaders that they must quit the Territory without delay and also give up General Pomeroy, a prisoner in their camp, which was all done; he also recognized the volunteers as the militia of Kansas, and empowering their officers to call them out whenever in their discretion the safety of Lawrence or other portions of the settlements required.

[Balance of letter was lost.]

NOTES.

From this singularly modest letter, but little idea can be gathered of the strange, almost solemn excitement created by the appearance of John Brown and his sons in that winter-chilled, beleaguered frontier town. Lawrence was the center of free-State sentiment and operations. The " Wakarusa War," of December, 1855, was the first attack in force by the Missourians in their vain attempt to enforce the slave code that they had framed. An eye witness in Lawrence, who has for thirty-seven years been a constant and even malicious critic of John Brown, his acts and memory, wrote in 1880 of the arrival in the Northern town of that band of " plain-living, high-thinking " farmers and fighters :

" It was near sunset, I should think, about the 3d of December (that was the date), when, in the distance, towards the South, a strange-looking object was seen approaching Lawrence. . . . ‘As it neared, it proved to be the skeleton of a horse covered with purely stuffed skin, wearily dragging a rather large one-horse lumber wagon. I think there were seven men standing in the box, which was made of wide, undressed, and weather-stained boards." Each man supported himself by a pole, "several feet in height, surmounted by a bayonet." These poles were "held in place by leather loops nailed to the side." Each man had a "Voltaic repeater strapped to his person, as also a short sword; at the same time supporting a musket at the position of order. "A formidable arsenal, well manned"; writes the pamphleteer, adding, with a sneer—"All but the horse."

The writer of the foregoing is Dr. George W. Brown, of Rockford, Illinois, who at the time of the "Wakarusa War," and until about 1858, was editor of the *Herald of Freedom.* He has of late years left the chief labor of assailing the memory of Capt. John Brown to others who find the task one that seems to suit them admirably,—Eli Thayer, of Massachusetts, and Charles Robinson, of Kansas. A writer of later days, whose work, however, shows the influence of Governor Robinson, Professor Spring of the Kansas State University, in his readable though by no means fair-minded work "Kansas," one of the "Commonwealth" series of State history, says of the "Shannon Agreement," which John Brown condemned, that:

"A single voice was raised in solemn and public protest against the peace. After the treaty and its stipulations became known, after speeches favorable to them were made, an unknown man—tall, slender, angular—his face clean shaved, somber, strongly lined, of Puritan tone and configuration; his blue gray eyes honest, inexorable, strange; unworldly intensities enveloping him like an atmosphere, mounted on a dry-goods box, and began to denounce the treaty as a foolish makeshift. . . . Since that day the name of this unknown man, plucked down with his speech mostly unspoken, has filled the post-horns of the world—Old John Brown."

SLAVES: AN ACT TO PUNISH OFFENSES AGAINST SLAVE PROPERTY.

Sec. 3. If any free person shall, by speaking, writing, or printing, advise, persuade, or induce any slaves to rebel, conspire against, or murder any citizen of this Territory, or shall bring into print, write, publish, or circulate, or cause to be brought into, printed, written, published, or circulated, or shall knowingly aid or assist in the bringing into, printing, writing, publishing, or circulating, in this Territory any book, pamphlet, paper, magazine, or circular for the purpose of exciting insurrection, rebellion, revolt, or conspiracy on the part of the slaves, free negroes, or mulattos against the citizens of the Territory or any part of them, such person shall be guilty of felony and suffer death.

Sec. 4. If any person shall entice, decoy, or carry away out of this Territory any slave belonging to another, with intent to deprive the owner thereof of the services of such slave, or with intent to effect or procure the freedom of such slave, he shall be adjudged guilty of grand larceny, and, on conviction thereof, shall suffer death, or be imprisoned at hard labor for not less than ten years.

Sec. 5. If any person shall aid or assist in enticing, decoying, persuading, or carrying away, or sending out of this Territory any slave, belonging to another, with intent to effect or procure the freedom of such slave, he shall be adjudged guilty of grand larceny, and, on conviction thereof, he shall suffer death, or be imprisoned at hard labor for not less than ten years.

Sec. 5. If any person shall aid or assist in enticing, decoying, persuading, or carrying away, or sending out of this Territory any slave belonging to another, with intent to effect or procure the freedom of such slave, or with intent to deprive the owner thereof of the services of such slave, he shall be adjudged guilty of grand larceny, and on conviction thereof, he shall suffer death, or be imprisoned at hard labor for not less than ten years.

Sec. 6. If any person shall entice, decoy, or carry away out of any State or other Territory of the United States any slave belonging to another, with intent to procure or effect the freedom of such slave, or to deprive the owners thereof of the services of such slave, and shall bring such slave into this Territory, he shall be adjudged guilty of grand larceny, in the same manner as if such slave had been enticed, decoyed, or carried away out of this Territory; and in such case the larceny may be charged to have been committed in any county of this Territory into or through which such slave shall have been brought by such person; and, on conviction thereof, the person offending shall suffer death, or be imprisoned at hard labor for not less than ten years.

Sec. 9. If any person print, write, introduce into, publish, or circulate, or cause to be brought into, printed, written, published, or circulated, or shall knowingly aid or assist in bringing into, printing, publishing, or circulating within this Territory any book, paper, pamphlet, magazine, handbill, or circular containing any statements, arguments, opinions, sentiment, doctrine, advice, or innuendo calculated to produce a disorderly, dangerous, or rebellious disaffection among the slaves of this Territory, or to induce such slaves to escape from the service of their masters, or resist their authority, he shall be guilty of felony, and be punished by imprisonment at hard labor for a term not less than five years.

Sec. 12. If any free person, by speaking or by writing, assert or maintain that persons have not the right to hold slaves in this Territory, or shall introduce into this Territory, print, publish, write, circulate, or cause to be printed, published, written, circulated, or introduced into this Territory any book, paper, magazine, pamphlet, or circular containing any denial of the right of persons to hold slaves in this Territory, such person shall be deemed guilty of felony, and punished by imprisonment at hard labor for a term not less than five years.

Sec. 13. No person who is conscientiously opposed to holding slaves, or who does not admit the right to hold slaves in this Territory, shall sit as a juror on the trial of any prosecution for any violation of any of the sections of this act.

JOHN BROWN'S SONS IN KANSAS.

In 1854, the four eldest sons of John Brown, named John, Jr., Jason, Owen, and Frederick (all children by a first wife), then living in Ohio, determined to remove to Kansas. John, Jr., sold his place, a very desirable little property near Vernon, in Trumbull County. Jason Brown had a very valuable collection of grape-vines, and also of choice fruit-trees, which he took up and shipped in boxes at a heavy cost. The other two sons held no landed property, but both were possessed of some valuable stock (as were also the two first named) derived from that of their father, which had been often noticed by liberal premiums, both in the State of New York and also of Ohio. The two first named, John and Jason, both had families. Owen had none. Frederick was engaged to be married, and was to return for his wife.

"In consequence of an extreme dearth in 1854 the crops in northern Ohio were almost an entire failure; and it was decided by the four brothers that the two youngest should take the teams and entire stock, cattle, and horses, and move them to southwestern Illinois to winter, and to have them on early in the spring, 1855. This was done at a very considerable expense, and with some loss of stock to John, Jr., some of his best stock having been stolen on the way. The wintering of the animals was attended with great expense, and with no little suffering to the two youngest brothers,—one of them, Owen, being to some extent a cripple from childhood by an injury of the right arm; and Frederick, though a very stout man, was subject to periodical sickness for many years, attended with insanity. It has been stated that he was idiotic; nothing could be more false. He had subjected himself to a most dreadful surgical operation but a short time before starting for Kansas, which had well-nigh cost him his life, and was but just through with his confinement when he started on his journey pale and weak. They were obliged to husk corn all winter, out of doors, in order to obtain fodder for their animals. Salmon Brown, a very strong minor son of the family, eighteen years old, was sent forward early in 1855, to assist the two last named, and all three arrived in Kansas early in the spring."

JOHN BROWN'S ACCOUNT OF THE BATTLE OF OSAWATOMIE, KANSAS, AUGUST, 1856.

"Early on the morning of the 30th of August, the enemy's scout approached to within a mile and a half of the western boundary of the town of Osawatomie. At this place my son Frederick, who was not attached to my force, had lodged with some four other young men from Lawrence, and a young man named Garrison from Middle Creek.

"The scouts, led by a pro-slavery preacher, named White, shot my son dead in the road, whilst he, as I have since ascertained, supposed them to be friendly. At the same time they butchered Mr. Garrison, and badly mangled one of the young men from Lawrence who came with my son, leaving him for dead. This was not far from sunrise. I had stopped during the night about two and a half miles from them, and nearly one mile from Osawatomie. I had no organized force, but only some twelve or fifteen new recruits, who were ordered to leave their preparations for breakfast, and follow me into the town as soon as this news was brought to me.

"As I had no means of learning correctly the force of the enemy, I placed twelve of the recruits in a log-house, hoping that we might be able to defend the town. I then gathered some fifteen more men together, whom we armed with guns, and we started in the direction of the enemy. After going a few rods, we could see them approaching the town in line of battle, about half a mile off, upon a hill west of the village. I then gave up all idea of doing more than to annoy, from the timber near the town, into which we were all retreated, and which was filled with a thick growth of underbrush, but had no time to recall the twelve men in the log-house, and so lost their assistance in the fight.

"At the point above named I met with Captain Cline, a very active young man, who had with him some twelve or fifteen mounted men, and persuaded him to go with us into the timber on the southern shore of the Osage, or Marais-des Cygnes, a little to the northwest of the village.   Here the men, numbering not more than thirty in all, were directed to scatter and secrete themselves as well as they could, and await the approach of the enemy.   This was done in full view of them, who must have seen the whole movement, and had to be done in the utmost haste.   I believe Captain Cline and some of his men were not even dismounted in the fight, but cannot assert positively. When the left wing of the enemy had approached to within common rifle shot, we commenced firing, and very soon threw the northern branch of the enemy's line into disorder.   This continued some fifteen or twenty minutes, which gave us an uncommon opportunity to annoy them.   Captain Cline and his men soon got out of ammunition, and retired across the river.

" After the enemy rallied, we kept up our fire, until, by the leaving of one and another, we had but six or seven left.   We then retired across the river.

" We had one man killed—a Mr. Powers, from Captain Cline's company—in the fight.   One of my men, a Mr. Partridge, was shot in crossing the river.   Two or three of the party who took part in the fight are yet missing, and may be lost or taken prisoners.   Two were wounded, viz., Dr. Updegraff and a Mr. Collis.

" I cannot speak in too high terms of them, and of many others I have not now time to mention.

" One of my best men, together with myself, was struck with a partially spent ball from the enemy in the commencement of the fight, but we were only bruised.   The loss I refer to is one of the missing men.   The loss of the enemy, as we learn by the different statements of our own as well as their people, was some thirty-one or two killed, and from forty to fifty wounded. After burning the town to ashes, and killing a Mr. Williams they had taken, whom neither party claimed, they took a hasty leave, carrying their dead and wounded with them.   They did not attempt to cross the river, nor to search for us, and have not since returned to look over their work.

" I give this in great haste, in the midst of constant interruptions. My second son was with me in the fight, and escaped unharmed. This I mention for the benefit of his friends.

" Old Preacher White, I hear, boasts of having killed my son. Of course, he is a lion. " JOHN BROWN.

"LAWRENCE, KANSAS, September 7th, 1856."

JOHN BROWN BEFORE THE MASSACHUSETTS LEGISLATURE IN 1857.

After an introduction, given by Mr. Frank B. Sanborn, he read the following statement " in a clear, ringing tone":

" I saw, while in Missouri, in the fall of 1855, large numbers of men going to Kansas to vote, and also returning, after they had so done, as they said.

" Later in the year, I, with four of my sons, was called out, and traveled, mostly on foot and during the night we helped to defend Lawrence, a distance of thirty-five miles, where we were detained, with some five hundred others, or thereabouts, from five to ten days—say an average of ten days—at a cost of not less than a dollar and a half per day as wages ; to say nothing of the actual loss and suffering occasioned to many of them by leaving their families sick, their crops not secured, their houses unprepared for winter, and many without houses at all. This was the case with myself and sons, who could not get houses built after returning. Wages alone would amount to seven thousand five hundred dollars ; loss and suffering cannot be estimated.

" I saw, at that time, the body of the murdered barber, and was present to witness his wife and other friends brought to see him with his clothes on, just as he was when killed.

" I, with six sons and a son-in-law, was called out, and traveled most of the way on foot, to try and save Lawrence, May 20th and 21st, and much of the way in the night. From that date, neither I, nor my sons, nor my son-in-law could do any work about our homes, but lost our whole time until we

left, in October ; except one of my sons, who had a few weeks
to devote to the care of his own and his brother's family, who
were then without a home.

"On or about the 30th of May, hundreds of men, like ourselves, lost their whole time, were imprisoned without other
crime than opposition to bogus legislation, and most barbarously treated for a time, one being held about one month, and
the other about four months. Both had their families on the
ground. After this, both of them had their houses burned,
and all their goods consumed by the Missourians. In this
burning all the eight suffered. One had his oxen stolen, in
addition."

Here Brown, laying aside his paper, said that he had now
at his hotel, and would exhibit to the committee, if they so
desired, the chains which one of his sons had worn, when he
was driven beneath the burning sun, by Federal troops, to a
distant prison, on a charge of treason. The cruelties he there
endured, added to the anxieties and sufferings incident to his
position, had rendered him, the old man said, as his eye
flashed and his voice grew sterner, " a maniac—yes, a maniac."

He paused a few seconds, wiped a tear from his eye, and
continued his narration :—

"At Black Jack the invading Missourians wounded three
free-state men, one of whom was my son-in-law ; and, a few
days afterwards, one of my sons was so wounded that he will
be a cripple for life.

"In August I was present, and saw the mangled and disfigured body of the murdered Hoyt, of Deerfield, Massachusetts, brought into our camp. I knew him well.

"I saw the ruins of many free-State men's houses in different parts of the Territory, together with grain in the stack,
burning, and wasted in other ways, to the amount, at least of
fifty thousand dollars.

"I saw several other free-state men, besides those I have
named, during the summer, who were badly wounded by the
invaders of the Territory.

"I know that for much of the time during the summer, the

travel over portions of the Territory was entirely cut off, and that none but bodies of armed men dared to move at all.

" I know that for a considerable time the mails on different routes were entirely stopped ; and, notwithstanding there were abundant troops in the Territory to escort the mails, I know that such escorts were not furnished as they ought to have been.

" I saw while it was standing, and afterwards saw the ruins of a most valuable house, the property of a highly civilized, intelligent, and exemplary Christian Indian, which was burned to the ground by the ruffians, because its owner was suspected of favoring the free-state men.   He is known as Ottawa Jones, or John T. Jones.

" In September last I visited a little free-state town called Staunton, on the north side of the Osage (or Marais-des-Cygnes, as it is sometimes called), from which every inhabitant had fled for fear of their lives, even after having built a strong log-house, or wooden fort, at a heavy expense, for their protection. Many of them had left their effects liable to be destroyed or carried off, not being able to remove them.   This was to me a most gloomy scene, and like a visit to a sepulcher.

" Deserted houses and corn fields were to be found in almost every direction south of the Kansas river.

" I have not yet told all I saw in Kansas.

" I once saw three mangled bodies, two of which were dead, and one alive, but with twenty bullet and buck-shot holes in him, after the two murdered men had lain on the ground, to be worked at by flies, for some eighteen hours. One of these young men was my own son."

The stern old man faltered.   He struggled long to suppress all exhibition of his feelings ; and then, but in a subdued tone, continued :

" I saw Mr. Parker, whom I well knew, all bruised about the head, and with his throat partly cut, after he had been dragged, sick, from the house of Ottawa Jones, and thrown over the bank of the Ottawa Creek for dead.

" About the 1st of September, I and five sick and wounded

sons, and a son-in-law, were obliged to lie on the ground, without shelter, for a considerable time, and at times almost in a state of starving, and dependent on the charity of the Christian Indian I have before named and his wife.

"I saw Dr. Graham, of Prairie City, who was a prisoner with the ruffians on the 2d of June, and was present when they wounded him in an attempt to kill him, as he was trying to save himself from being murdered by them during the fight at Black Jack.

" I know that numerous other persons, whose names I cannot now remember, suffered like hardships and exposures to those I have mentioned.

" I know well that on or about the 14th of September, 1856, a large force of Missourians and other ruffians, said by Governor Geary to be twenty-seven hundred in number, invaded the Territory, burned Franklin, and, while the smoke of that place was going up behind them, they, on the same day, made their appearance in full view of and within a mile of Lawrence; and I know of no reason why they did not attack that place, except that about one hundred free-state men volunteered to go out, and did go out on the open plain before that town, and give the offer of a fight, which, after getting scattered shots from our men they declined, and retreated back towards Franklin. I saw that whole thing. The Government troops at this time were at Lecompton, a distance of twelve miles only from Lawrence, with Governor Geary; and yet, notwithstanding runners had been dispatched to advise him in good time of the approach and setting out of the enemy (who had to march some forty miles to reach Lawrence), he did not, on that memorable occasion, get a single soldier on the ground until after the enemy had retreated to Franklin, and been gone for more than five hours. This is the way he saved Lawrence. And it is just the kind of protection the free-state men have received from the Administration from the first."

He concluded his remarks by denouncing the traitors to freedom.

The Chairman—"Captain Brown, I wish to ask you regarding

Buford's men. Did you ever mingle with them? And, if so, what did you see or hear?"

Captain Brown replied that he saw a great deal of them at first; that they spoke without hesitation before him, because he employed himself as surveyor; and as nearly all the surveyors were pro-slavery men, they probably thought he was "sound on the goose." They told him all their plans; what they intended to do; how they were determined to drive off the free-state men, and possess themselves of the Territory, and make it a slave State at all hazards—cost what it might. They said that the Yankees could not be whipped, coaxed, nor driven into a fight, and that one pro-slavery man could whip a dozen Abolitionists. They said that Kansas must be a slave State to save Missouri from Abolition; that both must stand or fall together. They did not hesitate to threaten that they would burn, kill, scalp, and drive out the entire free-state population of that Territory, if it were necessary to do so to accomplish their object.

The Chairman then asked who commanded the free-state men at Lawrence.

His answer was characteristic. He explained how bravely the free-state men had acted, and gave every one credit but himself. When again asked who commanded them, he said— No one; that he was asked to take the command, but refused, and only acted as their adviser!

In conclusion, he said, "We want good men, industrious men, men who respect themselves, who act only from the dictates of conscience—men who fear God too much to fear anything human."

The Chairman—"What is your opinion as to the probability of a renewal of the hostilities in Kansas—of another invasion? And what do you think would be the effect on the free-state men of an appropriation by Massachusetts?"

Captain Brown—"Whenever we heard, out in Kansas, what the North was doing for us, we were encouraged and strengthened to struggle on. As to the probability of another invasion, I do not know. We ought to be prepared for the worst.

Things do not look one iota more encouraging now than they did last year at this time.

AN IDEA OF THINGS IN KANSAS.

[*John Brown spoke in many New England meetings on Kansas affairs early in 1857. Mr. Sanborn gives the following as the "Notes" prepared for such addresses, pp. 243–46.*]

I propose, in order to make this meeting as useful and interesting as I can, to try and give a correct idea of the conditions of things in Kansas, as they were while I was there, and as I suppose they still are, so far as the great question at issue is concerned. And here let me remark that in Kansas the question is never raised of a man: Is he a Democrat? Is he a Republican? The questions there raised are, Is he a free-state man? or, Is he a pro-slavery man?

I saw while in Missouri, in the fall of 1855, large numbers on their way to Kansas to vote, and also returning after they had so done, as they said. I, together with four of my sons, was called out to help defend Lawrence in the fall of 1855, and traveled most of the way on foot, and during a dark night, a distance of thirty-five miles, where we were detained with some five hundred others, or thereabout, from five to fifteen days—say an average of ten days—at a cost of each per day of $1.50 as wages, to say nothing of the actual loss and suffering it occasioned; many of them leaving their families at home sick, their crops not secured, their houses unprepared for winter, and many of them without houses at all. This was the case with myself and all my sons, who were unable to get any house built after our return. The loss in that case, as wages alone, would amount to $7,500. Loss and suffering in consequence cannot be estimated. I saw at that time the body of the murdered barber, and was present when his wife and other friends were brought in to see him as he lay in the clothes he had on when killed,—no pleasant sight. I went in the spring of last year with some of my sons among the Buford men, in the character of a surveyor, to see and hear from them their business into the Territory; this took us from our work. I and numerous others, in the spring of last year, traveled some ten miles or over on foot to meet and advise as to what should be done to meet the gathering storm; this occasioned much loss of time. I also, with many others, about the same time traveled on foot a similar distance to attend a meeting of Judge Cato's court, to find out what kind of laws he intended to enforce; this occasioned further loss of time. I with six sons and a son-in-law was again called out to defend Lawrence, May 20th and 21st, and traveled most of the way on foot and during the night, being thirty-five miles. From that date none of us could do any work about our homes, but lost our whole time until we left, in October last, excepting one of my sons, who had a few weeks to devote to the care of his own and his mother's family, who had been burned out of their houses while the two men were prisoners.

From about the 20th of May of last year hundreds of men like ourselves lost their whole time, and entirely failed of securing any kind of crop whatever. I believe it safe to say that five hundred free-state men lost each one hundred and twenty days at $1.50 per day, which would be, to say nothing of attendant losses, $90,000. I saw the ruins of many free-state men's houses at different places in the Territory, together with stacks of grain wasted and burning, to the amount of, say $50,000; making in loss of time and destruction of property more than $150,000. On or about the 30th of May last, two of my sons, with several others, were imprisoned without other crime than opposition to bogus enactments, and most barbarously treated for a time,—one being held about a month, the other about four months. Both had their families in Kansas, and destitute of homes, being burned out after they were imprisoned. In this burning all the eight were sufferers, as we had all our effects at the two houses. One of my sons had his oxen taken from him at this time, and never recovered them. Here is the chain with which one of them was confined, after the cruelty, sufferings, and anxiety he underwent had rendered him a maniac—yes, a maniac.

On the 2d of June last, my son-in-law was terribly wounded (supposed to be mortally) and may prove a cripple for life. In August last I was present and saw the mangled and shockingly disfigured body of the murdered Hoyt, of Deerfield, Mass., brought into our camp. I knew him well. I saw several other free state men who were either killed or wounded, whose names I cannot now remember. I saw Dr. Graham, who was a prisoner with the ruffians on the 2d of June last, and was present when they wounded him, in an attempt to kill him, as he was trying to save himself from being murdered by them during the fight at Black Jack. I know that for much of the time during the last summer the travel over a portion of the Territory was entirely cut off, and that none but bodies of armed men dared to move at all. I know that for a considerable time the mails on different routes were entirely stopped, and that notwithstanding there were abundant United States troops at hand to escort the mails, such escorts were not furnished as they might or ought to have been. I saw, while it was standing, and afterwards saw the ruins of, a most valuable house full of good articles and stores, which had been burned by the ruffians for a highly civilized, intelligent, and most exemplary Christian Indian, for being suspected of favoring free-state men. He is known as Ottawa Jones, or John S. Jones. In September last I visited a beautiful little free state town called Stanton, on the north side of the Osage, or Marais des Cynges River, as it is called, from which every inhabitant had fled (being in fear of their lives), after having build them, at a heavy expense, a strong blockhouse or wooden fort, for their protection. Many of them had left their effects, liable to be destroyed or carried off, not being able to remove them.

This was a most gloomy scene, and like a visit to a vast sepulcher.

During last summer and fall deserted houses and corn fields were to be met with in almost every direction south of the Kansas river. I saw the burning of Osawatomie by a body of some four hundred ruffians, and of Franklin afterward, by some twenty-seven hundred men,—the first-named on August 30th,

the last-named, September 14th or 15th. Governor Geary had
been for some time in the Territory, and might have saved
Franklin with perfect ease. It would not have cost the
United States one dollar to have saved Franklin. I, with five
sick and wounded sons and son-in-law, was obliged for some
time to lie on the ground, without shelter. Our boots and
clothes worn out, and we were destitute of money, and at times
almost in a state of starvation, and dependent on the charities
of the Christian Indian and his wife, whom I before named. I
saw in September last a Mr. Parker, whom I well knew,
with his head all bruised over and his throat partly cut, having
before been dragged, while sick, out of the house of Ottawa
Jones, the Indian, when it was burned and left for dead over
the bank of the Ottawa Creek. I saw three mangled bodies
of three young men, two of which were dead and had lain on
the open ground for about eighteen hours for the flies to work
at, the other living with twenty buckshot and bullet-holes in
him. One of those two dead was my own son.

OLD JOHN BROWN'S FAREWELL.

TO THE PLYMOUTH ROCKS, BUNKER HILL MONUMENTS,
CHARTER OAKS, AND UNCLE TOM'S CABINS.

He has left for Kansas; has been trying since he came out
of the Territory to secure an outfit, or, in other words, the
means of arming and thoroughly equipping his regular minute-
men, who are mixed up with the people of Kansas. And he
leaves the States with a feeling of deepest sadness, that after
exhausting his own small means, and with his family and his
brave men suffering hunger, cold, nakedness, and some of them
sickness, wounds, imprisonment in irons, with extreme cruel
treatment, and others death; that, lying on the ground for
months in the most sickly, unwholsome, and uncomfortable
places, some of the time with sick and wounded, destitute of
any shelter, hunted like wolves, and sustained in part by

Indians; that after all this, in order to sustain a cause which every citizen of this "glorious Republic" is under equal moral obligation to do, and for the neglect of which he will be held accountable by God,—a cause in which every man, woman, and child of the entire human family has a deep and awful interest,—that when no wages are asked or expected, he cannot secure, amid all the wealth, luxury, and extravagance of this "heaven-exalted" people, even the necessary supplies of the common soldier. "How are the mighty fallen!"

I am destitute of horses, baggage-wagons, tents, harness, saddles, bridles, holsters, spurs, and belts; camp equipage, such as cooking and eating utensils, blankets, knapsacks, intrenching-tools, axes, shovels, spades, mattocks, crowbars; have not a supply of ammunition; have not money sufficient to pay freight and traveling expenses; and left my family poorly supplied with common necessaries.

BOSTON, April, 1857.

No. I.

DUTY OF THE SOLDIER.[1]

(Presented with respectful and kind feelings to the officers and soldiers of the United States army in Kansas.)

In the ancient Republics every man capable of bearing arms was, up to a certain period of his life, bound in duty to the public to fill his place in the ranks of the soldiery to secure his country against invasion or insult. The mode of warfare in remote times differed considerably from that adopted in the present day—man fought chiefly with those weapons which brought him into hand-to-hand collision with his enemy, hence

---

[1] This paper was first written in Kansas or Iowa in the fall of 1856. As finally printed it was probably revised by John Henri Kagi. I first saw it in November, 1857.

his military instruction was rather in the management of arms than the application of tactics, and the chiefs studied stratagem rather than strategy. When the war or expedition upon which he had been engaged was terminated, he returned to his civic occupations and his home, till some new exigency called him again into military service. The word *soldier* in ancient Republics was synonymous with *freeman*—for in assuming his armor the man did not engage to confine his mind in a strait-jacket. Indeed there are instances in ancient history in which the soldiery in camp was consulted on public affairs, and gave its vote on the great question of Right against Wrong—and in some cases the soldier was the first part of a nation to proclaim the supremacy of Right, Nevertheless in all military duties, those same intelligent soldiers desirous of conquering the foreign enemy showed, when in his presence, implicit obedience to their military chiefs.

The soldiery of the princes of antiquity was very different from the Republican warriors. The tyrants were necessitated to keep an armed force in constant readiness to uphold their authority at home as well as abroad, and they did exact that the myrmidons in their pay should unhesitatingly execute *all* the commands of their ministers with the same obedience with which the Republican soldiery attended to those orders only which were purely military. As the era of despotism extended and the limits of Liberty became proportionately circumscribed, the habit of obeying *all* commands, civil and military, became more usual among the soldiery.

Time rolled on till despotism, aided by priestcraft, corruption, and party rapacity, supplanted the Republics. The invention of gunpowder, though it overthrew the feudal system of the Barons, operated on the other hand against the People, for the increased precision and promptitude required in modern military maneuvers, necessitated a lengthened training for the soldiery, which served as a pretense for wicked rulers to inculcate in the minds of the soldiers the idea that they were *living machines*, Moreover, the cunning artifice of indirect taxation and of national loans enabled the despotic governments to maintain large permanent armies of those *living machines* to stifle Right and to perpetuate Wrong—for such the soldiers have proved themselves to be under despotism, and as such they are regarded by the oppressed populations: but *should the soldiery of a Republic be vile living machines?*

Two main points we have to analyze in this investigation— the first is Right, and the next is Authority.

Right is that which is good, true, honorable, just, humane, self-sacrificing—it is the precise opposite to Wrong. Right is immutable; as it was, so it is and so it always *must* be. Circumstances cannot change it. It never was right to lie, cheat, oppress, rob, or murder—it never can be right to do so —no legal subterfuge, no oratory, no public or private engagements, no theological interpretations, no arbitary laws, no government orders, no military commands can transform Wrong into Right. Oppression may trample under foot the devotees of Right—may calumniate, pillage, imprison, and even butcher them—yet that will not alter Right, though Wrong may be made more hideous. The weaker disciples of Right may quail and hesitate before dangers, privations, and sufferings — some indeed may abandon Right — yet Right itself cannot alter, though it may shine more beautiful under persecution. Between Right and Wrong there can be no compromise.

Authority is of two sorts: Legitimate and Illegitimate.

Legitimate Authority is based on Reason and Equity; it must spring from, and always be controlled by, the People; its object is the benefit of the People by the maintenance of justice, the diffusion of education and knowledge, the advancement of civilization, the repression of violence, the reclamation of vice and the development of Humanity. Though authority may be filched through a Party frenzied by some delusion, even that power would not be legitimate, for no portion of any nation can annul the *Rights of Man*—no majority can rightfully sacrifice the freedom and well-being of any one fellow man or posterity. Man cannot take or give that which is not his. The test, therefore, of Legitimate Authority is Right, and to maintain *that* authority soldiers are not required to be mere *living machines.*

Illegitimate Authority is founded on fraud and violence: it is created by a despot, an oligarchy, or the leaders of a party, and is used for the benefit of some usurpation. Under the plausible pretext of acting for the public good, of repelling some enemy, of checking party rancor, of maintaining law and order purposely disturbed, illegitimate authority has frequently been established in formerly happy communities, and the usurpation having seized the reins of government has hoped to perpetuate its domination by the distribution of lucrative offices, and by the hiring of *living machines.* The dominant party may boast, rejoice, and fatten, while mercenary scribes and orators flatter: but under such misrule the nation degenerates, violence becomes habitual, ignorance prevails, want nurtures crime, the tribunals become corrupt, vice revels and virtue is persecuted, the people, awaking under the smart of despotism, soon realize the difficulty of self-emancipation while ground down by the *living machines* set in motion by illegitimate authority. Will the soldiery of a Republic consent to become *living machines*, and thus sustain Wrong against Right?

It is self-evident that "There can exist no moral obligation to do that which is immoral—no virtuous obligation to do that which is vicious—no religious obligation to do that which is irreligious." It is also self evident that every citizen is in duty bound to sustain Right even though he thereby neglect temporarily some of his private business: he who regards his personal interests as of more importance to him than to exercise a watchfulness at all times for the public good and for the security of Right against Wrong, fails in an essential duty toward, the commonwealth. The Greeks decreed that all guilty of such neglect of duty were INFAMOUS: they were deprived of that citizenship which they had shown themselves unworthy to enjoy, their property, which they had preferred to the public welfare, was confiscated, and they were reduced to the lowest state of degradation.

THE BROWN PAPERS.

[Found in the carpet-bag captured at the Virginia hill-side school-house.]

Consisting of the Journal of the Constitutional Convention at Chatham, Canada, W. ; Brown's Declaration of Independence ; Kagi's Draft for a Provisional Army ; Correspondence and Plans of Brown's Men ; Letters from their friends, and from persons furnishing means ; Memoranda. Hints, and Suggestions ; Extracts from Letters, Diaries, and Journals ; Commissions issued under the Provisional Army regulations ; Lists of Members of the Provisional Convention and Government, etc., etc.—Copied from the Originals at Charlestown, by order of Executive Department of the State of Virginia.—November 16, 1859.

[Document No. I, Appendix to Message I, Documents relative to the Harper's Ferry Invasion.]

Copy of the Constitution, adopted at Chatham, May 8, 1858.

PROVISIONAL CONSTITUTION AND ORDINANCE FOR THE PEOPLE OF THE UNITED STATES.

PREAMBLE.

Whereas, slavery throughout its entire existence in the United States, is none other than a most barbarous, unprovoked, and unjustifiable war of one portion of its citizens upon another portion, the only conditions of which are perpetual imprisonment and hopeless servitude or absolute extermination ; in utter disregard and violation of those eternal and self-evident truths set forth in our Declaration of Independence : Therefore

We, citizens of the United States, and the Oppressed People, who, by a recent decision of the Supreme Court are declared to have no rights which the White Man is bound to respect ; together with all other people degraded by the laws thereof, Do, for the time being ordain and establish ourselves, the following PROVISIONAL CONSTITUTION and ORDINANCES, the better to protect our Persons, Property, Lives, and Liberties; and to govern our actions :

ARTICLE I.

QUALIFICATIONS FOR MEMBERSHIP.

All persons of mature age, whether Proscribed, oppressed, and enslaved Citizens, or of the Proscribed and oppressed races on the United States, who shall agree to sustain and enforce the Provisional Constitution and Ordinance of this organization, together with all minor children of such persons, shall be held to be fully entitled to protection under the same,

ARTICLE II.

BRANCHES OF GOVERNMENT.

The provisional government of this organization shall consist of three branches, viz.: Legislative, Executive, and Judicial.

ARTICLE III.

LEGISLATIVE.

The legislative branch shall be a Congress or House of Representatives, composed of not less than five, nor more than ten members, who shall be elected by all the citizens of mature age and of sound mind, connected with this organization ; and who shall remain in office for three years, unless sooner removed for misconduct, inability, or by death. A majority of such members shall constitute a quorum.

ARTICLE IV.

EXECUTIVE.

The executive branch of this organization shall consist of a President and Vice-President, who shall be chosen by the citizens or members of this organization, and each of whom shall hold his office for three years, unless sooner removed by death, or for inability or misconduct,

ARTICLE V.
JUDICIAL.

The judicial branch of this organization shall consist of one Chief-Justice of the Supreme Court, and of four Associate Judges of said Court; each constituting a Circuit Court. They shall each be chosen in the same manner as the President, and shall continue in office until their places have been filled in the same manner by election of the citizens. Said court shall have jurisdiction in all civil or criminal causes, arising under this constitution, except breaches of the Rules of War.

ARTICLE VI.
VALIDITY OF ENACTMENTS.

All enactments of the legislative branch shall, to become valid during the first three years, have the approbation of the President and of the Commander-in-Chief of the Army.

ARTICLE VII.
COMMANDER-IN-CHIEF.

A Commander-in-Chief of the army shall be chosen by the President, Vice-President, a majority of the Provisional Congress, and of the Supreme Court, and he shall receive his commission from the President, signed by the Vice-President, the Chief-Justice of the Supreme Court, and the Secretary of War: and he shall hold his office for three years, unless removed by death, or on proof of incapacity or misbehavior. He shall, unless under arrest (and till his place is actually filled as provided for by this constitution) direct all movements of the army, and advise with any allies. He shall, however, be tried, removed, or punished, on complaint to the President, by, at least, three general officers, or a majority of the House of Representatives, or of the Supreme Court; which House of Representatives (the President presiding); the Vice-President, and the members of the Supreme Court, shall constitute a court-martial, for his trial; with power to remove or punish, as the case may require; and to fill his place as above provided.

ARTICLE VIII.

OFFICERS.

A Treasurer, Secretary of State, Secretary of War, and Secretary of the Treasury, shall each be chosen for the first three years, in the same way and manner as the Commander-in-Chief; subject to trial or removal on complaint of the President, Vice-President, or Commander-in-Chief, to the Chief-Justice of the Supreme Court; or on complaint of the majority of the members of said court, or the Provisional Congress. The Supreme Court shall have power to try or punish either of those officers; and their places shall be filled as before.

ARTICLE IX.

SECRETARY OF WAR.

The Secretary of War shall be under the immediate direction of the Commander-in-Chief; who may temporarily fill his place, in case of arrest, or of any inability to serve.

ARTICLE X.

CONGRESS OR HOUSE OF REPRESENTATIVES.

The House of Representatives shall make ordinances for the appointment (by the President or otherwise) of all civil officers excepting those already named; and shall have power to make all laws and ordinances for the general good, not inconsistent with this Constitution and these ordinances.

ARTICLE XI.

APPROPRIATION OF MONEY, ETC.

The Provisional Congress shall have power to appropriate money or other property actually in the hands of the Treasurer, to any object calculated to promote the general good, so far as may be consistent with the provisions of this Constitution; and may in certain cases, appropriate, for a moderate compensation of agents, or persons not members of this organization, for important service they are known to have rendered.

ARTICLE XII.

SPECIAL DUTIES.

It shall be the duty of Congress to provide for the instant removal of any civil officer or policeman, who becomes habitually intoxicated, or who is addicted to other immoral conduct, or to any neglect or unfaithfulness in the discharge of his official duties. Congress shall also be a standing committee of safety, for the purpose of obtaining important information; and shall be in constant communication with the Commander-in-Chief; the members of which shall each, as also the President, Vice-President, members of the Supreme Court, and Secretary of State, have full power to issue warrants returnable as Congress shall ordain (naming witnesses, etc.) upon their own information, without the formality of a complaint. Complaint shall be made immediately after arrest, and before trial; the party arrested to be served with a copy at once.

ARTICLE XIII.

TRIAL OF PRESIDENT AND OTHER OFFICERS.

The President and Vice-President may either of them be tried, removed, or punished, on complaint made to the Chief-Justice of the Supreme Court, by a majority of the House of Representatives, which House, together with the Associate Judges of the Supreme Court, the whole to be presided over by the Chief-Justice in cases of the trial of the Vice-President, shall have full power to try such officers, to remove, or punish as the case may require, and to fill any vacancy so occurring, the same as in the case of the Commander-in-Chief.

ARTICLE XIV.

TRIAL OF MEMBERS OF CONGRESS.

The members of the House of Representatives may any and all of them be tried, and on conviction, removed or punished on complaint before the Chief-Justice of the Supreme Court, made by any number of members of said House, exceeding one-third, which House, with the Vice-President and Associate

Judges of the Supreme Court, shall constitute the proper tribunal, with power to fill such vacancies.

ARTICLE XV.

IMPEACHMENT OF JUDGES.

Any member of the Supreme Court, tried, convicted, or punished by removal or otherwise, on complaint to the President, who shall, in such case, preside; the Vice-President, House of Representatives, and other members of the Supreme Court, constituting the proper tribunal (with power to fill vacancies); on complaint of a majority of said House of Representatives, or of the Supreme Court; a majority of the whole having power to decide.

ARTICLE XVI.

DUTIES OF PRESIDENT AND SECRETARY OF STATE.

The President, with the Secretary of State, shall immediately upon entering on the duties of their office, give special attention to secure, from amongst their own people, men of integrity, intelligence, and good business habits and capacity; and above all, of first-rate moral and religious character and influence, to act as civil officers of every description and grade, as well as teachers, chaplains, physicians, surgeons, mechanics, agents of every discription, clerks, and messengers. They shall make special efforts to induce at the earliest possible period, persons and families of that description, to locate themselves within the limits secured by this organization; and shall, moreover, from time to time, supply the names and residence of such persons to the Congress, for their special notice and information, as among the most important of their duties, and the President is hereby authorized and empowered to afford special aid to such individuals, from such moderate appropriations as the Congress shall be able and may deem it advisable to make for that object. The President and Secretary of State, and in cases of disagreement, the Vice-President shall appoint all civil officers, but shall not have power to remove any officer. All removals shall be the result of a fair trial, whether civil or military.

ARTICLE XVII.

FURTHER DUTIES.

It shall be the duty of the President and Secretary of State, to find out (as soon as possible) the real friends, as well as the enemies of this organization in every part of the country; to secure among them, innkeepers, private postmasters, private mail-contractors, messengers, and agents: through whom may be obtained correct and regular information, constantly; recruits for the service, places of deposit and sale; together with all needed supplies: and it shall be matter of special regard to secure such facilities through the Northern States.

ARTICLE XVIII.

DUTIES OF THE PRESIDENT.

It shall be the duty of the President, as well as the House of Representatives, at all times, to inform the Commander-in-Chief of any matter that may require his attention, or that may affect the public safety.

ARTICLE XIX.

DUTY OF PRESIDENT—CONTINUED.

It shall be the duty of the President to see that the provisional ordinances of this organization, and those made by Congress, are promptly and faithfully executed; and he may in cases of great urgency call on the Commander-in-Chief of the army, or other officers for aid; it being, however, intended that a sufficient civil police shall always be in readiness to secure implicit obedience to law.

ARTICLE XX.

THE VICE-PRESIDENT.

The Vice-President shall be the presiding officer of the Provisional Congress; and in cases of tie shall give the casting vote.

ARTICLE XXI.
VACANCIES.

In case of death, removal, or inability of the President, the Vice-President, and next to him the Chief-Justice of the Supreme Court, shall be the President during the remainder of the term: and the place of Chief-Justice thus made vacant shall be filled by Congress from some of the members of said court; and places of the Vice-President and Associate Justice thus made vacant, filled by an election by the united action of the Provisional Congress and members of the Supreme Court. All other vacancies, not hertofore specially provided for, shall, during the first three years, be filled by the united action of the President, Vice-President, Supreme Court, and Commander-in-Chief of the Army.

ARTICLE XXII.
PUNISHMENT OF CRIMES.

The punishment of crimes not capital, except in case of insubordinate convicts or other prisoners, shall be (so far as may be) by hard labor on the public works, roads, etc.

ARTICLE XXIII.
ARMY APPOINTMENTS.

It shall be the duty of all commissioned officers of the army to name candidates of merit for office or elevation to the Commander-in-Chief, who, with the Secretary of War, and, in cases of disagreement, the President, shall be the appointing power of the army: and all commissions of military officers shall bear the signatures of the Commander-in-Chief and the Secretary of War. And it shall be the special duty of the Secretary of War to keep for constant reference of the Commander-in-Chief a full list of names of persons nominated for office, or elevation, by the officers of the army, with the name and rank of the officer nominating, stating distinctly but briefly the grounds for such notice or nomination. The Commander-in-Chief shall not have power to remove or punish any officer or soldier; but he may order their arrest and trial at any time, by court-martial.

ARTICLE XXIV.

COURTS-MARTIAL.

Courts-martial for Companies, Regiments, Brigades, etc., shall be called by the chief officer of each command, on complaint to him by any officer, or any five privates, in such command, and shall consist of not less than five nor more than nine officers, non-commissioned officers, and privates, one-half of whom shall not be lower in rank than the person on trial, to be chosen by the three highest officers in the command, which officers shall not be a part of such court. The chief officer of any command shall, of course, be tried by a court-martial of the command above his own. All decisions affecting the lives of persons, or office of persons holding commission, must, before taking full effect, have the signature of the Commander-in-Chief, who may also, on the recommendation of, at least, one-third of the members of the court-martial finding any sentence, grant a reprieve or commutation of the same.

ARTICLE XXV.

SALARIES.

No person connected with this organization shall be entitled to any salary, pay, or emolument, other than a competent support of himself and family, unless it be from an equal dividend, made of public property, on the establishment of peace, or of special provision by treaty ; which provision shall be made for all persons who may have been in any active civil or military service at any time previous to any hostile action for Liberty and Equality.

ARTICLE XXVI.

TREATIES OF PEACE.

Before any treaty of peace shall take full effect, it shall be signed by the President and Vice-President, the Commander-in-Chief, a majority of the House of Representatives, a majority of the Supreme Court, and majority of all general officers of the army.

ARTICLE XXVII.
DUTY OF THE MILITARY.

It shall be the duty of the Commander-in-Chief, and all officers and soldiers of the army, to afford special protection when needed, to Congress, or any member thereof ; to the Supreme Court, or any member thereof; to the President, Vice-President, Treasurer, Secretary of State, Secretary of Treasury, and Secretary of War ; and to afford general protection to all civil officers, other persons having right to the same.

ARTICLE XXVIII.
PROPERTY.

All captured or confiscated property, and all property the product of the labor of those belonging to this organization and of their families, shall be held as the property of the whole, equally, without distinction ; and may be used for the common benefit, or disposed of for the same object ; and any person, officer or otherwise, who shall improperly retain, secret, use, or needlessly destroy such property, or property found, captured, or confiscated, belonging to the enemy, or shall willfully neglect to render a full and fair statement of such property by him so taken or held, shall be deemed guilty of a misdemeanor and, on conviction, shall be punished accordingly.

ARTICLE XXIX.
SAFETY OR INTELLIGENCE FUND.

All money, plate, watches, or jewelry, captured by honorable warfare, found, taken, or confiscated, belonging to the enemy, shall be held sacred, to constitute a liberal safety or intelligence fund ; and any person who shall improperly retain dispose of, hide, use, or destroy such money or other article above named, contrary to the provisions and spirit of this article, shall be deemed guilty of theft, and, on conviction thereof, shall be punished accordingly. The Treasurer shall furnish the Commander-in-Chief at all times with a full statement of the condition of such fund and its nature.

Article XXX.

THE COMMANDER-IN-CHIEF AND THE TREASURY.

The Commander-in-Chief shall have power to draw from the Treasury the money and other property of the fund provided for in ARTICLE twenty-ninth, but his orders shall be signed also by the Secretary of War, who shall keep strict account of the same; subject to examination by any member of Congress, or general officer.

Article XXXI.

SURPLUS OF THE SAFETY OR INTELLIGENCE FUND.

It shall be the duty of the Commander-in-Chief to advise the President of any surplus of the Safety or Intelligence Fund; who shall have power to draw such surplus (his order being also signed by the Secretary of State) to enable him to carry out the provisions of Article Seventeenth.

Article XXXII.

PRISONERS.

No person, after having surrendered himself or herself a prisoner, and who shall properly demean himself or herself as such, to any officer or private connected with this organization, shall afterward be put to death, or be subject to any corporal punishment, without first having had the benefit of a fair and impartial trial: nor shall any prisoner be treated with any kind of cruelty, disrespect, insult, or needless severity: but it shall be the duty of all persons, male and female, connected herewith, at all times and under all circumstances, to treat all such prisoners with every degree of respect and kindness the nature of the circumstances will admit of; and to insist on a like course of conduct from all others, as in the fear of Almighty God, to whose care and keeping we commit our cause.

Article XXXIII.

VOLUNTARIES.

All persons who may come forward and shall voluntarily deliver up their slaves, and have their names registered on the Books of the organization, shall, so long as they continue at peace, be entitled to the fullest protection of person and property, though not connected with this organization, and shall be treated as friends, and not merely as persons neutral.

ARTICLE XXXIV.

NEUTRALS.

The persons and property of all non-slaveholders who shall remain absolute neutral, shall be respected so far as the circumstances can allow of it; but they shall not be entitled to any active protection.

ARTICLE XXXV.

NO NEEDLESS WASTE.

The needless waste or destruction of any useful property or article, by fire, throwing open of fences, fields, buildings, or needless killing of animals, or injury of either, shall not be tolerated at any time or place, but shall be promptly and properly punished.

ARTICLE XXXVI.

PROPERTY CONFISCATED.

The entire and real property of all persons known to be acting either directly or indirectly with or for the enemy, or found in arms with them, or found willfully holding slaves, shall be confiscated and taken, whenever and wherever it may be found, in either free or slave States.

ARTICLE XXXVII.

DESERTION.

Persons convicted, on impartial trial, of desertion to the enemy after becoming members, acting as spies, or of treacherous surrender of property, arms, ammunition, provisions, or supplies of any kind, roads, bridges, persons, or fortifications, shall be put to death and their entire property confiscated.

ARTICLE XXXVIII.

VIOLATION OF PAROLE OF HONOR.

Persons proven to be guilty of taking up arms after having been set at liberty on parole of honor, or, after the same, to have taken any active part with or for the enemy, direct or indirect, shall be put to death and their entire property confiscated.

Article XXXIX.

ALL MUST LABOR.

All persons connected in any way with this organization, and who may be entitled to full protection under it : shall be held as under obligation to labor in some way for the general good ; and persons refusing, or neglecting so to do, shall on conviction receive a suitable and appropriate punishment.

Article XL.

IRREGULARITIES.

Profane swearing, filthy conversation, indecent behavior, or indecent exposure of the person, or intoxication, or quarrelling, shall not be allowed or tolerated ; neither unlawful intercourse of the sexes.

Article XLI.

CRIMES.

Persons convicted of the forcible violation of any female prisoner shall be put to death.

Article XLII.

THE MARRIAGE RELATION—SCHOOLS—THE SABBATH.

The marriage relation shall be at all times respected ; and families kept together as far as possible ; and broken families encouraged to re-unite, and intelligence offices established for that purpose, schools and churches established, as soon as may be, for the purpose of religious and other instructions; and the first day of the week regarded as a day of rest and appropriated to moral and religious instruction and improvement ; relief to the suffering, instruction of the young and ignorant, and the encouragement of personal cleanliness ; nor shall any persons be required on that day to perform ordinary manual labor, unless in extremely urgent cases.

ARTICLE XLIII.

CARRY ARMS OPENLY.

All persons known to be of good character, and of sound mind and suitable age, who are connected with this organization, whether male or female, shall be encouraged to carry arms openly.

ARTICLE XLIV.

NO PERSON TO CARRY CONCEALED WEAPONS.

No person within the limits of the conquered territory, except regularly appointed policemen, express officers of the army, mail carriers, or other fully accredited messengers of the Congress, President, Vice-President, members of the Supreme Court, or commissioned officer of the army—and those only under peculiar circumstances—shall be allowed, at any time, to carry concealed weapons; and any person not specially authorized so to do, who shall be found so doing, shall be deemed a suspicious person, and may at once be arrested by any officer, soldier, or citizen, without the formality of a complaint or warrant, and may at once be subjected to thorough search, and shall have his or her case thoroughly investigated ; and be dealt with as circumstances, on proof, shall require.

ARTICLE XLV.

PERSONS TO BE SEIZED.

Persons within the limits of the territory holden by this organization, not connected with this organization, having arms at all, concealed or otherwise, shall be seized at once; or be taken in charge of some vigilant officer ; and their case thoroughly investigated : and it shall be the duty of all citizens and soldiers, as well as officers, to arrest such parties as are named in this and the preceding Section or Article, without the formality of complaint or warrant ; and they shall be placed in charge of some proper officer for examination, or for safe keeping.

Article XLVI.

THESE ARTICLES NOT FOR THE OVERTHROW OF GOV'M'T.

The foregoing Articles shall not be construed so as in any way to encourage the overthrow of any State Government of the United States : and look to no dissolution of the Union, but simply to Amendment and Repeal. And our flag shall be the same that our Fathers fought under in the Revolution.

Article XLVII.

NO PLURALITY OF OFFICES.

No two of the offices specially provided for, by this Instrument, shall be filled by the same person, at the same time.

Article XLVIII.

OATH.

Every officer, civil or military, connected with this organization, shall, before entering upon the duties of his office, make solemn oath or affirmation, to abide by and support this Provisional Constitution and these Ordinances. Also, every Citizen and Soldier, before being fully recognized as such, shall do the same.

SCHEDULE.

The President of this Convention shall convene, immediately on the adoption of this instrument, a convention of all such persons as shall have given their adherence, by signature, to the constitution, the President of this convention presiding, and issuing commissions to such officers elect : all such officers being thereafter elected in the manner provided in the body of this instrument.

BLANK FORM OF COMMISSION UNDER THE PROVISIONAL GOVERNMENT.

GREETING:

Whereas: has been chosen in accordance with the provisions of the schedule of the provisional constitution;

Therefore: by the authority vested in me by said instrument, I hereby commission the said   under said constitution.

Witness hand and the seal of the convention, at   this   day of   in the year eighteen hundred and fifty-eight.

· · · · · · · · · · · · · · · · ·

Pres. of the Convention.

JOURNAL OF THE PROVISIONAL CONVENTION HELD ON SATURDAY, MAY 8TH, 1858.

CHATHAM, CANADA WEST, Saturday, May 8th, 1858.

10 A. M.—Convention in persuance to call of John Brown and others, and was called to order by Mr. Jackson, on whose motion Mr. Wm. C. Monroe was chosen President:

When, on motion of Mr. Brown, Mr. J. H. Kagi was elected Secretary.

On motion of Mr. Delany, Mr. Brown then proceeded to state the object of the convention, at length, and then to explain the general features of the plan of action in the execution of the project in view by the Convention. Mr. Delany and others spoke in favor of the project and the plan, and both were agreed to by general consent.

Mr. Brown then presented a plan or organization, entitled "Provisional Constitution and Ordinances for the people of the United States," and moved the reading of the same.

Mr. Kinnard objected to the reading until an oath of secrecy be taken by each member of the Convention. Whereupon,

Mr. Delany moved that the following parole be taken by all members of the Convention: "I solemnly affirm that I will not in any way divulge any of the secrets of this convention, except to persons entitled to know the same, on the pain of forfeiting the respect and protection of this Organization;" which motion was carried.

The President then proceeded to administer the obligation, after which

The question was taken on the reading of plan proposed by Mr. Brown, and the same carried.

The plan was then carried by the Secretary. After which

On motion of Mr. Whipple, it was ordered that it be now read by articles, for consideration.

The articles from one to forty-five inclusive, were then read and adopted. On the reading of the forty-sixth, Mr. Reynolds moved to strike out the same. Reynolds spoke in favor, and Brown, Monroe, Owen Brown, Delany, Realf, Kinnard, and Kagi, against. The question was then taken and lost, there being but one vote in the affirmative.

The article was then adopted. The forty-seventh and forty-eighth Articles with the schedule, were then adopted in the same manner.

It was then moved by Mr. Delany that the Title and Preamble stand as read. Carried.

On motion of Mr. Kagi the Constitution as a whole was then unanimously adopted.

The Convention then, at 1½ P. M., adjourned, on motion of Mr. Jackson, till 3 o'clock.

3 P. M.—Journal read and approved.

On motion of Mr. Delany it was then ordered that those approving of the Constitution, as adopted, sign the same. Whereupon the names of all the members were appended. (See No. (91).)

After congratulatory remarks by Messrs. Kinnard and Delany, the convention on motion of Mr. Whipple, adjourned, at a quarter to 4.   J. H. KAGI.

Sec. of the Convention.

CHATHAM, CANADA WEST, Saturday, May 8th, 1858.

6 P. M.—In accordance with the obedience to the provisions of the schedule to the Constitution for the " proscribed and oppressed people " of the United States of America, to-day adopted at this place, a Convention was called by the President of the Convention framing that instrument, and met at the above-named hour, for the purpose of electing officers to fill

the offices specially established and named by said Consti
tution.

The Convention was called to order by Mr. M. R. Delany,
upon whose nomination Mr. Wm. C. Monroe was chosen President, and Mr. J. H. Kagi, Bell, Cook, and Monroe, was then
chosen to select candidates for the various offices to be filled,
for the consideration of the Convention.

On reporting progress and asking leave to set again, the
request was refused, and the Committee discharged.

On motion of Mr. Bell the Convention went into the election
of officers, in the following manner and order.

Mr. Whipple nominated John Brown for Commander-in-
Chief, who was, on the seconding of Mr. Delany, elected by
acclamation.

Mr. Realf nominated J. H. Kagi for Secretary of War, who
was elected in the same manner.

On motion of Mr. Brown the Convention then adjourned to
9 A.M. on Monday, the 10th.

————

9 A.M.—The proceedings of Convention of Saturday were
read and approved.

The President announced that the business before the Convention was the further election of officers.

Mr. Whipple nominated Thomas M. Kinnard for President.
In a speech of some length Mr. Kinnard declined.

Mr. Anderson nominated J. W. Loguen for the same office.
The nomination was afterwards withdrawn, Mr. Loguen not
being present, and it being announced that he would not serve
if elected.

Mr. Brown then moved to postpone the election of President
for the present.   Carried.

The Convention then went into the election of Members of
Congress. Messrs. Alfred M. Ellsworth and Osborn Anderson
were elected.

After which the Convention went into the election of Secretary of State, to which office Richard Realf was chosen.

Whereupon the Convention adjourned to 2½ P.M.

2 ½ P.M.—Convention again assembled, and went into a balloting for the election of Treasurer and Secretary of the Treasury. Owen Brown was elected as the former, and George B. Gill as the latter.

The following resolution was then introduced by Mr. Brown, and unanimously passed:

Resolved, that John Brown, J. H. Kagi, Richard Realf, L. F. Parsons, C. P. Tidd, E. Whipple, C. W. Moffet, John E. Cook, Owen Brown, Stewart Taylor, Osborn Anderson, A. M. Ellsworth, Richard Richardson, W. H. Leeman, and John Lawrence, be, and are hereby appointed a Committee to whom is delegated the power of the Convention to fill by election all the offices specially named in the Provisional Constitution which may be vacant after the adjournment of this Convention. The Convention then adjourned *sine die*.

(See No. (78).)
J. H. KAGI,
Sec. of the Convention.

.... 4th, 1859.

A DECLARATION OF LIBERTY BY THE REPRESENTATIVES OF THE SLAVE POPULATION OF THE UNITED STATES OF AMERICA.

" When in the course of Human events, it becomes necessary " for an oppressed People to Rise, and assert their Natural Rights, as Human Beings, as Native and Mutual Citizens of a free Republic, and break that odious yoke of oppression, which is so unjustly laid upon them by their fellow countrymen, " and to assume among the powers of Earth the same equal privileges to which the Laws of Nature, and nature's God entitle, them ; A moderate respect for the opinions of Mankind, requires that they should declare the causes which incite them to this Just & worthy action.

" We hold these truths to be Self Evident ; That all men are created Equal ; That they are endowed by the Creator with certain unalienable rights. That among these are Life, Liberty; & pursuit of happiness, " That nature hath freely given to all

Men, a full supply of Air, Water, and Land; for their susti-
nance, & mutual happiness. That No Man has any right to
deprive his fellow Man, of these Inherent rights in punishment
of crime. " That to secure these rights governments are insti-
tuted among men, deriving their Just powers from the consent
of the governed. That when any form of government, becomes
destructive to these ends, It is the right of the People, to alter
Amend, or Remoddel it, Laying its foundation on such Principles, & organizing its powers in such form as to them shall
seem most likely to affect the safety, & happiness " of the
Human Race. To secure equal rights, privileges, & Justice to
all; Irrespective of Sex; or Nation; To secure Fraternal
kindness to all Friends of Equal Moral privileges, to all who
honestly abandon their Despotic oppressive rule. We hold
this truth to be self evident: That it is the highest Privilege, &
Plain duty of Man; to strive in every reasonable way, to
promote the Happiness, Mental, Moral, & Physical elevation of
his fellow Man. And that People, or Clanish oppressors; who
wickedly violate this sacred principle; oppressing their fellow
Men, will bring upon themselves that certain and fearful retri-
bution, which is the Natural, & Necessary penalty of evil
Doing. " Prudence, indeed will dictate, that Governments long
established, should not be changed for light & transient
causes; But when a long train of abuses, & usurpations, pursuing invariably the same object; evince a design to perpetrate
an absolute Despotism; and most cruel bondage; It is then
Right, it is their Duty, to resist & change such Government,
& provide safeguards for their future Liberty." Such has been
the patient sufferance of the slaves of the United States, and
such is now the necessity which constrains them to Crush this
foul system of oppression.

" The history of Slavery in the United States, is a history of
injustice and cruelties inflicted upon the Slave in every con-
ceivable way, and in barbarity not surpassed by the most
savage Tribes. It is the embodiment of all that is Evil, and
ruinous to a Nation; and subversive of all Good. " In proof of
which; facts innumerable have been submitted to the People,

and have received the verdict and condemnation of a candid and Impartial World." Our Servants ; Members of Congress ; and other servants of the People, who receive exorbitant wages, from the People ; in return for their unjust Rule, "have refused to pass laws for the accommodation of large districts of People, unless that People, would relinquish the right of representation in the Legislation, a right inestimable of them, and formidable to tyrants only. Our President and other Leeches have called together legislative, or treasonable Bodies, at places unusual, uncomfortable, and distant from the depository of our public records ; for the sole purpose of fatigueing us into compliance with their measures. They have desolved Representative houses, for opposing with manly firmness, their invasions of the rights of the people.

" They have refused to grant Petitions presented by numerous and respectable Citizens, asking redress of grievances imposed upon us, demanding our Liberty and natural rights. With contempt they spurn our humble petitions ; and have failed to pass laws for our relief. " They have prevented in all possible ways, the administration of Justice to the Slave. They have made Judges like Taney dependent on their will alone, for the tenure of their office, and the amount and payment of their salaries. They have erected a Multitude of new offices, and Sent on Swarms of Blood Suckers, and Moths, to harass the People, and eat out their Substance. They have affected to render the Military, independent of, and superior to the power and wishes of the people, (the Civil power.) Claiming that knowledge is power, they have, (for their own safety,) kept us in total darkness, and Ignorance, inflicting base cruelties, for any attempt on our part to obtain knowledge. They have protected base Men, Pirates (engaged in a most Inhuman traffic ; The Foreign ; and Domestic Slave Trade.) " by mock trials, from punishment, for unprovoked murders which they have committed upon us, and free Citizens of the States. They have prevented by law, our having any Traffic or deal with our fellow Men ; Regardless of our wishes, they declare themselves invested with power to legislate for us in all cases whatsoever. They have abdicated government among us, by declaring us out of their protection, and waging a worse than cruel war upon us continually.

" The facts and full description of the enormous sin of Slavery, may be found in the General History of American Slavery, which is a history of repeated injuries, of base hypocracy ; A cursed treasonable, usurpation ; The most abominable provoking atrocities ; which are but a mockery of all that is Just, or worthy of any people. "Such cruelty, tyrany, and perfidy, has hardly a parallel, in the history of the most barbarous ages.

" Our Servants, or Law makers; are totally unworthy the name of Half Civilized Men. All their National acts, (which apply to slavery,) are false, to the words Spirit, and intention, of the Constitution of the United States, and the Declaration of Independence.

" They say by word & Act, That their own Children, or any faithful Citizen, may be legally robed of every Natural and Sacred Right, and that we had no rights whatever. They are a blot upon the character, the honor, of any Nation, which claims to have the least shadow or spark of Civilization above the lowest, most inferior Canibal Races. This is a slight though brief recital, of some of the enormous atrocities, of these Idle, haughty, tyranical, Arrogant Land Monopolists; slave holders are lords and masters, From which, Good Lord Deliver us. These are some of the facts, which we now, (after the lapse of 83 years, since the writing and signing of that Sacred Instrument, Honored and Adored by our Fathers, which declares that it is Self Evident that all Men are created Equal, Endowed by their Creator with certain inherent rights &c.") submit to the Decision of all Candid ; true Republican, Friends of Universal Freedom, and National Equality of Rights. All We Demand, is our Liberty, and the Natural rights and immunities of faithful Citizens of the United States. We will Obtain these rights or Die in the Struggle to obtain them. We make war upon oppression, we have no controversy with any Religious Sect, our intention is not to molest any Good Man,

whatever may be his religious belief. "The welfare of the
People ; Is the first Great Law." We hold these to be self
evident truths, That any Tribe, Rulers, or People, who Rob
and cruelly oppress their faithful Laboring Citizens, have within
themselves the Germ, of their own certain and fearful overthrow ; It is one of Nature's Immutable Laws; that "According to the measure that ye mete ; so shall it be measured to you
again." Herein is the secret of Security & true happiness, for
Individuals, and the only firm Basis, upon which Governments.
may be permanently Established ; where the Citizens, are Devoted to the greatest good of their fellow Men,The more humble.
benighted & oppressed they are, So much more sympathy, &
earnest effort for their relief, is demanded, striving earnestly to
promote the Safety and prosperity of their Nation ; & the
Human Race.

"It is a fixed Law of Nature, That any People or Nation,
whose steady purpose, & Constant Practice, is in accordance
with these principles ; Must go forward Progressing ; So long
as Man continues to Exist. For in Nature the Principle of
Reciprocity is Great.

"The Legitimate object of all Punishment, is to prevent
Crime." When any Punishment is inflicted more than is necessary to prevent Crime, it then ceases to be a Punishment; It
has then become a Barbarous Crime. A Sore Evil. "The
Natural Object of all Government is to Protect the right
Defend the Innocent. When any set of Usurpers, Tribe, or
community, fail to protect the right, but furnish protection &
encouragement to the Villian, by bestowing a Bounty, or Pre-
mium, upon the vile Thief, Rober, Libertine, Pirate ; & Woman
killing Slave Holder ; as a reward for their deeds of rascality
and Barbarism ; And inflict grievous cruelties upon the inocent,
Shooting and Butchering those most faithful, Citizens, who
have striven Manfully, for the relief of the down troden & oppressed of their country, Who fought bravely in support of the
Great Principles set forth in Our Declaration of Independence.
from the oppressive Rule of England. Encouraging in various
ways, by bribery and fraud, the most Fiendish acts of Bar-

barism, (like those Perpetrated within the limits of the United
States, at Blounts' Fort; in Florida and other Territories.)
under the Jurisdiction and guidance of Slave holding Authority, & in strict accordance with Slave holding Rules. They
have transcended their own limits, they have fairly outwitted
themselves; Their Slave Code is a Shame to any Nation, Their
Laws are no Laws, they themselves are no more than a Band
of Base Piratical Rulers. They are a curse to themselves, a
most lamentable Blot upon Society.

" In every stage of these oppressions, we have petitioned for
redress, in the most humble terms, Our repeated petitions have
been answered only by repeated Injury A Class of oppressors,
whose character is thus marked by every act which may define
a Tyranical Despotism, is unfit to rule any People. Nor have
we been wanting in attention, to our oppressors; We have
warned them from time to time, of attempts (made by their
headlong Blindness,) to perpetrate, extend, strengthen, and
revive the dieing eliments of this cursed Institution. We have
reminded them of our unhappy condition, and of their Cruelties.
We have appealed to their native Justice and magnanimity, we
have conjured them by the ties of our common nature, our
Brotherhood, & common Parentage, to disavow these usurpations, which have destroyed our Kindred friendship, and endangered their safety. " They have been Deaf to the voice of
Justice & Consanguinity. We must therefore acquiece in the
necessity, which denounces their tyrany & unjust rule over us.
Declaring that we will serve them no longer as slaves, knowing that the " Laborer is worthy of his hire." We therefore.
the Representatives of the circumscribed citizens of the United
States, of America in General Congress assembled, appealing
to the supreme Judge of the World, for the rectitude of our
intentions, Do in the name, & by authority of the oppressed
Citizens of the Slave States, Solemnly publish and Declare:
that the Slaves are, & of right ought to be as free & and independent as the unchangable Law of God, requires that All Men
Shall be. That they are absolved from all allegiance to those
Tyrants, who still presist in forcibly subjecting them to per-

petual "Bondage, and that all friendly connection between them & such Tyrants, is, & ought to be totally desolved, And that as free, & independent citizens of these states, they have a perfect right, a sufficient & just cause, to defend themselves against the tyrany of their oppressors. To solicit aid from & ask the protection of all true friends of humanity & reform, of whatever nation, & wherever found; A right to contract Alliances, & to do all other acts & things which free independent Citizens may of right do. And for the support of Declaration; with a firm reliance on the protection of Devine Providence; We mutually Pledge to each other, Our Lives, and Our Sacred Honor. Indeed; I tremble for my Country, when I reflect; that God is Just; And that his Justice; will not sleep forever" &c. &c. Nature is morning for its murdered, and Afflicted Children. Hung be the Heavens in Scarlet.

ARTICLES OF AGREEMENT FOR SHUBEL MOR-GAN'S COMPANY.

We, the undersigned, members of Shubel Morgan's Company, hereby agree to be governed by the following rules:

I. A gentlemanly and respectful deportment shall at all times and places be maintained towards all persons; and all profane and indecent language shall be avoided in all cases.

II. No intoxicating drinks shall be used as a beverage by any member, or be suffered in camp for such purpose.

III. No member shall leave camp without leave of the commander.

IV. All property captured in any manner shall be subjected to an equal distribution among the members.

V. All acts of petty or other thefts shall be promptly and properly punished, and restitution made as far as possible.

VI. All members, so far as able, shall contribute equally to all necessary labor in or out of camp.

VII. All prisoners who shall properly demean themselves shall be treated with kindness and respect, and shall be punished for crime only after trial and conviction, being allowed a hearing in defense.

VIII. Implicit obedience shall be yielded to all proper orders of the commander or other superior officers.

IX. All arms, ammunition, etc., not strictly private property, shall ever be held subject to, and delivered upon, the order of the commander.

Names.	Date, 1858.	Names.	Date, 1858.
Shubel Morgan,[1]	July 12.	E. W. Snyder,	July 15.
C. P. Tidd,	"	Elias J. Snyder,	"
J. H. Kagi,	"	John H. Snyder,	"
A. Wattles,	"	Adam Bishop,	"
Saml. Stevenson	"	Wm. Hairgrove,	"
J. Montgomery,[2]	"	John Mikel,	"
T. Homyer (Weiner?),[3]	"	Wm. Partridge,	"
Simon Snyder,	July 14.		

JOHN BROWN'S PARALLELS. [4]

TRADING POST, KANSAS, January, 1859.

GENTLEMEN—You will greatly oblige a humble friend by allowing the use of your columns while I briefly state two parallels, in my poor way.

Not one year ago eleven quiet citizens of this neighborhood

---

[1] A name assumed by Capt. John Brown in the conflicts of 1858-59, southeastern Kansas border.

[2] James Montgomery, one of the bravest partisans of the Kansas border, and during the Civil War colonel of a black regiment in South Carolina.

[3] In probability this name is meant for Theodore Weiner, the German-American citizen who was one of the eight that left the camp of the Pottawatomie Rifles the evening before the slaying of the Doyles, Wilkinson, and the man who always served with John Brown in Kansas as occasion offered. Mr. Sanborn states that this paper is in Kagi's handwriting.

[4] First published in the Lawrence, Kansas, *Tribune.*

—William Robertson, William Colpetzer, Amos Hall. Austin Hall, John Campbell, Asa Snyder, Thomas Stilwell, William Hairgrove, Asa Hairgrove, Patrick Ross, and B. L. Reed— were gathered up from their work and their homes by an armed force under one Hamilton, and without trial or opportunity to speak in their own defense were formed into line, and all but one shot,—five killed and five wounded. One fell unharmed, pretending to be dead. All were left for dead. The only crime charged against them was that of being free-state men. Now, I inquire what action has ever, since the occurrence in May last, been taken by either the President of the United States, the Governor of Missouri, the Governor of Kansas, or any of their tools, or by any pro-slavery or administration man, to ferret out and punish the perpetrators of this crime?

Now for the other parallel. On Sunday, December 19, a negro man called Jim came over the river to the Osage settlement, from Missouri, and stated that he, together with his wife, two children, and another negro man, was to be sold within a day or two, and begged for help to get away. On Monday (the following) night, two small companies were made up to go to Missouri and forcibly liberate the five slaves, together with other slaves. One of these companies I assumed to direct. We proceeded to the place, surrounded the buildings, liberated the slaves, and also took certain property supposed to belong to the estate. We, however, learned before leaving that a portion of the articles we had taken belonged to a man living on the plantation as a tenant, and who was supposed to have no interest in the estate. We promptly returned to him all we had taken. We then went to another plantation, where we found five more slaves, took some property and two white men. We moved all slowly away into the Territory for some distance, and then sent the white men back, telling them to follow us as soon as they chose to do so. The other company freed one female slave, took some property, and as I am informed, killed one white man (the master), who fought against the liberation.

Now for a comparison. Eleven persons are forcibly restored to their natural and inalienable rights, with but one man killed, and all " hell is stirred from beneath." It is currently reported that the Governor of Missouri has made a requisition upon the Governor of Kansas for the delivery of all such as were concerned in the last-named " dreadful outrage." The marshal of Kansas is said to be collecting a *posse* of Missouri (not Kansas) men at West Point, in Missouri, a little town about ten miles distant, to "enforce the laws." All pro-slavery, conservative, free-state, and doughface men and administration tools are filled with holy horror.

Consider the two cases, and the action of the administration party.   Repectfully yours,

JOHN BROWN.

HEADQUARTERS, WAR DEPARTMENT PROVISIONAL ARMY, HARPER'S FERRY, Oct. 10, 1859.

GENERAL ORDERS.
No. 1.
ORGANIZATION.

The Divisions of the Prov. Army and the coalition are hereby established as follows.

1.—COMPANY.

A company will consist of 56 privates, 12 non-com. off's. (8 corporals, 4 sergeants), 3 com. off. (2 Lieutenants, Captain) and a Surgeon.

The privates shall be divided into Bands or messes of 7 each numbering from 1 to 8, with a corporal to each, numbered like his Band. Two Bands will comprise a Section. Section will be numbered from 1 to 4. A Sergeant will be attached to each Section, and numbered like it.

Two Sections will comprise a Platoon. Platoons will be numbered 1 and 2 and each commanded by a lieutenant designed by like number.

2.—BATTALION.

The Battalion will consist of 4 companies complete.

The commissioned officers of the Battalion will be a Chief of

Battalion, and a 1st & 2nd major, one of whom shall be attached to each wing.

3.—THE REGIMENT.

The Regiment shall consist of 4 Battalions complete.

The commissioned officers of the Regiment will be a Colonel and 2 Lieutenant-Colonels, attached to the wings.

4.—THE BRIGADE.

The Brigade will consist of 4 Regiments complete.

The commissioned officers of the Brigade will be a General of Brigade.

5.—EACH GEN. STAFF.

Each of the above Divisions will be entitled to a General Staff, consisting of an adjutant, a commissary, a musician, and a surgeon.

6.—APPOINTMENT.

Non-commissioned officers will be chosen by those whom they are to command.

Commissioned officers will be appointed and commissioned by this Department.

The staff officers of each Division will be appointed by the respective commanders of the same.

(See No. (   ).—Transcriber.)

(The above document numbered " 2," is in the handwriting of J. H. Kagi. The erasures and cross-marks are copied from the original.—Note by transcriber.)[1]

RECOLLECTIONS OF THE JOHN BROWN RAID.

BY THE HON. ALEXANDER R. BOTELER, A VIRGINIAN WHO WITNESSED THE FIGHT.

[*This paper is in the whole so fair and candid in tone that it deserves a place in the record here made.*]

"On entering the room where John Brown was I found him alone, lying on the floor on his left side, and with his back

---

[1] From Sanborn's " Life and Letters of John Brown."

turned toward me. The right side of his face was smeared
with blood from the sword-cut on his head, causing his grim
and grizzly countenance to look like that of some aboriginal
savage with his war-paint on. Approaching him, I began the
conversation with the inquiry.

"'Captain Brown, are you hurt anywhere except on the
head?'

"'Yes, in my side,—here,' said he, indicating the place with
his hand.

"I then told him that a surgeon would be in presently to
attend to his wounds, and expressed the hope that they were
not very serious. Thereupon he asked me who I was, and on
giving him my name he muttered as if speaking to himself.

"'Yes, yes,—I know you now,—member of Congress—this
district.'

"I then asked the question:

"'Captain, what brought you here?'

"'To free your slaves,' was the reply.

"'How did you expect to accomplish it with the small force
you brought with you?'

"'I expected help.'

"'Where, whence, and from whom, Captain, did you expect it?'

"'Here and from elswhere,' he answered.

"'Did you expect to get assistance from whites here as well
as from the blacks?' was my next question.

"'I did,' he replied.

"'Then,' said I, 'you have been disappointed in not getting
it from either?'

"'Yes,' he muttered, 'I have—been—disappointed.'

"Then I asked him who planned his movement on Harper's
Ferry, to which he replied: 'I planned it all myself,' and upon
my remarking that it was a sad affair for him and the country,
and that I trusted no one would follow his example by undertaking a similar raid, he made no response. I next inquired if
he had any family besides the sons who had accompanied him
on his incursion, to which he replied by telling me he had a

wife and children in the State of New York at North Elba, and on my then asking if he would like to write to them and let them know how he was, he quickly responded:

"'Yes, I would like to send them a letter.'

"'Very well,' I said,' you will doubtless be permitted to do so. But, Captain,' I added, 'probably you understand that, being in the hands of the civil authorities of the State, your letters will have to be seen by them before they can be sent.'

"'Certainly,' he said.

"'Then, with that understanding,' continued I, 'there will, I'm sure, be no objection to your writing home; and although I myself have no authority in the premises, I promise to do what I can to have your wishes in that respect complied with.'

"'Thank you—thank you, sir,' said he, repeating his acknowledgment for the proferred favor and, for the first time, turning his head toward me.

"In my desire to hear him distinctly I had placed myself by his side, with one knee resting on the floor; so that, when he turned, it brought his face quite close to mine, and I remember well the earnest gaze of the gray eye that looked straight into mine. I then remarked:

"'Captain, we, too, have wives and children. This attempt of yours to interfere with our slaves, has created great excitement, and naturally causes anxiety on account of our families. Now, let me ask you: Is this failure of yours likely to be followed by similar attempts to create disaffection among our servants and bring upon our homes the horrors of a servile war?'

"'Time will show,' was his significant reply.

"Just then a Catholic priest appeared at the door of the room. He had been administering the last consolations of religion to Quinn, the marine, who was dying in the adjoining office; and the moment Brown saw him he became violently angry, and plainly showed, by the expression of his countenance, how capable he was of feeling 'hatred, malice, and all uncharitableness.'

"'Go out of here—I don't want you about me—go out!' was the salutation he gave the priest, who, bowing gravely, immediately retired. Whereupon I arose from the floor, and bidding Brown good-morning, likewise left him.

"In the entry leading to the room where Brown was, I met Major Russell, of the marine corps, who was going to see him, and I detailed to him the conversation I had just had. Meeting the major subsequently he told me that when he entered the apartment Brown was standing up—with his clothes unfastened —examining the wound in his side, and that, as soon as he saw him, forthwith resumed his former position on the floor; which incident tended to confirm the impression I had already formed, that there was a good deal of vitality left in the old man, notwithstanding his wounds,—a fact more fully developed that evening after I had left Harper's Ferry for home, when he had his spirited and historic talk with Wise, Hunter, and Vallandigham.

"Between the time of his raid and his execution I saw Brown several times, and was sitting near him in the court-room when the sentence of death was pronounced upon him, during which he was apparently the least interested person present. Of course, I did not witness his execution, as I had seen quite enough of horrors at Harper's Ferry, little dreaming of those, ten thousand times more terrible, which I was yet to witness as among the results of the John Brown raid."—*Century*.

PART II.

John Brown's Autobiography, Family Record, and other papers relating to John Brown and his family, with narratives of actions, etc., gathered from authentic sources.

JOHN BROWN'S AUTOBIOGRAPHY,

WRITTEN BY HIM TO HENRY L. STEARNS, SON OF GEORGE L. STEARNS, AND BEARING DATE RED ROCK, IOWA, JULY 7, 1857.

"John was born May 9th, 1800, at Torrington, Litchfield Co., Connecticut; of poor but respectable parents: a decendant on the side of his father of one of the company of the *Mayflower* who landed at Plymouth 1620. His mother was descended from a man who came at an early period to New England from Amsterdam, in Holland. Both his Father's & his Mother's Fathers served in the war of the revolution: His Father's Father; died in a barn at New York while in the service, in 1776.

"I cannot tell you of any thing in the first Four years of John's life worth mentioning save that at that *early age* he was tempted by Three large Brass Pins belonging to a girl who lived in the family & *stole them*. In this he was detected by his Mother; & after having a full day to think of the wrong: received from her a thorough whipping. When he was Five years old his Father moved to Ohio; then a wilderness filled with wild beasts, & Indians. During the long journey which was performed in part or mostly with an *ox team;* he was called on by turns to assist a boy Five years older (who had been adopted by his Father & Mother) & learned to think he could accomplish *smart things* in driving the Cows, and riding the horses. Sometimes he met with Rattle Snakes which were very large; & which some of the company generally managed to kill. After getting to Ohio in 1805 he was for some time rather afraid of the Indians, & of their Rifles; but this soon wore off: & he used to hang about them quite as much as was consistent with good manners; & learned a trifle of their talk. His Father learned to dress Deer Skins, & at 6 years old John was installed a young Buck Skin—He was perhaps rather observing as he ever after remembered the entire process of Deer Skin *dressing;* so that he could at any time dress his own leather such as Squirel, Raccoon, Cat, Wolf, or Dog Skins; & also learned to make Whip Lashes: which brought him some change at times; & was of considerable service in many ways. —At Six years old John began to be quite a rambler in the wild new country finding birds & Squirels, & sometimes a wild Turkey's nest. But about this period he was placed in the school of *adversity:* which my young friend was a most necessary part of his early training. You may *laugh* when you come to read about it; but these were *sore trials* to John: whose earthly treasures were very *few* & *small.* These were the beginning of a severe but *much needed course* of discipline which he afterwards was to pass through; & which it is to be hoped has learned him before this time that the Heavenly Father sees it best to take all the little things out of his hand which he has ever placed in them. When John was in his Sixth year a poor *Indian boy* gave him a Yellow Marble the first he had ever seen. This he thought a great deal of; & kept it a good while; but at last *he lost it* beyond recovery. *It took years to heal the wound;* & I *think* he cried at times about it. About Five months after this he caught a young Squirel tearing off his tail in doing it; & getting severely bitten at the same time himself. He however held *to the little bob tail* Squirel; & finally got him perfectly tamed, so that he almost idolized his pet. *This too be lost;* by its wandering away: or by getting killed : & for a year or Two John was *in mourning;* and looking at all the Squirels he could see to try & discover Bob tail, *if possible,* I must not neglect to tell you of a very *bad & foolish* habbit to which John was somewhat addicted. I mean *telling lies:* generally to screen himself from blame; or from punishment. He could not well endure to be reproached; & I now think had he been oftener encouraged to be entirely frank; *by making frankness a kind of atonement* for some of his faults; he would not have been so often guilty of this fault ; nor have been obliged to struggle *so long* in after life with *so mean* a habit.

John was *never quarrelsome;* but was *excessively* fond of the *hardest & roughest* kind of plays ; & could *never get enough* [of] them. Indeed when for a short time he was sometimes sent to School the opportunity it afforded to wrestle & Snow ball & run & jump & knock off old seedy wool hats; offered to him almost the only compensation for the confinement, & restraints of school. I need not tell you that with such a feeling & but little chance of going to school *at all:* he did not become much of a schollar. He would always choose to stay at home & work hard rather than be sent to school; & during the warm season might generally be seen *barefooted & bareheaded:* with Buck skin Breeches suspended often with one leather strap over his shoulder but sometimes with Two. To be sent off through the wilderness alone to very considerable distances was particularly his delight; & in this he was often indulged so that by the time he was Twelve years old he was sent off more than a Hundred Miles with companies of cattle ; & he would have thought his character much injured had he been obliged to be helped in any such job. This was a boyish kind of feeling but characteristic however.

" At Eight years old John was left a Motherless boy which loss was complete & permanent, for notwithstanding his Father again married to a sensible, inteligent, & on many accounts a very estimable woman: *yet be never addopted her in feeling :* but continued to pine after his own Mother for years. This

opperated very unfavourably uppon him : as he was both naturally fond of females ; & withall extremely diffident ; & deprived
him of a suitable connecting link between the different sexes ;
the want of which might under some circumstances have
proved his ruin.

"When the war broke out *with England,* his Father soon
commenced furnishing the troops with beef cattle, the collecting & driving of which *afforded* him some opportunity for the
chase (on foot) of wild steers & other cattle through the woods.
During this war he had some chance to form his own boyish
judgment of *men & measures :* & to become somewhat fa-
miliarly acquainted with some who have figured before the
country since that time. The effect of what he saw during the
war was to so far disgust him with military affairs that he
would neither train, *or drill ;* but paid fines ; & got along like
a Quaker untill his age finally has cleared him of Military duty.

"During the war with England a circumstance occurred that
in the end made him a most *determined Abolitionist :* & led
him to declare, *or Swear: Eternal war* with *Slavery.* He
was staying for a short time with a very gentlemanly landlord
once a United States Marshal who held a slave boy near his
own age very active, intelligent and good feeling ; & to whom
John was under considerable obligation for numerous little
acts of kindness. *The master* made a great pet of John :
brought him to table with his first company ; & friends ;
called their attention to every little smart thing he *said
or did :* & to the fact of his being more than a hundred
miles from home with a company of cattle alone ; while the
negro boy (who was fully if not more than his equal) was
badly clothed, poorly fed ; *& lodged in cold weather ; &*
beaten before his eyes with Iron Shovels or any other thing
that came first to hand. This brought John to reflect on the
wretched ; hopeless condition, of *Fatherless* & *Motherless* slave
children : for such children have neither Fathers nor Mothers
to protect, & provide for them. He sometimes would raise the
question *is God their Father ?*

"At the age of Ten years an old friend induced him to read

a little history; & offered him the free use of a good library; by which he acquired some taste for reading: which formed the principle part of his early education: & diverted him in a great measure from bad company. He by this means grew to be very fond of the company, & conversation of old & intelligent persons. He never attempted to dance in his life; nor did he even learn to know *one* of a pack of *cards* from *another*. He learned nothing of Grammar; nor did he get at school so much knowledge of common Arithmetic as the Four ground rules. This will give you some idea of the first Fifteen years of his life; during which time he became very strong & large of his age & ambitious to perform the full labour of a man; at almost any kind of hard work. By reading the lives of great, wise & good men their sayings, and writings; he grew to a dislike of vain & frivolous *conversation & persons ;* & was often greatly obliged by the kind manner in which older & more intelligent persons treated him at their houses: & in conversation ; which was a great relief on account of his extreme bashfulness.

"He very early in life became ambitious to excel in doing anything he undertook to perform. This kind of feeling I would recommend to all young persons both *male & female .* as it will certainly tend to secure admission to the company of the more intelligent ; & better portion of every community. By all means endeavor to excel in some laudable pursuit.

"I had like to have forgotten to tell you of one of John's misfortunes which set rather hard on him while a young boy. He had by some means *perhaps* by gift of his father become the owner of a little Ewe Lamb which did finely till it was about Two Thirds grown ; & then sickened & died. This brought another protracted *mourning season :* not that he felt the pecuniary loss so much : for that was never his disposition ; but so strong & earnest were his attachments.

"John had been taught from earliest childhood to 'fear God and keep his commandments'; & though quite skeptical he had always by turns felt much serious doubt as to his future well being ; & about this time became to some extent a convert to

Christianity & ever after a firm believer in the divine authenticity of the Bible. With this book he became very familiar, & possessed a most unusual memory of its entire contents.

" Now some of the things I have been *telling of ;* were just such as I would recommend to you : & I wd like to know that you had selected these out; & adopted them as part of your own plan of life; & I wish you to have *some definite plan*. Many seem to have none ; & others never stick to any that they do form. This was not the case with John. He followed up with *tenacity* whatever he set about so long as it answered his general purpose : & hence he rarely failed in some good decree to effect the things he undertook. This was so much the case that he *habitually expected to succeed* in his undertakings. With this feeling *should be coupled ;* the consciousness that our plans are right in themselves.

" During the period I have named John had acquired a kind of ownership to certain animals of some little value but as he had come to understand that the *title of minors* might be a little imperfect : he had recourse to various means in order to secure a more *independent ;* & perfect right of property. One of those means was to exchange with his Father for something of far less value. Another was trading with others persons for something his Father had never owned. Older persons have some times found difficulty with *titles*.

" From fifteen to Twenty years old, he spent most of his time working at the Tanner & Currier's trade keeping Bachelors hall ; & he was acting as Cook ; & for most of the time as forman of the establishment under his father. During this period he found much trouble with some of the bad habits I have mentioned & with some that I have not told you off : his conscience urging him forward with great power in this matter : but his close attention to *business;* & success in his management ; together with the way he got along with a company of men, & boys ; made him quite a favorite with the serious & more intelligent portion of older persons. This was so much the case ; & secured for him so many little notices from those he esteemed ; that his vanity was very much fed by it ; & he came forward to manhood quite full of self-conceit; & self-confident; notwithstanding his *extreme* bashfulness. A younger brother used sometimes to remind him of this: & to repeat to him *this expression* which you may somewhere find, 'A King against whom there is no rising up.' The habit so early formed of being obeyed rendered him in after life too much disposed to speak in an imperious & dictating way. From Fifteen years & upward he felt a good deal of anxiety to learn; but could only read & studdy a little; both for want of time; & on account of inflammation of the eyes. He however managed by the help of books to make himself tolerably well acquainted with common arithmetic; & Surveying; which he practiced more or less after he was Twenty years old.

"At a little past Twenty years led by his own inclination & *prompted also* by his Father, he married a *remarkably plain;* but neat industrious & economical girl; of excellent character; earnest piety; & good practical common sense; about one year younger than himself. This woman, by her mild, frank, & *more than all* else: by her very consistent conduct; acquired & ever while she lived maintained a most powerful; & good influence over him. Her plain but kind admonitions generally had the right effect; without arousing his haughty obstinate temper. John began early in life to discover a great liking to fine Cattle, Horses, Sheep, & Swine; & as soon as circumstances would enable him he began to be a practical *Shepherd: it being* a calling for which *in early* life he had a kind of *enthusiastic longing:* with the idea that as a business it bid fair to afford him the means of carrying out his greatest or principle object. I have now given you a kind of general idea of the early life of this boy; & if I believed it would be worth the trouble; or afford much interest to any good feeling person: I might be tempted to tell you something of his course in after life; or manhood. I do not say that I *will do it*.

"You will discover that in using up my *half sheets to save paper;* I have written Two pages, so that one does not follow the other as it should. I have no time to write it over; & but for unavoidable hindrances in traveling I can hardly say when

I should have written what I have.   With an honest desire for your best good, I subscribe myself,   Your Friend

J. Brown.

"P. S.   I had like to have forgotten to aknowledge your contribution in aid of the cause in which I serve.   God Allmighty *bless you ;* my son.   J. B."

THE JOHN BROWN FAMILY.

(Those living are given in roman, those who died in italics, and those who were slain are in capitals.)

Children by his wife Dianthe:—John Brown, Jr., born July 25, 1821, at Hudson, Ohio; married Wealthy C. Hotchkis, July, 1857; issue, son and daughter.   Lives at Put-in-Bay Island, Lake Erie, near Sandusky, Ohio, aged 73.   John served in the Kansas troubles and as a captain in the Union army.

Jason Brown, born Jan. 19, 1823, at Hudson ; married Ellen Sherbondy, July, 1847; living issue two sons ; Jason, 71 years of age, resides at South Pasadena, Cal.   Jason served in Kansas.

Owen Brown, born Nov. 4, 1824, at Hudson.   Never married, and died at Pasadena, a few years since, about 66 years of age.   *Owen* was in Kansas and at Harper's Ferry.

Frederick (first), Jan. 9, 1827, at Richmond, Pa.; died at four years of age, March 31, 1831.

Ruth, born Feb. 18, 1829, at Richmond, Pa.; married to Henry Thompson, Sept. 26, 1850, issue, living, three daughters, residing with her husband (brother of William and Dauphin Thompson, killed at Harper's Ferry, 1859) at South Pasadena, Cal.

FREDERICK (second), Dec. 31, 1830, at Richmond, Pa., unmarried, and slain at Osawatomie in a border-ruffian foray, August 30, 1856, in the twenty-sixth year of his life.

A son unnamed was buried with its mother, Aug. 10, 1832, at Richmond, Pa., three days after birth.

Children by his wife Mary :—*Sarah,* born May 11, 1834, at Richmond, Pa.; died in her ninth year, Sept. 23, 1843.

WATSON, born Oct. 7, 1835, at Franklin, Ohio; married *Isabella M. Thompson* (sister of Henry, William, and Dauphin). Sept. 1856; slain at Harper's Ferry. Oct. 18, 1859, in his twenty-seventh year. Their child died the next year. The widow was married again in 1864, to Salmon Brown, a cousin of Watson.

Salmon Brown, born Oct. 2, 1836, at Hudson, Ohio; married Abbie C. Hinckley, Oct. 15, 1857; he lives now in Washington near Tacoma, in his fifty-seventh year; has eight children. He served in Kansas, and as a lieutenant in the Civil War.

Charles, born Nov. 3, 1837, at Hudson; died in his fourth year, Sept. 11, 1841.

OLIVER, born March 9, 1839, at Franklin, Ohio; married *Martha E. Brewster*, April 7, 1858, slain in his twenty-first year at Harper's Ferry, Oct. 17, 1859; *Martha* died with her baby at North Elba in the following winter. OLIVER served in Kansas.

Peter, born 1840 in Ohio, at Hudson, and *Austin*, born 1842 at Richfield, Ohio, both died in September, 1843, and were buried in the same grave with their sister *Sarah* and brother *Charles*.

Amelie, born June, 1845, at Akron, Ohio, died October, 1848.

Ellen, born May, 1848, at Springfield, died in April 1849; also infant son, born and died at Akron, April and May, 1847.

Annie, born Dec, 7, 1843, at Richfield, Ohio; married Mr. Adams, mother of six living children, and resides at Petralia, Humboldt Co., Cal.

Sarah, born Sept. 11, 1846, at Akron, Ohio, lives in Santa Cruz Co., Cal., unmarried.

Ellen, born Sept. 25, 1854, at Akron, Ohio, married in California a Mr. Fablinger, and lives in Santa Cruz Co., that State.

The North Elba homestead is inhabited by Mr. Hinkley and family. He is a brother-in-law of Salmon Brown; his wife is a sister of William and Dauphin Thompson, killed at Harper's Ferry, and of Henry, Ruth Brown's husband, and Isabella, the wife of Watson Brown. The home and ground are now a trust, Miss Kate Field having raised the purchase money. Two of the California grandchildren died recently.

THE BROWN SETTLEMENT.

KANSAS LETTERS OF CAPTAINS JOHN BROWN AND JOHN BROWN, JR.

[From the archives of the Kansas Historical Society.]

BROWNSVILLE, BROWN CO., K. T., }
Friday Morning, June 22, 1855. }

DEAR FATHER—Day before yesterday we received a letter from you, dated Rockford, Illinois, 24th May, which for some unaccountable cause has been very long delayed on the road. We are exceedingly glad to hear from you, and that you still intend coming on. Our health is now excellent, and our crops, cattle, and horses look finely. We have now about twelve acres seed corn in the ground, more than one-fourth acre of white beans, two and one-half bushels seed potatoes planted, and once hoed; besides a good garden containing corn, potatoes, beets, cabbages, turnips, a few onions, some peas, cucumbers, melons, squashes, etc. Jason's fruit-trees, grape-vines, etc., that survived the long period of transportation, look very well; probably more than half he started with are living, with the exception of peaches; of these he has only one or two trees. As we arrived so late in the season we have but little expectation of harvesting much corn, and but few potatoes. The rainy season usually commences here early in April, or before, and continues from six to eight weeks, during which a great amount of rain falls. This year we had no rain of any consequence before the 12th or 15th of May. Since then have had two heavy rains, accompanied with some wind and most tremendous thunder and lightning. Have also had a number of gentle rains, continuing from one to twenty-four hours; but, probably, not more than half the usual fall of rain has yet come. As the season last year was irregular in this respect, probably this will be to some extent. We intend to keep our garden, beans, and some potatoes watered if we can, so as to have something if our corn should be a failure. As it is, the prospect is middling fair, and the ground is plowed, ready for early planting next year. Old settlers· here say, that people should calculate on having the spring's sowing and planting all done by the middle of April. In that case their crops are most abundant. The prairies are covered with grass, which begins to wave in the wind most beautifully. Shall be able to cut any quantity of this, and it is of far better quality than I had any idea.

In answer to your question, good oxen are from $50 to $60 per yoke; have been higher. Common cows from $15 to $25 each; probably will not be higher. Heifers in proportion. Limited demand as yet for fine stock, very best horses from $100 to $150 each; average good to fair, $75 to $80. No great demand now for cattle or horses. A good, strong buggy would sell well, probably a Sumberee best. Mr. Adair has had several chances to sell his. Very few Sumberee buggies among the settlers. White beans, $5 per bushel; corn-meal, $1.75 per bushel, of fifty lbs., tending downward. Flour, $7 per hundred lbs. Dried apples, twelve and a half cents per lb. Bacon, twelve to fourteen cents here. Fresh beef, five to six cents per lb. Inclosed is a slip, cut from a late number of the *Kansas Tribune*, giving the markets there. It differs some from what it is in this section. It is the paper published at Lawrence by the Speers. I have no doubt, it would be much cheaper and healthier for you to come in the way you propose, with a covered lumber buggy and one horse or mule, especially from St. Louis here. The navigation of the Missouri River, except by the light-draft boats recently built for the Kansas River, is a horrid business in a low stage of water, which is a considerable portion of the year. You will be able to see much more of the country on your way, and if you carry provisions along it is altogether the cheaper mode of traveling, besides such a conveyance is just what you want here to carry on the business of surveying. You can have a good road here " whithersoever " you may wish to go. Flour, white beans, and dried fruit will doubtless continue for some

time to come to be high. It is believed that a much larger
emigration will arrive here this fall than before. Should you
buy anything to send by water, you can send it either
to Lawrence, thirty-five miles north of us, or to Kansas
City, Mo., care of Walker & Chick, sixty miles northeast
of us.

A surveyor would soon find that great numbers are holding
more land, and especially timber, than can be covered by 160
acres, or even 320 ; that great numbers are holding claims for
their friends, so that I have no doubt people will find a sufficient amount of timber yet for a long time. Owing to the
rapid settlement of the country by squatters it does not open a
good field for land speculators.

The land on which we are located was ceded by the Pottawatomie Indians to the Government. The Ottawa lands are
soon to be sold, each person of the tribe receiving and choos-
ing 200 acres, the remainder open to preëmption after their
choice is made. The Peoria lands have been bargained for
by the Government and are to be sold to the highest bidder,
without reservation. But Missourians have illegally gone on
to these Peoria lands intending to combine and prevent their
going higher than $1.25 per acre, and then claim, if they go
higher, a large amount for improvements, thus cheating the
Indians. The Ottawas intend to divide into families and cultivate the soil and the habits of civilized life as many of them
are now doing. They are a fine people. The Peorias are well
advanced and might do the same but for a bad bargain with
the Government.

There is a town site recently laid out, on the space marked
Village Plat ;[1] as there are two or three in view it is uncertain
which will be taken. The semicircle is over ground sloping
every way, and affording a view in every way of from twenty to
thirty miles in every direction except one small point in the

---

[1] A nicely drawn plat accompanied this letter, which is now in
the archives of the Kansas State Historical Society.

direction of Osawatomie. The view from this ground is beautiful beyond measure.

The timbered lands on Middle Creek are covered with claims, the claimants, many of them from Ohio, Illinois, and the East, and are mostly free-state folks. There are probably twenty families within five or six miles of us.

Day before yesterday Owen and I ran the Peoria line east to see if there might not be found a patch of timber on some of the numerous small streams which put into the Osage and which would be south of the Peoria line. We found on a clear little stream sufficient timber for a log-house, and wood enough to last a hundred families for two or three years, perhaps more, and until we could buy and raise more. Here a good claim could be made by some one. The prairie land which would be included is of the very best I have ever seen; plenty of excellent stone on and adjoining it. Claims will soon be made here that will have no more than two or three acres of timber, and after these are exhausted prairie claims will be taken, the claimants depending on buying their timber. Already this is the case, and many are selling off twenty, thirty, and forty acres from their timber claims to those who have none.

(From John Brown, Jr.) [*Not signed.*]

JOHN BROWN ON THE ROAD.

SCOTT CO., IOWA, 4th Sept., 1855, in morning.

DEAR WIFE AND CHILDREN ALL—I am writing in our tent, about twenty miles west of the Mississippi, to let you know that we are all in good health and how we get along. We had some delay at Chicago on account of our freight not getting on as we expected; while there we bought a stout young horse that proves to be a very good one; but he has been unable to travel fast for several days from having taken the distemper. We think he appears quite us well as he has done this morning and we hope he will not fail us. Our load is heavy, so that we have to walk most of the time; indeed, all the time the last day. The roads are mostly very good and

we can make some progress if our horse does not fail us. We
fare very well on crackers, herring, boiled eggs, prairie-chick-
ens, tea, and sometimes a little milk. Have three chickens
now cooking for our breakfast. We shoot enough of them on
the wing as we go along to supply us with fresh meat.
Oliver succeeds in bringing them down quite as well as any of
us. Our expenses before we got away from Chicago had been
very heavy; since then very light; so that we hope that our
money will not entirely fail us; but we shall not have any of
account left when we get through. We expect to go direct
through Missouri, and if we are not obliged to stop on account
of our horse, shall soon be there. We mean to write you often
when we can. We got to Rock Island too soon for any letter
from you; but shall not be too early at Kansas City, where we
hope to hear from you. The country through which we have
traveled from Chicago, has been mostly very good; the worst
fault is the want of living streams of water.

With all the comforts we have along our journey, I think—
could I hope in any other way to answer the end of my being—
I would be quite content to be at North Elba. I have directed
the sale of the cattle in Connecticut, and to have the balance
sent in a New York draft payable to Watson's order, which I
hope will make you all quite comfortable. Watson should get
something more at Elizabethtown than the mere face of the
draft. He will need to write his name across the back of the
draft when he sells it; about two inches from the top end
would be the proper place. I want you to make the most of
the money you get, as I expect to be very poor about money
from any other source. Commend you all to the mercy and
infinite grace of God, I bid you all good-bye for this time.

Your affectionate husband and father,   JOHN BROWN.

ARRIVAL IN KANSAS.

OSAWATOMIE, K. T., Oct. 13th, 1855, Saturday Evening.

DEAR WIFE AND CHILDREN, EVERY ONE—We reached
the place where the boys are located one week ago, last night;

at least Henry and Oliver did; I, being tired, staid behind in
our tent a mile or two back. As the mail goes from here early
Monday morning we could get nothing here in time for that
mail. We found all more or less sick, or feeble but Wealthy
and Johnny. All at Brownville appear now to be mending.
All sick or feeble here at Mr. Adair's. Fever and ague and
chill fever seem to be very general. Oliver has had a turn of
the ague since he got here, but has got it broken. Henry has
had no return since first breaking it. We met with no difficulty in passing through Missouri, but from the sickness of our
horse and our heavy load; the horse has entirely recovered.
We had between us all sixty cents in cash when we arrived.
We found our folks in a most uncomfortable situation, with no
houses to shelter one of them, no hay or corn-fodder of any
account secured, shivering over their little fires, all exposed to
the dreadfully cutting winds, morning and evening, and the
stormy days. We have been trying to help them all in our
power and hope to get them more comfortable soon. I think
much of their ill health is owing to most unreasonable exposure. Mr. Adair's folks would be quite comfortable if they
were well. One letter from wife and Anne to Salmon of
August 10th, and one from Ruth to John of September 19th is
all I have seen from any of you since getting here. Henry
found one from Ruth which he has not shown me. Need I
write that I shall be glad to hear from you? I did not write
while in Missouri, because I had no confidence in your getting
my letter. We took up little Austin and brought him on here ·
which appears to be a great comfort to Jason and Ellen. We
were all out a good part of last night, helping to keep the
prairie fires from destroying everything; so that I am almost
blind to-day, or I would write you more.

Sabbath eve, October 14th. I notice in your letter to Salmon
your trouble about the means of having the house made more
comfortable for the winter, and I fondly hope you have been
relieved of that scare before now by funds from Mr. Hulbert,
of Winchester, Ct., from the sale of the cattle there. Write me
all about your situation, for if disappointed from that source I

shall make every effort to relieve you in some other way. Last
Tuesday was an election day with free-state men in Kansas,
and, hearing that there was a prospect of difficulty we all turned
out most thoroughly armed (except Jason who was too feeble),
but no enemy appeared; nor have I heard of any disturbance
in any part of the Territory. Indeed, I believe Missouri is fast
becoming discouraged about making Kansas a slave State, and
think the prospect of its becoming free is brightening every
day. Try to be cheerful; and always "hope in God," who will
not leave nor forsake them who put their trust in Him. Try to
comfort and encourage each other all you can. You are all very
dear to me; and I humbly trust we may be kept and spared to
meet again on earth; but if not; let us all endeavor earnestly
to secure admission to that eternal home where will be no
more bitter separations; "where the wicked shall cease from
troubling, and the weary be at rest." We shall probably spend
a few days more in helping the boys to provide some kind of
shelters for winter, and I mean to write you often. May the God
of infinite mercy bless, comfort, and save you all; for Christ's
sake.

Your affectionate husband and father,

JOHN BROWN.

SETTLERS' PRIVATIONS.

BROWNSVILLE, KANSAS TERRITORY, Nov. 2d, 1855.

DEAR WIFE AND CHILDREN, EVERY ONE—We last week
received Watson's letters too late to answer till now; I feel
grateful to learn that you were all then well; and I think I
fully sympathize with you in all the hardships and discourage-
ments you have to meet, but you may be agreed that you are
not *alone* in having trials to meet. I believe, I wrote you that
we found all more or less unwell here but Wealthy and Tonny;
without any sort of a place where a *stout man* even could protect himself from the cutting cold winds and storms which pre-
vail here, the winds I mean in particular much more than in any
place where we have ever lived; and that no crops of hay or

anything raised had been taken care of; with corn wasting by cattle and horses; without fence; and I may add without any meat; and Jason's folks without any sugar or any kind of bread-stuffs but corn ground with great labor in a hand-mill about two miles off. Since I wrote, Wealthy, Tonny, Ellen, and myself have escaped being sick; some have had the ague but lightly; but Jason and Oliver have had a hard time of it, and are yet feeble. They appear some better just now. Under existing circumstances we have made but little progress, but we have made a little. We have got a shanty three logs high, chinked, and mudded, and roofed with our tent, and a chimney so far advanced that we can keep a fire in it for Jason. John has his shanty a little better fixed than it was, but miserable enough now, and we have got their little crop of beans secured, which, together with a johnny cake, mush, and milk pumpkins, and squashes, constitute our fare.

[*Unsigned.*]

RENEWAL OF STRIFE.

OSAWATOMIE, KANSAS TERRITORY, Feb. 1, 1856.

DEAR WIFE AND CHILDREN, EVERY ONE— Your and Watson's letter to the boys and myself of December 30th and January 1st were received by last mail. We are all very glad to hear again of your welfare, and I am particularly grateful when I am noticed by a letter from *you*. I have just taken out two letters for Henry, one of which I suppose is from Ruth. Salmon and myself are so far on our way home from Missouri, and only reached Mr. Adair's last night. They are all well. and we know of nothing but all are well at the boys' shanties. The weather continues very severe and it is now nearly six weeks that the snow has been almost constantly driven (like dry sand) by the fierce winds of Kansas. Mr. Adair has been collecting ice of late from the Osage River, which is nine and one-half inches thick, of perfect clear, solid ice, formed under the snow. By means of the sale of our horse and wagon, our present wants are tolerably well met, so that if health is con-

tinued to us we shall not probably suffer much. The idea of
again visiting those of my dear family at North Elba is so calculated to unman me, that I seldom allow my thoughts to dwell
upon it, and I do not think best to write much about it. "Suf-
fice to say," that God is *abundantly* able to keep both us and
you, and *in Him let us all trust.* We have just learned of
some *new* and shocking outrages at Leavenworth, and that
free-state people there have fled to Lawrence, which place is
again threatened with an attack. *Should* that take place, we
may soon again be called upon to "buckle on our armor,"
which by the help of God we will do, when I suppose Henry
and Oliver will have a chance. *My judgement is* that we shall
have no general disturbance until warmer weather. *I have
more to say,* but not time now to say it, so farewell for this
time. *Write.*

Your affectionate husband and father,

JOHN BROWN.

BORDER–RUFFIAN RUMORS.

BROWN STATION, KANSAS TERRITORY, 7th April, 1856.

DEAR WIFE AND CHILDREN, EVERY ONE—I wrote you
last week enclosing New York draft for thirty dollars, made
payable to Watson, twenty dollars of which were to be given
to Ruth in part payment for the spotted cow; the balance to
be used as circumstances might require. I would have sent
you more, but I had no way to do it, and money is very scarce
with me indeed. Since I wrote last three letters have been
received by the boys from Ruth, dated March 5th and 9th, and
one of some date from Watson. The general tone of those
letters I like exceedingly. We do not want you to borrow
trouble about us, but trust us to the mercy of " Him who feeds
the young ravens when they cry." I have, *as usual*, but little
to write. We are doing off a house for Orson Day,[1] which we
hope to get through with soon, *after which* we shall probably
soon leave this neighborhood, but will advise you further when

---

[1] Brother to Mrs. Brown.

we do leave. It may be that Watson can manage to get a little money for shearing sheep if you do not get any from Connecticut. I still hope that you will get help from that source. We have no wars as yet, but we have abundance of "rumors." We still have frosty nights, but the grass starts a little. There are none of us complaining much just now, all being able to do something. John has just returned from Topeka, not having met with any difficulty, but we hear that preparations are making in the United States Court for numerous arrests of free-state men. For one I have no desire (all things considered) to have the slave-power cease from its acts of aggression. "Their foot shall slide in due time." No more now; may God bless and keep you all.   Your affectionate husband and father.

_____ [*Not signed.*]

FROM THE PRISONERS' CAMP NEAR LECOMPTON.

MONDAY MORNING, September 8, 1856.

DEAR FATHER AND BROTHER—Colonel Blood has just handed me your letter, for which I am most grateful. Having before heard of Frederick's death and that you were missing, my anxiety on your account has been most intense. Though my dear brother I shall never see again here, yet I thank God you and Jason still live. Poor Frederick has perished in a good cause, the success of which cause, I trust, will yet bring joy to millions. My "circumstances" and prospects are much the same as when I last wrote to you. The trial of Mr. Williams and myself is before Cato, in Olathe, I believe the 4th. Don't know whether or not the others will get any trial here. Judge Lecompte is reported sick, and as no notice of the names of the jurors and witnesses has been served on them, it looks as if the intention is to hold them over to another term. Wealthy has the chills and fever almost every day. She succeeds in checking it only a short time. It would afford us a great satisfaction to see you and Jason. He and I have no doubt you could come up with some one without any risk. If Governor Geary should not release us I think still of going with you, when you think it best, to some place out of reach of re-arrest. I can, I have no doubt, succeed in making my escape to you from here, where W. and Johnny might join us. There is some talk of our being remanded to Leavenworth soon. If we are, I suppose, the difficulty of escape would be very much increased. I AM ANXIOUS TO SEE YOU BOTH, in order to perfect some plan of escape, in case it should appear best. Come up, if you *consistently* can. The battle of Osawatomie is considered here as *the great fight* so far, and considering the enemies' loss, it is certainly a great victory for us ; certainly a very dear burning of the town for them. This has proved most unmistakably that "Yankees" WILL "fight." Every one I hear speaking of you is loud in your praise. The Missourians in this region show signs of great fear. Colonel Cook was heard to say that, " if our party were prudent in view of their success, there was nothing to prevent our having everything our own way."

Hoping to see you both soon, I am as ever your affectionate son and brother,

(On margin)   J. BROWN, JR., in prison.

AN INTERVIEW WITH JOHN BROWN AND KAGI.

[First written by Richard J. Hinton for and published in the " Public Life of John Brown" by James Redpath, Boston, 1860, under the caption " Some Shadows Before."]

" On Sunday I held a very interesting conversation with John Brown, which lasted nearly the whole afternoon. The purport of it was, on his part, inquiries as to various public men in the Territory, and the condition of political affairs. He was very particular in his inquiries as to the movements and character of Captain Montgomery. The massacre of the Marais des Cygnes was then fresh in the minds of the people. I remember an expression which he used. Warmly giving utterance to my detestation of slavery and its minions, and impatiently wishing for some effectual means of injuring it, Captain Brown said, most impressively : ' Young men must learn to wait Patience is the hardest lesson to learn. I have waited for twenty years to accomplish my purpose.'

"In the course of the conversation he reminded me of a message that I had sent him in 1857, and hoped I meant what I then said, for he should ask the fulfillment of that promise, and that perhaps very soon; and further added that he wanted to caution me against rash promises. Young men were too apt to make them, and should be very careful. The promise given was of great importance, and I must be prepared to stand by or disavow it now. My answer need not be stated. In this conversation he gave me no definite idea of his plans, but seemed generally bent on ascertaining the opinions and characters of our men of anti-slavery reputation.

"Kagi, at the same time, gave me to understand that their visit to Kansas was caused by a betrayal of their plans, by a Colonel Forbes, to the administration, and that they wished to give a different impression from what these disclosures had, by coming to the west. Both stated they intended to stay some time, and that night (Sunday) Captain Brown announced they would go south in the morning, to see Captain Montgomery, and visit his own relatives at Osawatomie.

"A few weeks later I rode to Mr. Adair's house at Osawatomie and met Captain Brown again. My account of that interview follows:

"Captain Brown had been quite unwell, and was then somewhat more impatient and nervous in his manner than I had before observed. Soon after my arrival, he again engaged in conversation as to various public men in the Territory. Of his own treatment at the hands of ambitious leaders, to which I had alluded in bitter terms, he said: 'They acted up to their instincts, As politicians, they thought every man wanted to lead, and, therefore, supposed I might be in the way of their schemes. While they had this feeling, of course, they opposed me. Many men did not like the manner in which I conducted warfare, and they too opposed me. Committees and councils could not control my movements, therefore they did not like me. But politicians and leaders soon found that I had different purposes, and forgot their jealousy. They have been kind to me since.'

"The conviction was expressed that trouble would break out again in southern Kansas. At this time I had mentioned my intention of embarking in a newspaper enterprise. Captain Brown, in an impressive manner, expressed a wish that I should not enter into any entangling engagements, referring to my letter of 1857. He said that he thought all engagements should be considered sacred, and liked my adhering to the one I had at the time. That was the reason he had not sent to me; but now he hoped I would keep myself free. In this connection he used words which I have often thought of since.

"'For twenty years,' he said, 'I have never made any business arrangement which would prevent me at any time answering the call of the Lord. I have kept my business in such condition that in two weeks I could always wind up my affairs, and be ready to obey the call. I have permitted nothing to be in the way of my duty, neither my wife, children, nor worldly goods. Whenever the occasion offered, I was ready. The hour is very near at hand, and all who are willing to act should be ready.'

"I was not at this time aware of his precise plans, but had a general conception of his purpose. All through that conversation I had the impression that those blue-gray eyes, mild yet inflexible, and beaming with the steady light of a holy purpose, were searching my soul, and that my whole being was as transparent to him as the bosom of one of his own Adirondack lakes. I shall never forget the look or the expression with which he said: 'Young men should have a purpose in life, and adhere to it through all trials. They would be sure to succeed if their purpose is such as to deserve the blessing of God.'

"After dinner Kagi had some conversation with the Captain apart. He then asked me if I would walk down to the Marais des Cygnes, 'as he was going to fish.' I acquiesced, and we started. About half way to the river we stopped and sat on a fence. Kagi asked me what I supposed was the plan of Cap-

tain Brown. My answer was, that I thought it had a reference
to the Indian Territory and the Southwestern States. He
shook his head, and gradually unfolded the whole of their
plans. . . . A full account of the conversation in Canada
was given, as well as of the organization, its extent and objects,
thereby effected. The mountains of Virginia were named as
the place of refuge, and as a country admirably adapted to
carrying on a guerilla warfare. In the course of the conversation, Harper's Ferry was mentioned as a point to be seized—
but not held—on account of the arsenal. The white members
of the company were to act as officers of different guerilla
bands, which, under the general command of John Brown,
were to be composed of Canadian refugees and the Virginia
slaves who would join them. A different time of the year was
mentioned for the commencement of the warfare from that
which has lately been chosen. It was not anticipated that the
first movement would have any other appearance to the masters than a slave stampede, or local outbreak at most. The
planters would pursue their chattels and be defeated. The
militia would then be called out, and would also be defeated.
It was not intended that the movement should appear to be of
large dimensions, but that, gradually increasing in magnitude,
it should, as it opened, strike terror into the heart of the slave
States by the amount of organization it would exhibit, and the
strength it gathered. They anticipated, after the first blow
had been struck, that, by the aid of the freed and Canadian
negroes who would join them, they could inspire confidence in
the slaves, and induce them to rally. No intention was expressed of gathering a large body of slaves, and removing them
to Canada. On the contrary, Kagi clearly stated, in answer to
my inquiries, that the design was to make the fight in the
mountains of Virginia, extending it to North Carolina and
Tennessee, and also to the swamps of South Carolina, if possible. Their purpose was not the expatriation of one or a
thousand slaves, but their liberation in the States wherein they
were born, and were held in bondage. 'The mountains and
the swamps of the South were intended by the Almighty,' said

John Brown to me afterwards, ' for a refuge for the slave, and a defense against the oppressor.'

"Kagi spoke of having marked out a chain of counties extending continuously through South Carolina, Georgia, Alabama, and Mississippi. He had traveled over a large portion of the region indicated, and from his own personal knowledge, and with the assistance of the Canadian negroes who had escaped from those States, they had arranged a general plan of attack. The counties he named were those which contained the largest proportion of slaves, and would, therefore, be the best in which to strike. The blow struck at Harper's Ferry was to be in the spring, when the planters were busy, and the slaves most needed. The arms in the arsenal were to be taken to the mountains, with such slaves as joined. The telegraph wires were to be cut and railroad tracks torn up in all directions. As fast as possible, other bands besides the original one were to be formed, and a continuous chain of posts established in the mountains. They were to be supported by provisions taken from the farms of the oppressors. They expected to be speedily and constantly reinforced ; first, by the arrival of those men, who in Canada, were anxiously looking and praying for the time of deliverance, and then by the slaves themselves. The intention was to hold the egress to the free States as long as possible, in order to retreat when that was advisable. Kagi, however, expected to retreat southward, not in the contrary direction. The slaves were to be armed with pikes, scythes, muskets, shot-guns, and other simple instruments of defense; the officers, white or black, and such of the men as were skilled and trustworthy, to have the use of the Sharpe's rifles and revolvers. They anticipated procuring provisions enough for subsistence by forage, as also arms, horses, and ammunition. Kagi said one of the reasons that induced him to go into the enterprise was a full conviction that at no very distant day forcible efforts for freedom would break out among the slaves, and that slavery might be more speedily abolished by such efforts than by any other means. He knew by observation in the South, that in no point was the system so vulnerable as in its fear of a slave rising. Believing that such a blow would be soon struck, he wanted to organize it so as to make it more effectual, and also, by directing and controlling the negroes, to prevent some of the atrocities that would necessarily arise from the sudden upheaving of such a mass as the Southern slaves. The constitution adopted at Chatham was intended as the framework of organization among the emancipationists, to enable the leaders to effect a more complete control of their forces. Ignorant men, in fact, all men, were more easily managed by the forms of law and organization than without them. This was one of the purposes to be subserved by the Provisional Government. Another was to alarm the (slave-holding) oligarchy by discipline and the show of organization. In their terror they would imagine the whole North was upon them pell-mell, as well as all their slaves. Kagi said John Brown anticipated that by a system of forbearance to non-slave-holders many of them might be induced to join them.

"In answer to an inquiry, Kagi stated that no politician, in the Republican or any other party, knew of their plans, and but few of the Abolitionists. It was no use talking, he said, of anti-slavery action to non-resistant agitators. That there were men who knew John Brown's general idea is most true; but, south of the Canadian Provinces and of North Elba, there were but few who were cognizant of the mode by which he intended to mould those ideas into deeds.

"After a long conversation, the substance of which I have given, we returned to the house. I had some further conversation with Brown, mostly upon his movements, and the use of arms. An allusion to the terror inspired by the fear of slaves rising, was the fact that Nat Turner with fifty men held a portion of Virginia for several weeks. The same number well organized and armed, can shake the system out of the State. . . . Much more was said which I cannot recall. The afternoon had more than half passed before I left for my destination. I rode over the prairies till sunset; and in the glory of the grand ideas which had been opened to me, it seemed as if the whole earth had become broader, and the heavens more vast."

RICHARD REALF'S ACCOUNT OF CAPTAIN BROWN'S PLANS,

AS GIVEN IN HIS TESTIMONY BEFORE THE UNITED STATES SENATE HARPER'S FERRY INVESTIGATION COMMITTEE, 1860.

" John Brown stated that for twenty or thirty years the idea had possessed him like a passion of giving liberty to the slaves ; that he made a journey to England, during which he made a tour upon the European continent, inspecting all fortifications, and especially all earthwork forts which he could find, with a view of applying the knowledge thus gained, with modifications and inventions of his own, to a mountain warfare in the United States. He stated that he had read all the books upon insur-rectionary warfare, that he could lay his hands on, the Roman warfare, the successful opposition of the Spanish chieftains during the period when Spain was a Roman province,—how, with ten thousand men, divided and subdivided into small com-panies, acting simultaneously, yet separately, they withstood the whole consolidated power of the Roman Empire through a number of years. In addition to this he had become very familiar with the successful warfare waged by Schamyl, the Circassian chief, against the Russians ; he had posted himself in relation to the war of Tousaint L'Ouverture ; he had become thoroughly acquainted with the wars in Hayti and the islands round about ; and from all these things he had drawn the con-clusion,—believing, as he stated there he did believe, and as we all (if I may judge from myself) believed,—that upon the first intimation of a plan formed for the liberation of the slaves, they would immediately rise all over the Southern States. He sup-posed that they would come into the mountains to join him, where he proposed to work, and that by flocking to his stand-ard they would enable him (making the line of mountains which cuts diagonally through Maryland and Virginia, down through the Southern States into Tennessee and Alabama, the base of his operations) to act upon the plantations on the plains lying on each side of that range of mountains ; that we should be able to establish ourselves in the fastnesses. And if any hostile action were taken against us, either by the militia of the States, or by the armies of the United States, we purposed to defeat the militia first, and next, if possible, the troops of the United States; and then organize the free blacks under the provisional constitution, which would carve out for the locality of its jurisdiction all that mountainous region in which the blacks were to be established, in which they were to be taught the useful and mechanical arts, and all the business of life. Schools were also to be established, and so on. The negroes were to be soldiers."

THREE REMARKABLE INTERVIEWS.

William A. Phillips, of Salina, Kansas, who died recently at Washington, went in 1855 from central or southern Illinois. He practised law, edited a newspaper, and was the author of several books. Among the stalwart free-soilers of Whig leanings in those early days, he had been for some time a contributor to the *New York Tribune*, so he naturally became its correspondent in Kansas. The work he did there was of an admirable character, clean, faithful, courageous, yet conservative in temper. He was from the first an active supporter of the Topeka Constitution movement, hoping to use the " Squatter Sovereignty " idea, which he no more than any of us believed in, as a means of aiding the actual majority of settlers to maintain their civic rights against the organized assaults of the slave-power. Charles Robinson was made Governor under that effort. It was Phillips's pen that wrote most of the free-state papers, the addresses to the country, and the messages of Dr. Robinson. He was much esteemed, and thereby managed to hold-in most of the younger and ardent men, correspondents and others, from extreme and radical action, Captain Brown had a great regard for Colonel Phillips. (He served as such in the Union army, and was for six years in Congress after the war, in June 1856.) The interviews from which these extracts are taken, were originally published in the *Atlantic Monthly*.

"We placed our two saddles together, so that our heads lay only a few feet apart. He spread his blanket on the wet grass, and we lay together upon it, mine was spread over us. Previous to doing this he had stationed a couple of guards. It was past eleven o'clock, and we lay there until two in the morning, scarcely time enough for sleep, indeed we slept none. He seemed as little disposed to sleep as I was, and we talked, or rather he did, for I said little more than enough to keep him going. I soon found that he was a very thorough astronomer, and he enlightened me on a good many matters in the starry firmament above us. He pointed out the different constellations and their movements. 'Now,' he said, 'it is midnight,' and he pointed to the finger marks of his great clock in the sky.

"In his ordinary moods the man seemed so rigid, stern, and unimpressible when I first knew him that I never thought a poetic and impulsive nature lay behind that cold exterior. The whispering of the wind on the prairie was full of voices to him, and the stars as they shone in the firmament of God seemed to inspire him. 'How admirable is the symmetry of the heavens,' he said, 'how grand and beautiful. Everything moves in sublime harmony in the government of God. Not so with us poor creatures. If one star is more brilliant than others, it is continually shooting in some erratic way into space.'

"He discussed and criticised both parties in Kansas. Of the pro-slavery men he spoke in bitterness. He said that slavery besotted everything, and made men more brutal and coarse. Nor did the free state men escape his sharp censure. He said that we had many noble and true men, but that we had too many broken down politicians from the older States. 'These men,' he said, 'would rather pass resolutions than act, and they criticised all who did real service.' 'A professional politician,' he went on, 'you never could trust; for even if he had convic tions, he was always ready to sacrifice his principles for his advantage.'

"One of the most interesting things in his conversation that night, and one that marked him as a theorist (and perhaps to some extent he might be styled a visionary), was his treatment of our forms of social and political life. He thought society ought to be organized on a less selfish basis; for, while material interests gained something by the deification of pure selfishness, men and women lost much by it. He said that all great reforms, like the Christian religion, were based on broad, generous, self-sacrificing principles. He condemned the sale of land as a chattel, and thought that there was an infinite number of wrongs to right before society would be what it should be, but that in our country slavery was the 'sum of all villainies,' and its abolition the first essential work. If the American people did not take courage, and end it speedily, human freedom and republican liberty would soon be empty names in these United States. (John Brown evidently saw beyond the defeat even of chattel slavery.)

"The second interview occurred, I think, in February, 1857. When I reached Mr. Whitman's (where the Captain stopped) I found him, and with him Kagi and 'Whipple' (that is Stevens), and Cook; in fact, most[1] of the men who were with him at Harper's Ferry. He took me to an apartment where we could be alone, and then he first inquired as to the condition of the free-state cause. He was very apprehensive that many of the free-state leaders would jeopardize the principles of the party in order to get power. He asked earnestly many questions about the free-state leaders. One very good man he criticised for several things he had done, and in response to my assur-

---

[1] The only others, besides one of Brown's sons, who were present at Mr. Whitman's, besides the three named, were Richard Realf and Luke F. Parsons, who did not go to Harper's Ferry. C. W. Moffett, of Montour, Iowa, joined them at Topeka, Kansas, and at Tabor, Iowa, they met Charles W. Tidd and Wm. H. Leeman, who were left watching the arms, etc., there.

ances about him he used one of his striking comparisons. He took out a large pocket-compass, and unscrewing its brass lid laid it down on the table before me, and pointing at the needle fixed his eyes on me, while he said:

"'You see that needle; it wabbles about and is mighty unsteady, but *it wants to point to the north*. Is he like that needle?'

"He told me that some friends in the East had raised for him and placed in his hands a very large sum of money, in all nearly five thousand dollars. He had picked his company, and would like a few more, if he could get the right kind of men. He had spent some time in Iowa and some on the Kansas border. He was drilling and educating his company, and training them to hardship and to be perfectly faithful and reliable. He desired, he said, to get my advice as to the best way of using his force and resources, so as to advance the great interests of freedom and humanity.

"He suggested that it was only fair, as Missouri had undertaken to make a slave State of Kansas, and failed, that Kansas should make a free State of Missouri, and proceeded at length to show, in the most logical manner, that it was not for the interests of Kansas to have a powerful slave State so close to it, and that the process of putting an end to slavery there was exceedingly simple. He said that he intended to spend some time near Tabor, Iowa, where he expected to be joined by others, who would need discipline and organization; and that he expected also to visit Canada, with the view of studying personally its suitability for receiving and protecting negro emigration. And so we parted on that occasion."

THE PROPHETIC INTERVIEW AND THE LAST.

John Brown's movements in 1859 are all well known, and the last interview to which Colonel Phillips refers, must have been in the earlier part of January, 1859, as John Brown was then in Lawrence for a day or two, preparing to bring about the successful removal of his eleven bond people he had brought out of Missouri on the preceding Christmas Eve, These fugitives had been left on the Pottawatomie, Lykens Co., and under the protection of Dr. (afterwards Major-General) James G. Blunt, and three citizens of that vicinity. The fact that Kagi called on Phillips, asking the latter to call on the Captain, also serves to fix the date. He was found at the Whitney House. At the time a price was on John Brown's head. Phillips says:

"He sketched the history of American slavery from its beginnings in the colonies, and referred to the States that were able to shake it off. He said the founders of the Republic were all opposed to slavery, and that the whole spirit and genius of the American Constitution antagonized it, and contemplated its early overthrow. . . . This remained the dominant sentiment for the first quarter of a century of the Republic. Afterwards slavery became more profitable, and as it did the desire grew to extend and increase it. The condition of the enslaved negroes steadily became worse, and the despotic necessities of a more cruel system constantly pressed on the degraded slaves. Gradually the pecuniary interests that rested on slavery seized the power of the Government. Public opinion opposed to slavery was placed under ban. Then began an era of political compromises, and men full of professions of love of country were willing, for peace, to sacrifice everything for which the Republic was founded.

"'And now,' he went on, 'we have reached a point where nothing but war can settle the question. Had they succeeded in Kansas, they would have gained a power that would have given them permanently the upper hand, and it would have been the death-knell of republicanism in America. They are checked, but not beaten. They never intend to relinquish the machinery of this Government into the hands of the opponents of slavery. It has taken them more than half a century to get it, and they know its significance too well to give it up. If the Republican party elects its President next year, there will be war. The moment they are unable to control they will go out. and as a rival nation alongside, they will get the countenance and aid of the European nations, until American republicanism and freedom are overthrown.'

" I have endeavored to quote him, but it is quite impossible to quote such a conversation accurately. I well remember all its vital essentials and its outlines. He had been more observant than he had credit for being. The whole powers of his mind (and they were great) had been given to one subject. He told me that a war was at that very moment contemplated in the cabinet of President Buchanan; that for years the army had been carefully arranged, as far as it could be, on a basis of Southern power; that arms and the best of troops were being concentrated, so as to be under control of its interests if there was danger of having to surrender the Government; that the Secretary of the Navy was then sending our vessels away on long cruises, so that they would not be available, and that the treasury would be beggared before it got into Northern hands.

" All this has a strangely prophetic look to me now; then it simply appeared incredible, or the dream and vagary of a man who had allowed one idea to carry him away. I told him he surely was mistaken, and had confounded every-day occurrences with treacherous designs.

" 'No,' he said, and I remember this part distinctly,—'no, the war is not over. It is a treacherous lull before the storm. We are on the eve of one of the greatest wars in history, and I fear slavery will triumph, and there will be an end of all aspirations for human freedom. For my part, I drew my sword in Kansas when they attacked us, and I will never sheathe it until this war is over. Our best people do not understand the danger. They are besotted. They have compromised so long that they think principles of right and wrong have no more any power on this earth.'

" My impression then was that it was his purpose to carry on incursions on the borders of the free and slave States, and I said to him,—

" 'Let us suppose that all you say is true. If we keep companies on the one side, they will keep them on the other. Trouble will multiply; there will be collision, which will produce the very state of affairs you deprecate. That would lead to war, and, to some extent, we should be responsible for it.

Better trust events. If there is virtue enough in this people to deserve a free government, they will maintain it.'

"'You forget the fearful wrongs that are carried on in the name of government and law.'

"'I do not forget them,—I regret them.'

"'I regret and will remedy them with all the power that God has given me.'

"He then went on to tell me of Spartacus and his servile war, and was evidently familiar with every step in the career of the great gladiator. I reminded him that Spartacus and Roman slaves were warlike people in the country from which they were taken, and were trained to arms in the arena, in which they slew or were slain, and that the movement was crushed when the Roman legions were concentrated against it. The negroes were a peaceful, domestic, inoffensive race. In all their sufferings they seemed to be incapable of resentment or reprisal.

"'You have not studied them right,' he said, 'and you have not studied them long enough. Human nature is the same everywhere.' He then went on in a very elaborate way to explain the mistakes of Spartacus, and tried to show me how he could easily have overthrown the Roman empire. The pith of it was that the leader of that servile insurrection, instead of wasting his time in Italy until his enemies could swoop on him, should have struck at Rome ; or, if not strong enough for that, he should have escaped to the wild northern provinces, and there have organized an army to overthrow Rome.

"I told him that I feared he would lead the young men with him into some desperate enterprise, where they would be imprisoned and disgraced.

"He rose : 'Well,' he said, 'I thought I could get you to understand this. I do not wonder at it. The world is very pleasant to you ; but when your household gods are broken, as mine have been, you will see all this more clearly'

"I rose then, somewhat offended, and said 'Captain, if you thought this, why did you send for me?' and walked to the door.

"He followed me, and laid his hand on my shoulder, and when I turned to him he took both my hands in his. I could see that tears stood on his hard, bronzed cheeks. 'No,' he said, 'we must not part thus. I wanted to see you and tell you how it appeared to me. With the help of God, I will do what I believe to be best.' He held my hands firmly in his stern, hard hands, leaned forward, and kissed me on the cheek, and I never saw him again."

RICHARD A. DANA'S ACCOUNT OF THE NORTH ELBA HOME, ITS HEAD, AND FAMILY.

[*From the Atlantic, July, 1871.*]

"A near turn in the road brought us in sight of a log-house and half-cleared farm, while, had we gone to the right, we should have found it seven miles to the nearest dwelling.

"Three more worn, wearied, hungry, black-fly bitten travelers seldom came to this humble, hospitable door. The people received us with cheerful sympathy, and, while we lay down on the grass, under the shadow of the house, where a smutch kept off the black-flies, prepared something for our comfort. The master of the house had gone down to the settlements, and was expected back before dark. His wife was rather an invalid, and we did not see much of her at first. There were a great many sons and daughters—I never knew how many; one a bonny, buxom young woman of some twenty summers, with fair skin and red hair, whose name was Ruth, and whose good humor, hearty kindness, good sense and helpfulness, quite won our hearts. She would not let us eat much at a time, and cut us resolutely off from the quantities of milk and cool water we were disposed to drink, and persuaded us to wait until something could be cooked for us, more safe and wholesome for faint stomachs; and we were just weak enough to be submissive subjects to this backwoods queen. A man came along in a wagon, and stopped to water his horses, and they asked him if he had seen anything of Mr. Brown below—which it seemed was the name of the family. Yes; he had seen him. He would be along in an hour or so. 'He has two negroes along with him,' said the man, in a confidential, significant tone, 'a man and a woman.' Ruth smiled, as if she understood him. Mr. Aikens told us that the country about here belonged to Gerrit Smith; that negro families, mostly fugitive slaves, were largely settled upon it, trying to learn farming; and that Mr. Brown was a strong Abolitionist and a kind of king among them. This neighborhood was thought to be one of the termini of the underground railroad.

"The farm was a mere recent clearing. The stumps of trees stood out, blackened by burning, and crops were growing among them, and there was a plenty of felled timber. The dwelling was a small log-house of one story in height, and the outbuildings were slight. The whole had the air of a recent enterprise, on a moderate scale, although there were a good many neat cattle and horses. The position was a grand one for a lover of mountain effects; but how good for farming I could not tell. Old White Face, the only exception to the uniform green and brown and black hues of the Adirondack hills, stood plain in view, rising at the head of Lake Placid, its white or pale-gray side caused, we were told, by a landslide. All about were the distant highest summits of the Adirondacks.

"Late in the afternoon a long buckboard wagon came in sight, and on it were seated a negro man and woman, with bundles; a tall, gaunt, dark-complexioned man walked before, having his theodolite and other surveyor's instruments with him, while a youth followed by the side of the wagon. The team turned into the sheds, and the man entered the house. This was 'father.' The sons came out and put up the cattle, and soon we were asked in to the meal. Mr. Brown came forward and received us with kindness: a grave, serious man he seemed, with a marked countenance and a natural dignity of manner—that dignity which is unconscious, and comes from a superior habit of mind.

"We were all ranged at a long table, some dozen of us, more or less; and these two negroes and one other had their places with us. Mr. Brown said a solemn grace. I observed that he called the negroes by their surnames, with the prefixes of Mr. and Mrs. The man was 'Mr. Jefferson,' and the woman 'Mrs. Wait.' He introduced us to them in due form, 'Mr. Dana, Mr. Jefferson,' 'Mr. Metcalf, Mrs. Wait.' It was plain they had not been so treated or spoken to often before, perhaps never until that day, for they had all the awkardness of field hands on a plantation; and what to do on the introduction, was quite beyond their experience. There was an unrestricted supply of Ruth's best bread, butter, and corn-cakes, and we had some meat and tea, and a plenty of the best of milk. We had some talk with Mr. Brown, who interested us very much. He told us he came here from the western part of Massachusetts. As some persons may distrust recollections, after very striking intervening events, I ask pardon for taking an extract from a journal I was in the habit of keeping at those times:—

"'The place belonged to a man named Brown, originally from Berkshire in Massachusetts, a thin, sinewy, hard-favored, clear-headed, honest-minded man, who had spent all his days as a frontier farmer. On conversing with him, we found him well informed on most subjects, especially in the natural sciences. He had books, and had evidently made a diligent use of them. Having acquired some property, he was able to keep a good farm, and had confessedly the best cattle and best farming utensils for miles round. His wife looked superior to the poor place they lived in, which was a cabin, with only four rooms. She appeared to be out of health. He seemed to have an unlimited family of children, from a cheerful, nice, healthy woman of twenty or so, and a full sized red-haired son, who seemed to be foreman of the farm, through every grade of boy and girl, to a couple that could hardly speak plain.

"'How all these, and we three and Mr. Jefferson and Mrs. Wait, were to be lodged here, was a problem; but Aikens said he had seen as much done here before. However, we were not obliged to test the expanding capacities of the house, for a man was going down to Osgood's, by whom we sent a message, and in an hour or two the smiling face of Tommy appeared behind his mules, and we took leave of our kind entertainers.

"'In these regions it is the custom for farmers to receive travelers; and, while they do not take out licenses as innholders, or receive strictly pay for what they furnish, they always accept something in the way of remuneration from the traveler. When we attempted to leave something with Ruth, which was intended to express our gratitude and good will, we found her inflexible. She would receive the bare cost of what we had taken, if we wished it, but nothing for attentions, or house-room, or as gratuity. We had some five-dollar bills and some bills of one dollar each. She took one of the one-dollar bills and went into the garret, and returned with some change. It was too piteous. We could not help smiling, and told her we should feel guilty of highway robbery if we took her silver. She consented to keep the one dollar, for three of us,—one meal apiece and some extra cooking in the morning, —as we seemed to think that was right. It was plain this family acted on a principle in the smallest matters. They knew pretty well the cost price of the food they gave; and if the traveler preferred to pay, they would receive that, but nothing more. There was no shamefacedness about the money transaction either. It was business or nothing; and if we preferred to make it business, it was to be upon a rule.'

"After a day spent on Lake Placid, and in ascending White Face, we returned to Osgood's, and the next day we took the road in our wagon on our return to Westport. We could not pass the Browns' house without stopping. I find this entry in my journal:—

"'June 29, Friday.—After breakfast, started for home. . . . We stopped at the Browns' cabin on our way, and took an affectionate leave of the family that had shown us so much kindness. We found them at breakfast, in the patriarchal style. Mr. and Mrs. Brown and their large family of children with the hired men and women, including three negroes, all at the table together. Their meal was neat, substantial, and wholesome.'

"It seems as if those few days of ours in the Adirondacks, in 1849, had been passed under a spell which held my senses from knowing what we saw. All is now become a region of peculiar sacredness. That plain, bare farm, amid the blackened stumps, the attempts at scientific agriculture under such disadvantages, the simple dwelling, the surveyor's tools, the setting of the little scene amid grand, awful mountain ranges, the negro colony and inmates, the family bred to duty and principle, and held to them by a power recognized as being from above,—all these now come back on my memory with a character nowise changed, indeed, in substance, but, as it were, illuminated. The widow, bearing homeward the body from the Virginia scaffold, with the small company of stranger friends, crossed the lake, as we had done, to Westport; and thence, along that mountain road, but in midwinter, to Elizabethtown; and thence, the next day, to the door of that dwelling. The scene is often visited now by sympathy or curiosity, no doubt, and master pens have made it one of the most marked in our recent history."

[*Letters and papers relating to Kansas, the Pottawatomie affair, George L. Stearns, the Chatham Convention, with reminiscences of a member of the John Brown party.*]

THE POTTAWATOMIE SLAYING.

HON. CHARLES A. FOSTER, OF OSAWATOMIE, FORMERLY THE LEADING FREE-STATE LAWYER IN SOUTHERN KANSAS.

"QUINCY, MASS., Nov. 10, 1892.

"MY DEAR HINTON—Very soon after my arrival at Osawatomie, I became acquainted with some of the sons of John Brown, viz., John, Jr., Owen, Jason, and Frederick. It came about in this way: About the time—July 2, 1855—a delegate meeting was called at Lawrence to take action in relation to the meeting of what we called the 'Border Ruffian Legislature.' On my way to that meeting I had to pass the place where the Brown boys had taken up claims, and when I reached there I found them just starting, and so joined them, and after the meeting was over, returned in their company. I formed a very high opinion of them and we became firm friends. John, Jr., had brought with him some Morgan horses for breeding purposes; Jason proposed to engage in fruit; Owen in sheep husbandry, and Frederick in fine cattle.

"During the rest of the summer they frequently called at my house, and as my profession at that time was to be the law, and I having for those times and that place a fairly good law library, John Brown, Jr., proposed when he had got a little more settled to take up the study of the law.

"You are more or less knowing to the current of events during the balance of the summer and fall of that year. I was a delegate to the 'Big Springs Convention,' at which the free-state party was formally organized, and was also elected assistant secretary of the 'Topeka Convention.' Previous, however, to the meeting of the last-named body the election was held by the 'Free-State party' for delegates to that convention, and for Reiche as delegate to Congress.

"At the close of that election I took the returns from my town to Lawrence. Upon my return trip I stopped at the Brown settlement, and John, Jr., said that his father was going to town and would keep me company. This was the first intimation I had had that he was in the Territory. We were accordingly introduced to each other; we freely conversed upon the various interests and the events that were pressing around us. In opinions and convictions, I soon found, he was more radical than any person whom I had met. I left him at Mr. Adair's house, and I do not remember of seeing him again until some time the next spring. In my intercourse with him he reminded me more fully of the Scotch Covenanters described by Sir Walter Scott.

"At the time of the 'Wakarusa War' (December, 1855), I was not able to accompany those who went to the assistance of the people of Lawrence; but, you know that John Brown, with all his family, went, and came home disgusted with the manner in which that difficulty was settled. In the meantime, John Brown, Jr., had been elected a member of the House of the famous ' Topeka Legislature,' and attended its first session and helped to organize the same. He returned home, and, until the breaking out of the trouble in the spring of 1856, I saw but little of the family.

"In the spring of 1856, as you know, began the Southern immigration under Buford and others. A company of Alabamians came into our neighborhood; I frequently saw many of them in our town; after a little they moved up Pottawatomie Creek in the vicinity of where Dr. Gilpatrick, Judge Hanway, the Wilkinsons, Doyles, and Shermans lived. A word about the Shermans: they were either Dutch or German. Henry Sherman, or Dutch Henry, as he was called, had strayed into the country some years before its settlement, and had been taken into the employment of Mr. Jones, ' Ottawa Jones ' as he was known all over the country. Jones was an educated, intelligent, Christian Indian who had married a white lady who had come out from Maine as a missionary teacher. Jones had a fine farm, good buildings, and for those times the best herd of cattle in the Territory. Dutch Henry staid with Jones for several years, had been saving, and finally moved south to Pottawatomie Creek, buying from Jones some of his cattle. A remarkable increase of his stock took place while the herd of Jones decreased in about the same proportions. Soon after Henry moved South his brother joined him, and both of them became at once active pro-slavery men.

"Soon after the arrival of the Alabamians on the Creek, we began to hear of loss of horses and stock of free-state men, and also threats that the free-state men would soon be driven out and their claims taken by the Southern immigrants. Then we received news of the proposed attack on Lawrence, and a call was made upon us for assistance. Previous to this, however, a raid had been made into our town soon after midday by a band from Missouri, who hurriedly gathered up such arms, money, jewelry, etc., as they could lay their hands upon.

" In response to the call for help from Lawrence, a company was formed of about forty men, and Oscar V. Dayton was chosen commander, and we started on our way. On arrival near the Brown settlement, we met a company under the command of John Brown, Jr., which had been raised on Pottawatomie Creek. We joined forces, and John Brown, Jr., was placed in command. Mr. Dayton was made second. Soon after this junction of forces, I had a long talk with H. H. Williams, who left Pottawatomie Creek the last man; he told me that an old man named Morse, who had sold all the lead and powder he had in his little store to the free-state men, had been visited by the Doyles, Wilkinson, the elder, and Dutch Henry, who threatened to hang him and all other free-state men left on the creek. Williams told him to notify all the free state men to join together for protection, and as soon as the party returned the disturbers would be taken care of. The first night the two companies camped on the prairie, and in the morning resumed our march; soon after we met John Brown and his sons going south.

" In 1883, after reading Professor Spring's article, I wrote to H. H. Williams, asking him for his recollections, and I have his letter before me, from which I copy.

" ' January 20, 1883.

" ' DEAR SIR—Your letter of the 15th inst. came yesterday, and in reply would say, that I have read the article referred to, written by L. W. Spring; in fact, have it before me now to refer to, and, except a little high coloring and a few minor points, it is correct. I don't know who the young surveyor referred to is, I saw them grinding their sabres, but don't recollect who was turning the grindstone. The scout referred to as carrying the news of the threats made to old man Morse and others, is myself. James Townsley lived near the forks of Pottawatomie, now near the corner of Miami, Franklin, Ander-

son, and Linn counties. In the party that left Ottawa Creek
to go and straighten things on the Pottawatomie, and which
we met at Jones's on our return, was old John Brown, three
sons, and one son-in-law, Winer, and Townsley; August Bondi
was not of the party, and he may have been the young surveyor referred to.

"'When this party met us, a short conference was had, and
we learned for the first time that Lawrence had been destroyed. Robinson, Deitzler, and Brown had been carried
prisoners to Lecompton.

"' The two parties separated, one company continuing on the
way towards Lawrence, and John Brown, going south. That day
we reached "Baldwin City," on the Sante Fé Road, and sent a
committee, of which I was one, into Lawrence, to learn the
situation of affairs, and also to learn what was to be the future
line of action.   Early the next morning—Sunday—we took up
our return march, and in the afternoon stopped for a short
time at "Prairie City," and here for the first time we learned
of what was called the "Pottawatomie Massacre." In the
form in which the news reached us, we were struck with
amazement and repudiated the act.

"'After an interview with John Brown, Jr., and the commander of a Company of U. S. dragoons, we resumed our
march, and that night camped at Ottawa Jones's. About eleven
o'clock I, being on guard near the house, heard the approach
of a wagon, and soon the old man and his party entered the
camp.   I found Frederick and questioned him about the affair,
and he replied:

"'"I can't tell you anything now, but when you hear the
whole story you will be satisfied that everything is all right."

"'We separated and I never saw any of the party again.

"'On the morning we resumed our march and arrived at
home that afternoon. We found everybody denouncing the
act, and in a few days the country was overrun by Missourians
and all the pro-slavery men of that section. John Brown, Jr.,
and Jason were arrested and carried to Lecompton.'

"Now, there are two questions to be met: First, was the

old man there and assisting? Second, was the act justifiable?

" In 1860, in a talk with Capt. Sam. Walker, he said : ' Old man Brown never lied, he told me himself that he was there, and I believe him.' Dr. T. H. Webb told me that Brown said to him that he was not there : 'but that, if that was murder, he (Brown) was guilty of murder, for he approved of the acts, and if he had been there he would have assisted.' F. B. Sanborn, whose life of Brown I have not read, before writing the same, went over the whole ground, talked with all the witnesses then living whom he could reach, copied from Judge Hanway's diary, made at the time, and told me that the only conclusion he could arrive at was, that the old man was there in command.

" Second. Was the party justified in their act? I will only answer by giving the information as I received it at that and subsequent times.

"After the excitement had subsided we began to gather facts. When the parting of the two companies took place, which I have previously related, John Brown and his party started for home, the first place they struck was the cabin of his son-in-law, which he found empty, next John Brown, Jr.'s, which he also found empty ; a neighbor informed them that the houses had been visited by the party from Pottawatomie, who had threatened to burn them over their heads ; the women being alarmed, found a yoke of cattle, yoked them to a cart, put their valuables into it with the children, and drove down to Mr. Adair's house, where we found them upon our return. The party, leaving Middle Creek, proceeded on their way to Pottawatomie ; coming in sight of where Winer's house should be, they found it burned with a small stock of goods which it contained ; a little further on they found the house of August Bondi also burned, and he soon after appearing told them it was the party who that night were killed, together with ' Dutch Henry ' and Judge Wilson, who had done the work. You now have all the facts within my recollection. One incident more which occurred in 1857 : A land sale of Indian Lands was had at Paola during the fall of that year ; the election for members of the Legislature was to take place ; the Free-State party had agreed to go into the election ; in view of this fact during the sale, notice was given out that on the morrow Gov. Walker, Sec. Stanton, and ex-Governor Bigler, of Pennslyvania, would address the people on the issues of the day.

" I was importuned to go over and reply to them ; this I at first promptly refused to do, as I, a young man, did not consider myself able to cope with gentlemen of such great ability ; but I finally consented. In my reply to the argument that we should vote for the Democratic candidates, I said among other things, ' that we did not like that kind of Democracy, that if they would come over to Osawatomie I would show them the graves of five men killed in cold blood, the ruins of thirty cabins, all done by Kansas Democrats ; ' upon which Judge Wilson stepped forward and said : ' Bro. Foster, how is it about the men your friend John Brown killed up Pottawatomie ? ' I replied, ' Judge Wilson, you are the last man in this world who should ask that question ; you know that if you had not been an unworthy member of a world-wide secret fraternity you would have paid the penalty of your crimes with your life that night, but you got warning in time and escaped.' Then was the time for him and his friend to have disclaimed, but he slunk away without a reply and was heard of no more."

FROM HON. JAMES HANWAY,
SHERMANSVILLE, K. T.

[*The writer of this letter, addressed in December, 1859, to the present author, was one of John Brown's sincere friends and a citizen of Kansas of high repute and character. He died full of honor and respected by all, within the past three years.*]

" Presuming you are well acquainted with the leading incidents in the life of John Brown, during the difficulties in Kansas, I, therefore, pass over these events and will only relate a

few items, which came more immediately under my own observation—to show his character and his motives which led him
onwards.

"I was in the military company which marched to the
rescue of Lawrence in May, 1856, from Pottawatomie Creek.
I became acquainted with our hero in the spring of that year.
While our company was camped on Ottawa Creek, waiting
orders from headquarters, a movement was set on foot by
John Brown, Jr., and others, to form a company of their own
and march back to the Pottawatomie Creek. Only a few knew
what the object of this new movement was, but the general
opinion in camp was that old Brown would undertake some
'rash' enterprise, and bring trouble on the free-state cause;
therefore several individuals were deputized to talk to Brown
and caution him to act with discretion. An old gent approached
Brown and inquired if he (Brown) had concluded to undertake
some new enterprise. Yes, was the response. Well, sir, said
the old gent to Brown, I hope you will act with great caution.
At this Brown, who was packing up his camp fixtures, instantly
stood erect and said, 'Caution, caution, sir, I am eternally
tired of hearing that word caution, it is nothing but the words
of cowardice.'

"On another occasion some one was questioning the bold-
ness of his movements, and he said, ' I would rather my body
was ground into the earth than yield to the despotism of the
slave-power.' In regard to the exit of the three Doyles, Wm.
Sherman, and Wilkinson (the postmaster), who lived on the
Pottawatomie Creek, I could perhaps give you the correct facts
in connection with this 'tragedy'—but I presume you know
them. However, I can give you Brown's opinion of this event.
In conversation with him, he remarked (about a year ago) that
it was a just act, to take the lives of those five pro-slavery
ruffians. That it had saved the lives of many good men, that
he knew it was the intention of the border ruffians to 'clear'
the Creek of every free-state man, by driving them off by
threats, burning and taking of human life. You, perhaps, are
aware that John Brown was a surveyor.

"This gave him an excellent opportunity to gain information. He *run his compass* into the pro-slavery camps. The ruffians took it for granted that *all* surveyors were pro-slavery and opposed to the 'abolitionists,' and believing that the administration would only employ those faithful to the slavery cause. John Brown received the information directly from these pro-slavery banditti; and he only took the advance step upon them, and thus blasted their hellish designs. The old settlers, almost unanimously, justify this tragic act, and they feel as if a debt of thanks was due to John Brown and his confederates in checking the hand of border ruffianism in that section of the country.

"*Before* this Pottawatomie tragedy took place, a man known by the name of Squire Morse, an old, inoffensive man, was notified to leave in three days or they (the Doyles) would burn down his house and store—other individuals received information of like character.

"Last year there was a common report that Martin White, of Mo., had been shot and killed. Of course everybody thought that old Brown had taken revenge on Martin White for the murderous act of shooting Frederick Brown a few hours before the Osawatomie fight. The old man was asked if he knew whether M. White had been thus disposed of. He replied, he believed that White was still living, that he knew many persons suppose that he (Brown) had sought revenge, etc. 'People,' says he, ' mistake my objects. I would not hurt one hair of his head. I would not go one inch to take his life; I do not harbor the feeling of revenge. *I act from a principle.* My aim and object is to restore human rights.'

"After the battle of Osawatomie he called at the house containing the corpse of his son Frederick. He requested permission to be left alone. For one hour he devoted to silent meditation, then left, to gather together his scattered men who had been with him in the fight, leaving to his friends the performance of the rite of sepulture. You must deny the error of Geary, that Frederick Brown was *insane.* He certainly was not insane. He was very excitable in debate and a man of good argumentive power.

" Dec. 10.—I have, since writing the above, endeavored to get other matter, but have not been able to gain any thing new. We have just heard of the execution of John Brown. He has many warm friends in Kansas, and, however they may regret his late movement, they admire his bold and heroic conduct during his imprisonment. John Brown is the Oliver Cromwell of America. I think that Brown possessed more humanity in his character than Cromwell."

A SECRET FREE-STATE ORDER.

[*Mr. James F. Legate, still a prominent citizen and public man in Kansas, writes me copiously in relation to the Pottawatomie slaying and events that led thereto. Part of what he said I have retained as confidential, as I understand he proposes to use such information in a book of his own, but the following is so thoroughly a part of the record of the period, that I may be pardoned for presenting it here with other matter.*]

FORMING THE DANITES.

In the fall of 1855, meetings for consultations were frequently held in the house of Charles Robinson, on the hill where the State University now stands. Murder and arson were of frequent occurrence; all the time Robinson under the dictation of our Boston friends, was counseling peace and non-resistance, till it became tiresome to some of us who were young and thoughtless. I had lived South, in Mississippi, for six years, and I felt I knew the Southern mind too well to believe that they would respect us as "peace men in time of war," and that was war.

At one of those meetings, just after an old man whose name has escaped my memory, had been seized and robbed and brutally treated by the border ruffians, while returning from Westport, Robinson gave a lecture on a peaceful bearing towards those men, I replied by saying, "I thought I knew the Southern mind better than he did—I did not believe they would respect us as worthy to be called American citizens, to endure these great wrongs without trying to put a stop to them, and the only way to do that was to retaliate in kind—if they burned a free-state man's house, burn two pro-slavery men's houses—if they robbed a free-state man, we must rob two pro-slavery men—if a free-state man was killed, we must kill two pro-slavery men." This seemed to strike all present with wonderful force, or rather it was giving language to thoughts that were in the discontented brain of the young men of those days. Even Robinson was "almost persuaded," but clung with wonderful tenacity to his instructions. Lane heard of what I had said, and fawned all over me for my "noble utterances," as he styled them. He corralled the spirit of unrest panting to do and dare anything, the tendency of which would be to put a stop to those border-ruffian crimes; so a secret society was formed, the purposes of which were to retaliate against the ruffians for the crimes they were committing. . . . James H. Lane was a member and a leader. John Speer, Charles Robinson, Captain Shore, and many others, whose names I cannot recall, were members. Charles Robinson, however, soon failed to attend, becoming more earnest in his Boston theory of non-resistance. The society had not much more than a year's duration, because Lane was continually calling meetings, and would invariably have a long paper of "whereas" Bill Smith, a "pro-slavery hell hound" had been guilty of stealing free-state men's horses, or burning some one's house, or some crime of less grade, and then, " Therefore Resolved " that Bill Smith shall be brought before this body of men, his case investigated and adjudicated, and the decree shall be executed by one or more men appointed by the commander of this council, or of some sub-council. Lane's "Whereases " killed the society. This society had its birth because of the murder of Dow, Barber, and the robbery and house-burning that were frequent in those days.

Robinson's Kansas Conflict is a burlesque on history. It

belittles himself—he makes the Kansas conflict a war waged
by murderers, thieves, and cutthroats for free-Kansas, against
a law-abiding. Christian community, who were simply holding
colored men in happy bondage. He makes the heroes of Kansas, who risked everything for free Kansas, murderers and
thieves, and the murderers and thieves who risked everything for
slavery in Kansas, heroes and patriots. His services in behalf
of free Kansas deserve and will receive in history the highest
encomium, but his later conduct will remain a stain upon his
memory through all the annals of time. Robinson could not
control the spirit of unrest, which permeated the young blood
of the free-state settlers. Lane came and seeing at a glance the
situation seized the leadership of these young spirits, who
were thirsting to do or dare anything that would redound to the
freedom of Kansas. Robinson was a safe counselor. Lane
was "one of the boys," always sharing or pretending to share
their danger, but always absorbing all their glory. Lane ultimately was completely successful; Robinson failed as a
popular man. Robinson has ever since had the unhappy
faculty of getting on the wrong side at the right time.

John Brown never had any faith in making Kansas a free
State, and preserving slavery in Missouri He felt his life's
mission was to destroy slavery, and that it never could be
destroyed but by means of war between the free and slave
States; whatever he did was designed to bring about a war, so
that by it the slave chattel should become a human being and
be possessed of all the God-given rights of an American
citizen. He religiously believed that God had sent him as a
special messenger to win freedom for the downtrodden slaves
in this land, and he was equally certain that it would not be
done only by war. Whatever he did or said was done and said
as "Thus said the Lord," and his attack upon Harper's Ferry
and his death upon the gallows did more to prepare the mind
of the South that war was a necessity, and commenced the conflict which ended slavery, than all things else combined. He
was prophetic in his theory and utterances, as subsequent
events so clearly demonstrate. He cannot be blotted out of

history, or proved to be a bad man. He gave his life freely
that liberty to the slaves might become a living fact. The good
that men do should never die, but that which is bad in good
men should be permitted to die with them.

STATEMENT BY JOHN EDWIN COOK

OF HIS CONNECTION WITH CAPTAIN JOHN BROWN.

[*This paper, usually stigmatized as a " Confession," was prepared by Captain Cook while in prison and on trial
for his life at Charlestown, Va., during the month of
November, 1859. It was prepared under the pressure
brought upon him by his counsel, Hon. Daniel W. Voorhees,
and his brother-in law, Lieutenant-Governor Willard of
Indiana, who seriously hoped thereby to save Cook's life.
For one, involved as I was, I never regarded the paper as
an offense, but rather as a weakness. Cook told nothing
that Governor Wise and his advisers did not know, when
the paper was read in court. R. J. H.*]

THE STATEMENT.

I became acquainted with Capt. John Brown in his camp on
Middle Creek, Kansas Territory, just after the battle of Black
Jack, and was with him in said camp until it was broken up
and his company disbanded by Col. Sumner, of the First
Cavalry, United States Army.

I next saw him at the convention at Topeka, which was on
the 4th of July, 1856. I next met him some days afterward in
Lawrence. Did not see him again until the fall of 1857, when
I met him at the house of E. B. Whitman, about four miles
from Lawrence, K. T., which, I think, was about the 1st of
November following. I was told that he intended to organize
a company for the purpose of putting a stop to the aggressions
of the pro-slavery men. I agreed to join him, and was asked

if I knew of any other young men who were perfectly reliable whom I thought would join also. I recommended Richard Realf, L. F. Parsons, and R. J. Hinton. I received a note on the next Sunday morning, while at breakfast in the Whitney House, from Capt. Brown, requesting me to come up that day, and to bring Realf, Parsons, and Hinton with me. Realf and Hinton were not in town, and therefore I could not extend to them the invitation. Parsons and myself went and had a long talk with Capt. Brown.

A few days afterward I received another note from Capt. Brown, which read, as near as I can recollect, as follows:

"DATE —— ——.

"CAPT. COOK:—Dear Sir—You will please get everything ready to join me at Topeka by Monday night next. Come to Mrs. Sheridan's, two miles south of Topeka, and bring your arms, ammunition, clothing, and other articles you may require. Bring Parsons with you, if he can get ready in time. Please keep very quiet about this matter. Yours, etc.,

"JOHN BROWN."

I made all my arrangements for starting at the time appointed. Parsons, Realf, and Hinton could not get ready. I left them at Lawrence, and started in a carriage for Topeka. Stopped at the hotel over night, and left early next morning for Mrs. Sheridan's, to meet Capt. Brown. Staid a day and a half at Mrs. S.'s—then left for Topeka, at which place we were joined by "Whipple," Moffett, and Kagi. Left Topeka for Nebraska City, and camped at night on the prairie northeast of Topeka. Here, for the first, I learned that we were to leave Kansas to attend a military school during the winter. It was the intention of the party to go to Ashtabula county, Ohio. Next morning I was sent back to Lawrence to get a draft of $80 cashed, and to get Parsons, Realf, and Hinton to go back with me. I got the draft cashed. Captain Brown had given me orders to take boat to St. Joseph, Mo., and stage from there to Tabor, Iowa, where he would remain for a few days. I had to wait for Realf for three or four days; Hinton could not leave at that time. I started with Realf and Parsons on a stage for Leavenworth. The boats had stopped running on account of the ice. Staid one day in Leavenworth and then left for Weston, where we took stage for St. Joseph, and from thence to Tabor. I found C. P. Tidd and Leeman at Tabor. Our party now consisted of Captain John Brown, Owen Brown, A. D. Stevens ("Whipple"), Charles Moffett, C. P. Tidd, Richard Robertson, Richard Realf, L. F. Parsons, Wm. Leeman and myself. We stopped some days at Tabor, making preparations to start. Here we found that Captain Brown's ultimate destination was the State of Virginia. Some warm words passed between him and myself in regard to the plan, which I had supposed was to be confined entirely to Kansas and Missouri. Realf and Parsons were of the same opinion with me. After a good deal of wrangling we consented to go on, as we had not the means to return, and the rest of the party were so anxious that we should go with them. At Tabor we procured teams for the transportation of about 200 Sharp's rifles, which had been taken on as far as Tabor, one year before, at which place they had been left awaiting the order of Captain Brown. There were, also, other stores, consisting of blankets, clothing, boots, ammunition, and about two hundred revolvers of the Massachusetts Arms patent, all of which we transported across the State of Iowa to Springdale, and from there to Liberty, at which place they were shipped for Ashtabula county, Ohio, where they remained till brought to Chambersburg, Pa., and were from there transported to a house in Washington county, Md., which Captain Brown had rented for six months, and which was situated about five miles from Harper's Ferry. It was the intention of Captain Brown to sell his teams in Springdale, and with the proceeds to go on with the rest of the company to some place in Ashtabula county, Ohio, where we were to have a good military instructor during the winter; but he was disappointed in the sale. As he could not get cash for the teams, it was decided we should remain in the neighborhood of Springdale, and that our instructor, Col. H. Forbes, should be sent on. We stopped in Pedee (Springfield), Iowa, over winter, at Mr. Maxson's, where we pursued a course of military studies. Col. H. Forbes and Captain Brown had some words, and he (Col. F.) did not come on ; consequently A. D. Stevens was our drillmaster. The people of the neighborhood did not know of our purpose. We remained at Pedee till about the middle of April, when we left for Chatham, Canada, *via* Chicago and Detroit. We staid about two weeks in Chatham—some of the party staid six or seven weeks. We left Chatham for Cleveland, and remained there until late in June. In the meantime, Captain Brown went East on business; but previous to his departure he had learned that Colonel Forbes had betrayed his plans to some extent. This, together with the scantiness of his funds, induced him to delay the commencement of his work, and was the means, for the time being, of disbanding the party. He had also received some information which called for his immediate attention in Kansas. I wished to go with him, but he said that I was too well known there, and requested me and some others to go to Harper's Ferry, Va., to see how things were there, and to gain information. While we were in Chatham he called a convention, the purpose of which was to make a complete and thorough organization. He issued a written circular, which he sent to various persons in the United States and Canada. The circular, as near as I can recollect, read as follows :

"CHATHAM, May —, 1858.

" MR.——:—Dear Sir—We have issued a call for a very quiet convention at this place, to which we shall be happy to see any true friends of freedom, and to which you are most earnestly invited to give your attendance. Yours respectfully,

" JOHN BROWN."

As the names were left blank I do not know to whom they were sent, though I wrote several of them. I learned, however, that one was sent to Frederick Douglass, and I think Gerrit Smith also received one. Who the others were sent to I do not know. Neither Douglass nor Smith attended the convention. I suppose some twenty-five or thirty of these circulars were sent, but as they were directed by Captain Brown or J. H. Kagi I do not know the names of the parties to whom they were addressed. I do know, however, that they were sent to none save those whom Captain Brown knew to be radical abolitionists. I think it was about ten days from the time the circulars were sent that the convention met. The place of meeting was in one of the negro churches in Chatham. The convention, I think, was called to order by J. H. Kagi. Its object was then stated, which was to complete a thorough organization and the formation of a constitution. The first business was to elect a president and secretary. Elder Monroe, a colored minister, was elected President, and J. H. Kagi, Secretary. The next business was to form a constitution. Captain Brown had already drawn up one, which, on motion, was read by the Secretary. On motion it was ordered that each article of the constitution be taken up and separately amended and passed, which was done. On motion, the constitution was then adopted as a whole. The next business was to nominate a Commander-in-Chief, Secretary of War, and Secretary of State. Captain John Brown was unanimously elected Commander-in-Chief; J. H. Kagi, Secretary of War, and Richard Realf, Secretary of State. Elder Monroe was to act as President until another was chosen. A. M. Chapman, I think, was to act as Vice-President. Doctor M. K. Delany was one of the Corresponding Secretaries of the organization, There were some others from the United States, whose names I do not now remember. Most of the delegates to the Convention were from Canada. After the constitution was adopted, the members took their oath to support it. It was then signed by all present. During the interval between the call for the convention and its assembling, regular meetings were held at Barbour's Hotel, where we were stopping, by those who were known to be true to the cause, at which meetings plans were laid and discussed. There were no white men at the convention save the members of our company. Men and money had both been promised from Chatham and other parts of Canada. When the convention broke up, news was received that Col. H. Forbes, who had joined in the movement, had given information to the government. This, of course, delayed the time of attack. A day or two afterward most of our party took the boat to Cleveland—Jno. H. Kagi, Richard Realf, Wm. H. Leeman, Richard Robertson, and Capt. Brown remaining. Capt. B., however, started in a day or two for the East. Kagi, I think, returned to some other town in Canada, to set up the type and to get the constitution printed, which he completed before he went to Cleveland. We remained in Cleveland for some weeks, at which place, for the time being, the company disbanded. Capt. Brown had had the plan of the insurrection in contemplation for several years—in fact, told me that it had been the chief aim of his life to carry out and accomplish the abolition of slavery.

In his trip East he did not realize the amount of money that he expected. The money had been promised *bona fide*, but owing to the tightness of the money market they failed to comply with his demands. The funds were necessary to the accomplishment of his plans. I afterwards learned that there was a lack of confidence in the success of his scheme. It was, therefore, necessary that a movement should be made in another direction to demonstrate the practicability of his plan. This he made about a year ago by his invasion of Missouri, and the taking of about a dozen slaves, together with horses, cattle, etc., into Kansas, in defiance of the United States marshal and his posse. From Kansas he took them to Canada *via* Iowa City and Cleveland. At the latter place he remained some days, and, I think, disposed of his horses there. It seems that the United States marshal was afraid to arrest him, and this was all that was wanting to give confidence to the wavering in the practicability of his plan and its ultimate success. He came to Harper's Ferry about the last of June, though I did not see him till late in July or the early part of August, when we met on Shenandoah street, Harper's Ferry, opposite Tearney's store. I do not know who were his aiders or abettors, but have heard him mention in connection with it the names of Gerrit Smith, of New York; Howe, of Boston, and

Sanborn and Thaddeus Hyatt, of New York city. What connection, and how far connected with his plan, I do not know,
but I know he wrote a letter a few weeks previous to his attack,
to some gentlemen in Boston, which read, as near as I can recollect, as follows:—

"DATE —— ——.

"GENTLEMEN—I have got nearly all my machines on, and
shall be ready to start them in a few days, unless prevented by
a special Providence. Everything is working well. I shall
want all the funds you promised me in a few days. Yours,
truly,   "CALM & STILL."

In the mean time the men who had engaged to go with him
had most of them arrived at Chambersburg, Pa., and been
sent to the place which he had rented in Washington county,
Md., about five miles from Harper's Ferry. The greater part
of the men kept out of sight during the day, for fear of attract-
ing attention. The arms, munitions, etc., were carted from
Chambersburg to his rendezvous. The spear-heads and guards
came in strong boxes, and the shafts passed for fork handles.
They were put together by our own men, at the house where
most of them were found. Letters of importance came to the
Chambersburg post-office, and were sent by some of our own
party to headquarters. The letters of minor importance came
to the Ferry to J. Smith & Sons. All allusions to our business
were made in such a blind way, that they would not have been
understood by any outside parties, even should they have been
miscarried. The attack was made sooner than it was intended,
owing to some friends in Boston writing a letter finding fault
with the management of Captain Brown, and what to them
seemed his unnecessary delay and expense. I do not know
who those persons were, or how far they were cognizant of his
(Captain Brown's) plans; but I do know that Dr. Howe gave
Captain Brown a breech-loading carbine and a pair of muzzle-
loading pistols, all of Government manufacture. They were
left either at the house of Captain Brown, or at the school-
house, where most of the arms were conveyed. At what time

and for what purpose they were given to Captain Brown, I do not know. It was supposed that Col. Hugh Forbes was dead. I was told by Captain Brown that when on East, he had been told by Thaddeus Hyatt, of New York, that some of the negroes at that place had informed him (Hyatt) that Forbes had "gone up"—a phrase which Captain Brown and the rest of our company understood to mean that he had been killed. I do not think that Forbes had any cognizance of our plans from the time of our leaving Pedee, a year ago, last April. Previous to his quarrel with Captain Brown, we considered that he would hold a place next to Brown in command. I do not know the present whereabouts of Luke F. Parsons or Charles Moffett. The last I heard of Parsons was through Captain Brown, who informed me that Parsons had started for Pike's Peak, and that he (Brown) thought he would be pretty tolerably peaked before he got there. A short time before the attack on Harper's Ferry, Captain Brown requested me to find out in some way, without creating suspicion, the number of male slaves on or near the roads leading from the Ferry, for a distance of eight or ten miles, and to make such memoranda that it would be unintelligible to others, but in such a manner that I could make it plain to him and the rest of the company. He gave me two dollars to pay my expenses with. I took the road from Harper's Ferry to Charlestown, under the plea of gaining statistics for a work to be published by John Henri, and to decide a wager between him and Mr. Smith. I did not go on any other road. A few days after this, Captain Brown sent his wagon over by his son Oliver and Jeremiah Anderson, to bring my wife and myself to his house. They gave me a note from him, which, as near as I can recollect, read as follows:—

"MR. COOK:—Dear Sir—You will please get everything ready to come with your wife to my house this morning. My wagon will wait for you. I shall take your wife to Chambersburg, and shall start early to-morrow morning. Be as expeditious as possible. Be very careful not to say or do anything which will awaken any suspicion. You can say your wife is going to make a visit to some friends of her's in the country. Be very careful that you do not let any of our plans leak out. Yours, etc.,   J. SMITH."

My wife and myself accordingly left Harper's Ferry that night, accompanied by Oliver Brown and Jeremiah Anderson, for Captain Brown's House in Washington county, Md.

The next day, after dinner, Captain Brown and his son Watson, together with my wife and child, started for Chambersburg. When Captain Brown returned, he told me that he had got her a good boarding-place in Chambersburg, at Mrs. Ritner's, and that she liked her boarding-place very well.

There were some six or seven in our party who did not know anything of our constitution, and, as I have since understood, were also ignorant of the plan of operations, until the Sunday morning previous to the attack. Among this number were Edwin Coppoc, Barclay Coppoc, Francis J. Merriam, Shields Green, John Copeland, and Leary.

The constitution was read to them by A. D. Stevens, and the oath afterwards administered by Captain Brown. Sunday evening, previous to our departure, Captain Brown made his final arrangements for the capture of Harper's Ferry, and gave to his men their orders. In closing, he said:—

"And now, gentlemen, let me press this one thing on your minds. You all know how dear life is to you, and how dear your lives are to your friends; and, in remembering that, consider that the lives of others are as dear to them as yours are to you; do not, therefore, take the life of any one if you can possibly avoid it, but if it is necessary to take life in order to save your own, then make sure work of it."

After taking the town, I was placed under Capt. Stevens, who received orders to proceed to the house of Col. Lewis Washington and to take him prisoner, and to bring his slaves, horses, and arms, and as we came back to take Mr. Altstadt and his slaves, and to bring them all to Capt. Brown at the armory. When we returned, I staid a short time in the engine-house to get warm, as I was chilled through. After I got warm, Capt. Brown ordered me to go with C. P. Tidd, who was to take William H. Leeman, and, I think, four slaves with him, in Col. Washington's large wagon, across the river, and to take Terrence Burns and his brother and their slaves prisoners. My orders were to hold Burns and brother as prisoners at their own house, while Tidd and the slaves who accompanied him were to go to Capt. Brown's house and to load in the arms and bring them down to the school house, stopping for the Burnses and their guard. William H. Leeman remained with me to guard the prisoners. On return of the wagon, in compliance with orders, we all started for the school-house. When we got there, I was to remain, by Capt. Brown's orders, with one of the slaves to guard the arms, while C. P. Tidd, with the other negroes, was to go back for the rest of the arms, and Burns was to be sent with William H. Leeman to Capt. Brown at the Armory. It was at this time that William Thompson came up from the Ferry and reported that everything was all right, and then hurried on to overtake William H. Leeman. A short time after the departure of Tidd I heard a good deal of firing and became anxious to know the cause, but my orders were strict to remain in the school-house and guard the arms, and I obeyed the orders to the letter. About four o'clock in the evening C. P. Tidd came with the second load. I then took one of the negroes with me and started for the ferry. I met a negro woman a short distance below the school-house, who informed me they were fighting hard at the ferry. I hurried on till I came to the lock kept by George Hardy, about a mile above the bridge, where I saw his wife and Mrs. Elizabeth Read, who told me that our men were hemmed in, and that several of them had been shot. I expressed my intention to try to get to them, when Mrs. Hardy asked me to try to get her husband released from the engine-house. I told her I would. Mrs. Read begged of me not to go down to the ferry. She said I would be shot. I told her I must make an attempt to save my comrades, and passed on down the road. A short distance below the lock I met two boys whom I knew, and they told me that our men were all hemmed in by troops from Charleston, Martinsburg, Hagers-town, and Shepherdstown. The negro who was with me had been very much frightened at the first report we received, and as the boys told me the troops were coming up the road after us soon, I sent him (the negro) back to inform Tidd, while I hastened down the road. After going down opposite the ferry, I ascended the mountain in order to get a better view of the position of our opponents.

I saw that our party were completely surrounded, and as I saw a body of men on High street firing down upon them— they were about a half a mile distant from me—I thought I would draw the fire upon myself; I therefore raised my rifle and took the best aim I could and fired. It had the desired effect, for the very instant the party returned it. Several shots were exchanged. The last one they fired at me cut a small limb I had hold of just below my hand, and gave me a fall of about fifteen feet, by which I was severely bruised and my flesh somewhat lacerated. I descended from the mountain and passed down the road to the Crane on the bank of the canal, about fifty yards from Mr. W.'s store. I saw several heads behind the door-post looking at me; I took a position behind the Crane, and, cocking my rifle, beckoned to some of them to come to me; after some hesitation, one of them approached, and then another, both of whom knew me. I asked them if there were any armed men in the store. They pledged me their word and honor that there were none. I then passed down to the lock-house, and went down the steps to the lock, where I saw William McGreg, and questioned him in regard to the troops on the other side. He told me that the bridge was filled by our opponents, and that all of our party were dead but seven; that two of them were shot while trying to escape across the river. He begged me to leave immedi-ately. After questioning him in regard to the position and number of the troops, and from what sources he received his information, I bade him good night, and started up the road at a rapid walk. I stopped at the house of an Irish family, at the foot of the hill, and got a cup of coffee and some eatables.

I was informed by them that Captain Brown was dead; that
he had been shot about four o'clock in the afternoon. At the
time I believed the report to be true. I went on up to the
school-house, and found the shutters and door closed; called
to Tidd and the boys, but received no answer; cocked my
rifle, and then opened the door; it was dark at the time. Some
of the goods had been placed in the middle of the floor, and, in
the dark, looked like men crouching. I uncocked my rifle
and drew my revolver, and then struck a match; saw that
there was no one in the school-house; went into the bushes
back of the school-house, and called for the boys. Receiving
no answer, I went across the road into some pines, and again
called, but could find no one. I then started up the road
towards Captain Brown's house; I saw a party of men coming
down the road; when within about fifty yards, I ordered them
to halt; they recognized my voice and called me; I found them
to be Charles P. Tidd, Owen Brown, Barclay Coppoc, F. J.
Merriam, and a negro who belonged to Washington or Alstadtt.
They asked me the news, and I gave the information I received
on the canal lock and on the road. It seemed that they thought
it would be sheer madness in them to attempt a rescue of our
comrades, and it was finally determined to return to the house
of Captain Brown. I found that Tidd, before leaving the
school-house to go for Brown, Coppoc, and Merriam, had
stationed the negroes in a good position in the timber back of
the school-house. On his return, however, they could not be
found. We, therefore, left for Captain Brown's house. Here
we got a few articles which would be necessary, and then went
over into the timber on the side of the mountain, a few yards
beyond the house, where the spears were kept. Here we laid
down and went to sleep. About three o'clock in the morning
one of our party awakened and found that the negro had left
us. He immediately aroused the rest of the party, and we
concluded to go to the top of the mountain before light. Here
we remained for a few hours, and then passed over to the other
side of the mountain, where we waited till dark, and then
crossed the valley to the other range beyond.

I have forgotten to state previously, that before I left Captain Brown in Cleveland, O., he gave me orders to trust no one with our secret, and to hold no conversation with the slaves, which orders I obeyed with but a single exception, which I here mention.   The exception to which I allude is simply this : I met a party of four negroes, two free and two slave, near Bolivar, Jefferson County, Va.   I asked them if they had ever thought about their freedom.   They replied, " they thought they ought to be free," but expressed doubts that they ever would be.   I told them that time might come before many years, but for the present to keep dark and look for the good time coming, and left them.

I see from some of the newspapers, that I have been represented as Captain Brown's chief aid.   This is incorrect.   Kagi was second in command, Stevens third, Hazlitt fourth. Further than this, I do not know that Captain Brown had made known any preference as to superiority or rank.   Edward Coppoc and Dauphin Thomas were the only lieutenants he commissioned.   Owen Brown, Barclay Coppoc, and F. J. Merriam were not at the Ferry during the time the attack was made, but remained by order of Captain B. to take charge of the premises, and to guard the arms left at Brown's house, in case of an attack.   I do not know of any person in the Ferry or its neighborhood who knew of our plan, save our own party, and they were pledged to keep it secret.

Richard Realf, one of our original party, and our Secretary of State, came from Chatham to Cleveland, a few days before Captain Brown's arrival from the East.   Soon after his arrival he (Captain B.) sent Realf to New York city, at which place he embarked for England, for the purpose of carrying out the plans of Captain Brown.   Realf was born and raised in England.   He is a peasant's son, but his native talents brought him into the notice of some of the nobility, who took charge of him, and made arrangements to give him a finished education. He was taken into the family of Lady Noel Byron, where he made his home while pursuing his studies.   Falling in love with a young lady of noble birth, who was a relative of Lady

Byron, he was censured by Lady B. for his presumption. He became offended at her interference, and finally left Lady B. to work his own way in the world.   About this time the Chartist move was made, Realf joined, and the result was he was obliged to seek safety by emigrating to America.   He made his home some years in New York city.   A part of the time he was there he was engaged as assistant superintendent of the Five-Points Mission.   He is well known as an author and a poet.   He gave up his situation as assistant-superintendent, and went to Kansas in the summer or fall of 1856.   I first met him in Lawrence, Kan.   No word was received of him, to my knowledge, after he left for England, to which place he went in his own capacity and that of our Secretary of State, to solicit funds for the support of our organization.   He proposed to deliver a course of lectures in various parts of England, the net proceeds of which were to be given to carry out Captain Brown's plan.   He is a man of rare talents, and a powerful and fluent speaker.   He is about twenty-eight years of age. Mr. Kagi, I believe, got a letter from some one in England a few months ago, stating that Realf had sailed for this country, and that he had quite a sum of money with him ; but further than that we have been unable to find any trace of him. Captain Brown and the rest of our company who knew him think that he is dead.

At the time Mr. Alstadtt was taken, I was not at his house, put in the carriage with Col. Lewis Washington, opposite the house.   I do not think any arms were placed in the hands of his slaves till they arrived at the musket armory.   I did not see any of the spears on our way from the Ferry to Col. Washington's—there were none taken out to my knowledge. After stopping about half an hour at the engine-house to get warm, I was called out by Captain Brown, and then saw, for the first time, the slaves with the spears in their hands.   I do not know who gave them the spears, but it was some of our party, and probably by the order of Captain Brown.

The negro who was with me on Monday evening, when I left the school-house for the Ferry, was armed with a double-

barreled shotgun, and, I think, a revolving pistol of the Massachusetts arms manufacture.   Who delivered him the arms I
do not know.   He was under my control till I sent him back to
report to Tidd that the troops were coming up.   He obeyed
orders while with me.

I was commissioned as a captain on the Sunday of the insurrection, at the same time the others were, and with them took
the oath prescribed in Article 48 of the Constitution.

George B. Gill joined us before leaving Iowa, in the spring,
as did Stewart Taylor.   JOHN E. COOK.

THE CHATHAM, CANADA, CONVENTION.

FROM ONE OF THE COLORED MEMBERS THEREOF.

[*Martin R. Delany, M. D., afterwards Major and Brigadier-
General, United States Colored Volunteers, gives in a
biographical volume*[1] *the following interesting account of
his meeting John Brown and of the Chatham Convention.*]

" In April, prior to his departure for Africa, while making
final completions for his tour, on returning home from a professional visit in the country, Mrs. Delany informed him that
an old gentleman had called to see him during his absence.
She described him as having a long, white beard, very gray
hair, a sad but placid countenance; in speech he was peculi-
arly solemn; she added, ' He looked like one of the old prophets. He would neither come in nor leave his name, but promised
to be back in two weeks' time.'   Unable to obtain any infor-

---

[1] " Life and Public Services of Martin R. Delany, Sub-Assis-
tant Commissioner, Bureau of Refugees, Freedmen, and Abandoned Lands, and late Major 104th United States Colored Troops."
By Frank A. Rollins (Mrs. Whipple), Boston: Lee & Sheppard.
1868. pp. 85-90.

mation concerning his mysterious visitor, the circumstance would have probably been forgotten, had not the visitor returned at the appointed time; and not finding him at home a second time, he left a message to the effect that he would call again '*in four days, and must see him then.*' This time the interest in the visitor was heightened, and his call was eagerly awaited. At the expiration of that time, while on the street, he recognized his visitor, by his wife's description, approaching him, accompanied by another gentleman; on the latter introducing him to the former, he exclaimed, 'Not Capt. John Brown of Osawatomie!' not thinking of the grand old hero as being east of Kansas, especially in Canada, as the papers had been giving such contradictory accounts of him during the winter and spring.

"'I am sir,' was the reply; 'and I have come to Chatham expressly to see you, this being my third visit on the errand. I must see you at once, sir,' he continued, with emphasis, 'and that, too, in private, as I have much to do and but little time before me. If I am to do nothing here, I want to know it at once.' Going directly to the private parlor of a hotel near by, says Major Delany, he at once revealed to me that he desired to carry out a great project in his scheme of Kansas emigration, which, to be successful, must be aided and countenanced by the influence of a general convention or council. *That* he was unable to effect in the United States, but had been advised by distinguished friends of his and mine, that, if he could but see me, his object could be attained at once. On my expressing astonishment at the conclusion to which my friends and himself had arrived, with a nervous impatience, he exclaimed, 'Why should you be surprised? Sir, the people of the Northern States are cowards; slavery has made cowards of them all. The whites are afraid of each other, and the blacks are afraid of the whites. You can effect nothing among such people,' he added, with decided emphasis. On assuring him if a council were all that was desired, he could readily obtain it, he replied, 'That is all; but that is a great deal to me. It is men I want, and not money; money I can get plentiful enough, but no men. Money can come without being seen, but men are afraid of identification with me, though they favor my measures. They are cowards, sir! cowards!' he reiterated. He then fully revealed his designs. With these I found no fault, but fully favored and aided in getting up the convention.

"The convention, when assembled, consisted of Captain John Brown, his son Owen, eleven or twelve of his Kansas followers, all young white men, enthusiastic and able, and probably sixty or seventy colored men, whom I brought together.

"His plans were made known to them as soon as he was satisfied that the assemblage could be confided in, which conclusion he was not long in finding, for with few exceptions the whole of these were fugitive slaves, refugees in her Britannic majesty's dominion. His scheme was nothing more than this: To make Kansas, instead of Canada, the terminus of the Underground Railroad; instead of passing off the slave to Canada, to send him to Kansas, and there test, on the soil of the United States territory, whether or not the right of freedom would be maintained where no municipal power had authorized.

"He stated that he had originated a fortification so simple, that twenty men, without the aid of teams or ordnance, could build one in a day that would defy all the artillery that could be brought to bear against it. How it was constructed he would not reveal, and none knew it except his great confidential officer, Kagi (the secretary of war in his contemplated provisional government), a young lawyer of marked talents and singular demeanor.

"Major Delany stated that he had proposed, as a cover to the change in the scheme, as Canada had always been known as the terminus of the Underground Railroad, and pursuit of the fugitive was made in that direction, to call it the Subterranean Pass Way,[1] where the initials would stand S. P. W., to

---

[1] The "Subterranean Pass Way" title was used by John Brown as early as 1850, This is proved by a daguerreotype of that period, in which John Brown appears with John Thomas, of Springfield, Mass. The latter, a colored man, holds in his hand a banneret marked "S. P. W."—Subterranean Pass Way.—R. J. H.

note the direction in which he had gone when not sent to Canada. He further stated that the idea of Harper's Ferry was never mentioned, or even hinted in that convention.

"Had such been intimated, it is doubtful of its being favorably regarded. Kansas, where he had battled so valiantly for freedom, seemed the proper place for his vantage-ground, and the kind and condition of men for whom he had fought, the men with whom to fight. Hence the favor which the scheme met of making Kansas the terminus of the Subterranean Pass Way, and there fortifying with these fugitives against the border slaveholders, for personal liberty, with which they had no right to interfere. Thus it is clearly explained that it was no design against the Union, as the slaveholders and their satraps interpreted the movement, and by this means would anticipate their designs.

"This also explains the existence of the constitution for a civil government found in the carpet-bag among the effects of Captain Brown, after his capture in Virginia, so inexplicable to the slaveholders, and which proved such a nightmare to Governor Wise, and caused him, as well as many *wiser* than himself, to construe it as a contemplated overthrow of the Union. The constitution for a provisional government owes its origin to these facts.

"Major Delany says, ' The whole matter had been well considered, and at first a state government had been proposed, and in accordance a constitution prepared. This was presented to the convention ; and here a difficulty presented itself to the minds of some present, that, according to American jurisprudence, negroes, having no rights respected by white men, consequently could have no right to petition, and none to sovereignty.

"Therefore it would be mere mockery to set up a claim as a fundamental right, which in itself was null and void.

"To obviate this, and avoid the charge against them as lawless and unorganized, existing without government, it was proposed that an independent community be established within and under the government of the United States, but without the state sovereignty of the compact, similar to the Cherokee nation of Indians, or the Mormons. To these last named, references were made, as parallel cases, at the time. The necessary changes and modification were made in the constitution, and with such it was printed.

"Captain Brown returned after a week's absence, with a printed copy of the corrected instrument, which, perhaps, was the copy found by Governor Wise.

" During the time this grand old reformer of our time was preparing his plans, he often sought Major Delany, desirous of his personal coöperation in carrying forward his work. This was not possible for him to do, as his attention and time were directed entirely to the African Exploration movement, which was planned prior to his meeting Captain Brown, as before stated. But as Captain Brown desired that he should give encouragement to the plan, he consented, and became president of the permanent organization of the Subterranean Pass Way, with Mr. Isaac D. Shadd, editor of the *Provincial Freeman*, as secretary.

" This organization was an extensive body, holding the same relation to his movements as a state or national executive committee hold to its party principles, directing their adherence to fundamental principles.

" This, he says, was the plan and purpose of the Canada Convention, whatever changed them to Harper's Ferry was known only to Captain Brown, and perhaps to Kagi, who had the honor of being deeper in his confidence than any one else. Mr. Osborn Anderson, one of the survivors of that immortal band, and whose statement as one of the principal actors in that historical drama cannot be ignored, states that none of the men knew that Harper's Ferry was the point of attack until the order was given to march."

GEORGE LUTHER STEARNS AND JOHN BROWN.

[A manuscript sent to the author of this volume by his widow, Mrs. Mary E. Stearns.]

" The passage of the Fugitive-Slave Bill, in 1850, followed by the virtual repeal of the Missouri Compromise, under the name of the Kansas-Nebraska Act, in 1854, alarmed all sane people for the safety of republican institutions; and the excitement reached a white heat when, on the 22d of May, 1856, Charles Sumner was murderously assaulted in the Senate chamber by Preston S. Brooks, of South Carolina, for words spoken in debate: the celebrated speech of the 19th and 20th of May, known as ' The Crime Against Kansas.' That same week the town of Lawrence in the Territory of Kansas was sacked and burned in the interest of the slave-power. The atrocities committed by the ' border ruffians ' upon the free-state settlers sent a thrill of terror through all law-abiding communities. In Boston the citizens gathered in Faneuil Hall to consider what could be done, and a committee was chosen, with Dr. S. G. Howe as chairman, for the relief of Kansas, called the ' Kansas Relief Committee.' After some $18,000 or $20,000 had been collected, chiefly in Boston, and forwarded to Kansas, the interest flagged, and Mr. Stearns, who had been working with that committee, saw the need of more energetic action; so one day he went to Dr. Howe, and told him he was ready to give *all* of his time, and much of his money, to push forward the work. Dr. Howe, seeing that here was the man for the hour, immediately resigned, and Mr. Stearns was chosen unanimously chairman of the ' Massachusetts State Kansas Committee,' which took the place of the one first organized. In the light of subsequent history it is difficult to believe the apathy and blindness which failed to recognize the significance of this attack upon Kansas by the slave-holding power. Only faithful watchmen in their high towers could see that it was the first battle-ground between two conflicting systems of freedom and slavery, which was finally to culminate in the War.

of the Rebellion. 'Working day and night without haste or rest,' failing in no effort to rouse and stimulate the community, still Mr. Stearns found that a vitalizing interest was wanting. When Governor Reeder was driven in disguise from the Territory, he wrote to him to come to Boston and address the people. He organized a mass-meeting for him in Tremont Temple, and for a few days the story he related stimulated to a livelier activity the more conservative people, who were inclined to think the reports of the free-state men much exaggerated. Soon, however, things settled back into the old sluggish way, so that for three consecutive committee-meetings the *chairman* was the only person who presented himself at the appointed time and place. Nothing daunted, he turned to the country towns, and at the end of five months he had raised by his personal exertions, and through his agents the sum of $48 000. Women formed societies all over the State for making and furnishing clothing and various supplies, which resulted in an addition of some $20,000 or $30,000 more. In January, 1857, this species of work was stopped, by advices from Kansas that no more contributions were needed, except for *defense*. At this juncture Mr. Stearns wrote to John Brown, that if he would come to Boston and consult with the friends of freedom, he would pay his expenses. They had never met, but 'Osawatomie Brown' had become a cherished household name during the anxious summer of 1856. Arriving in Boston, they were introduced to each other in the street by a Kansas man, who chanced to be with Mr. Stearns' on his way to the committee-rooms in Nilis's Block, School street. Captain Brown made a profound impression on all who came within the sphere of his moral magnetism. Emerson called him 'the most ideal of men, for he wanted to put all his ideas into action.' His absolute superiority to all selfish aims and narrowing pride of opinion touched an answering chord in the self-devotion of Mr. Stearns. A little anecdote illustrates the modest estimate of the work he had in hand. After several efforts to bring together certain friends to meet Captain Brown at his home, in Medford, he found that Sunday was the only day that would serve their several conveniences, and being a little uncertain how it might strike his ideas of religious propriety, he prefaced his invitation with something like an apology. With characteristic promptness came the reply: 'Mr. Stearns, I have a little ewe-lamb that I want to pull out of the ditch, and the Sabbath will be as good a day as any to do it.'

"It was this occasion which furnished to literature one of the most charming bits of autobiography. Our oldest son, Harry, a lad of eleven years, was an observant listener, and drank eagerly every word that was said of the cruel wrongs in Kansas, and of slavery everywhere. When the gentlemen rose to go, he privately asked his father if he might be allowed to give all his spending money to John Brown. Leave being granted, he bounded away, and, returning with his small treasure, said : ' Captain Brown, will you buy something with this money for those poor people in Kansas, and some time will you write to me and tell me *what sort of a little boy you were ?* ' ' Yes, my son, I will, and God bless you for your kind heart.'[1] The autobiography has been printed many times, but never before with the key which unlocked it.

"It may not be out of place to describe the impression he made upon the writer on this first visit. When I entered the parlor, he was sitting near the hearth, where glowed a bright, open fire. He rose to greet me, stepping forward with such an erect, military bearing, such fine courtesy of demeanor and grave earnestness, that he seemed to my instant thought some old Cromwellian hero suddenly dropped down before me ; a suggestion which was presently strengthened by his saying (proceeding with the conversation my entrance had interrupted), 'Gentlemen, I consider the Golden Rule and the Declaration of Independence one and inseparable ; and it is better that a whole generation of men, women, and children should be swept away than that this crime of slavery should exist one day longer.' These words were uttered like rifle balls ; in such

---

[1] This was in the last days of 1856.

emphatic tones and manner that our little Carl, not three years old, remembered it in manhood as one of his earliest recollections. The child stood perfectly still, in the middle of the room, gazing with his beautiful eyes on this new sort of man, until his absorption arrested the attention of Captain Brown, who soon coaxed him to his knee, tho' the look of awe and childlike wonder remained. His dress was of some dark brown stuff, quite coarse, but its exactness and neatness produced a singular air of refinement. At dinner, he declined all dainties, saying that he was unaccustomed to luxuries, even to partaking of butter.

" The 'friends of freedom,' with whom Mr. Stearns had invited John Brown to consult, were profoundly impressed with his sagacity, integrity, and devotion; notably among these were R. W. Emerson, Theodore Parker, H. D. Thoreau, A. Bronson Alcott, F. B. Sanborn, Dr. S. G. Howe, Col. T. W. Higginson, Gov. Andrew, and others. In February (1857) he appeared before a committee of the State Legislature, to urge that Massachusetts should make an appropriation in money in aid of those persons who had settled in Kansas from her own soil. The speech is printed in Redpath's 'Life.'[1] He obtained at this time from the Massachusetts State Kansas Committee, some two hundred Sharpe's rifles, with which to arm one hundred mounted men for the defense of Kansas, who could also be of service to the peculiar property of Missouri.[2] In those dark days of slave-holding supremacy, the friends of freedom felt justified in aiding the flight of its victims to free soil whenever and wherever opportunity offered. The Fugitive-Slave Law was powerless before the law written on the enlightened consciences of those devoted men and women. These rifles had been forwarded previously to the National Committee at Chicago, for the defense of Kansas, but for some unexplained reasons had never proceeded farther than Tabor, in the State of Iowa.

---

[1] This speech failed to secure any financial aid.—M. E. S.

[2] The committee also authorized him to draw on Patrick J. Jackson (their treasurer) for $500.

Later on, Mr. Stearns, in his individual capacity, authorized Captain Brown to purchase two hundred revolvers from the Massachusetts Arms Company, and paid for them from his private funds, thirteen or fifteen hundred dollars. During the summer of 1857, he united with Mr. Amos A. Lawrence and others in paying off the mortgage, held by Mr. Gerrit Smith, on his house and farm at North Elba, N. Y., he paying two hundred and sixty dollars. It would be difficult to state the entire amount of money Mr. Stearns put into the hands of John Brown for anti-slavery purposes and his own subsistence. He kept no account of what he gave. In April or May, 1857, he gave him a check for no less a sum than seven thousand dollars. Early in 1858, Hon. Henry Wilson wrote to Dr. S. G. Howe that he had learned John Brown was suspected of the intention of using those arms in other ways than for the defense of Kansas; and, by order of the committee, Mr. Stearns wrote (under date May 14, 1858) to Brown not to use them for any other purpose, and to hold them subject to his order, as chairman of said committee. When the operations of the Massachusetts State Kansas Committee virtually ceased, in June or July, 1858, it happened that this committee were some four thousand dollars in debt to Mr. Stearns, for advances of money from time to time to keep the organization in existence; and it was voted to make over to the chairman these two hundred Sharpe's rifles as part payment of the committee's indebtedness. They were of small account to Mr. Stearns. He knew them to be in good hands, and troubled himself no further about them, either the rifles or the revolvers, although keeping up from time to time a correspondence with his friend upon the all-engrossing subject.

"In February of 1859, John Brown was in Boston, and talked with some of his friends about the feasibility of entrenching himself, with a little band of men, in the mountains of Virginia, familiar to him from having surveyed them as engineer in earlier life. His plan was to open communication with the slaves of neighboring plantations, collect them together, and send them off in squads, as he had done in Missouri, 'without

snapping a gun.' Mr. Stearns had so much more faith in John
Brown's opposition to *Slavery*, than in any theories he advanced
of the *modus operandi*, that they produced much less impression on his mind than upon some others gifted with more
genius for details. *'From first to last,'* he believed in John
Brown. His plans or theories might be feasible, or they
might not. If the glorious old man wanted money to try his
plans, he should have it. His plans might fail; probably would,
but *he* could never be a failure. There he stood, unconquerable, in the panoply of divine Justice. Both of these men were
of the martyr type. No thought or consideration for themselves,
for *history*, or the estimation of others, ever entered into their
calculations. It was the service of *Truth* and *Right* which
brought them together, and in that service they were ready
to die.

"In the words of an eminent writer:[1] 'A common spirit
made these two men recognize each other at first sight; and
the power of both lay in that inability to weigh difficulties
against duty, that instant step of thought to deed, which makes
individuals fully possessed by the idea of the age, the turning-
points of its destiny; hands in the right place for touching
the match to the train it has laid, or for leading the public will
to the heart of its moral need. They knew each other as
minute-men upon the same watch; as men to be found *in* the
breach before others knew where it was; they were one in
pity, one in indignation, one in moral enthusiasm, burning
beneath features set to patient self-control; one in simplicity,
though of widely different culture; one in religious inspiration,
though at the poles of religious thought. The old frontiersman
came from his wilderness toils and agonies to find within the
merchant's mansion of art and taste, by the side of Bunker Hill,
a perfect sympathy: the reverence of children, tender interest
in his broken household, free access to a rich man's resources,
and even a valor kindred with his own.'

---

[1] Samuel Johnson, the accomplished Oriental scholar, in *The
Radical*, 1867. A faithful friend of the slave.

" The attack upon Harper's Ferry was a 'side issue,' to quote the words of John Brown, Jr., and a departure from his father's original plan. It certainly took all his friends by surprise. In his letter of Nov. 15, 1859 (while in prison), to his old schoolmaster, the Rev. H. L. Vaill, are these words: I am not as yet, in the *main*, at all disappointed. I have been a good deal disappointed as it regards *myself* in not keeping up to my own plans; but I now feel entirely reconciled to that even: for God's plan was infinitely better, no doubt, or I should have kept my own. Had Samson kept to his determination of not telling Delilah wherein his great strength lay, he would probably never have overturned the house. *I did not tell Delilah*, but I was induced to act very *contrary to my better judgment*.[1]

*   *   *   *   *   *   *

" It is idle to endeavor to explain, by any methods of the *understanding*, any rules of worldly wisdom, or prudence, this influx of the divine will, which has made John Brown already an ideal character. 'The wind bloweth where it listeth. and we hear the sound thereof; but know not whence it cometh, or whither it goeth.' So is every one that is born of the Spirit. Man works in the midst of laws which execute themselves, more especially if, by virtue of obedience, he has lost sight of all selfish aims, and perceives that truth and right alone can claim allegiance. Emerson says: ' Divine intelligence carries on its administration by good men; that great men are they who see that the spiritual are greater than any material forces; and that really there never was anything great accomplished but under religious impulse.

" The deadly *Atheism* of Slavery was rolling its car of Juggernaut all over the beautiful republic, and one pure soul was inspired to confront it by a practical interpretation of the Golden Rule.

" That Virginia would hang John Brown was a foregone conclusion. The Moloch of Slavery would have nothing less.

---

[1] The italics are Brown's.

His friends exerted themselves to secure the best counsel which could be induced to undertake the *formality* of a defense, foremost among whom was Mr. Stearns. A well-organized plan was made to rescue him, conducted by a brave man from Kansas, Col. James Montgomery, but a message came from the prisoner, that he should not feel at liberty to walk out if the doors were left open ; a sense of honor to his jailer (Captain Avis) forbidding anything of the kind.

"Not a little anxiety was felt lest certain of his adherents might be summoned as witnesses, whose testimony would lessen the chances of acquittal, and possibly involve their own lives. John A. Andrew (afterward Governor Andrew) gave it as his opinion, after an exhaustive search of the records, that Virginia would have no right to summon these persons from Massachusetts, but subsequently changed his opinion and urged Mr. Stearns to take passage to Europe, sending him home one day to pack his valise. The advice was opposed to his instincts, but he considered that his wife should have a voice in the matter, who decided, 'midst many tears and prayers that, if slavery required another victim, he must be ready.

"With Dr. Howe it was quite different. He became possessed with a dread that threatened to overwhelm his reason. He was in delicate health, and constitutionally subject to violent attacks of nervous headache. One day he came to Medford, and insisted that Mr. Stearns should accompany him to Canada, urging that if he remained here he should be insane, and that Mr. Stearns, of all his friends, was the only one who would be at all satisfactory to him. This request, or rather demand, Mr. Stearns promptly declined. How well I remember his agitation, walking up and down the room, and finally entreating Mr. Stearns, for 'friendship's sake,' to go and take care of him. I can recall no instance of such self-abnegation in my husband's self-denying career. He did not *stoop to an explanation*, even when Dr. Howe declared in his presence, some months later, 'that be never did anything in his life he so much wished to take back.' I had hoped that Dr. Howe would himself have spared *me* from making this contribution to the truth of history.

"On the 2d of December, Mr. Stearns yearned for the solitude of his own soul, in communion of spirit, with the friend
who, on that day, 'would make the gallows glorious like the
Cross'; and he left Dr. Howe and took the train for Niagara
Falls. There, sitting alone beside the mighty rush of water,
he solemnly consecrated his remaining life, his fortune, and all
that was most dear to the *cause* in whose service John Brown
had died.

"How well and faithfully he kept his vow may partly be
seen in his subsequent efforts in recruiting the colored troops
at a vital moment in the terrible War of the Rebellion, which so
swiftly followed the sublime apotheosis of 'Old John Brown.'"

[NOTE.—Two points in Mrs. Stearns's valuable paper require an
explanation. The testimony is overwhelming that "Harper's
Ferry," and the mountain section to which it is the key, was John
Brown's original and continued objective. He was "diverted" to
Kansas, and at times discussed other points of attack, but always
returned to the West Virginia Alleghenies and Harper's Ferry.
The plans John Brown did not keep "up to" were his early
return to the mountains. His failure to do that ended in defeat
and, in the end, a greater victory. The other reference is the
statement Col. James Montgomery was to have "conducted"
a "well organized plan" for the "rescue" of John Brown. No
such plan was formed. James Montgomery did not propose nor
consent to lead one. A rescue of Aaron D. Stevens and Albert
Hazlett was, however, planned in about the middle of January,
1860. In attempting to carry it out, the writer went to Kansas
and induced James Montgomery and others there to come East.
Montgomery was to be the leader. After the plan was abandoned,
on the advice of Montgomery himself, coupled with a protest
from both Stevens and Hazlett against attempting it, because it
would involve the life of Captain Avis and others, James Montgomery visited Boston and there met Mr. and Mrs. Stearns. This
was in the middle of March, 1860. I give more details in the
chapter relating to the John Brown men.—R. J. H.]

REMINISCENCES OF GEORGE B. GILL.

[A MEMBER OF JOHN BROWN'S COMMAND FROM 1856 TO
THE SPRING OF 1859, AND SELECTED BY THE CHATHAM
CONVENTION TO SERVE AS SECRETARY OF THE TREAS-
URY, UNDER THE PROVISIONAL FORM OF GOVERNMENT
PREPARED BY JOHN BROWN AND ADOPTED AT CHATHAM,
CANADA, WEST, MAY THE 11TH AND 12TH, 1858.]

[*Mr. George B. Gill, now living in the neutral strip, Territory of Oklahoma, who was a faithful and able member of
the original John Brown party, prevented only by severe
sickness from being at Harper's Ferry, has furnished me
with a large amount of manuscript notes, for the preparation of which I am, as well as the truth of history
itself, greatly indebted.   These original notes will all be
deposited with other material by me in the Kansas State
Historical Society to form an important part, I trust,
of its very valuable collection.   I have made large use of
Mr. Gill's data in the body of this book, but have deemed
that what follows was more appropriately to be placed in
this Appendix, and duly credited as a whole to its author,
to whom again I return my grateful thanks for all his
aid.   I am sure, too, that the reader of this volume will
be gratified at the opportunity and insight this paper
affords as to the manner of men that traveled with John
Brown from Kansas to Harper's Ferry.—R. J. Hinton.*]

Those who wintered at Mr. William Maxon's. in eastern
Iowa, and who had connected themselves with Brown, were
Kagi, Stevens, Realf, Parsons, Tidd, Leeman, Moffett, Cook,
Owen Brown, and Richard Richardson (Col.). Of these Kagi,
Realf, and Cook were more or less addicted to literary persuits.
Springdale, a village of Quaker origin, noted for its lyceums
and debating clubs, was but a short distance from their ren-
dezvous.

Never before, nor since, has that community been so mentally
feasted as they were that winter.   Realf, with fiery eloquence,

would hold his audience spellbound; Kagi with calm, logical deductions would be invincible, and Cook would hold an inter-mediate position—comic, poetic, or mirthful, as the occasion demanded.

While not noted in public debates, Owen Brown and Stevens were not to be dispised in private discussion. Owen with his calm, orderly, and honest ways, Stevens with his fine, rich voice, and passionate thoughts made life worth living in their boarding-house and all around them. Their boarding-house would sometimes remind one of a boiling, seething, roaring Vesuvius. A stranger would have supposed a battle imminent, but in a moment there would come a cheery, hearty laugh. They were earnest men, and as liberal towards others as they were positive in their own convictions. The people around Springdale were intensely anti-slavery. It soon became an open secret that these men were waiting and preparing to strike a blow whose rebound would probably be death to the heroes that gave it. Details were not known, nor even surmised, yet sympathetic instructions were so correctly formed that no sur-prise was felt when the sacrifice was made.

In their home at Mr. Maxon's they amused themselves at intervals in singing. Several of them had superior voices, and when on some patriotic refrain would make the welkin ring. Mr. Maxon lived in the extreme west edge of Iowa Township, in Cedar County, and adjoining Springdale Township. The majority of the people in Iowa Township were as rabidly pro-slavery as they were intensely anti-slavery in Springdale Town-ship. On learning the character of Mr. Maxon's boarders, the pro-slavery citizens of Iowa Township held an indignation meeting and passed resolutions denying the fact of Mr. Maxon being a resident of Iowa Township, alleging that he was a citizen of Springdale Township. Mr. Maxon accepted the change proudly. Brown paid one dollar per week to Mr. Maxon for each man boarded, a rate at which he probably lost money. The original intention was to familiarize themselves with mili-tary tactics and drill, but the instructor that they had expected had proven a failure in all ways. Stevens undoubtedly was

very capable of instructing them in drill, but the original pro
gramme was never fully carried out, except in a mental way,
by reading and discussing. This, however, was very thorough.
Not alone, however, in military discipline and strategy, but in
all things, theological or philosophical. No question too
abstruse, none too prominent. Some genius among them, Owen
Brown, whittled out some wooden swords with which they
practiced. Whenever any one of them who had been accustomed
to manual labor could get work to do, husking corn or similar
labor, they would gladly seize hold of it.

I think that it must have been in the early winter of 1857
that Brown came to Springdale with his men. I had come
from Kansas much earlier, and was living at West Liberty
(some seven miles from Springdale or about ten miles from
Maxon's), when I became cognizant of the fact of their being
in that locality. How I found it out I do not now remember,
neither do I now remember as to who I was acquainted with
previous to that time, with the exception of Realf. I knew
Brown slightly. Some of the others I had seen but was really
not acquainted with them. The two Coppocs and Steward
Taylor were old Iowa acquaintances. I was well enough acquainted with Brown to be recognized by him when I took
Steward Taylor up to introduce him. In April (1858), Brown
returned from the East, and preparations for an advance forward
were made, Parsons leaving Springdale in advance of the others
in order that Parsons might visit his people, a few days, somewhere in Illinois. I should have said that Kagi and Tidd accompanied Parsons to his home there previous to the balance
of the party leaving Springdale. From Attalissa, the point at
which they expected to take the cars, there came a characteristic letter from Kagi, telling that they had come in sight of the
station and train just in time ' to give the lie to that old adage'
that distance lends enchantment to the view ; they being too
late. At 11.45 A.M., on Tuesday, April 27, 1858, we left Springdale for West Liberty, where we boarded the cars at three P.M.,
and crossed the Mississippi, at Davenport, just as the sun was
setting. Our company then consisted of John Brown, Owen

Brown, A. D. Stevens, Moffett, Taylor, Leeman, Realf, Cook, myself, and Richardson, a colored man. During the process of changing cars, at Rock Island, some demonstrations were made towards arresting our colored man as a 'runaway nigger.' We were speedily relieved of this by the conductor taking him by the arm and pushing him into the car and immediately starting the train. We were passing for a company of surveyors returning from the West. After starting, the conductor came around congratulating himself as to how nicely he had given them the slip. Arriving at Chicago at five o'clock on the morning of the 28th, we stopped at the Massasoit House. We ate our breakfast all right, but just previous to going into dinner the landlord informed the old patriarch that our colored man would have to wait and eat with the servants. The old man would not accept the proposition, but, instead, gave the landlord a little of his terse logic, and left. We dined at the Adams House, where the conditions were altogether suitable, caste and color, accidental and otherwise, not being considered. Leaving Chicago at 4.30 o'clock in the afternoon, we reached Detroit at 6 o'clock A.M. on the 29th, taking up quarters at the villa tavern; Parsons, Kagi, and Tidd arrived next day. Nothing of any importance was done until Saturday, May 8th, with the exception of sending out a few notes to friends, inviting them to a proposed convention. This body convened on Saturday, May 8th (1858). It had 26 in attendance, 14 colored and 12 white. Another session was held on Monday. William Charles Monroe was made president and John Henri Kagi was secretary.

[*Mr. Gill wrote in this paper a brief résumé of the convention proceedings, which is, however, used in the general narrative with due credit. He then resumes the story of the movements of the party up to the early part of 1859.*]

On Tuesday, May 11th, at 9 A.M., Stevens, Tidd, Parsons, Owen Brown, Taylor, Cook, Moffett, and myself left, on the steamer *Swan*, for Detroit, destination being Cleveland. We arrived there at 5 A.M., on the 12th, and stopped for breakfast at the Bennett House. After breakfast, we engaged board at 85 Water street. From Chatham, Brown went East. Kagi went down to St. Catherine's to set up the work of the convention, including commissions, in James M. Bell's (colored) printing-office, Kagi doing the work himself. Between that time and the 21st of June we were compelled to resort to various expedients to maintain ourselves, our money being about all gone. I had loaned the little that I had to various members of the party, some to Brown himself. Parsons had quite a little supply, but had distributed his in the same way. Times were hard, and business that we could do was not to be found. I concluded to take a little trip up to Sandusky city to see Reynolds, a member of the convention, and to take in Oberlin, Berlin Heights, and Milan, on the way. I persuaded Steward Taylor to accompany me. The trip and style of traveling was too much for Steward; after walking half-way and lying out one night he took the back track, and arrived at Cleveland worn out in body and spirit. At Milan, I discovered rumors of John Brown's hidden arms and the locality that they were stored in; in fact, exactly where they were stored. My object in wishing to see Mr. Reynolds, who was a colored man (very little colored, however), was in regard to a military organization which, I had understood, was in existence among the colored people. He assured me that such was the fact, and that its ramifications extended through most, or nearly all, of the slave States. He himself, I think, had been through many of the slave States visiting and organizing. He referred me to many references in the Southern papers, telling of this and that favorite slave being killed or found dead. These, he asserted, must be taken care of, being the most dangerous element they had to contend with. He also asserted that they were only waiting for Brown, or some one else, to make a successful initiative move when their forces would be put in motion. None but colored persons could be admitted to membership, and, in part to corroborate his assertions, took me to the room in which they held their meetings and used as their arsenal. He showed me a fine collection of arms. He gave me this under the pledge of secrecy which we gave to each other at the Chatham Convention.

On my return to Cleveland he passed me through the organization, first to J. J, Pierce, colored, at Milan, who paid my bill over night at the Eagle Hotel, and gave me some money, and a note to E. Moore, at Norwalk, who in turn paid my hotel bill and purchased a railroad ticket through to Cleveland for me. At Cleveland I found that Realf and Leeman had arrived from Chatham. Realf had rented a room and established a kind of headquarters. Stevens, Tidd, and Owen Brown were working for the Shakers, some six or seven miles from Cleveland, receiving the munificent sum of fifty cents per day; more, however, than they could get anywhere else. I went out, thinking that perhaps I might get something to do; they then had all the help they needed. I suggested that I would work for my board, if they would let me do so. They said that they never turned any one away. From June 1st to June 21st I worked in company with Owen, mostly on repairing a dam, Stevens and Tidd leaving soon after I arrived. Steward Taylor worked for some one in the vicinity of Cleveland. Moffet had a married sister living in Cleveland with whom he stopped. Parsons paid his board. Just what Cook, Leeman, and the others were doing this time I cannot now remember, but they were, however, within call.

On June 21, 1858, we were notified that Brown had returned from the East and wanted us. On leaving, the Shaker superintendent handed me several dollars. I inquired as to what it was for. He said that it was to pay me for my work. Yes, but I told him I had agreed to work for my board. His answer was: "Keep the money, the laborer is worthy of his hire." On meeting Brown, he explained to us that the friends on whom he relied for money were, as he expressed it, in a panic on account of Forbes,[1] and that nothing could be done for the pres-

---

[1] Col. Hugh Forbes, the Englishman, originally employed as military instructor, and who wrote denouncing Brown to antislavery friends.

ent. He planned for us as well as he could considering the
financial basis.   Kagi, Tidd, and himself were to go directly to
Kansas by way of St. Louis.   Stevens and myself were to go
by the way of Iowa, and there raise some funds, and come on
to Kansas as soon as we could.   Realf was to go to New York
and watch the movements of Forbes   Owen wns to go out to
Jason's, at Akron, taking either Leeman or Taylor, or both,
with him, though it seems to me that Taylor was afterwards
reported in Illinois.   Moffett was already at home in Cleveland, but afterwards worked west to Iowa.   I am of the
opinion that both Moffett and Parsons had lost faith in the
movement.

Brown reasoned out a necessity for himself and some others
to go to Kansas, and, if possible, to make some demonstration
as an offset to Forbes's revelations, either made or threatened.
This was the true meaning of his return to Kansas.   By going
to Kansas, discredit would naturally follow Forbes's evidence,
making it so unreliable and worthless that neither friend nor foe
would be influenced by it.

Cook was to go to Harper's Ferry.   To me this does not
admit of a single doubt.   He did all in his power to persuade
me to go along, but just then I did not have entire faith in the
scheme being carried to a successful conclusion, or even an
attempt made to execute it for a long time.   The condition of
the treasury also made it objectionable to me, and I also feared
a lack of reserve on the part of Cook.   I am satisfied that
Brown furnished Cook with money to go with, and remember
distinctly of the caution and advice given him by Brown.   I do
not think that Brown first suggested his going, but, after being
suggested by Cook, I am confident that Brown acquiesced in
his going.   This I say emphatically, and feel that, if Brown
had been correctly reported, that there never would have been
any denial.

Brown, Kagi, and Tidd must have reached Kansas about
June 24, 1858 ; Stevens and myself reached Iowa on the 25th.
I reached Kansas about the 10th of August, Stevens somewhat
later.   Brown I found was in Linn County ; getting my cue

from William A. Phillips, I found Kagi and Tidd at Augustus Wattles's, and, in company with Kagi, found the old man quite sick at John Jones's (the Ottawa Indian).

[*The balance of Mr. Gill's paper has been made use of in the chapter on Events in Kansas from September, 1858, to January, 1859.—R. J. H.*]

INDEX

INDEX.

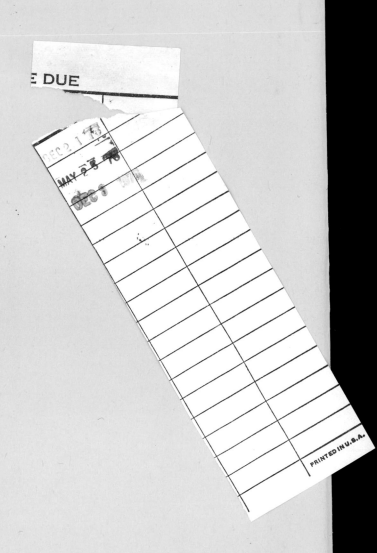

E DUE

DEC 2 1 78

MAY 23 79

DEC 9 1971

PRINTED IN U.S.A.

JOHN BROWN
AND
HIS MEN

Richard J. Hinton

ARNO PRESS and THE NEW YORK TIMES

NEW YORK 1968

General Editor
WILLIAM LOREN KATZ